MW00511659

GO!
with Microsoft®

Access 2007
Volume 1

Shelley Gaskin, Kris Townsend, and Suzanne Marks

PEARSON

Prentice
Hall

Upper Saddle River, New Jersey

This book is dedicated to my students, who inspire me every day, and to my husband, Fred Gaskin.
—Shelley Gaskin

This book is dedicated to the students at Spokane Falls Community College. Their adventures, joys, and frustrations guide my way.
—Kris Townsend

This book is dedicated with much love to my husband Phil, who is my everything; and to my children Jeff and Laura, who are the center of my universe.
—Suzanne Marks

Library of Congress Cataloging-in-Publication Data

Gaskin, Shelley.
   Go! with. Access / Shelley Gaskin, Kris Townsend and Suzanne Marks.
      p. cm.
   ISBN 0-13-513040-9
   1. Microsoft Access. 2. Database management. I. Marks, Suzanne. II. Title.
   QA76.9.D3G3864 2007
   005.75'65--dc22

2007023980

Vice President and Publisher: Natalie E. Anderson
Associate VP/Executive Acquisitions Editor, Print: Stephanie Wall
Executive Acquisitions Editor, Media: Richard Keaveny
Product Development Manager: Eileen Bien Calabro
Editorial Project Manager: Laura Burgess
Development Editor: Ginny Munroe
Editorial Assistant: Becky Knauer
Executive Producer: Lisa Strite
Content Development Manager: Cathi Profitko
Media Project Manager: Alana Myers
Production Media Project Manager: Lorena Cerisano
Director of Marketing: Margaret Waples
Senior Marketing Manager: Jason Sakos
Marketing Assistants: Angela Frey, Kathryn Ferranti
Senior Sales Associate: Rebecca Scott

Senior Managing Editor: Cynthia Zonneveld
Managing Editor: Camille Trentacoste
Production Project Manager: Wanda Rockwell
Production Editor: GGS Book Services
Photo Researcher: GGS Book Services
Manufacturing Buyer: Natacha Moore
Production/Editorial Assistant: Sandra K. Bernales
Design Director: Maria Lange
Art Director/Interior Design: Blair Brown
Cover Photo: Courtesy of Getty Images, Inc./Marvin Mattelson
Composition: GGS Book Services
Project Management: GGS Book Services
Cover Printer: Phoenix Color
Printer/Binder: RR Donnelley/Willard

Microsoft, Windows, Word, PowerPoint, Outlook, FrontPage, Visual Basic, MSN, The Microsoft Network, and/or other Microsoft products referenced herein are either trademarks or registered trademarks of Microsoft Corporation in the U.S.A. and other countries. Screen shots and icons reprinted with permission from the Microsoft Corporation. This book is not sponsored or endorsed by or affiliated with Microsoft Corporation.

Credits and acknowledgments borrowed from other sources and reproduced, with permission, in this textbook are as follows or on the appropriate page within the text.

Page 2: Index Stock Imagery, Inc.; page 98: Getty Images, Inc. – Liaison; page 300: PhotoEdit Inc.; pages 380 and 460: iStock.

Copyright © 2008 by Pearson Education, Inc., Upper Saddle River, New Jersey, 07458. All rights reserved. Printed in the United States of America. This publication is protected by Copyright and permission should be obtained from the publisher prior to any prohibited reproduction, storage in a retrieval system, or transmission in any form or by any means, electronic, mechanical, photocopying, recording, or likewise. For information regarding permission(s), write to the Rights and Permissions Department.

10 9 8 7 6 5 4 3 2
ISBN 10: 0-13-513040-9
ISBN 13: 978-0-13-513040-7

Contents in Brief

Table of Contents

Letter from the Editor

Dear Instructors and Students,

The primary goal of the *GO!* Series is two-fold. The first goal is to instructors teach the course they want in less time. The second goal provide students with the skills to solve business problems using the computer as a tool, for both themselves and the organization for which they might be employed.

The *GO!* Series was originally created by Series Editor Shelley Gaskin and published with the release of Microsoft Office 2003. Her ideas came from years of using textbooks that didn't meet all the needs of today's diverse classroom and that were too confusing for students. Shelley continues to enhance the series by ensuring we stay true to our vision of developing quality instruction and useful classroom tools.

But we also need your input and ideas.

Over time, the *GO!* Series has evolved based on direct feedback from instructors and students using the series. *We are the publisher that listens.* To publish a textbook that works for you, it's critical that we continue to listen to this feedback. It's important to me to talk with you and hear your stories about using *GO!* Your voice can make a difference.

My hope is that this letter will inspire you to write me an e-mail and share your thoughts on using the *GO!* Series.

Stephanie Wall
Executive Editor, *GO!* Series
stephanie_wall@prenhall.com

GO! System Contributors

We thank the following people for their hard work and support in making the GO! System all that it is!

Additional Author Support

Coyle, Diane	Montgomery County Community College
Fry, Susan	Boise State
Townsend, Kris	Spokane Falls Community College
Stroup, Tracey	Amgen Corporation

Instructor Resource Authors

Amer, Beverly	Northern Arizona University	Paterson, Jim	Paradise Valley Community College
Boito, Nancy	Harrisburg Area Community College	Prince, Lisa	Missouri State
Coyle, Diane	Montgomery County Community College	Rodgers, Gwen	Southern Nazarene University
Dawson, Tamara	Southern Nazarene University	Ruymann, Amy	Burlington Community College
Driskel, Loretta	Niagara County Community College	Ryan, Bob	Montgomery County Community College
Elliott, Melissa	Odessa College		
Fry, Susan	Boise State	Smith, Diane	Henry Ford Community College
Geoghan, Debra	Bucks County Community College	Spangler, Candice	Columbus State Community College
Hearn, Barbara	Community College of Philadelphia	Thompson, Joyce	Lehigh Carbon Community College
Jones, Stephanie	South Plains College	Tiffany, Janine	Reading Area Community College
Madsen, Donna	Kirkwood Community College	Watt, Adrienne	Douglas College
Meck, Kari	Harrisburg Area Community College	Weaver, Paul	Bossier Parish Community College
Miller, Cindy	Ivy Tech	Weber, Sandy	Gateway Technical College
Nowakowski, Tony	Buffalo State	Wood, Dawn	
Pace, Phyllis	Queensborough Community College	Weissman, Jonathan	Finger Lakes Community College

Super Reviewers

Brotherton, Cathy	Riverside Community College	Maurer, Trina	Odessa College
Cates, Wally	Central New Mexico Community College	Meck, Kari	Harrisburg Area Community College
		Miller, Cindy	Ivy Tech Community College
Cone, Bill	Northern Arizona University	Nielson, Phil	Salt Lake Community College
Coverdale, John	Riverside Community College	Rodgers, Gwen	Southern Nazarene University
Foster, Nancy	Baker College	Smolenski, Robert	Delaware Community College
Helfand, Terri	Chaffey College	Spangler, Candice	Columbus State Community College
Hibbert, Marilyn	Salt Lake Community College	Thompson, Joyce	Lehigh Carbon Community College
Holliday, Mardi	Community College of Philadelphia	Weber, Sandy	Gateway Technical College
Jerry, Gina	Santa Monica College	Wells, Lorna	Salt Lake Community College
Martin, Carol	Harrisburg Area Community College	Zaboski, Maureen	University of Scranton

Technical Editors

Janice Snyder
Joyce Nielsen
Colette Eisele
Janet Pickard
Mara Zebest
Lindsey Allen
William Daley
LeeAnn Bates

Student Reviewers

Allen, John	Asheville-Buncombe Tech Community College	Erickson, Mike	Ball State University
		Gadomski, Amanda	Northern Michigan University
Alexander, Steven	St. Johns River Community College	Gyselinck, Craig	Central Washington University
Alexander, Melissa	Tulsa Community College	Harrison, Margo	Central Washington University
Bolz, Stephanie	Northern Michigan University	Heacox, Kate	Central Washington University
Berner, Ashley	Central Washington University	Hill, Cheretta	Northwestern State University
Boomer, Michelle	Northern Michigan University	Innis, Tim	Tulsa Community College
Busse, Brennan	Northern Michigan University	Jarboe, Aaron	Central Washington University
Butkey, Maura	Central Washington University	Klein, Colleen	Northern Michigan University
Christensen, Kaylie	Northern Michigan University	Moeller, Jeffrey	Northern Michigan University
Connally, Brianna	Central Washington University	Nicholson, Regina	Athens Tech College
Davis, Brandon	Northern Michigan University	Niehaus, Kristina	Northern Michigan University
Davis, Christen	Central Washington University	Nisa, Zaibun	Santa Rosa Community College
Den Boer, Lance	Central Washington University	Nunez, Nohelia	Santa Rosa Community College
Dix, Jessica	Central Washington University	Oak, Samantha	Central Washington University
Moeller, Jeffrey	Northern Michigan University	Oertii, Monica	Central Washington University
Downs, Elizabeth	Central Washington University	Palenshus, Juliet	Central Washington University

...higan University
...ton University
... University
...ate University
...nity College
...shington University
Washington University

Shanahan, Megan | Northern Michigan University
Teska, Erika | Hawaii Pacific University
Traub, Amy | Northern Michigan University
Underwood, Katie | Central Washington University
Walters, Kim | Central Washington University
Wilson, Kelsie | Central Washington University
Wilson, Amanda | Green River Community College

	Houston Community College
	Agatston Consulting Technical College
...der, Melody	Ball Sate University
...ndro, Manuel	Southwest Texas Junior College
...i, Farha	Lander University
Amici, Penny	Harrisburg Area Community College
Anderson, Patty A.	Lake City Community College
Andrews, Wilma	Virginia Commonwealth College, Nebraska University
Anik, Mazhar	Tiffin University
Armstrong, Gary	Shippensburg University
Atkins, Bonnie	Delaware Technical Community College
Bachand, LaDonna	Santa Rosa Community College
Bagui, Sikha	University of West Florida
Beecroft, Anita	Kwantlen University College
Bell, Paula	Lock Haven College
Belton, Linda	Springfield Tech. Community College
Bennett, Judith	Sam Houston State University
Bhatia, Sai	Riverside Community College
Bishop, Frances	DeVry Institute—Alpharetta (ATL)
Blaszkiewicz, Holly	Ivy Tech Community College/Region 1
Branigan, Dave	DeVry University
Bray, Patricia	Allegany College of Maryland
Brotherton, Cathy	Riverside Community College
Buehler, Lesley	Ohlone College
Buell, C	Central Oregon Community College
Byars, Pat	Brookhaven College
Byrd, Lynn	Delta State University, Cleveland, Mississippi
Cacace, Richard N.	Pensacola Junior College
Cadenhead, Charles	Brookhaven College
Calhoun, Ric	Gordon College
Cameron, Eric	Passaic Community College
Carriker, Sandra	North Shore Community College
Cannamore, Madie	Kennedy King
Carreon, Cleda	Indiana University—Purdue University, Indianapolis
Chaffin, Catherine	Shawnee State University
Chauvin, Marg	Palm Beach Community College, Boca Raton
Challa, Chandrashekar	Virginia State University
Chamlou, Afsaneh	NOVA Alexandria
Chapman, Pam	Wabaunsee Community College
Christensen, Dan	Iowa Western Community College
Clay, Betty	Southeastern Oklahoma State University
Collins, Linda D.	Mesa Community College
Conroy-Link, Janet	Holy Family College
Cosgrove, Janet	Northwestern CT Community
Courtney, Kevin	Hillsborough Community College
Cox, Rollie	Madison Area Technical College
Crawford, Hiram	Olive Harvey College

Crawford, Thomasina	Miami-Dade College, Kendall Campus
Credico, Grace	Lethbridge Community College
Crenshaw, Richard	Miami Dade Community College, North
Crespo, Beverly	Mt. San Antonio College
Crossley, Connie	Cincinnati State Technical Community College
Curik, Mary	Central New Mexico Community College
De Arazoza, Ralph	Miami Dade Community College
Danno, John	DeVry University/Keller Graduate School
Davis, Phillip	Del Mar College
DeHerrera, Laurie	Pikes Peak Community College
Delk, Dr. K. Kay	Seminole Community College
Doroshow, Mike	Eastfield College
Douglas, Gretchen	SUNYCortland
Dove, Carol	Community College of Allegheny
Driskel, Loretta	Niagara Community College
Duckwiler, Carol	Wabaunsee Community College
Duncan, Mimi	University of Missouri-St. Louis
Duthie, Judy	Green River Community College
Duvall, Annette	Central New Mexico Community College
Ecklund, Paula	Duke University
Eng, Bernice	Brookdale Community College
Evans, Billie	Vance-Granville Community College
Feuerbach, Lisa	Ivy Tech East Chicago
Fisher, Fred	Florida State University
Foster, Penny L.	Anne Arundel Community College
Foszcz, Russ	McHenry County College
Fry, Susan	Boise State University
Fustos, Janos	Metro State
Gallup, Jeanette	Blinn College
Gelb, Janet	Grossmont College
Gentry, Barb	Parkland College
Gerace, Karin	St. Angela Merici School
Gerace, Tom	Tulane University
Ghajar, Homa	Oklahoma State University
Gifford, Steve	Northwest Iowa Community College
Glazer, Ellen	Broward Community College
Gordon, Robert	Hofstra University
Gramlich, Steven	Pasco-Hernando Community College
Graviett, Nancy M.	St. Charles Community College, St. Peters, Missouri
Greene, Rich	Community College of Allegheny County
Gregoryk, Kerry	Virginia Commonwealth State
Griggs, Debra	Bellevue Community College
Grimm, Carol	Palm Beach Community College
Hahn, Norm	Thomas Nelson Community College
Hammerschlag, Dr. Bill	Brookhaven College
Hansen, Michelle	Davenport University
Hayden, Nancy	Indiana University—Purdue University, Indianapolis

Hayes, Theresa	Broward Community College	Lord, Alexandria	Asheville Buncombe Tech
Helfand, Terri	Chaffey College	Lowe, Rita	Harold Washington College
Helms, Liz	Columbus State Community College	Low, Willy Hui	Joliet Junior College
Hernandez, Leticia	TCI College of Technology	Lucas, Vickie	Broward Community College
Hibbert, Marilyn	Salt Lake Community College	Lynam, Linda	Central Missouri State University
Hoffman, Joan	Milwaukee Area Technical College	Lyon, Lynne	Durham College
Hogan, Pat	Cape Fear Community College	Lyon, Pat Rajski	Tomball College
Holland, Susan	Southeast Community College	MacKinnon, Ruth	Georgia Southern University
Hopson, Bonnie	Athens Technical College	Macon, Lisa	Valencia Community College, West Campus
Horvath, Carrie	Albertus Magnus College		
Horwitz, Steve	Community College of Philadelphia	Machuca, Wayne	College of the Sequoias
Hotta, Barbara	Leeward Community College	Madison, Dana	Clarion University
Howard, Bunny	St. Johns River Community	Maguire, Trish	Eastern New Mexico University
Howard, Chris	DeVry University	Malkan, Rajiv	Montgomery College
Huckabay, Jamie	Austin Community College	Manning, David	Northern Kentucky University
Hudgins, Susan	East Central University	Marcus, Jacquie	Niagara Community College
Hulett, Michelle J.	Missouri State University	Marghitu, Daniela	Auburn University
Hunt, Darla A.	Morehead State University, Morehead, Kentucky	Marks, Suzanne	Bellevue Community College
		Marquez, Juanita	El Centro College
Hunt, Laura	Tulsa Community College	Marquez, Juan	Mesa Community College
Jacob, Sherry	Jefferson Community College	Martyn, Margie	Baldwin-Wallace College
Jacobs, Duane	Salt Lake Community College	Marucco, Toni	Lincoln Land Community College
Jauken, Barb	Southeastern Community	Mason, Lynn	Lubbock Christian University
Johnson, Kathy	Wright College	Matutis, Audrone	Houston Community College
Johnson, Mary	Kingwood College	Matkin, Marie	University of Lethbridge
Johnson, Mary	Mt. San Antonio College	McCain, Evelynn	Boise State University
Jones, Stacey	Benedict College	McCannon, Melinda	Gordon College
Jones, Warren	University of Alabama, Birmingham	McCarthy, Marguerite	Northwestern Business College
Jordan, Cheryl	San Juan College	McCaskill, Matt L.	Brevard Community College
Kapoor, Bhushan	California State University, Fullerton	McClellan, Carolyn	Tidewater Community College
Kasai, Susumu	Salt Lake Community College	McClure, Darlean	College of Sequoias
Kates, Hazel	Miami Dade Community College, Kendall	McCrory, Sue A.	Missouri State University
		McCue, Stacy	Harrisburg Area Community College
Keen, Debby	University of Kentucky	McEntire-Orbach, Teresa	Middlesex County College
Keeter, Sandy	Seminole Community College	McLeod, Todd	Fresno City College
Kern-Blystone, Dorothy Jean	Bowling Green State	McManus, Illyana	Grossmont College
		McPherson, Dori	Schoolcraft College
Keskin, Ilknur	The University of South Dakota	Meiklejohn, Nancy	Pikes Peak Community College
Kirk, Colleen	Mercy College	Menking, Rick	Hardin-Simmons University
Kleckner, Michelle	Elon University	Meredith, Mary	University of Louisiana at Lafayette
Kliston, Linda	Broward Community College, North Campus	Mermelstein, Lisa	Baruch College
		Metos, Linda	Salt Lake Community College
Kochis, Dennis	Suffolk County Community College	Meurer, Daniel	University of Cincinnati
Kramer, Ed	Northern Virginia Community College	Meyer, Marian	Central New Mexico Community College
Laird, Jeff	Northeast State Community College	Miller, Cindy	Ivy Tech Community College, Lafayette, Indiana
Lamoureaux, Jackie	Central New Mexico Community College		
		Mitchell, Susan	Davenport University
Lange, David	Grand Valley State	Mohle, Dennis	Fresno Community College
LaPointe, Deb	Central New Mexico Community College	Monk, Ellen	University of Delaware
		Moore, Rodney	Holland College
Larson, Donna	Louisville Technical Institute	Morris, Mike	Southeastern Oklahoma State University
Laspina, Kathy	Vance-Granville Community College		
Le Grand, Dr. Kate	Broward Community College	Morris, Nancy	Hudson Valley Community College
Lenhart, Sheryl	Terra Community College	Moseler, Dan	Harrisburg Area Community College
Letavec, Chris	University of Cincinnati	Nabors, Brent	Reedley College, Clovis Center
Liefert, Jane	Everett Community College	Nadas, Erika	Wright College
Lindaman, Linda	Black Hawk Community College	Nadelman, Cindi	New England College
Lindberg, Martha	Minnesota State University	Nademlynsky, Lisa	Johnson & Wales University
Lightner, Renee	Broward Community College	Ncube, Cathy	University of West Florida
Lindberg, Martha	Minnesota State University	Nagengast, Joseph	Florida Career College
Linge, Richard	Arizona Western College	Newsome, Eloise	Northern Virginia Community College Woodbridge
Logan, Mary G.	Delgado Community College		
Loizeaux, Barbara	Westchester Community College	Nicholls, Doreen	Mohawk Valley Community College
Lopez, Don	Clovis-State Center Community College District	Nunan, Karen	Northeast State Technical Community College

Odegard, Teri — Edmonds Community College
Ogle, Gregory — North Community College
Orr, Dr. Claudia — Northern Michigan University South
Otieno, Derek — DeVry University
Otton, Diana Hill — Chesapeake College
Oxendale, Lucia — West Virginia Institute of Technology

Paiano, Frank — Southwestern College
Patrick, Tanya — Clackamas Community College
Peairs, Deb — Clark State Community College
Prince, Lisa — Missouri State University-Springfield Campus
Proietti, Kathleen — Northern Essex Community College
Pusins, Delores — HCCC
Raghuraman, Ram — Joliet Junior College
Reasoner, Ted Allen — Indiana University—Purdue
Reeves, Karen — High Point University
Remillard, Debbie — New Hampshire Technical Institute
Rhue, Shelly — DeVry University
Richards, Karen — Maplewoods Community College
Richardson, Mary — Albany Technical College
Rodgers, Gwen — Southern Nazarene University
Roselli, Diane — Harrisburg Area Community College
Ross, Dianne — University of Louisiana in Lafayette
Rousseau, Mary — Broward Community College, South
Samson, Dolly — Hawaii Pacific University
Sams, Todd — University of Cincinnati
Sandoval, Everett — Reedley College
Sardone, Nancy — Seton Hall University
Scafide, Jean — Mississippi Gulf Coast Community College
Scheeren, Judy — Westmoreland County Community College
Schneider, Sol — Sam Houston State University
Scroggins, Michael — Southwest Missouri State University
Sever, Suzanne — Northwest Arkansas Community College
Sheridan, Rick — California State University-Chico
Silvers, Pamela — Asheville Buncombe Tech
Singer, Steven A. — University of Hawai'i, Kapi'olani Community College
Sinha, Atin — Albany State University
Skolnick, Martin — Florida Atlantic University
Smith, T. Michael — Austin Community College
Smith, Tammy — Tompkins Cortland Community Collge
Smolenski, Bob — Delaware County Community College
Spangler, Candice — Columbus State
Stedham, Vicki — St. Petersburg College, Clearwater
Stefanelli, Greg — Carroll Community College
Steiner, Ester — New Mexico State University
Stenlund, Neal — Northern Virginia Community College, Alexandria
St. John, Steve — Tulsa Community College

Sterling, Janet — Houston Community College
Stoughton, Catherine — Laramie County Community College
Sullivan, Angela — Joliet Junior College
Szurek, Joseph — University of Pittsburgh at Greensburg
Tarver, Mary Beth — Northwestern State University
Taylor, Michael — Seattle Central Community College
Thangiah, Sam — Slippery Rock University
Thompson-Sellers, Ingrid — Georgia Perimeter College
Tomasi, Erik — Baruch College
Toreson, Karen — Shoreline Community College
Trifiletti, John J. — Florida Community College at Jacksonville
Trivedi, Charulata — Quinsigamond Community College, Woodbridge
Tucker, William — Austin Community College
Turgeon, Cheryl — Asnuntuck Community College
Turpen, Linda — Central New Mexico Community College
Upshaw, Susan — Del Mar College
Unruh, Angela — Central Washington University
Vanderhoof, Dr. Glenna — Missouri State University-Springfield Campus
Vargas, Tony — El Paso Community College
Vicars, Mitzi — Hampton University
Villarreal, Kathleen — Fresno
Vitrano, Mary Ellen — Palm Beach Community College
Volker, Bonita — Tidewater Community College
Wahila, Lori (Mindy) — Tompkins Cortland Community College
Waswick, Kim — Southeast Community College, Nebraska
Wavle, Sharon — Tompkins Cortland Community College
Webb, Nancy — City College of San Francisco
Wells, Barbara E. — Central Carolina Technical College
Wells, Lorna — Salt Lake Community College
Welsh, Jean — Lansing Community College Nebraska
White, Bruce — Quinnipiac University
Willer, Ann — Solano Community College
Williams, Mark — Lane Community College
Wilson, Kit — Red River College
Wilson, Roger — Fairmont State University
Wimberly, Leanne — International Academy of Design and Technology
Worthington, Paula — Northern Virginia Community College
Yauney, Annette — Herkimer County Community College
Yip, Thomas — Passaic Community College
Zavala, Ben — Webster Tech
Zlotow, Mary Ann — College of DuPage
Zudeck, Steve — Broward Community College, North

About the Authors

Shelley Gaskin, Series Editor, is a professor of business and computer technology at Pasadena City College in Pasadena, California. She holds a master's degree in business education from Northern Illinois University and a doctorate in adult and community education from Ball State University. Dr. Gaskin has 15 years of experience in the computer industry with several Fortune 500 companies and has developed and written training materials for custom systems applications in both the public and private sector. She is also the author of books on Microsoft Outlook and word processing.

Kris Townsend is an Information Systems instructor at Spokane Falls Community College in Spokane, Washington, where he teaches computer applications, Internet programming, and digital forensics. Kris received his BA in Education and his BA in Business from Eastern Washington University with majors in Mathematics and Management Information Systems, respectively. He received his MA in Education from City University with an emphasis in Educational Technology. Kris has also worked as a public school teacher and as a systems analyst for a public school assessment department. In addition to teaching and authoring, Kris enjoys working with wood, snowboarding, and camping. He commutes to work by bike and enjoys long road rides in the Palouse country south of Spokane.

Suzanne Marks is a faculty member in Business Technology Systems at Bellevue Community College, Bellevue, Washington. She holds a bachelor's degree in business education from Washington State University, and was project manager for the first IT Skills Standards in the United States.

Visual Walk-Through of the *GO!* System

The *GO!* System is designed for ease of implementation on the instructor side and ease of understanding on the student. It has been completely developed based on professor and student feedback.

The *GO!* System is divided into three categories that reflect how you might organize your course—**Prepare**, **Teach**, and **Assess**.

Prepare

GO!

Because the GO! System was designed and written by instructors like yourself, it includes the tools that allow you to Prepare, Teach, and Assess in your course. We have organized the GO! System into these three categories that match how you work through your course and thus, it's even easier for you to implement.

To help you get started, here is an outline of the first activities you may want to do in order to conduct your course.

There are several other tools not listed here that are available in the GO! System so please refer to your GO! Guide for a complete listing of all the tools.

Prepare
1. Prepare the course syllabus
2. Plan the course assignments
3. Organize the student resources

Teach
4. Conduct demonstrations and lectures

Assess
5. Assign and grade assignments, quizzes, tests, and assessments

PREPARE

1. Prepare the course syllabus

A syllabus template is provided on the IRCD in the **go07_syllabus_template** folder of the main directory. It includes a course calendar planner for 8-week, 12-week, and 16-week formats. Depending on your term (summer or regular semester) you can modify one of these according to your course plan, and then add information pertinent to your course and institution.

2. Plan course assignments

For each chapter, an Assignment Sheet listing every in-chapter and end-of-chapter project is located on the IRCD within the **go01_go!office2007intro_instructor_resources_by_chapter** folder. From there, navigate to the specific chapter folder. These sheets are Word tables, so you can delete rows for the projects that you choose not to assign or add rows for your own assignments—if any. There is a column to add the number of points you want to assign to each project depending on your grading scheme. At the top of the sheet, you can fill in the course information.

Transitioning to GO! Office 2007   Page 1 of 1

NEW

Transition Guide

New to *GO!*–We've made it quick and easy to plan the format and activities for your class.

GO! with Microsoft Office 2007 Introductory
SAMPLE SYLLABUS (16 weeks)

I. COURSE INFORMATION

Course No.:   Semester:
Course Title: Credits:
Course Hours:

Instructor: Office:
Office Hours:
Email: Phone:

II. TEXT AND MATERIALS
Before starting the course, you will need the following:

> GO! with Microsoft Office 2007 Introductory by Shelley Gaskin, Robert L. Ferrett, Alicia Vargas, Suzanne Marks ©2007, published by Pearson Prentice Hall. ISBN 0-13-167990-6

> Storage device for saving files (any of the following: multiple diskettes, CD-RW, flash drive, etc.)

III. WHAT YOU WILL LEARN IN THIS COURSE
This is a hands-on course where you will learn to use a computer to practice the most commonly used Microsoft programs including the Windows operating system, Internet Explorer for navigating the Internet, Outlook for managing your personal information and the four most popular programs within the Microsoft Office Suite (Word, Excel, PowerPoint and Access). You will also practice the basics of using a computer, mouse and keyboard. You will learn to be an intermediate level user of the Microsoft Office Suite.

Within the Microsoft Office Suite, you will use Word, Excel, PowerPoint, and Access. Microsoft Word is a word processing program with which you can create common business and personal documents. Microsoft Excel is a spreadsheet program that organizes and calculates accounting-type information. Microsoft PowerPoint is a presentation graphics program with which you can develop slides to accompany an oral presentation. Finally, Microsoft Access is a database program that organizes large amounts of information in a useful manner.

Syllabus Template

Includes course calendar planner for 8-,12-, and 16-week formats.

Assignment Sheet

One per chapter. Lists all possible assignments; add to and delete from this simple Word table according to your course plan.

File Guide to the *GO!* Supplements

Tabular listing of all supplements and their file names.

NEW

Assignment Planning Guide

Description of *GO!* assignments with recommendations based on class size, delivery mode, and student needs. Includes examples from fellow instructors.

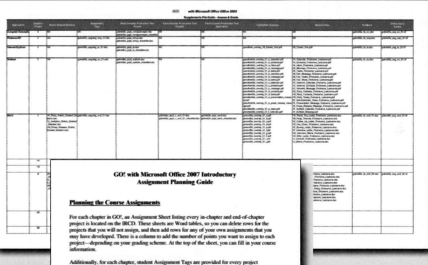

GO! with Microsoft Office 2007 Introductory
Assignment Planning Guide

Planning the Course Assignments

For each chapter in GO!, an Assignment Sheet listing every in-chapter and end-of-chapter project is located on the IRCD. These sheets are Word tables, so you can delete rows for the projects that you will not assign, and then add rows for any of your own assignments that you may have developed. There is a column to add the number of points you want to assign to each project—depending on your grading scheme. At the top of the sheet, you can fill in your course information.

Additionally, for each chapter, student Assignment Tags are provided for every project (including Problem Solving projects)—also located on the IRCD. These are small scoring checklists on which you can check off errors made by the student, and with which the student can verify that all project elements are complete. For campus classes, the student can attach the tags to his or her paper submissions. For online classes, many GO! instructors have the student include these with the electronic submission.

Deciding What to Assign

Front Portion of the Chapter—Instructional Projects: The projects in the front portion of the chapter, which are listed on the first page of each chapter, are the instructional projects. Most instructors assign all of these projects, because this is where the student receives the instruction and engages in the active learning.

End-of-Chapter—Practice and Critical Thinking Projects: In the back portion of the chapter (the gray pages), you can assign on a prescriptive basis; that is, for students who were challenged by the instructional projects, you might assign one or more projects from the two Skills Reviews, which provide maximum prompting and a thorough review of the entire chapter. For students who have previous software knowledge and who completed the instructional projects easily, you might assign only the Mastery Projects.

You can also assign prescriptively by Objective, because each end-of-chapter project indicates the Objectives covered. So you might assign, on a student-by-student basis, only the projects that cover the Objectives with which the student seemed to have difficulty in the instructional projects.

The five Problem Solving projects and the You and GO! project are the authentic assessments that pull together the student's learning. Here the student is presented with a "messy real-life situation" and then uses his or her knowledge and skill to solve a problem, produce a product, give a presentation, or demonstrate a procedure. You might assign one or more of the Problem

GO! Assignment Planning Guide   Page 1 of 1

Student Data Files

Music School Records discovers, launches, and and develops the careers of young artists in classical, jazz, and contemporary music. Our philosophy is to not only shape, distribute, and sell a music product, but to help artists create a career that can lats a lifetime. too often in the music industry, artists are forced to fit their music to a trend that is short-lived. Music School Records doesn't just follow trends, we take a long-term view of the music industry and help our artists develop a style and repertiore that is fluid and flexible and that will appeal to audiences for years and even decades.

The music industry is constantly changing, but over the last decade the changes have been enormous. New forms of entertainment such as DVDs, video games, and the Internet mean there are more competition for the leisure dollar in the market. New technologies give consomers more options for buying and listening to music, and they are demanding high quality recordings. Young consomers are comfortable with technology and want the music they love when and where they want it, no matter where they are or what they are doing.

Music School Records embraces new technologies and the sophisticated market of young music lovers. We believe that providing high quality recordings of truly talented artists make for more discerning listeners who will cherish the gift of music for the rest of their lives. The expertise of Music School Records includes:

- Insight into our target market and the ability to reach the desired audience
- The ability to access all current sources of music income
- A management team with years of experience in music commerce
- Innovative business strategies and artist development plans
- Investment in technology infrastructure for high quality recordings and business services
- Initiative and proactive management of artist careers

Online Study Guide for Students

Interactive objective-style questions based on chapter content.

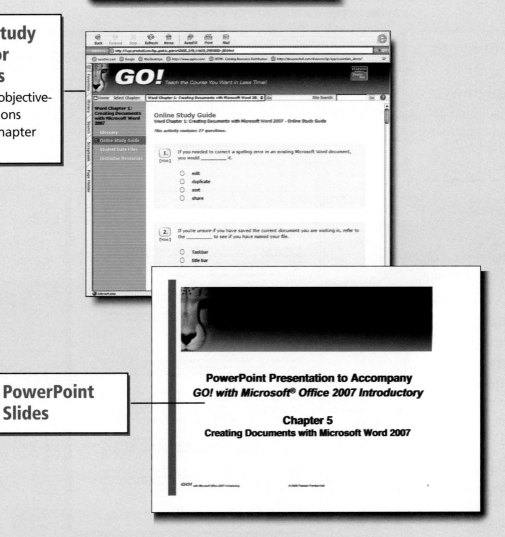

PowerPoint Slides

Learning Objectives and Student Outcomes

Objectives are clustered around projects that result in student outcomes. They help students learn how to solve problems, not just learn software features.

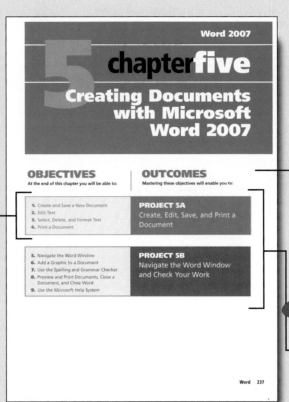

Project-Based Instruction

Students do not practice features of the application; they create real projects that they will need in the real world. Projects are color coded for easy reference and are named to reflect skills the students will be practicing.

A and B Projects

Each chapter contains two instructional projects—A and B.

Each chapter opens with a story that sets the stage for the projects the student will create; the instruction does not force the student to pretend to be someone or make up a scenario.

Each chapter has an introductory paragraph that briefs students on what is important.

Visual Summary

Shows students upfront what their projects will look like when they are done.

Project Summary

Stated clearly and quickly in one paragraph.

NEW

File Guide

Clearly shows students which files are needed for the project and the names they will use to save their documents.

Objective

The skills the student will learn are clearly stated at the beginning of each project and color coded to match projects listed on the chapter opener page.

Teachable Moment

KEY FEATURE

GO!

Expository text is woven into the steps—at the moment students need to know it—not chunked together in a block of text that will go unread.

NEW

Screen Shots

Larger screen shots.

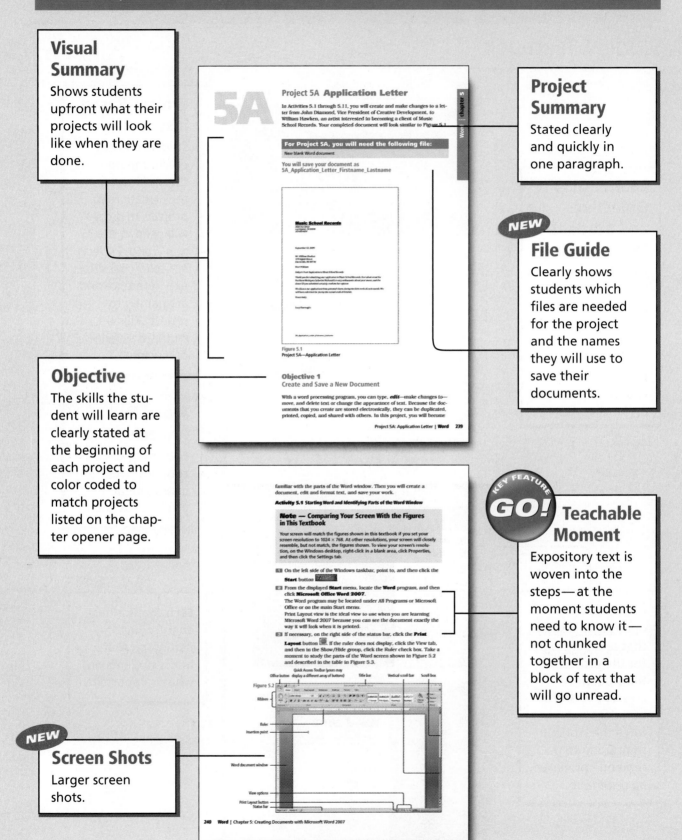

Steps

Color coded to the current project, easy to read, and not too many to confuse the student or too few to be meaningless.

GO! KEY FEATURE

Sequential Pagination

No more confusing letters and abbreviations.

GO! KEY FEATURE Microsoft Procedural Syntax

All steps are written in Microsoft Procedural Syntax to put the student in the right place at the right time.

End-of-Project Icon

All projects in the *GO! Series* have clearly identifiable end points, useful in self-paced or on-line environments.

Press [Enter] two more times.

In a business letter, insert two blank lines between the date and the inside address, which is the same as the address you would use on an envelope.

Type **Mr. William Hawken** and then press [Enter].

The wavy red line under the proper name *Hawken* indicates that the word has been flagged as misspelled because it is a word not contained in the Word dictionary.

On two lines, type the following address, but do not press [Enter] at the end of the second line:

123 Eighth Street
Harrisville, MI 48740

Note — Typing the Address

Include a comma after the city name in an inside address. However, for mailing addresses on envelopes, eliminate the comma after the city name.

On the **Home tab**, in the **Styles group**, click the **Normal** button.

The Normal style is applied to the text in the rest of the document. Recall that the Normal style adds extra space between paragraphs; it also adds slightly more space between lines in a paragraph.

Press [Enter]. Type **Dear William:** and then press [Enter].

This salutation is the line that greets the person receiving the letter.

Type **Subject: Your Application to Music School Records** and press [Enter]. Notice the light dots between words, which indicate spaces and display when formatting marks are displayed. Also, notice the extra space after each paragraph, and then compare your screen with Figure 5.6.

The subject line is optional, but you should include a subject line in most letters to identify the topic. Depending on your Word settings, a wavy green line may display in the subject line, indicating a potential grammar error.

Note — Space Between Lines in Your Printed Document

The Cambria font, and many others, uses a slightly larger space between the lines than more traditional fonts like Times New Roman. As you progress in your study of Word, you will use many different fonts and also adjust the spacing between lines.

From the **Office** menu, click **Close**, saving any changes if prompted to do so. Leave Word open for the next project.

Another Way | **To Print a Document**

To Print a document:

• From the Office menu, click Print to display the Print dialog box (to be covered later), from which you can choose a variety of different options, such as printing multiple copies, printing on a different printer, and printing some but not all pages.

• Hold down [Ctrl] and then press [P]. This is an alternative to the Office menu command, and opens the Print dialog box.

• Hold down [Alt], press [F], and then press [P]. This opens the Print dialog box.

End **You have completed Project 5A**

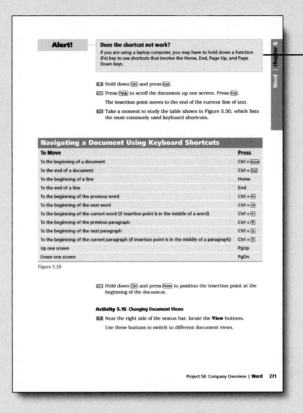

Alert box
Draws students' attention to make sure they aren't getting too far off course.

Another Way box
Shows students other ways of doing tasks.

More Knowledge box
Expands on a topic by going deeper into the material.

Note box
Points out important items to remember.

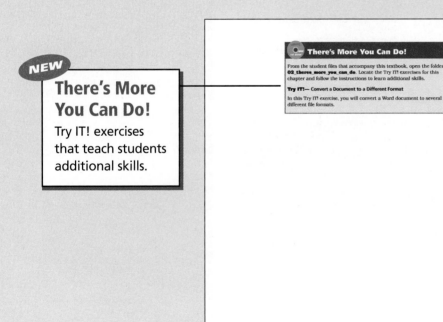

NEW

There's More You Can Do!
Try IT! exercises that teach students additional skills.

End-of-Chapter Material

Take your pick! Content-based or Outcomes-based projects to choose from. Below is a table outlining the various types of projects that fit into these two categories.

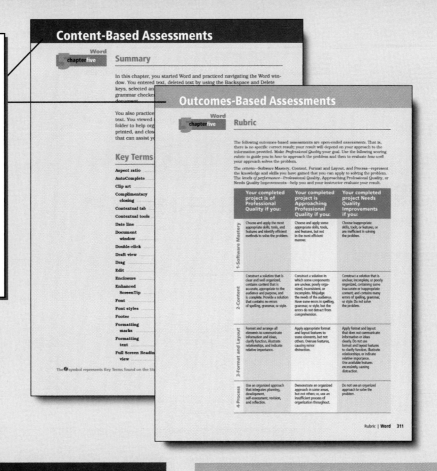

Content-Based Assessments
(Defined solutions with solution files provided for grading)

Project Letter	Name	Objectives Covered
N/A	Summary and Key Terms	
N/A	Multiple Choice	
N/A	Fill-in-the-blank	
C	Skills Review	Covers A Objectives
D	Skills Review	Covers B Objectives
E	Mastering Excel	Covers A Objectives
F	Mastering Excel	Covers B Objectives
G	Mastering Excel	Covers any combination of A and B Objectives
H	Mastering Excel	Covers any combination of A and B Objectives
I	Mastering Excel	Covers all A and B Objectives
J	Business Running Case	Covers all A and B Objectives

Outcomes-Based Assessments
(Open solutions that require a rubric for grading)

Project Letter	Name	Objectives Covered
N/A	Rubric	
K	Problem Solving	Covers as many Objectives from A and B as possible
L	Problem Solving	Covers as many Objectives from A and B as possible.
M	Problem Solving	Covers as many Objectives from A and B as possible.
N	Problem Solving	Covers as many Objectives from A and B as possible.
O	Problem Solving	Covers as many Objectives from A and B as possible.
P	You and GO!	Covers as many Objectives from A and B as possible
Q	GO! Help	Not tied to specific objectives
R	* Group Business Running Case	Covers A and B Objectives

* This project is provided only with the *GO! with Microsoft Office 2007 Introductory* book.

Objectives List

Most projects in the end-of-chapter section begin with a list of the objectives covered.

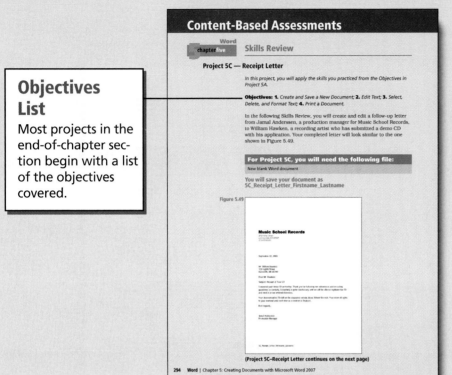

Content-Based Assessments

Word
chapter five **Skills Review**

Project 5C — Receipt Letter

In this project, you will apply the skills you practiced from the Objectives in Project 5A.

Objectives: 1. Create and Save a New Document; **2.** Edit Text; **3.** Select, Delete, and Format Text; **4.** Print a Document.

In the following Skills Review, you will create and edit a follow-up letter from Jamal Anderssen, a production manager for Music School Records, to William Hawken, a recording artist who has submitted a demo CD with his application. Your completed letter will look similar to the one shown in Figure 5.49.

For Project 5C, you will need the following file:
New blank Word document

You will save your document as
5C_Receipt_Letter_Firstname_Lastname

Figure 5.49

(Project 5C–Receipt Letter continues on the next page)

294 **Word** | Chapter 5: Creating Documents with Microsoft Word 2007

End of Each Project Clearly Marked

Clearly identified end points help separate the end-of-chapter projects.

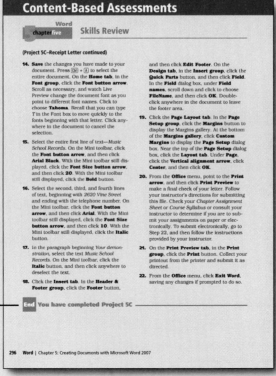

Content-Based Assessments

Word
chapter five **Skills Review**

(Project 5C–Receipt Letter continued)

14. Save the changes you have made to your document. Press Ctrl + A to select the entire document. On the **Home tab**, in the **Font group**, click the **Font button arrow**. Scroll as necessary, and watch Live Preview change the document font as you point to different font names. Click to choose **Tahoma**. Recall that you can type T in the Font box to move quickly to the fonts beginning with that letter. Click anywhere in the document to cancel the selection.

15. Select the entire first line of text—*Music School Records*. On the Mini toolbar, click the **Font button arrow**, and then click **Arial Black**. With the Mini toolbar still displayed, click the **Font Size button arrow**, and then click **20**. With the Mini toolbar still displayed, click the **Bold** button.

16. Select the second, third, and fourth lines of text, beginning with *2620 Vine Street* and ending with the telephone number. On the Mini toolbar, click the **Font button arrow**, and then click **Arial**. With the Mini toolbar still displayed, click the **Font Size button arrow**, and then click **10**. With the Mini toolbar still displayed, click the **Italic** button.

17. In the paragraph beginning *Your demonstration*, select the text *Music School Records*. On the Mini toolbar, click the **Italic** button, and then click anywhere to deselect the text.

18. Click the **Insert tab**. In the **Header & Footer group**, click the **Footer** button,

and then click **Edit Footer**. On the **Design tab**, in the **Insert group**, click the **Quick Parts** button, and then click **Field**. In the **Field** dialog box, under **Field names**, scroll down and click to choose **FileName**, and then click **OK**. Double-click anywhere in the document to leave the footer area.

19. Click the **Page Layout tab**. In the **Page Setup group**, click the **Margins** button to display the Margins gallery. At the bottom of the **Margins gallery**, click **Custom Margins** to display the **Page Setup** dialog box. Near the top of the **Page Setup** dialog box, click the **Layout tab**. Under **Page**, click the **Vertical alignment arrow**, click **Center**, and then click **OK**.

20. From the **Office** menu, point to the **Print arrow**, and then click **Print Preview** to make a final check of your letter. Follow your instructor's directions for submitting this file. Check your *Chapter Assignment Sheet* or *Course Syllabus* or consult your instructor to determine if you are to submit your assignments on paper or electronically. To submit electronically, go to Step 22, and then follow the instructions provided by your instructor.

21. On the **Print Preview tab**, in the **Print group**, click the **Print** button. Collect your printout from the printer and submit it as directed.

22. From the **Office** menu, click **Exit Word**, saving any changes if prompted to do so.

End **You have completed Project 5C**

296 **Word** | Chapter 5: Creating Documents with Microsoft Word 2007

Teach (continued)

NEW

Rubric

A matrix that states the criteria and standards for grading student work. Used to grade open-ended assessments.

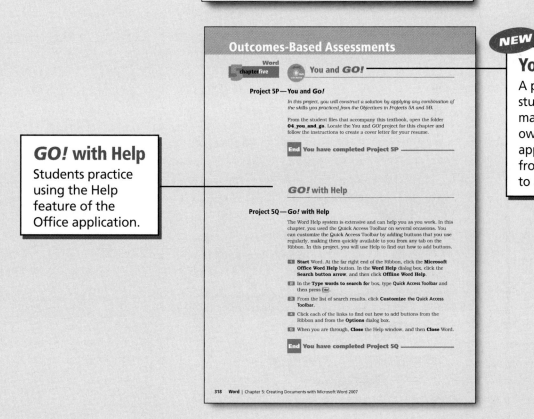

GO! with Help

Students practice using the Help feature of the Office application.

NEW

You and GO!

A project in which students use information from their own lives and apply the skills from the chapter to a personal task.

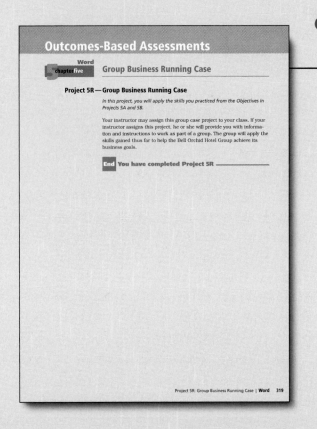

Group Business Running Case

A continuing project developed for groups that spans the chapters within each application.

Student CD includes:

- Student Data Files
- There's More You Can Do!
- Business Running Case
- You and *GO!*

Companion Web site

An interactive Web site to further student leaning.

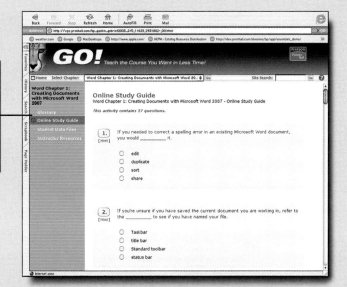

Online Study Guide

Interactive objective-style questions to help students study.

Annotated Instructor Edition

The Annotated Instructor Edition contains a full version of the student textbook that includes tips, supplement references, and pointers on teaching with the *GO!* instructional system.

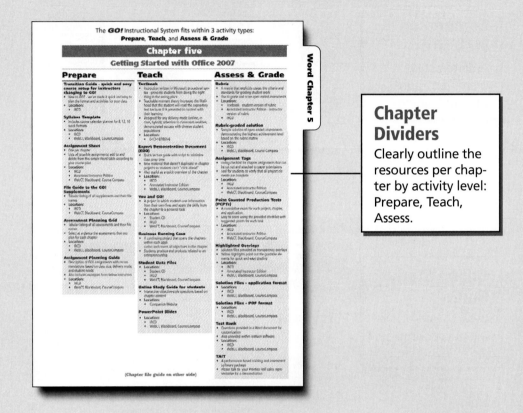

Chapter Dividers

Clearly outline the resources per chapter by activity level: Prepare, Teach, Assess.

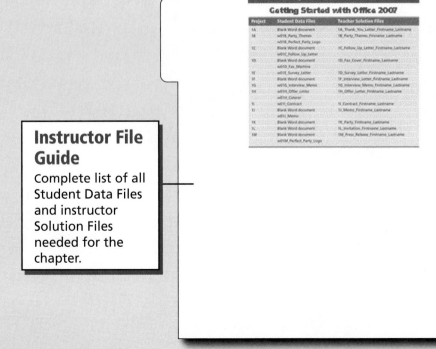

Instructor File Guide

Complete list of all Student Data Files and instructor Solution Files needed for the chapter.

Helpful Hints, Teaching Tips, Expand the Project

References correspond to what is being taught in the student textbook.

NEW

Full-Size Textbook Pages

An instructor copy of the textbook with traditional Instructor Manual content incorporated.

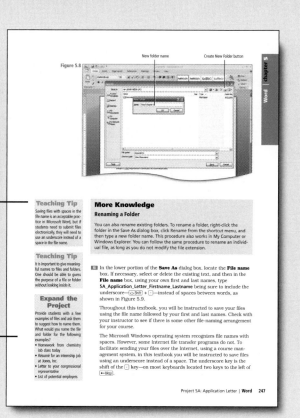

Teaching Tip

Saving files with spaces in the file name is an acceptable practice in Microsoft Word, but if students need to submit files electronically, they will need to use an underscore instead of a space in the file name.

Teaching Tip

It is important to give meaningful names to files and folders. One should be able to guess the purpose of a file or folder without looking inside it.

Expand the Project

Provide students with a few examples of files and ask them to suggest how to name them. What would you name the file and folder for the following examples?
- Homework from chemistry lab class today
- Résumé for an internship job at Jones, Inc.
- Letter to your congressional representative
- List of potential employers

More Knowledge

Renaming a Folder

You can also rename existing folders. To rename a folder, right-click the folder in the Save As dialog box, click Rename from the shortcut menu, and then type a new folder name. This procedure also works in My Computer or Windows Explorer. You can follow the same procedure to rename an individual file, as long as you do not modify the file extension.

In the lower portion of the **Save As** dialog box, locate the **File name** box. If necessary, select or delete the existing text, and then in the **File name** box, using your own first and last names, type **5A_Application_Letter_Firstname_Lastname** being sure to include the underscore—Shift + _ —instead of spaces between words, as shown in Figure 5.9.

Throughout this textbook, you will be instructed to save your files using the file name followed by your first and last names. Check with your instructor to see if there is some other file-naming arrangement for your course.

The Microsoft Windows operating system recognizes file names with spaces. However, some Internet file transfer programs do not. To facilitate sending your files over the Internet, using a course management system, in this textbook you will be instructed to save files using an underscore instead of a space. The underscore key is the shift of the _ key—on most keyboards located two keys to the left of Bksp.

Project 5A: Application Letter | Word 247

End-of-Chapter Concepts Assessments

contain the answers for quick reference.

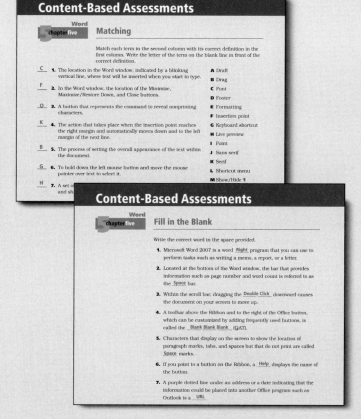

Content-Based Assessments

Word chapter five

Matching

Match each term in the second column with its correct definition in the first column. Write the letter of the term on the blank line in front of the correct definition.

_C_ **1.** The location in the Word window, indicated by a blinking vertical line, where text will be inserted when you start to type.

_F_ **2.** In the Word window, the location of the Minimize, Maximize/Restore Down, and Close buttons.

_O_ **3.** A button that represents the command to reveal nonprinting characters.

_K_ **4.** The action that takes place when the insertion point reaches the right margin and automatically moves down and to the left margin of the next line.

_B_ **5.** The process of setting the overall appearance of the text within the document.

_G_ **6.** To hold down the left mouse button and move the mouse pointer over text to select it.

_H_ **7.** A set of ...

A Draft
B Drag
C Font
D Footer
E Formatting
F Insertion point
G Keyboard shortcut
H Live preview
I Point
J Sans serif
K Serif
L Shortcut menu
M Show/Hide ¶

Content-Based Assessments

Word chapter five

Fill in the Blank

Write the correct word in the space provided.

1. Microsoft Word 2007 is a word _Right_ program that you can use to perform tasks such as writing a memo, a report, or a letter.

2. Located at the bottom of the Word window, the bar that provides information such as page number and word count is referred to as the _Space_ bar.

3. Within the scroll bar, dragging the _Double Click_ downward causes the document on your screen to move up.

4. A toolbar above the Ribbon and to the right of the Office button, which can be customized by adding frequently used buttons, is called the _Blank Blank Blank_ (QAT).

5. Characters that display on the screen to show the location of paragraph marks, tabs, and spaces but that do not print are called _Space_ marks.

6. If you point to a button on the Ribbon, a _Help_ displays the name of the button.

7. A purple dotted line under an address or a date indicating that the information could be placed into another Office program such as Outlook is a _URL_

NEW

Rubric

A matrix to guide the student on how they will be assessed is reprinted in the Annotated Instructor Edition with suggested weights for each of the criteria and levels of performance. Instructors can modify the weights to suit their needs.

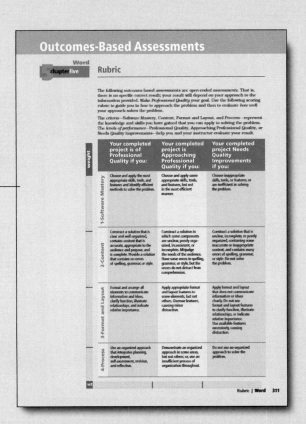

Assignment Tags

NEW

Scoring checklist for assignments. Now also available for Problem-Solving projects.

Highlighted Overlays

Solution files provided as transparency overlays. Yellow highlights point out the gradable elements for quick and easy grading.

GO! with Microsoft® Office 2007

Assignment Tags for GO! with Office 2007
Word Chapter 5

Name:	Project:	5A	Name:	Project:	5B
Professor:	Course:		Professor:	Course:	
Task	Points	Your Score	Task	Points	Your Score
Center text vertically on page	2		Insert the file w05B_Music_School_Records	4	
Delete the word "really"	1		Insert the Music Logo	4	
Delete the words "try to"	1		Remove duplicate "and"	2	
Replace "last" with "first"	1		Change spelling and grammar errors (4)	8	
Insert the word "potential"	1		Correct/Add footer as instructed	2	
Replace "John W. Diamond" with "Lucy Burrows"	2		Circled information is incorrect or formatted incorrectly		
Change entire document to the Cambria font	2				
Change the first line of text to Arial Black 20 pt. font	2				
Bold the first line of text	2				
Change the 2nd through 4th lines to Arial 10 pt.	2				
Italicize the 2nd through 4th lines of text	2				
Correct/Add footer as instructed	2				
Circled information is incorrect or formatted incorrectly					
Total Points	20	0	**Total Points**	20	0
Name:	Project:	5C	Name:	Project:	5D
Professor:	Course:		Professor:	Course:	
Task	Points	Your Score	Task	Points	Your Score
Add four line letterhead	2		Insert the file w05D_Marketing	4	
Insert today's date	1		Bold the first two title lines	2	
Add address block, subject line, and greeting	2		Correct spelling of "Marketing"	2	
Add two-paragraph body of letter	2		Correct spelling of "genres"	2	
Add closing, name, and title	2		Correct all misspellings of "allready"	2	
In subject line, capitalize "receipt"	1		Correct grammar error "are" to "is"	2	
Change "standards" to "guidelines"	1		Insert the Piano image	4	
Insert "quite"	1		Correct/add footer as instructed	2	
Insert "all"	1		Circled information is incorrect or formatted incorrectly		
Change the first line of text to Arial Black 20 pt. font	2				
Bold the first line of text	1				
Change the 2nd through 4th lines to Arial 10 pt.	1				
Italicize the 2nd through 4th lines of text	1				
Correct/add footer as instructed	2				
Circled information is incorrect or formatted incorrectly					
Total Points	20	0	**Total Points**	20	0

Music School Records

20 point Arial Black, bold and underline

2620 Vine Street
Los Angeles, CA 90028
323-555-0028

10 point Arial, italic

September 12, 2009

Mr. William Hawken
123 Eighth Street
Harrisville, MI 48740

Text vertically centered on page

Body of document changed to Cambria font, 11 point

Dear William:

Subject: Your Application to Music School Records

Thank you for submitting your application to Music School Records. Our talent scout for Northern Michigan, Catherine McDonald, is very enthusiastic about your music, and the demo CD you submitted certainly confirms her opinion.

Word "really" deleted

We discuss our applications from potential clients during the first week of each month. We will have a decision for you by the second week of October.

Yours Truly,

Words "try to" deleted

Lucy Burroughs

Point-Counted Production Tests (PCPTs)

A cumulative exam for each **project**, **chapter**, and **application**. Easy to score using the provided checklist with suggested points for each task.

GO! with Microsoft® Office 2007 Introductory

Point-Counted Production Test—Project for GO! with Microsoft® Office 2007 Introductory Project 5A

Instructor Name: _____
Course Information: _____

1. Start Word 2007 to begin a new blank document. Save your document as 5A_Cover_Letter_Firstname_Lastname Remember to save your file frequently as you work.

2. If necessary, display the formatting marks. With the insertion point blinking in the upper left corner of the document to the left of the default first paragraph mark, type the current date (you can use AutoComplete).

3. Press Enter three times and type the inside address:

   Music School Records
   2820 Vine Street
   Los Angeles, CA 90028

4. Press Enter three times, and type Dear Ms. Burroughs:

   Press Enter twice, and type Subject: Application to Music School Records

   Press Enter twice, and type the following text (skipping one line between paragraphs):

   I read about Music School Records in Con Brio magazine and I would like to inquire about the possibility of being represented by your company.

   I am very interested in a career in jazz and am planning to relocate to the Los Angeles area in the very near future. I would be interested in learning more about the company and about available opportunities.

   I was a member of my high school jazz band for three years. In addition, I have been playing in the local coffee shop for the last two years. My demo CD, which is enclosed, contains three of my most requested songs.

   I would appreciate the opportunity to speak with you. Thank you for your time and consideration. I look forward to speaking with you about this exciting opportunity.

5. Press Enter three times, and type the closing Sincerely, Press enter four times, and type your name.

6. Insert a footer that contains the file name.

7. Delete the first instance of the word very in the second body paragraph, and insert the word modern in front of jazz.

Copyright © 2008 Pearson Prentice Hall

Page 1 of 1

Test Bank

Available as TestGen Software or as a Word document for customization.

Chapter 5: Creating Documents with Microsoft Word 2007

Multiple Choice:

1. With word processing programs, how are documents stored?

   A. On a network

   B. On the computer

   C. Electronically

   D. On the floppy disk

Answer: C   **Reference:** Objective 1: Create and Save a New Document   **Difficulty:** Moderate

2. Because you will see the document as it will print, _____ view is the ideal view to use when learning Microsoft Word 2007.

   A. Reading

   B. Normal

   C. Print Layout

   D. Outline

Answer: C   **Reference:** Objective 1: Create and Save a New Document   **Difficulty:** Moderate

3. The blinking vertical line where text or graphics will be inserted is called the:

   A. cursor.

   B. insertion point.

   C. blinking line.

   D. I-beam.

Answer: B   **Reference:** Objective 1: Create and Save a New Document   **Difficulty:** Easy

Music School Records

Music School Records discovers, launches, and develops the careers of young artists in classical, jazz, and contemporary music. Our philosophy is to not only shape, distribute, and sell a music product, but to help artists create a career that can last a lifetime. Too often in the music industry, artists are forced to fit their music to a trend that is short-lived. Music School Records does not just follow trends, we take a long-term view of the music industry and help our artists develop a style and repertoire that is fluid and flexible and that will appeal to audiences for years and even decades.

The music industry is constantly changing, but over the last decade, the changes have been enormous. New forms of entertainment such as DVDs, video games, and the Internet mean there is more competition for the leisure dollar in the market. New technologies give consumers more options for buying and listening to music, and they are demanding high quality recordings. Young consumers are comfortable with technology and want the music they love when and where they want it, no matter where they are or what they are doing.

Music School Records embraces new technologies and the sophisticated market of young music lovers. We believe that providing high quality recordings of truly talented artists make for more discerning listeners who will cherish the gift of music for the rest of their lives. The expertise of Music School Records includes:

- Insight into our target market and the ability to reach the desired audience
- The ability to access all current sources of music income
- A management team with years of experience in music commerce
- Innovative business strategies and artist development plans
- Investment in technology infrastructure for high quality recordings and business services

pagexxxix_top.docx

Solution Files–Application and PDF format

Online Assessment and Training

my**it**lab is Prentice Hall's new performance-based solution that allows you to easily deliver outcomes-based courses on Microsoft Office 2007, with customized training and defensible assessment. Key features of my**it**lab include:

A *true* "system" approach: my**it**lab content is the same as in your textbook.
Project-based *and* skills-based: Students complete real-life assignments.
Advanced reporting *and* gradebook: These include student click stream data.
***No* installation required:** my**it**lab is completely Web-based. You just need an Internet connection, small plug-in, and Adobe Flash Player.

Ask your Prentice Hall sales representative for a demonstration or visit:

www.prenhall.com/myitlab

1 chapterone

Getting Started with Access Databases and Tables

OBJECTIVES

At the end of this chapter you will be able to:

1. Start Access and Create a New Blank Database
2. Add Records to a Table
3. Rename Table Fields in Datasheet View
4. Modify the Design of a Table
5. Add a Second Table to a Database
6. Print a Table
7. Create and Use a Query
8. Create and Use a Form
9. Create and Print a Report
10. Close and Save a Database

11. Create a Database Using a Template
12. Organize Database Objects in the Navigation Pane
13. Create a New Table in a Database Created with a Template
14. View a Report and Print a Table in a Database Created with a Template
15. Use the Access Help System

OUTCOMES

Mastering these objectives will enable you to:

PROJECT 1A
Create a New Blank Database

PROJECT 1B
Create a Database from a Template

Texas Lakes Medical Center

Texas Lakes Medical Center is an urban hospital serving the city of Austin and surrounding Travis County, an area with a population of over 1 million people. Texas Lakes is renowned for its cardiac care unit, which is rated among the top 10 in Texas. The hospital also offers state-of-the-art maternity and diagnostic services, a children's center, a Level II trauma center, and a number of specialized outpatient services. Physicians, nurses, scientists, and researchers from around the world come together at Texas Lakes to provide the highest quality patient care.

Getting Started with Access Databases and Tables

Do you have a collection of belongings that you like, such as a coin or stamp collection, a box of favorite recipes, or a stack of music CDs? Do you have an address book with the names, addresses, and phone numbers of your friends, business associates, and family members? If you collect something, chances are you have made an attempt to keep track of and organize the items in your collection. If you have an address book, you have probably wished it was better organized. A program like Microsoft Office Access can help you organize and keep track of information.

Microsoft Office Access 2007 is a program to organize a collection of related information about a particular topic, such as an inventory list, a list of people in an organization, or the students who are enrolled in classes in a college. Whether you use Access for personal or business purposes, it is a powerful program that helps you organize, search, sort, retrieve, and present information about a particular subject in an organized manner.

Project 1A **Doctor and Patient Contact Information**

In Activities 1.1 through 1.14, you will assist June Liu, Chief Administrative Officer at Texas Lakes Medical Center, in creating a new database for tracking the contact information for doctors and patients. June has a list of doctors and their contact information and a list of patients and their contact information. Using June's lists, you will create an Access database to track this information and use it to prepare a report. Your results will look similar to Figure 1.1.

For Project 1A, you will need the following file:

New blank Access database

You will save your database as
1A_Contact_Information_Firstname_Lastname

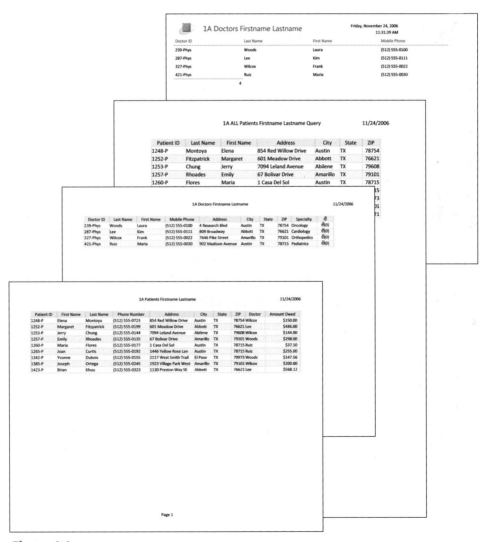

Figure 1.1
Project 1A—Contact Information

Objective 1
Start Access and Create a New Blank Database

A *database* collects and organizes *data*—facts about people, events, things, or ideas—related to a particular topic or purpose. Data that has been organized in a useful manner is referred to as *information*.

Many databases start as a simple list on paper, in a Word document, or in an Excel spreadsheet. As the list grows bigger and the data becomes more difficult to keep track of, it is a good idea to transfer the data to a database management system (*DBMS*) such as Access.

Examples of data that could be in a database include the titles and artists of all the CDs in a collection or the names and addresses of all the doctors and patients at a medical facility. A database includes not only the data, but also the tools for organizing the data in a way that is useful to you.

The first step in creating a new database from data that you already have is to plan your database on paper. Determine what information you want to track, and then ask yourself, *What questions should this database be able to answer for me?*

For example, in the Contact Information database for the Texas Lakes Medical Center, the questions to be answered may include:

• How many doctors and patients are there at the Texas Lakes Medical Center?

• Which and how many patients live in Austin?

• Is any doctor or patient listed twice?

• Which and how many patients have a balance owed?

Activity 1.1 Starting Access, Creating and Naming a Folder, and Creating a Database from a New Blank Database

There are two methods to create a new Access database: create a new database using a *template*—a preformatted database designed for a specific purpose—or create a new *blank database*. A blank database has no data and has no database tools; you create the data and the tools as you need them. In this activity, you will create a new blank database.

Regardless of which method you use, you must name and save the database before you can create any *objects* in the database. Objects are the basic parts of a database; you will create objects to store your data and work with your data. Think of an Access database as a container for the database objects that you will create.

1 On the left side of the Windows taskbar, click the **Start** button

【 start 】, determine where the **Access** program is located, point to **Microsoft Office Access 2007**, and then click one time to open the program. Take a moment to compare your screen with Figure 1.2 and study the parts of the Microsoft Access window described in the table in Figure 1.3.

From this Access starting point, you can open an existing database, start a new blank database, or begin a new database from one of the available database templates.

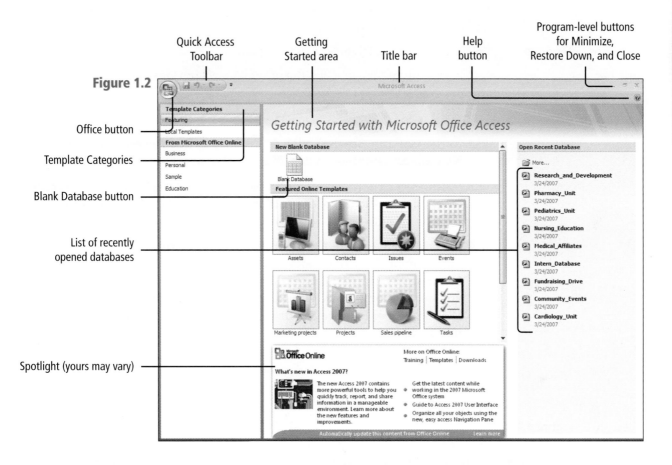

Figure 1.2

The Access Getting Started Screen

Window Part	Description
Blank Database button	Starts a new blank database.
Getting Started area	Contains the starting point to begin a New Blank Database or view new information from Microsoft Office Online.
Help button	Displays the Access Help window.
Open Recent Database	Displays a list of the most recently opened databases on the computer at which you are working.
Office button	Displays a menu of commands related to things you can do *with* a database, such as opening, saving, printing, or managing.
Program-level buttons for Minimize, Restore Down, and Close	Minimizes, restores, or closes the Access program.

(Continued)

Window Part	Description
Quick Access Toolbar	Displays buttons to perform frequently used commands with a single click. Frequently used commands in Access include Save, Undo, and Redo. You can add commands that you use frequently to the Quick Access Toolbar.
Spotlight	Displays the latest online content, such as new templates, articles about Access, and tips from Microsoft's Web site.
Template Categories	Displays a list of available database templates.
Title bar	Displays the program name and the program-level buttons.

Figure 1.3

2 In the **Getting Started with Microsoft Office Access** area, under **New Blank Database**, click **Blank Database**.

3 In the lower right portion of the screen, to the right of the **File Name** box, point to the **open file folder icon** to display the words *Browse for a location to put your database*, and then click the file folder icon.

4 In the displayed **File New Database** *dialog box*—a window containing commands or that asks you to make a decision—click the **Save in arrow**. From the displayed list, navigate to the drive where you are storing your projects for this chapter, for example, *Removable Disk (J:) drive*. Be sure the drive name and letter display in the **Save in** box, and then compare your screen with Figure 1.4.

File New Database dialog box   Create New Folder button

Figure 1.4

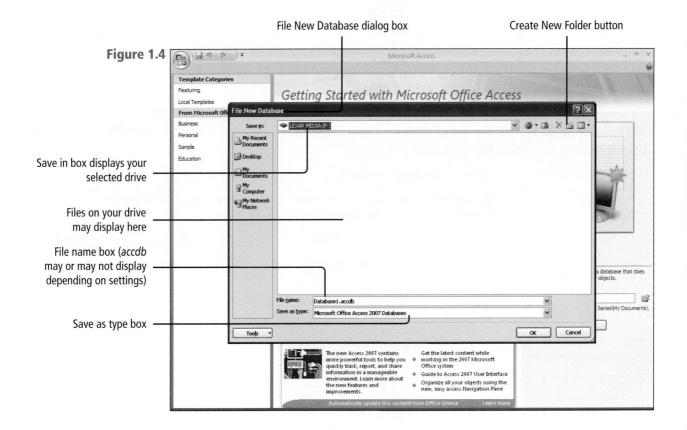

Save in box displays your selected drive

Files on your drive may display here

File name box (*accdb* may or may not display depending on settings)

Save as type box

5 In the upper right corner of the **File New Database** dialog box, click the **Create New Folder** button ⬚. In the displayed **New Folder** dialog box, type **Access Chapter 1** and then click **OK**. At the bottom of the dialog box, in the **File name** box, select the existing text, and then type **1A_Contact_Information_Firstname_Lastname** Press Enter, and then compare your screen with Figure 1.5.

Text that you select is replaced by new text that you type. The Microsoft Windows operating system recognizes file names with spaces. However, some Internet file transfer programs do not. To facilitate sending your files over the Internet, in this textbook you will save files using an underscore rather than a space. On most keyboards, the underscore key is the shift of the hyphen key, which is to the right of the zero key.

Figure 1.5

.accdb file extension

File Name box with your database name

Drive and folder where your database is stored

Create button

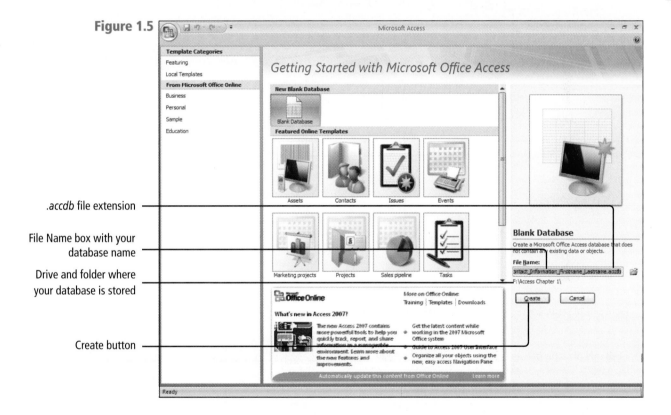

6 In the lower right corner, click the **Create** button, compare your screen with Figure 1.6, and then take a moment to study the screen elements described in the table in Figure 1.7.

Access creates the new database and opens a ***table*** named *Table1*. A table is the Access object that stores your data organized in an arrangement of columns and rows. Recall that *object* is the term used to refer to the parts of an Access database that you will use to store and work with your data.

Table objects are the foundation of your Access database because tables store the actual data.

Note — Comparing Your Screen with the Figures in This Textbook

Your screen will match the figures shown in this textbook if you set your screen resolution to 1024 × 768. At other resolutions, your screen will closely resemble, but not match, the figures shown. To view your screen's resolution, on the Windows desktop, right-click in a blank area, click Properties, and then click the Settings tab.

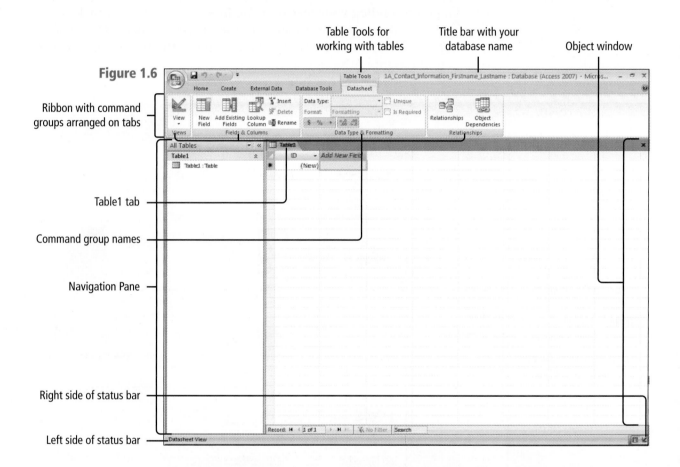

Table Tools for working with tables

Title bar with your database name

Object window

Figure 1.6

Ribbon with command groups arranged on tabs

Table1 tab

Command group names

Navigation Pane

Right side of status bar

Left side of status bar

Parts of the Access Window

Window Part	Description
Command group names	Contains groups of related command buttons associated with the selected command tab.
Left side of status bar	Indicates the active view and the status of actions occurring within the database.
Navigation Pane	Displays the database objects; from here you open the database objects to display in the object window at the right.
Object window	Displays the open table object.
Ribbon with command groups arranged on tabs	Groups the commands for performing related database tasks on tabs.
Right side of status bar	Provides buttons to switch between Datasheet View and Design View.
Table Tools for working with tables	Provides tools for working with a table object; Table Tools display only when a table is displayed.
Table1 tab	Enables you to select the table object.
Title bar with your database name	Displays the name of your database.

Figure 1.7

7 Leave your database open for the next activity.

Objective 2
Add Records to a Table

After you have saved and named the database, the next step is to plan and create the tables in which to record your data. Recall that tables are the foundation of your database because the actual data is stored there.

Limit the data in each table to one subject. For example, think of all the data at your college; there is likely one table for student information, another table for course information, another table for classroom information, and so on.

Within each table, create columns that are broken down into the smallest usable part. For example, instead of a complete address, break the address down into a part for the street address, a part for the city, a part for the state, and a part for the postal code. With small usable parts, you can, for example, find all of the people who live in a particular city or state or postal code.

To answer all the questions you want your database to answer, in this project you will create a database with two tables. One table will list the names and contact information for patients at Texas Lakes Medical Center and the other table will list the names and contact information for doctors at Texas Lakes Medical Center.

Activity 1.2 Adding Records to a Table

In a table object, each column contains a category of data called a *field*. Fields are categories that describe each piece of data stored in the table. You can add the field names, which display at the top of each column of the table, before or while you are entering your data. Each row in a table contains a **record**—all of the categories of data pertaining to one person, place, thing, event, or idea. Your *table design* refers to the number of fields, the names of fields, and the type of content within a field, for example numbers or text.

There are two ways to view a table—in **Datasheet view** or in **Design view**. Datasheet view displays the table data organized in a format of columns and rows similar to an Excel spreadsheet. Design view displays the underlying structure of the table object.

When you buy a new address book, it is not very useful until you fill it with names, addresses, and phone numbers. Likewise, a new database is not useful until you **populate**, or fill, a table with data. You can populate a table with records by typing data directly into the table.

In this activity, you will populate a table in Datasheet view that will list contact information for patients at Texas Lakes Medical Center.

1 Look at your screen and notice that the Datasheet view for a table displays. Then, take a moment to study the elements of the table object window as shown in Figure 1.8.

When you create a new blank database, only one object—a new blank table—is created. You will create the remaining database objects as you need them.

Because you have not yet named this table, the Table tab indicates the default name *Table1*. Access creates the first field and names it *ID*. In the ID field, Access will assign a unique sequential number—each number incremented by one—to each record as you type it into the table.

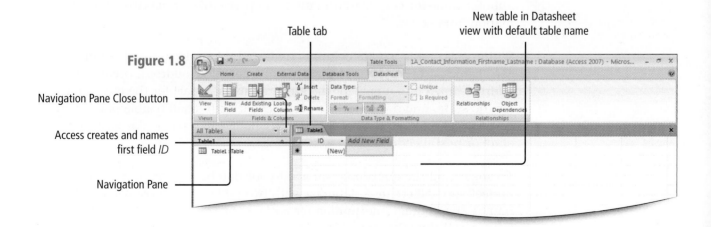

Figure 1.8

Table tab

New table in Datasheet view with default table name

Navigation Pane Close button

Access creates and names first field *ID*

Navigation Pane

2 In the **Navigation Pane**, click the **Open/Close** button ⟪ to collapse the **Navigation Pane** into a narrow bar at the left side of your screen.

Collapsing the Navigation Pane in this manner gives you more screen space in which to work with your database.

3 In the second column, click in the **cell**—the box formed by the inter-section of a row and a column—under *Add New Field*, type **Elena** and then press [Tab] or [Enter]. Click in the **ID** field. On the **Datasheet tab**, in the **Data Type & Formatting group**, click the **Data Type arrow**, and then click **Text**. Type **1248-P** and then to the right of *Elena*, click in the **Add New Field** cell, and type **L** Press [Tab]. Compare your screen with Figure 1.9.

As soon as information is entered, Access assigns the name *Field1* to the field and enters an AutoNumber of 1 in the ID field. The ID field is automatically created by Access. By default, Access creates this field for all new tables and sets the data type for the field to **AutoNumber**, which sequentially numbers each entry. Changing the ID field data type from *AutoNumber* to *Text* lets you enter a custom patient number. As you enter data, Access assigns Field names as *Field1*, *Field2*, and so on; you can rename the fields when it is conve-nient for you to do so.

The pencil icon in the **record selector box**—the small box at the left of a record in Datasheet view which, when clicked, selects the entire record—indicates that a new record is being entered.

Field named *Field1*

Figure 1.9

Pencil icon indicates a new record is being entered

Record selector box

First patient ID is *1248-P*

First name of first patient entered

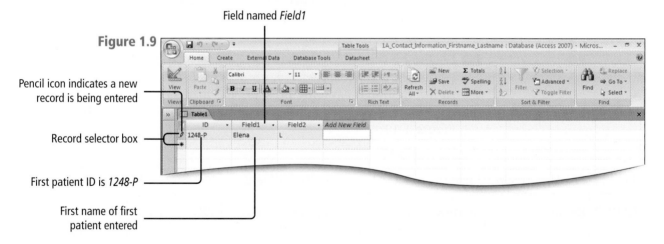

4 With the insertion point positioned in the fourth column, in the cell under *Add New Field*, type **Montoya** and then press [Tab] or [Enter].

5 Type **(512) 555-0723** and then press [Enter]. Type **854 Red Willow Drive** and then press [Enter] to form *Field5*.

Do not be concerned if the data does not completely display in the column. As you progress in your study of Access, you will adjust the column widths so that you can view the data.

6 Type **Austin** and then press [Enter] to form *Field6*. Type **TX** and then press [Enter] to form *Field7*.

7 Type **78754** and then press [Enter] to form *Field8*. Type **Wilcox** and then press [Enter] to form *Field9*. Type **150** and then press [Enter] two times. Compare your screen with Figure 1.10.

To move across the row, you can press [Tab] or [Enter]. Pressing [Enter] two times moves the insertion point to the next row to begin a new record. As soon as you move to the next row, the record is saved— you do not have to take any specific action to save the record.

First record entered

Figure 1.10

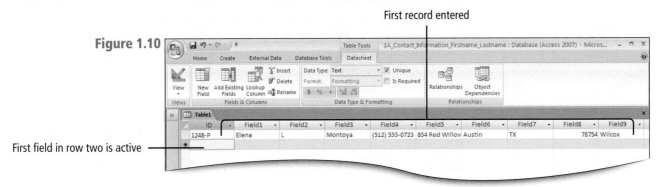

First field in row two is active

Note — Correct Typing Errors by Using Techniques Similar to Documents and Worksheets

If you make a mistake while entering data, you can correct the error by using [←Bksp] to remove characters to the left, [Delete] to remove characters to the right, or select the text you want to replace and type the correct information. You can also press [Esc] to exit out of a new record.

8 Beginning with the record for *Margaret E Fitzpatrick*, and using the technique you just practiced, enter the contact information for three additional patients, pressing [Enter] as necessary after entering the information in *Field10*. Then compare your screen with Figure 1.11.

ID	Field1	Field2	Field3	Field4	Field5	Field6	Field7	Field8	Field9	Field10
1248-P	Elena	L	Montoya	(512) 555-0723	854 Red Willow Drive	Austin	TX	78754	Wilcox	150
1252-P	Margaret	E	Fitzpatrick	(512) 555-0199	601 Meadow Drive	Abbott	TX	76621	Lee	486
1253-P	Jerry	R	Chung	(512) 555-0144	7094 Leland Avenue	Abilene	TX	79608	Wilcox	144
1257-P	Emily	A	Rhoades	(512) 555-0135	67 Bolivar Drive	Amarillo	TX	79101	Woods	298

Field 10 out of view (your screen may
vary in how many columns are shown)

Figure 1.11

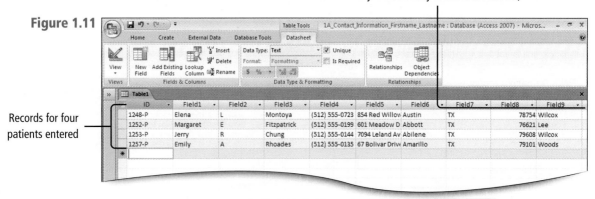

Records for four
patients entered

More Knowledge
Format for Typing Telephone Numbers in Access

Access does not require any specific format for entering telephone numbers
in a database. The examples in this project use the format used in Microsoft
Outlook. Using such a format facilitates easy transfer of Outlook information
to and from Access.

Objective 3
Rename Table Fields in Datasheet View

Recall that each column in a table contains a category of data called a
field, and that field names display at the top of each column of the table.
Recall also that each row contains a *record*—all of the data pertaining to
one person, place, thing, event, or idea—and that each record is broken
up into small parts—the *fields*.

Activity 1.3 Renaming the Fields In a Table in Datasheet View

In this activity, you will rename fields in your table to give the fields more
meaningful names.

1 At the top of the second column, point to the text *Field1* to display

the ⬇ pointer and click. Compare your screen with Figure 1.12.

Figure 1.12

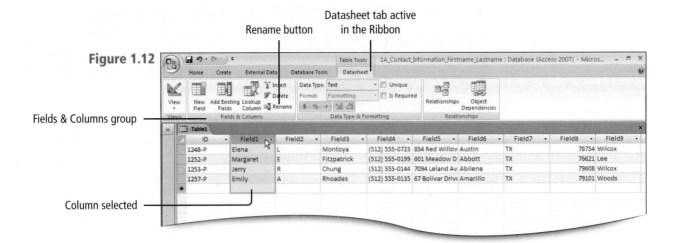

Fields & Columns group

Column selected

■2■ On the Ribbon, notice that **Table Tools** display above the **Datasheet tab**. In the **Fields & Columns group**, click the **Rename** button, and notice that the text *Field1* is selected.

■3■ Type **First Name** as the field name, and then press [Enter]. Point to the text *Field2*, click to select the column, and then in the **Fields & Columns group**, click the **Rename** button. Type **Middle Initial** and then press [Enter].

■4■ Point to the text *Field3* and *double-click* to select the text. With the text selected, type **Last Name** and then press [Enter]. Point to the text *Field4* and right-click. From the displayed shortcut menu, click **Rename Column**, and then type **Phone Number** and press [Enter].

■5■ Using any of the techniques you just practiced, rename the remaining fields as follows, and then compare your screen with Figure 1.13.

Field5	**Address**
Field6	**City**
Field7	**State/Province**
Field8	**ZIP/Postal Code**
Field9	**Doctor**
Field10	**Amount Owed**

Fields renamed

Figure 1.13

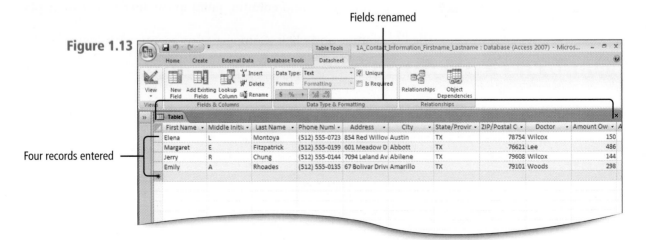

Four records entered

Activity 1.4 Changing the Data Type of a Field in Datasheet View

Data type is the characteristic that defines the kind of data that can be entered into a field, such as numbers, text, or dates. A field in a table can have only one data type. Based on the data you type into a field, Access assigns a data type, but you can change the data type if another type more accurately describes your data. In this activity, you will change the data type of fields.

1 In any of the four records that you have entered, click in the **ID field**. On the Ribbon, on the **Datasheet tab**, in the **Data Type & Formatting group**, notice that in the **Data Type** box, *Text* displays. Compare your screen with Figure 1.14.

Recall that the ID field has been changed from *AutoNumber*, which sequentially numbers each entry to *Text* so that a custom ID number for patients can be assigned.

Text indicated
as Data Type

Datasheet tab is active

Figure 1.14

Data Type box

ID field

Data Type & Formatting group

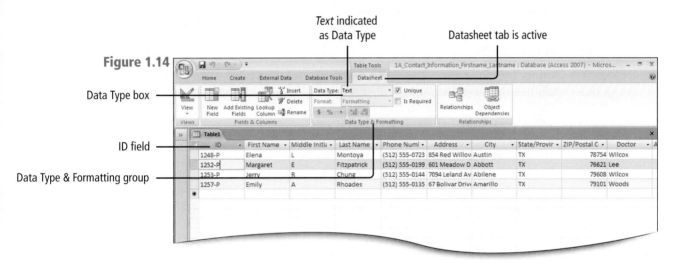

2 In any record, click in the **Last Name** field, and then on the **Datasheet tab**, notice that the **Data Type** indicates *Text*. Click the **Data Type arrow** to display a list of data types as shown in Figure 1.15 and take a moment to study the table in Figure 1.16 that describes the different data types.

Data Type arrow

Figure 1.15

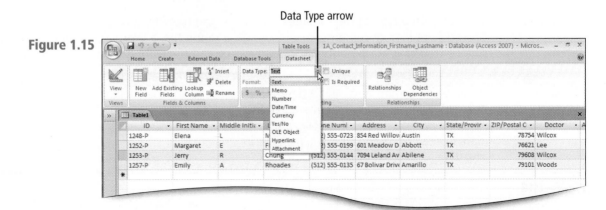

Data Type	Description	Example
AutoNumber	Available in Design view. A unique sequential or random number assigned by Access as each record is entered and that cannot be updated.	An inventory item number, such as 1, 2, 3 or a randomly assigned employee number, such as 3852788.
Text	Text or combinations of text and numbers; also numbers that are not used in calculations. Limited to 255 characters or length set on field, whichever is less. Access does not reserve space for unused portions of the text field. This is the default data type.	An inventory item such as a computer, or a phone number or postal code that is not used in calculations, and which may contain characters other than numbers.
Memo	Lengthy text or combinations of text and numbers up to 65,535 characters or limitations of database size.	Description of a product or information pertaining to a patient.
Number	Numeric data used in mathematical calculations with varying field sizes.	A quantity, such as 500.
Date/Time	Date and time values for the years 100 through 9999.	An order date, such as 11/10/2009 3:30 P.M.
Currency	Monetary values and numeric data that can be used in mathematical calculations involving data with one to four decimal places. Accurate to 15 digits on the left side of the decimal separator and to 4 digits on the right side. Use this data type to store financial data and when you do not want Access to round values.	An item price, such as $8.50.
Yes/No	Contains only one of two values—Yes/No, True/False, or On/Off. Access assigns -1 for all Yes values and 0 for all No values.	Whether an item was ordered—Yes or No.
OLE Object	An object created by programs other than Access that is linked to or embedded in the table. *OLE* is an abbreviation for *object linking and embedding*, a technology for transferring and sharing information among programs.	A graphics file, such as a picture of a product, a sound file, a Word document, or an Excel spreadsheet stored as a bitmap image.
Hyperlink	Web or email addresses.	An email address, such as dwalker@txlakemed.org or a Web page, such as *www.txlakemed.org*.
Attachment	Any supported type of file—images, spreadsheet files, documents, charts. Similar to email attachments.	A graphics file, such as a picture of a product, a sound file, a Word document, or an Excel spreadsheet stored as a bitmap image—same as OLE Object.
Lookup Wizard	Available in Design view. Not a data type, but will display on data type menu. Links to fields in other tables to display a list of data instead of having to manually type in the data.	Link to another field in another table.

Figure 1.16

3 Click the **Data Type arrow** again to close the list without changing the data type. In any record, click in the **Address** field, and notice that the **Data Type** box indicates *Text*.

As described in the table in Figure 1.16, Access assigns a data type of *Text* to combinations of letters and numbers.

4 Scroll to the right as necessary, in any record click in the **Amount Owed** field, and then in the **Data Type** box, notice that Access assigned the data type of *Number*. Click the **Data Type arrow** to the right of *Number*, and then from the displayed list, click **Currency**.

Based on your typing, Access determined this data type to be *Number*. However, Amount Owed refers to a monetary value, so the data type must be defined as *Currency*. When you click the Currency data type, Access automatically adds a U.S. dollar sign ($) and two decimal places to all the fields in the column. Compare your screen with Figure 1.17.

Data Type box indicates *Currency*

Amount Owed field data type changed to *Currency*

Figure 1.17

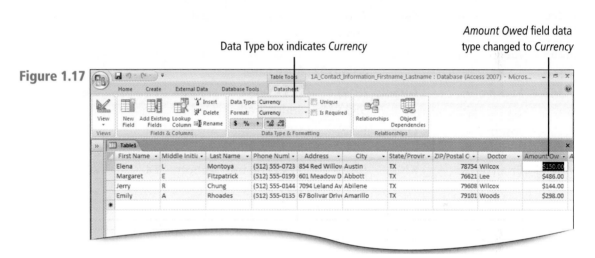

5 Scroll to the left as necessary, and in any record, click in the **ID** field.

In a database, each record should, in some way, be different from all the other records. What is important is that the number is unique; no other record in the table will be assigned this number.

You are probably familiar with unique numbers. For example, at your college, no two students have the same Student ID number, although they could have the same name, such as *David Michaels*.

When records in a database have *no* unique number, for example the CDs in your personal collection probably have no unique number, the AutoNumber data type is a useful way to automatically create a unique number so that you have a way to ensure that every record is unique.

6 Change the name of the **ID** field to **Patient ID**. In the new record row, which is indicated by an asterisk (*) in the record selector box on the left, click in the **Patient ID** field, and then type the records shown in the following list. When you are finished, compare your screen with Figure 1.18.

Recall that you need not be concerned if the data does not completely display in the column. Also, as soon as you move to the next row, the record is saved—you do not have to take any specific action to save the record. Correct typing mistakes using ordinary methods you have practiced in this and other programs.

Patient ID	First Name	Middle Initial	Last Name	Phone Number	Address	City	State/ Province	ZIP/ Postal Code	Doctor Name	Amount Owed
1260-P	Maria	S	Flores	(512) 555-0177	1 Casa Del Sol	Austin	TX	78715	Ruiz	37.50
1265-P	Joan	M	Curtis	(512) 555-0192	1446 Yellow Rose Lane	Austin	TX	78715	Ruiz	255
1342-P	Yvonne	L	Dubois	(512) 555-0155	2117 West Smith Trail	El Paso	TX	79973	Woods	147.56
1385-P	Joseph	C	Ortega	(512) 555-0245	1923 Village Park West	Amarillo	TX	79101	Wilcox	200
1423-P	Brian	K	Khuu	(512) 555-0323	1130 Preston Way SE	Abbott	TX	76621	Lee	568.12

Figure 1.18

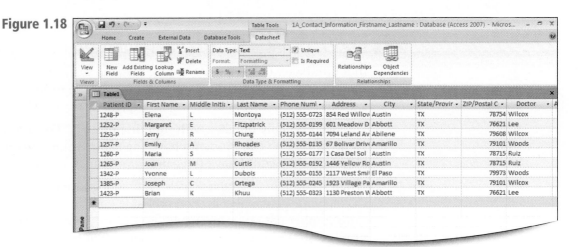

7 On the **Quick Access Toolbar**, click the **Save** button 🖫.

The Save As dialog box displays. Recall that an individual record is saved as soon as you move to another row in the table. However, because you have changed the table *design* by changing field names and data types, Access will prompt you to save the design changes made to the table.

Here you can also give the table a more meaningful name if you want to do so. In the Table Name box, a suggested name of *Table1* displays and is selected—yours may differ depending on the number of tables you have attempted to create in this database.

You will likely want to give your table a name that describes the information it contains. You can use up to 64 characters (letters or numbers), including spaces, to name a table.

8 In the **Save As** dialog box, in the **Table Name** box and using your first and last name, type **1A Patients Firstname Lastname** and then click **OK**. Compare your screen with Figure 1.19.

The table tab displays the new table name.

When you save objects within a database, it is not necessary to use underscores. Your name is included as part of the object name so that you and your instructor will be able to identify your printouts and electronic files.

Table name

Figure 1.19

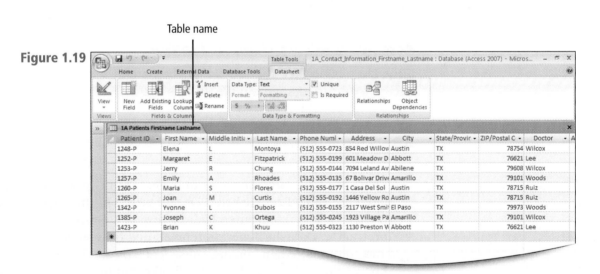

More Knowledge

Changing the Table Name

If you type the table name incorrectly or need to change the name of a table, click the Close button ⊠ in the upper right corner of the object window to close the table. Open the Navigation Pane, right-click the table name, and then from the displayed shortcut menu, click Rename. The table name will display in edit mode so that you can type the new name or edit it as you would any selected text.

Objective 4
Modify the Design of a Table

When you create and populate a new table in Datasheet view, the data that you type for the first record determines the number and content of the fields in the table. Recall that the number and names of the fields and the data type of each field is referred to as the *table design*. After you have created a table, you may find that you need to make changes to the design of the table by adding or deleting fields, or changing the order of the fields within a table. You can modify a table in Datasheet view, but you may prefer to modify the table in Design view where you have additional options.

Activity 1.5 Deleting a Field in Design View

June Liu has decided that a field for the patient's middle initial is not necessary for the Patients table. In this activity, you will delete the Middle Initial field in Design view.

1 On the **Datasheet tab**, in the **Views group**, click the **View button arrow**.

There are four common views in Access, but two that you will use often are Datasheet view and Design view. On the displayed list, Design view is represented by a picture of a pencil, a ruler, and a protractor. Datasheet view is represented by a small table of rows and columns. When you see these icons on the View button, you will know that clicking the button will take you to the view represented by the icon.

2 From the displayed list, click **Design View**, and then take a moment to study Figure 1.20.

Design view displays the underlying structure of your table. Each field name is listed, along with its data type. A column to add a Description—information about the data in the field—is provided. At the bottom of the Design view window, you can make numerous other decisions about how each individual field will look and behave. For example, you can set a specific field size.

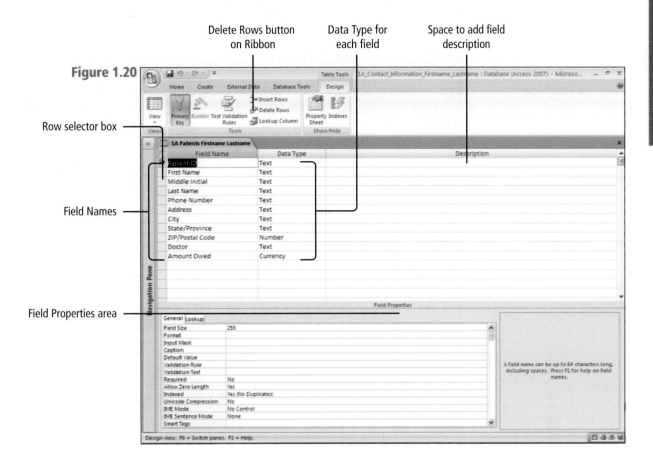

Figure 1.20

Delete Rows button on Ribbon

Data Type for each field

Space to add field description

Row selector box

Field Names

Field Properties area

3 In the **Field Name** column, to the left of **Middle Initial**, point to the row selector box to display the ➡ pointer, and then click to select—outline in orange—the entire row. Then, on the **Design tab**, in the **Tools group**, click the **Delete Rows** button, read the message in the displayed dialog box, and then click **Yes**.

If the field is deleted, both the field and its data will be deleted; you cannot undo this action. If you change your mind after deleting the field, you will have to add the field back into the table and then reenter the data for that field in each record.

More Knowledge

Choosing the Proper View To Make Changes

You can make design changes in Datasheet view or Design view. Design view provides more flexibility in the types of design changes you can make, and you will become familiar with these as you progress in your study of Access.

Activity 1.6 Modifying a Field Size and Description in Design View

In a database, there is typically more than one person entering data. For example, at your college there are likely numerous Registration Assistants who enter and modify student and course information every day.

When you design your database, there are things you can do to help yourself and others to always enter accurate data. Two ways to ensure accuracy are to restrict what can be typed in a field and to communicate information within the database itself. In this activity, you will modify fields to control the data entry process to ensure greater accuracy.

1 With your table still displayed in **Design view**, in the **Field Name** column, click anywhere in the **State/Province** field name. In the lower portion of the screen, under **Field Properties**, click in the **Field Size** box, select the text *255*, and then type **2** Compare your screen with Figure 1.21.

This action limits the size of the State/Province field to no more than two characters—the size of the two-letter state abbreviations provided by the United States Postal Service. **Field properties** are characteristics of a field that control how the field will display and how the data can be entered in the field. Using this portion of the Design view screen, you can define properties for each field.

The default field size for a text field is 255. By limiting the field size property to 2, you ensure that only two characters can be entered for each state. A primary goal of any database is to ensure the accuracy of the data that is entered. Setting the proper data type for the field and limiting the field size are two ways to help to reduce errors.

Field Properties Field Size changed to 2

Figure 1.21

State/Province field selected

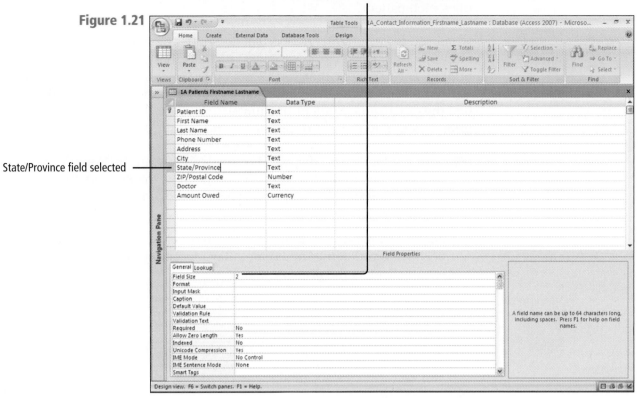

2 In the **State/Province** field name row, click in the **Description** column, and then type **Two-character state abbreviation**

Descriptions for fields in a table are not required. Include a description if the field name does not provide an obvious description of the field. Information typed in the description area displays in the status bar of the Datasheet view when the field is active. In this manner, the description communicates additional information to individuals who are entering data.

3 For the **Amount Owed** field name, click in the **Description** column, and then type **Outstanding balance**

4 On the **Quick Access Toolbar**, click the **Save** button [image], and then click **Yes** when the warning dialog box appears. Leave your table in Design view for the next activity.

The changes you have made to the fields and their properties will help to ensure accurate data entry and provide communication to users of the database. The warning indicates that if more than two characters are currently present in the State/Province field, the data could be lost because the field was not previously restricted to two characters.

Activity 1.7 Setting a Primary Key and Saving a Table

A **primary key** is the field that uniquely identifies a record in a table. For example, in a college registration system, your Student ID number uniquely identifies you—no other student at the college has your exact student number. In your 1A Patients table, the Patient ID uniquely identifies each patient.

When you create a table, Access will designate the first field as the primary key field. Good database design dictates that you establish a primary key to ensure that you do not enter the same record more than once. You can imagine the confusion if another student at your college had the exact same Student ID number as you do. The function of a primary key is to prevent duplicate records within the same table.

1 With your table still displayed in **Design view**, in the **Field Name** column, click to place your insertion point in the **Patient ID** box. To the left of the box, notice the small icon of a key as shown in Figure 1.22.

Access automatically designates the first field as the primary key field. However, using the Primary Key button on the Ribbon, you can set any field as the primary key.

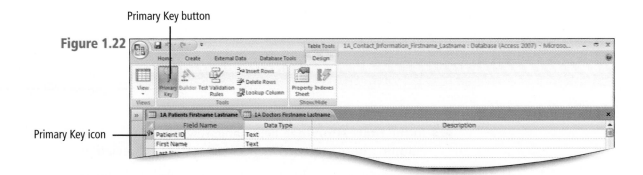

Figure 1.22

Primary Key button

Primary Key icon

2 On the **Design tab**, in the **Views group**, notice that the **View** button contains a picture of a Datasheet, indicating that clicking the button will return you to Datasheet view. Click the **View** button; if prompted, click **Yes** to save the changes you have made to the design of your table.

Objective 5
Add a Second Table to a Database

Access includes a **table template**—a pre-built table format for common topics such as contacts, issues, and tasks. You can use the table template as it is or customize it to suit your needs. Using a table template is a fast way to add an additional table to your database.

Activity 1.8 Adding a Second Table to a Database

In this activity, you will add a second table in your database. The table will contain contact information for the doctors at the medical center. You will create the table using a table template specifically designed for contact information.

1 With your **1A Patients** table displayed in Datasheet view, on the Ribbon, click the **Create tab**. In the **Tables group**, click **Table Templates**, and then from the displayed list, click **Contacts**. Compare your screen with Figure 1.23.

A new table with predefined fields displays in the object window. Your 1A Patients table is still open—its tab is visible—but is behind the new table. The Contacts Table Template most closely matches the business need to track doctor information.

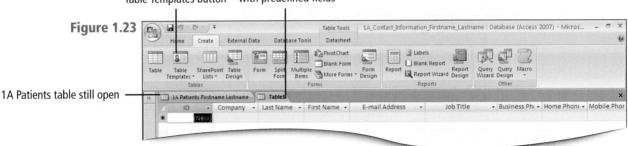

Figure 1.23

Table Templates button

New Table1 added with predefined fields

1A Patients table still open

2 On the Ribbon, click the **Datasheet tab** to display the groups of Datasheet commands. In the second column, point to the **Company** field name, click to select the field, and then on the **Datasheet tab**, in the **Fields & Columns group**, click **Delete**. Alternatively, right-click on the selected field name, and from the displayed shortcut menu, click Delete Column.

You can delete fields in Design view, in the manner you did in a previous activity, or you can delete fields directly in Datasheet view as you have done here.

3 Point to the **E-mail Address** field, and then with your ▼ pointer displayed, drag to the right to select both the **E-mail Address** field and the **Job Title** field. Right-click over the selected field names, and then from the displayed shortcut menu, click **Delete Column**.

4 Using the techniques you have just practiced, delete the following fields: **Business Phone**, **Home Phone**, **Fax Number**, **Country/Region**, **Web Page**, and **Notes**.

The field that displays a paperclip is the *Attachments* field. Recall that an attachment field can contain a graphics file such as a picture, a sound file, a Word document, or an Excel spreadsheet. In the future, June may attach a picture and a biography of each doctor to this field, so do not delete it.

5 On the **Datasheet tab**, in the **Views group**, click the **View** button to switch to **Design view**. In the **Save As** dialog box, in the **Table Name** box, type **1A Doctors Firstname Lastname** and then click **OK**.

This action will save the changes you have made to the design of the table—deleting fields—and provide a more meaningful table name. Your table displays in Design view, where you can see the names of each field and the data types assigned to the fields.

6 In the **Field Name** column, click anywhere in the **Attachments** box, and then on the **Design tab**, in the **Tools group**, click **Insert Rows**. In the newly inserted field name box, type **Specialty** In the **Description** box, type **Medical field specialty** and then compare your screen with Figure 1.24.

Description for new field

Figure 1.24

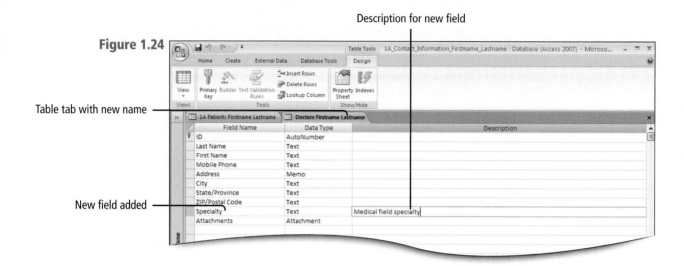

Table tab with new name

New field added

7 In the **Field Name** column, click in the **ID** box, and then replace the text with **Doctor ID** Press Tab to move to the **Data Type** column, click the arrow, and then from the displayed list, click **Text**. Press Tab to move to the **Description** column, and then type **Physician ID Number**

Because the medical center assigns a unique ID number to each doctor, you will use that number as the Primary Key instead of the AutoNumber generated by Access. Recall that AutoNumber is useful only when no other unique number for a record is available.

8 Click in the **State/Province** box, and then in the lower portion of the screen, under **Field Properties**, change the **Field Size** to **2** Compare your screen with Figure 1.25.

Description for Doctor ID

Figure 1.25

Doctor ID Data Type set to *Text*

Doctor ID field name

Descriptions added for two fields

State/Province Field Size changed to 2

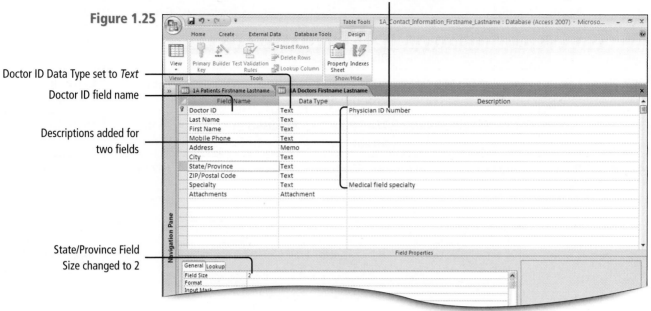

9 On the **Design tab**, in the **Views group**, click the **View** button to switch to Datasheet view—the picture of a datasheet reminds you that clicking the button will switch you to Datasheet view. Click **Yes** to save the changes you have made to the design of your table.

Activity 1.9 Adding Records to a Second Table

In this Activity, you will add the records for the doctors' contact information.

1 With your **1A Doctors** table displayed in Datasheet view, beginning in the first row under **Doctor ID**, use the techniques you have practiced to enter the following four records, and then compare your screen with Figure 1.26.

As you type in the Doctor ID field, *Physician ID Number* displays in the status bar. As you type in the Specialty field, *Medical field specialty* displays in the status bar.

Doctor ID	Last Name	First Name	Mobile Phone	Address	City	State/ Province	ZIP/Postal Code	Specialty
239-Phys	Woods	Laura	(512) 555-0100	4 Research Blvd	Austin	TX	78754	Oncology
287-Phys	Lee	Kim	(512) 555-0111	809 Broadway	Abbott	TX	76621	Cardiology
327-Phys	Wilcox	Frank	(512) 555-0022	7646 Pike Street	Amarillo	TX	79101	Orthopedics
421-Phys	Ruiz	Maria	(512) 555-0030	902 Madison Avenue	Austin	TX	78715	Pediatrics

Figure 1.26

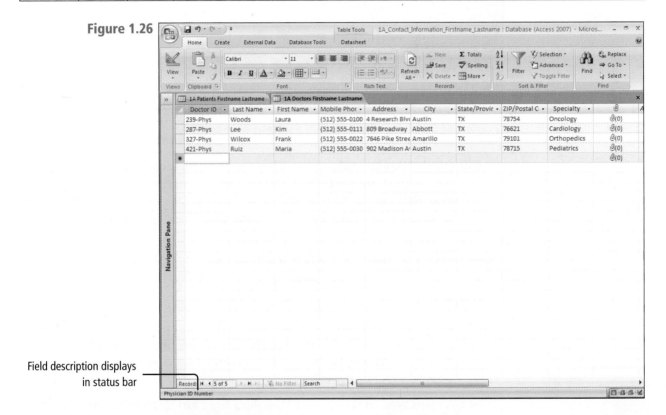

Field description displays
in status bar

Objective 6
Print a Table

A printed table is not as professional looking as a formal report, but there are times when you may want to print your table in this manner as a quick reference or to proofread the data you have entered.

Activity 1.10 Adjusting Column Widths and Printing a Table

1 In the object window, click the tab for your **1A Patients** table.

By clicking the tabs along the top of the object window, you can display open objects so that you can work with them.

In the table, you can see that all of the columns are the same width regardless of the amount of data that is entered in the field or the field size that was set. If you print the table as currently displayed, some of the fields in some records may not fully display. Thus, it is recommended that you adjust the column widths.

2 Change the field name of the **State/Province** field to **State** and change the name of the **ZIP/Postal Code** field to **ZIP**

3 In the row of field names, point to the right boundary of the **Address** field to display the ⊬ pointer, and then compare your screen with Figure 1.27.

Pointer positioned on right boundary of Address field

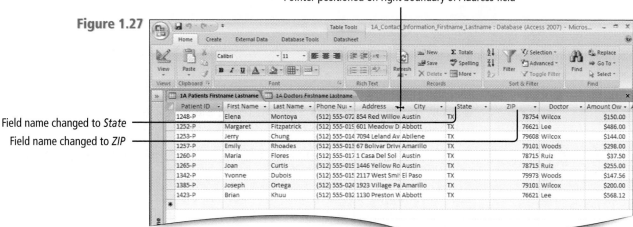

Figure 1.27

Field name changed to *State*

Field name changed to *ZIP*

4 With your ⊬ pointer positioned as shown in Figure 1.27, double-click the right boundary of the **Address** field.

The column width of the Address field widens to fully display the field name and the longest entry in the column. In this manner, the width of a column can be increased or decreased to fit its contents.

5 In the field headings row, point to the right border of the **City** field, and then with the ⊬ pointer, hold down the left mouse button and drag to the left to visually narrow the column width to accommodate only the widest entry in that column.

Adjusting the width of columns does not change the data contained in the table's records. It changes only your view of the data.

Another Way — **To Adjust Column Widths**

You can select multiple columns, and then in the heading area, double-click the right boundary of any selected column to adjust all widths, in a manner similar to an Excel spreadsheet. Or, you can select one or more columns, right-click over the selection, from the displayed menu click Column Width, and then in the Column Width dialog box, click Best Fit.

6 Using any of the techniques you have practiced or described above, adjust all the column widths, and then compare your screen with Figure 1.28.

All column widths adjusted to fit longest entry in the column

Figure 1.28

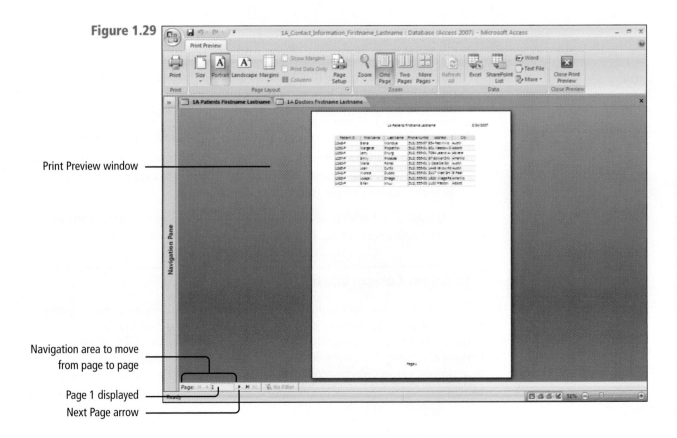

7 On the **Quick Access Toolbar**, click **Save** to save the changes you have made to the table's design—changing the column widths.

If you forget to save the table, Access will remind you to save when you close the table.

8 In the upper left corner of your screen, click the **Office** button. From the displayed menu, point to the **Print** button, click **Print Preview**, and then compare your screen with Figure 1.29.

Figure 1.29

Print Preview window

Navigation area to move from page to page

Page 1 displayed

Next Page arrow

9 In the navigation area in the lower left of your screen, click the **Next Page arrow**, point to the displayed data at the top of the page to display the 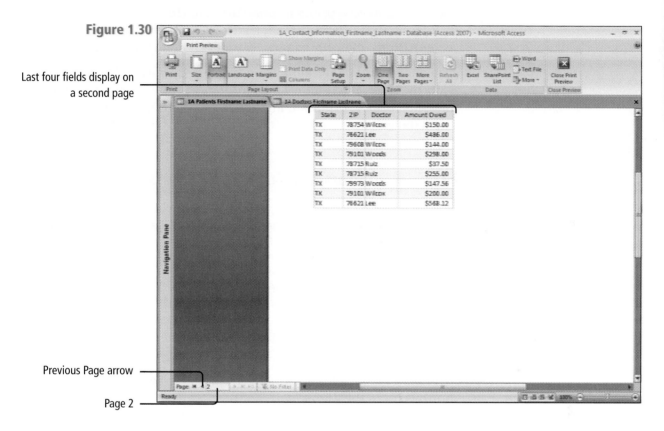 pointer, click one time to zoom in, and then compare your screen with Figure 1.30.

The second page of the table displays the last four field columns.

Figure 1.30

Last four fields display on a second page

Previous Page arrow

Page 2

10 On the Ribbon, in the **Zoom group**, click the **Zoom** button to zoom back to Fit to Window view. In the **Page Layout group**, click the **Margins** button. In the displayed **Margins gallery**, point to **Wide**, and then compare your screen with Figure 1.31.

Wide gallery choice

Figure 1.31

Margins button

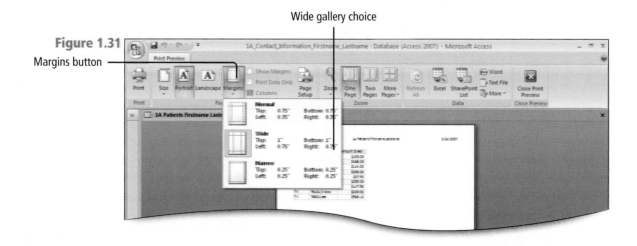

11 Click **Wide**. Then, in the **Page Layout group**, click the **Landscape** button.

The orientation of the printout changes, and the navigation arrows are inactive because all of the fields and all of the records display on one page. Additionally, the table name and current date display at the top of the page, and the page number displays at the bottom.

By default, Access prints in *portrait orientation*—the printed page is taller than it is wide. An alternate orientation is *landscape orientation*—the printed page is wider than it is tall.

The change in orientation from portrait to landscape is not saved with the table. Each time you want to print, you must check the margins, page orientation, and other print parameters to ensure that the data will print as you intend.

Note — Headers and Footers in Access Objects

The headers and footers in Access tables and queries are controlled by default settings; you cannot add additional information or edit the information. The object name displays in the center of the header area with the date on the right—that is why adding your own name to the object name is helpful to identify your paper or electronic results. The page number displays in the center of the footer area. The headers and footers in Access reports and forms, however, are more flexible; you can add to and edit the information.

12 On the right side of the status bar, just to the right of the **View** buttons, drag the **Zoom** slider to the right—or click the **Zoom In** button—until you have zoomed to approximately **120%**, as shown in Figure 1.32.

To *zoom* means to increase or to decrease the viewing area of the screen. You can zoom in to look closely at a particular section of a document, and then zoom out to see a whole page on the screen. You can also zoom to view multiple pages on the screen.

Figure 1.32

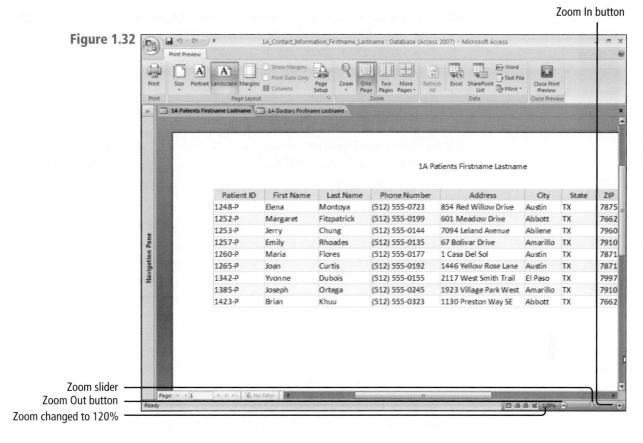

Zoom slider
Zoom Out button
Zoom changed to 120%

13 Drag the **Zoom** slider to the left—or click the **Zoom Out** button—until you have zoomed to approximately **50%**, as shown in Figure 1.33.

Figure 1.33

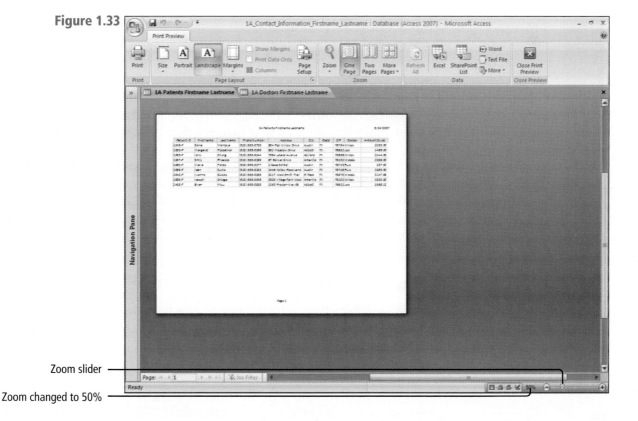

Zoom slider

Zoom changed to 50%

14 Check your *Chapter Assignment Sheet* or *Course Syllabus*, or consult your instructor, to determine whether you are to submit the printed pages that are the results of this project. If you are submitting your work on paper, on the **Print Preview tab**, in the **Print group**, click the **Print** button, and then in the displayed **Print** dialog box, click **OK**. To submit electronically, click Close Print Preview, and then follow the directions provided by your instructor.

15 In the **Close Preview group**, click the **Close Print Preview** button. At the far right edge of the object window, click the **Close Object** button ☒ to close your **1A Patients** table. If prompted to do so, click Yes to save any unsaved design changes.

16 With your **1A Doctors** table displayed, change the name of the **State/Province** field to **State** and the name of the **ZIP/Postal Code** field to **ZIP** Then, adjust all the column widths to accommodate the longest line in the column, including the **Attachments** column, which displays a paperclip icon.

17 Display the table in **Print Preview**. Change the **Margins** to **Wide** and the orientation to **Landscape**. Print if you are directed to do so, or submit your work electronically.

18 Click **Close Print Preview**, and then at the far right of the object window, click the **Close Object** button ☒ . Click **Yes** to save the changes you made to the layout—changing the column widths.

All of your database objects—the 1A Patients table and the 1A Doctors table—are closed, and the object window is empty.

Objective 7
Create and Use a Query

A *query* is a database object that retrieves specific data from one or more tables and then, in a single datasheet, displays only the data you specified. Because the word *query* means *to ask a question*, you can think of a query as a question formed in a manner that Access can interpret.

One type of query in Access is a *select query*. A select query, also called a *simple select query*, retrieves (selects) data from one or more tables and makes it available for use in the format of a datasheet. A select query is used to create subsets of data that you can use to answer specific questions; for example, *Which patients live in Austin, TX?*

Activity 1.11 Using the Simple Query Wizard To Create a Query

The table or tables from which a query gets its data are referred to as the query's *data source*. In the following activity, you will create a simple select query using a *wizard*. A wizard is a feature in Microsoft Office programs that walks you step by step through a process.

The process involves choosing the data source, and then indicating the fields you want to include in the query result. The query—the question that you want to ask—is *What is the name, complete mailing address, and Patient ID of every patient in the database?*

1 On the Ribbon, click the **Create tab**, and then in the **Other group**, click the **Query Wizard** button. In the **New Query** dialog box, click **Simple Query Wizard**, and then click **OK**. Compare your screen with Figure 1.34.

Figure 1.34

Simple Query Wizard dialog box

Tables/Queries arrow

Add Field button

No database objects display in object window; all are closed

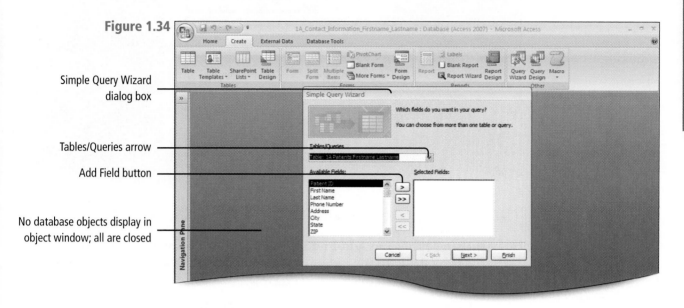

2 Click the **Tables/Queries arrow**, and then click your **Table: 1A Patients**.

To create a query, first choose the data source—the tables or queries from which you will select the data you want. To find the name and complete mailing address of every patient, you will need the 1A Patients table.

3 Under **Available Fields**, click **Patient ID**, and then click the **Add Field** button ![>] to move the field to the **Selected Fields** list on the right. Using the same technique, add the **Last Name** field to the list. Alternatively, double-click the field name to move it to the Selected Fields list. Compare your screen with Figure 1.35.

Recall that the second step is to choose the fields that you want to include in your resulting query.

Figure 1.35

Two fields added to Selected Fields list

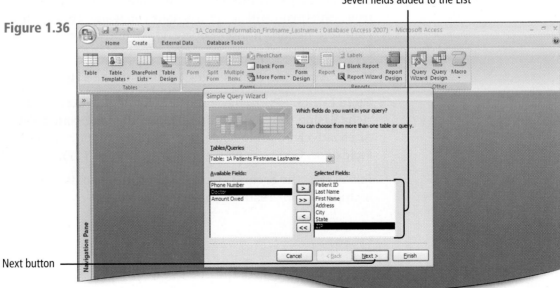

4 Using either the **Add Field** button **>** or double-click, add the following fields to the **Selected Fields** list: **First Name**, **Address**, **City**, **State**, **ZIP**. Compare your screen with Figure 1.36.

Choosing these seven fields will give you the query result that you want—it will answer the question, *What is the name, address, and Patient ID of every patient in the database?*

Seven fields added to the List

Figure 1.36

Next button

5 In the lower right corner, click the **Next** button. Be sure that the option for **Detail (shows every field of every record)** is selected, and then in the lower right corner, click the **Next** button. Click in the **What title do you want for your query?** box, and then edit as necessary so that the query name, using your own first and last name, is **1A ALL Patients Firstname Lastname Query** Compare your screen with Figure 1.37.

Name of query

Figure 1.37

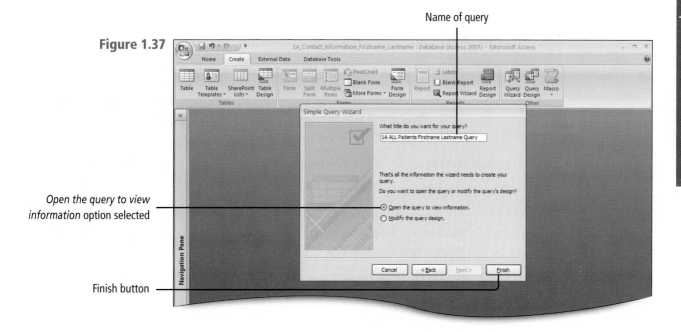

Open the query to view information option selected

Finish button

▣ Click **Finish**.

Access **runs** the query—performs the actions indicated in your query design by searching the table of records included in the query, finding the records that match the criteria, and then displaying the records in a datasheet—so that you can see the results. In this manner, a select query *selects*—pulls out and displays—*only* the information from the table that you requested.

In the object window, Access displays every patient record in Datasheet view, but displays only the seven fields that you included in the Selected Fields list in the query wizard.

▣ Display the query in **Print Preview**, and then print or submit electronically as directed. Click **Close Print Preview**; leave the query object open.

Objective 8
Create and Use a Form

A *form* is an Access object with which you can enter data, edit data, or display data from a table or a query. Think of a form as a window through which you and others can view and work with the data. In a form, the fields are laid out in a visually attractive format on the screen, which makes working with the database more pleasant and more efficient.

One type of Access form displays only one record in the database at a time. Such a form is useful not only to the individual who performs the data entry—typing in the actual records—but also to anyone who has the job of viewing information in a database.

For example, when you visit the Records office at your college to obtain a transcript, someone displays your record on a screen. For the viewer, it is much easier to look at one record at a time, using a form, than to look at all the student records in the database table.

Activity 1.12 Creating a Form

The Form command on the Ribbon creates a form that displays all the fields from the underlying data source (table) on the form, and does so one record at a time. You can use this new form immediately, or you can modify it. Records that you edit or create by using a form automatically update the underlying table or tables.

1 In the upper right corner of the object window, click the **Close Object** button ⊠ to close your query. Then, at the top of the **Navigation Pane**, click the **Open** button ⧉. Point to your **1A Patients** table, and then right-click to display a shortcut menu as shown in Figure 1.38.

In the Navigation Pane, a table displays a datasheet icon and a query displays an icon of two overlapping datasheets.

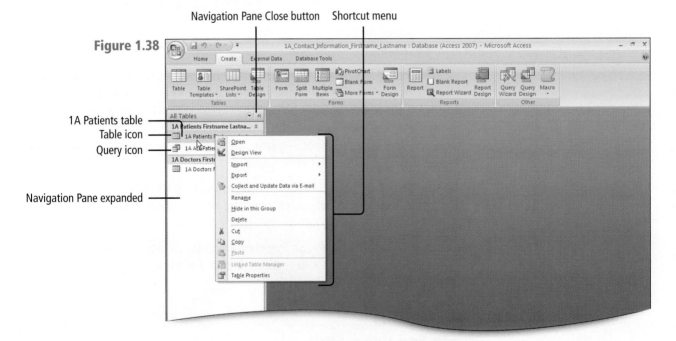

Figure 1.38

Navigation Pane Close button   Shortcut menu

1A Patients table
Table icon
Query icon

Navigation Pane expanded

2 From the displayed menu, click **Open** to display the table in the object window, and then in the upper right corner of the **Navigation Pane**, click the **Close** button ⧉ to maximize your screen space.

3 Notice that there are 10 fields in your table. On the Ribbon, click the **Create tab**, and then in the **Forms group**, click the **Form** button. Compare your screen with Figure 1.39.

Access creates a form based on the currently selected object—your 1A Patients table. Access creates the form in a simple top-to-bottom format, with all the fields in the table lined up in a single column.

The form displays in Layout view, which means you can make modifications to the form on this screen. The data for the first record in the table—for *Elena Montoya*—displays in each field.

Figure 1.39

Form object tab displays red form icon

Layout View button active

First record, for Elena Montoya, displays

Next record button

Total number of records

Navigation buttons to move among records

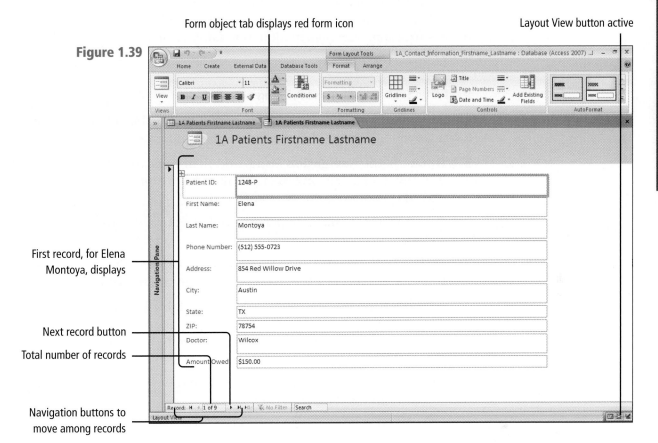

4 In the lower right corner of the screen, at the right edge of the status bar, notice that the **Layout View** button ⊞ is active, indicating the form is displayed in Layout view.

5 At the right edge of the status bar, click the **Form View** button 🖼. Alternatively, on the Home tab, in the Views group, click the View button, which displays an icon of a form indicating the Form view.

In this view, you can view the records, but you cannot change the layout of the form.

6 In the navigation area, click the **Next record** button ▶ three times.

The fourth record—for *Emily Rhoades*—displays. The navigation buttons are useful to scroll among the records to select any single record you need to display.

7 On the **Quick Access Toolbar**, click the **Save** button 🖫. In the displayed **Save As** dialog box, accept the default name for the form—

1A Patients Firstname Lastname—by clicking **OK**. **Close** ✖ the form object.

Your 1A Patients Firstname Lastname table remains open in the object window.

Objective 9
Create and Print a Report

A *report* is a database object that displays the fields and records from a table or a query in an easy-to-read format suitable for printing. Create reports to summarize information in a database in a professional-looking manner.

Activity 1.13 Creating and Printing a Report

In this activity, you will create a report that lists mobile phone contact information for doctors at Texas Lakes Medical Center.

1 **Open** ⟩⟩ the **Navigation Pane**, and then open your **1A Doctors** table by double-clicking the table name or by right-clicking and clicking Open from the shortcut menu.

Your 1A Doctors table displays in Datasheet view in the object window.

2 **Close** ⟨⟨ the **Navigation Pane**. Click the **Create tab**, and then in the **Reports group**, click **Report**. Compare your screen with Figure 1.40.

A report displays each of the fields in the table laid out in a report format suitable for printing. The report displays in Layout view, which means you can make quick changes to the design of the report on this screen.

Dotted lines indicate how the report would be broken across pages if you print in the current layout.

Report Layout Tools available

Figure 1.40

Report object tab displays a Report icon

Dotted line indicates page break if printed in current layout

Layout View button active

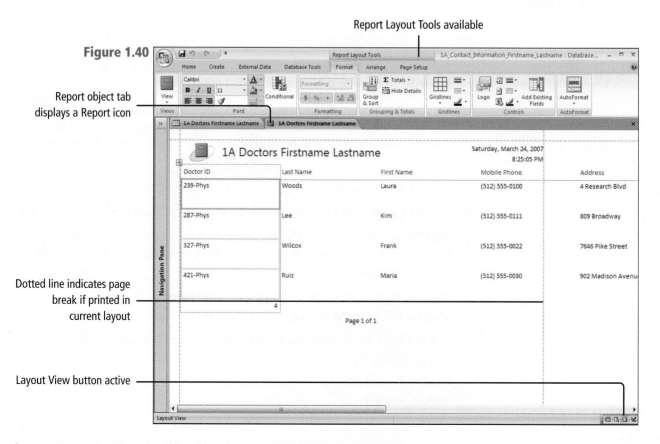

3 Scroll to the right as necessary, point to the **Address** field, right-click, and then from the displayed shortcut menu, click **Delete**.

The Address field and data are deleted and the report readjusts to accommodate the deletion.

4 Use the same technique to delete the following fields on the report layout: **City**, **State**, **ZIP**, **Specialty**, and **Attachments**.

This report will provide June with a quick list of each doctor and his or her ID and mobile phone number.

5 Click the **Page Setup tab**, and then in the **Page Layout group**, click **Landscape**. Scroll to the left, and then compare your screen with Figure 1.41.

Figure 1.41

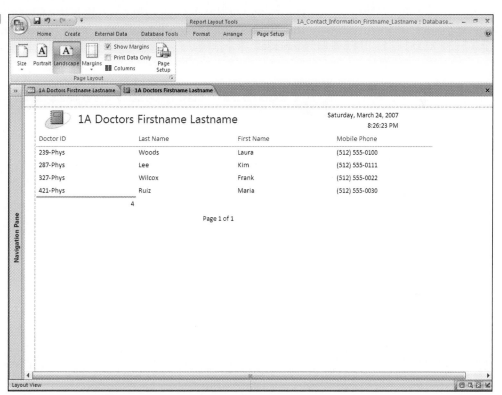

6 If you are submitting your results from this Project on paper, from the **Office** menu, point to the **Print** button, click **Print Preview**, and then in the **Print group**, click **Print**. To submit electronically, follow the directions provided by your instructor.

7 Click the **Close Print Preview** button. Click the **Close Object** button to close the report. In the **Microsoft Office Access** dialog box, click **Yes** to save the report. In the **Save As** dialog box, click **OK** to accept the report name.

8 **Close** all the open objects so that there are no objects displayed in the object window.

Objective 10
Close and Save a Database

When you close an Access table, any changes made to the records are saved automatically. If you have changed the design of the table, or have changed the layout of the Datasheet view, such as adjusting the column widths, you will be prompted to save your changes. At the end of your Access session, close your database, and then close Access.

Activity 1.14 Closing and Saving a Database

1 Be sure all objects are closed.

2 From the **Office** menu , click **Close Database**, and then at the right edge of the Access title bar, click the **Close** button [×] to close the Access program. Alternatively, from the Office menu, click Exit Access.

End **You have completed Project 1A** ────────────

Project 1B Health Seminars

In Activities 1.15 through 1.21, you will assist June Liu, Chief Administrative Officer, in creating a database to store information about community health seminars presented by Texas Lakes Medical Center. You will use a database template that tracks event information. You will add seminar information to the database and print a page displaying the results. Your printout will look similar to Figure 1.42.

For Project 1B, you will need the following file:

New Access database using the Events template

You will save your database as
1B_Health_Seminars_Firstname_Lastname

Location	On Site/Off Site	Seating Capacity	Room Arrangement	Visual Equipment
Dogwood Room	On Site	50	Classroom	Computer Projector
Jefferson High School	Off Site	150	Theater	Computer Projector
Sandbox Preschool	Off Site	20	Classroom	White Board
Yellow Rose Room	On Site	20	U-Shape Table	Computer Projector

1B Seminar Locations Firstname Lastname — 11/24/2006

Page 1

Figure 1.42
Project 1B—Health Seminars

Objective 11
Create a Database Using a Template

A database template contains pre-built tables, queries, forms, and reports to perform a specific task, such as tracking a large number of events. For example, your college probably holds a large number of events, such as athletic contests, plays, lectures, concerts, and club meetings. Using a predefined template, your college Activities Director could quickly establish a database to manage such events.

The advantage of using a template to start a new database is that you do not have to create the objects—all you need to do is enter your data and modify the pre-built objects to suit your needs.

The purpose of the database in this project is to track the health seminars offered by Texas Lakes Medical Center. The questions to be answered may include:

- *What seminars will be offered and when will they be offered?*

- *In what Medical Center rooms or community locations will the seminars be held?*

- *Which seminar rooms have a computer projector for PowerPoint presentations?*

Activity 1.15 Creating a New Database Using a Template

In this activity, you will create a new database using the Events template.

1 **Start** Access. On the left side of the screen, under **Template Categories**, click **Local Templates**. Compare your screen with Figure 1.43.

Available Local Templates

Figure 1.43

Local Templates

Events template

Under **Local Templates**, click **Events**. In the lower right portion of your screen, to the right of the **File Name** box, click the **file folder icon**, and then navigate to your **Access Chapter 1** folder that you created in Project 1A.

At the bottom of the **File New Database** dialog box, delete any text in the **File name** box, and then, using your own information, type **1B_Health_Seminars_Firstname_Lastname** and press Enter.

In the lower right corner of your screen, click the **Create** button.

Your 1B Health Seminars database is created, and the name displays in the title bar.

Directly below the Ribbon, on the **Message Bar**, check to see if a **Security Warning** displays.

Note

If no Security Warning displays, skip the next step and move to Activity 1.16.

On the **Message Bar**, click the **Options** button. In the displayed **Microsoft Office Security Options** dialog box, click the **Enable this content** option button, and then click **OK** or press Enter. Compare your screen with Figure 1.44.

Databases provided by Microsoft are safe to use on your computer.

Figure 1.44

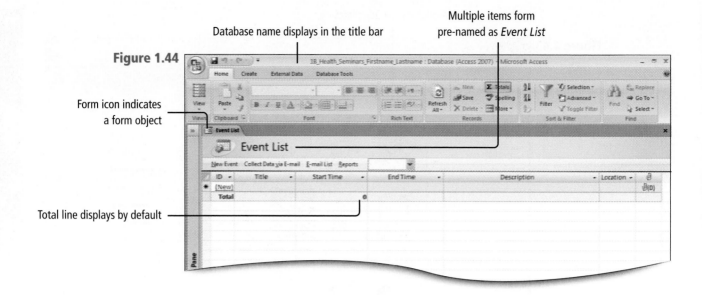

Database name displays in the title bar

Multiple items form pre-named as *Event List*

Form icon indicates a form object

Total line displays by default

Activity 1.16 Building a Table by Entering Records in a Multiple Items Form

The purpose of a form is to simplify the entry of data into a table—either for you or for others who enter data. In Project 1A, you created a simple form, in which you can display or enter records in a table one record at a time.

The Events template creates a ***multiple items form***, a form in which you can display or enter *multiple* records in a table, but still with an easier and more simplified screen than typing directly into the table itself.

1 Click in the first empty **Title** field. Type **Repetitive Stress Injuries** and then press Tab. In the **Start Time** field, type **3/9/09 7p** and then press Tab.

Access formats the date and time. As you enter dates and times, a small calendar displays to the right of the field, which you can click to select a date instead of typing.

2 In the **End Time** field, type **3/9/09 9p** and then press Tab. In the **Description** field, type **Workplace Health** and then press Tab. In the **Location** field, type **Yellow Rose Room** and then press Tab three times to move to the new record row. Compare your screen with Figure 1.45.

Because the seminars have no unique number, the AutoNumber feature of Access is useful to assign a unique number to each seminar.

First record entered

Figure 1.45

Access formats date and time ──

Link bar ──

AutoNumber creates a unique number ──

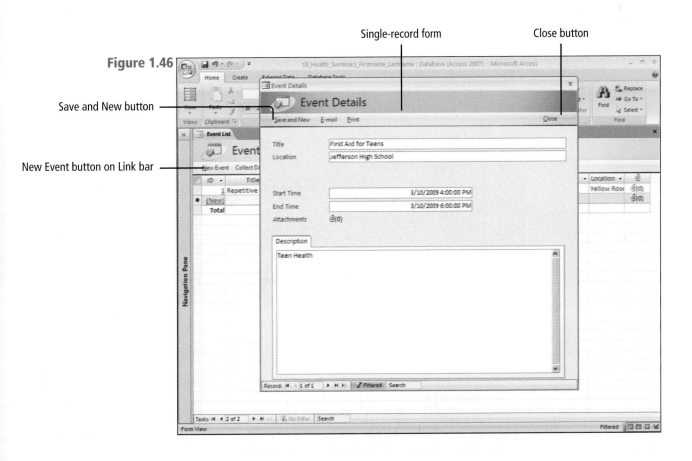

3 In the **Link bar**, just above the field names, click **New Event**.

A single-record form displays, similar to the simple form you created in Project 1A.

4 Using Tab to move from field to field, enter the following record— press Tab three times to move from the **End Time** field to the **Description** field. Compare your screen with Figure 1.46.

Title	Location	Start Time	End Time	Description
First Aid for Teens	**Jefferson High School**	**3/10/09 4p**	**3/10/09 6p**	**Teen Health**

Single-record form   Close button

Figure 1.46

Save and New button ──

New Event button on Link bar ──

5 In the upper right corner of the single-record form, click **Close**, and notice that the new record displays in your Multiple Items form. Using either the rows on the Multiple Items form or the New Event single-record form, enter the following records, and then compare your screen with Figure 1.47:

<table>
<tr><td>Alert!</td><td colspan="2">Does a single record form open?
When entering records in the multiple items form, pressing [Enter] three times at the end of a row to begin a new record may display the single-record New Event form. If you prefer to use the multiple items form, close the single record form and continue entering records, using the [Tab] key to move from field to field.</td></tr>
</table>

ID	Title	Start Time	End Time	Description	Location
3	**Safety on the Job**	**3/18/09 2p**	**3/18/09 4p**	**Workplace Health**	**Yellow Rose Room**
4	**Nutrition for Toddlers**	**3/19/09 1p**	**3/19/09 3p**	**Child Health and Development**	**Sandbox Preschool**
5	**Stay Healthy While You Travel**	**4/6/09 9a**	**4/6/09 11a**	**Life Style and Health**	**Dogwood Room**
6	**Work Smart at Your Computer**	**4/8/09 11a**	**4/8/09 12:30p**	**Workplace Health**	**Dogwood Room**
7	**Be Heart Smart**	**4/14/09 7p**	**4/14/09 9p**	**Life Style and Health**	**Yellow Rose Room**

Figure 1.47

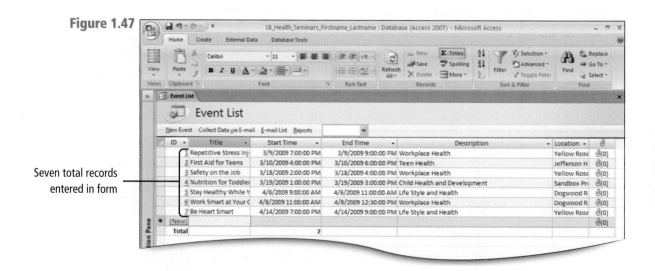

Seven total records entered in form

Objective 12
Organize Database Objects in the Navigation Pane

Use the Navigation Pane to organize your database objects, to open them for use, and to perform common tasks like renaming an object. So far, your databases have had only a few objects, but databases can have a large number of tables and other objects. Thus, the Navigation Pane will become your tool for organizing your database objects.

Activity 1.17 Organizing Database Objects in the Navigation Pane

The Navigation Pane groups and displays your database objects, and can do so in predefined arrangements. In this activity, you will group your database objects using the **Tables and Views category**, an arrangement that groups objects by the table to which they are related. Because all of your data must be stored in one or more tables, this is a useful arrangement.

1 **Open** >> the **Navigation Pane**. At the top of the **Navigation Pane**, click the **Navigation arrow** ⊙ , and then from the displayed list, in the **Navigate To Category** section, click **Tables and Related Views**.

Click the **Navigation arrow** ⊙ to display the list again, and then in the **Filter By Group** section, point to **All Tables**. Compare your screen with Figure 1.48.

Figure 1.48

All Tables displays

Tables and Related Views selected

All Tables selected

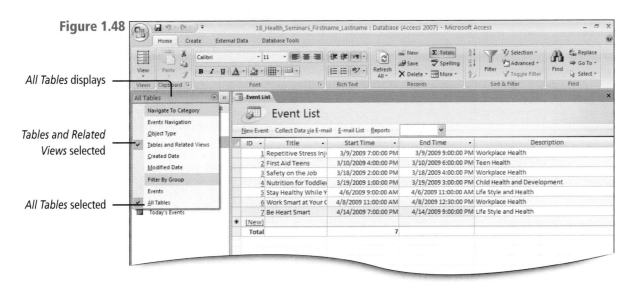

2 Click **All Tables** to close the list, and then confirm that *Events* displays in the blue bar at the top of the **Navigation Pane**. Compare your screen with Figure 1.49.

The icons to the left of the objects listed in the Navigation Pane indicate that the Events template created a number of objects for you—among them, one table titled *Events*, five reports, two forms, and one query. The Event List Multiple Items form, which is currently displayed in the object window, is included in the list.

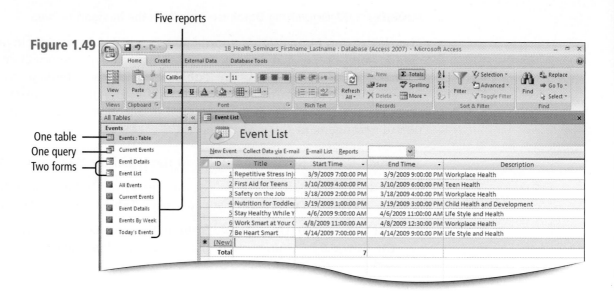

Five reports

Figure 1.49

One table
One query
Two forms

3 In the **Navigation Pane**, point to the **Events** *table*, and then right-click to display a shortcut menu. On the shortcut menu, click **Open**. Alternatively, double-click the table name to open it in the object window.

The Events table becomes the active object in the object window. Use the Navigation Pane to open objects for use.

The seven records that you entered using the Multiple Items *form* display in the *table*. Recall that the purpose of a form is to make it easy to get records into a table. Tables are the foundation of your database because your data must be stored in a table. You can enter records directly into a table in the manner you did in Project 1A, or you can use a simple form or a Multiple Items form to enter records.

4 In the object window, click the **Event List** form tab to bring it into view and make it the active object.

Recall that a form presents a more user-friendly screen with which to enter records into a table.

5 In the **Navigation Pane**, right-click the report named **Current Events**, and then click **Open**. Alternatively, double-click the report name to open it. Compare your screen with Figure 1.50.

An advantage of using a template to begin a database is that many objects, such as attractively formatted reports, are already designed for you.

Current Events report preformatted
and designed by the template

Figure 1.50

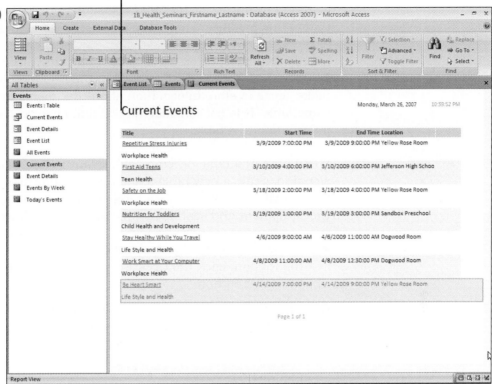

6 In the object window, **Close** ☒ the **Current Events** report.

7 From the **Navigation Pane**, open the **Events By Week** report.

In this predesigned report, the events are displayed by week. These are among the reports that are predesigned and come with the template. After you enter your records, these preformatted reports are instantly available to you.

8 In the object window, **Close** ☒ the **Events By Week** report. Then **Close** ☒ the remaining two open objects. Leave the **Navigation Pane** fully displayed.

There are no open objects in your object window.

Objective 13
Create a New Table in a Database Created with a Template

The Events template created only one table—the *Events* table. Although the database was started from a template and contains many necessary objects, you can add additional objects as you need them.

Create a new table in a database when you begin to see repeated information. Repeated information is a good indication that an additional table is needed. For example, in the Events database, both the Yellow Rose Room and the Dogwood Room are listed more than one time.

Activity 1.18 Creating a New Table and Changing Its Design

June has information about the various locations where seminars are held. For example, for the Yellow Rose Room, she has information about the seating arrangements, number of seats, and audio-visual equipment.

In your database, three seminars are currently scheduled in the Yellow Rose Room and two are scheduled in the Dogwood Room. It would not make sense to store information about the rooms multiple times in the same table. It is *not* considered good database design to have duplicate information in a table.

When data in a table becomes redundant in this manner, it is usually a signal to create a new table to contain the information about the topic. In this activity, you will create a table to track the seminar locations and the equipment and seating arrangements in each location.

1 **Close** ⟪ the **Navigation Pane** to maximize your screen space. On the Ribbon, click the **Create tab**, and then in the **Tables group**, click the **Table** button.

2 Click in the cell under **Add New Field**, type **Yellow Rose Room** and then press Tab. Type **On Site** and then press Tab. Type **20** and then press Tab. Type **U-Shape Table** and then press Tab. Type **Computer Projector** and then press Tab three times. Compare your screen with Figure 1.51.

Access will assign an AutoNumber in the ID field.

Figure 1.51

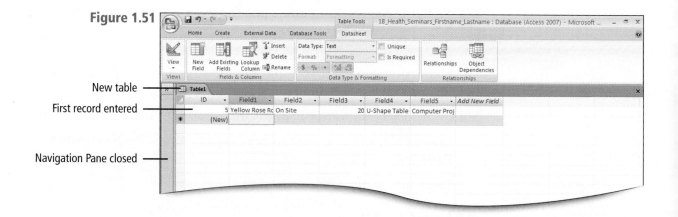

New table ——

First record entered ——

Navigation Pane closed ——

3 Point to the text *Field1*, right-click, and then from the displayed shortcut menu, click **Rename Column**. Type **Location** Point to the text *Field2*, double-click, and then type **On Site/Off Site** Point to and click *Field3*, click the **Datasheet tab**, and then in the **Fields & Columns group**, click **Rename**. Type **Seating Capacity** Using any of the techniques you have practiced, change *Field4* to **Room Arrangement** and *Field5* to **Visual Equipment**

4 In the **Views group**, click the **View** button to switch to **Design view**. **Save** the table as **1B Seminar Locations Firstname Lastname** and then click **OK**.

5 In **Design view**, in the **Field Name** column, click in the **Location** box. Then on the **Design tab**, in the **Tools group**, click the **Primary Key** button.

The key icon moves to the left of the Location field. Recall that the Primary Key is the field that contains a unique identifier for the record. In the Seminar Locations table, the Location name is unique; no other record will have the same Location name.

6 Point to the **row selector box** for the **ID** field to display the pointer, and then click to select the entire row. On the **Design tab**, in the **Tools group**, click the **Delete Rows** button, and then click **Yes** in the warning box.

Because the Location name will serve as the primary key field, the ID field is not necessary.

7 On the Ribbon, in the **Views group**, click the **View** button, which by its icon indicates that you will return to the Datasheet view of the table. Click **Yes** to save the changes you have made to the table design.

8 Enter the remaining records in the table:

Location	On Site/ Off Site	Seating Capacity	Room Arrangement	Visual Equipment
Jefferson High School	Off Site	150	Theater	Computer Projector
Dogwood Room	On Site	50	Classroom	Computer Projector
Sandbox Preschool	Off Site	20	Classroom	White Board

9 Point to the field name *Location* to display the ⬇ pointer, hold down the left mouse button, and then drag across to select all of the columns, as shown in Figure 1.52.

All the columns selected

Figure 1.52

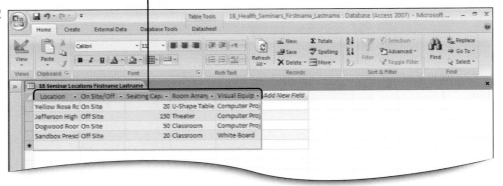

10 Point to any of the selected field names in the top row, right-click, and then from the displayed shortcut menu, click **Column Width**. In the displayed **Column Width** dialog box, click **Best Fit**. Alternatively, with the columns selected, in the field heading row, point to the right boundary of any of the selected rows to display the ⬌ pointer, and then double-click to apply Best Fit to all of the selected columns.

All of the columns widths are adjusted to accommodate the longest entry in the column.

11 Click in any record to cancel the selection of the columns. **Open** ⟩⟩ the **Navigation Pane**, locate the name of your new table, and then compare your screen with Figure 1.53.

Recall that as it is currently arranged, the Navigation Pane organizes the objects by table name. The Events table is listed first, followed by its associated objects, and then the Seminar Locations table is listed. Currently, there are no other objects associated with the Seminar Locations table.

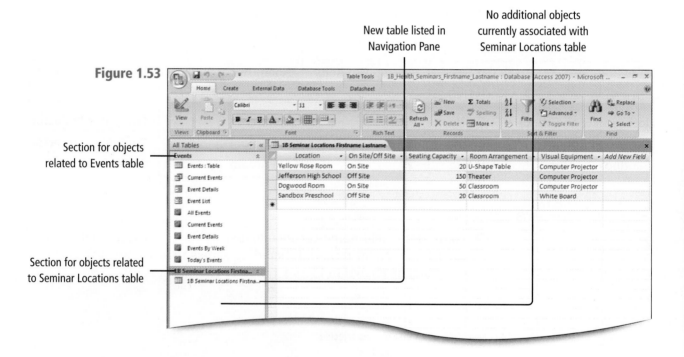

Figure 1.53

No additional objects currently associated with Seminar Locations table

New table listed in Navigation Pane

Section for objects related to Events table

Section for objects related to Seminar Locations table

12 In the object window, **Close** ✕ your **1B Seminar Locations** table, and then click **Yes** to save the layout changes you made to the column widths. Leave the **Navigation Pane** open.

Objective 14
View a Report and Print a Table in a Database Created with a Template

Recall that an advantage to starting a new database with a template is that many report objects are already created for you.

Activity 1.19 Viewing a Report

1 From the **Navigation Pane**, open the **All Events** report. Compare your screen with Figure 1.54.

The All Events report displays in an attractively arranged pre-built report.

All Events report

Figure 1.54

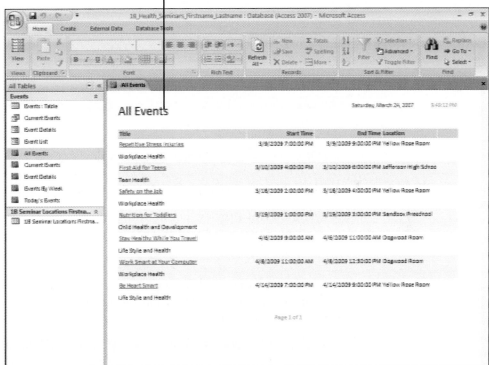

2 **Close** ☒ the **All Events** report.

3 Open the **Event Details** report and compare your screen with Figure 1.55.

The Event Details report displays in a pre-built report. Each report displays the records in the table in different useful formats.

Event Details report

Figure 1.55

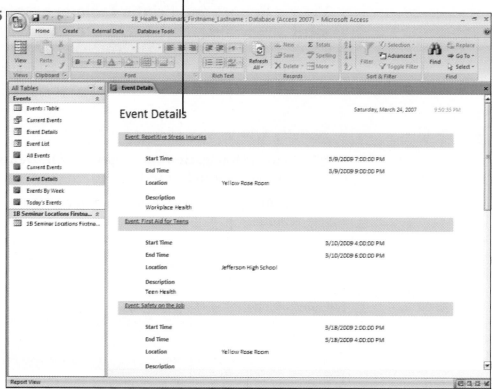

4 Close **[X]** the **Event Details** report.

Activity 1.20 Printing a Table

Use the Print Preview command to determine if a table will print on one page, or if you need to adjust column widths, margins, or the direction the data displays on the page.

Recall that there will be occasions when you want to print your table for a quick reference or for proofreading. For more formal-looking information, print a report.

1 From the **Navigation Pane**, open your **1B Seminar Locations**

table. Display the **Office** menu 🔲, point to the **Print** button, and then click **Print Preview**.

The table displays in the Print Preview window so you can see how it will look when it is printed. The name of the table displays at the top of the page. The navigation area at the bottom of the window displays *1* in the Pages box, and the right-pointing arrow—the Next arrow—is active. Recall that when you are in the Print Preview window, the navigation arrows are used to navigate from one page to the next, rather than from one record to the next.

2 In the navigation area, click the **Next Page** arrow.

The second page of the table displays the last field column. Whenever possible, try to print all of the fields horizontally on one page. Of course, if you have many records you may need more than one page to print all of the records.

3 On the **Print Preview tab**, in the **Page Layout group**, click **Margins**, and then click **Wide**. Then, click the **Landscape** button and compare your screen with Figure 1.56.

Table in landscape orientation

Figure 1.56

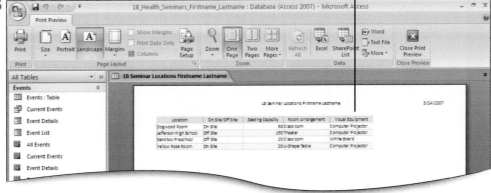

4 Check your *Chapter Assignment Sheet* or *Course Syllabus*, or consult your instructor, to determine whether you are to submit the printed pages that are the results of this project. To submit your work on paper, on the **Print Preview tab**, in the **Print group**, click the **Print** button. To submit electronically, close the Print Preview and follow the directions provided by your instructor.

5 On the **Print Preview tab**, click **Close Print Preview**. Close your **1B Seminar Locations** table.

6 Close any open objects, and then **Close** ❮❮ the **Navigation Pane**.

From the **Office** menu 🔘, click **Close Database**. From the **Getting Started** screen, display the **Office** menu 🔘, and then click **Exit Access**.

Objective 15
Use the Access Help System

Access has a Help feature to assist you when performing a task in Access or to get more information about a particular topic in Access. You can activate the Help feature by clicking the Help button or by pressing F1.

Activity 1.21 Using the Access Help System

1 **Start** Access. In the upper right corner of the Access window, click the **Help** button 🔘. In the **Access Help** window, click the **Search arrow**, and then under **Content from this computer**, click **Access Help**.

2 Click in the **Search** box, type **database design** and then press Enter. In the list that displays, click **Database design basics**.

This information is an informative overview of how to design a database from the beginning—from the stage where you are just writing your ideas on paper. If desired, print this information by clicking the Print button.

3 In the upper right corner of the Help window, click the **Close** button ⊠ to close the Help window.

End **You have completed Project 1B** ———————————————

There's More You Can Do!

From My Computer, navigate to the student files that accompany this textbook. In the folder **02_theres_more_you_can_do_pg1_36**, locate and open the folder for this chapter. Open and print the instructions for this project, which are provided to you in Adobe PDF format.

Try IT! 1—Convert a Database to a Different Format

In this Try IT! exercise, you will convert an Access 2007 database to a database that others can view and edit in Access 2002 or Access 2003.

Content-Based Assessments

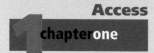

Summary

Microsoft Office Access is a database management system that uses various objects—tables, forms, queries, reports—to organize a database. Data is stored in tables in which you establish fields, set the data type and field size, and create a primary key. Data from a database can be reported and printed.

Key Terms

The ⊙ symbol represents Key Terms found on the Student CD in the 02_theres_more_you_can_do folder for this chapter.

Content-Based Assessments

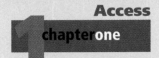

Access
chapterone

Matching

Match each term in the second column with its correct definition in the first column. Write the letter of the term on the blank line in front of the correct definition.

_____ **1.** An organized collection of facts about people, events, things, or ideas related to a particular topic or purpose.

_____ **2.** Facts about people, events, things, or ideas.

_____ **3.** Data that is organized in a useful manner.

_____ **4.** The basic parts of a database, which include tables, forms, queries, reports, and macros.

_____ **5.** The Access object that stores your data organized in an arrangement of columns and rows.

_____ **6.** The area of the Access window that displays and organizes the names of the objects in a database, and from where you open objects for use.

_____ **7.** The portion of the Access window that displays open objects.

_____ **8.** A category that describes each piece of data stored in a table.

_____ **9.** All of the categories of data pertaining to one person, place, thing, event, or idea.

_____ **10.** The number of fields, and the type of content within each field, in an Access table.

_____ **11.** The Access view that displays an object organized in a format of columns and rows similar to an Excel spreadsheet.

_____ **12.** The Access view that displays the underlying structure of an object.

_____ **13.** The action of filling a database table with records.

_____ **14.** The characteristic that defines the kind of data that can be entered into a field, such as numbers, text, or dates.

_____ **15.** An Access feature that sequentially numbers entered records creating a unique number for each field and which is useful for data that has no distinct field that is unique.

A AutoNumber

B Data

C Data type

D Database

E Datasheet view

F Design view

G Field

H Information

I Navigation Pane

J Object window

K Objects

L Populate

M Record

N Table

O Table design

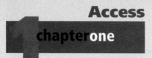

Fill in the Blank

Write the correct word in the space provided.

1. DBMS is an acronym for _____ _____ _____.

2. A preformatted database designed for a specific purpose is a database _____.

3. A database that has no data and has no database tools, in which you create the data and the tools as you need them, is referred to as a _____ database.

4. Characteristics of a field that control how the field will display and how data can be entered in a field are known as the _____ _____.

5. The field that uniquely identifies a record in a table is the _____ _____.

6. A pre-built table format for common topics such as contacts, issues, and tasks is a _____ _____.

7. A database object that retrieves specific data from one or more tables, and then displays the specified data in Datasheet view is a _____.

8. A type of query that retrieves data from one or more tables and makes it available for use in the format of a datasheet is a _____ query.

9. The table or tables from which a query gets its data is the _____ _____.

10. A feature in Microsoft Office programs that walks you step by step through a process is a _____.

11. The process in which Access searches a table of records included in a query, finds the records that match the criteria, and then displays the records in a datasheet is called _____.

12. An Access object with which you can enter new records into a table, edit existing records in a table, or display existing records from a table is a _____.

13. The Access object that displays data in a formatted manner for printing and publication is a _____.

14. The Access form object in which multiple records can be entered into or displayed from a table is a _____ _____ form.

15. An arrangement of objects in the Navigation Pane in which the objects are grouped by the table to which they are related is the _____ _____ _____ category.

Skills Review

Project 1C — Medical Center Departments

In this project, you will apply the skills you practiced from the Objectives in Project 1A.

Objectives: 1. *Start Access and Create a New Blank Database;* **2.** *Add Records to a Table;* **3.** *Rename Table Fields in Datasheet View;* **4.** *Modify the Design of a Table;* **5.** *Add a Second Table to a Database;* **6.** *Print a Table;* **7.** *Create and Use a Query;* **8.** *Create and Use a Form;* **9.** *Create and Print a Report;* **10.** *Close and Save a Database.*

In the following Skills Review, you will assist Kendall Walker, the CEO of Texas Lakes Medical Center, in creating a database to store information about the Departments and Department Directors at Texas Lakes Medical Center. Your printed results will look similar to those in Figure 1.57.

For Project 1C, you will need the following file:

New blank Access database

You will save your database as
1C_Departments_Firstname_Lastname

Figure 1.57

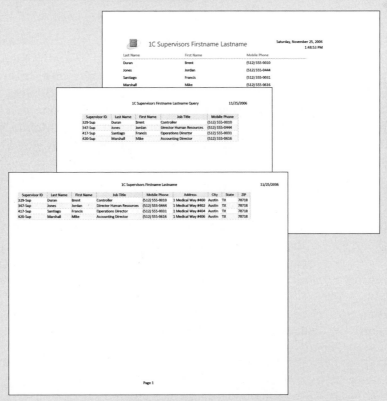

(Project 1C–Medical Center Departments continues on the next page)

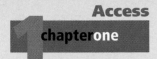

Skills Review

(Project 1C–Medical Center Departments continued)

1. **Start** Access and create a new **Blank Database**. In the lower right portion of the screen, click the **file folder icon**, navigate to your Access Chapter 1 folder, and then save the database as **1C_Departments_Firstname_Lastname** Press Enter. In the lower right corner, click the **Create** button.

2. In the **Navigation Pane**, click the **Close** button to collapse the **Navigation Pane** and maximize your screen space. Click in the first **Add New Field** box, type **Accounting** and then click in the **ID** field. To assign custom Department IDs, on the **Datasheet tab**, in the **Data Type & Formatting group**, click the **Data Type arrow**, and then click **Text**. Type **1212-D** and then click in the next **Add New Field** box to the right of *Accounting*, and complete the entry of this record and the next record as follows.

ID	Field1	Field2	Field3	Field4	Field5	Field6	Field7	Field8	Field9	Field10
1212-D	Accounting	Jennifer	R	Lee	(512) 555-0987	1 Medical Way #216	Austin	TX	78718	Duran
1233-D	Employee Benefits	Mike	M	Hernandez	(512) 555-0344	1 Medical Way #214	Austin	TX	78718	Duran

3. Point to the text *ID*, and then click to select the column. On the **Datasheet tab**, in the **Fields & Columns group**, click the **Rename** button, type **Dept ID** and press Enter. Point to the text *Field1*, right-click, and from the displayed menu, click **Rename Column**. Type **Department** and press Enter. Point to the text *Field2* and double-click. With the text selected, type **Director First Name** and press Enter. Using any of these techniques, rename *Field3* as **Director Middle Initial** Rename *Field4* as **Director Last Name** Rename *Field5* as **Mobile Phone** Rename *Field6* as **Address** Rename *Field7* as **City** Rename *Field8* as **State** Rename *Field9* as **ZIP** Rename *Field10* as **Supervisor**

4. Enter the following additional records:

Dept ID	Department	Director First Name	Director Middle Initial	Director Last Name	Mobile Phone	Address	City	State	ZIP	Supervisor
1259-D	Emergency Room	Paul	S	Roberts	(512) 555-0234	1 Medical Way #212	Austin	TX	78718	Marshall
1265-D	Nursing Services	Andrea	T	McMillan	(512) 555-0233	1 Medical Way #302	Austin	TX	78718	Jones

(Project 1C–Medical Center Departments continues on the next page)

(Project 1C–Medical Center Departments continued)

1313-D	Finance	Beth	N	Crosby	(512) 555-0266	1 Medical Way #301	Austin	TX	78718	Duran
1355-D	Physician Services	Laura	O	Klein	(512) 555-0277	1 Medical Way #146	Austin	TX	78718	Jones
1459-D	Facilities	Mario	B	Bartello	(512) 555-0211	1 Medical Way #236	Austin	TX	78718	Santiago

5. On the **Datasheet tab**, in the **Views group**, click the **View button arrow**. From the displayed list, click **Design View**. To save the changes you made to the field names and data types, and to give the table a more meaningful name, save the table, using your own first and last name, as **1C Departments Firstname Lastname** and then click **OK**.

6. In the **Field Name** column, click the row selector box to the left of the **Director Middle Initial** field name to select the entire row. Then, on the **Design tab**, in the **Tools group**, click the **Delete Rows** button, read the message in the displayed dialog box, and then click **Yes**. For this table, Kendall decides that having the Director's middle initial is not necessary.

7. With your table still displayed in Design view, in the **Field Name** column, click in the **Dept ID** box. To the left of the box, notice the small icon of a key representing the primary key. Recall that the primary key is the field that uniquely identifies each individual record—no two records in the database will have the same Dept ID.

8. In the **Field Name** column, click in the **State** field, and then in the **Field Properties** area, set the **Field Size** to **2** In the **Description** column, click in the **Address** row, and then type **Include the Room number** Recall that descriptions entered here will display in the status bar when entering records using a form. This will communicate additional information to the person entering data about how to enter data in the field.

9. Click the **View** button to return to Datasheet view, and then click **Yes** two times to save the changes you have made to the design of your table—deleting a field, adding a description, and changing a field property.

10. With your **1C Departments** table displayed in Datasheet view, notice that in the **Supervisor** field, several names are repeated. Thus, it would not make sense to include information about these individuals multiple times in the same table. Recall that when you see repeated information, it is likely that an additional table should be added to your database. On the Ribbon, click the **Create tab**. In the **Tables group**, click **Table Templates**, and then from the displayed list, click **Contacts**.

11. Click the **Datasheet tab** to display the groups of Datasheet commands. In the second column, point to the text *Company*, click to select the field, and then on the **Datasheet tab**, in the **Fields & Columns group**, click **Delete**.

(Project 1C–Medical Center Departments continues on the next page)

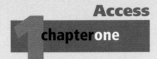
(Project 1C–Medical Center Departments continued)

12. Delete the **E-mail Address** field. With your mouse, drag to the right to select the **Business Phone** field and **Home Phone** field. Right-click over the field names, and then from the displayed shortcut menu, click **Delete Column**. Delete the **Fax Number** field. Then, delete the fields **Country/Region**, **Web Page**, **Notes**, and **Attachments** (the field with the paper clip icon).

13. On the **Datasheet tab**, in the **Views group**, click the **View** button to switch to **Design view**. To save the changes you made to the field arrangement and to give the table a more meaningful name, save the table, using your own first and last name, as **1C Supervisors Firstname Lastname** and then click **OK**.

14. In the **Field Name** column, click the **ID** box, delete the text, and then type **Supervisor ID** Click in the **Data Type** box, click the **Data Type arrow**, and then from the displayed list, click **Text**. Click in the **Description** column, and type **Supervisor's ID number** The medical center assigns a unique ID number to each Supervisor, which you will use as the primary key instead of the AutoNumber.

15. In the **Field Name** column, click in the **State/Province** field, and then in the **Field Properties** area, set the **Field Size** to **2** Click the **View** button to switch to Datasheet view, and then click **Yes** to save the changes you have made to the design of your table—changing a field name, adding a description, and changing a field property.

16. With your **1C Supervisors** table displayed in Datasheet view, in the new record row which is indicated by an asterisk (*) in the record selector box on the left, click in the **Supervisor ID** field, and then add the following records:

Supervisor ID	Last Name	First Name	Job Title	Mobile Phone	Address	City	State/Province	ZIP/Postal Code
329-Sup	Duran	Brent	Controller	(512) 555-0010	1 Medical Way #400	Austin	TX	78718
347-Sup	Jones	Jordan	Director Human Resources	(512) 555-0444	1 Medical Way #402	Austin	TX	78718
417-Sup	Santiago	Francis	Operations Director	(512) 555-0031	1 Medical Way #404	Austin	TX	78718
420-Sup	Marshall	Mike	Accounting Director	(512) 555-0616	1 Medical Way #406	Austin	TX	78718

17. Change the field name **State/Province** to **State** and **ZIP/Postal Code** to **ZIP** Select all of the columns, and then apply **Best Fit** either by double-clicking the right border of any selected column or by displaying the shortcut menu, clicking Column Width, and then clicking Best Fit. On the **Quick Access Toolbar**, click **Save** to save the changes you have made to the layout of the table.

(Project 1C–Medical Center Departments continues on the next page)

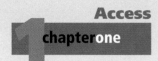

(Project 1C–Medical Center Departments continued)

18. From the **Office** menu, point to the **Print** button, and then click **Print Preview**. In the **Page Layout group**, click the **Margins** button, and then click **Normal**. Click the **Landscape** button. If you are submitting paper results, click the **Print** button, and in the displayed **Print** dialog box, click **OK**. To submit electronically, follow the directions provided by your instructor. Click **Close Print Preview**.

19. **Close** your **1C Supervisors** table and **Close** your **1C Departments** table. Click the **Create tab**, and then in the **Other group**, click **Query Wizard**. In the **New Query** dialog box, click **Simple Query Wizard**, and then click **OK**. Click the **Tables/Queries arrow**, and then click your **Table: 1C Supervisors**. Under **Available Fields**, click **Supervisor ID**, and then click the **Add Field** button to move the field to the **Selected Fields** list on the right. Add the **Last Name**, **First Name**, **Job Title**, and **Mobile Phone** fields to the **Selected Fields** list. Recall that you can also double-click a field name to move it.

This query will answer the question *What is the Supervisor ID, name, job title, and mobile phone number of every Supervisor in the database?* Click the **Next** button. Be sure that the option **Open the query to view information** is selected. Click **Finish**. Display the query in Print Preview, use the default margins and orientation, and then print or submit electronically. Close the Print Preview.

20. **Close** your query. **Open** the **Navigation Pane**, click to select your **1C Supervisors** table. You need not open the table, just select it. **Close** the **Navigation Pane**. On the Ribbon, click the **Create tab**, and then in the **Forms group**, click **Form**. The form displays in Layout view, in which you can make changes to the layout of the form. Because no changes are necessary, on the **Home tab**, in the **Views group**, click the **View button arrow**, and then from the displayed list, click **Form View**. From the **Office** menu, click **Save** to save your newly designed form, and then click **OK** to accept the default name. **Close** the form object. Recall that you typically create forms to make data entry easier for the individuals who enter new records into your database.

21. **Open** the **Navigation Pane**, locate your **1C Supervisors** table—recall that a table displays a small icon of a datasheet, a query displays a small icon of two datasheets, and a form displays a red form icon. Open the table either by double-clicking the table name or right-clicking and clicking Open from the shortcut menu. **Close** the **Navigation Pane**. On the **Create tab**, in the **Reports group**, click **Report**.

22. Point to the **Supervisor ID** column heading, right-click, and then click **Delete**. Delete the **Job Title**, **Address**, **City**, **State**, and **ZIP** fields from the report layout. From the **Office** menu, display **Print Preview**. In the **Page Layout group**, click the **Margins** button, and then click **Wide**. Click the **Landscape** button. If you are submitting paper results, click the **Print** button. To submit electronically, follow the instructions provided by your instructor. Click **Close Print Preview**.

23. **Close** your **1C Supervisors** report, and then click **Yes** to save the design changes. In the **Save As** dialog box, click **OK** to save the report with the default name. If necessary, close any remaining objects and close the Navigation Pane. From the **Office** menu, click **Exit Access**.

End You have completed Project 1C

Content-Based Assessments

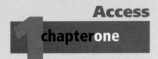

Project 1D — Benefits Fair

In this project, you will apply the skills you practiced from the Objectives in Project 1B.

Objectives: 11. *Create a Database Using a Template;* **12.** *Organize Database Objects in the Navigation Pane;* **13.** *Create a New Table in a Database Created with a Template;* **14.** *View a Report and Print a Table in a Database Created with a Template.*

In the following Skills Review, you will assist Sharon Fitzgerald, the Human Resources Director at Texas Lakes Medical Center, in creating a database to store information about the Employee Benefits Fair at Texas Lakes Medical Center. Your printed result will look similar to Figure 1.58.

For Project 1D, you will need the following file:

New Access database using the Events Template

You will save your database as
1D_Benefits_Fair_Firstname_Lastname

Figure 1.58

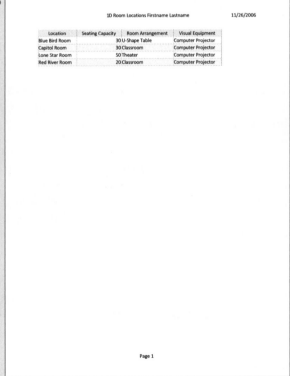

(Project 1D–Benefits Fair continues on the next page)

(Project 1D–Benefits Fair continued)

1. **Start** Access, under **Template Categories**, click **Local Templates**, and then click **Events**. In the lower right portion of the screen, click the **file folder icon**, navigate to your Access Chapter 1 folder, and then save the database as **1D_Benefits_Fair_Firstname_Lastname** Press Enter. In the lower right corner, click the **Create** button. If necessary, to the right of the **Security Warning**, click **Options**, click **Enable this content**, and then click **OK**.

2. Recall that a template opens with a pre-built Multiple Items form into which you can enter records to build a table. In the Event List Multiple Items form, enter the following records, pressing Tab to move across the row:

ID	Title	Start Time	End Time	Description	Location
1	Medical Plan	5/1/09 8a	5/1/09 5p	Health Benefits	Lone Star Room
2	Eye Care Plan	5/1/09 9a	5/1/09 3p	Health Benefits	Red River Room
3	Prescription Plan	5/1/09 8a	5/1/09 8p	Health Benefits	Lone Star Room
4	Pension Plan	5/1/09 10a	5/1/09 7:30p	Retirement Benefits	Capitol Room
5	Life Insurance Plan	5/1/09 1p	5/1/09 5p	Life Insurance Benefits	Blue Bird Room
6	Deferred Compensation Plan	5/1/09 10a	5/1/09 3p	Compensation Benefits	Red River Room

3. In the **Link bar**, just above the Field names, click **New Event**, and then enter the following record using the single record form. Recall that you can also use this form to enter records into a table:

Title	Location	Start Time	End Time	Description
Dental Plan	Blue Bird Room	5/1/09 8a	5/1/09 5p	Health Benefits

4. **Close** the single record form. **Close** the **Event List** form. **Open** the **Navigation Pane**. At the top of the **Navigation Pane**, click the **Navigation arrow**. In the **Navigate To Category** section, click **Tables and Related Views**. Click the **Navigation arrow** again, and then in the **Filter By Group** section, notice that **All Tables** is selected. Recall that this arrangement organizes the database objects by the table to which they are related.

5. From the **Navigation Pane**, right-click the **Events** table, and then click **Open**—or double-click the table name to open it. This is the table that was built from the records you entered into the form. Rather than enter information about the Locations multiple times in this table, you will create another table for the Location information. **Close** the **Events** table, and then **Close** the **Navigation Pane**.

(Project 1D–Benefits Fair continues on the next page)

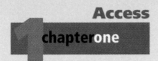

(Project 1D–Benefits Fair continued)

6. On the Ribbon, click the **Create tab**, and then in the **Tables group**, click **Table**. Enter the fol-
    lowing records, pressing Tab or Enter to move across the row. Recall that Access will assign
    unique numbers; your assigned numbers may vary.

ID	Field1	Field2	Field3	Field4
4	Blue Bird Room	30	U-Shape Table	Computer Projector
5	Red River Room	20	Classroom	Computer Projector
6	Capitol Room	30	Classroom	Computer Projector

7. Point to the text *Field1* and click to select the column. On the **Datasheet tab**, in the **Fields &
    Columns group**, click **Rename**, and then type **Location** Point to the text *Field2*, right-click,
    and then from the displayed menu, click **Rename Column**. Type **Seating Capacity** Point to the
    text *Field3* and double-click. With the text selected, type **Room Arrangement** Using any of these
    techniques, rename *Field4* as **Visual Equipment**

8. Enter one additional record as follows:

ID	Location	Seating Capacity	Room Arrangement	Visual Equipment
7	Lone Star Room	50	Theater	Computer Projector

9. On the **Home tab**, in the **Views group**, click the **View button arrow**, and then click **Design
    View**. **Save** the table as **1D Room Locations Firstname Lastname** and then click **OK**.

10. In the **Field Name** column, click in the **Location** box, and then on the **Design tab**, click the
    Primary Key button. Point to the row selector box for the **ID** field, and then click to select the
    entire row. On the **Design tab**, click **Delete Rows**, and then click **Yes**. The Location name will
    serve as the primary key for this table. In the **Views group**, click the **View** button, and then
    click **Yes** to save the changes you made to the table design.

11. On the field name row, drag across to select all of the columns. Right-click over any column
    heading, click **Column Width**, and then in the displayed **Column Width** dialog box, click
    Best Fit.

12. **Close** the **1D Room Locations** table, and then click **Yes** to save the layout changes you made
    to the column widths. From the **Navigation Pane**, open the **All Events** report. Open the **Event
    Details** report. The pre-built reports are arranged in various useful formats. **Close** both
    reports.

13. From the **Navigation Pane**, open your **1D Room Locations** table. From the **Office** menu,
    point to the **Print** button, and then click **Print Preview**. Check your *Chapter Assignment Sheet*
    or *Course Syllabus*, or consult your instructor, to determine whether you are to submit the

(Project 1D–Benefits Fair continues on the next page)

Content-Based Assessments

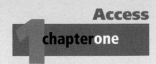

Skills Review

(Project 1D–Benefits Fair continued)

printed page. If you are submitting your work on paper, on the **Print Preview tab**, in the **Print group**, click **Print**. To submit electronically, follow the directions provided by your instructor.

14. Close Print Preview, and then **Close** your **1D Room Locations** table. **Close** the **Navigation Pane**. Be sure all database objects are closed. From the **Office** menu, click **Exit Access**.

 End **You have completed Project 1D** —————————————————————————

Content-Based Assessments

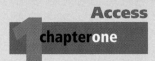
Mastering Access

Project 1E—Orthopedic Supplies

In this project, you will apply the skills you practiced from the Objectives in Project 1A.

Objectives: 1. *Start Access and Create a New Blank Database;* **2.** *Add Records to a Table;* **3.** *Rename Table Fields in Datasheet View;* **4.** *Modify the Design of a Table;* **5.** *Add a Second Table to a Database;* **6.** *Print a Table;* **7.** *Create and Use a Query;* **8.** *Create and Use a Form;* **9.** *Create and Print a Report;* **10.** *Close and Save a Database.*

In the following Mastering Access assessment, you will assist Kelley Martin, the Orthopedics Director of Texas Lakes Medical Center, in creating a database to store information about medical suppliers and supplies. Your printed results will look similar to those shown in Figure 1.59.

For Project 1E, you will need the following file:

New blank Access database

You will save your database as
1E_Orthopedic_Supplies_Firstname_Lastname

Figure 1.59

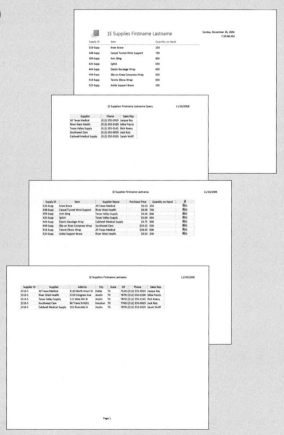

(Project 1E–Orthopedic Supplies continues on the next page)

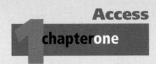

(Project 1E–Orthopedic Supplies continued)

1. **Start** Access, create a new **Blank Database**, use the **open folder icon** to navigate to your chapter folder, and then name the new database **1E_Orthopedic_Supplies_Firstname_Lastname** Close the **Navigation Pane**, and then beginning in the first new field, add the following records:

ID	Field1	Field2	Field3	Field4	Field5	Field6	Field7	Field8	Field9
9	1312-S	All Texas Medical	6120 North Acorn Dr	Dallas	TX	75201	(512) 555-0929	Jacque Ray	14-O
10	1313-S	River West Health	5150 Congress Ave	Austin	TX	78701	(512) 555-0100	Mike Frantz	16-R

2. Rename *Field1* as **Supplier ID** Rename *Field2* as **Supplier** Rename *Field3* as **Address** Rename *Field4* as **City** Rename *Field5* as **State** Rename *Field6* as **ZIP** Rename *Field7* as **Phone** Rename *Field8* as **Sales Rep** Rename *Field9* as **Sales Code**

3. Click **View** to open the table in **Design view**. Name the table **1E Suppliers Firstname Lastname** Set the **Supplier ID** field as the **Primary Key**, and then delete the **ID** field. Set the **Field Size** for the **State** field to **2** Return to **Datasheet view**, save the changes, and then, beginning with *Supplier ID 1314-S*, enter the following records:

Supplier ID	Supplier	Address	City	State	ZIP	Phone	Sales Rep	Sales Code
1312-S	All Texas Medical	6120 North Acorn Dr	Dallas	TX	75201	(512) 555-0929	Jacque Ray	14-O
1313-S	River West Health	5150 Congress Ave	Austin	TX	78701	(512) 555-0100	Mike Frantz	16-R
1314-S	Texas Valley Supply	121 West 6th St	Austin	TX	78701	(512) 555-0145	Rich Keeny	12-R
1315-S	Southwest Care	80 Travis St #101	Houston	TX	77002	(512) 555-0929	Jack Ruiz	14-O
1316-S	Caldwell Medical Supply	192 Riverside Dr	Austin	TX	78701	(512) 555-0329	Sarah Wolff	16-O

4. **Delete** the **Sales Code** field. Apply **Best Fit** to all of the columns to accommodate their data and column headings. If you are submitting printed pages, display the **Print Preview**, change the margins to **Wide**, change the orientation to **Landscape**, and then print the table. For electronic submissions, follow your instructor's directions. **Close Print Preview**, and then on the **Quick Access Toolbar**, **Save** the changes you have made to your table.

(Project 1E–Orthopedic Supplies continues on the next page)

Content-Based Assessments

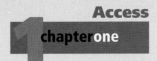
(Project 1E–Orthopedic Supplies continued)

5. Close your **1E Suppliers** table. Create a second table using the **Table Templates Assets** template to record the information about the orthopedic supplies that have been purchased by the medical center. Delete the following fields from the template: **Category, Condition, Acquired Date, Current Value, Location, Manufacturer, Model, Comments**, and **Retired Date**.

6. Rename the **Description** field as **Supplier Name** and then rename the **ID** field as **Supply ID** From the **Datasheet tab**, set the **Data Type** for the **Supply ID** field to **Text**. From the **Home tab**, switch to **Design view**, save the table as **1E Supplies Firstname Lastname** and then in the **Field Name** column, insert a new row above **Attachments**. Name the new field **Quantity on Hand** Click the **Supply ID** field, and then change its **Field Size** to **8** Return to **Datasheet view**, save your changes, and then add the following records:

Supply ID	Item	Supplier Name	Purchase Price Each	Quantity on Hand
323-Supp	Knee Brace	All Texas Medical	9.50	250
346-Supp	Carpal Tunnel Wrist Support	River West Health	8	700
399-Supp	Arm Sling	Texas Valley Supply	8	800
425-Supp	Splint	Texas Valley Supply	5	650
444-Supp	Elastic Bandage Wrap	Caldwell Medical Supply	9.75	900
449-Supp	Slip-on Knee Compress Wrap	Southwest Care	16.25	500
519-Supp	Tennis Elbow Wrap	All Texas Medical	28	600
525-Supp	Ankle Support Brace	River West Health	9.50	300

7. Select all the columns, and then apply **Best Fit**. Display the table in **Print Preview**, and then select **Wide** margins and **Landscape** orientation. If you are submitting printed pages, print the table. To submit electronically, follow the directions provided by your instructor.

8. **Close Print Preview, Close** the **1E Supplies** table, and then save the changes. On the **Create tab**, use the **Query Wizard** to create a **Simple Query** based on the **1E Suppliers** table. The query will answer the question *What is the name of every supplier, their phone number, and their Sale Rep's name?* Add the **Supplier** field, **Phone** field, and **Sales Rep** field. Title the query as **1E Suppliers Firstname Lastname Query** Print and then close the query.

9. From the **Navigation Pane**, select your **1E Supplies** table—you do not need to open the table, just be sure that it is selected. **Create** a **Form** based on the table, click the **View button arrow**

(Project 1E–Orthopedic Supplies continues on the next page)

Content-Based Assessments

(Project 1E–Orthopedic Supplies continued)

and then click **Form View**. When needed, the form can be used to enter or view records one record at a time.

10. **Close** the form, and then save it with the default name. **Create** a **Report** based on your **1E Supplies** table. Delete the **Supplier Name** field, the **Purchase Price** field, and the **Attachments** field from the report. In **Print Preview**, set the **Margins** to **Wide** and the orientation to **Landscape**. If you are submitting printed pages, print the table. To submit electronically, follow the directions provided by your instructor.

11. **Close Print Preview**, close and save the report with the default name. Close any open objects, close the **Navigation Pane**, and then from the **Office** menu, click **Exit Access**.

 You have completed Project 1E ——————————————————————————

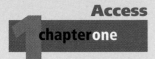

Mastering Access

Project 1F—Fundraisers

In this project, you will apply the skills you practiced from the Objectives in Project 1B.

Objectives: 11. *Create a Database Using a Template;* **12.** *Organize Database Objects in the Navigation Pane;* **13.** *Create a New Table in a Database Created with a Template;* **14.** *View a Report and Print a Table in a Database Created with a Template.*

In the following Mastering Access project, you will assist Kirk Shaw, the Development Director for Texas Lakes Medical Center, in creating a database to store information about the various fundraising events held throughout the year. Your printed results will look similar to those shown in Figure 1.60.

For Project 1F, you will need the following file:

New Access database using the Events Template

**You will save your database as
1F_Fundraisers_Firstname_Lastname**

Figure 1.60

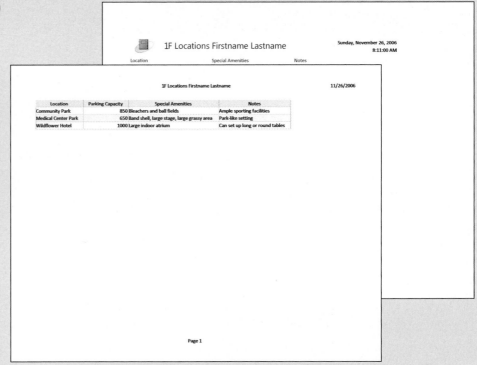

(Project 1F–Fundraisers continues on the next page)

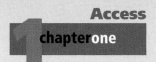
(Project 1F—Fundraisers continued)

1. **Start** Access, and then from **Local Templates**, create a new database using the **Events** database template. In the lower right portion of the screen, click the **file folder icon**, navigate to your Access Chapter 1 folder, and then name the new database **1F_Fundraisers_Firstname_Lastname** In the lower right corner, click the **Create** button. If necessary, to the right of the **Security Warning**, click **Options**, click **Enable this content**, and then click **OK**.

2. To build the Event List table, enter the following records using either the displayed Multiple Items form or the single record form, which is available by clicking New Event in the Link bar:

ID	Title	Start Time	End Time	Description	Location
1	**Heart Ball**	**2/14/09 6p**	**2/14/09 11p**	**Gala Ball**	**Wildflower Hotel**
2	**Auto Raffle**	**3/30/09 4p**	**3/30/09 6p**	**Raffle**	**Medical Center Park**
3	**Spring Book Sale**	**4/5/09 8a**	**4/5/09 8p**	**New and Used Book Sale**	**Wildflower Hotel**
4	**Softball Contest**	**6/10/09 11a**	**6/10/09 6p**	**Softball games**	**Community Park**
5	**Taste of Texas**	**8/28/09 11a**	**8/28/09 11p**	**Food and music festival**	**Community Park**
6	**Holiday Kids Fair**	**12/15/09 1p**	**12/15/09 7p**	**Children's Rides and Games**	**Medical Center Park**

3. **Close** the **Event List** form. **Open** the **Navigation Pane**, and then using the **Navigation arrow**, arrange the **Navigation Pane** by **Tables and Related Views.** From the **Navigation Pane**, open the **Events** table that you created by entering records in the form. Select all the columns in the table, apply **Best Fit**, and then **Close** the table and save the changes to the layout. **Close** the **Navigation Pane**, and then **Create** a second **Table**. Enter the following records. Recall that Access will assign unique ID numbers; yours may vary.

ID	Field 1	Field 2	Field 3	Field 4
4	**Wildflower Hotel**	**1000**	**Large indoor atrium**	**Can set up long or round tables**
5	**Community Park**	**850**	**Bleachers and ball fields**	**Ample sporting facilities**
6	**Medical Center Park**	**650**	**Band shell, large stage, large grassy area**	**Park-like setting**

4. Rename *Field1* as **Location** Rename *Field2* as **Parking Capacity** Rename *Field3* as **Special Amenities** Rename *Field4* as **Notes** Display the table in **Design view**, and then name it **1F Locations Firstname Lastname** Set the **Location** field as the **Primary Key**—no two locations will have the same name. Delete the **ID** field row.

5. Return to Datasheet view, save the design changes, select all the table columns, and then apply **Best Fit**. Display the table in **Print Preview**; select **Wide** margins and **Landscape**

(Project 1F—Fundraisers continues on the next page)

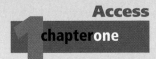

(Project 1F—Fundraisers continued)

orientation. If you are submitting printed pages, print the table. To submit electronically, follow the directions provided by your instructor. **Close** the table and save the changes to the layout.

6. Be sure your **1F Locations** table is still active, **Create** a **Report** based on the table. In the report, delete the **Parking Capacity** field, and then display the report in **Print Preview**. Select **Landscape** orientation, **Wide** margins, and then **Print** the report. To submit electronically, follow the directions provided by your instructor.

7. **Close Print Preview**, **Close** the report, save the changes to the design, and then accept the default report name. Close and save any open objects, and then **Exit** Access.

 You have completed Project 1F ————————————————

Content-Based Assessments

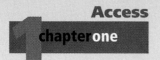
Mastering Access

Project 1G — Gift Shop

In this project, you will apply skills you practiced from the Objectives in Projects 1A and 1B.

Objectives: 1. *Start Access and Create a New Blank Database;* **2.** *Add Records to a Table;* **3.** *Rename Table Fields in Datasheet View;* **4.** *Modify the Design of a Table;* **5.** *Add a Second Table to a Database;* **6.** *Print a Table;* **7.** *Create and Use a Query;* **8.** *Create and Use a Form;* **9.** *Create and Print a Report;* **10.** *Close and Save a Database;* **12.** *Organize Database Objects in the Navigation Pane.*

In the following Mastering Access project, you will assist Scott Williams, the Gift Shop Manager of Texas Lakes Medical Center, in creating a database to store information about gift items in the shop's inventory. Your printed results will look similar to those shown in Figure 1.61.

For Project 1G, you will need the following file:

New Access database

**You will save your database as
1G_Gift_Shop_Firstname_Lastname**

Figure 1.61

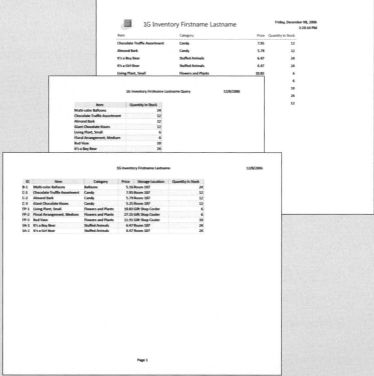

(Project 1G—Gift Shop continues on the next page)

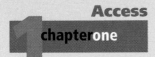

(Project 1G—Gift Shop continued)

1. **Start** Access, create a new **Blank Database**, and then store it in your Access Chapter 1 folder as **1G_Gift_Shop_Firstname_Lastname**

2. **Close** the **Navigation Pane**. Change the **ID** field **Data Type** to **Text**. Enter the following records:

ID	Field1	Field2	Field3	Field4	Field5
C-1	Chocolate Truffle Assortment	Candy	7.95	Room 107	12
C-2	Almond Bark	Candy	5.79	Room 107	12
SA-1	It's a Boy Bear	Stuffed Animals	6.47	Room 107	24
SA-2	It's a Girl Bear	Stuffed Animals	6.47	Room 107	24
FP-1	Living Plant, Small	Flowers and Plants	10.83	Gift Shop Cooler	6
FP-2	Floral Arrangement, Medium	Flowers and Plants	27.15	Gift Shop Cooler	6
FP-3	Bud Vase	Flowers and Plants	11.91	Gift Shop Cooler	10
B-1	Multi-color Balloons	Balloons	5.16	Room 107	24
C-3	Giant Chocolate Kisses	Candy	5.25	Room 107	12

3. Rename *Field1* as **Item** Rename *Field2* as **Category** Rename *Field3* as **Price** Rename *Field4* as **Storage Location** Rename *Field5* as **Quantity in Stock** Select all the table columns, and then apply **Best Fit**. On the **Quick Access Toolbar**, **Save** the table, and name it **1G Inventory Firstname Lastname** Display the table in **Print Preview**, set the margins to **Wide** and the orientation to **Landscape**. If you are submitting printed pages, click **Print**; or submit electronically as directed by your instructor. **Close Print Preview**; close the table and save any changes.

4. **Create** a second **Table** to record the information about the storage of inventory categories. Add the following records to the new table. Recall that Access will assign unique ID numbers; yours may vary.

ID	Field1	Field2	Field3
3	Candy	Room 107	North Zone 1
4	Stuffed Animals	Room 107	South Zone 2
5	Flowers and Plants	Gift Shop Coolers	Cooler 1
6	Balloons	Room 107	East Zone 3

(Project 1G–Gift Shop continues on the next page)

Content-Based Assessments

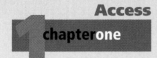
(Project 1G–Gift Shop continued)

5. Rename *Field1* as **Category** Rename *Field2* as **Storage Location** Rename *Field3* as **Location Detail** Switch to Design view, name the table **1G Categories Firstname Lastname** Set the **Category** field as the **Primary Key**—each category of inventory items is unique. Delete the **ID** field. Switch back to Datasheet view and save the changes. Select all the columns, and then apply **Best Fit**. **Close** your **1G Categories** table, and then save the changes to the layout.

6. **Create**, using the **Query Wizard**, a **Simple Query** based on your **1G Inventory** table. Include only the **Item** and **Quantity in Stock** fields in the query result. The query will answer the question *How many of each item do we currently have in stock?* Accept the default name, and then print and close the query.

7. **Create** a **Report** based on your **1G Inventory** table. Delete the **ID** field and the **Storage Location** field. Display the report in **Print Preview**, set the margins to **Wide** and the orientation to **Landscape**. If you are submitting printed pages, print the table. To submit electronically, follow the directions provided by your instructor. Close the report, save the design changes, and then accept the default name. **Close** any open objects and close the **Navigation Pane**. From the **Office** menu, **Exit Access**.

 You have completed Project 1G

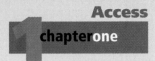

Project 1H—Recruiting Events

In this project, you will apply skills you practiced from the Objectives in Projects 1A and 1B.

Objectives: 2. *Add Records to a Table;* **6.** *Print a Table;* **7.** *Create and Use a Query;* **10.** *Close and Save a Database;* **11.** *Create a Database Using a Template;* **12.** *Organize Database Objects in the Navigation Pane;* **13.** *Create a New Table in a Database Created with a Template;* **14.** *View a Report and Print a Table in a Database Created with a Template.*

In the following Mastering Access project, you will assist Serge Juco, Vice President of Human Resources, in creating a database to track recruiting events that are scheduled to attract new employees to careers at the medical center. Your printed results will look similar to those shown in Figure 1.62.

For Project 1H, you will need the following file:

New Access database using the Events Template

You will save your database as
1H_Recruiting_Events_Firstname_Lastname

Figure 1.62

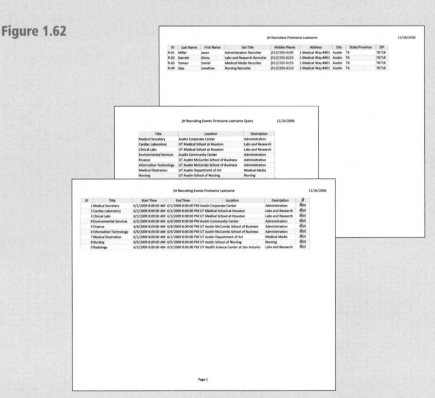

(Project 1H–Recruiting Events continues on the next page)

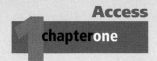
(Project 1H–Recruiting Events continued)

1. **Start** Access and then from **Local Templates**, create a new database based on the **Events** template. In your Access Chapter 1 folder, name the new database **1H_Recruiting_Events_Firstname_Lastname** In the lower right corner, click the **Create** button. If necessary, to the right of the **Security Warning**, click **Options**, click **Enable this content**, and then click **OK**.

2. In the **Multiple Items** form, enter the following records to build the Event List table; if you prefer, use the New Event single record form available on the Link bar:

ID	Title	Start Time	End Time	Description	Location
1	Medical Secretary	6/1/09 8a	6/1/09 8p	Administration	Austin Corporate Center
2	Cardiac Laboratory	6/2/09 8a	6/2/09 8p	Labs and Research	UT Medical School at Houston
3	Clinical Labs	6/2/09 8a	6/2/09 8p	Labs and Research	UT Medical School at Houston
4	Environmental Services	6/3/09 8a	6/4/09 8p	Administration	Austin Community Center
5	Finance	6/4/09 8a	6/4/09 8p	Administration	UT Austin McCombs School of Business
6	Information Technology	6/5/09 8a	6/5/09 8p	Administration	UT Austin McCombs School of Business
7	Medical Illustration	6/1/09 8a	6/1/09 8p	Medical Media	UT Austin Department of Art
8	Nursing	6/5/09 8a	6/5/09 8p	Nursing	UT Austin School of Nursing
9	Radiology	6/3/09 8a	6/3/09 8p	Labs and Research	UT Health Science Center at San Antonio

3. **Close** the form, and then display the **Navigation Pane**. Using the **Navigation arrow**, organize the objects by **Tables and Related Views**. Point to the **Events** table, right-click, click **Rename**, and then type **1H Recruiting Events Firstname Lastname** and press [Enter] to rename the table.

4. **Open** the table; recall that the table was built by typing records into the Multiple Items form. Leave the Attachments field because Serge may decide to attach job description brochures for each event. The AutoNumber ID will serve as the primary key—the unique identifier for each record. **Close** the **Navigation Pane**. Select all the columns and apply **Best Fit**. Display the table in **Print Preview**, set the margins to **Normal** and the orientation to **Landscape**. Print if

(Project 1H–Recruiting Events continues on the next page)

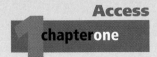

Access

Mastering Access

(Project 1H–Recruiting Events continued)

you are submitting paper results; or, follow your instructor's directions for electronic submission. **Close Print Preview**, and then **Close** the table, saving the changes to the layout.

5. **Create** a new table using the **Contacts Table Template**. Delete the **Company** field. Delete the **E-mail Address** field. Delete the **Business Phone** and **Home Phone** fields. Delete the **Fax Number** field. Delete the **Country/Region**, **Web Page**, **Notes**, and **Attachments** fields. Click in the first **ID** field, from the **Datasheet tab**, change the **Data Type** of the **ID** field to **Text**, and then enter the following records:

ID	Last Name	First Name	Job Title	Mobile Phone	Address	City	State/ Province	ZIP/ Postal Code
R-01	Miller	Jason	Administration Recruiter	(512) 555-0195	1 Medical Way #401	Austin	TX	78718
R-02	Garrett	Ginny	Labs and Research Recruiter	(512) 555-0223	1 Medical Way #401	Austin	TX	78718
R-03	Yeman	Daniel	Medical Media Recruiter	(512) 555-0155	1 Medical Way #401	Austin	TX	78718
R-04	Zeja	Jonathan	Nursing Recruiter	(512) 555-0122	1 Medical Way #401	Austin	TX	78718

6. **Close** the table, save the changes, and then name the table **1H Recruiters Firstname Lastname Create**, using the **Query Wizard**, a **Simple Query** based on your **1H Recruiting Events** table. Add the appropriate fields to the query to answer the question *What is the title, location, and description of all the recruiting events?* Accept the default name for the query. Print and then close the query.

7. From the **Navigation Pane**, open your **1H Recruiters** table. Change the name of the **ZIP/Postal Code** field to **ZIP** Select all the columns in the table and apply **Best Fit**. Display the table in **Print Preview**, set the margins to **Normal** and the orientation to **Landscape** and then either print or submit electronically.

8. **Close Print Preview**, and then **Close** the table, saving the layout changes. From the **Navigation Pane**, open the **All Events** report. Then, open the **Events By Week** report. Recall that one advantage of starting a database from a database template is that many objects, such as attractively arranged reports, are provided.

9. **Close** the reports and any other open objects. **Close** the **Navigation Pane**. From the **Office** menu, **Exit Access**.

End **You have completed Project 1H**

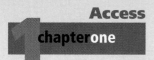

Project 1I— Facility Expansion

In this project, you will apply all the skills you practiced from the Objectives in Projects 1A and 1B.

Objectives: 1. *Start Access and Create a New Blank Database;* **2.** *Add Records to a Table;* **3.** *Rename Table Fields in Datasheet View;* **4.** *Modify the Design of a Table;* **5.** *Add a Second Table to a Database;* **6.** *Print a Table;* **7.** *Create and Use a Query;* **8.** *Create and Use a Form;* **9.** *Create and Print a Report;* **10.** *Close and Save a Database;* **11.** *Create a Database Using a Template;* **12.** *Organize Database Objects in the Navigation Pane;* **13.** *Create a New Table in a Database Created with a Template;* **14.** *View a Report and Print a Table in a Database Created with a Template.*

In the following Mastering Access project, you will assist Jerry Lopez, the Budget Director, in creating a database to store information about the facility expansion at Texas Lakes Medical Center and in creating a separate database to store information about public events related to the expansion. Your printed results will look similar to the ones shown in Figure 1.63.

For Project 1I, you will need the following files:

New Access database
New Events database

You will save your databases as
1I_Facility_Expansion_Firstname_Lastname
1I_Public_Events_Firstname_Lastname

Figure 1.63

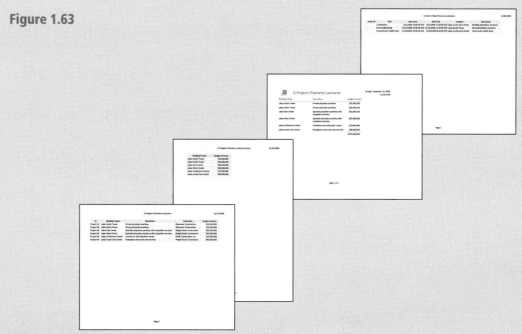

(Project 1I—Facility Expansion continues on the next page)

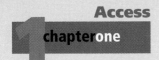

Mastering Access

(Project 1I—Facility Expansion continued)

1. **Start** Access, create a new **Blank Database**, and store it in your Access Chapter 1 folder as 1I_Facility_Expansion_Firstname_Lastname

2. **Close** the **Navigation Pane**. Change the **ID** field **Data Type** to **Text**. Enter the following records:

ID	Field1	Field2	Field3	Field4
Project-01	Lakes South Tower	Private physician practices	Glenmore Construction	30,000,000
Project-02	Lakes North Tower	Private physician practices	Glenmore Construction	30,000,000
Project-03	Lakes East Center	Specialty physician practices with outpatient services	Wright Rosen Contractors	60,000,000
Project-04	Lakes West Center	Specialty physician practices with outpatient services	Wright Rosen Contractors	60,000,000
Project-05	Lakes Conference Center	Conference and education center	Wells Construction, Inc.	10,000,000
Project-06	Lakes Acute Care Center	Emergency and acute care services	Wright Rosen Contractors	80,000,000

3. Rename *Field1* as **Building Project** Rename *Field2* as **Description** Rename *Field3* as **Contractor** Rename *Field4* as **Budget Amount** Change the **Data Type** of the **Budget Amount** field to **Currency**. Apply **Best Fit** to all the columns in the table. **Save** the table as **1I Projects Firstname Lastname** In **Print Preview**, set the margins to **Wide** and the orientation to **Landscape**. If you are submitting printed pages, click **Print**; or submit electronically as directed by your instructor. **Close Print Preview** and then close your **1I Projects** table.

4. **Create** a second **Table** to record the information about the contractors for the facility expansion. Add the following records to the new table. Recall that Access will assign unique ID numbers; your numbers may vary.

ID	Field1	Field2	Field3
3	Glenmore Construction	Bob Ballard	(512) 555-0900
4	Wright Rosen Contractors	Lisa Li	(512) 555-0707
5	Wells Construction, Inc.	Frank Levin	(512) 555-0444

(Project 1I—Facility Expansion continues on the next page)

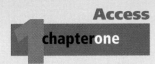

(Project 1I—Facility Expansion continued)

5. Rename *Field1* as **Contractor** Rename *Field2* as **Project Manager** Rename *Field3* as **Phone Number** Switch to **Design view**, name the table **1I Contractors Firstname Lastname** Set the **Contractor** field as the **Primary Key**—each contractor name is unique. Delete the **ID** field. Switch back to **Datasheet view** and save the changes. Apply **Best Fit** to all the columns. **Close** your **1I Contractors** table and save the changes to the layout—the column widths.

6. **Create**, using the **Query Wizard**, a **Simple Query** based on your **1I Projects** table. Include only the appropriate fields to answer the question *For each Building Project, what is the Budget Amount?* Accept the default name, display the query in **Print Preview**, and then print or submit electronically. **Close Print Preview**, and then close the query.

7. In the **Navigation Pane**, select your **1I Projects** table. **Create** a **Form**, close the **Navigation Pane**, view and then **Close** the form. Save and accept the default name.

8. **Open** your **1I Projects** table from the **Navigation Pane**. With the table open, **Create** a **Report**. Delete the **ID** field and the **Contractor** field. Display the report in **Print Preview**, set the margins to **Wide** and the orientation to **Landscape**. If you are submitting printed pages, print the report. To submit electronically, follow the directions provided by your instructor. **Close Print Preview**, close the report, save the changes, and accept the default name. **Close** any open objects and close the **Navigation Pane**. From the **Office** menu, click **Close Database**.

9. From the **Local Templates**, create a new database using the **Events template**. Create the database in your chapter folder and name it **1I_Public_Events_Firstname_Lastname** If necessary, enable the content.

10. To build the Events table, enter the following records using either the displayed Multiple Items Event List form or the single record form, which is available by clicking New Event in the Link bar:

Title	Start Time	End Time	Description	Location
Dedication	12/1/09 10a	12/1/09 11a	Building dedication ceremony	Lakes Acute Care Center
Groundbreaking	11/15/09 10a	11/15/09 11a	Groundbreaking ceremony	Lakes South Tower
Community Health Expo	11/30/09 10a	11/30/09 9p	Community Health Expo	Lakes Conference Center

11. **Close** the **Event List** form. **Open** the **Navigation Pane**, and then using the **navigation arrow**, arrange the **Navigation Pane** by **Tables and Related Views**. From the **Navigation Pane**, point to the **Events** table and right-click. From the shortcut menu, click **Rename**, type **1I Events Table Firstname Lastname** and then press Enter. Then open the table. Recall that the table was created by entering records in the form. Change the field name **ID** to **Event ID** Delete the **Attachments** field. Select all the columns in the table, apply **Best Fit**, and then display the table in **Print Preview**. Set the margins to **Normal** and the orientation to **Landscape**. Print or submit electronically, **Close Print Preview**, and then close the table and save the changes to the layout.

12. If necessary, close the Navigation Pane and close any open objects. Close the database and exit Access.

End **You have completed Project 1I**

Content-Based Assessments

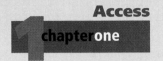

Business Running Case

Project 1J — Business Running Case

In this project, you will apply the skills you practiced in Projects 1A and 1B.

From My Computer, navigate to the student files that accompany this textbook. In the folder **03_business_running_case_pg37_86**, locate and open the folder for this chapter. Open and print the instructions for this project, which are provided to you in Adobe PDF format. Follow the instructions and use the skills you have gained thus far to assist Jennifer Nelson in meeting the challenges of owning and running her business.

 You have completed Project 1J ────────────

Outcomes-Based Assessments

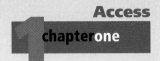

Rubric

The following outcomes-based assessments are *open-ended assessments*. That is, there is no specific correct result; your result will depend on your approach to the information provided. Make *Professional Quality* your goal. Use the following scoring rubric to guide you in *how* to approach the problem and then to evaluate *how well* your approach solves the problem.

The *criteria*—Software Mastery, Content, Format and Layout, and Process—represent the knowledge and skills you have gained that you can apply to solving the problem. The *levels of performance*—Professional Quality, Approaching Professional Quality, or Needs Quality Improvements—help you and your instructor evaluate your result.

	Your completed project is of Professional Quality if you:	Your completed project is Approaching Professional Quality if you:	Your completed project Needs Quality Improvements if you:
1-Software Mastery	Choose and apply the most appropriate skills, tools, and features and identify efficient methods to solve the problem.	Choose and apply some appropriate skills, tools, and features, but not in the most efficient manner.	Choose inappropriate skills, tools, or features, or are inefficient in solving the problem.
2-Content	Construct a solution that is clear and well organized, contains content that is accurate, appropriate to the audience and purpose, and is complete. Provide a solution that contains no errors of spelling, grammar, or style.	Construct a solution in which some components are unclear, poorly organized, inconsistent, or incomplete. Misjudge the needs of the audience. Have some errors in spelling, grammar, or style, but the errors do not detract from comprehension.	Construct a solution that is unclear, incomplete, or poorly organized, containing some inaccurate or inappropriate content; and contains many errors of spelling, grammar, or style. Do not solve the problem.
3-Format and Layout	Format and arrange all elements to communicate information and ideas, clarify function, illustrate relationships, and indicate relative importance.	Apply appropriate format and layout features to some elements, but not others. Overuse features, causing minor distraction.	Apply format and layout that does not communicate information or ideas clearly. Do not use format and layout features to clarify function, illustrate relationships, or indicate relative importance. Use available features excessively, causing distraction.
4-Process	Use an organized approach that integrates planning, development, self-assessment, revision, and reflection.	Demonstrate an organized approach in some areas, but not others; or, use an insufficient process of organization throughout.	Do not use an organized approach to solve the problem.

Outcomes-Based Assessments

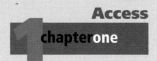

Problem Solving

Project 1K — Public Seminars

In this project, you will construct a solution by applying any combination of the skills you practiced from the Objectives in Projects 1A and 1B.

For Project 1K, you will need the following files:

New Access database
a1K_Public_Seminars (Word document)

You will save your database as
1K_Public_Seminars_Firstname_Lastname

Texas Lakes Medical Center has developed a series of public health seminars. The information about the seminars is located in your student files, in the Word document **a1K_Public_Seminars**. Using the data in the Word document and a new database created from the Events database template, enter the data into the Multiple Items form. Each seminar will begin at 7 p.m. and end at 9 p.m. After entering the records, in the Navigation Pane, point to the name of the table that was created as a result of entering the records into the Multiple Items form, click Rename, and then name the table **1K Seminars Firstname Lastname** Open the table, apply Best Fit to the table's columns, and then display and modify the Print Preview so that that all the columns fully display on a single sheet. Print the table or submit electronically. Close the database.

 End You have completed Project 1K ————————————

Outcomes-Based Assessments

Problem Solving

Project 1L — Media Contacts

In this project, you will construct a solution by applying any combination of the skills you practiced from the Objectives in Projects 1A and 1B.

> **For Project 1L, you will need the following files:**
>
> New Access database
> a1L_Media_Contacts (Word document)

You will save your database as
1L_Media_Contacts_Firstname_Lastname

The Public Relations Department at Texas Lakes Medical Center maintains a list of media contacts who receive e-mail notification when press releases regarding the Medical Center are issued. The information about the media contacts is located in your student files, in the Word document **a1L_Media_Contacts**. Create a new blank database, and then close the default Table1. Create a new table using the Contacts table template, and then use the data in the Word document to enter the records. Delete the unneeded fields from the table. As necessary, rename fields to match those in the Word document. Change the data type of the ID field to Text, and use the IDs provided. Close the table, and save it as **1L Media Contacts Firstname Lastname** Create a report and delete the Media ID column. In Page Setup or Print Preview, use narrow margins and landscape orientation to arrange the report. Print or submit the report electronically. Close the database.

 End **You have completed Project 1L** —————————

Outcomes-Based Assessments

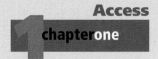

Problem Solving

Project 1M—Billing Rates

In this project, you will construct a solution by applying any combination of the skills you practiced from the Objectives in Projects 1A and 1B.

> **For Project 1M, you will need the following files:**
>
> New Access database
> a1M_Billing_Rates (Word document)
>
> **You will save your database as**
> **1M_Billing_Rates_Firstname_Lastname**

Physicians at Texas Lakes Medical Center have varying billing rates. The information about the physician names and billing rates is located in your student files, in the Word document **a1M_Billing_Rates**. Create a new blank database. Create a table with the Physician IDs and billing rates. For the rates, change data type to Currency. Apply Best Fit to the columns, save and name the table **1M Rates Firstname Lastname** and then print the table, or submit electronically as directed. From the table, create a query indicating only the Physician ID and the rate, and print or submit the query electronically. Create a second table using the Contacts table template, enter the names and phone numbers of the physicians, and delete unneeded columns. Apply Best Fit to the columns, save and name the table **1M Physicians Firstname Lastname** Print the table or submit electronically. Close the database.

 You have completed Project 1M ⎯⎯⎯⎯⎯⎯⎯

Outcomes-Based Assessments

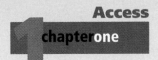

Problem Solving

Project 1N—Training

In this project, you will construct a solution by applying any combination of the skills you practiced from the Objectives in Projects 1A and 1B.

For Project 1N, you will need the following files:

New Access database
a1N_Training (Word document)

You will save your database as
1N_Training_Firstname_Lastname

Texas Lakes Medical Center has developed a series of training seminars to increase the skills of staff members in making public presentations and in dealing with the media. The information about the seminars is located in your student files, in the Word document **a1N_Training**. Using the data in the Word document and a new database created from the Events database template, enter the data into the Multiple Items form. Each seminar will begin at 8:30 a.m. and end at 11:30 a.m. After entering the records, in the Navigation Pane, point to the name of the table that was created as a result of entering the records into the Multiple Items form, click Rename, and then name the table **1N Training Firstname Lastname** Open the table, apply Best Fit to the table's columns, and then display and modify the Print Preview so that that all the columns fully display on a single sheet. Print the table or submit electronically. Close the database.

 End You have completed Project 1N ——————

Outcomes-Based Assessments

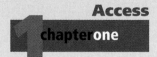

Problem Solving

Project 10 — Nurses

In this project, you will construct a solution by applying any combination of the skills you practiced from the Objectives in Projects 1A and 1B.

> **For Project 10, you will need the following files:**
>
> New Access database
> a10_Nurses (Word document)
>
> **You will save your database as**
> **10_Nurses_Firstname_Lastname**

The Nursing Supervisor at Texas Lakes Medical Center maintains a list of nurses and the departments to which they are assigned. The information about the nurses is located in your student files, in the Word document **a10_Nurses**. Create a new blank database, and then close the default Table1. Create a new table using the Contacts table template, and then use the data in the Word document to enter the records. Use the Department data for the Company field, and change the field name accordingly. Delete the unneeded fields from the table. Change the ID field name to Emp#, and use the Employee numbers provided. Close the table, and save it as **10 Nurses Firstname Lastname** Based on the table, create a report and print it or submit the report electronically. Close the database.

End You have completed Project 10 ————————

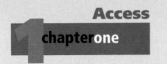 **You and GO!**

Project 1P — You and GO!

In this project, you will construct a solution by applying any combination of the skills you practiced from the Objectives in Projects 1A and 1B.

From My Computer, navigate to the student files that accompany this textbook. In the folder **04_you_and_go_pg87_102**, locate and open the folder for this chapter. Open and print the instructions for this project, which are provided to you in Adobe PDF format. Follow the instructions to create a personal inventory database for insurance purposes.

End **You have completed Project 1P** ————————————

GO! with Help

Project 1Q — GO! with Help

1 **Start** Access and in the upper right corner, click the **Help** button . Click the **Search arrow**, and then under **Content from this computer**, click **Access Help**. In the **Search** box, type **Help** and then press Enter.

2 From the displayed list, scroll down as necessary, and then locate and click **What's new in Microsoft Office Access 2007?** Maximize the displayed window. Scroll through and read all the various features of Microsoft Access 2007.

3 If you want to do so, print a copy of the information by clicking the printer button at the top of the Access Help window. **Close** [X] the Help window, and then exit Access.

End **You have completed Project 1Q** ————————————

Outcomes-Based Assessments

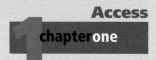

Group Business Running Case

Project 1R — Group Business Running Case

In this project, you will apply the skills you practiced from the Objectives in Projects 1A and 1B.

Your instructor may assign this group case project to your class. If your instructor assigns this project, he or she will provide you with information and instructions to work as part of a group. The group will apply the skills gained thus far to help the Bell Orchid Hotel Group achieve its business goals.

 You have completed Project 1R

chaptertwo

Sort and Query a Database

OBJECTIVES

At the end of this chapter you will be able to:

1. Open an Existing Database
2. Create Table Relationships
3. Sort Records in a Table
4. Create a Query in Design View
5. Create a New Query from an Existing Query
6. Sort Query Results
7. Specify Criteria in a Query

8. Create a New Table by Importing an Excel Spreadsheet
9. Specify Numeric Criteria in a Query
10. Use Compound Criteria
11. Create a Query Based on More Than One Table
12. Use Wildcards in a Query
13. Use Calculated Fields in a Query
14. Group Data and Calculate Statistics in a Query

OUTCOMES

Mastering these objectives will enable you to:

PROJECT 2A
Sort and Query a Database

PROJECT 2B
Create a Database Table from an Excel Spreadsheet and Create Complex Queries

Florida Port Community College

Florida Port Community College is located in St. Petersburg, Florida, a coastal port city located near the Florida High Tech Corridor. With 60 percent of Florida's high tech companies and a third of the state's manufacturing companies located in the St. Petersburg and Tampa Bay areas, the college partners with businesses to play a vital role in providing a skilled workforce. The curriculum covers many areas including medical technology, computer science, electronics, aviation and aerospace, and simulation and modeling. The college also serves the community through cultural, athletic, and diversity programs, and provides adult basic education.

Sort and Query a Database

To convert data into meaningful information, you must manipulate the data in a way that you can answer questions. For example, you might ask the question, *What are the names and addresses of students who are enrolled in the Business Information Technology program and who has a grade point average of 3.0 or higher?* With such information, you could send the selected students information about scholarships that might be available to them.

Questions concerning the data in database tables can be answered by sorting the data or by creating a query. Access queries enable you to isolate specific data in database tables by limiting the fields that display and by setting conditions that limit the records to those that match specified conditions. You can also use a query to create calculations. In this chapter, you will sort Access database tables. You will also create and modify queries in an Access database.

Project 2A Instructors and Courses

Port Florida Community College uses sorting techniques and queries to locate information about data in their databases. In Activities 2.1 through 2.13, you will assist Lydia Barwari, Dean, in locating information about the records in the Instructors and Courses database in the Business Information Technology Department. Your completed queries and report will look similar to those in Figure 2.1.

For Project 2A, you will need the following file:

a2A_Instructors_and_Courses

You will save your database as
2A_Instructors_and_Courses_Firstname_Lastname

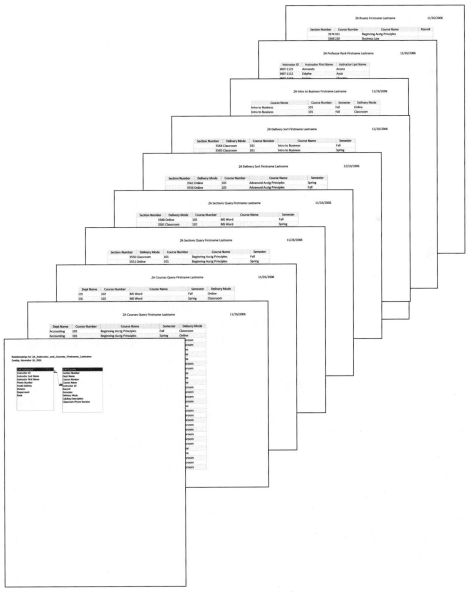

Figure 2.1
Project 2A—Instructors and Courses

Objective 1
Open an Existing Database

In other Microsoft Office 2007 applications, when you open a file, your computer loads the program and the file into random access memory (RAM). When you save and close, the file is transferred to a permanent storage location that you designate, such as a removable USB flash drive or your hard disk drive.

Because database files are typically very large, the entire database file is *not* loaded to RAM; rather, you work with the file from its permanent storage location. For this reason, Access does not have a Save As command with which you can save an entire database file with a new name. Thus, to work with the student files that accompany this textbook, you will use commands within your Windows operating system to copy the file to your chapter folder, and then rename the file before opening it.

Activity 2.1 Renaming and Opening an Existing Database

In this activity, you will use My Computer to copy a database file to a new storage location and then rename the database.

1 On the left side of the Windows taskbar, click **Start** [*start*] , and then click **My Computer**. Navigate to the location where you are storing your projects for this chapter.

2 On the menu bar, click **File**, point to **New**, and then click **Folder**.

A new folder is created, the words *New Folder* display highlighted in the folder's name box, and the insertion point is blinking. Recall that within Windows, highlighted text will be replaced by your typing.

3 Type **Access Chapter 2** and press Enter to rename the folder.

4 Navigate to the location where the student files that accompany this textbook are located, and then click one time to select the file **a2A_Instructors_and_Courses**. Point to the selected file name, and then right-click to display a shortcut menu. On the displayed shortcut menu, click **Copy**.

5 Navigate to and open the Access Chapter 2 folder you created in Step 3. In an open area, right-click to display a shortcut menu, and then click **Paste**.

The database file is copied to your folder and is selected.

6 Right-click the selected file name, and then from the displayed shortcut menu, click **Rename**. As shown in Figure 2.2, and using your own first and last name, type **2A_Instructors_and_Courses_Firstname_Lastname**

Alert!

Does your system display file extensions?

If the Windows operating system on the computer at which you are working is set to display file extensions, be sure to type the new file name in front of the extension, for example: 2A_Instructors_and_Courses_Firstname_Lastname.accdb

Access Chapter 2
indicated in the title bar

Figure 2.2

Your folder name

Your name here

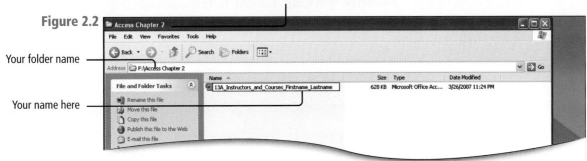

7 Press [Enter] to save the file with the new name. On the title bar, click the **Close** button ☒ to close the **My Computer** window.

Alert!

Does a Confirm File Rename message display?

If the file you have copied has a Read-only property applied, a message box will display to alert you when you attempt to rename a file. In the message box, click Yes to rename the file. Then, right-click the file name, and from the shortcut menu click Properties. In the displayed Properties dialog box, on the General tab under Attributes, click to clear the Read-only check mark. Click OK to accept the change, and then close the dialog box.

Activity 2.2 Opening an Existing Database and Resolving Security Alerts

The **Message Bar** is the area directly below the Ribbon that displays information such as security alerts when there is potentially unsafe, active content in an Office 2007 document that you open. Settings that determine which alerts display on your Message Bar are set in the Access **Trust Center**. The Trust Center is an area of the Access program where you can view the security and privacy settings for your Access installation.

You may or may not be able to change the settings in the Trust Center, depending upon decisions made within your organization's computing environment. To display the Trust Center, from the Office menu, in the lower right corner click Access Options, and then click Trust Center.

1 **Start** Access. From the **Office** menu 🗔, click **Open**. In the displayed **Open** dialog box, click the **Look in arrow**, and then navigate to your Access Chapter 2 folder.

2 Locate the database file that you saved and renamed with your name in Activity 2.1. Click your **2A_Instructors_and_Courses_Firstname_Lastname** database file one time to select it, and then, in the lower right corner, click the **Open** button. Alternatively, double-click the name of the database to open it.

The database window opens, and the database name displays in the title bar.

3 Directly below the Ribbon, on the **Message Bar**, check to see if a **Security Warning**, similar to the one shown in Figure 2.3, displays.

Database name in title bar

Figure 2.3

Security Warning message

Message Bar

Options button

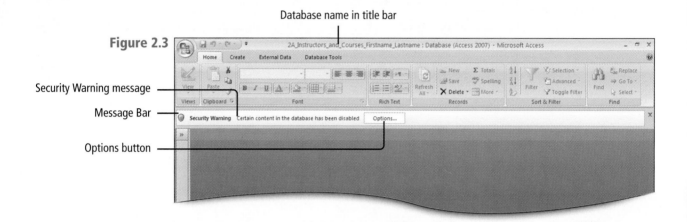

4 On the **Message Bar**, click the **Options** button. In the displayed **Microsoft Office Security Options** dialog box, click the **Enable this content** option button, and then click **OK** or press [Enter].

When working with the student files that accompany this textbook, repeat these actions each time you see this security warning. Databases provided with this textbook are safe to use on your computer.

Objective 2
Create Table Relationships

Access databases are **relational databases** because the tables in the database can relate—actually *connect*—to other tables through **common fields**. Common fields are fields that contain the same data in more than one table.

After you have set up a table for each different subject in your database, you must provide a way to bring that data back together again when you need to create meaningful information. To do this, place common fields in tables that are related and then define table **relationships**. A relationship is an association that you establish between two tables based on common fields. After the relationship is established, you can create a query, a form, or a report that displays information from more than one table.

Activity 2.3 Creating Table Relationships and Enforcing Referential Integrity

In this activity, you will connect a field in one table with a field in another table to create a relationship. The common field between the two tables is Instructor ID; that is, Instructor ID is the field that appears in both tables. By connecting this information, you could identify the name, and not just the Instructor ID, of an instructor for a course section.

1 **Open** ⏩ the **Navigation Pane**. At the top of the **Navigation Pane**, click the **Navigation Pane menu arrow** ⏷, and then look at the displayed menu to verify that the objects are organized by **Tables and Related Views**. Click outside the menu to close it, and then compare your screen with Figure 2.4.

Two objects, the *2A Instructors* table and the *2A Courses* table, display in the Navigation Pane.

No objects open in
the object window

Figure 2.4

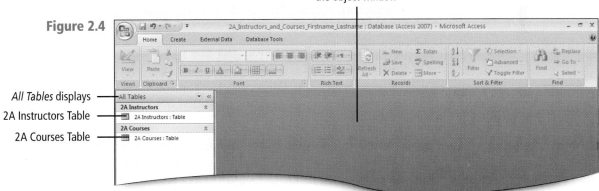

All Tables displays

2A Instructors Table

2A Courses Table

2 By right-clicking and clicking **Open**, or by double-clicking, open the **2A Instructors** table and take a moment to examine its contents. Then, open the **2A Courses** table and examine its contents.

In the 2A Instructors table, Instructor ID is the primary key field, which ensures that each individual instructor will appear in the table only one time. In the 2A Courses table, Section Number is the primary key. Each course's record includes the Instructor ID of the instructor who teaches the course.

Because *one* instructor can teach *many* different courses, *one* instructor's Instructor ID number can appear *many* times in the 2A Courses table. Thus, the relationship between each instructor and the courses is referred to as a ***one-to-many relationship***. This is the most common type of relationship in Access.

3 **Close** ✖ both tables so that the object window is empty; leave the **Navigation Pane** displayed. On the Ribbon, click the **Database Tools tab**. In the **Show/Hide group**, click the **Relationships** button to open the Relationships window and display the **Relationship Tools** on the Ribbon.

4 On the **Design tab**, in the **Relationships group**, click the **Show Table** button to display the **Show Table** dialog box. In the **Show Table** dialog box, in the list of table objects, click **2A Courses**, and then at the bottom of the dialog box, click **Add**.

5 In the **Show Table** dialog box, point to the **2A Instructors** table, double-click to add the table to the **Relationships** window, and then click **Close** to close the **Show Table** dialog box.

Use either technique to add a table to the Relationships window. A *field list*—a list of the field names in a table—for each of the two table objects displays and each table's primary key is identified. Although this database currently has only two tables, larger databases can have many tables.

6 In the **2A Courses** field list, position your mouse pointer over the lower right corner of the field list to display the 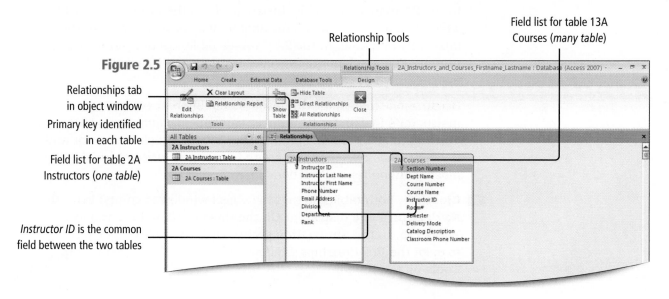 pointer, and then drag downward and to the right as necessary to display the names of each field completely.

Because you can now view the entire list, the scroll bar on the right is removed. Expanding the field list in this manner enables you to see all of the available fields.

7 Using the same technique, use the ⬉ pointer to resize the **2A Instructors** field list as necessary so that all of the field names are completely visible. Then, by pointing to the title bar of each field list and dragging, position the expanded field lists approximately as shown in Figure 2.5.

Recall that *one* instructor can teach *many* courses. By arranging the tables in this manner on your screen, the *one table* is on the left and the *many table* is on the right.

Recall that the primary key in each table is the field that uniquely identifies the record in each table. For example, in the Instructors table, each instructor is uniquely identified by the Instructor ID. In the Courses table, each course section offered is uniquely identified by the Section Number.

Relationship Tools

Field list for table 13A Courses (*many table*)

Figure 2.5

Relationships tab in object window

Primary key identified in each table

Field list for table 2A Instructors (*one table*)

Instructor ID is the common field between the two tables

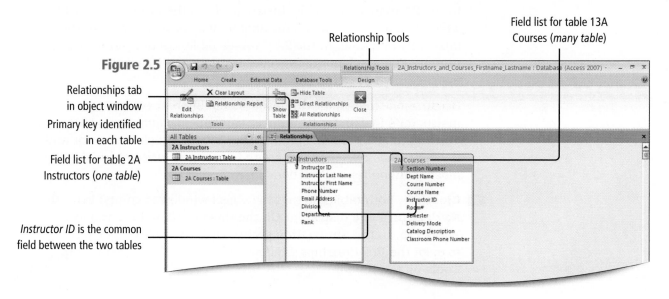

Note — Highlighted Field Does Not Matter

As you rearrange the two field lists in the Relationships window, the high-lighted field indicates which field list and which field is active. This is of no consequence for completing the activity. It simply indicates which of the field lists you moved last.

 In the **2A Instructors** field list, point to **Instructor ID**, hold down the left mouse button, and then drag to the right to the **2A Courses** field list until your mouse pointer is on top of **Instructor ID** as shown in Figure 2.6. Then release the mouse button.

As you drag, a small graphic displays to indicate that you are drag-ging the Instructor ID primary key from the Instructors table to the Instructor ID field in the Courses table. The Edit Relationships dialog box displays.

A table relationship works by matching data in two fields—typically two fields with the same name in both tables.

Icon indicates you are dragging the
primary key field to another table

Figure 2.6

 Point to the title bar of the **Edit Relationships** dialog box, and then drag the dialog box below the two field lists as shown in Figure 2.7.

Both tables include the Instructor ID field—that is the common field between the two tables. By dragging, you created the one-to-many relationship. In the Instructors table, Instructor ID is the primary key. In the Courses table, Instructor ID is referred to as the **_foreign key_** field. The foreign key is the field that is included in the related table so the field can be joined with the primary key in another table.

The field on the _one_ side of the relationship is typically the primary key. Recall that _one_ instructor can teach _many_ courses. Thus, _one_ instructor record in the Instructors table can be related to _many_ course records in the Courses table.

Figure 2.7

2A Courses table indicated on
the right as Related Table/Query

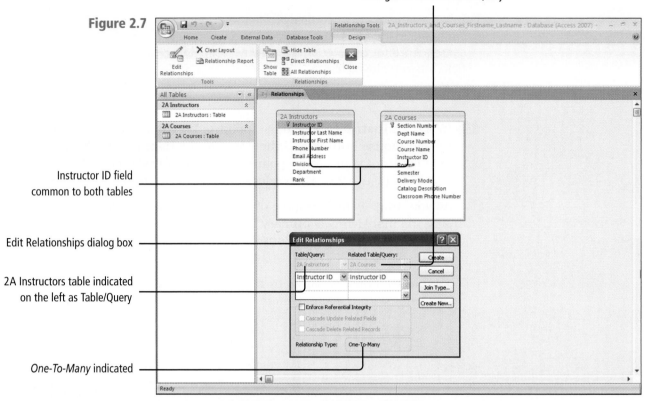

Instructor ID field
common to both tables

Edit Relationships dialog box

2A Instructors table indicated
on the left as Table/Query

One-To-Many indicated

Another Way ─── **To Create a Table Relationship**

With the tables displayed in the Relationships window, rather than dragging
one field into another field list, instead, click the Edit Relationships button on
the Ribbon, click Create New, and then in the Create New dialog box, designate the Left and Right tables and fields that will create the relationship.

---

10 In the **Edit Relationships** dialog box, click to select the **Enforce
Referential Integrity** check box—as you progress in your study of
Access, you will use the Cascade options.

Referential integrity is a set of rules that Access uses to ensure
that the data between related tables is valid. Enforcing referential
integrity ensures that a course cannot be added to the 2A Courses
table with the name of an instructor who is *not* included in the 2A
Instructors table. In this manner, you ensure that you do not have
courses listed in the 2A Courses table with no corresponding
instructor in the 2A Instructors table. Similarly, you will not be able
to delete an Instructor from the 2A Instructors table if there is a
course listed for that instructor in the 2A Courses table.

11 In the upper right corner of the **Edit Relationships** dialog box, click
the **Create** button, and then compare your screen with Figure 2.8.

A *join line*—the line joining two tables—displays between the two
tables. On the line, *1* indicates the *one* side of the relationship, and
the infinity symbol (∞) indicates the *many* side of the relationship.
These symbols display when referential integrity has been enforced.

Common field in both tables

Figure 2.8

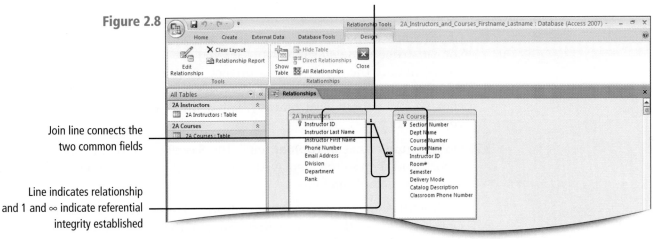

Join line connects the two common fields

Line indicates relationship and 1 and ∞ indicate referential integrity established

More Knowledge

Fields in a Relationship

To create a relationship, the two connected fields must have the same data type and the same field size, but they need not have the exact same field name.

Activity 2.4 Printing a Relationship Report

Table relationships provide a map of how your database is organized, and you can print this information as a report. In this activity, you will print your relationship report.

1 With the **Relationships** window open, on the **Design tab**, in the **Tools group**, click **Relationship Report** to create the report and display it in Print Preview. On the displayed **Print Preview tab**, in the **Page Layout group**, click **Margins**, and then click **Normal**. Compare your screen with Figure 2.9.

Print Preview tab

Figure 2.9

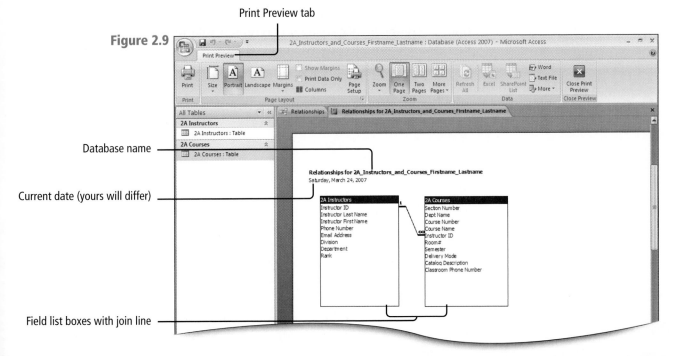

Database name

Current date (yours will differ)

Field list boxes with join line

2 Check your *Chapter Assignment Sheet* or *Course Syllabus*, or consult your instructor, to determine whether you are to submit the printed pages that are the results of this project. To print, on the **Print Preview tab**, in the **Print group**, click the **Print** button, and then click **OK**. To submit electronically, follow the directions provided by your instructor.

3 On the **Quick Access Toolbar**, click the **Save** button ⊟ to save the report, and then in the displayed **Save As** dialog box, click **OK** to accept the default name.

The report name displays in the Navigation Pane under *Unrelated Objects*. Because the report is just a map of the relationships, and not a report containing actual records, it is not associated with either of the tables.

4 Click **Close Print Preview**. In the object window, **Close** ☒ the **Relationships** report, and then **Close** ☒ the **Relationships** window.

Note

The report may briefly display in the Design view (with dotted grid lines) as you close the report.

---

5 In the **Navigation Pane**, open your **2A Instructors** table. On the left side of the table, in the first record, point to the **plus sign**, and then click one time. Compare your screen with Figure 2.10.

Plus signs to the left of a record in a table indicate that related records exist in a *related* table. In the first record for *Julie Adeeb*, you can see that related records exist in the Courses table. The relationship displays because you created a relationship between the two tables using the Instructor ID field.

Figure 2.10

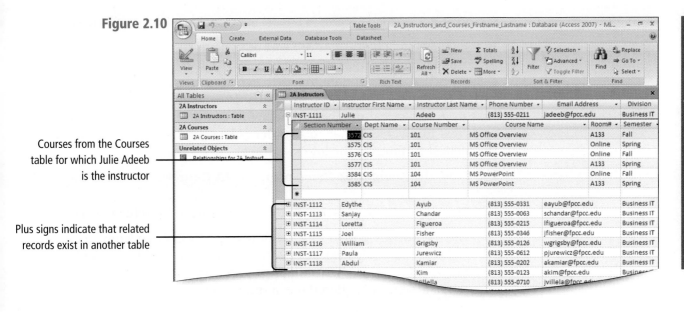

Courses from the Courses table for which Julie Adeeb is the instructor

Plus signs indicate that related records exist in another table

6 **Close** ☒ the **2A Instructors** table.

More Knowledge

Other Types of Relationships: One-to-One and Multiple One-to-Many

There are other relationships that can be created using the same process in the Relationships window. The type of relationship is determined by the placement of the primary key field. A one-to-one relationship exists between two tables when a record in one table is related to a single record in a second table. In this case, both tables use the same field as the primary key. This is most often used when data is placed in a separate table because access to the information is restricted. You can also create multiple one-to-many relationships between tables in a database simply by adding more tables to the Relationships window and creating a join line between the tables based on their common field. A primary key field from one table can be joined to the same field in more than one table.

Objective 3
Sort Records in a Table

Sorting is the process of arranging data in a specific order based on the value in each field. For example, you could sort the names in your address book alphabetically by each person's last name, or you could sort your CD collection by the date of purchase.

Initially, records in an Access table display in the order in which they are entered into the table. After a primary key is established, the records are displayed in order based on the primary key field.

Activity 2.5 Sorting Records in a Table in Ascending or Descending Order

In the following activity, you will sort records in the Courses table to determine which courses in the Business IT Division will be offered each semester. You can sort data in either **ascending order** or **descending order**. Ascending order sorts text alphabetically (A to Z) and sorts numbers from the lowest number to the highest number. Descending order sorts text in reverse alphabetical order (Z to A) and sorts numbers from the highest number to the lowest number.

1 From the **Navigation Pane**, open the **2A Courses** table, and then

Close ⌐«⌐ the **Navigation Pane** to maximize your screen space.

The records are sorted in ascending order by Section Number, which is the primary key field. Recall that the primary key is the field whose value uniquely identifies each record in a table—each section of a course that is offered has a unique section number.

2 At the top of the **Dept Name** column, click the **Dept Name arrow**. In the displayed list, click **Sort A to Z**, and then compare your screen with Figure 2.11.

To sort records in a table, click the arrow to the right of the field name in the column on which you want to sort, and then choose the sort order you prefer. After a field is sorted in ascending or descending order, a small arrow in the field name indicates its sort order.

The records display in alphabetical order by Dept Name. Because like names are now grouped together, you can quickly scroll the length of the table and see how many courses are offered by each department.

Ascending button selected

Figure 2.11

Small arrow indicates order in which field is sorted

Records sorted alphabetically by Dept Name

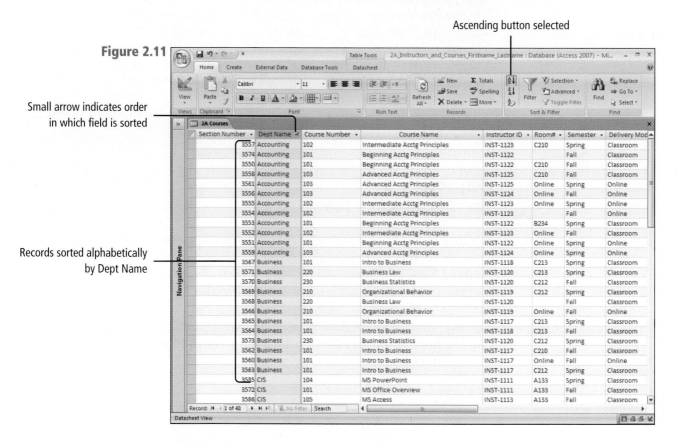

3 In the **Sort & Filter group**, click the **Clear All Sorts** button 🔀 to clear all the sorts and return the records to the default sort order, which is by the primary key field—*Section Number*. Scroll to the right if necessary, click the **Semester arrow**, and then click **Sort Z to A**.

The records in the table are sorted by semester in reverse alphabetical order; thus *Spring* courses are listed before *Fall* courses. The small arrow in the Field name points downward indicating a descending sort, and in the Ribbon, the Descending button is selected.

Activity 2.6 Sorting Records in a Table on Multiple Fields

To sort a table on two or more fields, first identify the fields that will act as the ***outermost sort field*** and the ***innermost sort field***. The outermost sort field is the first level of sorting, and the innermost sort field is the second level of sorting. After you identify your outermost and innermost sort fields, sort the innermost field first, and then sort the outermost field.

Lydia Barwari, the Dean, would like to view the course names in alphabetical order by delivery mode, with online classes listed first. Access enables you to sort on two or more fields in a table in this manner.

1 Click the **Clear All Sorts** button 🔀 to clear any sorts from the previous activity. In the **Delivery Mode** column, click any record. In the

Sort & Filter group, click the **Descending** button 🔽.

The records are sorted in descending alphabetical order by Delivery Mode, with Online courses listed before Classroom courses.

2 Point anywhere in the **Course Name** column, and then right-click. From the displayed shortcut menu, click **Sort A to Z**. Notice the first four records in the **Course Name** column, for *Advanced Acctg Principles*, and then compare your screen with Figure 2.12.

The records are sorted first by Course Name—the *outermost* sort field—and then within a specific Course Name grouping, the sort continues in descending alphabetical order by Delivery Mode—the *innermost* sort field.

In this manner, you can perform a sort on multiple fields using both ascending and descending order.

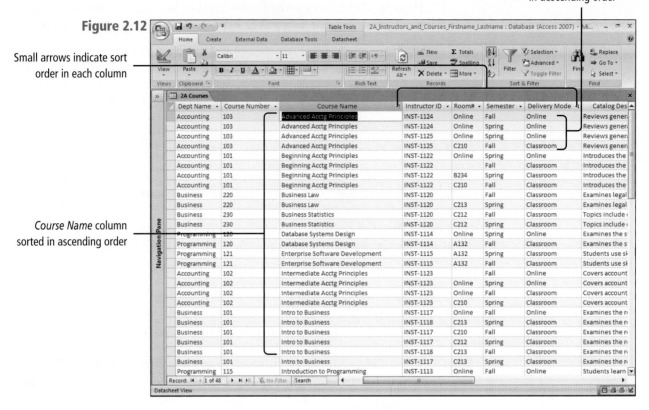

Figure 2.12

Within each *Course Name*, *Online* and *Classroom* sorted in descending order

Small arrows indicate sort order in each column

Course Name column sorted in ascending order

3 In the **Sort & Filter group**, click the **Clear All Sorts** button. In

the object window, **Close** ✖ the table, and then click **No**; you need not save any changes made to the design.

Objective 4
Create a Query in Design View

Recall that a ***select query*** is a database object that retrieves (selects) specific data from one or more tables and then displays the specified data in datasheet view. A query answers a question such as *Which instructors are teaching CIS courses in the Fall semester?* Unless a query has already been set up to ask this question, you must create a new query.

Individuals who use databases rarely need to see all of the records in all of the tables. That is why a query is so useful; it creates a subset of records according to your specifications and then displays only those records—and does so in a useful manner.

Activity 2.7 Creating a New Select Query in Design View

Previously, you practiced creating a query using the Query Wizard. In this chapter, you will create queries in Design view, in which you can create queries that are more complex. Recall that the table or tables from which a query selects its data is referred to as the **data source**.

1 On the Ribbon, click the **Create tab**, and then in the **Other group**, click the **Query Design** button. Compare your screen with Figure 2.13.

A new query opens in Design view and the Show Table dialog box displays. The Show Table dialog box lists all of the tables in the database.

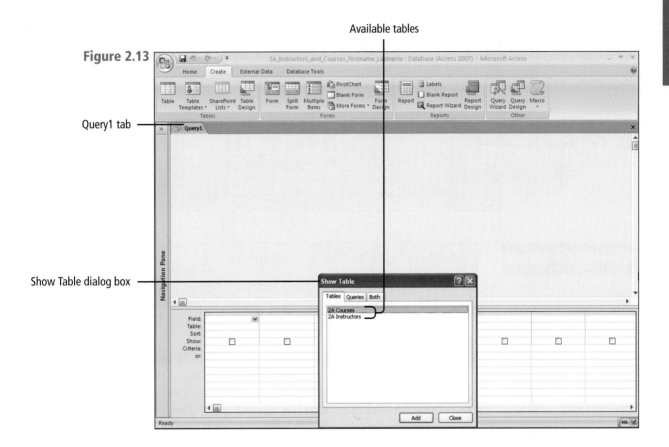

Available tables

Figure 2.13

Query1 tab

Show Table dialog box

2 In the **Show Table** dialog box, click **2A Courses**, click the **Add** button, and then **Close** the **Show Table** dialog box. Compare your screen with Figure 2.14.

A field list for the 2A Courses table displays in the upper pane of the Query window. The Section Number field is indicated as the primary key field in this table. The Query window has two parts: the **table area** (upper pane) displays the field lists for tables that are used in the query, and the **design grid** (lower pane) displays the design of the query.

Figure 2.14

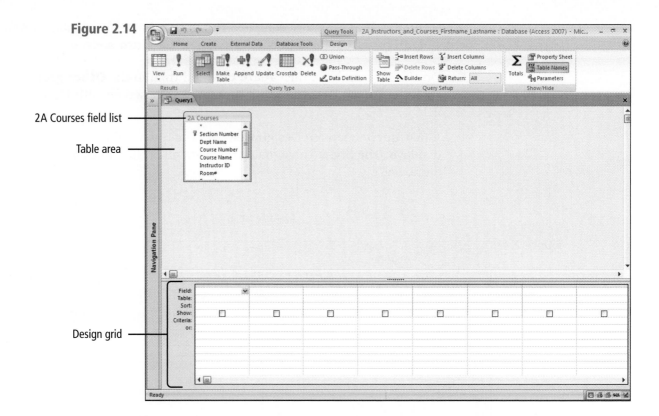

2A Courses field list

Table area

Design grid

Another Way — **To Add a Table to the Query Window**

You can also double-click a table name in the Show Table dialog box to add it to the Query window.

---

3 Point to the lower right corner of the field list to display the ⤡ pointer, and then drag down and to the right to expand the height and width of the field list as necessary to view all of the field names. In the **2A Courses** field list, double-click **Dept Name**, and then look at the design grid.

The Dept Name field displays in the design grid in the Field row. By designing a query in Design view, you can limit the fields that display in the result by placing only the fields you want in the design grid.

4 In the **2A Courses** field list, point to **Course Number**, hold down the left mouse button, and then drag down into the design grid until you are pointing to the **Field** row in the next available column. Release the mouse button, and then compare your screen with Figure 2.15.

This is another way to add field names to the design grid. As you drag the field, a small rectangular shape attaches to the mouse pointer. When you release the mouse button, the field name displays in the Field row.

Figure 2.15

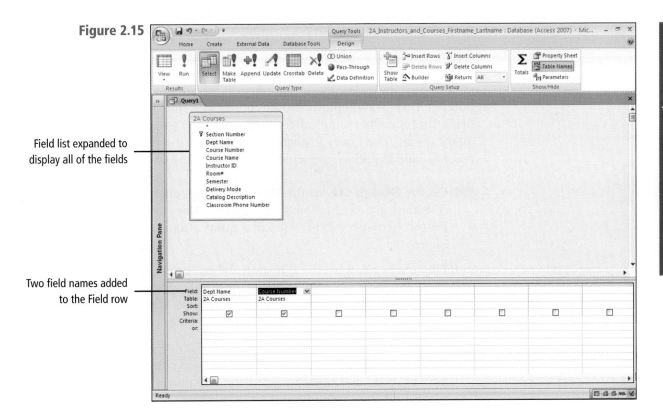

Field list expanded to display all of the fields

Two field names added to the Field row

5 In the **Field** row of the design grid, click in the third column, and then click the **arrow** that displays. From the displayed list, click **Course Name** to add this field to the design grid, which is another way to add a field to the design of the query.

6 Using one of the methods you just practiced, add the **Semester** field as the fourth column in the design grid, and then add the **Delivery Mode** field as the fifth column in the design grid. Compare your screen with Figure 2.16.

Figure 2.16

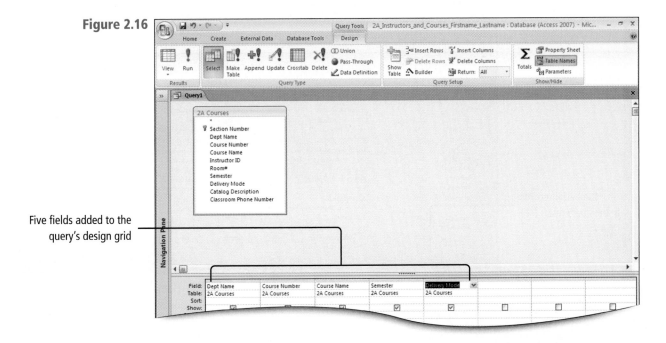

Five fields added to the query's design grid

Activity 2.8 Running, Saving, Printing, and Closing a Query

After you create a query, you *run* it to see the results. When you run a query, Access looks at the records in the table (or tables) you have included in the query, finds the records that match the specified conditions (if any), and displays those records in a datasheet view. Only the fields that have been included in the query design are displayed in the query result. The query is always run against the current table of records, and therefore presents the most up-to-date information.

1 On the **Design tab**, in the **Results group**, click the **Run** button. Alternatively, on the Design tab, in the Results group, click the View button to display the results of a query. Compare your screen with Figure 2.17.

This query answers the question, *What is the Dept Name, Course Number, Course Name, Semester, and Delivery Mode of all the courses in the table?* Think of a query as a subset of the records in one or more tables, arranged in datasheet view, according to the conditions that you specify.

The five fields that you specified display in columns, the records display in rows, and navigation buttons display at the bottom of the window in the same manner as in a table.

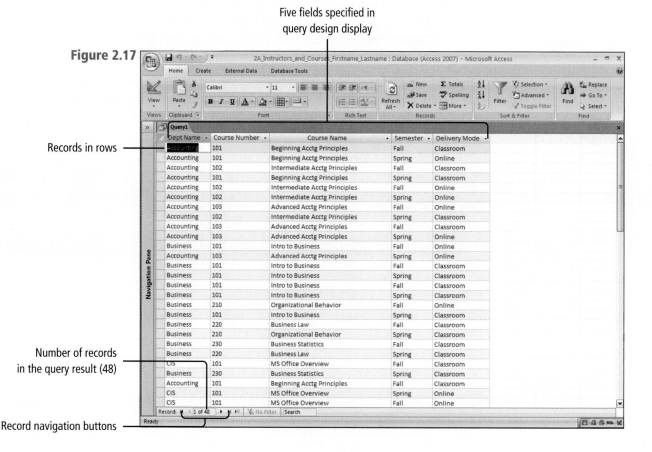

Figure 2.17

2 On the **Quick Access Toolbar**, click the **Save** button 🖫 to display the **Save As** dialog box. Type **2A Courses Query Firstname Lastname** and then click **OK**.

It is not necessary to save all queries, but save your queries if it is likely that you will need to ask the same question again. Doing so will save you the effort of creating the query again to answer the same question.

3 From the **Office** menu 🖭, point to the **Print** button, and then click **Print Preview**. In the **Page Layout group**, click the **Landscape** button. In the **Zoom group**, click the **Two Pages** button to see how your query will print on two pages. If you are printing your assignments on paper, click the **Print** button, and then in the displayed **Print** dialog box, click **OK**. To submit electronically, follow the directions provided by your instructor.

Two pages will print. Queries are created to answer questions and to create information from the data contained in the tables. Queries are typically created as a basis for a report. As you have just done here, however, the actual query result can be printed in a manner similar to tables and other database objects.

4 Click the **Close Print Preview** button. In the object window, **Close** ☒ the query. **Open** ⯮ the **Navigation Pane**, and then compare your screen with Figure 2.18.

The query is saved and closed. The new query name displays in the Navigation Pane under the table with which it is associated—the *Courses* table. When you save a query, only the design of the query is saved. The records still reside in the table object. Each time you open the query, Access runs it again and displays the results based on the data stored in the associated table(s). Thus, the results of a query always reflect the latest information in the associated tables.

Figure 2.18

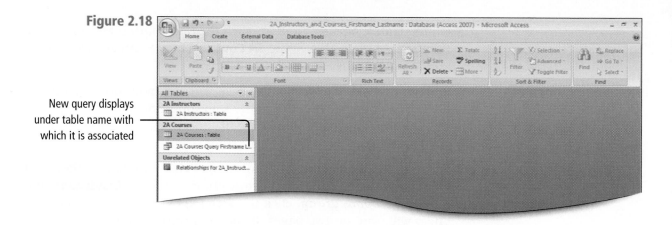

New query displays
under table name with
which it is associated

Objective 5
Create a New Query from an Existing Query

In this activity, you will begin with an existing query, save it with a new name, and then create a new query from the existing one.

Activity 2.9 Creating a New Query from an Existing Query

1 From the **Navigation Pane**, open your **2A Courses Query** by either double-clicking the name or right-clicking and clicking Open.

The query opens in the Datasheet view, which is the view used to display the records in a query result.

2 From the **Office** menu [icon], click **Save As**, which will save the current database object—a query—as a new object. In the **Save As** dialog box, edit as necessary to name the new query **2A Sections Query Firstname Lastname** and then click **OK**. On the **Home tab**, in the **Views group**, click the **View** button to switch to Design view. Compare your screen with Figure 2.19.

A new query, based on a copy of your 2A Courses Query, is created and displays in the object window and is added to the Navigation Pane. Your query displays in Design view.

Figure 2.19

New *2A Sections* query in object window

New query *2A Sections* displays in Navigation Pane

Selection bar in design grid

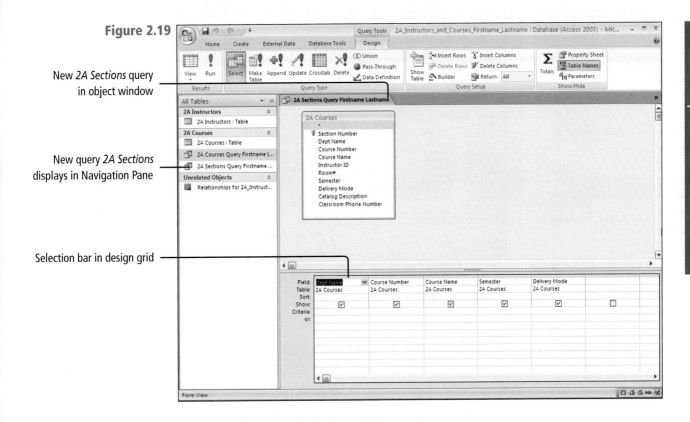

3 **Close** the **Navigation Pane**. In the design grid, point to the thin gray selection bar above the **Dept Name** field until the ⬇ pointer displays. Click to select the **Dept Name** column, and then press Delete.

The Dept Name field is removed from the design grid and the Delivery Mode field moves to the fourth column in the design grid. This action deletes the field from the query design only—it has no effect on the underlying 2A Courses table.

4 Using a similar technique, from the gray selection bar, select the **Delivery Mode** column. Then, point to the **selection bar** at the top of the selected column to display the ↖ pointer, and drag to the left to position **Delivery Mode** in the first column.

To rearrange fields in the query design, first select the field you want to move, and then drag it to a new position in the design grid.

5 From the field list, add the **Section Number** field as the fifth column in the design grid. Then using the technique you just practiced, select and move the **Section Number** field to the first column in the design grid. Compare your screen with Figure 2.20.

Figure 2.20

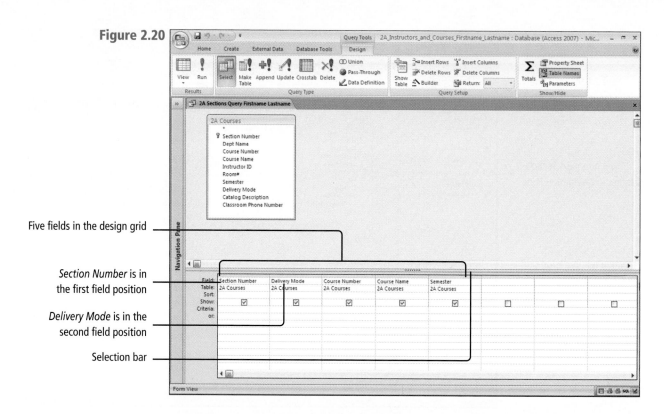

Five fields in the design grid

Section Number is in
the first field position

Delivery Mode is in the
second field position

Selection bar

6 On the **Query Tools Design tab**, in the **Results group**, click the **Run**
button. The result of the query displays five fields in the new
arrangement. Compare your screen with Figure 2.21.

This query answers the question, *What is the Section Number,
Delivery Mode, Course Number, Course Name, and Semester of every
course?* Recall that you can think of a query as a subset of the
records in one or more tables, arranged in datasheet view, according
to the conditions that you specify.

Figure 2.21

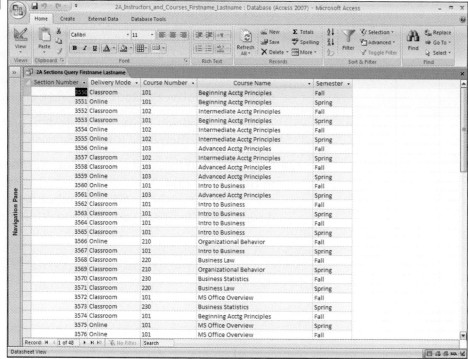

7 From the **Office** menu 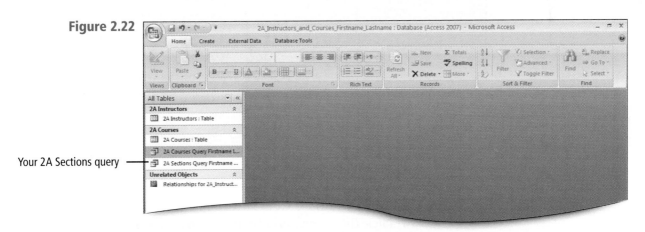, point to the **Print** button, and then click **Print Preview**. On the **Print Preview tab**, in the **Page Layout group**, click **Landscape**. In the **Zoom group**, click the **Two Pages** button to view how your query will print on two pages. If you are printing on paper, in the **Print group**, click the **Print** button. In the displayed **Print** dialog box, click **OK**. To submit electronically, follow your instructor's directions.

8 Click the **Close Print Preview** button. In the object window, **Close** ✕ the query, and then click **Yes** to save the changes to the design. **Open** ≫ the **Navigation Pane**, and then compare your screen with Figure 2.22.

The query is saved and closed. The new query name displays in the Navigation Pane under the table with which it is associated. Recall that when you save a query, only the design of the query is saved. The records still reside in the respective table objects.

Each time you open the query, Access runs it again and displays the results based on the records stored in the associated table(s).

Figure 2.22

Your 2A Sections query

Objective 6
Sort Query Results

You can sort the results of a query. Because the results of a query are formatted like a table in Datasheet view, the process for sorting is similar to sorting in a table. Records can be sorted in ascending or descending order. Data in a query can be sorted from the Datasheet view or from the Design view.

Activity 2.10 Sorting Query Results

In this activity, you will open an existing query, save it with a new name, and then sort the query results in a new arrangement.

1 From the **Navigation Pane**, open your **2A Sections Query**. From the **Office** menu , click **Save As**. In the **Save As** dialog box, edit as necessary to name the query **2A Delivery Sort Firstname Lastname** and then click **OK**.

Access creates a new query, based on a copy of your 2A Sections Query.

2 **Close** 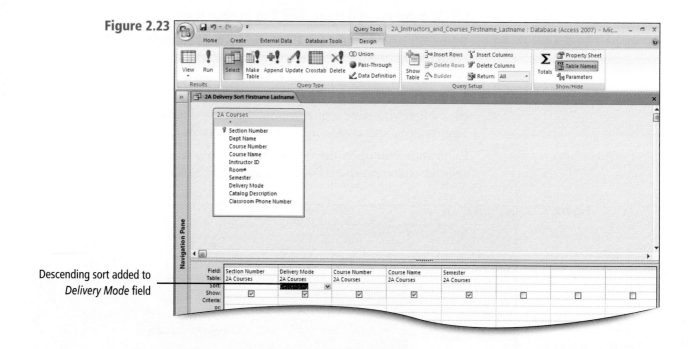 the **Navigation Pane**, and then in the **Views group**, click the **View** button to switch to Design view. In the design grid, in the **Sort** row, click in the **Delivery Mode** field to place the insertion point there and display an arrow. Click the **Sort arrow**, and then in the displayed list, click **Descending**. Compare your screen with Figure 2.23.

Figure 2.23

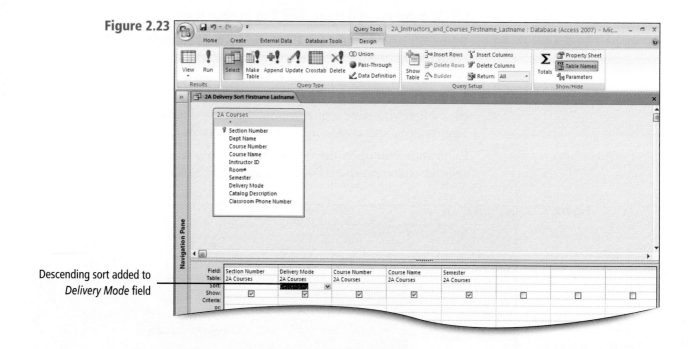

Descending sort added to *Delivery Mode* field

3 In the **Sort** row, under **Course Name**, click to display the **Sort arrow**, click the arrow, and then click **Ascending**.

4 On the **Design tab**, in the **Results group**, click the **Run** button, and then compare your screen with Figure 2.24.

Fields that have a Sort designation are sorted from left to right. That is, the sorted field on the left becomes the outermost sort field, and the sorted field on the right becomes the innermost sort field. Thus, the records are sorted first in descending alphabetical order by the Delivery Mode field—the leftmost indicated sort field. Then in the Course Name field, within the Online records, the Course Names are sorted in ascending alphabetical order.

Figure 2.24

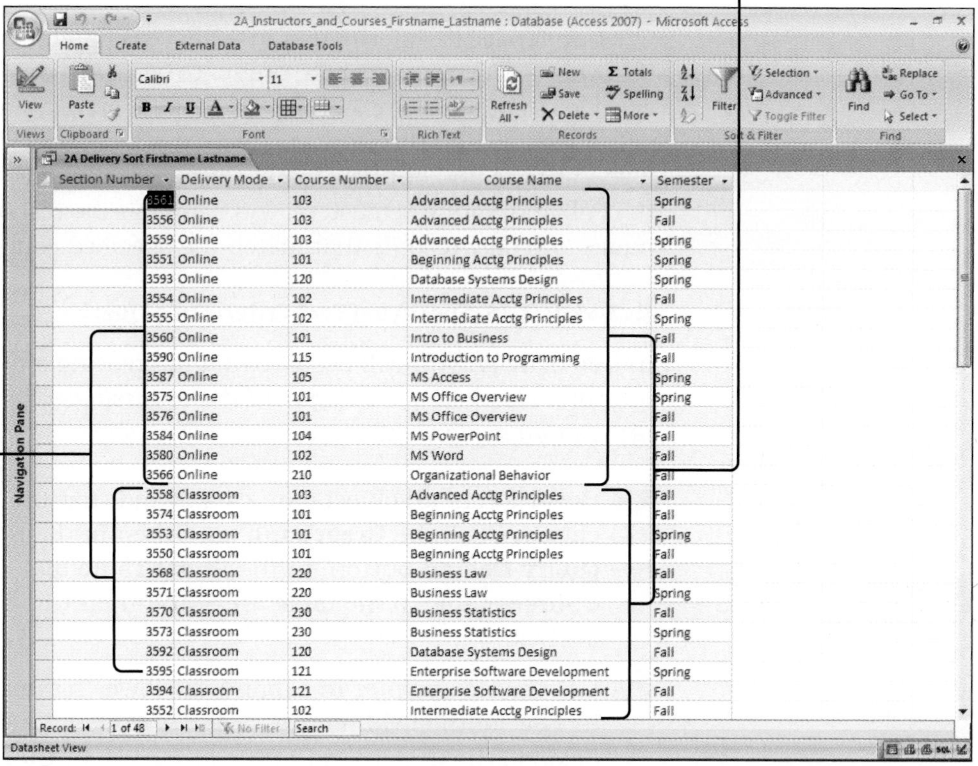

Within Course Name, records sorted in ascending order

Within Delivery Mode, records sorted in descending order

5 From the **Office** menu, point to the **Print** button, and then click **Print Preview**. On the **Print Preview tab**, in the **Page Layout group**, click **Landscape**. In the **Zoom group**, click the **Two Pages** button to view the layout of the pages. If you are printing on paper, in the **Print group**, click the **Print** button. In the displayed **Print** dialog box, click **OK**. To submit electronically, follow your instructor's directions.

6 Click the **Close Print Preview** button. **Close** [X] the query, and then click **Yes** to save the changes to this query's design.

More Knowledge
Sorting

If you add a sort order to the *design* of a query, it remains as a permanent part of the query design. If you use the sort buttons in the Datasheet view, it will override the sort order of the query design, and can be saved as part of the query. A sort order designated directly in datasheet view will not display in the Sort row of the query design grid.

Objective 7
Specify Criteria in a Query

Queries can locate information in an Access database based on **_criteria_** that you specify as part of the query. Criteria are conditions that identify the specific records you are looking for. Criteria enable you to ask a more specific question, and therefore you will get a more specific result. For example, if you want to find out how many _Business Law_ courses will be offered in the Fall and Spring semesters, you can limit the results to a specific course name, and only records that match the specified course name will display.

Activity 2.11 Specifying Text Criteria in a Query

In this activity, you will assist Lydia in creating a query to answer the question _How many sections of Intro to Business will be offered in the Fall and Spring semesters?_

1 Be sure that all objects are closed and that the **Navigation Pane** is closed. Click the **Create tab**, and then in the **Other group**, click the **Query Design** button. In the **Show Table** dialog box, **Add** the **2A Courses** table to the table area, and then **Close** the **Show Table** dialog box.

2 Use the ⬉ pointer to expand the lower right corner of the field list to view all the field names. Using any technique, add the following fields to the design grid in the order listed: **Course Name**, **Course Number**, **Semester**, and **Delivery Mode**.

3 In the **Criteria** row of the design grid, click in the **Course Name** field, type **Intro to Business** and then press Enter. Compare your screen with Figure 2.25.

Access places quote marks around your criteria. Use the Criteria row to specify the criteria that will limit the results of the query to your exact specifications. Access adds quote marks to text criteria in this manner to indicate that this is a **_text string_**—a sequence of characters—that must be matched.

Figure 2.25

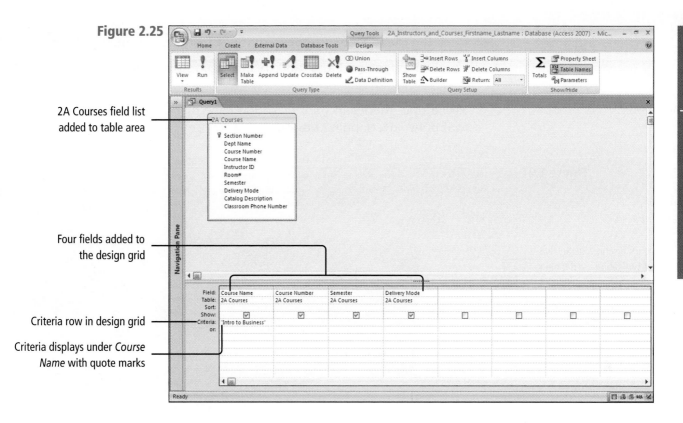

2A Courses field list
added to table area

Four fields added to
the design grid

Criteria row in design grid

Criteria displays under *Course
Name* with quote marks

---

4 **Run** the query, and then compare your screen with Figure 2.26.

Six records display that meet the specified criteria—records that
have *Intro to Business* in the Course Name field.

Figure 2.26

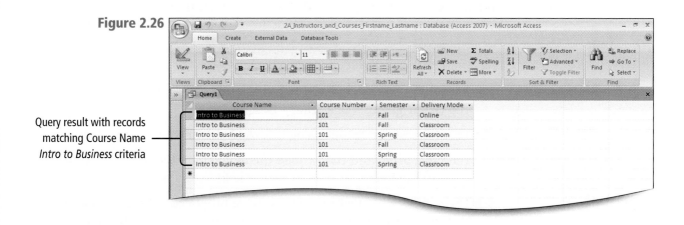

Query result with records
matching Course Name
Intro to Business criteria

---

5 On the **Quick Access Toolbar**, click the **Save** button , and then
in the **Save As** dialog box, type **2A Intro to Business Firstname
Lastname** and then click **OK**.

6 From the **Office** menu , point to the **Print** button, and then click
Print Preview. If you are printing your assignments on paper, in the
Print group, click the **Print** button. In the displayed **Print** dialog
box, click **OK**. Or, submit electronically as directed.

7 Click the **Close Print Preview** button. **Close** $\boxed{\times}$ the query, **Open** $\boxed{\gg}$ the **Navigation Pane**, and then compare your screen with Figure 2.27.

Recall that queries in the Navigation Pane display a distinctive icon—that of two overlapping tables.

Figure 2.27

Queries display a distinctive icon of two tables overlapping

Four queries created based on 2A Courses table

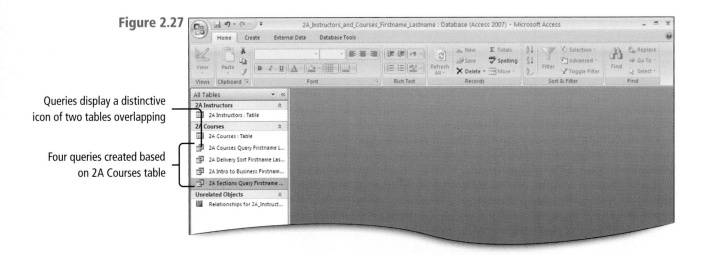

Activity 2.12 Specifying Criteria Using a Field Not Displayed in the Query Result

So far, all of the fields that you included in the query design have also been included in the query result. It is not required to have every field in the query actually display in the result. In fact, there will be times when you will want to prevent some fields from displaying in the result.

In this activity, you will assist Lydia in creating a query to answer the question, *Which instructors have a rank of Professor?*

1 **Close** $\boxed{\ll}$ the **Navigation Pane**. Click the **Create tab**, and then in the **Other group**, click **Query Design**.

2 From the **Show Table** dialog box, **Add** the **2A Instructors** table to the table area, and then **Close** the dialog box. Use the $\boxed{\nwarrow}$ pointer to expand the height and width of the field list as necessary.

3 Using any of the techniques you have practiced—double-clicking, dragging, or displaying the arrow, and then selecting in the list—add the following fields, in the order listed, to the design grid: **Instructor ID**, **Instructor First Name**, **Instructor Last Name**, and **Rank**.

4 In the **Sort** row, click in the **Instructor Last Name** field, click the **arrow**, and then click **Ascending**.

5 In the **Criteria** row, click in the **Rank** field, type **Professor** and then press Enter. Compare your screen with Figure 2.28.

When you press Enter, the insertion point moves to the next criteria box and quote marks are added around the text you entered. Recall that Access adds quote marks to text criteria to indicate that this is a text string—a sequence of characters—that must be matched.

Figure 2.28

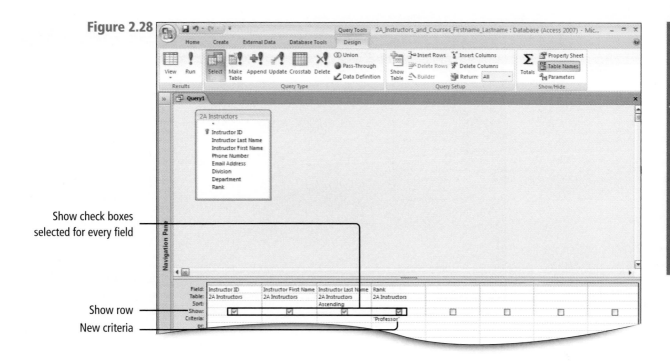

Show check boxes selected for every field

Show row

New criteria

---

6 In the design grid, in the **Show** row, notice that the check box is selected for every field. **Run** the query to view the result of the query.

Six records meet the criteria, and each of the six records displays *Professor* in the Rank column.

Alert! | **Do your query results differ?**

If you mistype the criteria, enter it under the wrong field, or make some other error, the result will display no records. This indicates that there are no records in the table that match the criteria as you entered it. If this occurs, return to the Design view and reexamine the query design. Verify that the criteria are typed on the Criteria row, under the correct field, and that it is spelled correctly. Then rerun the query.

7 On the **Home tab**, in the **Views group**, click the **View** button to return to Design view. In the design grid, under **Rank**, in the **Show** row, click to clear the check box, and then compare your screen with Figure 2.29.

Because it is repetitive and not particularly useful to have *Professor* display for each record in the query result, you can clear this check box so that the field does not display.

Figure 2.29

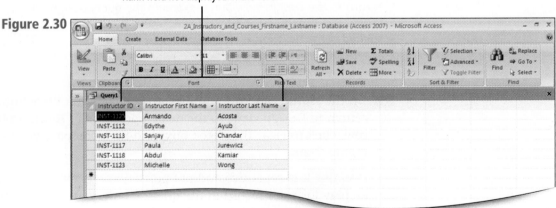

Show check box cleared for the Rank field

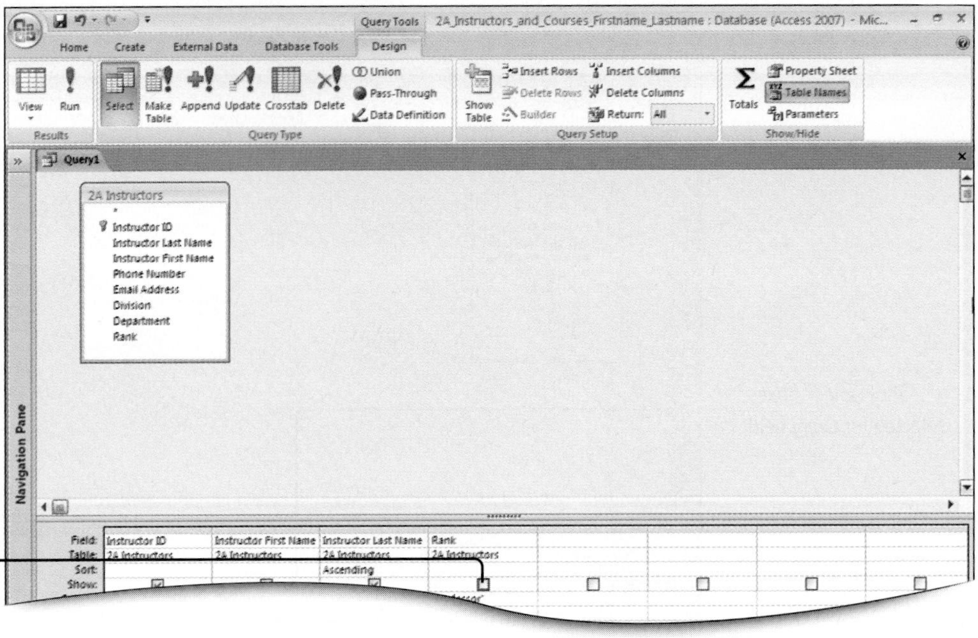

8 **Run** the query again, and then compare your screen with Figure 2.30.

The query results display the same six records, but the *Rank* field does not display. Although the Rank field was still included in the query criteria for the purpose of identifying specific records, it is not necessary to display the field in the result.

Clear the Show check box when necessary to avoid cluttering the query results with redundant data.

Rank field not displayed in the result

Figure 2.30

9 On the **Quick Access Toolbar**, click the **Save** button, and then in the **Save As** dialog box, type **2A Professor Rank Firstname Lastname** Click **OK**.

10 From the **Office** menu, point to the **Print** button, and then click **Print Preview**. If you are printing your assignments on paper, in the

Print group, click the **Print** button. In the displayed **Print** dialog box, click **OK**. To submit electronically, follow your instructor's directions.

11 Click the **Close Print Preview** button. **Close** ☒ the query, **Open** ⧄ the **Navigation Pane**, and then notice the query listed under the table with which it is associated—the 2A Instructors table.

Activity 2.13 Using Is Null Criteria To Find Empty Fields

Sometimes you must locate records where specific data is missing. You can locate such records by using **is null**—empty—as a criteria in a field. Additionally, you can display only the records where a value *has* been entered in a field by using **is not null** as a criteria, which will exclude records where the specified field is empty.

In this activity, you will help Lydia run a query to find out *Which course sections have not yet had a classroom assigned?*

1 **Close** ⧏ the **Navigation Pane**. Click the **Create tab**, and then in the **Other group**, click the **Query Design** button to begin a new query. **Add** the **2A Courses** table, and then **Close** the **Show Table** dialog box. Use the ⬉ pointer as necessary to expand the height and width of the field list.

2 Using any of the techniques you have practiced, add the following fields to the design grid in the order given: **Section Number**, **Course Number**, **Course Name**, and **Room#**.

3 On the **Criteria** row, click in the **Room#** field, type **Is Null** and press ⏎. Alternatively, type *is null* and Access will change the criteria to display with capital letters. Compare your screen with Figure 2.31.

The criteria *Is Null* examines the field and looks for records that do *not* have any values entered in the Room# field. In this manner, you can determine which courses still need to have a classroom assigned.

Figure 2.31

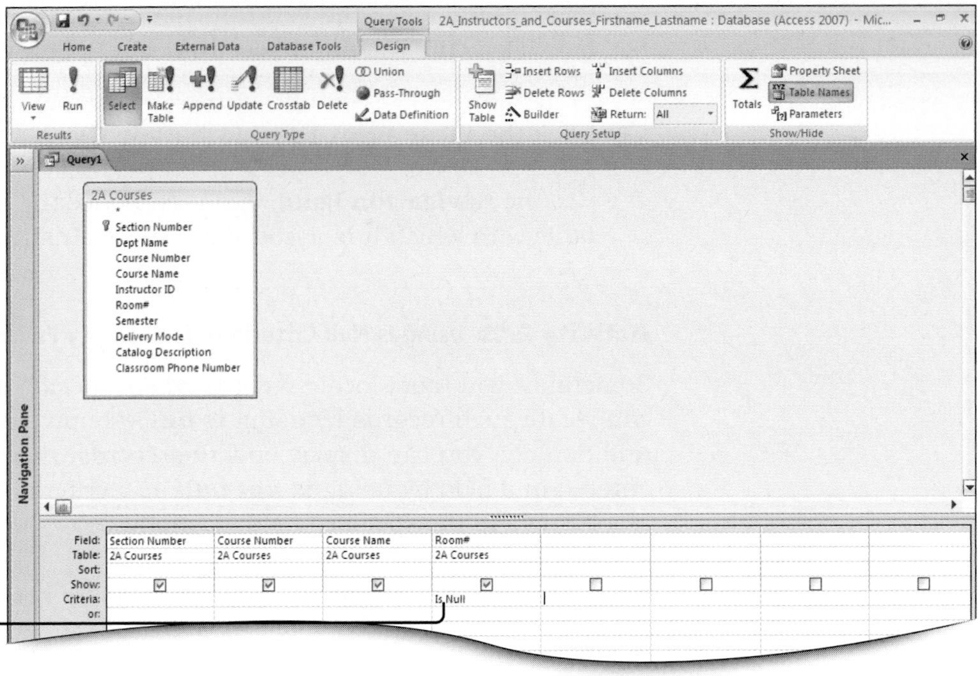

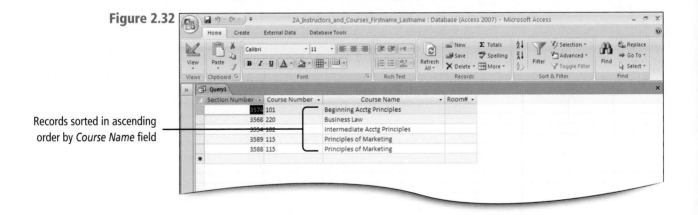

Is Null criteria added
to the Room# field

4 On the **Sort** row, click in the **Course Name** field, click the **Sort arrow**, and then click **Ascending**. **Run** the query to see the results, and then compare your screen with Figure 2.32.

Five course sections do not have a Room# assigned—the Room# field is empty for these course sections. The course names are sorted in ascending (alphabetical) order.

Figure 2.32

Records sorted in ascending
order by *Course Name* field

5 **Save** your query, and then in the **Save As** dialog box, type **2A Rooms Firstname Lastname** Click **OK**.

6 From the **Office** menu, point to the **Print** button, and then click **Print Preview**. If you are printing your assignments on paper, in the **Print group**, click the **Print** button. In the displayed **Print** dialog box, click **OK**. To submit electronically, follow your instructor's directions.

7 Click the **Close Print Preview** button, and then **Close** ☒ the query. **Open** ⟩⟩ the **Navigation Pane**, and then compare your screen with Figure 2.33.

Each query that you created displays under the table with which it is associated. The objects display in alphabetical order.

Figure 2.33

Query objects display, in alphabetical order, with table on which they are based

8 **Close** ⟨⟨ the **Navigation Pane** and be sure all objects are closed.

9 From the **Office** menu, click **Close Database**, and then at the right edge of the Access title bar, click the **Close** button ☒ to close the Access program. Alternatively, from the Office menu, click Exit Access.

End **You have completed Project 2A** ──────────

Project 2B **Athletes and Scholarships**

In Activities 2.14 through 2.25, you will assist Marcus Simmons, Athletic Director for Florida Port Community College, in developing and querying his Athletes and Scholarships database. In this database, Mr. Simmons tracks the scholarships awarded to student athletes. Your completed Relationships report and queries will look similar to those in Figure 2.34.

For Project 2B, you will need the following files:

a2B_Athletes_and_Scholarships
a2B_Athletes (Excel file)

You will save your database as
2B_Athletes_and_Scholarships_Firstname_Lastname

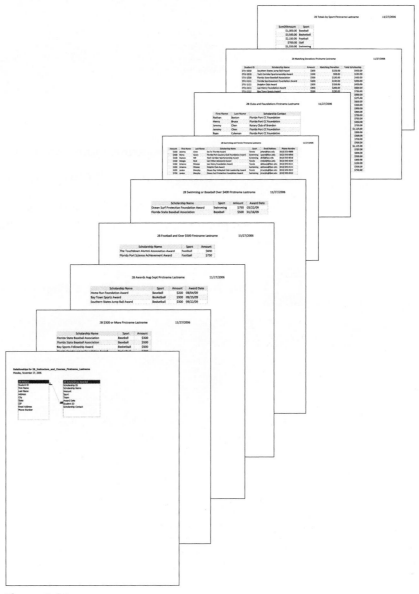

Figure 2.34
Project 2B—Athletes and Scholarships

Objective 8
Create a New Table by Importing an Excel Spreadsheet

Many users of Microsoft Office track their data in an Excel spreadsheet. The sorting and filtering capabilities of Excel are useful enough for a simple database where all the information can reside in one large table, which is the Excel spreadsheet itself.

Excel is limited as a database management program because it cannot support multiple tables nor can it *relate* the information so that you can retrieve information from multiple spreadsheets using a query. However, data in an Excel spreadsheet can easily become an Access table by importing the spreadsheet, because Excel's format of columns and rows is similar to that of an Access table.

Activity 2.14 Opening an Existing Database and Preparing To Import an Excel Spreadsheet

In this activity, you will open, rename, and save an existing database, and then examine an Excel spreadsheet that Mr. Simmons wants to bring into Access as a new table.

1 On the left side of the Windows taskbar, click **Start** ![start], and then click **My Computer**. Navigate to the location where the student files that accompany this textbook are stored, and then click one time to select the file **a2B_Athletes_and_Scholarships**.

2 Point to the selected file name, right-click to display a shortcut menu, and then click **Copy**. Navigate to and open the Access Chapter 2 folder you created in Project 2A. In an open area, right-click to display a shortcut menu, and then click **Paste**.

3 Right-click the selected file name, click **Rename**, and then using your own first and last name type **2B_Athletes_and_Scholarships_ Firstname_Lastname** Press Enter to save the new file name. On the title bar, **Close** ![X] the **My Computer** window.

4 **Start** Access. From the **Office** menu ![icon], click **Open**. In the displayed **Open** dialog box, click the **Look in arrow**, navigate to your Access Chapter 2 folder, and then open your **2B_Athletes_and_Scholarships** database file.

5 If necessary, on the **Message Bar**, click the **Options** button, and then in the **Microsoft Office Security Options** dialog box, click the **Enable this content** options button. Click **OK**.

6 **Open** ![»] the **Navigation Pane**, open the **2B Scholarships Awarded** table, **Close** ![«] the **Navigation Pane**, and then take a moment to examine the data in the table. Compare your screen with Figure 2.35.

In this table, Mr. Simmons tracks the name and amount of scholarships awarded to student athletes. In the table, the students are identified only by their Student ID numbers; the table's primary key is the Scholarship ID field.

Student ID of student receiving scholarship

Figure 2.35

Scholarship Name field

Amount field

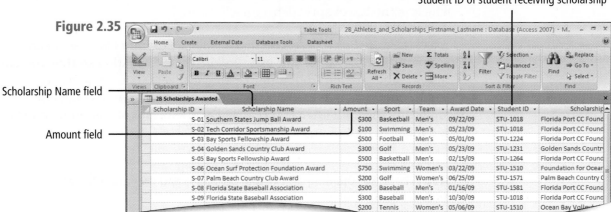

7 **Close** ☒ the table. From the Windows taskbar, click **Start** ⌗ start , and then locate and open **Microsoft Office Excel 2007**.

In Excel, from the **Office** menu 🗔, click **Open**, navigate to the location where the student files for this textbook are stored, and then open the file **a2B_Athletes**. Compare your screen with Figure 2.36.

Mr. Simmons created an Excel spreadsheet to store the names, addresses, and other information of all the student athletes. Because *one* athlete can receive *many* scholarships, Mr. Simmons can see that using Access, rather than Excel, and having two *related* tables of information, will enable him to track and query this information more efficiently.

Excel spreadsheet containing student information

Figure 2.36

Student ID field

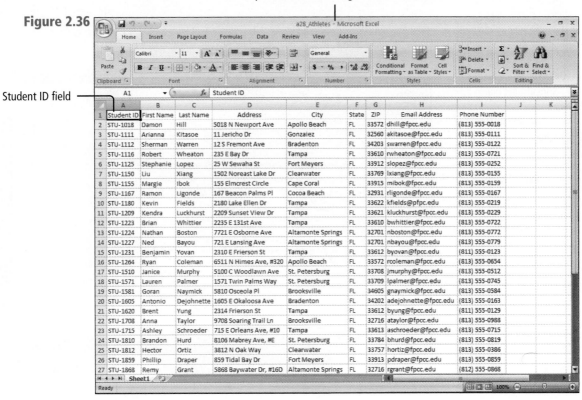

8 In the Excel spreadsheet, notice that in **row 1**, the column titles are similar to the field names in an Access table, and that each row contains the information for one student in a manner similar to a record in Access. Then, display the **Office** menu , and in the lower right corner of the menu, click **Exit Excel**.

Activity 2.15 Creating a New Table by Importing an Excel Spreadsheet

In this activity, you will create a new Access table by importing the Excel spreadsheet containing the names and addresses of the student athletes, create a one-to-many relationship between the new table and the 2A Scholarships Awarded table, enforce referential integrity, and then print a Relationship report.

1 Open the **Navigation Pane**. On the Ribbon, click the **External Data tab**, and then in the **Import group**, click **Excel**. In the displayed **Get External Data – Excel Spreadsheet** dialog box, to the right of the **File name** box, click the **Browse** button.

2 In the displayed **File Open** dialog box, click the **Look in arrow**, navigate to the location where the student files for this textbook are stored, and then click the Excel file **a2B_Athletes**. In the lower right corner, click **Open**, and then compare your screen with Figure 2.37.

Figure 2.37

Browse button

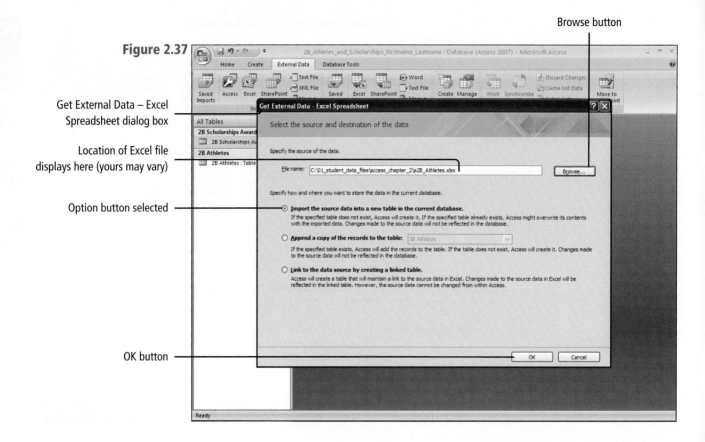

Get External Data – Excel Spreadsheet dialog box

Location of Excel file displays here (yours may vary)

Option button selected

OK button

3 Be sure the **Import the source data into a new table in the current database** option button is selected, and then in the lower right corner, click **OK**.

The Import Spreadsheet Wizard opens and displays the worksheet data.

4 In the upper portion of the **Import Spreadsheet Wizard**, click to select the **First Row Contains Column Headings** check box.

The Excel data in the lower portion of the dialog box is framed so that the first row of Excel column titles can become the Access table field names, and the remaining rows can become the individual records for the new Access table.

5 In the lower right corner, click **Next**. Notice that the first column is selected, and in the upper portion of the dialog box, the **Field Name** is indicated and the **Data Type** is indicated. Click anywhere in the **First Name** column, and then compare your screen with Figure 2.38.

Here you can review and change the field properties of each field (column).

Figure 2.38

Excel column titles become Field Names

Import Spreadsheet Wizard

Data type of selected field identified

Spreadsheet data displays

Excel rows become records

Next button

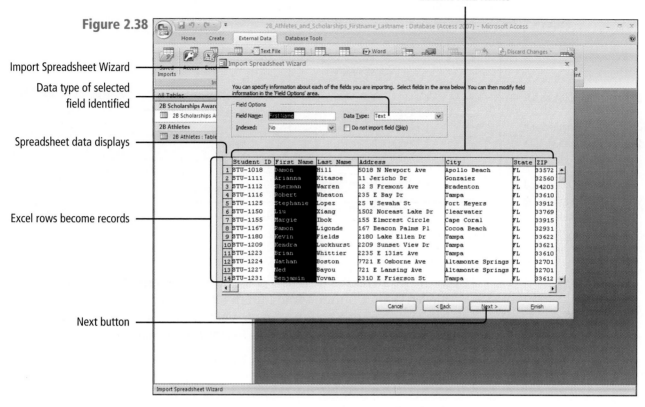

6 Under **Field Options**, make no changes for any of the fields, and then in the lower right corner, click **Next**. In the upper portion of the dialog box, click the **Choose my own primary key** option button, and then be sure that **Student ID** displays.

In the new table, Student ID will be the primary key. No two students will have the same Student ID. By default, Access selects the first field as the primary key.

7 In the lower right corner, click **Next**. In the **Import to Table** box, type **2B Athletes** and then click **Finish**. In the lower right corner of the **Get External Data – Excel Spreadsheet** dialog box, click **Close**.

That is all the information the Wizard needs to import your data. In the Navigation Pane, your new table displays.

8 On the Ribbon, click the **Database Tools tab**, and then in the **Show/Hide group**, click the **Relationships** button. On the **Design tab**, in the **Relationships group**, click **Show Table**. In the **Show Table** dialog box, **Add** the **2B Athletes** table, and then **Add** the **2B Scholarships Awarded** table. **Close** the **Show Table** dialog box.

9 Use the ⬉ pointer as necessary to expand the height and width of the field lists, position the field lists as necessary so that the **2B Athletes** table is on the left, and allow approximately 1 inch of space between the two field lists. Compare your screen with Figure 2.39.

Positioning the field lists in this manner is not required, but while studying Access, it makes it easier for you to view while creating the relationships.

Figure 2.39

Approximately 1 inch
between field lists

2B Scholarships Awarded
field list on right

2B Athletes field list on left

Imported table renamed and
displays in Navigation Pane

Each field list's height and
width expanded to view all
field names

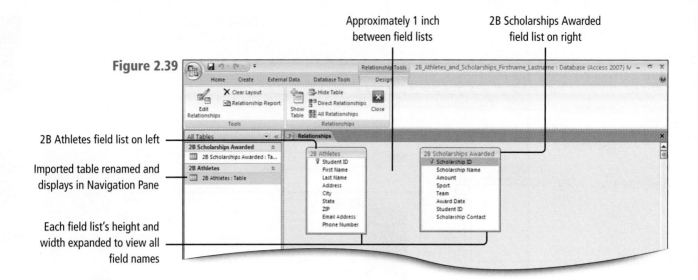

10 In the **2B Athletes** field list, point to the **Student ID** field, hold down the left mouse button, drag into the **2B Scholarships Awarded** field list, and then position the mouse pointer on top of the **Student ID** field near the bottom of the list. Release the mouse button.

11 Point to the title bar of the **Edit Relationships** dialog box, and then drag it below the two field lists. In the **Edit Relationships** dialog box, be sure that the **2B Athletes** table is indicated on the left, that the **2B Scholarships Awarded** table is indicated on the right, and that **Student ID** is indicated as the field for both the *Table* and the *Related Table*.

The two tables are related in a one-to-many relationship—*one* athlete can be awarded *many* scholarships. The common field between the two tables is the Student ID field. In the 2B Athletes table, Student ID is the primary key. In the 2B Scholarships Awarded table, Student ID is the foreign key.

12 In the **Edit Relationships** dialog box, select the **Enforce Referential Integrity** check box, click the **Create** button, and then compare your screen with Figure 2.40.

The one-to-many relationship is established, and the *1* and ∞ indicate that referential integrity is enforced. Enforcing referential integrity ensures that a scholarship cannot be awarded to a student whose name does not appear in the 2B Athletes table. Similarly, you will not be able to delete a student athlete from the 2B Athletes table if there is a scholarship listed for that student in the 2B Scholarships Awarded table.

Join line indicates relationship established using *Student ID* as common field

Foreign key field in the *many* table

Figure 2.40

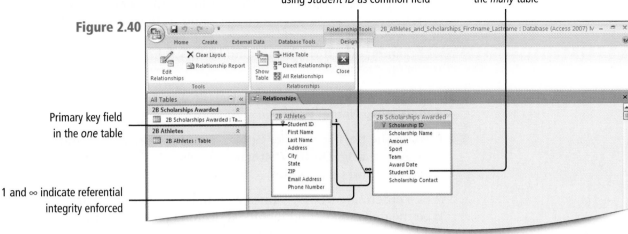

Primary key field in the *one* table

1 and ∞ indicate referential integrity enforced

13 On the **Design tab**, in the **Tools group**, click **Relationship Report**. On the displayed **Print Preview tab**, in the **Page Layout group**, click **Margins**, and then click **Normal**. Submit electronically as directed, or, if you are printing your assignments on paper, click the **Print** button, and then click **OK**. Click **Close Print Preview**. On the **Quick Access Toolbar**, click the **Save** button 🔲 to save the report. With the text in the **Save As** dialog box highlighted, type **2B Relationships Firstname Lastname** and then click **OK**.

14 **Close** ❎ the report and the Relationships window. From the **Navigation Pane**, open the **2B Athletes** table. On the left side of the table, in the first record, point to the **plus sign**, and then click one time.

In the first record—for *Damon Hill*—you can see that three related records exist in the 2B Scholarships Awarded table. The relationship displays because you created a relationship between the two tables using the Student ID field as the common field.

15 **Close** ❎ the **2B Athletes** table, and then **Close** « the **Navigation Pane**.

Objective 9
Specify Numeric Criteria in a Query

Criteria can be set for fields that contain numeric data. When you design your table, set the appropriate data type for fields that will contain numbers, currency, or dates so that mathematical calculations can be performed.

Activity 2.16 Specifying Numeric Criteria in a Query

Mr. Simmons wants to know *Which scholarships, and for which sport, are in the amount of $300?* In this activity, you will specify criteria in the query so that only the records of scholarships in the amount of $300 will display.

1 On the **Create tab**, in the **Other group**, click the **Query Design** button. In the **Show Table** dialog box, **Add** the **2B Scholarships Awarded** table, and then **Close** the **Show Table** dialog box. With the

[↖] pointer, adjust the height and width of the field list so that all of the fields display.

2 Add the following fields to the design grid in the order given: **Scholarship Name**, **Sport**, and **Amount**.

3 Click in the **Sort** row under **Sport**, click the **Sort arrow**, and then click **Ascending**. On the **Criteria** row, click in the **Amount** field, type **300** and then press [Enter]. Compare your screen with Figure 2.41.

When entering currency values as criteria in the design grid, do not type the dollar sign, and include a decimal point only if you are looking for a specific amount that includes cents—for example 300.50.

Figure 2.41

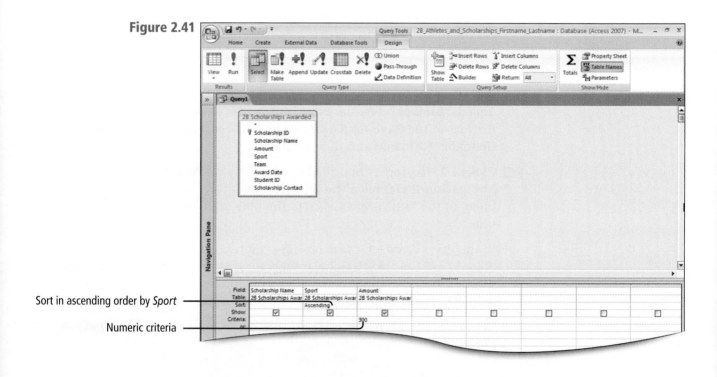

Sort in ascending order by *Sport*

Numeric criteria

4 On the **Design tab**, in the **Results group**, click the **Run** button to view the results. Alternatively, click the View button.

Five scholarships awarded were in the exact amount of $300. At the bottom of the datasheet, *1 of 5* displays to indicate the number of records that match the criteria.

5 On the **Home tab**, in the **Views group**, click the **View** button to return to Design view. Leave the query open in Design view for the next activity.

Activity 2.17 Using Comparison Operators

Comparison operators are symbols that evaluate each field value to determine if it is the same (=), greater than (>), less than (<), or in between a range of values as specified by the criteria.

If no comparison operator is specified, equal (=) is assumed. For example, in the previous activity, you created a query to display only records where the *Amount* was 300. The comparison operator of = was assumed, and Access displayed only records that had entries equal to 300.

In this activity, you will specify criteria in the query to display records from the 2B Scholarships Awarded table that have scholarships that are *greater* than $300 and then to display scholarships that are *less* than $300.

1 Be sure your query from the last activity is displayed in Design view. On the **Criteria** row, click in the **Amount** field, delete the existing criteria, type **>300** and then press [Enter]. Compare your screen with Figure 2.42.

Unlike a field with a data type of *Text*, Access does not add quote marks around criteria entered in a field that has a data type of *Number* or *Currency*.

Figure 2.42

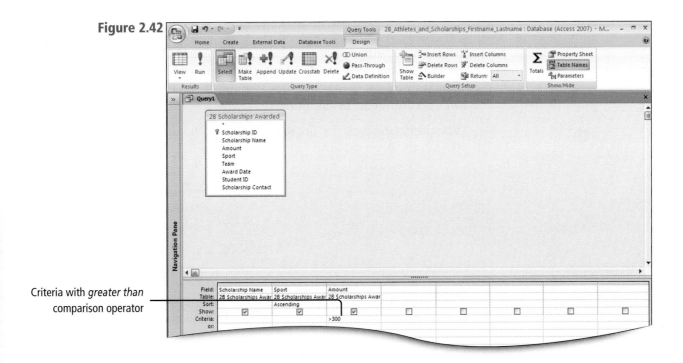

Criteria with *greater than* comparison operator

2 Click the **Design tab**, and then in the **Results group**, click the **Run** button.

Fourteen records match the criteria for an Amount that is greater than $300. The results show the records for which the Amount is *greater than* $300, but not *equal* to $300.

3 Click the **View** button to return to Design view. On the **Criteria** row, under **Amount**, delete the existing criteria, type **<300** Press Enter, and then on the **Design tab**, in the **Results group**, click the **Run** button.

Eleven records display and each has an Amount less than $300. The results show the records for which the Amount is *less than* $300, but not *equal to* $300.

4 Switch to Design view. On the **Criteria** row, click in the **Amount** field, delete the existing criteria, type **>=300** and then press Enter.

Note — Pressing Enter After Criteria Is Added

If you press Enter or click in another column or row in the query design grid after you have added your criteria, you can see how Access alters the criteria so it can interpret what you have typed. Sometimes, there is no change, such as when a number is added to a number or currency field. Other times, Access may capitalize a letter or add quote marks or other symbols to clarify the criteria. Whether or not you press Enter after criteria is added does not affect the query results. It is used in this text to help you see how the program behaves.

---

5 **Run** the query, and then compare your screen with Figure 2.43.

Nineteen records display, including the records for scholarships in the exact amount of $300. Thus, the displayed records include scholarships *equal to* or *greater than* $300. In this manner, comparison operators can be combined.

This query answers the question, *Which scholarships, and for which sport, have been awarded in the amount of $300 or more?*

Figure 2.43

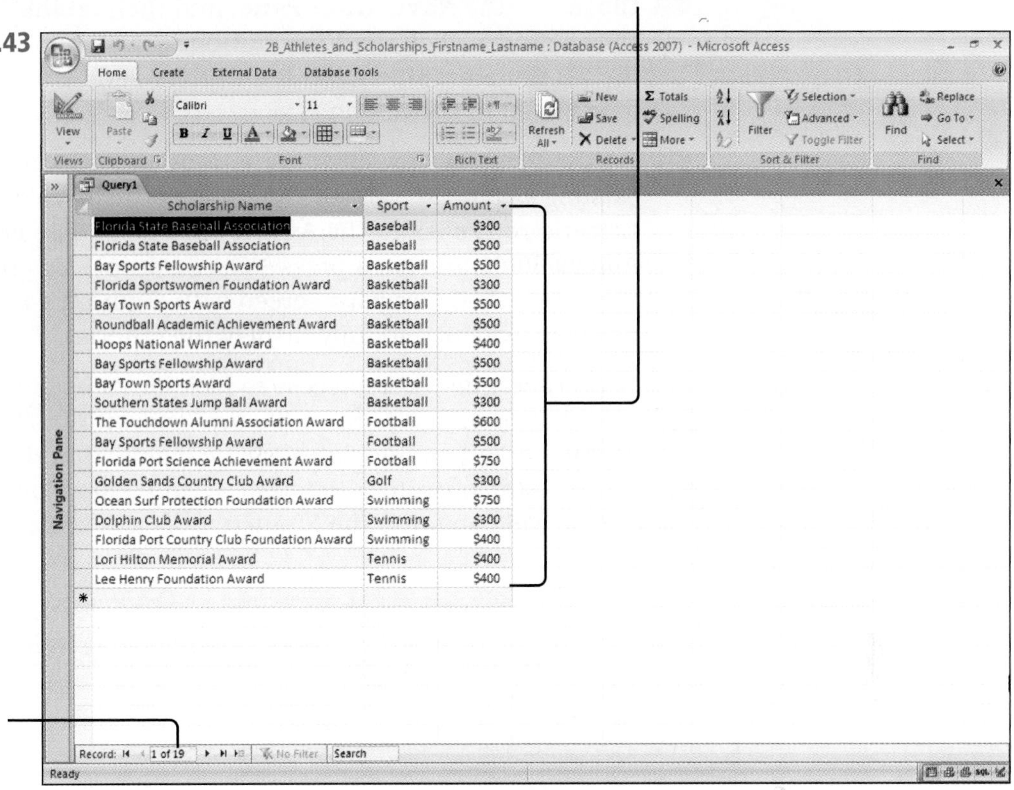

Records with a scholarship amount of $300 or more

Number of records that meet criteria

6 On the **Quick Access Toolbar**, click the **Save** button , and then in the **Save As** dialog box, type **2B $300 or More Firstname Lastname** Click **OK**.

7 From the **Office** menu , point to the **Print** button, and then click **Print Preview**. If you are printing your assignments on paper, in the **Print group**, click the **Print** button. In the displayed **Print** dialog box, click **OK**. To submit electronically, follow your instructor's directions.

8 Click the **Close Print Preview** button, and then **Close** ☒ the query.

Open » the **Navigation Pane**, and notice that your new query displays under the table from which it retrieved the records.

Activity 2.18 Using the Between. . . And Comparison Operator

The ***Between. . . And*** operator is a comparison operator that looks for values within a range. It is particularly useful when you need to locate records that are within a range of dates, for example, scholarships awarded between August 1 and September 30. In this activity, you will create a new query from an existing query, and then add criteria to look for values within a range of dates. The query will answer the question *Which scholarships were awarded between August 1 and September 30?*

1 From the **Navigation Pane**, open your **2B $300 or More** query.

From the **Office** menu , click **Save As**. In the **Save As** dialog box, type **2B Awards Aug-Sept Firstname Lastname** and then click **OK**.

2 **Close** the **Navigation Pane**, and then on the **Home tab**, in the **Views group**, click the **View** button to switch to Design view. From the **2B Scholarships Awarded** field list, add the **Award Date** as the fourth field in the design grid.

3 On the **Criteria** row, click in the **Amount** field, and then delete the existing criteria so that the query is not restricted by amount. On the **Criteria** row, click in the **Award Date** field, type **Between 08/01/09 And 09/30/09** and then press Enter. Access places quote marks around the dates. Compare your screen with Figure 2.44, where the column has been widened to fully display the criteria.

This criteria instructs Access to look for values in the Award Date field that begin with 08/01/09 and end with 09/30/09. Both the beginning and ending dates will be included in the query results. If you type the operators *Between. . . And*, using lowercase letters, Access will capitalize the first letter of each operator.

Figure 2.44

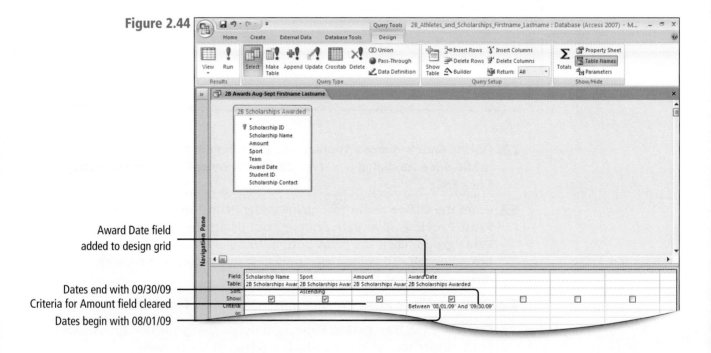

Award Date field added to design grid

Dates end with 09/30/09
Criteria for Amount field cleared
Dates begin with 08/01/09

4 **Run** the query and notice that three scholarships were awarded between the dates you specified in your criteria.

5 From the **Office** menu , point to the **Print** button, and then click **Print Preview**. If you are printing your assignments on paper, in the **Print group**, click the **Print** button. In the displayed **Print** dialog box, click **OK**. To submit electronically, follow your instructor's directions.

6 Click the **Close Print Preview** button. In the object window, **Close** ⊠ the query, and then click **Yes** to save the changes to the design.

Open » the **Navigation Pane**, and notice that your new query displays under the table from which it retrieved records.

Note — Widening Columns in the Query Grid

For a better view of your criteria, you can widen a column in the design grid using the same techniques that are used in a table. In the selection bar at the top of the column, point to the right border and double-click to expand the column to fully display the contents on the criteria row. You can also drag the right border to the width you want.

Objective 10
Use Compound Criteria

You can specify more than one condition—criteria—in a query; this is called **compound criteria**. Compound criteria enable you to create queries that are quite specific. Two types of compound criteria used in queries are AND and OR, which are **logical operators**. Logical operators allow you to enter criteria for the same field or different fields.

Activity 2.19 Using AND Criteria in a Query

Compound criteria that create an AND condition will display the records in the query result that meet *both* parts of the specified criteria. In this activity, you will help Mr. Simmons answer the question *Which scholar-ships over $500 were awarded for Football?* The results will match the criteria >$500 *and* Football.

1 **Close** ⟪ the **Navigation Pane**, and then from the **Create tab**, open a new query in Design view. **Add** the **2B Scholarships Awarded** table to the table area, **Close** the **Show Table** dialog box, and then adjust the height and width of the field list with the ⬉ pointer.

2 Add the following fields to the design grid in the order given: **Scholarship Name**, **Sport**, and **Amount**.

3 On the **Criteria** row, click in the **Sport** field, type **Football** and then press Tab. On the **Criteria** row, in the **Amount** field, type **>500** press Enter, and then compare your screen with Figure 2.45.

The AND condition is created by placing the criteria for both fields on the same line in the Criteria row. The results will display records that contain *Football* and an amount greater than *$500*.

Figure 2.45

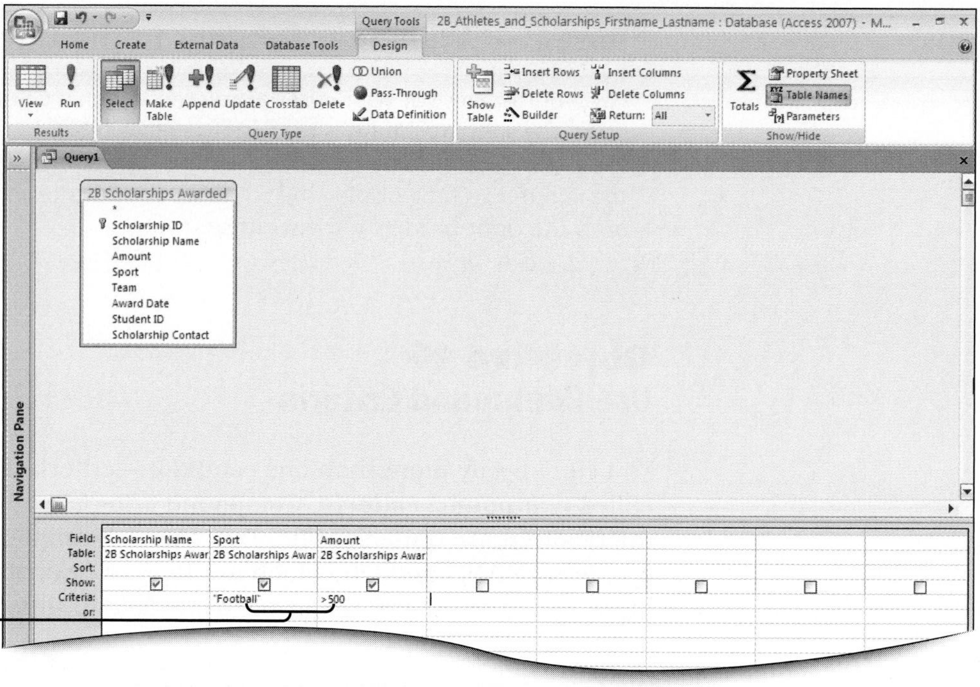

Criteria specified for
Sport and Amount

4 On the **Design tab**, in the **Results group**, click the **Run** button.

Two records display that match both conditions—Football in the Sport field and greater than $500 in the Amount field.

5 **Close** ☒ the query, click **Yes** to save changes to the query, and then in the **Save As** dialog box, type **2B Football and Over $500 Firstname Lastname** as the query name. Click **OK** or press Enter.

6 **Open** ⟫ the **Navigation Pane**, click one time to select the query you just named and saved, and then from the **Office** menu 🔘, point to the **Print** button and click **Print Preview**. If you are printing your assignments on paper, in the **Print group**, click the **Print** button. In the displayed **Print** dialog box, click **OK**. To submit electronically, follow your instructor's directions.

7 Click the **Close Print Preview** button, and then **Close** ⟪ the **Navigation Pane**.

You can print any selected object from the Navigation Pane in this manner—the object does not have to be displayed on your screen to print.

Activity 2.20 Using OR Criteria in a Query

Use the OR condition to specify multiple criteria for a single field, or multiple criteria on different fields when you want the records that meet either condition to display in the results. In this activity, you will help Mr. Simmons answer the question *Which scholarships over $400 were awarded in the sports of Baseball or Swimming?*

1 From the **Create tab**, open a new query in Design view. **Add** the **2B Scholarships Awarded** table, **Close** the dialog box, expand the field list, and then add the following four fields to the design grid in the order given: **Scholarship Name**, **Sport**, **Amount**, and **Award Date**.

2 On the **Criteria** row, click in the **Sport** field, and then type **Baseball**

3 In the design grid, locate the **or** row. On the **or** row, click in the **Sport** field, type **Swimming** and then press Enter. **Run** the query.

The query results display seven scholarship records whose Sport is either Baseball *or* Swimming. Use the OR condition in this manner to specify multiple criteria for a single field.

4 Return to Design view. Under **Sport**, on the **or** row, delete the text. Under **Sport**, click in the **Criteria** row, delete the existing text, and then type **Swimming Or Baseball** On the **Criteria** row, under **Amount**, type **>400** press Enter, and then compare your screen with Figure 2.46.

This is an alternative way to use the OR compound operator. Because criteria has been entered for two different fields, Access will return the records that are Baseball *or* Swimming and that have a scholarship awarded in an amount greater than $400.

In this manner, you can type multiple criteria for the same field on the Criteria row.

Figure 2.46

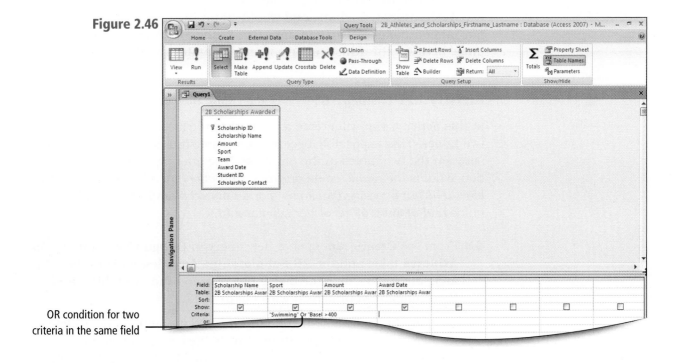

OR condition for two criteria in the same field

5 **Run** the query to display the two records that match the conditions.

6 **Close** ☒ the query, click **Yes** to save changes to the query, and then in the **Save As** dialog box, type **2B Swimming or Baseball Over $400 Firstname Lastname** as the query name. Click **OK** or press Enter.

7 Open **»** the **Navigation Pane**, click one time to select the query you just named and saved, and then from the **Office** menu
[icon], display the **Print Preview**. If you are printing your assignments on paper, in the **Print group**, click the **Print** button, and then click **OK**. To submit electronically, follow your instructor's directions.

8 Click the **Close Print Preview** button, and then **Close** **«** the **Navigation Pane**.

Objective 11
Create a Query Based on More Than One Table

In a relational database, you can retrieve information from more than one table. Recall that each table in a relational database contains all of the records about a single topic. Tables are joined by relating the primary key field in one table to a foreign key field in another table. This common field creates a relationship, which enables you to include data from more than one table in a query.

For example, the Athletes table contains all of the information about the student athletes—name, address, and so on. The Scholarships Awarded table includes the scholarship name, amount, award date, and so on. When an athlete receives a scholarship, only the Student ID field is included with the scholarship to identify who received the scholarship. It is not necessary to include, and would result in repeated information, if any other athlete information appeared in the Scholarships Awarded table, because the athlete information is contained in the Athletes table.

Activity 2.21 Creating a Query Based on More Than One Table

In this activity, you will create a query that retrieves information from two tables. This is possible because a relationship has been established between the two tables in the database. The query will answer the question *What is the name, email address, and phone number of student athletes who have received swimming or tennis scholarships, and what is the name and amount of his or her scholarship?*

1 From the **Create tab**, open a new query in Design view. **Add** the **2B Athletes** table and the **2B Scholarships Awarded** table to the table area, and then **Close** the dialog box. Expand the two tables, and then compare your screen with Figure 2.47.

The join line indicates the one-to-many relationship—one athlete can have many scholarships. Student ID is the common field in the two tables. Notice that Student ID is designated by a key in the Athletes table where it is the primary key field, but it is not designated by a key in the Scholarships Awarded table where it is the foreign key field.

Figure 2.47

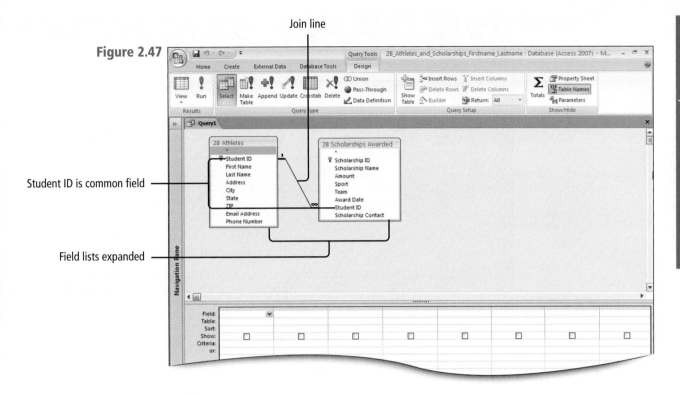

Join line

Student ID is common field

Field lists expanded

2 From the **2B Athletes** field list, add the following fields in the order given: **First Name**, **Last Name**, **Address**, **City**, **State**, and **ZIP**. On the **Sort** row, under **Last Name**, click to select **Ascending** to sort the records in alphabetical order by last name.

3 From the **2B Scholarships Awarded** field list, add **Scholarship Name**, **Sport**, and **Amount** to the design grid. On the **Criteria** row, under **Sport**, type **Swimming** On the **or** row, under **Sport**, type **Tennis** and then press Enter.

4 In the design grid, locate the second row—the **Table** row, and notice that for each field, the table from which the field was added is indicated. Compare your screen with Figure 2.48.

When using multiple tables in a query, this information is helpful, especially when some tables may include the same field names, such as address, but different data, such as a student's address or a coach's address.

Figure 2.48

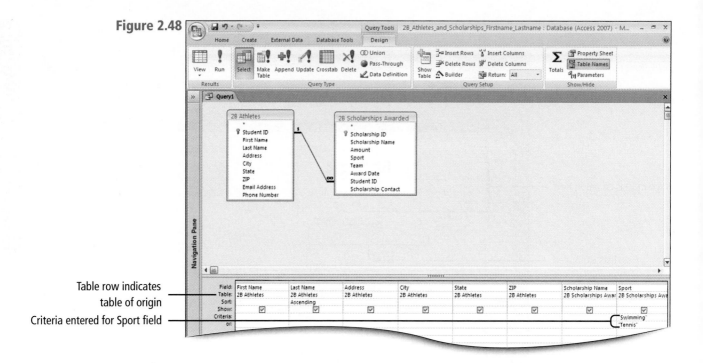

5 **Run** the query.

The names and addresses of eight student athletes display. Notice that the First Name and Last Name is included in the query results even though the common field—Student ID—was *not* included in the query design. Because Student ID is included in both tables, and a one-to-many relationship was created between the tables, you can display data from both tables in one query.

Two students—*Arianna Kitasoe* and *Janice Murphy*—received scholarships in both Swimming and Tennis. Recall that *one* student athlete can have *many* scholarships.

6 Return to Design view. From the **Athletes** field list, add **Phone Number** to the design grid. Point to **Email Address**, drag it to the design grid on top of **Amount**, and then release the mouse button.

When you release the mouse button, Email Address is inserted to the left of the Amount field.

7 In the design grid, select, by dragging in the gray selection bar, the **Address**, **City**, **State**, and **ZIP** fields, and then press Delete. In the design grid, select the **Amount** field, and then drag it to the first field position in the grid. Click outside of the grid to cancel the selection, and then compare your screen with Figure 2.49.

Phone Number is added as the last field in the design grid. The Address, City, State, and ZIP fields are deleted. The amount field is in the first position. In this manner, you can modify your query design.

Figure 2.49

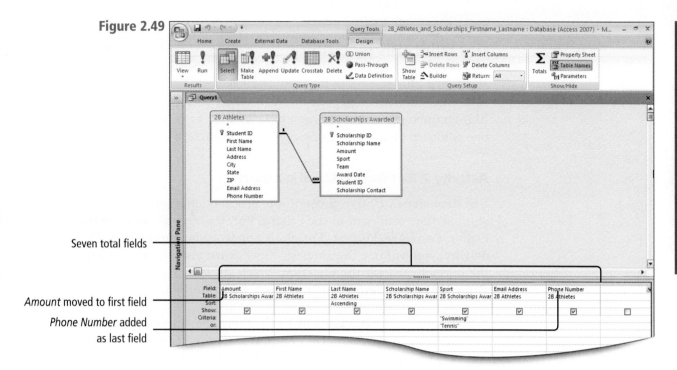

Seven total fields

Amount moved to first field

Phone Number added
as last field

8 **Run** the query again. Using techniques similar to that of a table, select all the columns in the query and apply **Best Fit** (with the columns selected, in the field heading row, point to the right boundary of any of the selected rows to display the 🔩 pointer, and then double-click to apply Best Fit to all of the selected columns).

9 On the **Quick Access Toolbar,** click the **Save** button 🔲, type **2B Swimming and Tennis Firstname Lastname** and then click **OK**. Display the query in **Print Preview**, set the **Margins** to **Normal**, and then change the orientation to **Landscape**. Print or submit electronically as directed.

10 **Close** the print preview, close the query, open the **Navigation Pane**, and notice that your new query displays under *both* tables from which it retrieved records.

In the Tables and Related Views arrangement of the Navigation Pane, any object that references a table will display with that table.

More Knowledge

Add a Table to the Table Area

To add another table to the table area, in the Query Setup group, click Show Table; or, right-click in the table area, and from the shortcut menu, click Show Table.

Objective 12
Use Wildcards in a Query

Wildcard characters in a query serve as a placeholder for one or more unknown characters in your criteria. When you are unsure of the particular character or set of characters to include in your criteria, you can use wildcard characters in place of the characters in the criteria.

Activity 2.22 Using a Wildcard in a Query

Use the asterisk (*) to represent any group of characters. For example, if you use the * wildcard in the criteria Fo*, the results would return Foster, Forrester, Forrest, Fossil, or any word beginning with *Fo*. In this activity, you will use the asterisk (*) wildcard and specify the criteria in the query to answer the question *Which student athletes received scholarships from local Rotary Clubs, country clubs, and foundations?*

1 **Close** ⟪ the **Navigation Pane**. From the **Create tab**, start a new query in Design view, add both tables to the table area, and then expand the field lists to view all the field names. Add the following fields to the design grid: **First Name** and **Last Name** from the **2B Athletes** table, and **Scholarship Contact** from the **2B Scholarships Awarded** table. On the **Sort** row, sort the query results in **Ascending** order by **Last Name**.

2 On the **Criteria** row, under **Scholarship Contact**, type **Rotary*** and then press Enter.

The wildcard character * is used as a placeholder to match any number of characters. When you press Enter, *Like* is added by Access at the beginning of the criteria. This is used to compare a sequence of characters and test whether or not the text matches a pattern.

Access will automatically insert expressions similar to this when creating queries.

3 **Run** the query to display the three student athletes who received scholarships from Rotary Clubs.

4 Return to the Design view. On the **or** row, under **Scholarship Contact**, type ***Country Club** and then press Enter.

The * can be used at the beginning or end of the criteria. The position of the wildcard determines the location of the unknown characters. Here you will search for records that end in *Country Club*.

5 **Run** the query to display a total of six records.

6 Return to Design view. In the next available row under **Scholarship Contact**, type ***Foundation*** press Enter, and then compare your screen with Figure 2.50.

In this manner, the query will return records that have the word *Foundation* anywhere—beginning, middle, or end—in the field. You can also see that you can combine many *or* criteria in a query.

Figure 2.50

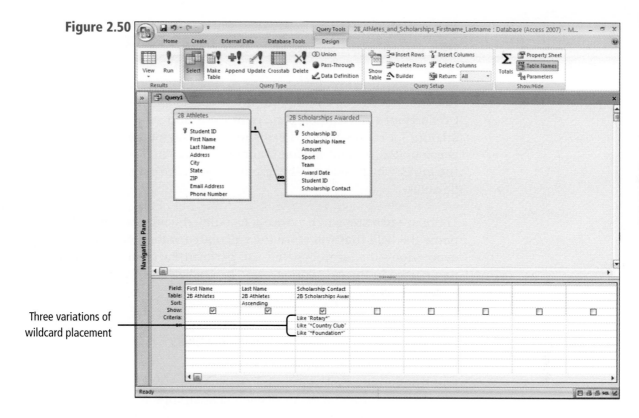

Three variations of
wildcard placement

7 **Run** the query to display a total of 28 records.

Twenty-eight scholarships were awarded from either a Country Club, a Rotary club, or a Foundation.

8 On the **Quick Access Toolbar**, click the **Save** button, and name the query **2B Clubs and Foundations Firstname Lastname** Display the **Print Preview**, and print your result if you are submitting paper assignments, or submit electronically as directed. **Close Print Preview**, **Close** the query ⊠, and then **Open** ≫ the **Navigation Pane**.

Because the query retrieved data from two tables, the query displays below each table's name.

> ## More Knowledge
>
> ### Search for a Single Unknown Character by Using the ? Wildcard
>
> The question mark (?) is another wildcard that is used to search for unknown single characters. For each question mark included in a criteria, any character can be inserted. For example, if you used *b?d* as a criteria, the query could locate bid, bud, bed or any three-character word beginning with *b* and ending with *d*. If *b??d* is entered as the criteria, the results could include bind, bend, bard or any four-character word beginning with *b* and ending with *d*.

Objective 13
Use Calculated Fields in a Query

Queries can create calculated values. For example, Florida Port Community College could multiply two fields together, such as Total Credit Hours and Tuition per Credit Hour and get a Total Tuition Due amount for each student. In this manner, the total amount of tuition due is calculated without having to include a specific field for this amount in the table, which reduces the size of the database and provides more flexibility.

There are two steps to produce a calculated field in a query. First, name the field that will store the calculated values. Second, write the expression—the formula—that will perform the calculation. Each field name used in the calculation must be enclosed within its own pair of square brackets.

Activity 2.23 Using Calculated Fields in a Query

For each scholarship received by college student athletes, the Florida Port Community College Alumni Association has agreed to donate an amount equal to 50 percent of each scholarship. In this activity, you will create a calculated field to determine the additional amount each scholarship is worth. The query will answer the question *What will the value of each scholarship be if the Alumni Association makes a matching 50% donation?*

1 **Close** « the **Navigation Pane**. From the **Create tab**, start a new query in Design view. **Add** the **2B Scholarships Awarded** table and expand the field list. Add the following fields to the design grid: **Student ID**, **Scholarship Name**, and **Amount**.

2 Click in the **Sort** row under **Student ID**, click the **Sort arrow**, and then click **Ascending**. In the **Field** row, right-click in the first empty column to display a shortcut menu, and then click **Zoom**.

The Zoom dialog box that displays gives you working space so that you can see the calculation as you type it. The calculation can also be typed directly in the empty Field box in the column.

3 In the **Zoom** dialog box, type **Matching Donation: [Amount]*0.5** and then compare your screen with Figure 2.51.

The first element, *Matching Donation*, is the new field name where the calculated amounts will display. Following that is a colon (:). A colon in a calculated field separates the new field name from the expression. *Amount* is in square brackets because it is an existing field name from the 2B Scholarships Awarded table. It contains the information on which the calculation will be performed. Following the square brackets is an asterisk (*), which in math calculations signifies multiplication. Finally, the percentage (50% or 0.5) is indicated.

Calculated value

Figure 2.51

New field name ———

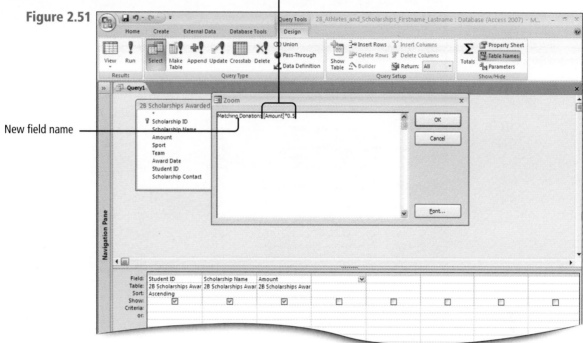

Alert!	**Does your screen differ?**
	If your calculations in a query do not work, carefully check the expression you typed. Spelling or syntax errors will prevent calculated fields from working properly.

---

4 In the **Zoom** dialog box, click **OK**, and then **Run** the query. Select all the columns and apply **Best Fit**. Compare your screen with Figure 2.52.

The query results display the three fields from the 2B Scholarships Awarded table plus a fourth field—Matching Donation—in which a calculated amount displays. Each calculated amount equals the amount in the Amount field multiplied by 0.5.

Figure 2.52

New calculated field created (50% of Amount)

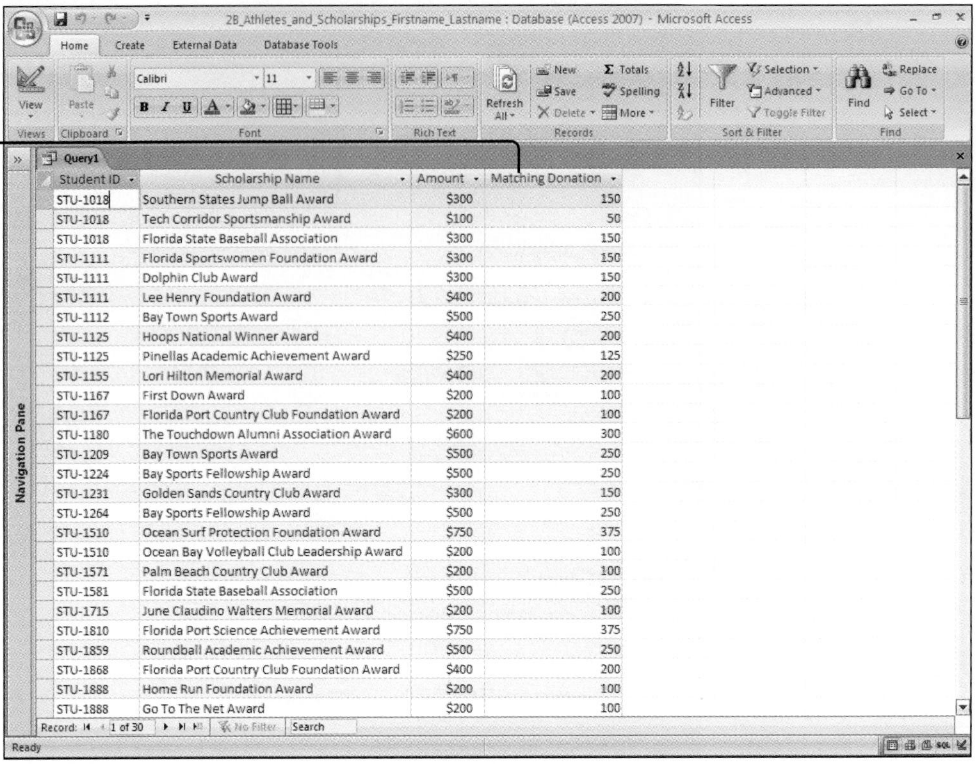

Student ID	Scholarship Name	Amount	Matching Donation
STU-1018	Southern States Jump Ball Award	$300	150
STU-1018	Tech Corridor Sportsmanship Award	$100	50
STU-1018	Florida State Baseball Association	$300	150
STU-1111	Florida Sportswomen Foundation Award	$300	150
STU-1111	Dolphin Club Award	$300	150
STU-1111	Lee Henry Foundation Award	$400	200
STU-1112	Bay Town Sports Award	$500	250
STU-1125	Hoops National Winner Award	$400	200
STU-1125	Pinellas Academic Achievement Award	$250	125
STU-1155	Lori Hilton Memorial Award	$400	200
STU-1167	First Down Award	$200	100
STU-1167	Florida Port Country Club Foundation Award	$200	100
STU-1180	The Touchdown Alumni Association Award	$600	300
STU-1209	Bay Town Sports Award	$500	250
STU-1224	Bay Sports Fellowship Award	$500	250
STU-1231	Golden Sands Country Club Award	$300	150
STU-1264	Bay Sports Fellowship Award	$500	250
STU-1510	Ocean Surf Protection Foundation Award	$750	375
STU-1510	Ocean Bay Volleyball Club Leadership Award	$200	100
STU-1571	Palm Beach Country Club Award	$200	100
STU-1581	Florida State Baseball Association	$500	250
STU-1715	June Claudino Walters Memorial Award	$200	100
STU-1810	Florida Port Science Achievement Award	$750	375
STU-1859	Roundball Academic Achievement Award	$500	250
STU-1868	Florida Port Country Club Foundation Award	$400	200
STU-1888	Home Run Foundation Award	$200	100
STU-1888	Go To The Net Award	$200	100

5 Notice the formatting of the **Matching Donation** field—there are no dollar signs, commas, or decimal places; you will adjust this formatting later. Return to Design view. On the **Field** row, in the first empty column, right-click, and then click **Zoom**.

6 In the **Zoom** dialog box, type **Total Scholarship: [Amount]+[Matching Donation]** and then click **OK**. **Run** the query to view the results. Apply **Best Fit** to the new column.

Total Scholarship is calculated by adding together the Amount field and the Matching Donation field. The Total Scholarship column includes dollar signs, commas, and decimal points, which carried over from the Amount field.

7 Return to Design view. On the **Field** row, click in the **Matching Donation** field. On the **Design tab**, in the **Show/Hide group**, click the **Property Sheet** button. Alternatively, right-click the Matching Donation field, and then click Properties.

The Property Sheet task pane displays on the right side of your screen. Here you can customize fields in a query, for example, the format of numbers in the field.

8 In the **Property Sheet** task pane, on the **General tab**, click the text *Format*, and then click the **arrow** that displays. Compare your screen with Figure 2.53.

A list of possible formats for this field displays.

Property Sheet   Format arrow

Figure 2.53

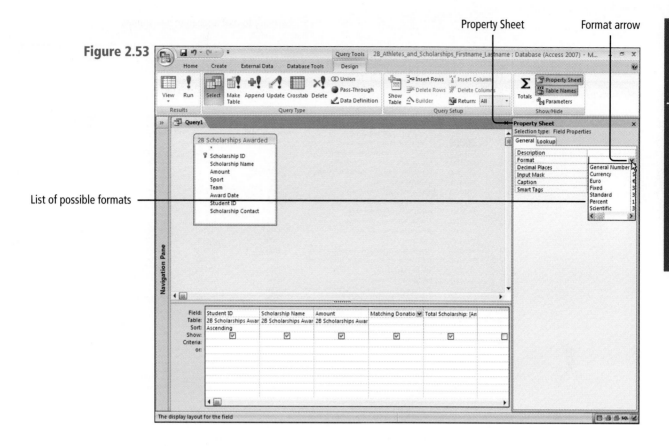

List of possible formats

[9] In the list of formats, click **Currency**, and then **Close** the **Property Sheet** task pane.

[10] **Run** the query to view the results. If necessary, select all the columns, and apply **Best Fit**. Click in any record to cancel the selection, and then compare your screen with Figure 2.54.

The Matching Donation column displays with currency formatting—a dollar sign, thousands comma separators, and two decimal places.

Figure 2.54

Currency format applied to all columns

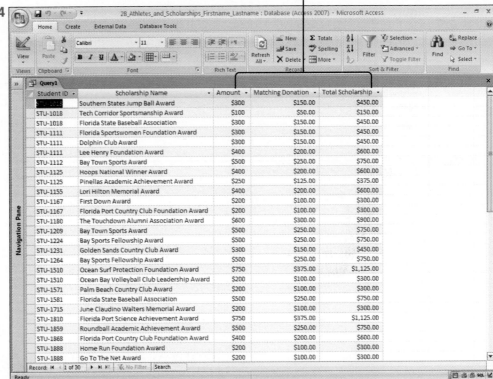

11 On the **Quick Access Toolbar**, click the **Save** button, and then name the query **2B Matching Donations Firstname Lastname** Display the **Print Preview**, change the **Orientation** to **Landscape**, and then print or submit electronically as directed. **Close Print Preview**, and then **Close** ☒ the query.

Objective 14
Group Data and Calculate Statistics in a Query

In Access queries, you can perform statistical calculations on a group of records. Calculations that are performed on a group of records are called *aggregate functions*. In the activities that follow, you will use AVG, SUM, MAX, and MIN functions. As you progress in your study of Access, you will use other functions.

Activity 2.24 Using the MIN, MAX, AVG and SUM Functions in a Query

In this activity, you will use the average, sum, maximum, and minimum functions in a query to examine the amounts of scholarships awarded. The last query will answer the question *What is the total amount of scholarships awarded?*

1 From the **Create tab**, create a new query in Design view. **Add** the **2B Scholarships Awarded** table, and then expand the field list. Add **Amount** to the design grid.

When you want to summarize a field, include only the field you want to summarize in the query, so that the aggregate function (sum, average, minimum, maximum, and so forth) is applied to that single field.

2 On the **Design tab**, in the **Show/Hide group**, click the **Totals** button to add a **Total** row as the third row in the design grid. Notice that in the design grid, on the **Total** row, under **Amount**, *Group By* displays.

Here you select the function—such as Avg, Sum, Min, or Max—that you want to use for this field.

3 In the **Total** row, under **Amount**, click in the **Group By** box, and then click the **arrow** to display the list of functions. Access supports the aggregate functions summarized in the table shown in Figure 2.55. Take a moment to review this table, and then compare your screen with Figure 2.56.

Aggregate Functions

Function Name	What It Does
Sum	Totals the values in a field.
Avg	Averages the values in a field.
Min	Locates the smallest value in a field.
Max	Locates the largest value in a field.
Count	Counts the number of records in a field.
StDev	Calculates the Standard Deviation on the values in a field.
Var	Calculates the Variance on the values in a field.
First	Displays the First value in a field.
Last	Displays the Last value in a field.
Expression	Creates a calculated field that includes an aggregate function.
Where	Limits records displayed to those that match a condition specified on the Criteria row.

Figure 2.55

List of aggregate functions   Totals button in the Show/Hide group

Figure 2.56

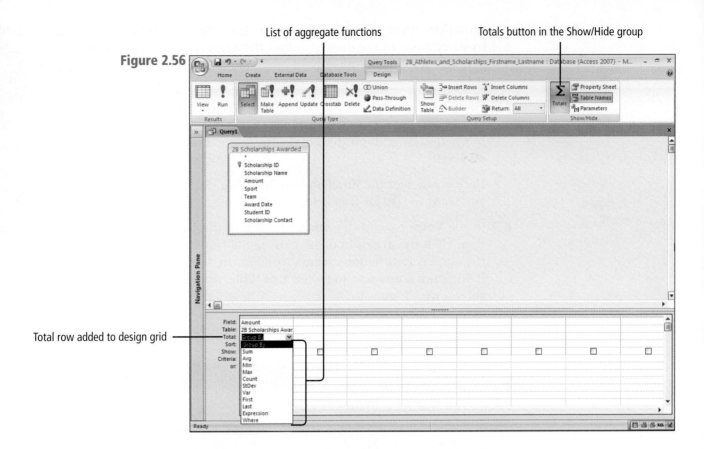

Total row added to design grid

4 From the list of functions, click **Min**, and then **Run** the query. Double-click the right boundary of the column heading to widen the column.

Access calculates the minimum (smallest) scholarship award—$100.00. The field name, *MinOfAmount* displays for the calculation. This query answers the question, *What is the minimum (smallest) scholarship amount awarded?*

5 Return to Design view. Using the technique you just practiced, select the **Max** function, and then **Run** the query.

The maximum (largest) scholarship amount is $750.00.

6 Switch to Design view, select the **Avg** function, and then **Run** the query.

The average scholarship amount awarded is $358.33.

7 Return to Design view. Select the **Sum** function. **Run** the query.

Access sums the Amount field for all records and displays a result of *$10,750.00*. The field name, SumOfAmount, displays. This query answers the question, *What is the total of all the scholarships awarded?*

Activity 2.25 Grouping Data in a Query

The aggregate functions can also be used to calculate totals by groups of data. For example, if you wanted to group (summarize) the amount of scholarships awarded to each student, you would include the Student ID field, in addition to the Amount field, and then group all of the records for each student together to calculate a total awarded to each student. Similarly, you could calculate how much money was awarded to each sport.

1 Switch to Design view. Add the **Student ID** field to the design grid.

On the Total row, under Student ID, *Group By* displays by default. The design of this query will group—summarize—the records by StudentID and calculate a total Amount for each student.

2 **Run** the query to display the results, apply **Best Fit** to the columns, click any record to deselect, and then compare your screen with Figure 2.57.

The query calculates totals for each student.

Figure 2.57

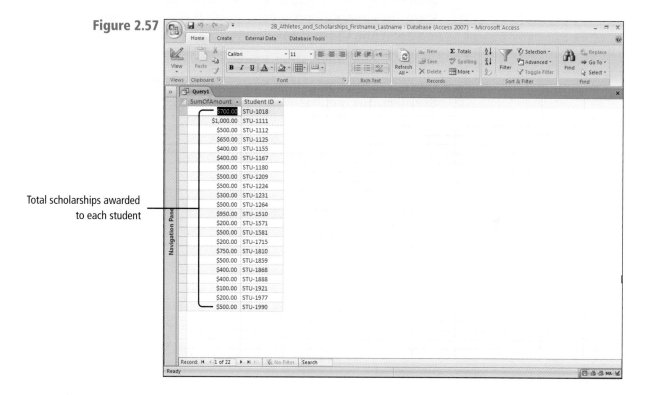

Total scholarships awarded to each student

3 Switch to Design view. In the design grid, select and delete the **Student ID** field, and then add the **Sport** field to the design grid. **Run** the query to see the results. Compare your screen with Figure 2.58.

Access summarizes the data by each sport. You can see that Basketball received the largest total Amount—$3,500.00.

Figure 2.58

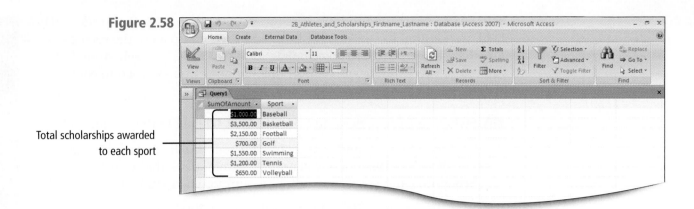

Total scholarships awarded
to each sport

4 On the **Quick Access Toolbar**, click the **Save** button, and then name the query **2B Totals by Sport Firstname Lastname** Display the **Print Preview**, and print your result if you are submitting paper assignments. **Close Print Preview**, close the query, and then

Open the **Navigation Pane** to view the queries you have created.

5 **Close** the **Navigation Pane**, close your **2B_Athletes_ Scholarships** database, and then **Close** Access.

End **You have completed Project 2B** ⸻

There's More You Can Do!

From My Computer, navigate to the student files that accompany this textbook. In the folder **02_theres_more_you_can_do_pg1_36**, locate and open the folder for this chapter. Open and print the instructions for this project, which are provided to you in Adobe PDF format.

Try IT! 1— Password Protect Your Database

In this Try IT! exercise, you will encrypt and password protect your database to conceal data and prevent unwanted users from opening your database.

Content-Based Assessments

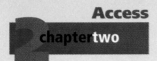

Summary

Importing an Excel spreadsheet is an efficient way to create new tables in an Access database. Sorting data in a table reorders the records based on one or more fields and is a quick way to alphabetize records or to find the highest or lowest amount in a numeric, currency, or date field. Use queries to ask complex questions about the data in a database in a manner that Access can interpret. Save queries so they can be run as needed against current records. By using queries, you can limit the fields that display, add criteria to restrict the number of records in the query result, create calculated values, and include data from more than one table.

Key Terms

Content-Based Assessments

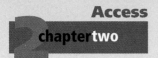

Access
chapter two

Matching

Match each term in the second column with its correct definition in the first column. Write the letter of the term on the blank line in front of the correct definition.

_____ **1.** The area directly below the Ribbon that displays information such as security alerts when there is potentially unsafe, active content in an Office 2007 document that you open.

_____ **2.** An area of the Access program where you can view the security and privacy settings for your Access installation.

_____ **3.** A type of database in which the tables in the database can relate or connect to other tables through common fields.

_____ **4.** Fields that contain the same data in more than one table.

_____ **5.** An association that is established between two tables using common fields.

_____ **6.** A relationship between two tables where one record in the first table corresponds to many records in the second table—the most common type of relationship in Access.

_____ **7.** A list of the field names in a table.

_____ **8.** The field that is included in the related table so that it can be joined to the primary key in another table for the purpose of creating a relationship.

_____ **9.** A set of rules that Access uses to ensure that the data between related tables is valid.

_____ **10.** In the Relationships window, the line joining two tables that visually indicates the related field and the type of relationship.

_____ **11.** The process of arranging data in a specific order based on the value in each field.

_____ **12.** A sorting order that arranges text in alphabetical order (A to Z) or numbers from the lowest to highest number.

_____ **13.** A database object that retrieves (selects) specific data from one or more tables and then displays the specified data in datasheet view.

_____ **14.** When sorting on multiple fields in datasheet view, the field that will be used for the first level of sorting.

_____ **15.** The table or tables from which a query selects its data.

A Ascending

B Common fields

C Data source

D Field list

E Foreign key

F Join line

G Message Bar

H One-to-many

I Outermost sort field

J Referential integrity

K Relational

L Relationship

M Select Query

N Sorting

O Trust Center

Content-Based Assessments

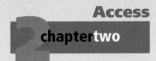
Fill in the Blank

Write the correct word in the space provided.

1. The upper pane of the Query window, which displays the field lists for tables that are used in the query is the _____.

2. The lower pane of the Query window, which displays the design of the query is the _____.

3. The process in which Access searches the records in the table(s) included in a query design, finds the records that match the specified criteria, and then displays those records in a datasheet is called _____.

4. Conditions that identify the specific records you are looking for are called _____.

5. Each time you open a saved query, Access _____ the query again and displays the results based on the data stored in the associated tables; thus, the results always reflect the latest information in the tables.

6. A sequence of characters, which when used in query criteria, must be matched, is referred to as a _____.

7. A criteria that searches for fields that are empty is called _____.

8. A criteria that searches for fields that are *not* empty is called _____.

9. Symbols that evaluate each field value to determine if it is the same (=), greater than (>), less than (<), or in between a range of values as specified by the criteria are referred to as _____.

10. In a(n) _____ condition, both parts of the query must be met.

11. In a(n) _____ condition, either part of the query must be met.

12. Multiple conditions in a query or filter are called _____.

13. In a query, a character that serves as a placeholder for one or more unknown characters is a _____.

14. Calculations that are performed on a group of records are called _____.

15. To locate the largest value in a group of records, use the _____ function.

Access

chaptertwo

Skills Review

Project 2C — Music Department

In this project, you will apply the skills you practiced from the Objectives in Project 2A.

Objectives: 1. *Open an Existing Database;* **2.** *Create Table Relationships;* **3.** *Sort Records in a Table;* **4.** *Create a Query in Design View;* **5.** *Create a New Query from an Existing Query;* **6.** *Sort Query Results;* **7.** *Specify Criteria in a Query.*

In the following Skills Review, you will assist Pascal Sanchez, Florida Port Community College Music Director, in using his database to answer various questions about the instruments in the Music Department's inventory. Your query results will look similar to those shown in Figure 2.59.

For Project 2C, you will need the following file:

a2C_Music_Department

You will save your database as
2C_Music_Department_Firstname_Lastname

Figure 2.59

(Project 2C–Music Department continues on the next page)

Content-Based Assessments

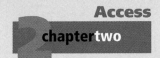

(Project 2C–Music Department continued)

1. From the student files that accompany this textbook, locate the file **a2C_Music_Department**. Copy and then paste the file to your Access Chapter 2 folder. Rename the file 2C_Music_Department_Firstname_Lastname **Start** Access, open your database, and then enable the content.

2. Click the **Database Tools tab**. In the **Show/Hide group**, click the **Relationships** button. On the **Design tab**, in the **Relationships group**, click the **Show Table** button. Click the **2C Student Musicians** table, and then at the bottom of the dialog box, click **Add**. Point to the **2C Instruments Inventory** table, and then double-click to add the table to the Relationships window. **Close** the **Show Table** dialog box. In each table, use the

pointer to resize the field list as necessary to display the table name and all the field names completely.

3. In your **2C Student Musicians** field list, point to **Student ID**, hold down the left mouse button, and then drag to the right to the **2C Instruments Inventory** field list until your mouse pointer is on top of **Student ID**. Release the mouse button, and then drag the **Edit Relationships** dialog box below the two field lists. The relationship between the two tables is a one-to-many relationship; *one* student can play *many* instruments. The common field is Student ID.

4. Click to select the **Enforce Referential Integrity** check box, and then click the **Create** button. With the **Relationships** window open, on the **Design tab**, in the **Tools group**, click **Relationship Report**. To print, on the **Print Preview tab**, in the **Print group**, click the **Print** button, and then click **OK**, or submit electronically as

directed. Click **Close Print Preview**. On the **Quick Access Toolbar**, click the **Save** button, and then in the displayed **Save As** dialog box, click **OK** to accept the default name. Close all open objects.

5. **Open** the 2C Instruments Inventory table, and then **Close** the **Navigation Pane**. In the **Condition** field, click any record. In the **Sort & Filter group**, click the **Descending** button to sort the records from *Poor* to *Excellent*. Point anywhere in the **Category** field, and then right-click. From the displayed shortcut menu, click **Sort A to Z**. The records are sorted first by **Category**, the outermost sort field, and then within categories, by **Condition**, the innermost sort field. In the **Sort & Filter group**, click the **Clear All Sorts** button. **Close** the table, and then click **No**; you need not save the changes to the design after viewing a sort.

6. Click the **Create tab**, and then in the **Other group**, click the **Query Design** button. From the **Show Table** dialog box, **Add** the 2C Instruments Inventory table, and then **Close** the **Show Table** dialog box. Use the pointer to adjust the height and width of the field list as necessary.

7. In the **2C Instruments Inventory** field list, double-click **Instrument ID** to add it to the design grid. In the **2C Instruments Inventory** field list, point to **Category**, hold down the left mouse button, and then drag down into the design grid until you are pointing to the **Field** row in the next available column. Release the mouse button. In the **Field** row of the design grid, click in the third column, and then click the **arrow** that displays. From the dis-

(Project 2C–Music Department continues on the next page)

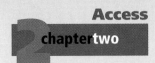
(Project 2C–Music Department continued)

played list, click **Instrument** to add this field to the design grid.

8. Using any technique, add the **Student ID** and **Condition** fields as the fourth and fifth field in the design grid. On the **Query Tools Design tab**, in the **Results group**, click the **Run** button. This query answers the question, *What is the Instrument ID, Category, Instrument, Student ID, and Condition of all the instruments in the inventory?* On the **Quick Access Toolbar**, click the **Save** button to display the **Save As** dialog box. Type **2C All Instruments Query Firstname Lastname** and then click **OK**.

9. From the **Office** menu, point to the **Print** button, and then click **Print Preview**. Click the **Print** button; or, submit electronically as directed. Click the **Close Print Preview** button. Leave the query open. From the **Office** menu, click **Save As**. In the **Save As** dialog box, type **2C Condition Query Firstname Lastname** and then click **OK**. Recall that you can create a new query based on an existing query in this manner.

10. On the **Home tab**, in the **Views group**, click the **View** button to switch to Design view. In the design grid, point to the thin gray selection bar above the **Student ID** field until the ↓ pointer displays. Click to select the **Student ID** column, and then press [Delete]. From the gray selection bar, select the **Instrument ID** column. Then, point to the selection bar at the top of the selected column to display the ℞ pointer, and drag to the right to position **Instrument ID** as the fourth (last) column.

11. **Run** the query. The results of the query display four fields in the new arrangement. This query answers the question, *What is* the Category, Instrument, Condition, and Instrument ID of every instrument in the inventory?* **Close** the query, and then click **Yes**. Open the **Navigation Pane**, select the query name, display the **Print Preview**, and then print or submit electronically as directed. Close the print preview.

12. **Open** your **2C All Instruments Query**, and then save it as **2C Instrument Sort Firstname Lastname** Switch to Design view. In the design grid, delete the **Student ID** field. In the **Category** field, click in the **Sort** row, click the **Sort arrow**, and then click **Descending**. Under **Condition**, click to display the **Sort arrow**, and then click **Ascending**. **Run** the query. This query answers the question *Within each category (with Category in descending alphabetical order), what instruments are in the inventory and what is the instrument's condition (with the condition listed in ascending alphabetic order)?* Print the query or submit electronically as directed. **Close** the query, and then click **Yes** to save the changes.

13. Close any open objects and close the **Navigation Pane**. **Create** a new query in Design view, and then **Add** the **2C Instruments Inventory** table. Add the following fields to the design grid: **Instrument ID**, **Category**, **Instrument**, and **Condition**. On the **Criteria** row of the design grid, under **Condition**, type **Fair** and then press [Enter]. **Run** the query. This query answers the question, *What is the Instrument ID, Category, and Instrument type of instruments that are in Fair condition?* Click the **Save** button, and then name the query **2C Fair Condition Firstname Lastname** Print or submit the query electronically, and then close the query.

(Project 2C–Music Department continues on the next page)

Content-Based Assessments

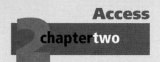

Skills Review

(Project 2C–Music Department continued)

14. Create a new query in Design view, **Add** the **2C Instruments Inventory** table, and then add the following fields to the design grid: **Category**, **Instrument**, and **Condition**. On the **Criteria** row, under **Category**, type **Woodwinds** and then press Enter. Under **Category**, click to clear the **Show** check box, and then **Run** the query. This query answers the question, *What is the condition of the woodwind instruments in the inventory?* Recall that if all results are of the same criteria, it is not necessary to display the field name of the criteria. **Save** the query with the name **2C Woodwinds Condition Firstname Lastname** Print or submit electronically as directed, and then close the query.

15. Create a new query in Design view, **Add** the **2C Student Musicians** table, and then add the following fields to the design grid

in the order listed: **First Name**, **Last Name**, **Email Address**, and **Phone Number**. On the **Criteria** row, under the **Phone Number** field, type **Is Null** and then press Enter. On the **Sort** row, click in the **Last Name** field, click the **Sort arrow**, and then click **Ascending**. **Run** the query. This query answers the question, *For which student musicians are phone numbers missing?* **Save** the query as **2C Missing Phone Numbers Firstname Lastname** Print or submit electronically as directed, and then close the query.

16. If necessary, close any open objects and close the **Navigation Pane**. From the **Office** menu, click **Close Database**, and then at the right end of the Access title bar, click the **Close** button to close the Access program. Alternatively, from the Office menu, click **Exit Access.**

End **You have completed Project 2C**

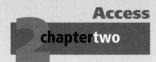

Skills Review

Project 2D — Concerts and Sponsors

In this project, you will apply the skills you practiced from the Objectives in Project 2B.

Objectives: 8. *Create a New Table by Importing an Excel Spreadsheet;* **9.** *Specify Numeric Criteria in a Query;* **10.** *Use Compound Criteria;* **11.** *Create a Query Based on More Than One Table;* **12.** *Use Wildcards in a Query;* **13.** *Use Calculated Fields in a Query;* **14.** *Group Data and Calculate Statistics in a Query.*

In the following Skills Review, you will assist Pascal Sanchez, College Music Director, in answering questions about concerts, sponsors, box office receipts, dates, and concert locations. Your query results will look similar to those shown in Figure 2.60.

For Project 2D, you will need the following files:

a2D_Concerts_Sponsors
a2D_Sponsors (Excel file)

You will save your database as
2D_Concerts_Sponsors_Firstname_Lastname

Figure 2.60

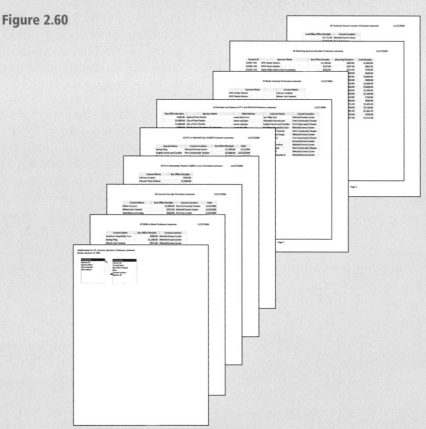

(Project 2D–Concerts and Sponsors continues on the next page)

Content-Based Assessments

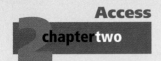
(Project 2D–Concerts and Sponsors continued)

1. From the student files that accompany this textbook, locate the file **a2D_Concerts_Sponsors**. Copy and paste the file to your Access Chapter 2 folder. Rename the file **2D_Concerts_Sponsors_Firstname_Lastname** Start Access, open your database, and then enable the content.

2. **Open** the **Navigation Pane**. On the Ribbon, click the **External Data tab**, and then in the **Import group**, click the **Excel** button. In the displayed **Get External Data – Excel Spreadsheet** dialog box, to the right of the **File name** box, click the **Browse** button. Navigate to the location where the student files for this textbook are stored, and then click the Excel file **a2D_Sponsors**. In the lower right corner, click **Open**. Be sure the **Import the source data into a new table in the current database** option button is selected, and then in the lower right corner, click **OK**.

3. In the upper portion of the **Import Spreadsheet Wizard**, click to select the **First Row Contains Column Headings** check box. In the lower right corner, click **Next**. Under **Field Options**, make no changes for any of the fields, and then in the lower right corner, click **Next**. In the upper portion of the dialog box, click the **Choose my own primary key** option button, and then be sure that **Sponsor ID** displays. Click **Next**. In the **Import to Table** box, type **2D Sponsors** and then in the lower right corner, click **Finish**. In the displayed dialog box, in the lower right corner, click **Close**. The imported Excel spreadsheet becomes the second table in the database.

4. Click the **Database Tools tab**, and then in the **Show/Hide group**, click the

Relationships button. On the **Design tab**, in the **Relationships group**, click **Show Table**. **Add** the **2D Concerts** table, and then **Add** the **2D Sponsors** table. Expand the height and width of the field lists and position the field lists as necessary so that the **2D Sponsors** table is on the left. In the **2D Sponsors** field list, point to the **Sponsor ID** field, hold down the left mouse button, drag into the **2D Concerts** field list, position the mouse pointer on top of the **Sponsor ID** field, and then release the mouse button. Click to select the **Enforce Referential Integrity** check box, and then click the **Create** button. A one-to-many relationship is established; *one* sponsor organization can sponsor *many* concerts.

5. On the **Design tab**, in the **Tools group**, click the **Relationship Report** button. On the displayed **Print Preview tab**, click **Print**; or, submit electronically as directed. Click the **Save** button, and then click **OK** to accept the default name. **Close Print Preview**, close all open objects, and then close the **Navigation Pane**.

6. On the **Create tab**, in the **Other group**, click the **Query Design** button. **Add** the **2D Concerts** table, and then add the following fields to the design grid in the order given: **Concert Name**, **Box Office Receipts**, and **Concert Location**. Click in the **Sort** row under **Concert Location**, click the **arrow**, and then click **Ascending**. On the **Criteria** row, under **Box Office Receipts**, type **800** and then press Enter. **Run** the query. Only one concert— *Southern Hospitality Tour*—had Box Office Receipts of exactly $800.

7. On the **Home tab**, in the **Views group**, click the **View** button to return to Design view. On the **Criteria** row, under **Box**

(Project 2D–Concerts and Sponsors continues on the next page)

Content-Based Assessments

(Project 2D–Concerts and Sponsors continued)

Office Receipts, delete the existing criteria, type **>800** and then press Enter. **Run** the query again. Eight concerts had Box Office Receipts greater than $800. Return to Design view, change the **Box Office Receipts** criteria to **<800** and then run the query. Eight concerts had Box Office Receipts less than $800. Return to Design view, change **Box Office Receipts** criteria to **>=800** and then run the query. Nine records meet the criteria. This query answers the question, *Which concerts had Box Office Receipts of $800 or more, what was the amount of the Box Office Receipts, and where was each concert held?* **Save** the query as **2D $800 or More Firstname Lastname** Print or submit electronically as directed. Leave the query open. From the **Office** menu, click **Save As**, and then type **2D Concerts Jan-Apr Firstname Lastname** and click **OK**.

8. Return to Design view. From the **2D Concerts** field list, add the **Date** as the fourth field in the design grid. On the **Criteria** row, under **Box Office Receipts**, delete the existing criteria so that the query is not restricted by receipts. Under **Concert Location**, in the **Sort** row, click the arrow, and then click **(not sorted)**. Under **Date**, in the **Sort** row, click the arrow, and then click **Ascending**. Under **Date**, in the **Criteria** row, type **Between 01/01/2009 And 04/30/2009** and then press Enter. **Run** the query; five records meet the criteria. This query answers the question, *What is the name, box office receipts, location, and date, in chronological order, of concerts held between January 1, 2009 and April 30, 2009?* Print or submit electronically as directed. **Close** the query, and click **Yes** to save the changes to the design.

9. Create a new query in Design view. From the **2D Concerts** table, add the following fields to the design grid in the order given: **Concert Name**, **Concert Location**, and **Box Office Receipts**. In the **Criteria** row, under **Concert Location**, type **Port Community Theater** and then press Tab. In the **Criteria** row under **Box Office Receipts**, type **<=1000** and then press Enter. **Run** the query; two records display. This query answers the question, *Which concerts that were held at the Port Community Theater had Box Office Receipts of $1,000 or less?* Return to Design view, and then in the **Concert Location** field, clear the **Show** check box. **Run** the query. Recall that if all the records have the same criteria in one of the fields, it is not necessary to display that field in the query results. **Save** the query and name it **2D Port Community Theater $1000 or Less Firstname Lastname** Print or submit electronically, and then close the query.

10. Create a new query in Design view. From the **2D Concerts** table, add the following four fields to the design grid in the order given: **Concert Name**, **Concert Location**, **Box Office Receipts**, and **Date**. On the **Criteria** row, under **Concert Location**, type **Port Community Theater** In the design grid, locate the **or** row. On the **or** row, under **Concert Location**, type **Mitchell Events Center** and then press Enter. **Run** the query. This query answers the question, *How many concerts were held at either the Port Community Theater or the Mitchell Events Center?* Twelve records meet the criteria. Return to Design view.

11. Under **Concert Location**, on the **or** row, delete the text. Under **Concert Location**, click in the **Criteria** row, delete the existing text, and then type **Port Community**

(Project 2D–Concerts and Sponsors continues on the next page)

Content-Based Assessments

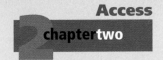
(Project 2D–Concerts and Sponsors continued)

Theater Or Mitchell Events Center On the **Criteria** row, under **Box Office Receipts**, type **>1000** and then press Enter. **Run** the query. Four records display. This query answers the question, *Which concerts held at either the Mitchell Events Center or the Port Community Theater had Box Office Receipts of more than $1,000 and on what dates were the concerts held?* **Save** the query as **2D PCT or Mitchell Over $1000 Firstname Lastname** Print or submit the query electronically as directed. Close the query.

12. Create a new query in Design view and add both tables. From the **2D Sponsors** field list, add the following fields: **Sponsor ID**, **Sponsor Name**, and **Phone Number**. On the **Sort** row, under **Sponsor Name**, click to select **Ascending** to sort the results in alphabetical order by Sponsor Name. From the **2D Concerts** field list, add **Concert Name**, **Concert Location**, **Box Office Receipts**, and **Date** to the design grid.

13. On the **Criteria** row, under **Concert Location**, type **Port Community Theater** On the **or** row, under **Concert Location**, type **Mitchell Events Center** and then press Enter. **Run** the query. Twelve records display. Return to the Design view. From the **Sponsors** field list, drag **Web Address** to the design grid on top of **Phone Number** and release the mouse button to insert the new field to the right of **Sponsor Name**. Select the **Sponsor ID** field and delete it.

14. In the design grid, select the **Box Office Receipts** field, and then drag it to the first field position in the grid. Delete the **Phone Number** and **Date** fields. **Run** the query. This query answers the question, *What were the box office receipts, sponsor name, sponsor Web address, concert name, and*

concert location of all concerts held at either the Port Community Theater or the Mitchell Events center, sorted alphabetically by sponsor name? Using techniques similar to that of a table, select all the columns in the query, and then apply **Best Fit**.

15. **Save** the query and name it **2D Receipts and Sponsors PCT and Mitchell Firstname Lastname** In **Print Preview**, change the orientation to **Landscape**, change the **Margins** to **Normal**, and then print the query or submit electronically as directed. Close the Print Preview and close the query. **Open** the **Navigation Pane** and notice that your new query displays under *both* tables from which it retrieved records. **Close** the **Navigation Pane**.

16. Create a new query in Design view, add both tables, and then add the following fields to the design grid: From the **2D Sponsors** table, add the **Sponsor Name** field. From the **2D Concerts** table, add the **Concert Name** field. On the **Criteria** row, under **Sponsor Name**, type **Florida*** and then press Enter. **Run** the query and widen the **Sponsor Name** column to view all of the data. Three sponsors have names that begin with *Florida*.

17. Return to Design view. On the **Criteria** row, under **Sponsor Name**, delete the text. On the **Criteria** row, under **Concert Name**, type ***Festival** and then press Enter. **Run** the query; five Concert Names end with the word *Festival*. Return to Design view. On the **Criteria** row, under **Sponsor Name**, type ***Radio*** and then press Enter. **Run** the query; two records have the word *Radio* somewhere in the Sponsor Name and the word *Festival* at the end of the Concert Name. This query answers the question, *Which radio stations are sponsor-*

(Project 2D–Concerts and Sponsors continues on the next page)

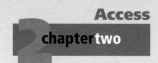

(Project 2D–Concerts and Sponsors continued)

ing Festival-type concerts? **Save** the query and name it **2D Radio Festivals Firstname Lastname** Print or submit the query electronically as directed, and then close the query.

18. Create a new query in Design view, add both tables, and then add the following fields to the design grid: **Concert ID**, **Sponsor Name**, and **Box Office Receipts**. Click in the **Sort** row under **Concert ID**, click the **Sort arrow**, and then click **Ascending**. Sponsors have indicated that they will donate an additional amount to the Music Department based on 50 % of the **Box Office Receipts**. On the **Field** row, right-click in the first empty column to display a shortcut menu, and then click **Zoom**. In the **Zoom** dialog box, type **Matching Donation: [Box Office Receipts]*0.5** In the **Zoom** dialog box, click **OK**, and then **Run** the query to view the new field— *Matching Donation*. Return to Design view.

19. In the **Field** row, in the first empty column, right-click, and then click **Zoom**. In the **Zoom** dialog box, type **Total Receipts: [Box Office Receipts]+[Matching Donation]** and then click **OK**. In the **Field** row, click in the **Matching Donation** field (fourth column), and then in the **Show/Hide group**, click the **Property Sheet** button. In the **Property Sheet** task pane, click in the white text box next to **Format**, click the **arrow** that displays, and then from the displayed list of formats, click **Currency**. **Close** the **Property Sheet** task pane.

20. **Run** the query to view the results. This query answers the question, *In ascending order by Concert ID, assuming each sponsor makes a matching 50% donation based on each concert's Box Office Receipts, what is the Sponsor Name, Box Office Receipts, Matching Donation, and Total Receipts for*

each concert? Select all the columns, and then apply **Best Fit**. **Save** the query and name it **2D Matching Sponsor Donation Firstname Lastname** In **Print Preview**, change the orientation to **Landscape**, and then print or submit the query electronically. Close the Print Preview and then close the query.

21. Create a new query in Design view, **Add** the **2D Concerts** table, and then add the **Box Office Receipts** field to the design grid. On the **Design tab**, in the **Show/Hide group**, click the **Totals** button to add a **Total** row as the third row in the design grid. On the **Total** row, under **Box Office Receipts**, click in the **Group By** box, and then click the **arrow** to display the list of functions. In the list of functions, click **Min**, and then **Run** the query. The lowest amount of Box Office Receipts for any concert was *$400.00*.

22. Return to Design view. Using the technique you just practiced, select the **Max** function, and then **Run** the query. The highest amount of Box Office Receipts for any concert was *$2,500.00*. Switch to **Design** view, select the **Avg** function, and then **Run** the query. The average Box Office Receipts for each concert was *$1,027.94*. Using the same technique, select the **Sum** function and **Run** the query. The total Box Office Receipts for all the concerts was *$17,475.00*.

23. Apply **Best Fit** to the **SumOfBox Office Receipts** column. Switch to Design view. Add the **Sponsor ID** field to the design grid. **Run** the query; concerts sponsored by SPONSOR-101 had the largest amount of Box Office Receipts—*$4,975.00*.

24. Switch to Design view. In the design grid, select and delete the **Sponsor ID** field from

(Project 2D–Concerts and Sponsors continues on the next page)

Content-Based Assessments

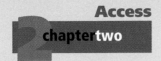
(Project 2D–Concerts and Sponsors continued)

the query design, and then add the **Concert Location** field to the design grid. **Run** the query. This query answers the question *What are the total Box Office Receipts for each concert location?* **Save** the query and name it **2D Totals by Concert Location Firstname Lastname** Print or sub-mit the query electronically. **Close** the query. From the **Office** menu, click **Close Database**, and then at the right end of the Access title bar, click the **Close** button to close the Access program. Alternatively, from the Office menu, click **Exit Access.**

 You have completed Project 2D ————————————————————

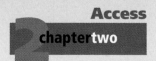
Mastering Access

Project 2E — Lab Administrators

In this project, you will apply the skills you practiced from the Objectives in Project 2A.

Objectives: 1. *Open an Existing Database;* **2.** *Create Table Relationships;* **3.** *Sort Records in a Table;* **4.** *Create a Query in Design View;* **5.** *Create a New Query from an Existing Query;* **6.** *Sort Query Results;* **7.** *Specify Criteria in a Query.*

In the following Mastering Access project, you will assist Stephanie Cannon, Computing Services Director at the college, in querying the database to answer questions about computer lab administrators and their skill specialties. Your query results will look similar to those shown in Figure 2.61.

For Project 2E, you will need the following file:

a2E_Lab_Administrators

You will save your database as
2E_Lab_Administrators_Firstname_Lastname

Figure 2.61

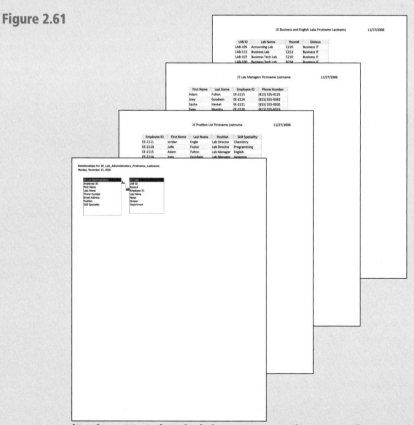

(Project 2E–Lab Administrators continues on the next page)

Content-Based Assessments

Access
chaptertwo

Mastering Access

(Project 2E–Lab Administrators continued)

1. From the student files that accompany this textbook, locate the file **a2E_Lab_Administrators**. Copy and paste the file to your Access Chapter 2 folder. Rename the file **2E_Lab_Administrators_Firstname_Lastname Start** Access, open your database, and then enable the content.

2. Open the database tables and examine their fields and records to become familiar with the data; then close the tables. Create a one-to-many relationship between the **2E Lab Administrators** table and the **2E Labs** table based on the **Employee ID** field and enforce referential integrity; *one* Lab Administrator can be responsible for *many* Labs. Create the **Relationship Report** and save it with the default name. Print the report, or submit electronically as directed, and then close all open objects.

3. Display the **2E_Lab_Administrators** table; close the **Navigation Pane**. Notice the + signs that indicate the relationships you created. Perform a multiple-field sort on the table as follows, and remember to sort *first* by the innermost sort field: sort the table in **Ascending** order by **Last Name** (*innermost* sort field) and then sort in **Descending** order by **Position** (*outermost* sort field). The result is that your table is sorted by Position, with Lab Managers listed first, Lab Directors second, and Lab Assistants third, and within each Position, the names are alphabetized by Last Name. After examining the organization of the data, **Clear All Sorts**, close the table, and do not save the changes.

4. Create a new query in Design view and add the **2E Lab Administrators** table. Add fields to the design grid so that your query

will answer the question, *What is the Employee ID, First Name, and Last Name of each Lab Administrator in alphabetical order by Last Name, and what is each Lab Administrator's Position and Skill Specialty if any?* **Run** the query, save it with the name **2E Position List Firstname Lastname** Print or submit the query electronically as directed. Leave the query open.

5. From the previous query, create a new query and name it **2E Lab Managers Firstname Lastname** Switch to Design view, and then edit the design so that the query will answer the question, *What is the First Name, Last Name, Employee ID, and Phone Number of those who have the Position of Lab Manager, sorted alphabetically by Last Name?* Display the fields in the order listed in the question, display *only* the fields listed in the question, and do *not* show the **Position** field in the query result. Six employees have the position of Lab Manager. Print or submit the query electronically; close the query, and then save any changes to the design.

6. Create a new query in Design view based on the **2E Labs** table to answer the question, *What is the LAB ID, Lab Name, and Room# of every lab in the Business IT Division and the English Division, sorted alphabetically by Lab Name?* Display the fields in the order listed in the question. Eight records meet the criteria. Save the query with the name **2E Business and English Labs Firstname Lastname** Print or submit electronically, and then close the query. Close the database, and then close Access.

End **You have completed Project 2E**

Content-Based Assessments

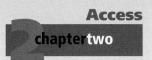
Mastering Access

Project 2F — Bookstore Inventory

In this project, you will apply the skills you practiced from the Objectives in Project 2B.

Objectives: 8. *Create a New Table by Importing an Excel Spreadsheet;* **9.** *Specify Numeric Criteria in a Query;* **10.** *Use Compound Criteria;* **11.** *Create a Query Based on More Than One Table;* **12.** *Use Wildcards in a Query;* **13.** *Use Calculated Fields in a Query;* **14.** *Group Data and Calculate Statistics in a Query.*

In the following Mastering Access project, you will assist Nancy Pelo, College Bookstore Manager, in using her database to answer questions about the bookstore inventory. Your query results will look similar to those shown in Figure 2.62.

For Project 2F, you will need the following files:

a2F_Bookstore_Inventory
a2F_Vendors (Excel file)

**You will save your database as
2F_Bookstore_Inventory_Firstname_Lastname**

Figure 2.62

(Project 2F–Bookstore Inventory continues on the next page)

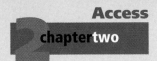

(Project 2F–Bookstore Inventory continued)

1. From the student files that accompany this textbook, locate the file **a2F_Bookstore_Inventory**. Copy and paste the file to your Access Chapter 2 folder. Rename the file **2F_Bookstore_Inventory_Firstname_Lastname Start** Access, open your database, and then enable the content.

2. From the student files that accompany this textbook, import the Excel spreadsheet **a2F_Vendors**. Use the first row of the spreadsheet as the column headings, and choose the **Vendor ID** column as the primary key. Name the table **2F Vendors**

3. Open the database tables and examine their fields and records to become familiar with the data; then close the tables. Create a one-to-many relationship between the **2F Vendors** table and the **2F Purchase Orders** table based on the **Vendor ID** field, and then enforce referential integrity; *one* Vendor can have *many* Purchase Orders. Create the **Relationship Report**, saving it with the default name. Print the report or submit electronically as directed, and then close all open objects.

4. Create a new query in Design view to answer the question, *What is the Vendor ID, Purchase Amount, Purchase Order Number, and Store Category for purchases greater than $10,000?* Display the fields in the order listed in the question. Eleven records meet the criteria. Save the query as **2F Purchases Over $10K Firstname Lastname** Print or submit electronically as directed; leave the query open.

5. Create a new query from the existing query and save it as **2F Purchases 1st Quarter Firstname Lastname** Redesign the query to answer the question, *In chronological order by Date Issued, which Purchase Order Numbers were issued between 01/01/2009 and 03/31/2009, for what amount, and to which Vendor ID?* Display the fields in the order listed in the question, display *only* the fields listed in the question, and do not restrict the purchase amount. Seventeen records meet the criteria. Print or submit electronically as directed; close the query and save the design changes.

6. Create a new query in Design view to answer the question, *Which Purchase Order Numbers issued for the Textbooks department had a Purchase Amount greater than $30,000 and for what amount?* Do *not* show the **Dept** field in the result. Two records meet the criteria. Save the query as **2F Textbook Orders Over $30K Firstname Lastname** Print or submit electronically as directed; close the query and save any changes.

7. Create a new query in Design view to answer the question, *Which Purchase Order Numbers were issued for either the Supplies Department or the Sundries Department and for what amount, with the amounts listed in descending order?* Display the results in the order listed in the question. Fourteen records meet the criteria. Save the query as **2F Supplies and Sundries Firstname Lastname** Print or submit electronically as directed; close the query and save any changes.

8. By using both tables, create a new query to answer the question, *Which Purchase Order Numbers were issued for either the Textbooks or Technology Department, sorted in Ascending order by Department name, and what is the Vendor Name and amount of each purchase order?* Apply **Best**

(Project 2F–Bookstore Inventory continues on the next page)

Content-Based Assessments

Mastering Access

(Project 2F–Bookstore Inventory continued)

Fit to the columns in the query result. Twelve records meet the criteria. Save the query as **2F Textbooks and Technology Firstname Lastname** Print or submit electronically as directed; close the query and save any changes.

9. Create a new query in Design view, and then by using a wildcard in the format of *C**, answer the following question: *What is the Vendor Name, Address, City, State, and Zip of all vendors in the cities of Clearwater, Cape Coral or Cocoa Beach, and who is their Sales Rep?* Five records meet the criteria. Apply **Best Fit** to the columns in the query result, and then save the query as **2F Rep Names Firstname Lastname** Print or submit electronically as directed; close the query and save any changes.

10. Create a new query in Design view, and then by using the **Sum** aggregate function, answer the question, *What are the total Purchase Order Amounts for each Department?* Apply **Best Fit** to the columns in the result, and then save the query as **2F Totals by Department Firstname**

Lastname Print or submit electronically as directed; close the query and save any changes.

11. The state government announced a reduction in the tax rate applied to college bookstore purchases of 1%. Create a query to answer the question, *For each Purchase Order Number, assuming the state reduces each Purchase Amount by 1%, what will be the Amount of Reduction and the New Purchase Amount?* (Hint: First compute the amount of the reduction, naming the new field **Amount of Reduction** Then calculate the new purchase amount, naming the new field **New Purchase Amount**) As necessary, change the properties of all the new fields so that the **Format** is **Currency** and the **Decimal Places** are set to **2**. Apply **Best Fit** to the columns in the query result. **Save** the query as **2F Cost Reduction Firstname Lastname** In **Print Preview**, set the orientation to **Landscape**. Print or submit electronically as directed; close the query and save any changes. Close the database and **Close** Access.

End **You have completed Project 2F**

Content-Based Assessments

Access

chaptertwo

Mastering Access

Project 2G—Grants and Organizations

In this project, you will apply the skills you practiced from the Objectives in Projects 2A and 2B.

Objectives: 1. *Open an Existing Database;* **2.** *Create Table Relationships;* **3.** *Sort Records in a Table;* **4.** *Create a Query in Design View;* **5.** *Create a new Query from an Existing Query;* **6.** *Sort Query Results;* **7.** *Specify Criteria in a Query;* **8.** *Create a New Table by Importing an Excel Spreadsheet;* **9.** *Specify Numeric Criteria in a Query;* **10.** *Use Compound Criteria;* **11.** *Create a Query Based on More Than One Table;* **12.** *Use Wildcards in a Query;* **13.** *Use Calculated Fields in a Query;* **14.** *Group Data and Calculate Statistics in a Query.*

In the following Mastering Access project, you will assist Peter Donahue, Director of Grants for the college, in using his database to answer questions about public and private grants awarded to college departments. Your query results will look similar to those shown in Figure 2.63.

> **For Project 2G, you will need the following files:**
>
> a2G_Grants_Organizations
> a2G_Organizations (Excel file)

**You will save your database as
2G_Grants_Organizations_Firstname_Lastname**

Figure 2.63

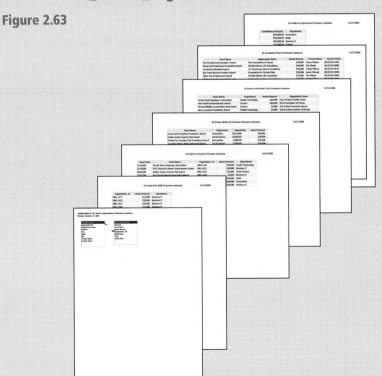

(Project 2G–Grants and Organizations continues on the next page)

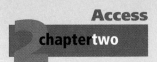

(Project 2G–Grants and Organizations continued)

1. From the student files that accompany this textbook, locate the file **a2G_Grants_Organizations**. Copy and paste the file to your Access Chapter 2 folder. Rename the file **2G_Grants_Organizations_Firstname_Lastname Start** Access, open your database, and then enable the content.

2. From the student files that accompany this textbook, import the Excel spreadsheet **a2G_Organizations**. Use the first row of the spreadsheet as the column headings, and then choose the **Organization ID** column as the primary key. Name the table **2G Organizations**

3. Open the database tables, and then examine their fields and records to become familiar with the data; then close the tables. Create a one-to-many relationship between the **2G Organizations** table and the **2G Grants Awarded** table based on the **Organization ID** field and enforce referential integrity; *one* Organization can give *many* Grants. Create the **Relationship Report**, saving it with the default name. Print the report or submit electronically as directed, and then close all open objects.

4. Create a new query in Design view to answer the question, *What is the Organization ID and Award Amount for grants greater than $10,000 and, in alphabetical order, to what Departments were the grants awarded?* Display the fields in the order listed in the question. Twelve records meet the criteria. Save the query as **2G Grants Over $10K Firstname Lastname** Print or submit electronically as directed; leave the query open.

5. Create a new query from the existing query and save it as **2G Grants 1st Quarter Firstname Lastname** Redesign the query to

answer the question, *In chronological order by Award Date, which Grants were awarded between 01/01/2009 and 03/31/2009, from which Organization ID, for what amount, and to which Department?* Display the fields in the order listed in the question, display *only* the fields listed in the question, sort *only* on one field, and do *not* restrict the amount. Seven records meet the criteria. Apply **Best Fit** to the columns in the query result. In **Print Preview**, set the print to **Landscape**, and then print or submit electronically as directed; close the Print Preview, close the query, and then save any design changes.

6. Create a new query in Design view to answer the question, *What are the names of privately funded grants awarded to either the Humanities or Social Science department, on what date were they awarded, and with the largest grants listed first, for what amount?* Display the results in the order listed in the question, and do not show the type of grant in the query result. Nine records meet the criteria. Save the query as **2G Private HMN and SS Grants Firstname Lastname** In **Print Preview**, set the print to **Landscape**, and then print or submit electronically as directed. Close the Print Preview; close the query, and then save any changes.

7. Create a new query in Design view using both tables to answer the question, *Which grants were awarded to either the Science or Health Technology department, for what amount, and, in alphabetical order, from which Organization Name?* Seven records meet the criteria. Apply **Best Fit** to the columns in the result. Save the query as **2G Science and Health Tech Firstname Lastname** In **Print Preview**, set the print to

(Project 2G–Grants and Organizations continues on the next page)

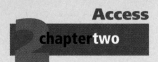

(Project 2G–Grants and Organizations continued)

Landscape, and then print or submit electronically as directed. Close the Print Preview, close the query, and then save any changes.

8. Using both tables, create a new query to answer the question, *Which grants were awarded from organizations that are Foundations, what is the name of the organization, what is the amount of the grant listed in descending order by amount, and what is the name and phone number of the organization contact?* Hint: Use a wildcard in the format of *Foundation* to find organization names containing the word *Foundation.* Fourteen records meet the criteria. Apply **Best Fit** to the columns in the result, and then save the query as **2G**

Foundation Grants Firstname Lastname Change the orientation to **Landscape**, set the **Margins** to **Normal**, and then print or submit electronically as directed; close the query, and then save any changes.

9. Create a new query in Design view, and then by using the **SUM** aggregate function, answer the question, *Listed from the largest amounts to the smallest, what are the total Award Amounts for each Department?* Apply **Best Fit** to the columns in the result, and then save the query as **2G Totals by Department Firstname Lastname** Print or submit electronically as directed; close the query, and then save any changes. Close the database, and then **Close** Access.

End **You have completed Project 2G** ————————————————————

Access

chaptertwo

Mastering Access

Project 2H — Events and Clients

In this project, you will apply skills you practiced from the Objectives in Projects 2A and 2B.

Objectives: 1. *Open an Existing Database;* **2.** *Create Table Relationships;* **4.** *Create a Query in Design View;* **5.** *Create a New Query from an Existing Query;* **7.** *Specify Criteria in a Query;* **8.** *Create a New Table by Importing an Excel Spreadsheet;* **9.** *Specify Numeric Criteria in a Query;* **10.** *Use Compound Criteria;* **11.** *Create a Query Based on More Than One Table;* **12.** *Use Wildcards in a Query;* **13.** *Use Calculated Fields in a Query;* **14.** *Group Data and Calculate Statistics in a Query*

In the following Mastering Access project, you will assist Peter Steinmetz, Facilities Manager at the college, in using his database to answer questions about facilities that the college rents to community and private organizations. Renting the facilities at times when they are not in use for college activities provides additional funding to maintain and staff the facilities. Your query results will look similar to those shown in Figure 2.64.

For Project 2H, you will need the following files:

a2H_Events_Clients
a2H_Rental_Clients (Excel file)

You will save your database as
2H_Events_Clients_Firstname_Lastname

Figure 2.64

(Project 2H–Events and Clients continues on the next page)

(Project 2H–Events and Clients continued)

1. From the student files that accompany this textbook, locate the file **a2H_Events_Clients**. Copy and paste the file to your Access Chapter 2 folder. Rename the file **2H_Events_Clients_Firstname_Lastname Start** Access, open your database, and then enable the content.

2. From the student files that accompany this textbook, import the Excel spreadsheet **a2H_Rental_Clients**. Use the first row of the spreadsheet as the column headings, and then choose the **Rental Client ID** column as the primary key. Name the table **2H Rental Clients**

3. Open the database tables, and then examine their fields and records to become familiar with the data; then close the tables. Create a one-to-many relationship between the **2H Rental Clients** table and the **2H Events** table based on the **Rental Client ID** field and enforce referential integrity; *one* Rental Client can have *many* Events. Create the **Relationship Report**, print or submit electronically as directed, and then save it with the default name. Close all open objects.

4. Create a new query in Design view to answer the question, *What is the Event Name, Rental Client ID, and Rental Fee for events with fees greater than or equal to $500, in ascending order by Rental Client ID, and in which Facility was the event held?* Display the fields in the order listed in the question. Eleven records meet the criteria. Save the query as **2H Fees $500 or More Firstname Lastname** Print or submit electronically as directed; leave the query open.

5. Create a new query from the existing query, and save it as **2H Afternoon Events**

Firstname Lastname Redesign the query to answer the question, *Which Events were held in the Afternoon between 07/01/2009 and 08/31/2009, in chronological order by date, what was the Rental Fee, and what was the Event ID?* Display the fields in the order listed in the question, but do *not* display the **Time** field in the result. Do *not* restrict the result by Rental Fee. Four records meet the criteria. Print or submit electronically as directed; close the query, and then save the design changes.

6. Create a new query in Design view to answer the question, *Which Events and Event Types were held in either the White Sands Music Hall or the Theater that had Rental Fees greater than $500?* Three records meet the criteria. Apply **Best Fit** to the columns, save the query as **2H White Sands and Theater Over $500 Firstname Lastname** Print or submit electronically as directed; close the query and save any changes.

7. Using both tables, create a new query in Design view to answer the question *Which Events were held on one of the sports Fields, for which Renter Name, and what was the Rental Fee in order of lowest fee to highest fee?* Hint: Use a wildcard with the word *Field*. Five records meet the criteria. Apply **Best Fit** to the columns in the result. Save the query as **2H Field Usage Firstname Lastname** Print or submit electronically as directed; close the query, and then save any changes.

8. Create a new query in Design view, and then by using the **Sum** aggregate function, answer the question *In descending order by total, what are the total Rental Fees for each Event Type?* As necessary, change the properties of all appropriate fields to

(Project 2H–Events and Clients continues on the next page)

Content-Based Assessments

Mastering Access

(Project 2H–Events and Clients continued)

display in **Currency** format with **0** decimal places. Apply **Best Fit** to the columns in the result, and then save the query as **2H Totals by Event Type Firstname Lastname** Print or submit electronically as directed; close the query, and then save any changes.

9. The college Alumni Association will donate money to the Building Fund in an amount based on 10% of total facility rental fees. Create a query to answer the question, *In ascending order by Event ID, what will the total of each Rental Fee be if the Alumni*

Association donates an additional 10% of each fee? Hint: First compute the amount of the donation and name the new field **Amount of Donation** Then calculate the new rental fee and name the new field **New Rental Fee Amount** As necessary, change the properties of the all appropriate fields to display in **Currency** format with **0** decimal places. Apply **Best Fit** to the columns in the query result. Save the query as **2H Alumni Donation Firstname Lastname** Print or submit electronically as directed; close the query, and then save any changes. Close the database, and then close Access.

End **You have completed Project 2H**

Project 2I — Students and Scholarships

In this project, you will apply the skills you practiced from all the Objectives in Projects 2A and 2B.

Objectives: 1. *Open an Existing Database;* **2.** *Create Table Relationships;* **3.** *Sort Records in a Table;* **4.** *Create a Query in Design View;* **5.** *Create a New Query From an Existing Query;* **6.** *Sort Query Results;* **7.** *Specify Criteria in a Query;* **8.** *Create a New Table by Importing an Excel Spreadsheet;* **9.** *Specify Numeric Criteria in a Query;* **10.** *Use Compound Criteria;* **11.** *Create a Query Based on More Than One Table;* **12.** *Use Wildcards in a Query;* **13.** *Use Calculated Fields in a Query;* **14.** *Group Data and Calculate Statistics in a Query.*

In the following Mastering Access project, you will assist Diane Nguyen, Director of Academic Scholarships, in using her database to answer questions about academic scholarships awarded to students. Your query results will look similar to those shown in Figure 2.65.

For Project 2I, you will need the following files:

a2I_Students_Scholarships
a2I_Students (Excel file)

You will save your database as
2I_Students_Scholarships_Firstname_Lastname

Figure 2.65

(Project 2I–Students and Scholarships continues on the next page)

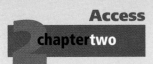

(Project 2I–Students and Scholarships continued)

1. From the student files that accompany this textbook, locate the file **a2I_ Students_Scholarships**. Copy and paste the file to your Access Chapter 2 folder. Rename the file **2I_Students_ Scholarships_Firstname_Lastname Start** Access, open your database, and then enable the content.

2. From the student files that accompany this textbook, import the Excel spreadsheet **a2I_Students**. Use the first row of the spreadsheet as the column headings, and then choose the **Student ID** column as the primary key. Name the table **2I Students**

3. Open the database tables and examine their fields and records to become familiar with the data; then close the tables. Create a one-to-many relationship between the **2I Students** table and the **2I Scholarships** table based on the **Student ID** field and enforce referential integrity; *one* student can have *many* scholarships. Create the **Relationship Report**, print or submit electronically as directed, and then save it with the default name. Close all open objects.

4. Display the **2I Students** table; notice the + signs that indicate the relationships you created. Perform a multiple-field sort on the table to sort students in alphabetic order by Last Name within groups of cities, and sort the City names in alphabetical order. Remember to sort *first* by the innermost sort field. After examining the sorted table, **Clear All Sorts**, close the table, and do not save the changes.

5. Create a new query in Design view, based on the **2I Scholarships Awarded** table, to answer the question, *In alphabetical order by Scholarship Name, what is the*

Scholarship Name, Amount, and Major for scholarships greater than or equal to $500? Display the fields in the order listed in the question. Ten records meet the criteria. Save the query as **2I Scholarships $500 or More Firstname Lastname** Print or submit electronically as directed; leave the query open.

6. Create a new query from the existing query, and then save it as **2I Scholarships 1st Quarter Firstname Lastname** Add the **2I Students** table to the table area, and then redesign the query to answer the question, *In chronological order by Award Date, which scholarships were awarded between 01/01/2009 and 03/31/2009, for what amount, and what was the name of the student?* Be sure the fields display in the order listed in the question, display *only* the fields listed in the question, do not restrict the amount, and sort only by date. Eight records meet the criteria. In **Print Preview**, set **Wide** margins and **Landscape** orientation. Print or submit electronically as directed; close the query, and then save the design changes.

7. Create a new query in Design view to answer the question, *Which scholarships were awarded for either CIS or Nursing majors for amounts greater than $100, listed in descending order by amount?* Four records meet the criteria. Save the query as **2I Nursing and CIS $100 and Over Firstname Lastname** Print or submit electronically as directed; close the query, and then save any changes.

8. Create a new query in Design view using only the 2I Students table, and then by using a wildcard, answer the question, *In alphabetical order by Last Name, what is the Student ID, First Name, Last Name, and*

(Project 2I–Students and Scholarships continues on the next page)

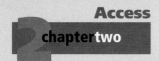
(Project 2I–Students and Scholarships continued)

City of all students in cities that begin with the letter B? Five records meet the criteria. Save the query as **2I Cities Firstname Lastname** Print or submit electronically as directed; close the query, and then save any changes.

9. Create a new query in Design view based on the **2I Students** table, and that includes all the table's fields, to answer the question *For which students is the Address missing?* Three students are missing addresses. Apply **Best Fit** to the columns, and save the query as **2I Missing Addresses Firstname Lastname** Print or submit electronically as directed; close the query, and then save any changes.

10. Create a new query in Design view, and then by using the **Sum** aggregate function, answer the question, *In descending order by amount, what are the total scholarship amounts for each Major?* Use the Property Sheet as necessary to display the sums with **0** decimal places. Apply **Best Fit** to the columns in the result, and then save the query as **2I Totals by Major Firstname Lastname** Print or submit electronically as

directed; close the query, and then save any changes.

11. For each academic scholarship received by students, the Board of Trustees of the college will donate an amount equal to 50% of each scholarship. By using a calculated field and both tables, answer the question, *In alphabetical order by scholarship name, and including the first and last name of the scholarship recipient, what will the value of each scholarship be if the Board of Trustees makes a matching 50% donation?* Hint: First compute the amount of the donation, and then name the new field **Donation** Then calculate the new scholarship value and name the new field **New Value** As necessary, change the properties of all the fields to display in **Currency** format with **0** decimal places. Apply **Best Fit** to the columns in the query result. Save the query as **2I Trustee Donation Firstname Lastname** Print in **Landscape** or submit electronically as directed. Close the query, and then save any changes. Close the database, and then close Access.

End **You have completed Project 2I**

Content-Based Assessments

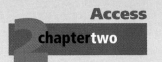

Business Running Case

Project 2J — Business Running Case

In this project, you will apply the skills you practiced in Projects 2A and 2B.

From My Computer, navigate to the student files that accompany this textbook. In the folder **03_business_running_case_pg37_86**, locate and open the folder for this chapter. Open and print the instructions for this project, which are provided to you in Adobe PDF format. Follow the instructions and use the skills you have gained thus far to assist Jennifer Nelson in meeting the challenges of owning and running her business.

 End **You have completed Project 2J** _____

Outcomes-Based Assessments

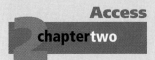

Rubric

The following outcomes-based assessments are *open-ended assessments*. That is, there is no specific correct result; your result will depend on your approach to the information provided. Make *Professional Quality* your goal. Use the following scoring rubric to guide you in *how* to approach the problem and then to evaluate *how well* your approach solves the problem.

The *criteria*—Software Mastery, Content, Format and Layout, and Process—represent the knowledge and skills you have gained that you can apply to solving the problem. The *levels of performance*—Professional Quality, Approaching Professional Quality, or Needs Quality Improvements—help you and your instructor evaluate your result.

	Your completed project is of Professional Quality if you:	Your completed project is Approaching Professional Quality if you:	Your completed project Needs Quality Improvements if you:
1-Software Mastery	Choose and apply the most appropriate skills, tools, and features and identify efficient methods to solve the problem.	Choose and apply some appropriate skills, tools, and features, but not in the most efficient manner.	Choose inappropriate skills, tools, or features, or are inefficient in solving the problem.
2-Content	Construct a solution that is clear and well organized, contains content that is accurate, appropriate to the audience and purpose, and is complete. Provide a solution that contains no errors of spelling, grammar, or style.	Construct a solution in which some components are unclear, poorly organized, inconsistent, or incomplete. Misjudge the needs of the audience. Have some errors in spelling, grammar, or style, but the errors do not detract from comprehension.	Construct a solution that is unclear, incomplete, or poorly organized, containing some inaccurate or inappropriate content; and contains many errors of spelling, grammar, or style. Do not solve the problem.
3-Format and Layout	Format and arrange all elements to communicate information and ideas, clarify function, illustrate relationships, and indicate relative importance.	Apply appropriate format and layout features to some elements, but not others. Overuse features, causing minor distraction.	Apply format and layout that does not communicate information or ideas clearly. Do not use format and layout features to clarify function, illustrate relationships, or indicate relative importance. Use available features excessively, causing distraction.
4-Process	Use an organized approach that integrates planning, development, self-assessment, revision, and reflection.	Demonstrate an organized approach in some areas, but not others; or, use an insufficient process of organization throughout.	Do not use an organized approach to solve the problem.

Outcomes-Based Assessments

Problem Solving

Project 2K — Student Refunds

In this project, you will construct a solution by applying any combination of the skills you practiced from the Objectives in Projects 2A and 2B.

For Project 2K, you will need the following files:

a2K_Student_Refunds
a2K_Student_Refunds (Word document)

**You will save your database as
2K_Student_Refunds_Firstname_Lastname**

Start Microsoft Word, and then from your student files, open the Word document **a2K_Student_Refunds**. Use the skills you have practiced in this chapter to assist Kathy Knudsen, the Associate Dean of Student Services, in answering questions about student refunds in your database **2K_Student_Refunds_Firstname_Lastname**. Save any queries that you create, include your name in the query title, and submit your queries as directed by your instructor. Record your answers to the questions in the Word document.

 You have completed Project 2K ——————

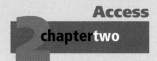

Problem Solving

Project 2L — Leave

In this project, you will construct a solution by applying any combination of the skills you practiced from the Objectives in Projects 2A and 2B.

For Project 2L, you will need the following files:

a2L_Leave
a2L_Leave (Word document)

You will save your database as
2L_Leave_Firstname_Lastname

Start Microsoft Word, and then from your student files, open the Word document **a2L_Leave**. Use the skills you have practiced in this chapter to assist Gabe Stevens, the Director of Human Resources, in answering questions about employee leave time in your database **2L_Leave_Firstname_Lastname**. Save any queries that you create, include your name in the query title, and submit your queries as directed by your instructor. Record your answers to the questions in the Word document.

End **You have completed Project 2L** ———————————

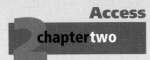

Problem Solving

Project 2M—Coaches

In this project, you will construct a solution by applying any combination of the skills you practiced from the Objectives in Projects 2A and 2B.

For Project 2M, you will need the following files:

a2M_Coaches
a2M_Coaches (Word document)

You will save your database as
2M_Coaches_Firstname_Lastname

Start Microsoft Word, and then from your student files, open the Word document **a2M_Coaches**. Use the skills you have practiced in this chapter to assist Marcus Simmons, the Athletic Director, in answering questions about the Coaches in your database **2M_Coaches_Firstname_Lastname**. Save any queries that you create, include your name in the query title, and submit your queries as directed by your instructor. Record your answers to the questions in the Word document.

End **You have completed Project 2M** ——————

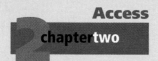

Problem Solving

Project 2N — Faculty Awards

In this project, you will construct a solution by applying any combination of the skills you practiced from the Objectives in Projects 2A and 2B.

For Project 2N, you will need the following files:

a2N_Faculty_Awards
a2N_Faculty_Awards (Word document)

You will save your database as
2N_Faculty_Awards_Firstname_Lastname

Start Microsoft Word, and then from your student files, open the Word document **a2N_Faculty_Awards**. Use the skills you have practiced in this chapter to assist Angela Ta, President of the Faculty Association, in answering questions about faculty awards in your database **2N_Faculty_Awards_Firstname_Lastname**. Save any queries that you create, include your name in the query title, and submit your queries as directed by your instructor. Record your answers to the questions in the Word document.

 You have completed Project 2N ————————————

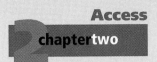

Problem Solving

Project 2O — Club Donations

In this project, you will construct a solution by applying any combination of the skills you practiced from the Objectives in Projects 2A and 2B.

> **For Project 2O, you will need the following files:**
>
> a2O_Club_Donations
> a2O_Club_Donations (Word document)

You will save your database as
2O_Club_Donations_Firstname_Lastname

Start Microsoft Word, and then from your student files, open the Word document **a2O_Club_Donations**. Use the skills you have practiced in this chapter to assist Kathy Durbin, Director of Student Activities, in answering questions about donations to student clubs in your database **2O_Club_Donations_Firstname_Lastname**. Save any queries that you create, include your name in the query title, and submit your queries as directed by your instructor. Record your answers to the questions in the Word document.

 End **You have completed Project 2O** ————————

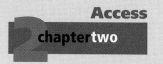

Access
chapter**two**

You and *GO!*

Project 2P —You and *GO!*

In this project, you will construct a solution by applying any combination of the Objectives found in Projects 2A and 2B.

From My Computer, navigate to the student files that accompany this textbook. In the folder **04_you_and_go_pg87_102**, locate and open the folder for this chapter. Open and print the instructions for this project, which are provided to you in Adobe PDF format. Follow the instructions to create queries for your personal database.

 End **You have completed Project 2P** ——————————————

GO! with Help

Project 2Q— *GO!* with Help

There are numerous wildcards that you can use in your queries. Use the Access Help system to find out more about wildcards in Access.

1 **Start** Access. Click the **Microsoft Office Access Help** button. Click the **Search arrow**, and then under **Content from this computer**, click **Access Help**. In the **Search box**, type **wildcards** and then press [Enter]. Scroll the displayed list as necessary, and then click **Using Wildcard Characters in String Comparisons**. Review the information shown in this topic.

2 If you would like to keep a copy of this information, click the **Print** button. Click the **Close** button [X] in the top right corner of the Help window to close the Help window, and then **Close** Access.

 End **You have completed Project 2Q** ——————————————

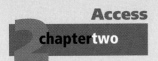

Group Business Running Case

Project 2R—Group Business Running Case

In this project, you will apply the skills you practiced from the Objectives in Projects 2A and 2B.

Your instructor may assign this group case project to your class. If your instructor assigns this project, he or she will provide you with information and instructions to work as part of a group. The group will apply the skills gained thus far to help the Bell Orchid Hotel Group achieve its business goals.

 You have completed Project 2R ────────

chapterthree

Forms, Filters, and Reports

OBJECTIVES

At the end of this chapter you will be able to:

1. Create a Form
2. Use a Form To Add and Delete Records
3. Create a Form by Using the Form Wizard
4. Modify a Form in Design View and in Layout View
5. Filter Records

OUTCOMES

Mastering these objectives will enable you to:

PROJECT 3A

Create Forms To Enter and Display Data in a Database

6. Create a Report by Using the Report Tool
7. Create a Report by Using the Blank Report Tool
8. Create a Report by Using the Report Wizard
9. Modify the Design of a Report
10. Print a Report and Keep Data Together

PROJECT 3B

Create Reports To Display Database Information

Baltimore Area Job Fair

The Baltimore Area Job Fair is a nonprofit organization that brings together employers and job seekers in the Baltimore and Washington, DC metropolitan areas. Each year the organization holds a number of targeted job fairs and the annual Greater Baltimore Job Fair draws over 1,000 employers in more than 70 industries and registers more than 4,000 candidates. Candidates pay a small registration fee. Employers pay to display and present at the fairs and to have access to candidate resumes. Candidate resumes and employer postings are managed by a state-of-the-art database system, allowing participants quick and accurate access to job data and candidate qualifications.

Forms, Filters, and Reports

You can both enter and view information directly in the database tables. However, for entering and viewing information, it is usually easier to use an Access form. You can design forms to display one record at a time, with fields placed in the same order to match a paper source document. When the form on the screen matches the pattern of information on the paper form, it is easier to enter the new information. In a form or table, you can also filter records to display only a portion of the total records based on matching specific values.

When viewing information, it is usually easier to view only one record at a time. For example, your college counselor can look at your college transcript in a nicely laid out form on the screen without seeing the records of other students at the same time.

In Access, reports summarize the data in a database in a professional looking manner suitable for printing. The design of a report can be modified so that the final report is laid out in a format that is useful to the person reading it. In this chapter, you will create and modify both forms and reports for Access databases.

Project 3A Candidate Interviews

Local employers and candidates who are seeking jobs get together at the two-day Greater Baltimore Job Fair. In Activities 3.1 through 3.10, you will assist Janna Sorokin, database manager for the Job Fair, in using an Access database to track the job candidates and the job interviews they have scheduled with employers during the fair event. Your completed database objects will look similar to those in Figure 3.1.

For Project 3A, you will need the following file:

a3A_Candidate_Interviews

You will save your database as
3A_Candidate_Interviews_Firstname_Lastname

3A Candidates Input Form

Candidate ID#:   22155
First Name   Firstname

3A Candidates

Candidate ID#:	22155
Candidate First Name:	Firstname
Candidate Last Name:	Lastname
College Major:	Business
Internships Completed:	Government
Phone Number:	(443) 555-0765
Registration Fee:	$10.00
Date Fee Collected:	10/10/2009

Figure 3.1
Project 3A—Candidate Interviews

Objective 1
Create a Form

A *form* is an Access object with which you can enter, edit, or display data from a table or a query. One typical use of a form is to control access to the data. For example, in a college registration system, you could design a form for Registration Assistants who could see and enter the courses scheduled and fees paid by an individual student. However, they could not see or enter grades or other personal information in the student's record. In this manner, think of a form as a window through which others see and reach your database.

Some Access forms display only one record at a time; other form types display multiple records at the same time. A form that displays only one record at a time is useful not only to the individual who performs the *data entry*—typing in the actual records—but also to anyone who has the job of viewing information in a database. For example, when you visit the Records office at your college to obtain a transcript, someone displays your record on a screen. For the viewer, it is much easier to look at one record at a time, using a form, than to look at all the student records in the database.

Activity 3.1 Creating a Form

There are various ways to create a form in Access, but the fastest and easiest is to use the *Form tool*. With a single mouse click, all the fields from the underlying data source (table or query) are placed on the form. Then you can use the new form immediately, or you can modify it in Layout view or in Design view.

The Form tool incorporates all the information, both the field names and the individual records, from an existing table or query and then instantly creates the form for you. Records that you edit or create using a form automatically update the underlying table or tables. In this activity, you will create a form, and then use it to add new interview records to the database.

1 By using the technique you practiced in Chapter 1, open **My Computer**, and then navigate to the location where you will store your projects for this chapter. Create a new folder and name it **Access Chapter 3**.

2 From the student files that accompany this text, locate the file **a3A_Candidate_Interviews**. Copy and then paste the file to the Access Chapter 3 folder you created in Step 1. Rename the file **3A_Candidate_Interviews_Firstname_Lastname** Close **My Computer**, start Access, open your **3A_Candidate_Interviews** database, and then if necessary, enable the content.

3 **Open** 〉〉 the **Navigation Pane**. Click the **Database Tools tab**, and then in the **Show/Hide group**, click the **Relationships** button. Compare your screen with Figure 3.2.

At the Job Fair event, *one* candidate can have interviews with *many* organizations. Thus, a one-to-many relationship has been established between the 3A Candidates table and the 3A Interviews table using Candidate ID# as the common field—the field that displays in both tables.

Join line with symbols indicating one-to-many
relationship and referential integrity

Figure 3.2

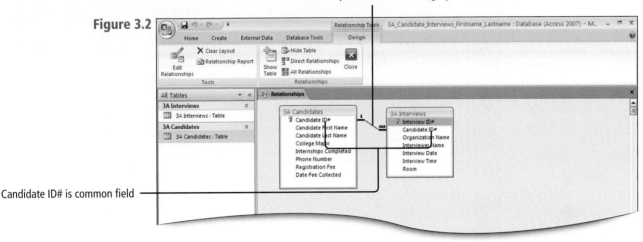

Candidate ID# is common field

4 In the **Relationships group**, click the **Close** button to close the **Relationships window**. From the **Navigation Pane**, open the **3A Interviews table**, and notice the seven fields—*Interview ID#, Candidate ID#, Organization Name, Interviewer Name, Interview Date, Interview Time,* and *Room.* **Close** ⊠ the **3A Interviews table**.

5 Be sure the **3A Interviews table** is still selected in the **Navigation Pane**. Click the **Create tab**, and then in the **Forms group**, click **Form. Close** « the **Navigation Pane**, and then compare your screen with Figure 3.3.

Access creates the form based on the currently selected object—the 3A Interviews table—and displays the form in **Layout view**. In Layout view, you can make design changes to the form while it is displaying data. For example, you can adjust the size of the text boxes to fit the data. You can use Layout view for many of the changes you might need to make to a form.

Access creates the form in a simple top-to-bottom layout, with all seven fields in the table lined up in a single column. The data for the first record in the table displays in the fields.

6 In the navigation area, click the **Next record** button ▶ four times.

Dotted lines indicate Layout View   Button indicates Layout View is active

Figure 3.3

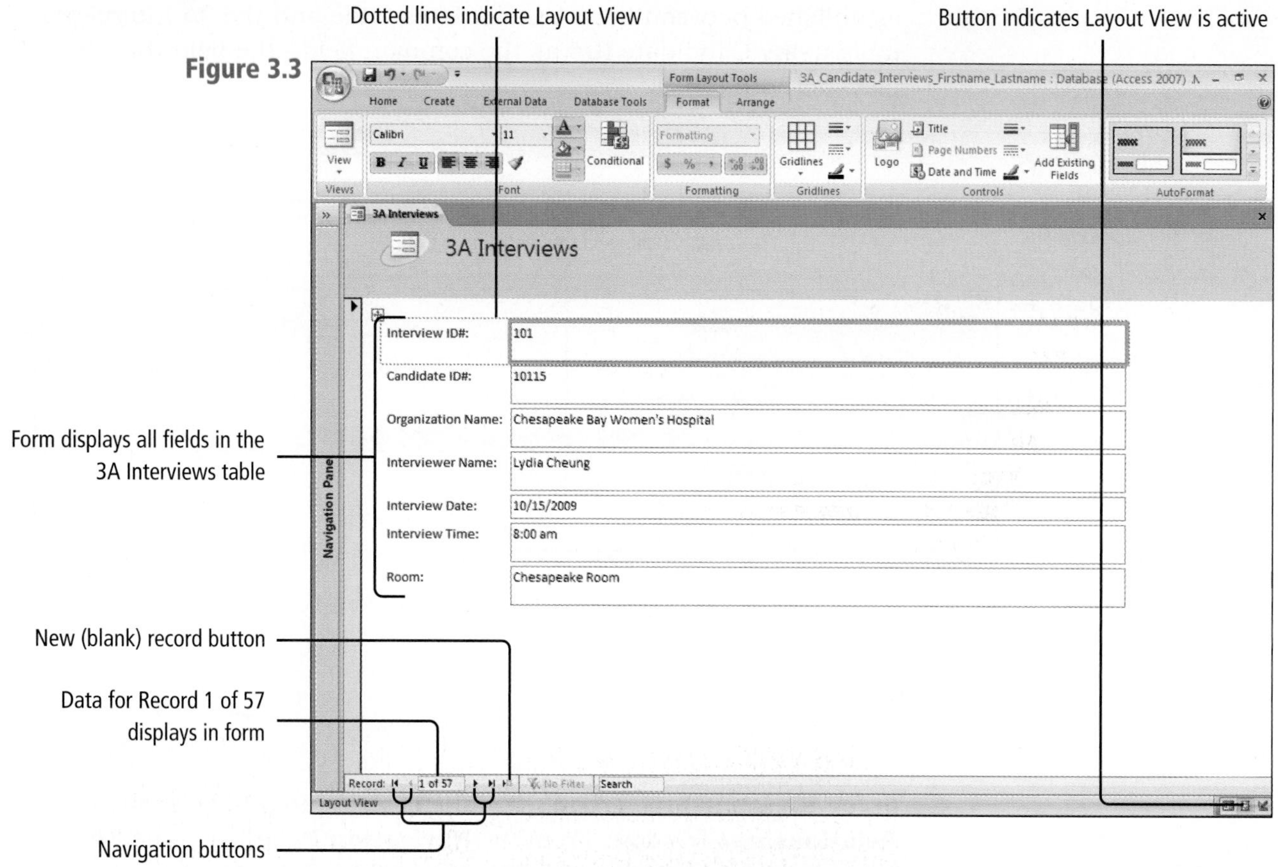

Form displays all fields in the
3A Interviews table

New (blank) record button

Data for Record 1 of 57
displays in form

Navigation buttons

The fifth record—for *Interview ID# 105*—displays. Use the navigation buttons to scroll among the records to display any single record you want to view.

7 In the navigation area, click the **Last record** button ▶⎸ to display the record for *Interview ID# 157*, and then click the **First record** button ⎸◀ to display the record for *Interview ID# 101*.

8 From the **Office** menu 🔵, click **Save** 💾 to save this form for future use. In the displayed **Save As** dialog box, edit as necessary to name the form **3A Interviews Form** and click **OK**. **Close** ✖ the form object.

9 **Open** ≫ the **Navigation Pane**, and notice that your new form displays under the table with which it is associated—the **3A Interviews table**. Notice also that your new form displays the form icon, which identifies it as a form.

10 From the **Navigation Pane**, select the **3A Candidates table**, click the **Create tab**, and then in the **Forms group**, click **Form**. **Close** ≪ the **Navigation Pane**, and then compare your screen with Figure 3.4.

If a record has related records in another table, the related records display in the form. You can scroll down and see that *Candidate ID#*

10115, for *Sally Marques*, has five interviews scheduled during the two-day Job Fair event.

Figure 3.4

14A Candidates form

Layout View button active

Candidate has related records
(interviews scheduled)

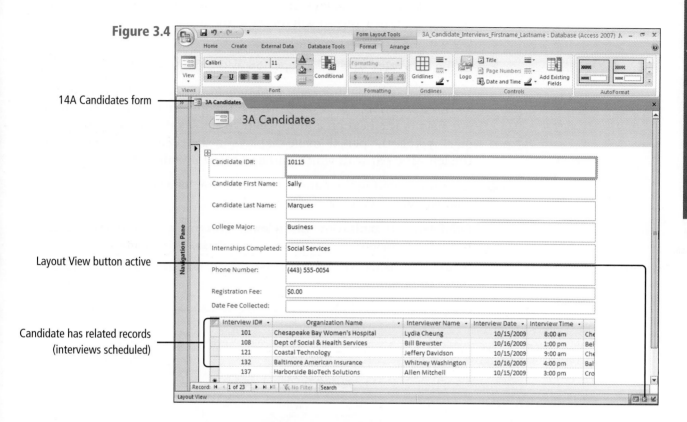

11 **Close** ❌ the **3A Candidates form**, click **Yes**, edit as necessary to name the form **3A Candidates Form** and then click **OK**.

Objective 2
Use a Form To Add and Delete Records

Adding and deleting records using a single-record form helps to prevent data entry errors, because the person performing the data entry is look-ing at only one record at a time. Recall that your database is useful only if the information is accurate—just like your personal address book is useful only if it contains accurate addresses and phone numbers.

Activity 3.2 Adding Records to a Table by Using a Form

Forms are based on, also referred to as *bound* to, the table where the records are stored. That is, when a record is entered in a form, the new record is added to the corresponding table. The reverse is also true—when a record is added to a table, the new record can be viewed in the corresponding form. In this activity, you will add a new record to the 3A Interviews table by using the form that you just created.

1 **Open** ⯈⯈ the **Navigation Pane**, and then open the **3A Interviews Form**. **Close** ⯇⯇ the **Navigation Pane**. In the navigation area at the bottom of the form, click the **New (blank) record** button 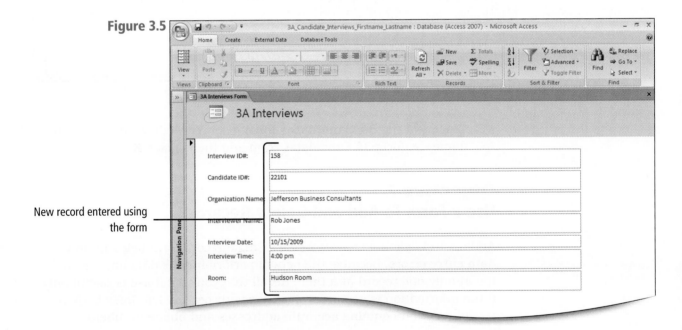.

A new blank form displays, indicated in the navigation area by *58 of 58*. Adding a new record will increase the number of records in the table to 58.

2 In the **Interview ID#** field, type **158** and then press Tab.

Use the Tab key to move from field to field in a form. This is known as the *tab order*—the order in which the insertion point moves from one field to the next on a form when you press the Tab key. After you start typing, the pencil image displays in the *record selector* bar at the left—the bar with which you can select an entire record.

3 Continue entering the data as shown in the following table, and then compare your screen with Figure 3.5.

Candidate ID#	Organization Name	Interviewer Name	Interview Date	Interview Time	Room
22101	Jefferson Business Consultants	Rob Jones	10/15/2009	4:00 pm	Hudson Room

Figure 3.5

New record entered using the form

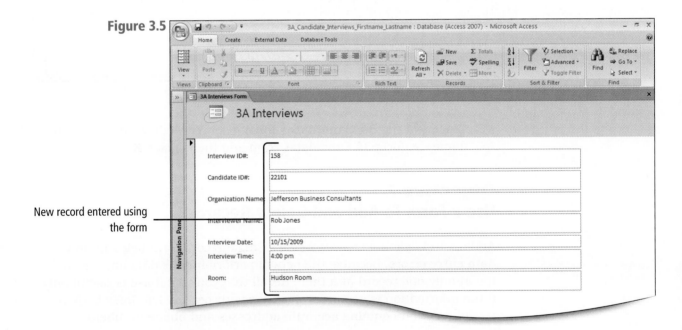

4 **Close** ✕ the **3A Interviews Form**—the new record is stored in the table. **Open** ≫ the **Navigation Pane**, open the **3A Candidates Form**, and then **Close** ≪ the **Navigation Pane**.

5 At the bottom of the screen, in the navigation area, click the **New (blank) record** button. In the displayed blank form, and using your own first and last name, fill in the form using the information in the following table:

Candidate ID#	Candidate First Name	Candidate Last Name	College Major	Internships Completed	Phone Number	Registration Fee	Date Fee Collected
22155	Firstname	Lastname	Business	Government	(443) 555-0765	$10.00	10/10/2009

6 **Close** ☒ the **3A Candidates Form**, **Open** ≫ the **Navigation Pane**, open the **3A Candidates table**, and then verify that your record as a candidate displays as the last record in the table. **Close** ☒ the table.

Activity 3.3 Deleting Records from a Table by Using a Form

You can delete records from a database table by using a form. In this activity, you will delete Interview ID# 103, because Jennifer Lee has notified Janna that she will be unable to meet with AAA Telecom at that time.

1 From the **Navigation Pane**, open the **3A Interviews Form**, click in the **Interview ID#** field, and then on the **Home tab**, in the **Find group**, click the **Find** button. Alternatively, press [Ctrl] + [F] to open the Find and Replace dialog box.

2 In the **Look In** box, notice that *Interview ID#* is indicated, and then in the **Find What** box, type **103** Click **Find Next** and then compare your screen with Figure 3.6 and confirm that the record for **Interview ID# 103** displays.

Record for *Interview ID# 103* displays

Figure 3.6

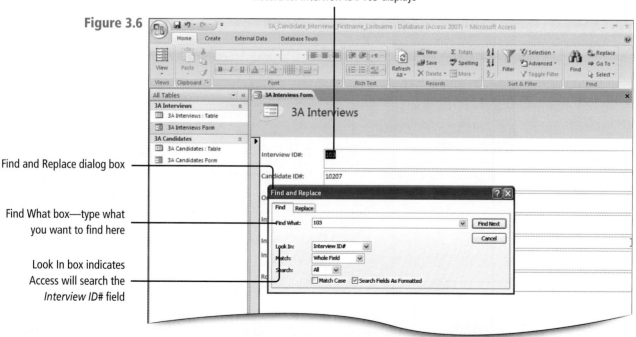

Find and Replace dialog box

Find What box—type what you want to find here

Look In box indicates Access will search the *Interview ID#* field

3 **Close** ⊠ the **Find and Replace** dialog box.

4 On the **Home tab**, in the **Records group**, click the **Delete button arrow**, and then in the displayed list, click **Delete Record** to delete the record for Interview ID# 103. Alternatively, press Delete on your keyboard.

The record is removed and a message displays alerting you that you are about to delete *1 record*. If you click Yes and delete the record, you cannot use the Undo button to reverse the action. If you delete a record by mistake, you must re-create the record by reentering the data.

5 Click **Yes** to delete the record, and then in the navigation area at the bottom of the screen, notice that the number of records in the table is *57*. **Close** ⊠ the form object.

6 From the **Navigation Pane**, open the **3A Interviews table**.

7 Examine the table and verify that the record for *Interview ID# 103* no longer displays—by default, tables are sorted in ascending order by their primary key field, which in this table is the **Interview ID#** field. Then, scroll down and verify that the new record you added for **Interview ID# 158** is included in the table. Compare your screen with Figure 3.7.

Your actions of adding and deleting records using the 3A Interviews Form updates the records stored in this 3A Interviews table.

Figure 3.7

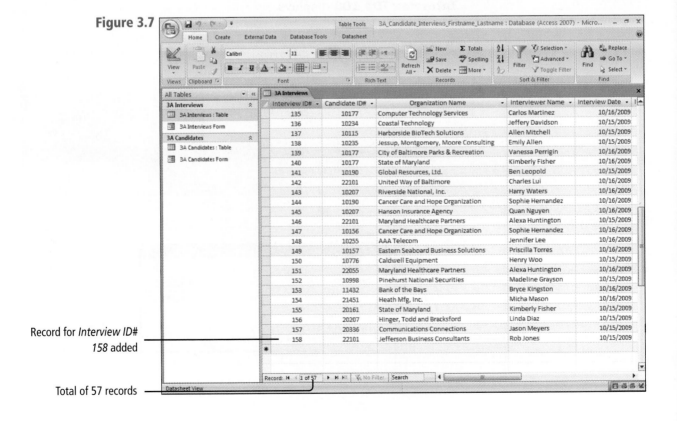

Record for *Interview ID# 158* added

Total of 57 records

8 **Close** ✕ the table.

Activity 3.4 Printing a Form

Like other Access objects, forms can be printed. If you click the Print button, *all* of the records will print in the form layout that you selected.

1 From the **Navigation Pane**, open the **3A Candidates Form**. Press Ctrl + F to display the **Find and Replace** dialog box. In the **Find What** box, type **22155** In the **Look In** box, be sure that *Candidate ID#* is indicated, and then click **Find Next** to display the record with your name. **Close** ✕ the dialog box.

2 From the **Office** menu 🗔, click the **Print** button. In the displayed **Print** dialog box, under **Print Range**, click the **Selected Record(s)** option button. In the lower left corner of the dialog box, click the **Setup** button.

3 In the displayed **Page Setup** dialog box, click the **Columns tab**, and then under **Column Size**, in the **Width** box, delete the existing text and type **7"** Compare your screen with Figure 3.8.

Column Width set to 7″

Figure 3.8

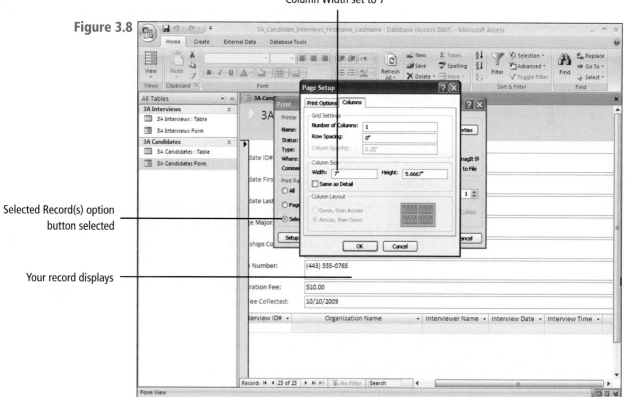

Selected Record(s) option button selected

Your record displays

4 Click **OK** two times to print only your record in the form layout, or submit electronically as directed.

5 **Close** ☒ the **3A Candidates Form**, and then **Close** ⤫ the **Navigation Pane**.

Objective 3
Create a Form by Using the Form Wizard

The Form tool creates an instant form in a simple top-to-bottom layout with all the fields lined up in a single column. The Form Wizard, on the other hand, creates a form quickly, but does so in a manner that gives you more flexibility in the design, layout, and number of fields included.

The design of the form should be planned for the individuals who use the form—either for entering new records or viewing records. For example, when your college counselor displays your information to answer a question for you, it is easier for her or him to view the information spread out in a logical pattern across the screen rather than in one long column.

Activity 3.5 Creating a Form by Using the Form Wizard

By using the Form Wizard to create your form, you control how the form looks by selecting the fields to include, the style to apply, and the layout. When candidates register to attend the Job Fair and view job openings from exhibiting employers, they fill out a paper form. To make it easier to enter candidates into the database, you will create an Access form that matches the layout of the paper form. This will make it easier for the person entering the data into the database.

1 **Open** ⏩ the **Navigation Pane**, and then click to select the **3A Candidates table**. On the **Create tab**, in the **Forms group**, click the **More Forms** button, and then in the displayed list, click **Form Wizard**.

The Form Wizard is an Access feature that walks you step by step through a process by asking questions. In the first screen of the Form Wizard, you select which fields you want on your form, and the fields can come from more than one table or query.

2 In the text box below **Tables/Queries**, click the **arrow** to display a list of available tables and queries from which you can create the form.

There are two tables from which you can create a new form.

3 In the displayed list, click **Table: 3A Candidates**. Compare your screen with Figure 3.9.

The field names from the 3A Candidates table display in the Available Fields box.

One Field button   Next button

Figure 3.9

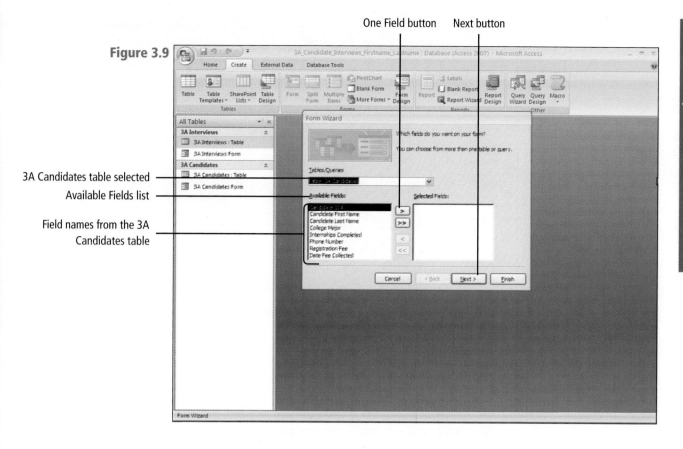

3A Candidates table selected

Available Fields list

Field names from the 3A
Candidates table

---

4 Using the **One Field** button [>], move the following fields to the
Selected Fields list: **Candidate First Name**, **Candidate Last Name**,
College Major, **Internships Completed**, and **Phone Number**.
Alternatively, double-click a field name to move it to the Selected
Fields box.

5 Click **Next**. Be sure **Columnar** is selected as the layout for your
form, and then click **Next**.

Here you select the style you would like for your form. The style controls the font, font size, font color, and background.

6 Click several of the styles to see how they are formatted, and then
scroll as necessary and click **Trek**. Click **Next** to move to the final
step; here you name your form. In the box at the top, edit as necessary to name the form **3A Candidates Input Form** and then click
Finish to close the wizard and create the form. Compare your screen
with Figure 3.10.

In the final step of the Form Wizard, when you name the form and
click Finish, the form is saved and added to the Navigation Pane.
Leave the new form open for the next activities.

Figure 3.10

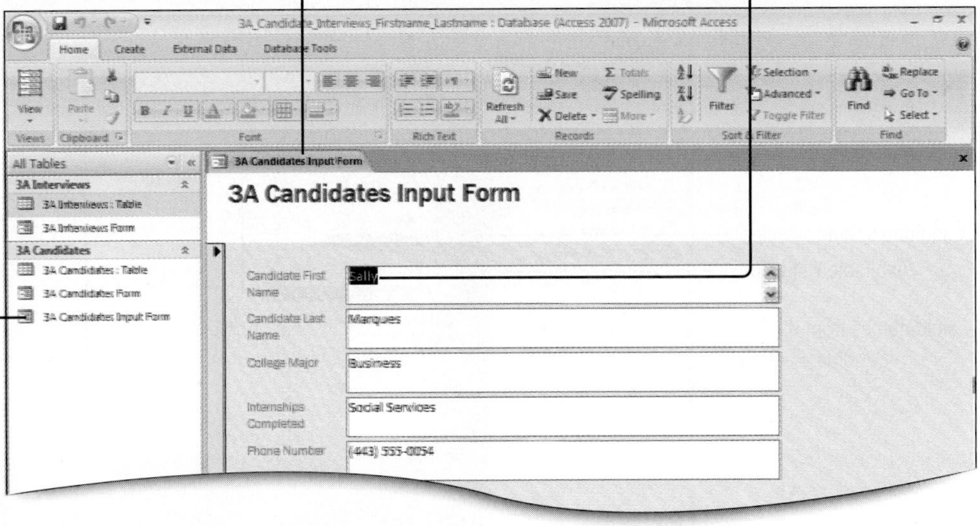
Completed form from wizard
Candidate Sally Marques
(first record in table) displays in form
New form displays in the
Navigation Pane
3A Candidates Input Form
Candidate First Name
Sally
Candidate Last Name
Marques
College Major
Business
Internships Completed
Social Services
Phone Number
(443) 555-0054

Objective 4
Modify a Form in Design View and in Layout View

After you create a form, Access provides tools with which you can make additional changes. For example, you can resize the fields on the form for easier viewing or more efficient data entry.

Activity 3.6 Modifying a Form in Design View

Design view presents a detailed view of the structure of your form. Because the form is not actually running when displayed in Design view, you cannot see the underlying data. However, some tasks, such as resizing sections, must be completed in Design view.

1 **Close** « the **Navigation Pane** and be sure your **3A Candidates Input Form** displays. In the lower right corner of your screen, on the right end of the status bar, click the **Design View** button. Alternatively, in the Views group, click the View button arrow, and then click Design View. Compare your screen with Figure 3.11.

A form is divided into three sections—***Form Header***, ***Detail***, and ***Form Footer***—each designated by a bar called a ***section bar***. ***Controls*** are objects on a form that display data, perform actions, and let you view and work with information; controls make the form easier to use for the person who is either using the form to enter data or to view data.

The most commonly used control is the ***text box control***, which typically displays data from the underlying table, in which case it is referred to as a ***bound control***—its source data comes from a table or query. Access places a ***label*** to the left of a text box control, which contains descriptive information that appears on the form, usually the field names. A control that does not have a source of data, for example a label that displays the title of the form, is an ***unbound control***.

Figure 3.11

Text box controls

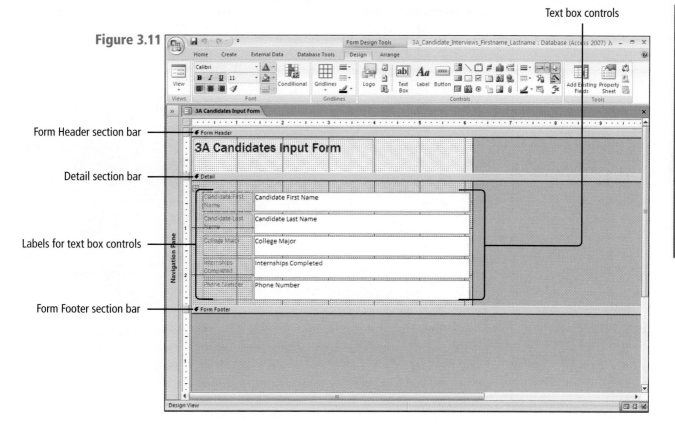

Form Header section bar

Detail section bar

Labels for text box controls

Form Footer section bar

Alert!

Does the field list display?

If the Field List pane displays on the right, in the upper right corner, click its Close button.

2 Point to upper edge of the **Detail section bar** to display the ✛ pointer, and then drag downward approximately **0.5 inches**. Compare your screen with Figure 3.12.

The Form Header expands—do not be concerned if your expanded Form Header area does not match Figure 3.12 exactly; you will adjust it later. The background grid is dotted and divided into 1-inch squares by horizontal and vertical grid lines to help you place and align controls on the form precisely. You can also use the vertical and horizontal rulers to guide the placement of a control on the form.

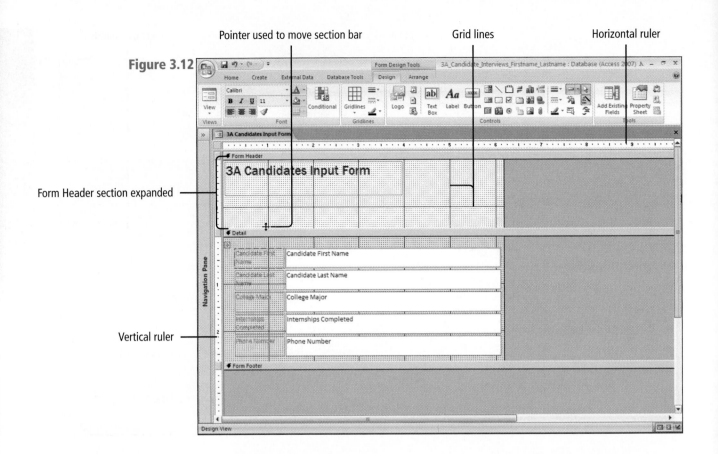

Figure 3.12

Pointer used to move section bar — Grid lines — Horizontal ruler

Form Header section expanded

Vertical ruler

Alert!

Are the rulers missing?

If the horizontal and vertical rulers do not display, on the Arrange tab, in the Show/Hide group, click Ruler.

---

3 In the **Form Header section**, click anywhere in the title *3A Candidates Input Form* to select it. On the **Design tab**, in the **Font group**, click the **Font Size arrow** [11 ▾], and then click **18**. Click the **Bold** button [B] to add bold emphasis to the text. Click the **Font Color arrow** [A ▾], and then under **Access Theme Colors**, in the second row, click the ninth color—**Access Theme 9**.

The label is selected as indicated by the orange border surrounding it. The border displays small boxes called **sizing handles**, which are used to resize the control.

4 On the right side of the selected label control, point to the **middle sizing handle** to display the [↔] pointer—or point to one of the other sizing handles to display a resize pointer—and then double-click to adjust the size of the label control. Compare your screen with Figure 3.13.

The size of the label resizes to fit the text as it has been reformatted.

Form Header text—*3A Candidates Input Form*—modified

Sizing handles indicate label is selected

Figure 3.13

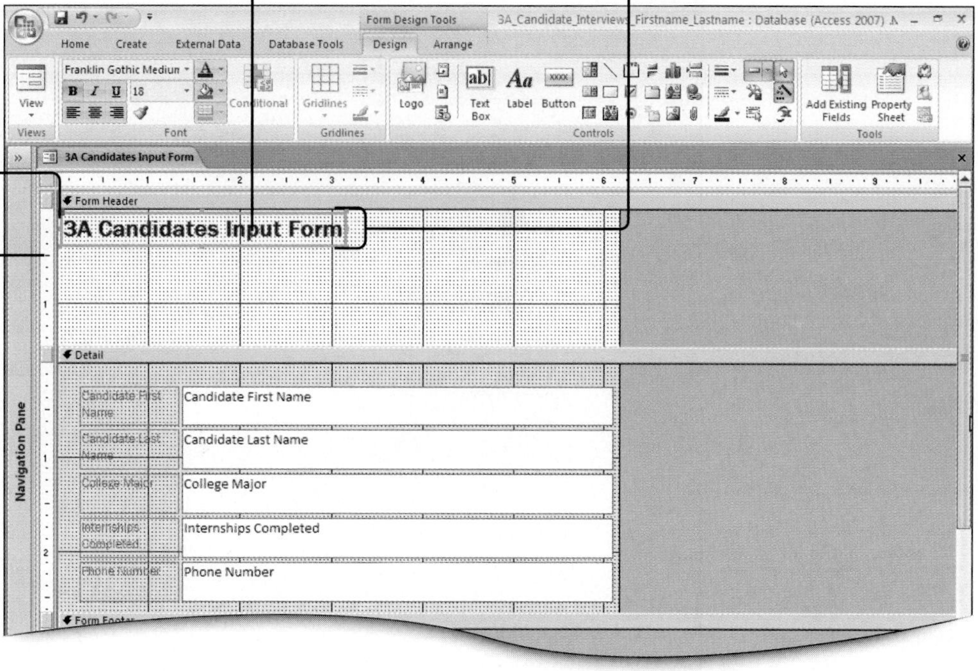

Label formatted and resized

0.50 inch on the vertical ruler

5 Point to the upper edge of the **Detail section bar** to display the pointer, and then drag upward until the bar is at **0.50 inch on the vertical ruler**—allowing approximately two rows of dots between the lower edge of the label control border and the upper edge of the **Detail section bar**.

6 At the bottom of the form, point to the lower edge of the **Form Footer section bar** to display the ⊕ pointer, and then drag downward approximately **0.50 inch** to expand this section of the form.

7 On the **Design tab**, in the **Controls group**, click the **Label** button. Position the plus sign of the pointer ⊞A in the **Form Footer** section at approximately **0.25 inch on the horizontal ruler** and even with the top edge of the section. Drag to the right to **5 inches on the horizontal ruler**, and then downward approximately **0.25 inch**. If you are not satisfied with your result, click Undo and begin again.

8 Using your own name, type **3A Candidates Input Form Firstname Lastname** and then press Enter. Point to a sizing handle to display one of the resize pointers, and then double-click to fit the control to the text you typed. On the right end of the status bar, click the **Form View** button ⊞. Compare your screen with Figure 3.14.

Form Footer text displays on the screen at the bottom of the form, and prints only on the last page when all the forms are printed as a group.

Form Header label modified

Figure 3.14

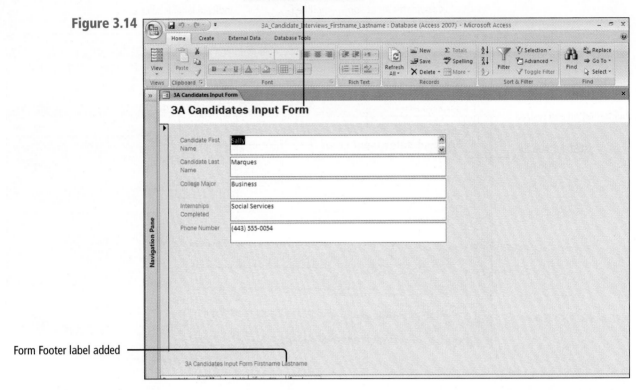

Form Footer label added

---

[9] On the **Quick Access Toolbar**, click the **Save** button ![save icon] to save the changes you have made to the design of your form. Leave the **3A Candidates Input Form** open for the next activity.

Activity 3.7 Adding, Resizing, and Moving Controls in Layout View

Use the Layout view to change the form's ***control layout***—the grouped arrangement of controls on a form in Layout view. Use Layout view to make quick changes to the form's design by adding or moving controls.

[1] In the lower right corner of your screen, at the right end of the status bar, click the **Layout View** button ![layout view icon].

On the Ribbon, the Format tab is selected. A dotted line surrounds the first control—label and text box—and the white text box is surrounded by a solid orange border. In the upper left corner, the ***layout selector*** displays, with which you can select and move the entire group of controls in this view.

[2] In the **Controls group**, click the **Add Existing Fields** button to display the **Field List** pane. Compare your screen with Figure 3.15.

Figure 3.15

First label and control selected

Field List pane displays

Layout selector

Layout View button in status bar selected

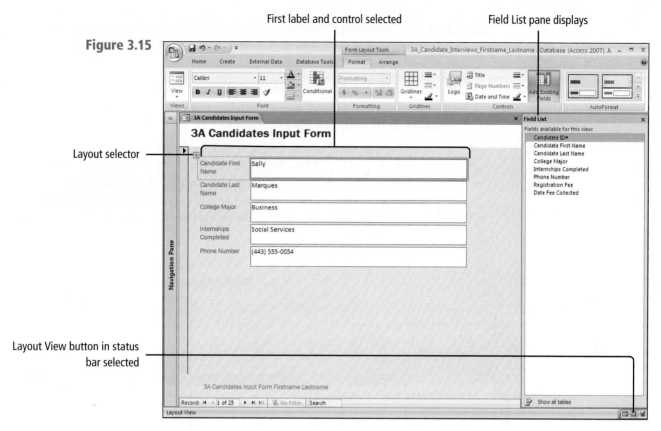

3 In the displayed **Field List**, point to **Candidate ID#**, hold down the left mouse button, and then drag until the pointer is in the upper portion of the *Candidate First Name* text box control and a thick orange line displays above the control. Release the mouse button, and then compare your screen with Figure 3.16. If you are not satisfied with your result, click Undo and begin again.

The Candidate ID# text box control is added to the form; recall that Access also places a label to the left of the text box. In this manner you can add a bound text box to a form by dragging a field from the Field List pane.

Candidate ID# text box control added to the form

Figure 3.16

Access adds label to the text box control

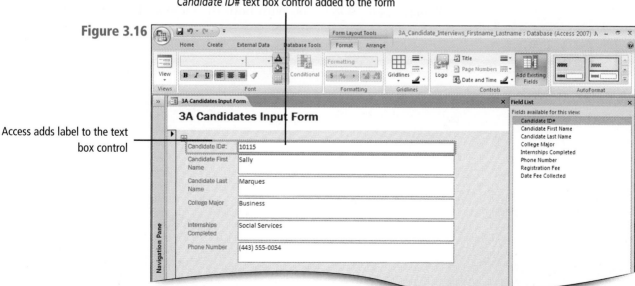

4 **Close** 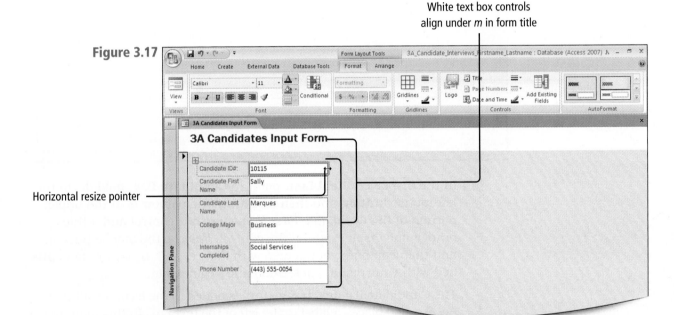 the **Field List** pane. Click the white text box control for **Candidate ID#**, which currently displays *10115*, to surround it with an orange border. Point to the right edge of the white text box control until the ⟷ pointer displays, and then drag to the left until all the white text box controls align under the *m* in the form title above. Compare your screen with Figure 3.17.

All six white text box controls are resized simultaneously. By decreasing the width of the text box controls, you have more space in which to rearrange the various form controls. In Layout view, because you can see your data, you can determine visually that the space you have allotted is adequate to display all records.

White text box controls
align under *m* in form title

Figure 3.17

Horizontal resize pointer

5 Click the white text box control for **Phone Number**, which currently displays *(443) 555-0054*. With both the label and the text box control selected, point to the white text box control until the 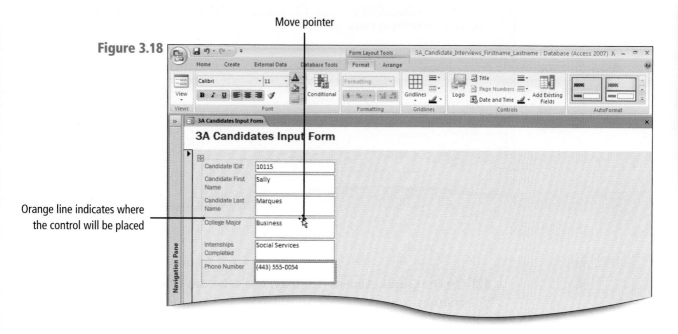 pointer displays, and then drag upward until a thick orange line displays above the text *College Major* as shown in Figure 3.18.

Figure 3.18

Move pointer

Orange line indicates where the control will be placed

6 Release the mouse button to place the **Phone Number control** above the **College Major control**.

7 Click the **Candidate First Name label** to select it. Click to the left of the word *First* to place the insertion point in the control, and then press ←Bksp as necessary to delete the text *Candidate* so that the label indicates *First Name*.

With the insertion point placed in the label, you can edit the label. The form label text does not have to match the field name of the associated table.

8 Using the technique you just practiced, edit the **Candidate Last Name label** to indicate *Last Name*. Then, click in a shaded area of the form so that no controls are selected and compare your screen with Figure 3.19.

Figure 3.19

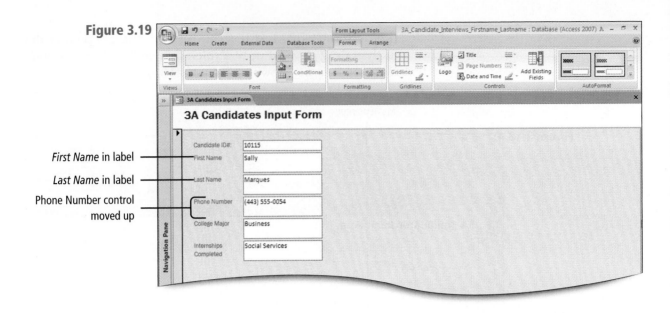

First Name in label ——
Last Name in label ——
Phone Number control moved up ——

3A Candidates Input Form

Candidate ID#:	10115
First Name	Sally
Last Name	Marques
Phone Number	(443) 555-0054
College Major	Business
Internships Completed	Social Services

9 On the **Quick Access Toolbar**, click the **Save** button 🖫 to save the changes you have made to the design of your form in Layout view.

Activity 3.8 Formatting and Aligning Controls in Layout View

1 With the form still displayed in Layout view, hold down ⇧Shift, and then click each of the **white text box controls**.

2 With the six text box controls selected, on the **Format tab**, in

Alert!

Do your controls change order when selecting?

If, when selecting all the controls, the controls change order, click Undo and select the controls again.

the **Font group**, click the **Fill/Back Color button arrow** 🖍▾. Under **Access Theme Colors**, in the second row, click the fourth color—**Access Theme 4**. Click the **Font Size button arrow** 11 ▾, and then click **12**.

3 Click in a shaded area of the screen to deselect all the **text box controls**. Hold down ⇧Shift, and then click each of the six labels to the left of the text box controls. With the six label controls selected, change the **Font Size** 11 ▾ to **12**, change the **Font Color** A ▾ to

Access Theme 9, and then apply **Bold** B . Click in a shaded area to deselect, and then compare your screen with Figure 3.20.

Text box controls formatted with Font Size 12 and Access Theme 4 fill color

Figure 3.20

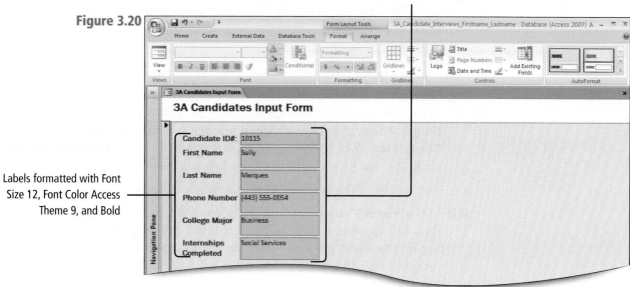

Labels formatted with Font Size 12, Font Color Access Theme 9, and Bold

4 Click the label **Internships Completed**. On the Ribbon, click the **Arrange tab**, and then in the **Tools group**, click the **Property Sheet** button. Compare your screen with Figure 3.21.

The *Property Sheet* for the selected label displays. Each control has an associated Property Sheet where you can make precision changes to the properties—characteristics—of selected controls.

Arrange tab selected

Property Sheet button in Tools group

Figure 3.21

Property Sheet for label

Label selected

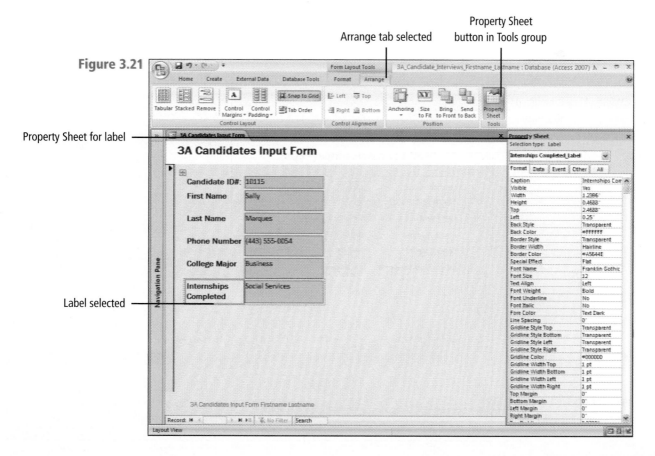

5 In the displayed **Property Sheet**, be sure the **Format tab** is selected. In the **Width** property box, point to the word *Width* and click to select its value to the right. Type **2** to replace the value, and then press Enter.

The width of all the labels changes to 2 inches.

6 Click in the shaded area to deselect the label. Hold down ⇧Shift, and then click to select the blue text box controls for **First Name**, **Last Name**, **Phone Number**, **College Major**, and **Internships Completed**. With the five text boxes selected, in the **Property Sheet**, click the word *Height*, type **0.3** and then press Enter.

The height of the selected text box controls decreases.

7 In the **Form Footer section**, click to select the label with your name that you created earlier. In the displayed **Property Sheet**, point to the text *Left* and click to select the value, and then change the **Left** property to **1** Press Enter to align the left edge of the label at 1 inch.

8 In the **Form Header section**, click anywhere in the title label text *3A Candidates Input Form*. In the **Property Sheet**, on the **Format tab**, change the **Left** property to **1** and then press Enter. Compare your screen with Figure 3.22.

Recall that each control has an associated Property Sheet on which you can change the properties—characteristics—of the control. Because this is a label that was added to the form, Access assigns it a number. The number on your property sheet may differ. The left edge of the label moves so that its left edge aligns at 1 inch. In this manner you can place a control in a specific location on the form.

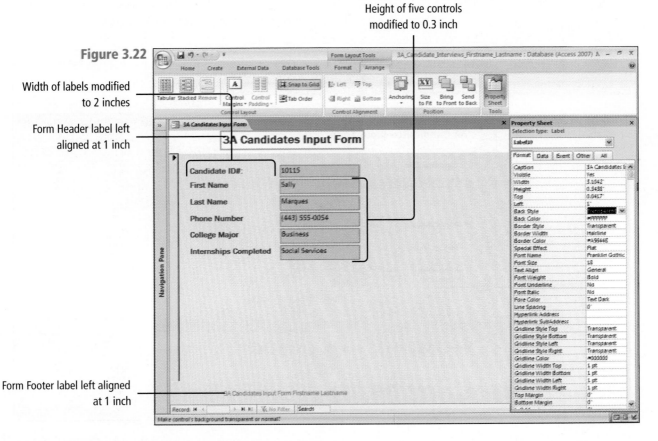

Figure 3.22

Height of five controls modified to 0.3 inch

Width of labels modified to 2 inches

Form Header label left aligned at 1 inch

Form Footer label left aligned at 1 inch

9 In the upper right corner of the **Property Sheet**, click the **Close** button ![X]. On the right side of the status bar, click the **Form View** ![icon] button. Compare your screen with Figure 3.23.

The form displays in Form view. Using these techniques, you can make a form attractive and easy to use for those who must use the form to view and enter records on a screen.

Figure 3.23

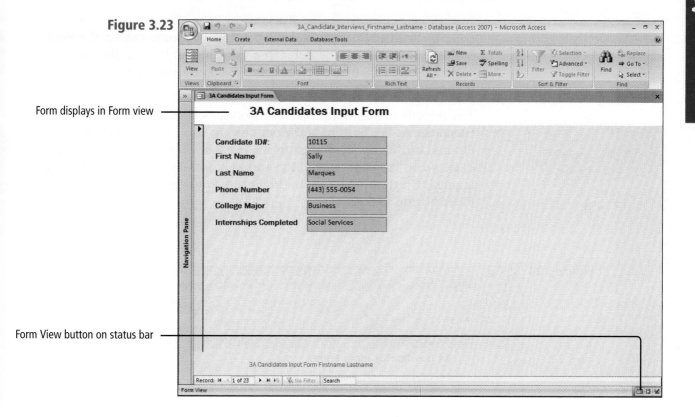

Form displays in Form view

Form View button on status bar

10 On the **Quick Access Toolbar**, click the **Save** button ![icon] to save the changes you have made to your form's design. In the navigation area, click the **Last record** button ![icon] to display the record containing your name. Then, from the **Office** menu ![icon], click **Print**. In the displayed **Print** dialog box, under **Print Range**, click the **Selected Record(s)** option button. Click **OK** to print, or submit electronically as directed.

11 **Close** ![X] the form, and if necessary, click **Yes** to save the changes.

Objective 5
Filter Records

Filtering records in a form is the process of displaying only a portion of the total records—a *subset*—based on matching specific values. Filters are commonly used to provide a quick answer, and the result is not generally saved for future use. For example, by filtering records in a form, you can quickly display a subset of records for students majoring in Business.

Activity 3.9 Filtering Data by Selection on One Field

Several interviewers at the Baltimore Job Fair would like to see records for candidates who are majoring in Business. Use the *Filter By Selection* command—which retrieves only the records that contain the value in the selected field—to temporarily remove the records that do *not* contain the value in the selected field.

1 **Open** >> the **Navigation Pane**, and then open the **3A Candidates Input Form**. **Close** << the **Navigation Pane**. In the displayed first record, click the **College Major** label. On the **Home tab**, in the **Sort & Filter group**, click the **Selection** button, and then in the displayed list, click **Equals "Business"**. Compare your screen with Figure 3.24.

Ten records match the contents of the selected College Major field—*Business*. At the bottom of the window, in the navigation area, a Filtered button displays next to the number of records. *Filtered* also displays on the right side of the status bar to indicate that a filter is applied. On the Home tab, in the Sort & Filter group, the Toggle Filter button is active.

Figure 3.24

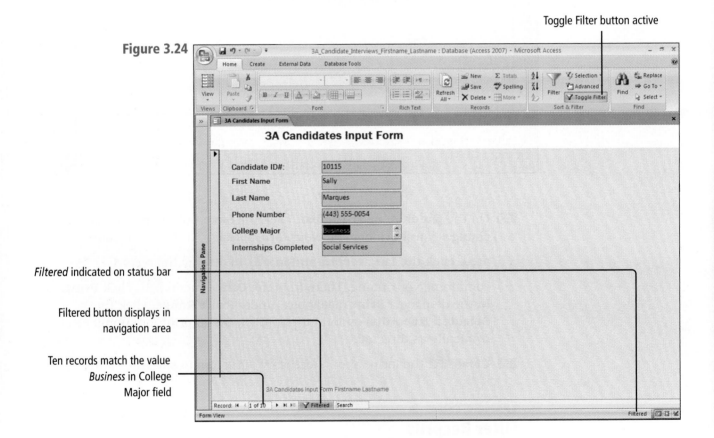

Toggle Filter button active

Filtered indicated on status bar

Filtered button displays in navigation area

Ten records match the value *Business* in College Major field

2 On the **Home tab**, in the **Sort & Filter group**, click the **Toggle Filter** button to remove the filter and activate all 23 records. Notice the **Unfiltered** button in the navigation area. Alternatively, click the Filtered button in the navigation area to remove a filter.

3 Be sure the first record—for Sally Marques—displays, and then click to place the insertion point in the blue **College Major** text box control to display up and down arrows. On the **Home tab**, in the **Sort & Filter group**, click the **Toggle Filter** button to reapply the filter, and then in the navigation area, click the **Last record** button ▶| to display the last of the ten records that match *Business*.

The record for *Candidate ID# 22155* displays—the record with your name.

4 In the **Sort & Filter group**, click the **Toggle Filter** button to remove the filter and activate all of the records. In the navigation area, click the **Next record** button ▶ one time to move to **Record 2**. In the **Phone Number** field, select the text *(410)* including the parentheses, which is the Area Code. On the **Home tab**, in the **Sort & Filter group**, click the **Selection** button, and then click **Begins with "(410)"**.

A new filter is applied that retrieves the fourteen records in which the *Phone Number* contains the (410) Area Code.

5 On the **Home tab**, in the **Sort & Filter group**, click the **Toggle Filter** button to remove the filter and activate all of the records.

Activity 3.10 Using Filter by Form

Use the *Filter By Form* command to filter the records in a form based on one or more fields, or based on more than one *value* in the same field. The Filter By Form command offers greater flexibility than the Filter by Selection command when you want an answer to a question that requires matching multiple values. In this activity, you will help Janna Sorokin determine how many candidates have a major of *Communications* or *Graphic Arts*, because several interviewers are interested in candidates with one of those two backgrounds.

1 With the **3A Candidates Input Form** still open, on the **Home tab**, in the **Sort & Filter group**, click the **Advanced** button, and then in the displayed list, click **Filter By Form**. Click the **Advanced** button again, and then click **Clear Grid**. Compare your screen with Figure 3.25.

The Filter by Form window displays; all the field names are included, but without any data. In the empty text box for each field, you can type a value or choose from a list of available values. The *Look for* and *Or* tabs display at the bottom.

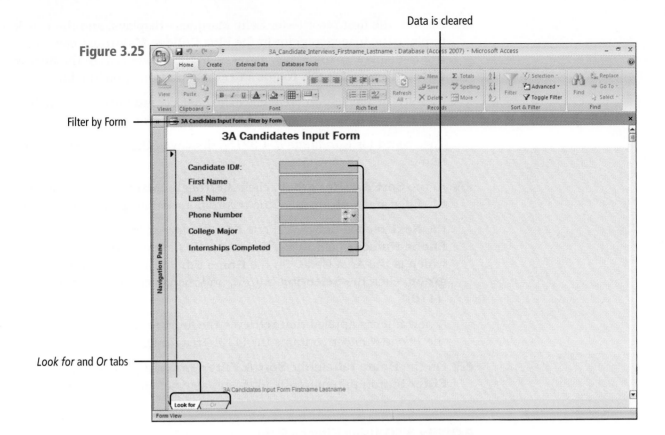

Figure 3.25

Data is cleared

Filter by Form

Look for and Or tabs

Click the blue **College Major** text box control. At the far right edge of the text box, click the larger **down arrow**, and then in the displayed list, click **Communications**. In the **Sort & Filter group**, click the **Toggle Filter** button, and then compare your screen with Figure 3.26.

As indicated in the navigation area, six candidate records indicate a College Major of *Communications*.

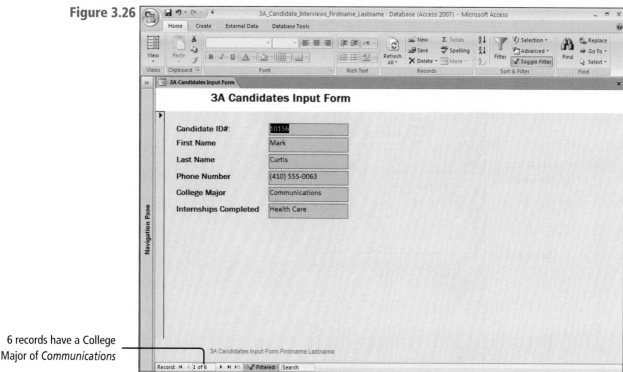

Figure 3.26

6 records have a College
Major of *Communications*

Note — Toggle Filter Button

On the Home tab, the Toggle Filter button is used to apply or remove a filter. If no filter has been created, the button is not active—it is dimmed. After a filter is created, this button becomes active. Because it is a toggle button used to apply or remove filters, the ScreenTip that displays for this button will alternate between Apply Filter—when a filter has been created but is not currently applied—and Remove Filter—when a filter has been applied.

3 Click in the blue **College Major** text box control again. In the **Sort & Filter group**, click the **Filter** button. From the displayed menu, click to select the **Graphic Arts** check box, and then click **OK**.

As indicated in the navigation area, eight candidate records have a College Major in either Communications *or* Graphic Arts. You have created an **OR condition**; that is, only records where one of two values—Communications *or* Graphic Arts—is present in the selected field are activated.

4 Click in the blue **College Major** text box control. In the **Sort & Filter group**, click the **Advanced** button, and then from the displayed menu, click **Clear All Filters**. Click the **Advanced** button again, and then from the displayed menu, click **Advanced Filter/Sort**. Use the ⬉ pointer to expand the field list so that you can view all of the field names. Compare your screen with Figure 3.27.

The Advanced Filter design grid displays. The design grid is similar to the query design grid.

Figure 3.27

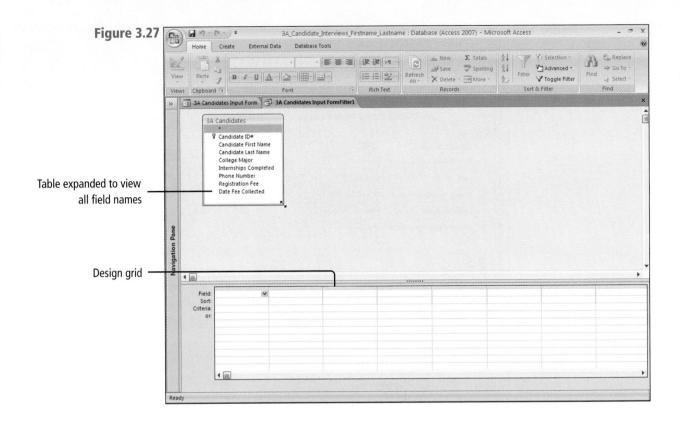

Table expanded to view all field names

Design grid

5 From the **3A Candidates table**, double-click the **College Major** field to add it to the design grid. Then, add the **Internships Completed** field to the design grid. In the **Criteria** row, in the **College Major** field, type **Business** In the **Criteria** row, in the **Internships Completed** field, type **Finance** and then press ⏎. In the **Sort & Filter group**, click **Toggle Filter**. Compare your screen with Figure 3.28.

As indicated in the navigation area, three records match the criteria. You have created an ***AND condition***; that is, only records where both values—Business *and* Finance—are present in the selected fields display. There are three Business majors who have completed an internship in Finance.

Figure 3.28

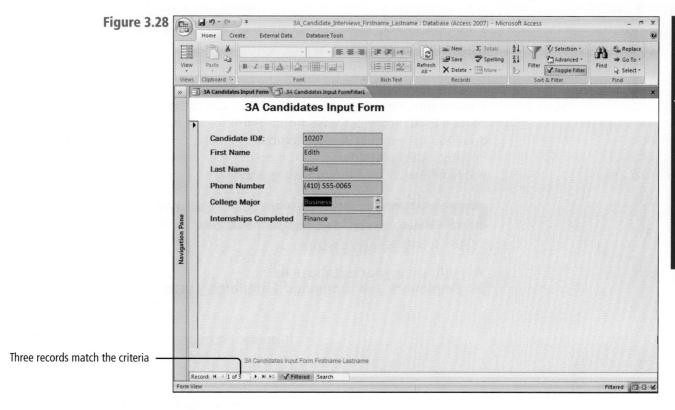

Three records match the criteria

6 In the **Sort & Filter group**, click the **Toggle Filter** button to unfilter the records. Close all open objects, from the **Office** menu 🔵 close the database, and then **Close** ⊠ Access.

End **You have completed Project 3A** ————————

Project 3B Employers and Job Openings

At the Job Fair event, employers post job openings and candidates can request interviews for jobs in which they are interested. In Activities 3.11 though 3.16, you will assist Janna Sorokin, database manager for the Job Fair, in using an Access database to track the employers and the job openings they plan to post at the event. Your completed database objects will look similar to those in Figure 3.29.

For Project 3B, you will need the following file:

a3B_Employers_Job_Openings

You will save your database as
3B_Employers_Job_Openings_Firstname_Lastname

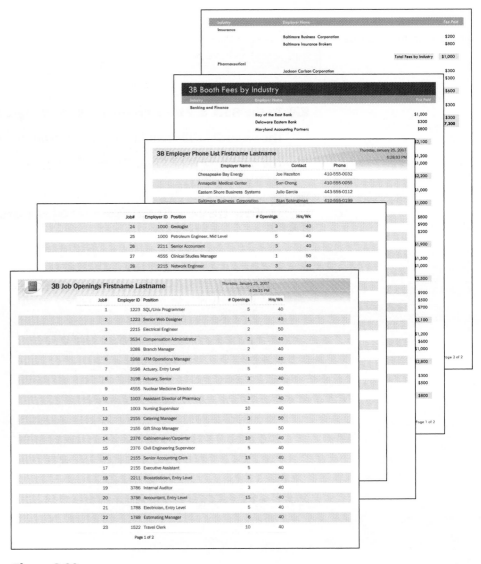

Figure 3.29
Project 3B—Employers and Job Openings

Objective 6
Create a Report by Using the Report Tool

A *report* is a database object that summarizes the fields and records from a table, or from a query, in an easy-to-read format suitable for printing. The report consists of information pulled from tables or queries, as well as information that is stored with the report's design, for example labels, headings, and graphics.

The tables or queries that provide the underlying data for a report are referred to as the report's *record source*. If the fields that you want to include in your report all come from the same table, then you can use the table as the report's record source.

Access provides three ways to create a report: by using the Report tool, the Blank Report tool, or the Report Wizard. After you create a report, you can modify the report in Layout view or in Design view.

Activity 3.11 Creating and Modifying a Report by Using the Report Tool and Layout View

The *Report tool*, which is the fastest way to create a report, generates a report immediately by displaying all the fields and records from the record source that you choose—the underlying table or query. This method of creating a report is useful as a way to quickly look at the underlying data in an easy-to-read format, after which you can save the report and then modify it in Layout view or in Design view.

In this activity, you will use the Report tool to create a report for Janna Sorokin that lists all the employers who are participating in the Job Fair, modify the report in Layout view, and then print the report.

1 Open **My Computer**. From the student files that accompany this text, locate the file **a3B_Employers_Job_Openings**. Copy and then paste the file to your Access Chapter 3 folder. Rename the file as **3B_Employers_Job_Openings_Firstname_Lastname** Close **My Computer**, start Access, open your **3B_Employers_Job_Openings** database, and then if necessary enable the content.

2 Click the **Database Tools tab**, and then in the **Show/Hide group**, click the **Relationships** button. Compare your screen with Figure 3.30.

At the Job Fair event, *one* employer can have *many* job openings. Thus, a one-to-many relationship has been established between the 3B Employers table and the 3B Job Openings table using Employer ID# as the common field—the field that displays in both tables.

Join line with symbols indicating one-to-many relationship

Figure 3.30

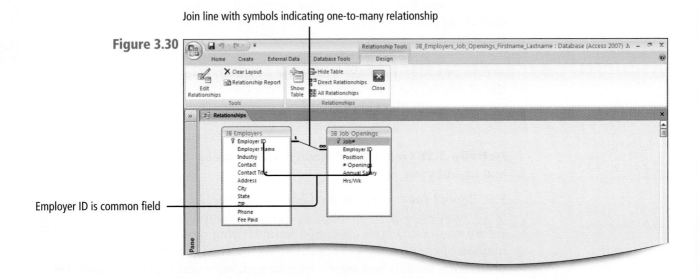

Employer ID is common field

3 In the **Relationships group**, click the **Close** button to close the **Relationships** window.

4 **Open** ⟩⟩ the **Navigation Pane**, click to select the **3B Job Openings table**, and then on the **Create tab**, in the **Reports group**, point to the **Report** button and read its ScreenTip. Click the **Report** button, and then **Close** ⟨⟨ the **Navigation Pane**. Compare your screen with Figure 3.31.

Access creates the 3B Job Openings report and displays it in Layout view. The report includes all the fields and all the records in the table. In Layout view, you can see the margins and page breaks in the report as the pages are currently set up.

Figure 3.31

All fields from table display in report

Dotted lines indicate margins ⎯

All records from table display in report ⎯

Report displays in Layout view ⎯

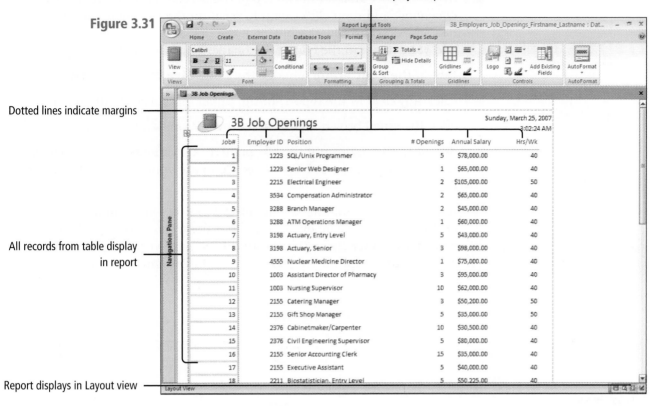

Click to select the field name **Annual Salary** to surround it with an orange border and to select the entire column. Right-click over the selected name, and then from the displayed shortcut menu, click **Delete**.

The Annual Salary field is deleted from the report.

Click to select the field name **# Openings** to surround it with an orange border and to select the entire column. On the **Format tab**, in the **Grouping & Totals group**, click the **Totals** button. In the displayed list, click **Sum**. Scroll down to view the last line of the report, and notice that Access summed the numbers in the field and that the total number of job openings is *182*.

Use Layout view in this manner to make quick changes to a report created with the Report tool. The Report tool is not intended to create a perfectly formatted formal report, but rather it is a way to quickly summarize the data in a table or query in an easy-to-read format suitable for printing and reading.

Click the **Page Setup tab**, and then in the **Page Layout group**, click the **Landscape** button. Click the **Format tab**, and then in the **AutoFormat group**, click the **AutoFormat** button. From the displayed gallery of formats, locate, and then click the **Trek** AutoFormat.

AutoFormat enables you to apply a predefined format to a report, which is another way to give a professional look to a report created quickly with the Report tool. Apply AutoFormat before performing other editing to the text of your report.

8 In the **Report Header** at the top of the screen, click the text *3B Job Openings*, and then click again to position the insertion point in the header. Alternatively, double-click the header. Edit as necessary to add your name to the end of the header text. On the **Format tab**, in the **Font group**, change the **Font Size** [11 ▼] to **16**.

9 Click any field in the report. In the upper left corner of the report, click the small brown **layout selector** button ⊞, and then drag it to the right until the ⊹ pointer is positioned approximately below the *O* in the word *Openings*. Compare your screen with Figure 3.32.

Recall that by using the layout selector button, you can move the entire layout of the labels and text box controls. In this manner, you can easily center the entire layout on the page visually, instead of opening and manipulating the controls in Design view.

Your name displays in Report Header   *Trek* AutoFormat applied

Figure 3.32

Report Header Font Size changed to 16 pt.

Layout centered horizontally on the page

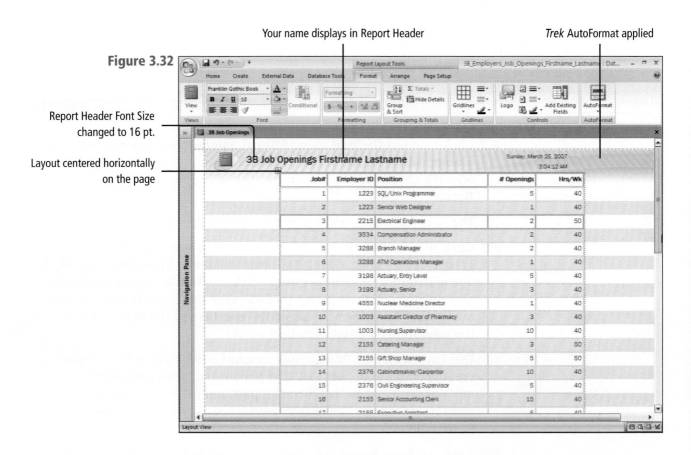

10 In the lower right corner of the screen, at the right edge of the status bar, click the **Print Preview** button ⊡. On the **Print Preview tab**, in the **Zoom group**, click the **Two Pages** button to view the two pages of your report.

11 To print your report, on the **Print Preview tab**, in the **Print group**, click **Print** to print the report. Or, submit electronically as directed.

12. On the **Print Preview tab**, in the **Close Preview group**, click the **Close Print Preview** button, and then **Close** ☒ the **3B Job Openings report**. In the displayed message box, click **Yes** to save changes to the design of the report. In the **Save As** dialog box, click **OK** to accept the default name—*3B Job Openings*.

Objective 7
Create a Report by Using the Blank Report Tool

Activity 3.12 Creating a Report by Using the Blank Report Tool

Use the ***Blank Report tool*** to create a report from scratch. This is an efficient way to create a report, especially if you plan to include only a few fields in your report.

In this activity, you will use the Blank Report tool to build a report that lists only the Employer Name, Contact, and Phone fields, which Janna will use as a quick reference for phoning various employers to verify the details of their Job Fair participation.

1. On the **Create tab**, in the **Reports group**, click the **Blank Report** button.

A blank report displays in Layout view, and the Field List pane displays.

2. In the **Field List** pane, if necessary click **Show all tables**, and then click the **plus sign (+)** next to the **3B Employers table**. Compare your screen with Figure 3.33.

The list of fields in the 3B Employers table displays.

Field List pane

Figure 3.33

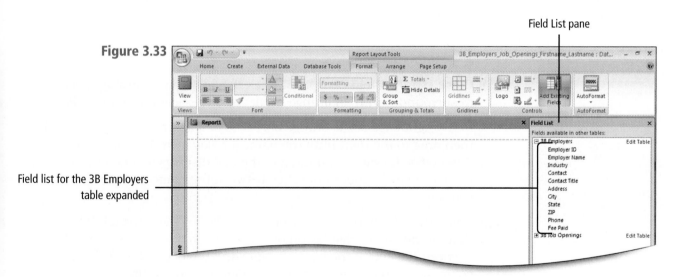

Field list for the 3B Employers table expanded

3. Point to the **Employer Name** field, right-click, and then click **Add Field to View**.

The Employer Name field and its associated records display as the first column of the report. In this manner, you build the report field by field, in the order you want the fields to display.

4 From the **Field List** pane, drag the **Contact** field into the blank report—anywhere to the right of **Employer Name**. Double-click the **Phone** field to add it as the third field in the report. Compare your screen with Figure 3.34.

You can use any of the techniques you just practiced when you want to include fields in a blank report.

Three fields added to the report

Figure 3.34

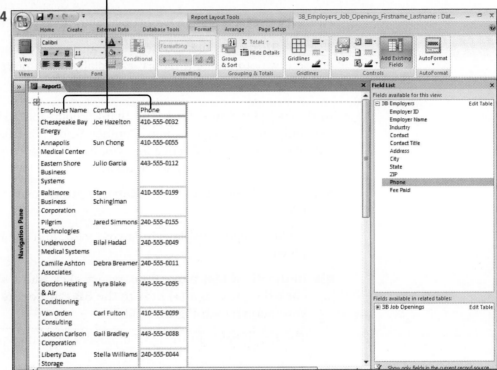

5 **Close** ✕ the **Field List** pane. Click the field name **Employer Name** to surround it with an orange border and to select the column. Point to the right edge of the orange border to display the ↔ pointer, and then drag to the right until the name for *Baltimore Management Association* (toward the bottom of the list) displays on one line and there is a small amount of space between the name and the next column.

6 Using the technique you just practiced, widen the **Contact** field so that all the names display on one line and some space is allowed between the end of the longest name and the beginning of the next column. Compare your screen with Figure Figure 3.35.

Figure 3.35

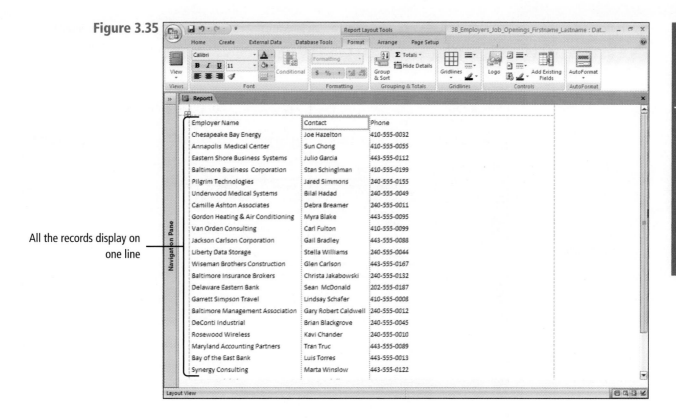

All the records display on one line

7 On the **Format tab**, in the **Controls group**, click the **Date & Time** button. In the displayed **Date and Time** dialog box, click **OK**.

In the **Controls group**, click the **Title** button, and then using your own name, type **3B Employer Phone List Firstname Lastname** In the **AutoFormat group**, click the **AutoFormat** button, and then apply the **Trek** AutoFormat. With the title still selected, in the **Font group**, change the **Font Size** 11 to **14**.

8 Click the field name **Employer Name** to select it, hold down ⌂Shift, and then click the **Contact** field name and the **Phone** field name. On the **Format tab**, in the **Font group**, click the **Center** button.

9 In the upper left corner of the report, click the small brown **layout selector** button, and then drag it to the right until the pointer is positioned approximately below the *P* in the word *Phone*—or to whatever position appears to center the group of controls horizontally between the dotted margin lines. Compare your screen with Figure 3.36.

Apply the AutoFormat first, and then edit other formatting. Recall that by using the layout selector button, you can move the entire

Figure 3.36

Field names formatted and centered over data

Date and Time inserted (yours will vary)

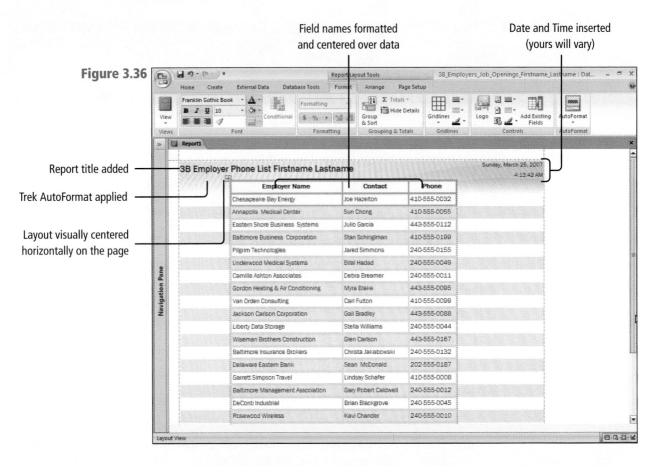

Report title added

Trek AutoFormat applied

Layout visually centered horizontally on the page

layout of the label and text box controls to easily center the entire layout on the page visually.

10 To print your report, on the status bar, click the **Print Preview** button ⬛. On the **Print Preview tab**, in the **Print group**, click **Print** to print the report. Or, submit electronically as directed.

11 On the **Print Preview tab**, in the **Close Preview group**, click the **Close Print Preview** button, and then **Close** ✖ the report. In the displayed message box, click **Yes** to save the changes to the design of the report. In the **Save As** dialog box, type **3B Employer Phone List** and then click **OK**.

12 **Open** ⏩ the **Navigation Pane**. Notice that in this Navigation Pane arrangement—Tables and Related Views—reports display below the table with which they are associated. Notice also that report objects display a small green notebook icon, which visually identifies them as reports. **Close** ⏪ the **Navigation Pane**.

Objective 8
Create a Report by Using the Report Wizard

Use the **Report Wizard** when you need flexibility and want to control the report content and design. The Report Wizard enables you to specify how the data is grouped and sorted, and you can use fields from more than one table or query, provided you have specified the relationships between the tables and queries beforehand.

The Report Wizard is similar to the Form Wizard; it creates a report by asking you a series of questions and then designs the report based on your answers.

Activity 3.13 Creating a Report by Using the Report Wizard

The Greater Baltimore Area Job Fair database includes data regarding employment information such as industry sectors, employers, job openings, and annual salaries. Based on the data that has been collected, Janna would like to have a report that shows groupings by industry, employer, and the total fees paid by employers for renting a booth at the Job Fair.

1 On the **Create tab**, in the **Reports group**, click **Report Wizard**.

The Report Wizard displays with its first question. Here you select the tables or queries from which you want to get information, and then select the fields that you want to include in the report. You can also choose from more than one table or query.

2 Click the **Tables/Queries arrow**, and then click **Table: 3B**

Employers. Using either the **One Field** button $\boxed{>}$ or by double-clicking the field name, move the following fields to the **Selected Fields** list in the order given: **Industry**, **Employer Name**, and **Fee Paid** (scroll down as necessary to find the *Fee Paid* field). Click **Next**.

The Report Wizard displays its second question. Here you decide if you want to add any grouping levels.

3 With **Industry** selected, click the **One Field** $\boxed{>}$ button, and then compare your screen with Figure 3.37.

Figure 3.37

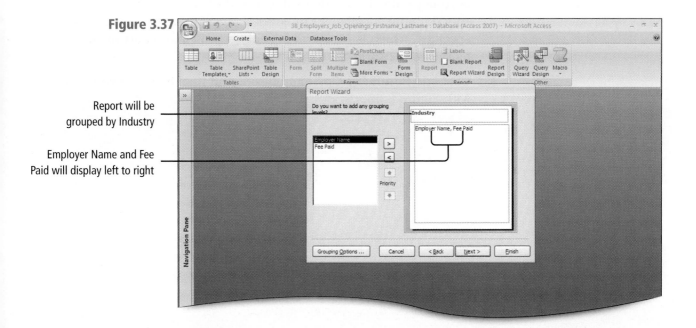

Report will be grouped by Industry

Employer Name and Fee Paid will display left to right

Grouping data helps you organize and summarize the data in your report. Grouping data in a report places all of the records that have the same data in a field together as a group—in this instance, each *Industry* will display as a group.

4 Click **Next**. In the **1** box, on the right, click the **arrow**, and then click **Employer Name**. Compare your screen with Figure 3.38.

Here you decide how you want to sort and summarize the information. You can sort on up to four fields. The Summary Options button displays because the data is grouped and contains numerical or

Select the fields you want to sort by here

Use to change the sort order from Ascending to Descending

Figure 3.38

Summary Options button displays because numerical or currency fields included

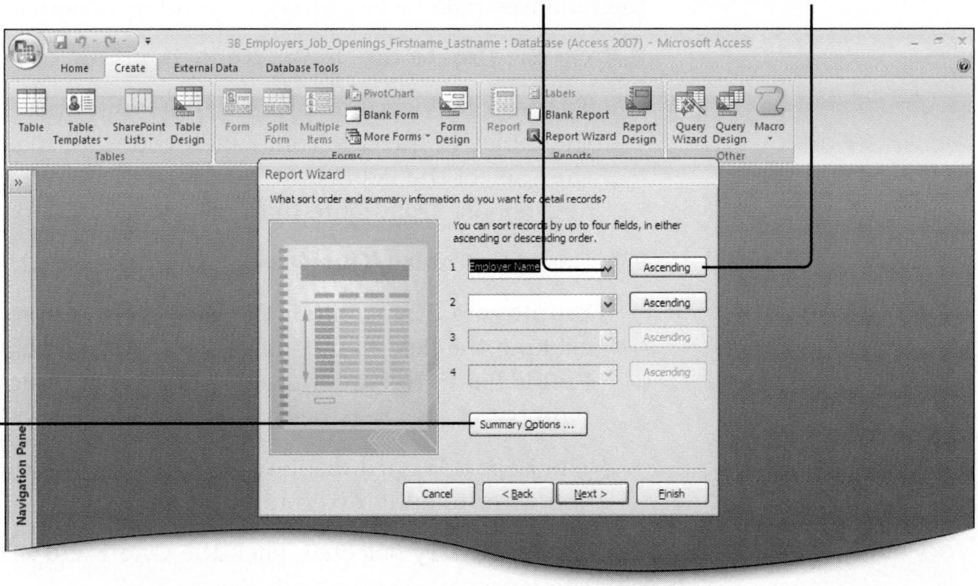

currency data. This action will cause the records in the report to be sorted alphabetically by Employer Name within the grouping option specified, which is *Industry.* Sorting records in a report presents a more organized report.

5 Click the **Summary Options** button, and then compare your screen with Figure 3.39.

Choose to show details and
summary or only summary information

Figure 3.39

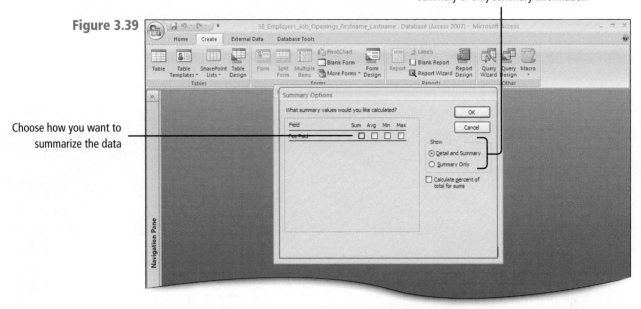

Choose how you want to
summarize the data

The Summary Options dialog box displays. Here you can choose to
display only summary information or to display both details—each
record—and the summary information. The Fee Paid field can be
summarized by selecting one of the four options displayed—Sum,
Avg, Min, or Max.

6 To the right of **Fee Paid**, select the **Sum** check box. Under **Show**, be
sure the **Detail and Summary** option button is selected, and then
click **OK**. Click **Next**.

Here you select the layout and the page orientation. The box on the
left displays a preview of the currently selected layout.

7 Click each **Layout** option button and view the options, and then
click the **Stepped** option button to select it as the layout for your
report. On the right side of the dialog box, under **Orientation**, be
sure **Portrait** is selected, and at the bottom be sure the **Adjust the
field width so all fields fit on a page** check box is selected.

8 Click **Next**. In the displayed list of styles, click one or more styles to
view the preview to the right.

9 Click the **Median** style, and then click the **Next** button. In the **What
title do you want for your report?** text box, name the report **3B
Booth Fees by Industry** and then click the **Finish** button. Compare
your screen with Figure 3.40.

The report is named and displays in Print Preview. This step also
saves the report with the name that you entered as the report title.

Each of the specifications you defined in the Report Wizard is
reflected in the report, although some data is not completely visible.
The records are grouped by Industry, and then within each Industry,

the Employer Names are alphabetized. In a manner similar to an Excel spreadsheet, numeric data that does not fit into the space may display as a series of # signs. Within each Industry grouping, the Fee Paid is summarized—the word *Sum* displays at the end of the grouping. However, some information is not fully displayed.

indicates data too wide for field

Figure 3.40

Report displays in Print Preview

Data grouped by Industry

Records sorted by Employer Name

Summary information included

Fees summed by Industry

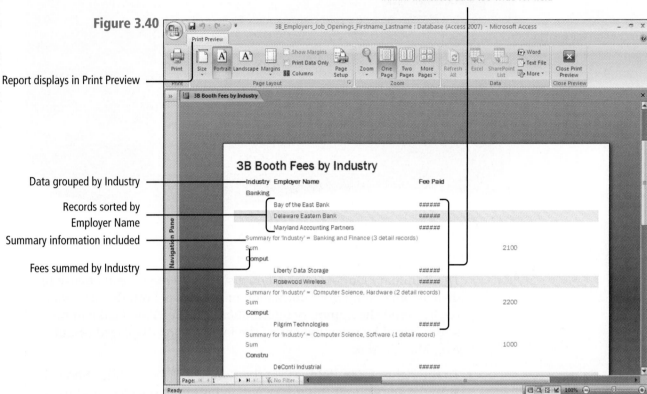

10 In the **Zoom group**, click the **Two Pages** button.

As currently formatted, the report will print on two pages.

11 In the lower right corner of your screen, on the status bar, click the **Layout View** button to switch to Layout view, and leave the report open in this view for the next activity.

Objective 9
Modify the Design of a Report

After a report is created, you can modify its design by using tools and techniques similar to those you used to modify the design of a form. You can change the format of controls, add controls, remove controls, or change the placement of controls in the report. Most report modifications can be made in Layout view.

Activity 3.14 Modifying a Report in Layout View

In your *3B Booth Fees by Industry* report, under the *Industry* heading, several of the industry names are truncated—not fully displayed.

Likewise, some of the amounts under Fee Paid are not fully displayed and display as # signs. You can modify the controls on a report to accommodate the data that displays.

In this activity, you will adjust the size and position of the controls so that the data is visible and attractively presented.

1 Be sure that your **3B Booth Fees by Industry** report displays in Layout view; if necessary click the Layout View button on the status bar.

2 In the upper left corner of the report, click to select the **Industry label control** to surround it with an orange border and to select the column. Point to the right side of the selected label control to display

Fees not fully displayed and display as ####

Figure 3.41

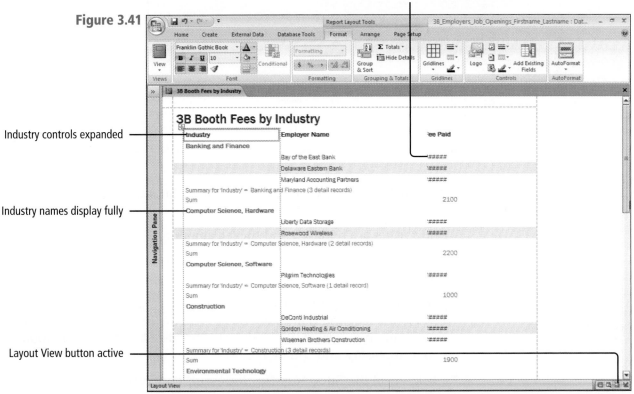

Industry controls expanded

Industry names display fully

Layout View button active

the ↔ pointer, and then drag to the right until the right edge is aligned under the *I* in *Industry* in the Report Header above. Compare your screen with Figure 3.41.

3 Click to select the **Fee Paid label control**, and then drag its right edge to the right just slightly inside the dotted margin. Then drag the left side of the control to the right to shorten the control and leave a

Left side of control shortened   Right side of control moved to right margin

Figure 3.42

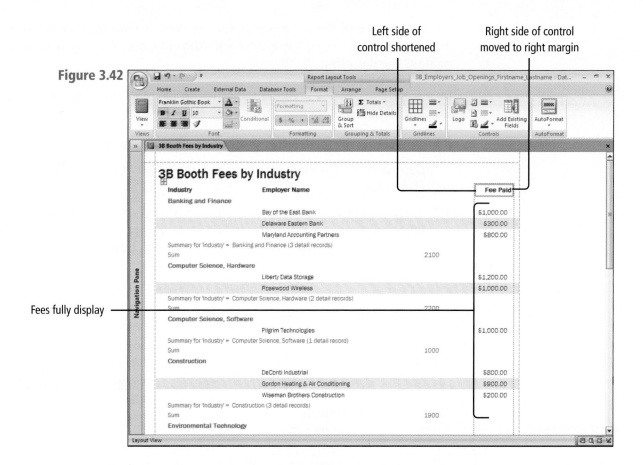

Fees fully display

small amount of space to the left of the dollar signs ($) in the fees. Compare your screen with Figure 3.42.

The # signs are removed and the fee amounts display fully.

4 Within each Industry grouping, notice the **Summary for 'Industry'** information.

Access includes a summary line that details what is being summarized (summed) and how many records are included in the total. Now that Janna has viewed the report, she has decided this information is not necessary and can be removed.

5 Click any of the **Summary for 'Industry' controls**.

The control that you clicked is surrounded by an orange border and all the others are surrounded by paler borders to indicate that all are selected.

6 Right-click any of the selected controls, and then from the displayed shortcut menu, click **Delete**. Alternatively, press [Del].

7 In the **Fee Paid** field, click any of the fee amounts to select these controls. Right-click any of the selected controls, and then from the displayed shortcut menu, click **Properties**. In the displayed **Property Sheet**, click the **Format tab**.

Property Sheet

Figure 3.43

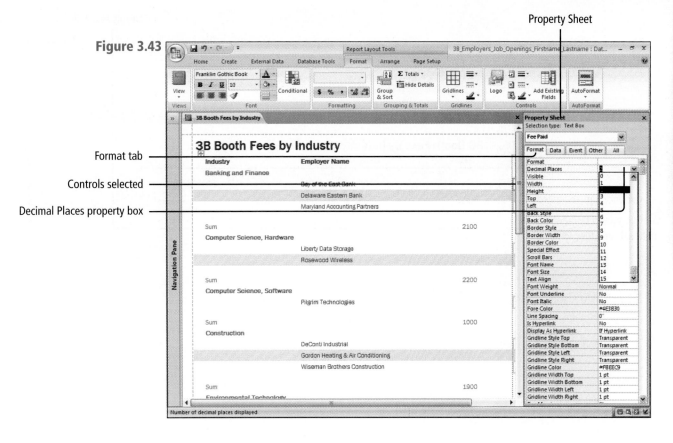

Format tab

Controls selected

Decimal Places property box

8 In the **Property Sheet**, on the **Format tab**, click the name of the second property—**Decimal Places**—and then click the **arrow** that displays. Compare your screen with Figure 3.43.

9 In the displayed list, click **0**. **Close** ☒ the **Property Sheet**.

The fees display with no decimal places.

10 In the **Banking and Finance grouping** of the report, to the right of the word *Sum*, click **2100** to select these controls. Point to any of the selected controls, right-click, and then from the displayed shortcut menu, click **Properties**.

These amounts would be more relevant if they included currency formatting to indicate that they are the sum of the fees paid within each industry grouping.

The summary controls are examples of *calculated controls*—controls that contain an expression—often a formula—that uses one or more fields from the underlying table or query.

11 In the **Property Sheet**, on the **Format tab**, click the name of the first property—**Format**—and then click the arrow that displays to the right.

12 In the displayed list of formats, click **Currency**. Click the **Decimal Places** property box, click the **arrow** that displays, and then click **0**.

Close ☒ the **Property Sheet**.

13 With the ↔ pointer, drag the right side of any of the selected controls to the right, just inside the dotted margin line. After you release the mouse button adjust as necessary so that the summed amounts

Figure 3.44

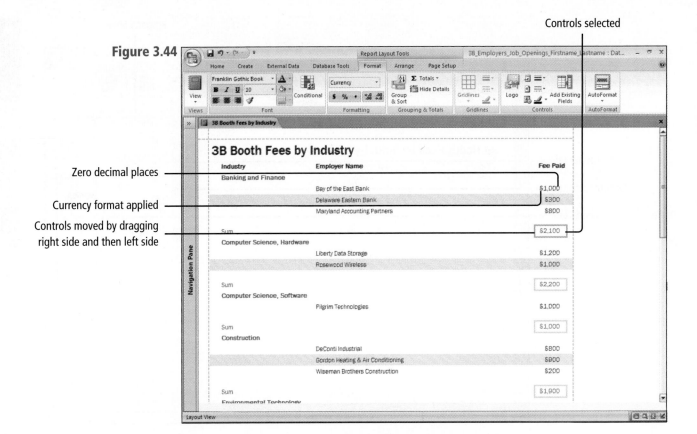

Controls selected

Zero decimal places

Currency format applied

Controls moved by dragging right side and then left side

display directly under the fees above. Then, shorten the control by dragging the left side to the right with just enough space to accommodate the data. Compare your screen with Figure 3.44.

14 On the left side of the report, click one of the **Sum** controls to select these controls, and then click again to place the insertion point inside the selected control. Alternatively, double-click to place the insertion point inside the control.

15 Delete the text, type **Total Fees by Industry** and then press Enter. Notice that the label is on the left side of the page, but the Fee Paid to which it refers is on the right.

The new text more clearly states what is being summed, however, the label would be more useful positioned next to the summary value.

16 Use the ↔ pointer to lengthen the right side of the control so that it

Figure 3.45

Access | chapter 3

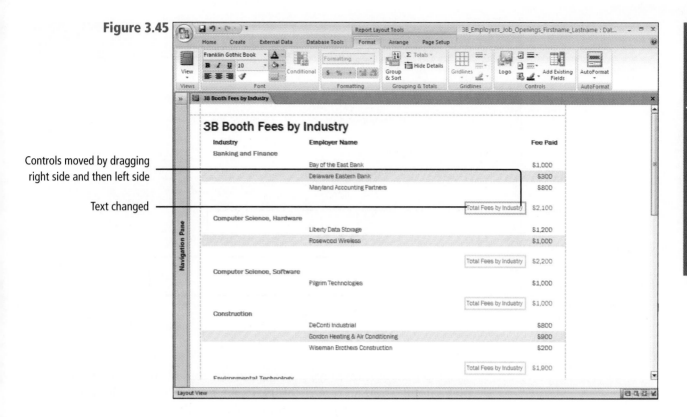

Controls moved by dragging right side and then left side

Text changed

is slightly to the left of the total amount, and then shorten the left side so that the control accommodates the text with no extra space. Compare your screen with Figure 3.45.

17 At the top of your report, click to select the **Industry label control**, hold down ⇧Shift, and then click the **Employer Name label control** and the **Fee Paid label control**. In the **Font group**, click the **Italic** button I , and then click the **Bold** button B .

18 Scroll downward to view the end of the report. Click to select the sum **17300**, which is the Grand Total for all fees paid. Using the techniques you have practiced, display the **Property Sheet** for this control and change its format to **Currency** with **0 Decimal Places**. **Close** X the **Property Sheet**, and then adjust each side of the control to position it below the other fees.

19 By adjusting the right and left sides of the control, move the text *Grand Total* to the immediate left of **$17,300**. Compare your screen with Figure 3.46.

The *Grand Total* amount is the ***report footer*** and displays at the end of the data. The current date and the page number information that display on the bottom of the page is the ***page footer***.

Figure 3.46

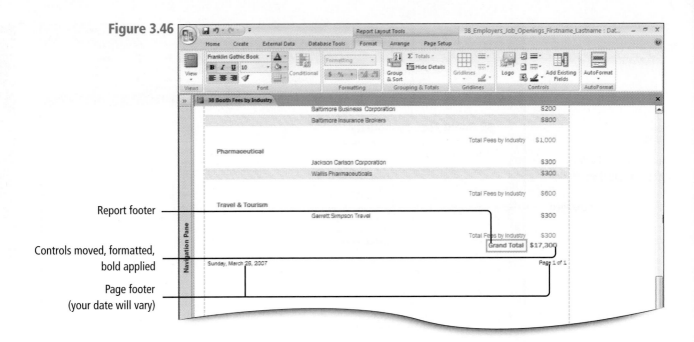

Report footer

Controls moved, formatted, bold applied

Page footer (your date will vary)

The report footer displays one time at the end of the data, and displays items such as report totals. It displays *only* if the data has been summarized. A page footer displays at the bottom of every page of the report.

20 On the **Quick Access Toolbar**, click **Save**. Leave your report open in Layout view for the next activity.

Activity 3.15 Modifying a Report in Design View

Design view gives you a more detailed view of the structure of your report. You can see the header and footer bands for the report, for the page, and for groups. In Design view, your report is not actually running, so you cannot see the underlying data while you are working. However some tasks, such as adding labels and images, are accomplished in Design view. In this activity you will add a label to the Page Footer section of your *3B Booth Fees by Industry* report and insert identifying information there.

1 Be sure that your **3B Booth Fees by Industry** report is displayed in Layout view. Press Ctrl + Home to display the top of the report. On the right end of the status bar, click the **Design View** button ![icon]. Compare your screen with Figure 3.47.

You can see that the Design view for a report is similar to the Design view of a form. You can also modify the layout of the report here, and use the dotted grid pattern to align controls. This report contains a **Report Header**, a **Page Header**, a **Group Header**, which in this instance is the *Industry* grouping, a Detail section that displays the data, a **Group Footer** (Industry), a Page Footer, and a Report Footer.

The Report Header displays information at the top of the *first page* of a report. The Page Header displays information at the top of *every page* of a report. The Group Header and Group Footer displays the field label by which the data has been grouped—*Industry* in this

Figure 3.47

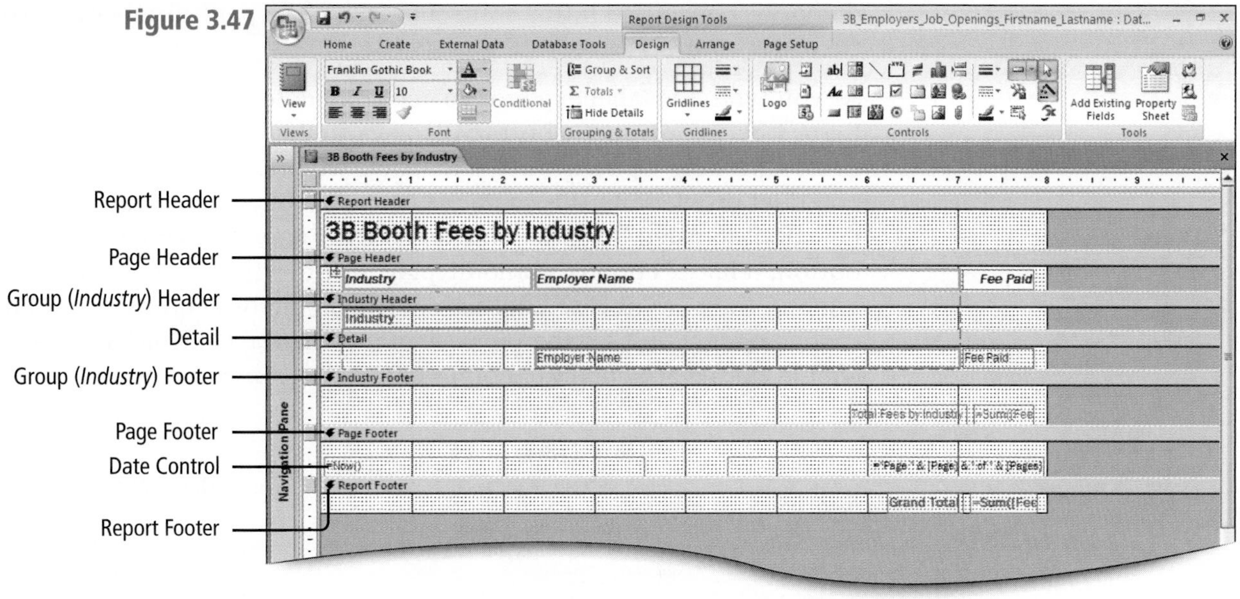

Report Header

Page Header

Group (*Industry*) Header

Detail

Group (*Industry*) Footer

Page Footer

Date Control

Report Footer

instance. If you do not group data in a report, the Group Header does not display. Similarly, if you do not summarize data, the Group Footer does not display.

2 Locate the **Page Footer** section of the report and examine the two controls in this section.

The **date control** on the left, identified as =*Now( )*, inserts the current date each time the report is opened. The **page number control** on the right, identified as =*"Page" & [Page] & "of"" & [Pages]*, inserts the page number, for example Page 1 of 2, in the report when the report is displayed in Print Preview or when you print the report. Both of these are examples of programming code that is used by Access to create controls in a report.

3 In the **Page Footer** section, click to select the **date control**. Shorten this control by dragging the right sizing handle to the left to **1.75 inches on the horizontal ruler**.

The Page Footer displays information at the bottom of *every page* in the report, including the page number and the current date inserted by those controls.

4 Click the **page number control** on the right. Shorten this control by dragging the left sizing handle to the right to **5.5 inches on the horizontal ruler**.

5 On the **Design tab**, in the **Controls group**, click the **Label** button **Aa**, and then in the **Page Footer** section, position the **+** portion of the pointer vertically in the middle of the section and horizontally at **2 inches on the horizontal ruler**. Click one time, and then using your own name, type **3B Booth Fees by Industry Firstname Lastname** Press Enter to select the control. If necessary, hold down Ctrl, and then press ↑ to align the top edge even with the other two controls, but do not be concerned if this control overlaps the page number control. Compare your screen with Figure 3.48.

As you type, the label expands to accommodate your typing. The Error Checking Options button displays to the left of the label. The Error Checking Options button displays when Access detects a potential problem. In this instance, the control you have added is a new unassociated label. If you clicked the Error Checking Options button, a list of options would display, one of which is to associate—attach—the new label to another control so the two controls could be treated as one unit for the purpose of moving the controls. This label should not be attached to another control so you can ignore this

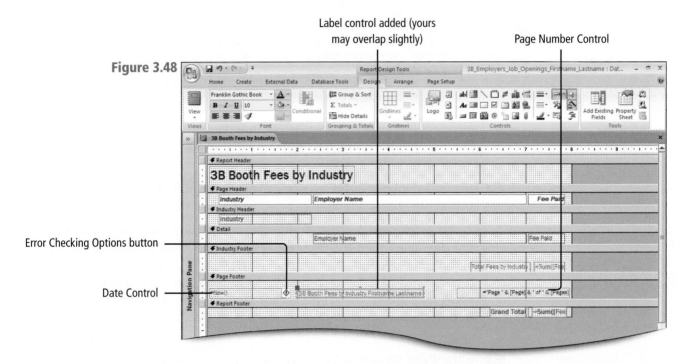

Figure 3.48

option button. A green triangle displays in the upper left corner of the affected control.

6 With the label control selected, on the **Design tab**, in the **Font group**, click the **Font Color button arrow** ▲▾, and then under **Access Theme Colors**, click **Access Theme 1**. On the **Quick Access Toolbar**, click **Save** 🖫. At the right edge of the status bar, click the **Report View** button 🔲. Scroll to the bottom of the page and compare your screen with Figure 3.49.

Figure 3.49

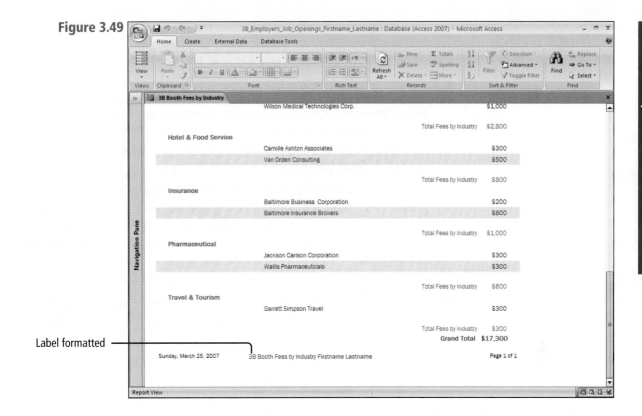

Label formatted

The new label displays with your name and the font color.

Objective 10
Print a Report and Keep Data Together

Before you print a report, examine the preview of the report to ensure that all of the labels and data are fully displayed, and to make sure that all of the data is properly grouped. Sometimes a page break occurs in the middle of a group of data, leaving the labels on one page and the data or totals on another page.

Activity 3.16 Keeping Data Together and Printing a Report

It is possible to keep the data in a group together so it does not break across a page unless, of course, the data itself exceeds the length of a page.

1 From the **Office** menu, point to the **Print** button, and then click **Print Preview**. In the **Zoom group**, click the **One Page** button. Click the **Zoom button arrow**, and then click **Zoom 100%**. Scroll to the bottom of the report to see where the first page ends, and then at the bottom of the screen, click the **Next Page** button and scroll to view the top of **Page 2**. Alternatively, in the Zoom group, click the Two Pages button to see a reduced view of the pages side by side.

This report prints on two pages. The data in the *Insurance* group is split between page 1 and 2, with one employer at the bottom of page 1 and the second employer at the top of page 2.

2 On the **Print Preview tab**, in the **Close Preview group**, click **Close Print Preview**. Click the **Layout View** button 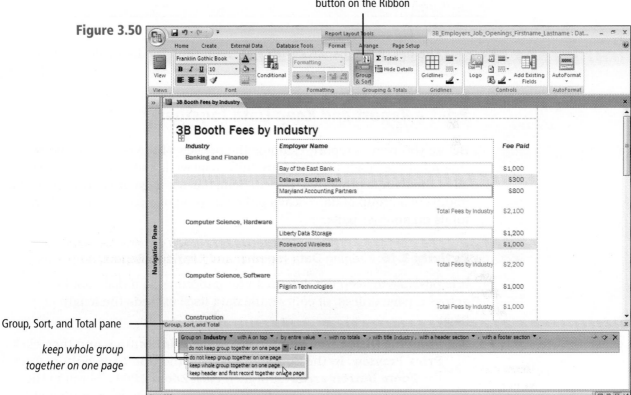 on the status bar. On the **Format tab**, in the **Grouping and Totals group**, point to the **Group & Sort** button, and then read its ScreenTip. Then click the **Group & Sort** button.

At the bottom of your screen, the ***Group, Sort, and Total pane*** displays. Here you can control how information is sorted and grouped. This pane gives you the most flexibility when you want to add or modify groups, sort orders, or totals options on a report. Layout view is the preferred view in which to accomplish such tasks, because you can see how your changes affect the display of the data.

3 In the **Group, Sort, and Total** pane, on the **Group on Industry bar**, click the **More** button, click the **arrow** to the right of **do not keep**

Group, Sort, and Total
button on the Ribbon

Figure 3.50

Group, Sort, and Total pane

keep whole group together on one page

group together on one page, and then point to **keep whole group together on one page**. Compare your screen with Figure 3.50.

4 Click **keep whole group together on one page**, and then click the **with A on top arrow**. In the displayed list, click **with A on top,** which indicates this field is sorting in ascending order. Compare your screen with Figure 3.51.

Figure 3.51

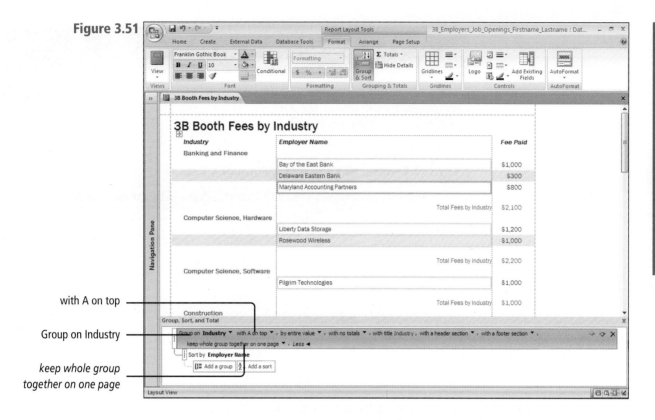

with A on top

Group on Industry

keep whole group together on one page

The *keep whole group together on one page* command will keep each employer together as a group, from the name in the group header, through the summary in the group footer.

5 On the Ribbon, in the **Grouping & Totals group**, click the **Group & Sort** button again to close the **Group, Sort & Total** pane. From the **Office** 🔲 menu, point to the **Print** button, and then click **Print Preview**. Display the top of **Page 2** to verify that the two records and total for the **Insurance** group display together as a group.

6 On the **Print Preview tab**, in the **Print group**, click the **Print** button to print the report. Or, submit electronically as directed.

7 On the **Print Preview tab**, in the **Close Preview group**, click the **Close Print Preview** button. **Close** ❌ the report, and then click **Yes** to save the changes to the design of your report. **Close** the database and close Access.

End You have completed Project 3B ————————

There's More You Can Do!

From My Computer, navigate to the student files that accompany this textbook. In the folder **02_theres_more_you_can_do_pg1_36**, locate and open the folder for this chapter. Open and print the instructions for this project, which are provided to you in Adobe PDF format.

Try IT! 1—Insert a Logo into a Form or a Report

In this Try IT! exercise, you will insert a logo into an Access form.

Content-Based Assessments

Summary

A form is a tool for either entering or viewing information in a database. Although you can both enter and view database information in the database table itself, using a form is easier because it can display one record at a time. The Form tool creates an instant form based on the fields in the table. Using the Form Wizard, you can create a customized form. Once created, a form can be modified in Layout view or in Design View.

Reports in Access summarize the data in a database in a professional-looking manner suitable for printing. The Report tool, the Blank Report tool, and the Report Wizard assist in report creation. The design of a report can be modified so that the final report is laid out in a format that is useful for the person reading it.

Key Terms

Content-Based Assessments

Matching

Match each term in the second column with its correct definition in the first column by writing the letter of the term on the blank line in front of the correct definition.

_____ **1.** An Access object with which you can enter, edit, or display data from a table or a query; a window for displaying and collecting information.

_____ **2.** The action of typing a record into a database.

_____ **3.** The Access tool that creates a form with a single mouse click, and that includes all the fields from the underlying data source (table or query).

_____ **4.** The Access view in which you can make changes to a form or to a report while the form is running, and in which the data from the underlying record source displays.

_____ **5.** The term used to describe objects and controls that are based on data that is stored in tables.

_____ **6.** The order in which the insertion point moves from one field to the next in a form when you press the Tab key.

_____ **7.** The bar on the left side of a form with which you can select the entire record.

_____ **8.** The detailed structured view of a form or report, and the view in which some tasks must be performed; only the controls, and not the data, are visible in this view.

_____ **9.** Information, such as a form's title, which displays at the top of the screen in Form view, and that is printed at the top of the first page when records are printed as forms.

_____ **10.** The section of a form or report that displays the records from the underlying table or query.

_____ **11.** Information at the bottom of the screen in Form view that is printed after the last detail section on the last page.

_____ **12.** In Design view, a gray bar in a form or report that identifies and separates one section from another; used to select the section and to change the size of the adjacent section.

_____ **13.** Objects on a form or report that display data, perform actions, and let you view and work with information.

_____ **14.** The graphical object on a form or report that displays the data from the underlying table or query.

_____ **15.** A control on a form or report that contains descriptive information, typically a field name.

A Bound

B Controls

C Data entry

D Design view

E Detail section

F Form

G Form footer

H Form header

I Form tool

J Label

K Layout view

L Record selector

M Section bar

N Tab order

O Text box control

Content-Based Assessments

Fill in the Blank

Write the correct answer in the space provided.

1. A control that does not have a source of data is an _____ control.

2. The small boxes around the edge of a control indicating the control is selected and that can be adjusted to resize the selected control are _____ handles.

3. The grouped arrangement of controls on a form or report is referred to as the _____ layout.

4. A small symbol that displays in the upper left corner of a selected control layout, and with which you can move the entire group of controls is the _____ _____.

5. A list of characteristics for controls on a form or report in which you can make precision changes to each control is the _____ Sheet.

6. The process of displaying only a portion of the total records (a subset) based on matching specific values is called _____.

7. An Access command that retrieves only the records that contain the value in the selected field is called _____ _____ _____.

8. An Access command that filters the records in a form based on one or more fields, or based on more than one value in the same field is called _____ _____ _____.

9. A condition in which only records where one of two values is present in the selected field is the _____ condition.

10. A condition in which only records where both specified values are present in the selected fields is a(n) _____ condition.

11. A database object that summarizes the fields and records from a table, or from a query, in an easy-to-read format suitable for printing is a(n) _____.

12. The tables or queries that provide the underlying data for a report are referred to as the _____ _____.

13. The Access feature that creates a report with one mouse click, and which displays all the fields and records from the record source that you choose is the _____ _____.

Content-Based Assessments

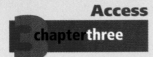

Fill in the Blank

14. An Access feature with which you can create a report from scratch by adding the fields you want in the order you want them to appear is the _____ _____ _____.

15. A control whose source of data is an expression—typically a formula—rather than a field is called a _____ control.

Content-Based Assessments

Skills Review

Project 3C—Counseling Sessions

In this project, you will apply the skills you practiced from the Objectives in Project 3A.

Objectives: 1. *Create a Form;* **2.** *Use a Form To Add and Delete Records;* **3.** *Create a Form by Using the Form Wizard;* **4.** *Modify a Form in Design View and in Layout View;* **5.** *Filter Records.*

At the Job Fair, various professional organizations schedule personal one-on-one counseling sessions with interested candidates to give them advice about opportunities in the fields they represent. Janna Sorokin, the database manager, has a database in which she is tracking the counseling sessions that have been scheduled thus far. Your completed database objects will look similar to those in Figure 3.52.

For Project 3C, you will need the following file:

a3C_Counseling_Sessions

You will save your database as
3C_Counseling_Sessions_Firstname_Lastname

Figure 3.52

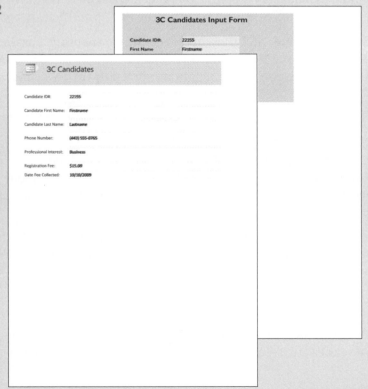

(Project 3C–Counseling Sessions continues on the next page)

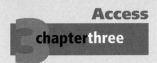

Access

Skills Review

(Project 3C–Counseling Sessions continued)

1. Open **My Computer** and navigate to the location where the student files that accompany this textbook are located. Click once to select the file **a3C_Counseling_Sessions**; copy and then paste the file to your chapter folder. Rename the file **3C_Counseling_Sessions_Firstname_Lastname**

2. Close **My Computer**, start Access, and then open your **3C_Counseling_Sessions** database. If necessary, enable the content. Click the **Database Tools tab**, and then in the **Show/Hide group**, click the **Relationships** button. Examine the one-to-many relationship, and then **Close** the Relationships window. *One* candidate can attend *many* counseling sessions.

3. From the **Navigation Pane**, select the **3C Counseling Sessions table**, and then on the **Create tab**, in the **Forms group**, click **Form**. **Close** the **Navigation Pane**. Click the **Next record** button four times to display the record for *Session ID# 105*. Click the **Last record** button to display the record for *Session ID# 132*, and then click the **First record** button to display the record for *Session ID# 101*. Recall that you can view records one at a time in this manner by using a form. On the **Quick Access Toolbar**, click the **Save** button. In the displayed **Save As** dialog box, edit as necessary to name the form **3C Counseling Sessions Form** and then click **OK**. As additional candidates schedule sessions, you can use this form to enter the data into the 3C Counseling Sessions table. **Close** the form object.

4. From the **Navigation Pane**, select the **3C Candidates table**, click the **Create tab**, and then in the **Forms group**, click **Form**. **Close** the **Navigation Pane**. Notice that the form displays the scheduled sessions for the first candidate's record. On the **Quick Access Toolbar**, click **Save**, name the form **3C Candidates Form** and then click **OK**. **Close** the form object. As new candidates register, you can use this form to enter the data into the Candidates table.

5. **Open** the **Navigation Pane**, and then open the **3C Counseling Sessions Form**. **Close** the **Navigation Pane**. Click the **New (blank) record** button. In the **Session ID#** field, type **133** and then press Tab. Continue entering the data as shown in the following table:

Candidate ID#	Counseling Session Host	Counselor
10776	Graphic Arts Professionals	Connie Rogers

6. **Close** the **3C Counseling Sessions Form**—the record is added to the associated table. **Open** the **Navigation Pane**, open the **3C Candidates Form**, and then **Close** the **Navigation Pane**. Click the **New (blank) record** button. Using your own first and last name, fill in the form using the information in the following table:

Candidate ID#	Candidate First Name	Candidate Last Name	Phone Number	Professional Interest	Registration Fee	Date Fee Collected
22155	Firstname	Lastname	(443) 555-0765	Business	$15.00	10/10/2009

7. **Close** the **3C Candidates form**, **Open** the **Navigation Pane**, open the **3C Candidates table**, and then verify that your record as a candidate displays as the last record in the table. **Close** the table.

(Project 3C–Counseling Sessions continues on the next page)

Content-Based Assessments

(Project 3C–Counseling Sessions continued)

8. From the **Navigation Pane**, open the **3C Counseling Sessions Form**. **Close** the **Navigation Pane**. Click in the **Session ID#** field, and then on the **Home tab**, in the **Find group**, click the **Find** button. In the **Look In** box, notice that *Session ID#* is indicated, and then in the **Find What** box, type **106** Click **Find Next**, and then confirm that the record for **Session ID# 106** displays. **Close** the **Find and Replace** dialog box.

9. On the **Home tab**, in the **Records group**, click the **Delete button arrow**, and then in the displayed list, click **Delete Record**. Click **Yes** to delete the record, and notice that the number of records in the table is *32*. **Close** the form object.

10. From the **Navigation Pane**, open the **3C Counseling Sessions table**. Examine the table and verify that the record for *Session ID# 106* no longer displays. Then, verify that the new record you added for **Session ID# 133** is included in the table. **Close** the table.

11. From the **Navigation Pane**, open the **3C Candidates Form**. **Close** the **Navigation Pane**. Press [Ctrl] + [F] to display the **Find and Replace** dialog box. In the **Find What** box, type **22155** In the **Look In** box, be sure that *Candidate ID#* is indicated, and then click **Find Next** to display the record with your name. **Close** the dialog box. With this record displayed, from the **Office** menu, click **Print**. In the displayed **Print** dialog box, under **Print Range**, click the **Selected Record(s)** option button. Click the **Setup** button, click the **Columns tab**, and then under **Column Size**, in the **Width** box, delete the existing text and type **7"** Click **OK** two times to print only your record in the form layout, or submit electronically as directed. **Close** the **3C Candidates form**.

12. **Open** the **Navigation Pane**, and then select the **3C Candidates table**. On the **Create tab**, in the **Forms group**, click the **More Forms button**, and then in the displayed list, click **Form Wizard**. Click the **Tables/Queries arrow**, and then in the displayed list, click **Table: 3C Candidates**. Move the following fields to the **Selected Fields** list in the order given: **Candidate First Name**, **Candidate Last Name**, **Professional Interest**, and **Phone Number**. Click **Next**. Be sure **Columnar** is selected, and then click **Next**. Click **Solstice**, click **Next**, name the form **3C Candidates Input Form** and then click **Finish** to close the wizard and create the form.

13. **Close** the **Navigation Pane** and be sure your **3C Candidates Input Form** displays. Click the **Design View** button; if necessary close the Field List pane. Point to the upper edge of the **Detail section bar** to display the 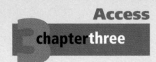 pointer, and then drag downward approximately **0.5 inch**. In the **Form Header section**, click in the title *3C Candidates Input Form* to select it. On the **Design tab**, in the **Font group**, click the **Font Size arrow**, and then click **18**. Click the **Bold** button. Click the **Font Color arrow**, and then under **Access Theme Colors**, click **Access Theme 9**.

14. Point to any **sizing handle** and double-click to fit the size of the label. Point to the upper edge of the **Detail section bar**, and then by using the 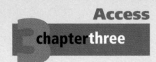 pointer, drag upward until the bar is at **0.50 inch on the vertical ruler**.

(Project 3C–Counseling Sessions continues on the next page)

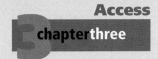
(Project 3C–Counseling Sessions continued)

15. Expand the lower edge of the **Form Footer section bar** approximately **0.50 inch**. On the **Design tab,** in the **Controls group**, click the **Label** button. Position the plus sign of the pointer in the **Form Footer** section at approximately **0.25 inch on the horizontal ruler** and even with the top edge of the section. Drag to the right to **5 inches on the horizontal ruler**, and then downward approximately **0.25 inch**. Using your own name, type **3C Candidates Input Form Firstname Lastname** and then press Enter. Double-click a sizing handle to fit the label to the text you typed. On the status bar, click the **Form View** button. On the **Quick Access Toolbar**, **Save** the changes you have made thus far.

16. On the status bar, click the **Layout View** button. In the **Controls group**, click the **Add Existing Fields** button to display the **Field List** pane. Point to **Candidate ID#**, and then drag to position the pointer in the upper portion of the white **Candidate First Name** text box control until a thick orange line displays above the control. Release the mouse button. **Close** the **Field List** pane. Click the white text box control for **Candidate ID#**, which currently displays *10115*, to surround it with an orange border. Point to the right edge of the white text box control, and then drag to the left until all of the white text box controls align under the *m* in the form title above.

17. Click the white text box control for **Phone Number**, which currently displays *(443) 555-0054*. With the control selected, drag upward with the 🔲 pointer until a thick orange line displays above **Professional Interest**. Release the mouse button to place the **Phone Number control** above the **Professional Interest control**. Click the **Candidate First Name label** to select it, and then click again to place the insertion point in the control. Edit the **Candidate First Name** and **Candidate Last Name** labels so that the labels indicate *First Name* and *Last Name*. On the **Quick Access Toolbar**, **Save** the changes you have made.

18. Click in a shaded area of the form to deselect any controls. Hold down ⇧Shift, and then click to select each of the five **white text box controls**. On the **Format tab**, in the **Font group**, click the **Fill/Back Color** button arrow. Under **Access Theme Colors**, click **Access Theme 3**. Click the **Font Size button arrow,** and then click **12**. Click in a shaded area of the screen to deselect all the controls. Using the technique you just practiced, select the five labels, change the **Font Size** to **11**, change the **Font Color** to **Access Theme 9**, and then apply **Bold**.

19. Click the **Professional Interest** label, right-click, and then click **Properties**. In the **Property Sheet**, on the **Format tab**, click **Width**, and then change the width to **1.75** Click in a shaded area to deselect. Hold down ⇧Shift, and then select the blue **First Name, Last Name, Phone Number**, and **Professional Interest** text box controls. In the Property Sheet, change the Height to **0.3** and then press Enter.

20. In the **Form Footer** section, click to select the label with your name. In the displayed **Property Sheet**, change the **Left** property to **1** and then press Enter. In the **Form Header** section, click anywhere in the label text *3C Candidates Input Form*. In the **Property Sheet**, change the **Left** property to **1** and then press Enter. **Close** the **Property Sheet**. On the status bar, click the **Form View** button. Click the **Last record** button to display the record containing your name. Then, from the **Office** menu, click **Print**. Under **Print Range**, click the

(Project 3C–Counseling Sessions continues on the next page)

Content-Based Assessments

Skills Review

(Project 3C—Counseling Sessions continued)

Selected Record(s) option button. Click **OK** to print, or submit electronically as directed. **Close** the form, and then click **Yes** to save the changes you have made.

21. From the **Navigation Pane**, open the **3C Candidates Input Form**. **Close** the **Navigation Pane**. In the displayed first record, click the **Professional Interest** label. On the **Home tab**, in the **Sort & Filter group**, click the **Selection** button, and then in the displayed list, click **Equals "Business"**. Ten records indicate *Business* in the Professional Interest field. On the **Home tab**, in the **Sort & Filter group**, click **Toggle Filter** to remove the filter and activate all 22 records. Notice the **Unfiltered** button in the navigation area.

22. Be sure the first record displays, and then click to place the insertion point in the **Professional Interest** text box control. On the **Home tab**, in the **Sort & Filter group**, click the **Toggle Filter** button to reapply the filter. In the navigation area, click the **Last record** button to display the tenth record that matches *Business*. In the **Sort & Filter group**, click the **Toggle Filter** button to reactivate all of the records. In the navigation area, click the **Next record** button one time to move to **Record 2**. In the **Phone Number** field, select the Area Code text *(443)* including the parentheses. On the **Home tab**, in the **Sort & Filter group**, click the **Selection** button, and then click **Begins With "(443)"**. Nine records contain this Area Code. On the **Home tab**, in the **Sort & Filter group**, click the **Toggle Filter** button to remove the filter and reactivate all 22 records.

23. With the **3C Candidates Input Form** still open, on the **Home tab**, in the **Sort & Filter group**, click the **Advanced** button, and then click **Filter By Form**. Click the **Advanced** button again, and then click **Clear Grid**. Click the **Professional Interest** text box control, click the **arrow** at the far right edge of the control, and then click **Nursing**. In the **Sort & Filter group**, click the **Toggle Filter** button. Click in the **Professional Interest** text box again. In the **Sort & Filter group**, click the **Filter** button. Click to select the **Biology** check box, and then click **OK**. Five records meet the OR condition; that is, five candidates have a Professional Interest of either Nursing *or* Biology.

24. Click the **Toggle Filter** button to remove all filters. Close the form object, close the database, and then close Access.

 You have completed Project 3C

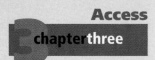

Project 3D — Workshops and Rooms

In this project, you will apply the skills you practiced from the Objectives in Project 3B.

Objectives: 6. *Create a Report by Using the Report Tool;* **7.** *Create a Report by Using the Blank Report Tool;* **8.** *Create a Report by Using the Report Wizard;* **9.** *Modify the Design of a Report;* **10.** *Print a Report and Keep Data Together.*

In the following Skills Review, you will create, modify, and print reports for Janna Sorokin regarding details about the Workshop rooms for the Job Fair. Your completed database objects will look similar to Figure 3.53.

For Project 3D, you will need the following file:

a3D_Workshops_Rooms

You will save your database as
3D_Workshops_Rooms_Firstname_Lastname

Figure 3.53

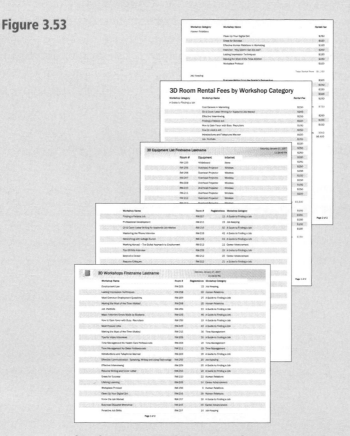

(Project 3D–Workshops and Rooms continues on the next page)

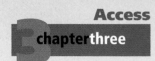
(Project 3D–Workshops and Rooms continued)

1. From the student files that accompany this text, locate the file **a3D_Workshops_Rooms**. Copy and then paste the file to your Access Chapter 3 folder. Rename the file as **3D_Workshops_Rooms_Firstname_Lastname Start** Access and open your **3D_Workshops_Rooms** database. If necessary, enable the content. Click the **Database Tools tab**, and then in the **Show/Hide group**, click the **Relationships** button to view the relationship between the two tables; one room can have many workshops. **Close** the Relationships window.

2. From the **Navigation Pane**, select the **3D Workshops table**. On the **Create tab**, in the **Reports group**, click the **Report** button, and then **Close** the **Navigation Pane**. Click to select the field name **Workshop #**, right-click over the selected name, and then click **Delete**. Click the **Rental Fee** field, and then delete it. Click to select the field name **Registrations**. On the **Format tab**, in the **Grouping & Totals group**, click the **Totals** button. In the displayed list, click **Sum**. Scroll to the bottom of the report; the total registrations for the various workshops is *988*.

3. Click the **Page Setup tab**, and then in the **Page Layout group**, click **Landscape**. Click the **Format tab**, and then in the **AutoFormat group**, click the **AutoFormat** button. Locate, and then click the **Trek** AutoFormat. In the **Report Header** at the top of the screen, double-click the header text *3D Workshops* to position the insertion point in the header. Edit as necessary to add your name to the end of the header text, and then on the **Format tab**, in the **Font group**, change the **Font Size** to **16**.

4. Click the **Workshop Name** field name, point to the right edge of the orange border to display the ⟷ pointer, and then drag to the right until each name displays on one line. Click the **Room #** field name, point to the right edge of the orange border to display the ⟷ pointer, and then drag to the left to set the column width to accommodate the longest entry with a small amount of space to the right. Click any record in the report. In the upper left corner of the report, click the small brown **layout selector** button, and then drag it to the right until the pointer is positioned approximately below the *D* in *3D* of the report header.

5. In the lower right corner of the screen, at the right edge of the status bar, click the **Print Preview** button. On the **Print Preview tab**, in the **Zoom group**, click the **Two Pages** button to view the two pages of your report. To print your report, on the **Print Preview tab**, in the **Print group**, click **Print** to print the report. Or, submit electronically as directed. On the **Print Preview tab**, in the **Close Preview group**, click the **Close Print Preview** button, and then **Close** the **3D Workshops** report. In the displayed message box, click **Yes** to save changes to the design of the report. In the **Save As** dialog box, edit the Report Name to indicate **3D Workshop Attendance Report** and then click **OK**.

6. On the **Create tab**, in the **Reports group**, click the **Blank Report** button. In the **Field List** pane, click **Show all tables**, and then click the **plus sign (+)** next to the **3D Rooms table**. Point to the **Room #** field, right-click, and then click **Add Field to View**. In the **Field List** pane, drag the **Equipment** field into the blank report—

(Project 3D–Workshops and Rooms continues on the next page)

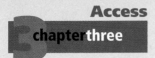
(Project 3D–Workshops and Rooms continued)

anywhere to the right of **Room #**. Double-click the **Internet** field to add it as the third field in the report. **Close** the **Field List** pane.

7. Click the **Equipment** field name, point to the right edge of the orange border to dis play the ⟷ pointer, and then drag to the right until the text *Overhead Projector* displays on one line and there is a small amount of space between the name and the next column. On the **Format tab**, in the **Controls group**, click the **Date & Time** button. In the displayed **Date and Time** dialog box, click **OK**. In the **Controls group**, click the **Title** button, and then using your own name, type **3D Equipment List Firstname Lastname** In the **AutoFormat group**, click the **AutoFormat** button, and then apply the **Trek** AutoFormat. With the title still selected, in the **Font group**, change the **Font Size** to **14**.

8. Click the field name **Room#**, hold down ⇧ Shift, click the **Equipment** and **Internet** field names, and then with the three field names selected, change the **Font Size** to **12** and apply **Bold**. By using the **layout selector** button, move the group of controls until the pointer is positioned approximately below the *t* in the word *List*—or to whatever position appears to be horizontally centered between the margins. From the status bar, click **Print Preview**, and then print the report or submit electronically as directed. **Close Print Preview**, and then **Close** the report. In the displayed message box, click **Yes** to save the changes to the design of the report. In the **Save As** dialog box, type **3D Equipment List** and then click **OK**.

9. On the **Create tab**, in the **Reports group**, click **Report Wizard**. Click the **Tables/Queries arrow**, and then click **Table: 3D Workshops**. Use the **One Field** button to move the following fields to the **Selected Fields** list in the order given: **Workshop Category**, **Workshop Name**, and **Rental Fee**. Click **Next**. With **Workshop Category** selected, click the **One Field** button to group the report by this field. Click **Next**. In the **1** box, on the right, click the **arrow**, and then click **Workshop Name** to sort by the name of the workshop. Click the **Summary Options** button. To the right of **Rental Fee**, select the **Sum** check box. Under **Show**, be sure the **Detail and Summary** option button is selected, and then click **OK**.

10. Click **Next**. Click the **Stepped** option button. On the right side of the dialog box, under **Orientation**, be sure **Portrait** is selected, and at the bottom be sure the **Adjust the field width so all fields fit on a page** check box is selected. Click **Next**. In the displayed list of styles, click the **Trek** style, and then click the **Next** button. In the **What title do you want for your report?** text box, name the report **3D Room Rental Fees by Workshop Category** and then click the **Finish** button. In the **Zoom Group**, click the **Two Pages** button, and then examine the report as currently formatted. Then, in the lower right corner of your screen, on the status bar, click the **Layout View** button.

11. Select the **Workshop Category label control**, and then widen the right side of the controls to align under the *t* in *Rental* in the Report Header above. Widen the right side of the **Rental Fee label**

(Project 3D–Workshops and Rooms continues on the next page)

Content-Based Assessments

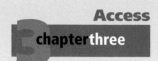
(Project 3D–Workshops and Rooms continued)

controls to just slightly inside the dotted margin. Then drag the left side of the control to the right to shorten the control and leave a small amount of space to accommodate the data.

12. Within each **Workshop Category group**, notice the **Summary for 'Workshop Category'** information. Click any of the **Summary for 'Workshop Category' controls**. Right-click any of the selected controls, and then from the displayed shortcut menu, click **Delete**. In the **Rental Fee** field, click any of the fee amounts to select these controls. Right-click any of the selected controls, and then from the displayed shortcut menu, click **Properties**. In the displayed **Property Sheet**, click the **Format tab**. In the **Property Sheet**, on the **Format tab**, click the name of the second property—**Decimal Places**—and then click the **arrow** that displays to the right of *Auto*. In the displayed list, click **0**. **Close** the **Property Sheet**. In any of the **Workshop Category groupings** of the report, to the right of the word *Sum*, click the dollar amount to select these controls. Point to any of the selected controls, right-click, and then from the displayed shortcut menu, click **Properties**. Change the number of decimal places to **0**, and then **Close** the **Property Sheet**.

13. By using the $\leftrightarrow$ pointer, move the right and then the left border to position the summed amounts directly under the fees above with just enough space to accommodate the data. On the left side of the report, click one of the **Sum** controls to select these controls, and then click again to place the insertion point inside the selected control. Alternatively, double-click to place the insertion point inside the control. Delete the text, type **Total Rental Fees**

and then press Enter. Move the controls to the immediate left of the summed amounts.

14. At the top of your report, click to select the **Workshop Category label control**, hold down ⇧ Shift, and then click the **Workshop Name**, and the **Rental Fee label control**. Apply **Italic**. Scroll down to view the end of the report. Click to select the sum **6400.00**, which is the Grand Total for all the rental fees. Display the **Property Sheet** for this control and change its format to **0 Decimal Places**. **Close** the **Property Sheet**, and then adjust each side of the control to position it below the other fees. From the **Format tab**, apply **Bold** formatting. By adjusting the right and left sides of the control, move the text *Grand Total* to the immediate left of **$6,400**, and then apply **Bold**. On the **Quick Access Toolbar**, click **Save** to save the changes you have made to your report thus far.

15. Press Ctrl + Home to display the top of the report, and then on the right end of the status bar, click the **Design View** button. Drag the upper edge of the **Page Header section bar** downward approximately **0.5 inch**. Click the **Report Header** *3D Room Rental Fees by Workshop Category*, and then change the **Font Size** to **26**. Double-click a sizing handle to fit the control to the larger text. Drag the **Page Header section bar** upward slightly to approximately **0.5 inch on the vertical ruler**.

16. In the **Page Footer** section, click to select the **date control**. Shorten this control by dragging the right sizing handle to the left to **1.75 inches on the horizontal ruler**. Click the **page number control** on the right. Shorten this control by dragging the

(Project 3D–Workshops and Rooms continues on the next page)

Content-Based Assessments

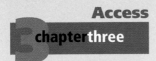

(Project 3D–Workshops and Rooms continued)

left sizing handle to the right to **5.5 inches on the horizontal ruler**. On the **Design tab**, in the **Controls group**, click the **Label** button, and then in the **Page Footer** section, position the plus sign portion of the pointer vertically in the middle of the section and horizontally at **2 inches on the horizontal ruler**. Click one time, and then using your own name, type **3D Rental Fees by Category Firstname Lastname** Press Enter to select the control. If necessary, hold down Ctrl, and then press ↑ to align the top edge even with the other two controls, but do not be concerned if this control overlaps the page number control. With the label control selected, on the **Design tab**, in the **Font group**, click the **Font Color button arrow**, and then under **Access Theme Colors**, click **Access Theme 9**. On the **Quick Access Toolbar**, click **Save**. Click the **Layout View** button.

17. On the status bar, click the **Print Preview** button. In the **Zoom group**, click the **Two Pages** button to view how your report is

currently laid out. Notice that the bottom of **Page 1** does not break at the end of a category. **Close** the **Print Preview**.

18. On the **Format tab**, in the **Grouping and Totals group**, click the **Group & Sort** button. In the **Group**, **Sort**, **and Total** pane, on the **Group on Workshop Category bar**, click the **More** button, click the arrow to the right of **do not keep group together on one page**, and then click **keep whole group together on one page**. Click the **with A on top arrow**. In the displayed list, click **with A on top**, which indicates this field is sorting in ascending order. In the **Grouping & Totals group**, click the **Group & Sort** button again to close the **Group**, **Sort & Total** pane.

19. On the status bar, click the **Print Preview** button. Print the report, or submit electronically as directed. **Close** the report, click **Yes** to save the changes to the design of your report. Close the database, and then close Access.

End **You have completed Project 3D**

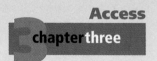

Access

chapter three

Mastering Access

Project 3E — Booth Duty

In this project, you will apply the skills you practiced from the Objectives in Project 3A.

Objectives: 1. *Create a Form;* **2.** *Use a Form To Add and Delete Records;* **3.** *Create a Form by Using the Form Wizard;* **4.** *Modify a Form in Design View and in Layout View;* **5.** *Filter Records.*

In the following Mastering Access assessment, you will assist Janna Sorokin, database manager for the Greater Baltimore Area Job Fair, in using a database to track the staff and booth duty schedule during the fair event. Your completed database objects will look similar to Figure 3.54.

For Project 3E, you will need the following file:

a3E_Booth_Duty

You will save your database as
3E_Booth_Duty_Firstname_Lastname

Figure 3.54

(Project 3E–Booth Duty continues on the next page)

Content-Based Assessments

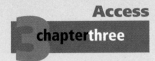

(Project 3E–Booth Duty continued)

1. From the student files that accompany this textbook, locate the file **a3E_Booth_Duty**. Copy and paste the file to your Access Chapter 3 folder. Rename the file **3E_Booth_Duty_Firstname_Lastname Start** Access and open your **3E_Booth_Duty** database. Enable the content. On the **Database Tools tab**, view the table relationships, and then **Close** the window. One staff member can be assigned many booth duties during the Job Fair event.

2. Based on the **3E Booth Duty table**, use the **Form** tool to create a new form. From the status bar, switch to Form view. Scroll through the records, and then after verifying that you can view the 48 records, **Save** and name the form **3E Booth Duty Form** Use the form to add the following new record:

Booth Duty ID#	BOOTH	STAFF ID#	Time Slot	Booth Location	Day
BD-49	BOOTH-I	STAFF-1109	8-12	South Hall	Day 1

3. Close the form, and then based on the **3E Staff table**, use the **Form** tool to create a new form. Switch to Form view, **Save** the form, name it **3E Staff Form** and then using your own first and last name, add the following new record:

STAFF ID#	Staff First Name	Staff Last Name	Phone Number	Title
STAFF-1119	Firstname	Lastname	(410) 555-0765	Assistant

4. After adding the record, display the **Print** dialog box, click the **Selected Record(s)** option button, click the **Setup** button, click the **Columns tab**, and then under **Column Size**, in the **Width** box, type **7"** Click **OK** two times to print only your record in the form layout, or submit electronically as directed. Close the **3E Staff Form**.

5. Open the **3E Staff table**, verify that your record as a staff member displays as the last record in the table, and then close the table. Open the **3E Booth Duty Form**. Display the **Find and Replace** dialog box, locate, and then delete the record for **Booth Duty ID# BD-06** Close the form. Open the **3E Booth Duty table**. Examine the table and verify that the record for **Booth Duty ID# BD-06** no longer displays. Then, look at the last record in the table, and verify that the new record that you added for **BOOTH-I** is included in the table. Close the table.

6. Based on the **3E Staff table**, use the **Form Wizard** to create a form. Add the following fields to the **Selected Fields** list in the order listed: **Staff First Name**, **Staff Last Name**, **Title**, and **Phone Number**. Select the **Columnar** layout and the **Trek** style for the form. Edit the title as necessary to name the form **3E Staff Input Form** and then click **Finish**.

(Project 3E–Booth Duty continues on the next page)

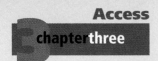

Mastering Access

(Project 3E–Booth Duty continued)

7. Switch to Design view. Expand the lower edge of the **Form Footer section bar** approximately **0.50 inch**, and then in the expanded **Form Footer section**, create a label, beginning at approximately **0.25 inch on the horizontal ruler** and even with upper edge of the section. Drag to the right to **5 inches on the horizontal ruler**, and then downward approximately **0.25 inch**. Using your own name, type **3E Staff Input Form Firstname Lastname** and then press Enter. Double-click a sizing handle to fit the control to the text you typed.

8. Switch to Layout view. Display the **Field List** pane, and then drag the **Staff ID#** field into the form slightly below the **Phone Number control**. Close the **Field List** pane. Adjust the white text box controls to align under the *m* in the form title. Move the **Phone Number** control above the **Title** control. Edit the **Staff First Name** and **Staff Last Name** labels to indicate *First Name* and *Last Name*.

9. Deselect all controls. Then, hold down ⇧ Shift and select all five **text box controls**. Apply a **Fill/Back Color** using **Access Theme 2**. Change the font size to **12**, and if necessary, widen the controls so that the phone number displays on one line. Deselect all the controls. Select all the labels, change the font size to **12**, change the font color to **Access Theme 8**, and then apply **Bold**.

10. Deselect all controls, and then select all the labels. From the **Arrange tab**, display the **Property Sheet**. Change the **Width** property for all of the labels to **1.25** Select all the text box controls, and then change the **Height** property for all the text box controls to **0.35** and the **Width** property to **1.25** Select the **Form Footer label**, hold down ⇧ Shift and click the **Form Header label**, and then change the **Left** property to **1** Close the **Property Sheet**. Switch to Form view. Click the **Last record** button to display the record containing your name. Display the **Print** dialog box, click the **Selected Record(s)** option button, and then click **OK** to print; or submit electronically as directed. **Close** the form and save the changes.

11. Open the **3E Staff Input Form**. In the displayed first record, click the **Title** label. In the **Sort & Filter group**, click the **Selection** button, and then in the displayed list, click **Equals "Associate"**. Six records contain the title *Associate*. In the **Sort & Filter group**, click **Toggle Filter** to remove the filter and activate all 19 records. Be sure the first record displays, and then click to place the insertion point in the **Title** text box control. Click the **Toggle Filter** to reapply the filter, and then in the navigation area, click the **Last record** button to display **Record 6**. In the **Phone Number** field, select the Area Code text *(410)*. Click the **Selection** button, and then click **Begins with "(410)"**. Four records meet the condition. Click the **Toggle Filter** button to remove the filter and reactivate all of the records. Close all the open objects, close the database, and then close Access.

End **You have completed Project 3E**

Content-Based Assessments

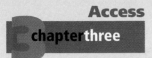
Mastering Access

Project 3F—Lectures and Presenters

In this project, you will apply the skills you practiced from the Objectives in Project 3B.

Objectives: 6. *Create a Report by Using the Report Tool;* **7.** *Create a Report by Using the Blank Report Tool;* **8.** *Create a Report by Using the Report Wizard;* **9.** *Modify the Design of a Report;* **10.** *Print a Report and Keep Data Together.*

In the following Mastering Access assessment, you will create reports for Janna Sorokin regarding information about the various informational lectures and presenters that will be conducted during the Job Fair event. Your completed database objects will look similar to Figure 3.55.

For Project 3F, you will need the following file:

a3F_Lectures_Presenters

You will save your database as
3F_Lectures_Presenters_Firstname_Lastname

Figure 3.55

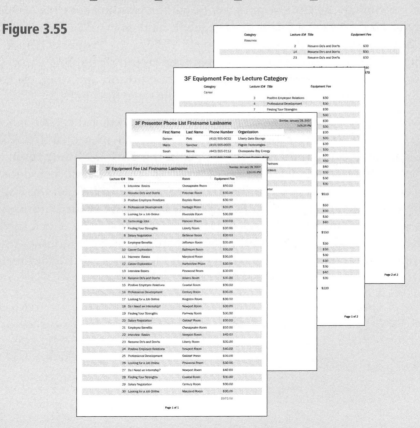

(Project 3F–Lectures and Presenters continues on the next page)

Content-Based Assessments

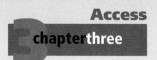

Access

chapter **three**   Mastering Access

(Project 3F—Lectures and Presenters continued)

1. From the student files that accompany this textbook, locate the file **a3F_Lectures_ Presenters**. Copy and then paste the file to your Access Chapter 3 folder. Rename the file as **3F_Lectures_Presenters_Firstname_ Lastname Start** Access, and then open your **3F_ Lectures_Presenters** database. Enable the content. On the **Database Tools tab**, view the table relationships, and then **Close** the window. One presenter can give many lectures during the Job Fair event.

2. Based on the **3F Lectures table**, use the **Report** tool to create a new report. Delete the following fields from the report: **Presenter ID**, **Lecture Date**, **Lecture Time**, and **Category**. At the bottom of the **Equipment Fee** column, notice that the Report tool automatically summed the column; the total is *$970.00*. Apply the **Trek** AutoFormat. Edit the Report Header text to indicate **3F Equipment Fee List Firstname Lastname** and then change the font size to **3**. Shorten the right side of the **Room** field leaving a small amount of space between the columns. Use the **layout selector** button to visually center the entire layout horizontally between the margins. Click the **Print Preview** button, click the **One Page** button, check your centering. Print the report, or submit electronically as directed. Close Print Preview, close the report, save, and then name the report **3F Equipment Fee List**

3. Based on the **3F Presenters table**, create a **Blank Report**. Add the following fields: **First Name**, **Last Name**, **Phone Number**, and **Organization**. Widen the **Organization** field until all the names display on one line. Click the **Date & Time** and **Title** buttons, and type **3F Presenter Phone List Firstname Lastname** as the report title. Apply the **Trek** AutoFormat, and then with the title still selected, change the

title's font size to **16**. Select the four field names, change the font size to **12**. Center the layout horizontally on the page. Check the layout in **Print Preview**. Print the report, or submit electronically as directed. Close Print Preview, close the report, save, and then name the report **3F Presenter Phone List**

4. Based on the **3F Lectures** table, create a report by using the **Report Wizard**, and then add the following fields in the order listed: **Category**, **Lecture ID#**, **Title**, and **Equipment Fee**. Group the report by **Category**, sort by **Lecture ID#** in **Ascending order**, and **Sum** the **Equipment Fee** field. Select the **Stepped** option, **Portrait** orientation, and **Trek** style. For the report title, type **3F Equipment Fee by Lecture Category** In **Print Preview**, click the **Two Pages** button, and notice that one category is split between two pages.

5. Switch to Layout view. Widen the right side of the **Category** field to accommodate the longest category name, which is *Job Search Techniques*. Shorten the right side of the **Title** field to accommodate the longest line with just a small amount of space between the columns. Click any of the **Lecture ID#** numbers, and in the **Font group**, click the **Center** button. Select the four field names, center them, and then apply **Italic**. By using the **layout selector** button, visually center the entire layout horizontally on the page.

6. Select and delete the **Summary for 'Category'** controls. In the **Career** grouping of the report, to the right of the word *Sum*, click **$510.00** to select these controls, right-click, and then click **Properties**. Change the number of **Decimal Places** to **0**.

(Project 3F—Lectures and Presenters continues on the next page)

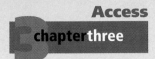

Access

chapterthree

Mastering Access

(Project 3F–Lectures and Presenters continued)

7. Select one of the amounts in the **Equipment Fee** field, display the **Property Sheet**, and then change the number of **Decimal Places** to **0**. Select the summed amount of **$510**, and then adjust as necessary so that the summed amounts display directly under the fee above with just enough space to accommodate the data. Change the font color to **Access Theme 10**. Select one of the **Sum** controls, place the insertion point inside the control, delete the text, type **Total Equipment Fees by Category** change the font color to **Access Theme 10**, and then press Enter. Position theses controls to the immediate left of the total amount.

8. At the end of the report, select the sum **$970.00**, which is the Grand Total for all equipment fees, change the number of decimal places to **0**, apply **Bold**, and then change the font color to **Access Theme 10**. Position the total directly below the other totals. Apply the same formatting to the text *Grand Total*, and then position this label to the immediate left of the total amount. **Save** the changes you have made to your report thus far.

9. Switch to Design view. In the **Page Footer** section, shorten the date control by moving its right edge to **1.75 inches on the**

horizontal ruler. Shorten the **page number control** by moving its left edge to **5.5 inches on the horizontal ruler**. In the **Page Footer section**, create a label, and then position the pointer at **2 inches on the horizontal ruler** and in the vertical center of the section. Click one time, and then using your own name, type **3F Equipment Fees by Category Firstname Lastname** and then press Enter. Double-click a sizing handle to fit the control. With the label control selected, change the font color to **Access Theme 9**.

10. Display the **Print Preview** in the **Two Pages** arrangement, notice the bottom of **Page 1**, and then close the Print Preview. Switch to Layout view. In the **Grouping and Totals group**, click the **Group & Sort** button. From the **Group, Sort, and Total** pane, choose to **keep whole group together on one page** and **with A on top arrow**. Close the pane, click **Print Preview**, display **Two Pages**, and then verify that the entire *Resumes* group displays at the top of **Page 2**.

11. Print the report or submit electronically as directed. Close the report, save your changes, close the database, and then close Access.

 You have completed Project 3F ————————————————

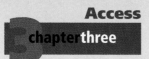

Mastering Access

Project 3G — Raffle Sponsors

In this project, you will apply skills you practiced from the Objectives in Projects 3A and 3B.

Objectives: 1. *Create a Form;* **2.** *Use a Form To Add and Delete Records;* **6.** *Create a Report by Using the Report Tool;* **7.** *Create a Report by Using the Blank Report Tool;* **10.** *Print a Report and Keep Data Together.*

In the following Mastering Access Assessment, you will assist Janna Sorokin, database manager for the Greater Baltimore Area Job Fair, in using a database to track raffle items and sponsors for the fair event. Your completed form and report will look similar to Figure 3.56.

For Project 3G, you will need the following file:

a3G_Raffle_Sponsors

You will save your database as 3G_Raffle_Sponsors_Firstname_Lastname

Figure 3.56

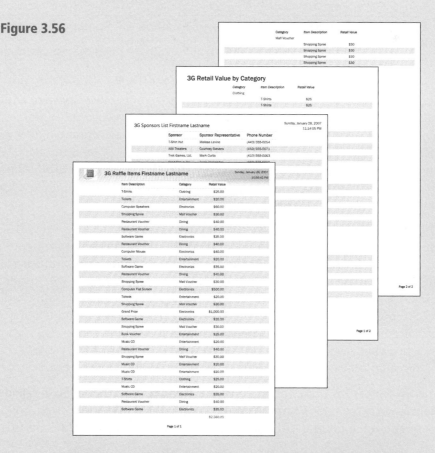

(Project 3G–Raffle Sponsors continues on the next page)

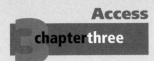

(Project 3G–Raffle Sponsors continued)

1. From the student files that accompany this textbook, locate the file **a3G_Raffle_Sponsors**. Copy and then paste the file to your Access Chapter 3 folder. Rename the file **3G_Raffle_Sponsors_Firstname_Lastname Start** Access, and then open your **3G_Raffle_Sponsors** database. Enable the content. On the **Database Tools tab**, view the table relationships, and then **Close** the window. One sponsor can provide many raffle items during the Job Fair event.

2. Based on the **3G Raffle Items table**, use the **Form** tool to create a form. Switch to Form view and scroll through the records. Add a new record as follows:

Raffle Item ID#	Item Description	Sponsor ID#	Provider's Item Code	Category	Retail Value
RAFF-31	Software Game	SP-1203	TG-79044	Electronics	35

3. Close the form, and then save it as **3G Raffle Items Form** Based on the **3G Sponsors table**, use the **Form** tool to create a form. Switch to Form view, and then scroll through the records. Add a new record as follows, using your own first and last name:

Sponsor ID#	Sponsor	Phone Number	Sponsor Representative
SP-1211	Baltimore Sweets	(410) 555-0765	Firstname Lastname

4. Close the form, and then save it as **3G Sponsors Form** Open the **3G Sponsors table**, verify that your record as a sponsor representative displays as the last record in the table, and then close the table. Open the **3G Raffle Items Form**. Use the **Find and Replace** dialog box to locate the record for **RAFF-02**, **Delete** the record for **RAFF-02**, and then **Close** the form. Open the **3G Raffle Items table**. Examine the table and verify that the record for *RAFF-02* no longer displays. Then scroll to **Record 31** and verify that the new record you added for **Sponsor ID# SP-1203** is included in the table. Close the table.

5. Based on the **3G Raffle Items** table, use the **Report** tool to create a new report. Apply the **Trek** AutoFormat to the report; recall that you should apply the AutoFormat first, and then edit other formatting. Delete the following fields: **Raffle Item ID#**, **Sponsor ID#**, and **Provider's Item Code**. At the bottom of the report, notice that the Report tool summed the **Retail Value** field; the total is *$2,380.00*. Add your name to the end of the Report Header text, and then change the font size to **16**. Shorten the right side of the **Category** field leaving a small amount of space between the columns. Use the **layout selector** button to visually center the layout horizontally on the page. Check your centering in print preview, and then print the report, or submit electronically as directed. Close, and then name the report **3G Retail Value List**

6. Based on the **3G Sponsors table**, create a **Blank Report**. Add the following fields: **Sponsor**, **Sponsor Representative**, and **Phone Number**. Apply the **Trek** AutoFormat to the report; recall that you should apply the AutoFormat first, and then edit other formatting. Widen

(Project 3G–Raffle Sponsors continues on the next page)

Content-Based Assessments

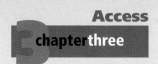
(Project 3G–Raffle Sponsors continued)

the **Sponsor** field until all the names display on one line. Click the **Date & Time** and **Title** buttons, and then as the report title, type **3G Sponsors List Firstname Lastname** Change the title's font size to **14**. Select the three field names, and then change the font size to **12**. Visually center the layout horizontally on the page. Check your centering in print preview, and then print the report; or, submit electronically as directed. Close, save, and then name the report **3G Sponsors List**

7. Based on the **3G Raffle Items** table, create a report by using the **Report Wizard**, and then add the following fields in the order listed: **Category**, **Item Description**, and **Retail Value**. Group the report by **Category**, sort by **Item Description** in **Ascending order**, and **Sum** the **Retail Value** field. Select the **Stepped** option, **Portrait** orientation, and **Trek** style. As the report title, type **3G Retail Value by Category** In **Print Preview**, click the **Two Pages** button, and then examine how the records break across the two pages.

8. Switch to Layout view. Widen the right side of the **Category controls** to accommodate the longest category name. Shorten the right side of the **Item Description controls** to accommodate the longest line and leave a small amount of space between the columns. Select the three field names and apply **Italic**. Visually center the layout horizontally.

9. Select, and then delete the **Summary for 'Category'** controls. Select any value in the **Retail Value** field, and then from the **Property Sheet**, change the **Decimal Places** to **0**. In the **Clothing** grouping of the report, to the right of the word *Sum*, click **$50.00** to select these controls. Change the number of **Decimal Places** to **0**, change the font color to **Access Theme 10**, and then align the total under the values above.

10. Select one of the **Sum** controls, change the text to **Total Retail Value by Category** align this control to the immediate left of the amount, and then change its font color to **Access Theme 10**.

11. At the end of the report, select the Grand Total **$2,380.00**, change the number of decimal places to **0**, apply **Bold**, and then change the font color to **Access Theme 10**. Position the total directly below the other totals. Apply the same formatting to the text *Grand Total*, and then position this label to the immediate left of the total amount. **Save** the changes you have made thus far.

12. Switch to Design view. In the **Page Footer** section, shorten the date control by moving its right edge to **1.75 inches on the horizontal ruler**. Shorten the **page number control** by moving its left edge to **5.5 inches on the horizontal ruler**. In the **Page Footer section**, create a label, and then position the pointer at **2 inches on the horizontal ruler** and in the vertical center of the section. Click one time, and then using your own name, type **3G Retail Values by Category Firstname Lastname** and then press ⏎. Double-click a sizing handle to fit the control. With the label control selected, change the font color to **Access Theme 9**.

13. Display the **Print Preview** in the **Two Pages** arrangement, notice the bottom of **Page 1**, and then close the Print Preview. Switch to Layout view. In the **Grouping and Totals group**, click the **Group & Sort** button. From the **Group, Sort, and Total** pane, choose to **keep whole group together on one page** and **with A on top arrow**. Close the pane, display the print

(Project 3G–Raffle Sponsors continues on the next page)

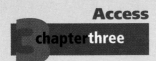

(Project 3G–Raffle Sponsors continued)

preview, display **Two Pages**, and then verify that the entire *Mall Voucher* group displays at the top of **Page 2**.

14. Print the report or submit electronically as directed. Close the report, save your changes, close the database, and then close Access.

 You have completed Project 3G

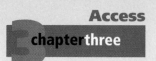

Mastering Access

Project 3H — Contractors and Facility Services

In this project, you will apply skills you practiced from the Objectives in Projects 3A and 3B.

Objectives: 1. *Create a Form;* **2.** *Use a Form To Add and Delete Records;* **6.** *Create a Report by Using Report Tool;* **7.** *Create a Report by Using the Blank Report Tool;* **8.** *Create a Report by Using the Report Wizard;* **10.** *Print a Report and Keep Data Together;* **9.** *Modify the Design of a Report*

In the following Mastering Access assessment, you will assist Janna Sorokin, database manager for the Greater Baltimore Area Job Fair, in using a database to track facility and staff services for the fair event. Your completed objects will look similar to Figure 3.57.

For Project 3H, you will need the following file:

a3H_Contractors_Facility_Services

**You will save your database as
3H_Contractors_Facility_Services_Firstname_Lastname**

Figure 3.57

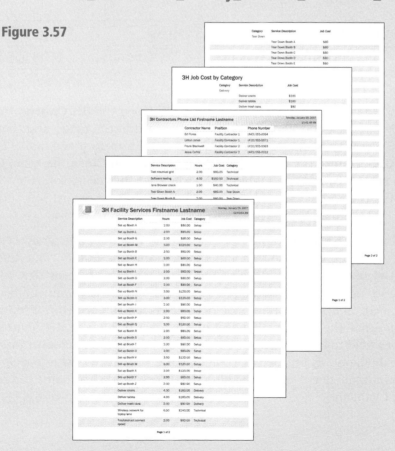

(Project 3H–Contractors and Facility Services continues on the next page)

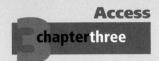

Access

Mastering Access

(Project 3H–Contractors and Facility Services continued)

1. From the student files that accompany this textbook, locate the file **a3H_Contractors_Facility_Services**. Copy and then paste the file to your Access Chapter 3 folder. Rename the file **3H_Contractors_Facility_Services_Firstname_Lastname** Start Access, and then open your **3H_Contractors_Facility_Services** database. Enable the content. On the **Database Tools tab**, view the table relationships, and then **Close** the window. One contractor can provide many facility services during the Job Fair event.

2. Based on the **3H Facility Services table**, use the **Form** tool to create a form. Switch to Form view, and then scroll through some of the 60 records. Add a new record as follows:

Job#	Date	Service Description	Contractor ID#	Hours	Job Cost	Category
JB-061	4/11/2009	Set up workroom	CO-3009	2	$80.00	Setup

3. Close the form, and then save it as **3H Facility Services Form** Based on the **3H Contractors table**, use the **Form** tool to create a form. Switch to Form view, and then scroll through the some of the 15 records. Add a new record as follows, using your own first and last name:

Contractor ID#	Contractor Name	Position	Phone Number
CO-3016	Firstname Lastname	Facility Contractor 1	(410) 555-0765

4. Close the form, and then save it as **3H Contractors Form** Open the **3H Contractors table**, verify that your record as a contractor displays as the last record in the table, and then close the table. Open the **3H Facility Services Form**. Use the **Find and Replace** dialog box to locate the record for **JB-003**, **Delete** the record for **JB-003**, and then **Close** the form. Open the **3H Facility Services table**. Examine the table and verify that the record for *JB-003* no longer displays. Then, scroll to the end of the table and verify that the new record you added for **JB-061** is included in the table. Close the table.

5. Based on the **3H Facility Services** table, use the **Report** tool to create a new report. Apply the **Trek** AutoFormat to the report; recall that you should apply the AutoFormat first, and then edit other formatting. Delete the following fields: **Job#**, **Date**, and **Contractor ID#**. At the bottom of the **Job Cost** column, notice that the total job cost is *$5,440.00*. Add your name to the end of the Report Header text. Shorten the right side of the **Service Description** field leaving a small amount of space between the columns (longest line is toward the bottom). Shorten the right side of the **Category** field to accommodate the data. Use the **layout selector** button to visually center the controls horizontally on the page. Display the **Print Preview** to check your centering. Print the report, or submit electronically as directed. Close, and then name the report **3H Job Cost List Firstname Lastname**

(Project 3H–Contractors and Facility Services continues on the next page)

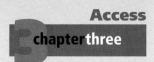
(Project 3H–Contractors and Facility Services continued)

6. Based on the **3H Contractors table**, create a **Blank Report**. Add the following fields: **Contractor Name**, **Position**, and **Phone Number**. Widen the **Position** field until all the positions display on one line. Click the **Date & Time** and **Title** buttons, and then as the title, type **3H Contractors Phone List Firstname Lastname** With the title still selected, apply the **Trek** AutoFormat, and then change the title's font size to **14**. Select the three field names, and then change the font size to **12**. Visually center the controls horizontally on the page. Display **Print Preview** to check your centering. Print the report, or submit electronically as directed. Close, and then name the report **3H Contractors Phone List Firstname Lastname**

7. Based on the **3H Facility Services table**, create a report by using the **Report Wizard**. Select the following fields in the order given: **Category**, **Service Description**, and **Job Cost**. Group the report by **Category**, sort by **Service Description** in **Ascending order**, and **Sum** the **Job Cost** field. Select the **Stepped** option, **Portrait** orientation, and **Trek** style. For the report title, type **3H Job Cost by Category** In **Print Preview**, click the **Two Pages** button and examine your report.

8. Switch to Layout view. Widen the right side of the **Category controls** to accommodate the longest category name, which is *Technical*. Shorten the right side of the **Service Description controls** to accommodate the longest line, and leave a small amount of space between the columns (the longest line is at the bottom of the list). Select the three field names, and then apply **Italic**. Visually center the layout horizontally.

9. Select, and then delete the **Summary for 'Category'** controls. Select any value in the **Job Cost** field, right-click, click **Properties**, and then change the number of **Decimal Places** to **0**. In the **Delivery** grouping of the report, to the right of the word *Sum*, click the value displayed as ##### to select these controls. Change the number of **Decimal Places** to **0**, change the font color to **Access Theme 10**, and then align the total under the values above.

10. Select one of the **Sum** controls, place the insertion point inside the control, delete the text, type **Total Job Cost by Category** and then press Enter. Align this control to the immediate left of the amount, and then change its font color to **Access Theme 10**. Be sure you have aligned the amount properly so that each Category's amount displays completely.

11. At the end of the report, expand if necessary, and then select the Grand Total sum that displays as #####, change the number of decimal places to **0**, apply **Bold**, and then change the font color to **Access Theme 10**. Position the total directly below the other totals. Apply the same formatting to the text *Grand Total*, and then position this label to the immediate left of the total amount. **Save** the changes you have made thus far.

12. Switch to Design view. In the **Page Footer** section, shorten the date control by moving its right edge to **1.75 inches on the horizontal ruler**. Shorten the **page number control** by moving its left edge to **5.5 inches on the horizontal ruler**. In the **Page Footer section**, create a label, and then position the pointer at **2 inches on the horizontal ruler** and in the vertical center of the section. Using your own name, type **3H Job Cost by Category Firstname Lastname** and then press Enter. Double-click a sizing handle to fit the control. With the label control selected, change the font color to **Access Theme 9**.

(Project 3H–Contractors and Facility Services continues on the next page)

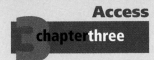

(Project 3H—Contractors and Facility Services continued)

13. Display the **Print Preview** in the **Two Pages** arrangement, notice how the groups flow from the bottom of **Page 1**, and then close the Print Preview. Switch to Layout view. In the **Grouping and Totals group**, click the **Group & Sort** button. From the **Group, Sort, and Total** pane, choose to **keep whole group together on one page** and **with A on top arrow**. View the Print Preview again, display **Two Pages**, and then verify that the entire *Tear Down* group displays on **Page 2**.

14. Print the report or submit electronically as directed. Close the Print Preview, close the report, save your changes, close the database, and then close Access.

 You have completed Project 3H ⎯⎯⎯⎯⎯⎯⎯⎯⎯⎯⎯⎯⎯⎯⎯⎯⎯⎯⎯⎯

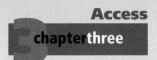

Mastering Access

Project 3I — Career Bookstore

In this project, you will apply all the skills you practiced from the Objectives in Projects 3A and 3B.

Objectives: 1. *Create a Form;* **2.** *Use a Form To Add and Delete Records;* **3.** *Create a Form by Using the Form Wizard;* **4.** *Modify a Form in Design View and in Layout View;* **5.** *Filter Records;* **6.** *Create a Report by Using the Report Tool;* **7.** *Create a Report by Using the Blank Report Tool;* **8.** *Create a Report by Using the Report Wizard;* **9.** *Modify the Design of a Report;* **10.** *Print a Report and Keep Data Together.*

In the following Mastering Access assessment, you will assist Janna Sorokin, database manager for the Greater Baltimore Area Job Fair, in using a database to track publishers and book titles for the books that are for sale at the Career Bookstore during the Job Fair event. Your completed objects will look similar to Figure 3.58.

For Project 3I, you will need the following file:

a3I_Career_Bookstore

**You will save your database as
3I_Career_Bookstore_Firstname_Lastname**

Figure 3.58

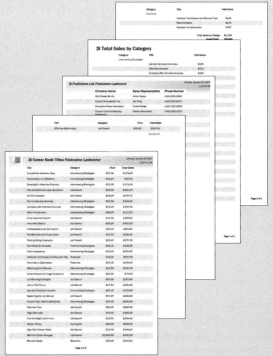

(Project 3I–Career Bookstore continues on the next page)

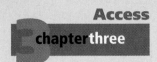

(Project 3I–Career Bookstore continued)

1. From the student files that accompany this textbook, locate the file **a3I_Career_Bookstore**. Copy and then paste the file to your Access Chapter 3 folder. Rename the file **3I_Career_Bookstore_Firstname_Lastname Start** Access, and then open your **3I_Career_Bookstore** database. Enable the content. Examine the data in the two tables. On the **Database Tools tab**, view the table relationships, and then **Close** the window. One publisher can provide many career book titles during the Job Fair event.

2. Based on the **3I Career Book Titles table**, use the **Form** tool to create a form. Switch to Form view, and then scroll through the records. Add a new record as follows:

Title ID #	Title	Author	Publisher ID#	Category	Price	Total Sales
T-33	Effective Networking	Jean Flowers	PUB-100	Job Search	20	200

3. Close the form, and then save it as **3I Career Book Titles Form** Based on the **3I Publishers table**, use the **Form** tool to create a form. Switch to Form view, and then scroll through the records. Add a new record as follows, using your own first and last name:

Publisher ID#	Phone Number	Sales Representative	Company Name	Title
PUB-111	(410) 555-0765	Firstname Lastname	Associated Publishers	Sales Associate

4. Close the form, and then save it as **3I Publishers Form** Open the **3I Publishers table**, verify that your record as a Sales Associate displays as the last record in the table, and then close the table. Open the **3I Career Book Titles Form**. Use the **Find and Replace** dialog box to locate the record for **T-05**, **Delete** the record for **T-05**, and then close the form. Open the **3I Career Book Titles table**. Examine the table and verify that the record for *T-05* no longer displays. Then scroll to **Record 33** and verify that the new record you added for **Title ID# T-33** is included in the table. Close the table.

5. Based on the **3I Career Book Titles table**, use the **Report** tool to create a new report. Apply the **Trek** AutoFormat to the report; recall that you should apply the AutoFormat first, and then edit other formatting. Delete the following fields: **Title ID#**, **Author**, and **Publisher ID#**. At the bottom of the report, notice that the Report tool summed the **Total Sales** field, the total is *$9,945.00*. Add your name to the end of the Report Header text, and then change the font size to **16**. Shorten the right side of the **Category** field leaving a small amount of space between the columns. Use the **layout selector** button to visually center the layout horizontally on the page. Click the **Print Preview** button to check your centering. Print the report, or submit electronically as directed. Close, and then name the report **3I Total Sales**

6. Based on the **3I Publishers table**, create a **Blank Report**. Add the following fields: **Company Name**, **Sales Representative**, and **Phone Number**. Widen the **Company Name** field until all the names display on one line. Click the **Date & Time** and **Title** buttons, and then as the

(Project 3I–Career Bookstore continues on the next page)

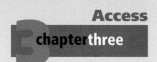

(Project 3I–Career Bookstore continued)

report title, type **3I Publishers List Firstname Lastname** With the title still selected, apply the **Trek** AutoFormat, and then change the title's font size to **14**. Select the three field names, change the font size to **12**. Check your centering in print preview, and then print the report; or, submit electronically as directed. Close, save, and then name the report **3I Publishers List**

7. Based on the **3I Career Book Titles table**, create a report by using the **Report Wizard**, and add the following fields in the order listed: **Category**, **Title,** and **Total Sales**. Group the report by **Category**, sort by **Title** in **Ascending order**, and then **Sum** the **Total Sales** field. Select the **Stepped** option, **Portrait** orientation, and **Trek** style. As the report title, type **3I Total Sales by Category** In **Print Preview**, click the **Two Pages** button, and then examine how the records break across the two pages.

8. Switch to Layout view. Widen the right side of the **Category controls** to accommodate the longest category name. Shorten the right side of the **Title controls** to accommodate the longest line and leave a small amount of space between the columns. Select the three field names and apply **Italic**. Visually center the layout horizontally.

9. Select, and then delete the **Summary for 'Category'** controls. Select any value in the **Total Sales** field, right-click, click **Properties**, and then change the **Decimal Places** to **0**. In the **Interviewing Strategies** grouping of the report, to the right of the word *Sum*, click **$3,600.00** to select these controls. Change the number of **Decimal Places** to **0**, change the font color to **Access Theme 10**, and then align the total under the values above.

10. Select one of the **Sum** controls, change the text to **Total Sales by Category** align this control to the immediate left of the amount, and then change its font color to **Access Theme 10**.

11. At the end of the report, select the sum **$9,945.00**, which is the Grand Total, change the number of decimal places to **0**, apply **Bold**, and then change the font color to **Access Theme 10**. Position the Grand Total directly below the other totals. Apply the same formatting to the text *Grand Total*, and then position this label to the immediate left of the Grand Total amount. **Save** the changes you have made to your report thus far.

12. Switch to Design view. In the **Page Footer** section, shorten the date control by moving its right edge to **1.75 inches on the horizontal ruler**. Shorten the **page number control** by moving its left edge to **5.5 inches on the horizontal ruler**. In the **Page Footer section**, create a label, and then position the pointer at **2 inches on the horizontal ruler** and in the vertical center of the section. Click one time, and then using your own name, type **3I Total Sales by Category Firstname Lastname** and then press Enter. Double-click a sizing handle to fit the control. With the label control selected, change the font color to **Access Theme 9**.

13. Display the **Print Preview** in the **Two Pages** arrangement, notice the flow between the bottom of **Page 1** and the top of **Page 2**, and then close the Print Preview. Switch to Layout view. In the **Grouping and Totals group**, click the **Group & Sort** button. From the **Group, Sort, and Total** pane, choose to **keep whole group together on one page** and **with A on top arrow**. Close the pane, click **Print Preview**, display **Two Pages**, and then verify that the entire *Resumes* group displays at the top of **Page 2**. Print the report or submit electronically as directed. Close, and then save the report.

(Project 3I–Career Bookstore continues on the next page)

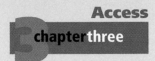

(Project 3I–Career Bookstore continued)

14. Open the **3I Publishers Form**. In the displayed first record, click the **Title** label. In the **Sort & Filter group**, click the **Selection** button, and then in the displayed list, click **Equals "Sales Representative"**. Six records contain the title *Sales Representative*. In the **Sort & Filter group**, click **Toggle Filter** to remove the filter and activate all 12 records. Be sure the first record displays, and then click to place the insertion point in the **Title** text box control. Click the **Toggle Filter** to reapply the filter, and then in the navigation area, click the **Last record** button to display the sixth record in the filtered group. In the **Phone Number** field, select the Area Code text *(443)*. Click the **Selection** button, and then click **Begins with "(443)"**. Four records meet the condition. Click the **Toggle Filter** button to remove the filter and reactivate all of the records. Close all the open objects, close the database, and then close Access.

End **You have completed Project 3I**

Content-Based Assessments

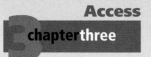

Business Running Case

Project 3J — Business Running Case

In this project, you will apply the skills you practiced in Projects 3A and 3B.

From My Computer, navigate to the student files that accompany this textbook. In the folder **03_business_running_case_pg37_86**, locate and open the folder for this chapter. Open and print the instructions for this project, which are provided to you in Adobe PDF format. Follow the instructions and use the skills you have gained thus far to assist Jennifer Nelson in meeting the challenges of owning and running her business.

End **You have completed Project 3J** ————————————

Rubric

The following outcomes-based assessments are *open-ended assessments*. That is, there is no specific correct result; your result will depend on your approach to the information provided. Make *Professional Quality* your goal. Use the following scoring rubric to guide you in *how* to approach the problem and then to evaluate *how well* your approach solves the problem.

The *criteria*—Software Mastery, Content, Format and Layout, and Process—represent the knowledge and skills you have gained that you can apply to solving the problem. The *levels of performance*—Professional Quality, Approaching Professional Quality, or Needs Quality Improvements—help you and your instructor evaluate your result.

	Your completed project is of Professional Quality if you:	Your completed project is Approaching Professional Quality if you:	Your completed project Needs Quality Improvements if you:
1-Software Mastery	Choose and apply the most appropriate skills, tools, and features and identify efficient methods to solve the problem.	Choose and apply some appropriate skills, tools, and features, but not in the most efficient manner.	Choose inappropriate skills, tools, or features, or are inefficient in solving the problem.
2-Content	Construct a solution that is clear and well organized, contains content that is accurate, appropriate to the audience and purpose, and is complete. Provide a solution that contains no errors of spelling, grammar, or style.	Construct a solution in which some components are unclear, poorly organized, inconsistent, or incomplete. Misjudge the needs of the audience. Have some errors in spelling, grammar, or style, but the errors do not detract from comprehension.	Construct a solution that is unclear, incomplete, or poorly organized, containing some inaccurate or inappropriate content; and contains many errors of spelling, grammar, or style. Do not solve the problem.
3-Format and Layout	Format and arrange all elements to communicate information and ideas, clarify function, illustrate relationships, and indicate relative importance.	Apply appropriate format and layout features to some elements, but not others. Overuse features, causing minor distraction.	Apply format and layout that does not communicate information or ideas clearly. Do not use format and layout features to clarify function, illustrate relationships, or indicate relative importance. Use available features excessively, causing distraction.
4-Process	Use an organized approach that integrates planning, development, self-assessment, revision, and reflection.	Demonstrate an organized approach in some areas, but not others; or, use an insufficient process of organization throughout.	Do not use an organized approach to solve the problem.

Outcomes-Based Assessments

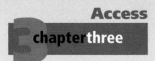

Problem Solving

Project 3K — Candidates and Offers

In this project, you will construct a solution by applying any combination of the Objectives found in Projects 3A and 3B.

> **For Project 3K, you will need the following file:**
>
> a3K_Candidates_Offers

You will save your database as
3K_Candidates_Offers_Firstname_Lastname

Copy the student file **a3K_Candidates_Offers** to your Access Chapter 3 folder and rename it **3K_Candidates_Offers_Firstname_Lastname** Michael Dawson, Executive Director of the Baltimore Area Job Fair, would like one form and two reports created from the Job Fair database. Mr. Dawson wants a report listing the Organization Name and Offer Amount of each job offered to a candidate as a result of the Job Fair. Create and save the report as **3K Offers Firstname Lastname** Print the report or submit electronically as directed. Mr. Dawson also wants a report of the names, college majors, and phone numbers of the candidates. Save the report as **3K Candidates Firstname Lastname** Print the report or submit electronically as directed. Using the skills you have practiced in this chapter, create an attractive, easy-to-follow input form that can be used to update candidate records. Using your own information, add a new record as Candidate ID# 22102. Save the form as **3K Candidate Update Firstname Lastname** For the report that you added, print or submit electronically.

 You have completed Project 3K ————————

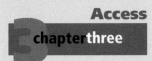

Problem Solving

Project 3L—Applicants and Job Openings

In this project, you will construct a solution by applying any combination of the Objectives found in Projects 3A and 3B.

> **For Project 3L, you will need the following file:**
>
> a3L_Applicants_Job_Openings
>
> **You will save your database as**
> **3L_Applicants_Job_Openings_Firstname_Lastname**

Copy the file **a3L_Applicants_Job_Openings** to your Access Chapter 3 folder and rename it **3L_Applicants_Job_Openings_Firstname_ Lastname** Janice Strickland, Employer Coordinator, wants to know which types of positions have the most openings so she can highlight them on the Job Fair Web site. Sort the records in the table so you can provide Janice with the appropriate information, print the table in the sorted order, save the table as **3L Table Sort Firstname Lastname** or submit electronically; save the changes to the table's design. Janice also needs an input form for Job Fair applicants so she can update the database if needed. Save the form as **3L Applicant Input Form Firstname Lastname** Print the form, or submit electronically. Create an Applicant input form, and using your own information, add a new record as Applicant ID# 4600. Janice needs a report with applicant contact information so she can send updates about new job openings. Create an attractive, easy-to-read applicant contact information report. Include a Report Header with **3L Applicant Contact Information Firstname Lastname** Save and print the report, or submit electronically.

End **You have completed Project 3L** ——————————

Outcomes-Based Assessments

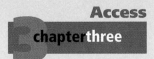
Problem Solving

Project 3M—Candidates and Activities

In this project, you will construct a solution by applying any combination of the Objectives found in Projects 3A and 3B.

> **For Project 3M, you will need the following file:**
>
> a3M_Candidates_Activities

**You will save your database as
3M_Candidates_Activities_Firstname_Lastname**

Copy the file **a3M_Candidates_Activities** to your Access Chapter 3 folder and rename it **3M_Candidates_Activities_Firstname_Lastname** Janice Strickland, Employer Coordinator, wants a report that shows the room where each activity is being held so that she can give the Activity Coordinators their room assignments. Create an attractive, easy-to-read report that shows the Meeting Room for each Activity. Include your name in the report heading, save the report as **3M Activity Meeting Rooms Firstname Lastname** and then print the report or submit electronically. Then create a Candidate Input Form for adding information for new candidates. Using your own information, as STU-2049 add a new record to the form. Save as **3M Candidate Input Form Firstname Lastname** and then print the STU-2049 record or submit electronically.

End **You have completed Project 3M** _____

Outcomes-Based Assessments

Problem Solving

Project 3N—Donors and Gifts

In this project, you will construct a solution by applying any combination of the Objectives found in Projects 3A and 3B.

For Project 3N, you will need the following file:

a3N_Donors_Gifts

You will save your database as
3N_Donors_Gifts_Firstname_Lastname

Copy the file **a3N_Donors_Gifts** to your Access Chapter 3 folder and rename it **3N_Donors_Gifts_Firstname_Lastname** Michael Dawson, Executive Director of the Baltimore Area Job Fair, wants a Donor Gifts Report so he can determine the total retail value of gift items distributed during the Job Fair. Create a report grouped by Category and sorted by Item Description that includes the Retail Value totals. Include the Grand Total of the Retail Value of the gift items. Create a footer with the project name (3N Donors and Gifts) and your name in the footer. Save the report as **3N Gift Retail Value Firstname Lastname** Mr. Dawson also needs a donor list with phone numbers so he can call the donor representatives and thank them for participating in the Job Fair. Create a report with the date and a report title that includes the project name and your name. Save the report as **3N Donor List Firstname Lastname** Print or submit the reports electronically.

End **You have completed Project 3N**

Outcomes-Based Assessments

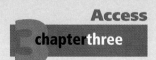

Problem Solving

Project 3O—Food Services Staffing

In this project, you will construct a solution by applying any combination of the Objectives found in Projects 3A and 3B.

For Project 3O, you will need the following file:

a3O_Food_Services_Staffing

You will save your database as
3O_Food_Services_Staffing_Firstname_Lastname

Copy the file **a3O_Food_Services_Staffing** to your Access Chapter 3 folder and rename it **3O_Food_Services_Staffing_Firstname_Lastname** Roy McLean, Food Services Manager for the Baltimore Area Job Fair, would like a report created with Food Service staff contact information. He needs the report for calling staff members when the schedule changes. Create an attractive, easy-to-read staff contact report. Include the project name (3O Food Services Staffing) and your name in the report heading. Save the report as **3O Staff Contact Firstname Lastname** Print or submit electronically.

 You have completed Project 3O ⎯⎯⎯⎯⎯⎯

Outcomes-Based Assessments

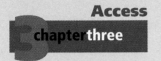
Project 3P — You and *GO!*

In this project, you will construct a solution by applying any combination of the skills you practiced from the Objectives in Projects 3A and 3B.

From My Computer, navigate to the student files that accompany this textbook. In the folder **04_you_and_go_pg87_102**, locate and open the folder for this chapter. Open and print the instructions for this project, which are provided to you in Adobe PDF format. Follow the instructions to create forms and reports for your personal database.

 End **You have completed Project 3P** ────────

GO! with Help

Project 3Q — *GO!* with Help

In addition to creating single-record forms, you can create a multiple items form. Use the Access Help system to find out how to create a form that displays multiple records.

1 **Start** Access. Click the **Microsoft Office Access Help**

button 🔘. Click the **Search arrow**, and then under **Content from this computer**, click **Access Help**. In the **Search box**, type **create a form** and then press Enter. Scroll the displayed list as necessary, and then click **Create a form**. Under **What do you want to do?**, click **Create a form that displays multiple records by using the Multiple Items tool**.

2 If you would like to keep a copy of this information, click the **Print**

button 🖶. Click the **Close** button ☒ in the top right corner of the Help window to close the Help window, and then close Access.

 End **You have completed Project 3Q** ────────

Outcomes-Based Assessments

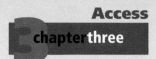

Group Business Running Case

Project 3R — Group Business Running Case

In this project, you will apply the skills you practiced from the Objectives in Projects 3A and 3B.

Your instructor may assign this group case project to your class. If your instructor assigns this project, he or she will provide you with information and instructions to work as part of a group. The group will apply the skills gained thus far to help the Bell Orchid Hotel Group achieve its business goals.

 You have completed Project 3R ————————

chapterfour

Designing and Building a Relational Database

OBJECTIVES

At the end of this chapter, you will be able to:

1. Customize Table Fields
2. Structure Data Input
3. Validate Data Input

4. Create Indexes and Change Sort Order
5. Create Relationships Between Tables
6. Create Forms and Reports with Related Tables

OUTCOMES

Mastering these objectives will enable you to:

PROJECT 4A
Structure and validate data in a database

PROJECT 4B
Build and work with related tables

MIS Technical Training Institute

MIS Technical Training Institute (MISTTI) offers training for working professionals needing skills in the management of information systems. Training centers are located in Portland, Oregon and Boise, Idaho where there is a high demand for their classes. All classes are taught by industry experts who have worked in the field that they teach. Classes cover database administration, server management, and network administration, and are offered in weekly sessions Wednesdays through Saturdays. The company is developing a database that they can use to track classes, students, and instructors.

Designing and Building a Relational Database

Access provides many tools that help ensure the data can be entered into tables with accuracy and speed. Values from a list or another table can be looked up so that the user needs only to click the appropriate choice. Fields such as phone numbers can conform to a pre-defined format. Rules can be created that validate the data as it is entered and provide an error message if the entry breaks this rule.

A database is more effective if information is divided into subject-based tables instead of using a single table. Information in two tables can be related using fields common to both tables. If a customer's phone number is changed, it needs to be changed only in one table's record. All the tables related to the customer table will be able to access the correct phone number. In this chapter, you will modify field properties to provide consistent data and relate tables to create a relational database. You will then create forms, queries, and reports that take advantage of these properties and relationships.

Project 4A **Classes**

The MIS Technical Training Institute needs a database that will track its class offerings and the instructors who will teach them. In Activities 4.1 through 4.12, you will design two tables in the MISTTI database—one for instructors, and the other for class offerings. You will design the tables to automate data entry for the company. You will test your changes by entering sample data into each table. Your final output will be a form and a report that will look similar to Figure 4.1.

For Project 4A, you will need the following files:

a04A_Classes
a04A_Patel
a04A_Booth

You will save your database as
4A_Classes_Firstname_Lastname

Figure 4.1
Project 4A—Classes

Objective 1
Customize Table Fields

The information in a database is only as accurate as the data entered into it. Access provides many ways to improve the accuracy of data entry. By changing *field properties*, many data entry errors can be avoided. Recall that field properties provide additional control over how data is stored, entered, or displayed. The types of available field properties depend on that field's *data type*. Recall that this attribute determines what kind of data will be stored in that field. Field properties ensure that data is entered consistently and correctly from record to record. Access can provide values for the user to choose from and even tell the user when the data they have entered does not conform to the rules you specified for that field.

Before creating a table, designers often plan the field properties that are needed for each field. A designer needs to know:

- Will the field name be understood by the person entering the data?

- What are the rules of the business to which the data needs to conform?

- Can the field be left blank?

- Does the data need to conform to a standard format, such as (555) 555-5555 or $0.53?

- Is there a default value that should display automatically?

- Can the values be looked up from a list?

Activity 4.1 Adding Captions to Fields

Sometimes table names and field names should not contain spaces. This is often the case when Web designers plan to use the database to create a dynamic Web site, but it makes the field names harder to understand for the *end-user*. End-users are the people who enter the data using forms and who use the information found in queries and reports. One way to make field names more user-friendly is to use the *Caption property*—alternate display text for database objects. The end users will see the caption's value instead of the field name. In this activity, you will change the Caption property for several fields.

> ## Note — Comparing Your Screen with the Figures in This Textbook
>
> Your screen will match the figures shown in this textbook if you set your screen resolution to 1024 x 768. At other resolutions, your screen will closely resemble, but not match, the figures shown. To view your screen's resolution, on the Windows desktop, right-click in a blank area, click Properties, and then click the Settings tab.

1 Navigate to the location where you are storing the student files for this project. Right-click **a04A_Classes**, and then click **Copy** from the shortcut menu.

2 Navigate to the location where you are saving your files for this project, such as your USB drive. Right-click a blank area and from the shortcut menu, point to **New**, and then click **New Folder**. Type **Access Chapter 4** and press Enter.

3 Open the folder you just created, right-click, and then click **Paste** from the shortcut menu. Right-click the pasted file, and then click **Rename**. Rename the file **4A_Classes_Firstname_Lastname**

4 Open **4A_Classes_Firstname_Lastname** in Access 2007. If necessary, in the Message bar, click **Options**. Click **Enable this content**, and then click **OK**.

5 In the **Navigation Pane**, click the **Open** button ▶, right-click **Instructors**, and then click **Design View**.

The field properties for InstructorID display in the lower half of the screen.

6 Under **Field Properties**, click in the **Field Size** textbox, and replace *255* with **5**

7 Click in the **Caption** text box, type **ID** and compare your screen with Figure 4.2.

Two field properties for the InstructorID field have changed.

Figure 4.2

InstructorID field active ⎯⎯⎯

Field Size property ⎯⎯⎯
Caption property ⎯⎯⎯

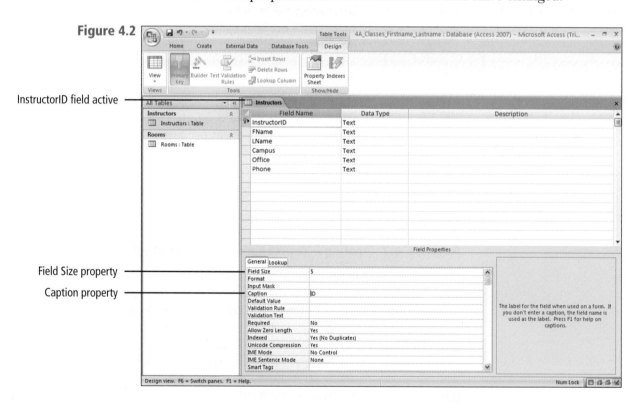

8 Using the method you just practiced, change the Caption property for the following fields:

Field	Caption
FName	First Name
LName	Last Name

9 On the Quick Access toolbar, click the **Save** button 🖫. In the **Views group**, click the **View button arrow**, and then click **Datasheet View.** Compare your screen with Figure 4.3.

In the column headers, the captions that you entered display in place of the field names.

Figure 4.3

ID, First Name, and
Last Name captions

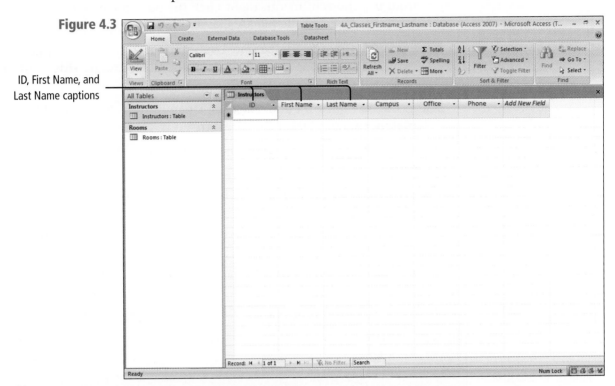

10 With the insertion point in the first empty **ID** field, type **1** and then press (Tab). Type your first name and press (Tab). Continue in this manner to fill in the rest of the record:

Last Name	Campus	Office	Phone
Lastname	Boise	218A	(208) 555-4988

11 Leave the table open for the next activity.

Activity 4.2 Creating a Yes/No Field and Set a Default Value

Recall that Access provides ten different data types that can be assigned to a field. Each data type is used to store different types of values such as text, numbers, and dates and times. The *Yes/No data type* is assigned to a field that will hold only one of two values. These values are typically Yes/No, True/False, or On/Off. In this activity, you will create a Yes/No field that determines if an instructor works full-time or part-time.

1 Switch the **Instructors** table to Design View. In the **Field Name** column, click in the empty row below Phone, type **Full-Time** and then press (Tab).

2 In the **Data Type** box, click the **arrow**. Click **Yes/No**, press (Tab), and then compare your screen with Figure 4.4.

The properties available for a Yes/No field data type display.

Figure 4.4

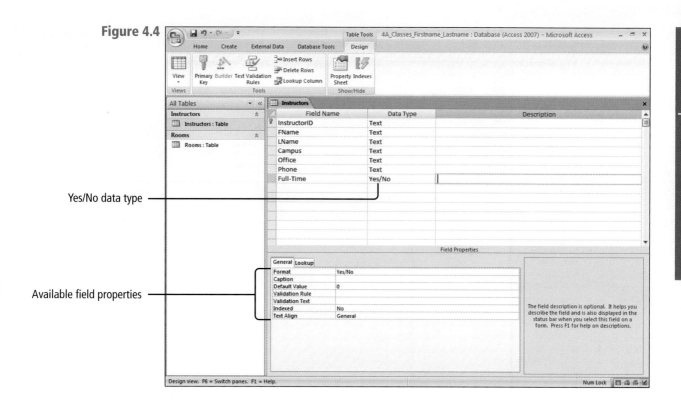

Yes/No data type

Available field properties

■ Click in the **Default Value** text box and replace the *0* with **Yes**

Default values are the values that display in a new record before data is entered. The default value can be changed to a different value during data entry.

■ **Save** 🖫 the table, switch to Datasheet View, and then compare your screen with Figure 4.5.

The Yes/No field displays as a check box. In the row for the next record, it is checked by default.

Figure 4.5

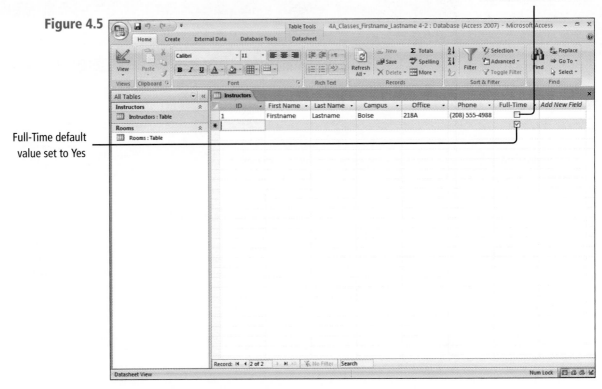

Full-Time default
value set to Yes

5 Using the datasheet, add the following instructors:

ID	First Name	Last Name	Building	Office	Phone	Full-Time
2	Margarita	Patel	Boise	218B	(208) 555-4989	Yes(checked)
3	Joey	Booth	Portland	105	(503) 555-2595	No(unchecked)
4	Carlton	Serrano	Portland	107	(503) 555-2598	Yes(checked)
5	Ernest	Hickman	Boise	218A	(208) 555-4985	No(unchecked)

6 Leave the table open for the next activity.

Activity 4.3 Creating and Populating an Attachment Field

The *Attachment data type* is used to store pictures, Office files, and even small executable programs. In Access 2007, attachments are the preferred data type for storing digital images. In this activity, you will add an attachment field and add two instructor images to the field.

1 In the **Instructors** table, switch to Design View.

2 In the **Field Name** column, below **Full-Time**, type **Attachments** and press Tab. Click the **Data Type arrow** to view the available data types, and then click **Attachment**.

The Attachment data type is assigned. This data type has only two field properties.

3 Under **Field Properties**, in the **Caption** text box, type **Photo**

4 **Save** 💾 the table and switch to Datasheet View. Compare your screen with Figure 4.6.

For each record, the attachment field shows the caption that you entered and displays an attachment icon. The zeroes indicate the number of attachments for that record.

Attachment icon

Figure 4.6

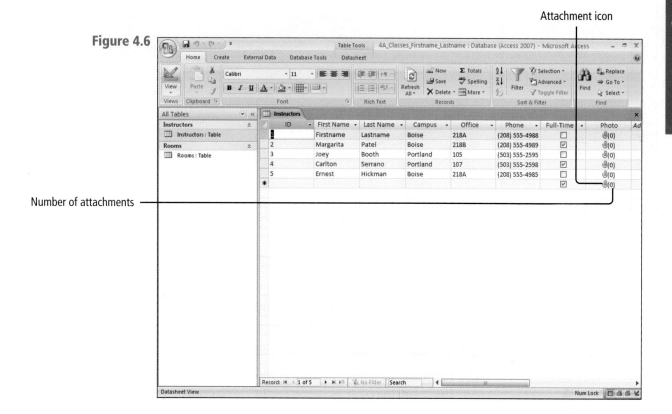

Number of attachments

5 In the record for *Margarita Patel*, double-click the **Photo** attachment field.

The Attachments dialog box displays.

6 In the **Attachments** dialog box, click **Add**. In the displayed **Choose File** dialog box, navigate to the student files for this project and click **a04A_Patel**. Click **Open**.

In Attachments, the file is listed as an attached file. More than one file can be attached to a single attachment field.

7 In the **Attachments** dialog box, click **OK** and compare your screen with Figure 4.7.

The Photo field for Margarita shows that one file is attached.

Figure 4.7

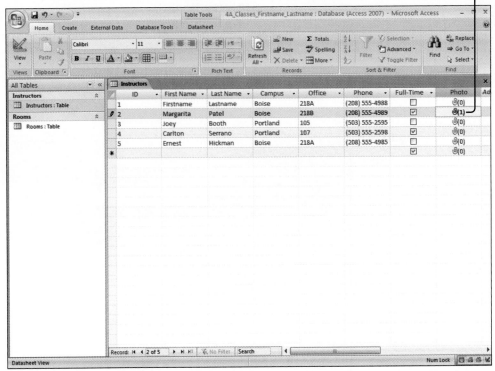

☐ For the photo field for *Joey Booth*, attach the file **a04A_Booth**, located in the student files for this project.

☐ **Save** 🔲 and close ✖ the table.

☐ Click the **Create tab**. In the **Navigation Pane**, be sure the **Instructors** table is selected. In the **Reports group**, click **Report**, and then compare your screen with Figure 4.8.

A report is created based on the Instructors table. The report displays in Layout View, and the Report Layout Tools contextual tabs display.

Figure 4.8

Report Layout Contextual tabs

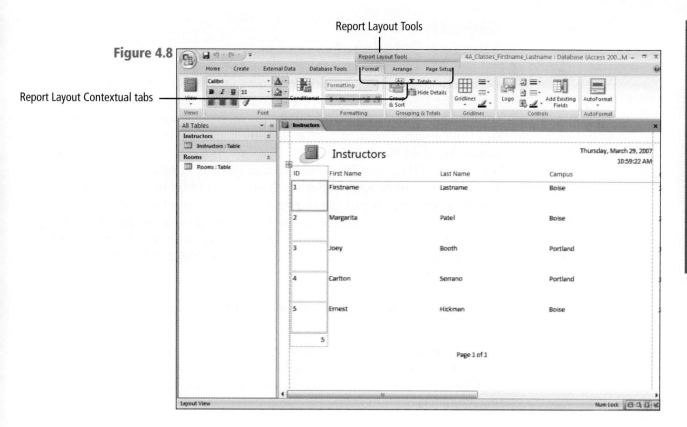

11 In the **AutoFormat group**, click the **AutoFormat button**, and then click the **Civic** AutoFormat—the last choice in the first row.

12 Near the **ID** column header, click the **Layout Selector** button. Click the **Arrange tab**, and then in the **Position group**, click the **Size to Fit** button.

The report now fits on a single page, but some columns are too narrow.

13 Click any phone number so that the column is selected. Place the pointer over the orange border on the right of the **Phone** column.

When the pointer displays, drag to the right so that the phone numbers display on a single line.

14 Click the **Layout Selector** button. In the **Control Layout group**, click the **Control Padding button arrow**, and then click **Wide**.

The controls widen to better fill the page.

15 Display the **Office** menu, point to **Print**, and then click **Print Preview**. Check with your instructor for directions about printing. If your instructor has asked you to print this project, click the **Print** button.

16 **Save** your report. In the **Save As** dialog box, using your name, type **Instructors Firstname Lastname** and then click **OK**. **Close** the report.

Objective 2
Structure Data Input

Certain field properties help the end-user enter data efficiently and cor-rectly. The Lookup data type can be assigned to fields that will contain a common set of values. A Lookup data type, or **lookup field,** retrieves val-ues from another table or a value list. In forms and reports, the retrieved values are then displayed in a list from which the user can quickly select a value. Entering data in a consistent manner is critical if that field will ever be searched or sorted. For fields such as phone numbers, states, and zip codes, the **Input Mask property** can be used to control the structure of the data entered in the field. For example, an input mask can require that all phone numbers be entered as (555) 555-5555. With such an input mask in place, for example, 555.555.5555 could not be entered by mistake.

Activity 4.4 Creating a Lookup Field from a Typed List

Lookup fields are set manually or by using the Lookup Wizard. Whenever possible, you should use the **Lookup Wizard**. The Lookup Wizard fills in the correct field properties needed to perform a lookup. In this activity, you will add a lookup field that displays the times that classes are offered in a combo box.

1 Be sure that the database **4A_Classes_Firstname_Lastname** is still open. On the **Create tab**, in the **Tables group**, click the **Table Design** button.

2 Using the techniques you have practiced, add the following fields with these data types and field size properties:

Field Name	Data Type	Field Size
Code	Text	8
ClassNumber	Text	7
ClassName	Text	100

3 Click anywhere in the **Code row**, and then in the **Tools group**, click the **Primary Key** button. **Save** 🔲 the table with the name **Sections Firstname Lastname**

4 Below **ClassName**, add a new field named **StartTime** In the field just created, click the **Data Type arrow**, and then click **Lookup Wizard**.

5 Click the **I will type in the values that I want** option button, click **Next**, and then compare your screen with Figure 4.9.

A table displays with an **append row** below Col1. The append row is the row where new records or values are entered.

Figure 4.9

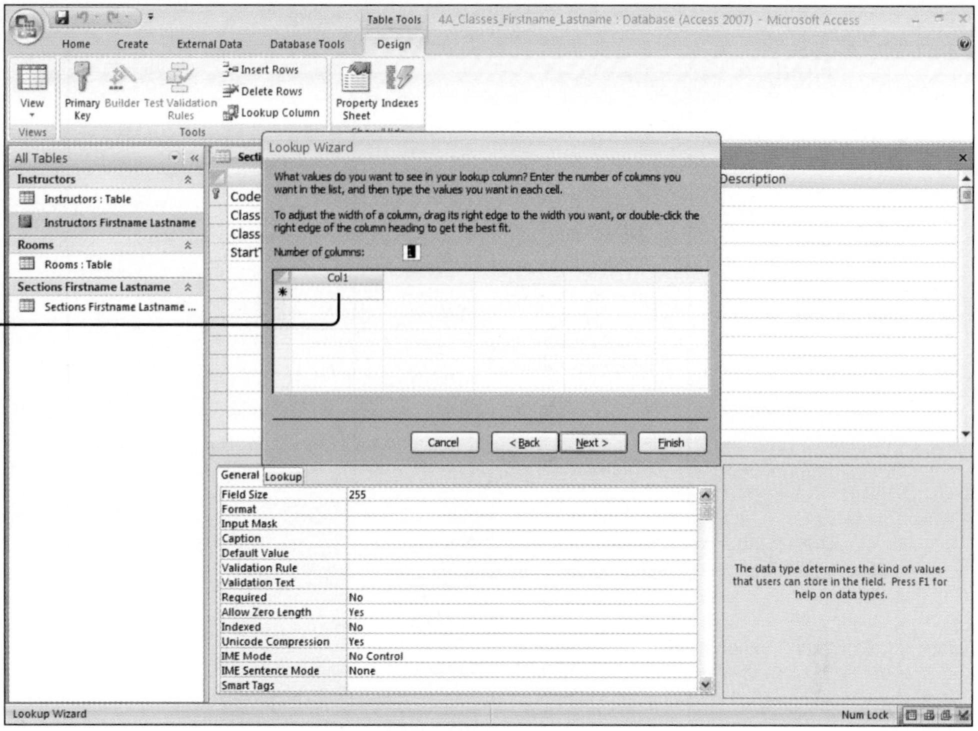

Append row

6 Click in the append row under the **Col1** column header, type **9:00 AM** and press [Tab]. Type the following values using [Tab] to move to the next append row:

Col1 Value
1:00 PM
5:00 PM

7 When you are done typing the values, click **Next**, and then click **Finish**.

Although not yet visible, several field properties for StartTime have been changed.

8 Under **Field Properties**, click the **Lookup tab**, and then compare your screen with Figure 4.10.

Three properties have been changed by the Lookup Wizard. The Display Control has been changed to a *combo box*. A combo box provides an arrow that when clicked displays a list of items from which the user can choose. Combo boxes enable the user to enter a value that is not provided in the list. A lookup field can also be displayed as a *list box*. A list box displays several values without having to click an arrow. Unlike combo boxes, the user cannot add a value that is not in the list. If the Display Control is set to Text Box, all lookup properties for the field will be removed. The Row Source Type determines if the lookup should be performed on a table or a typed list. The *row source property* specifies the name of a table or query or the typed list that actually stores the list of values to be looked up.

Figure 4.10

Display control   Row Source

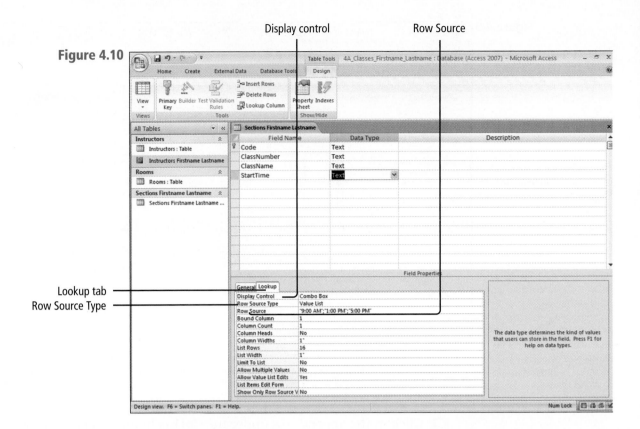

Lookup tab
Row Source Type

⏹**9** **Save** 🖫 the table and switch to Datasheet View. In the append row, click in the **StartTime** field, and then click the **arrow**.

The three values from the typed list display in the combo box.

⏹**10** Press Esc to close the combo box without selecting any value and leave the table open for the next activity.

Activity 4.5 Creating a Lookup Field with Multiple Columns

Recall that lookup fields can also store values in a table. A **_multiple column lookup field_** enables you to see more than one column of data from the table that stores the lookup values. For example, a field can look up the Customer IDs from another table, and then display the customer names and phone numbers in a combo box or list box. In this activity, you will add a lookup field that displays the room number and campus in a list box.

1 With the **Sections** table open in Datasheet View, click in the field below the **Add New Field** column header.

2 Click the **Datasheet tab**. In the **Fields & Columns group**, click the **Lookup Column** button.

You can start the Lookup Wizard in both Design and Datasheet Views.

3 Be sure the **I want the lookup column to look up the values in a table or query** option button is selected, and then click **Next**.

The wizard asks which table or query should be used.

4 Click **Table: Rooms** and click **Next**. Click the **Move All** button ⏵⏵, and then compare your screen with Figure 4.11.

Because two fields were selected, both will display in the combo box or list box.

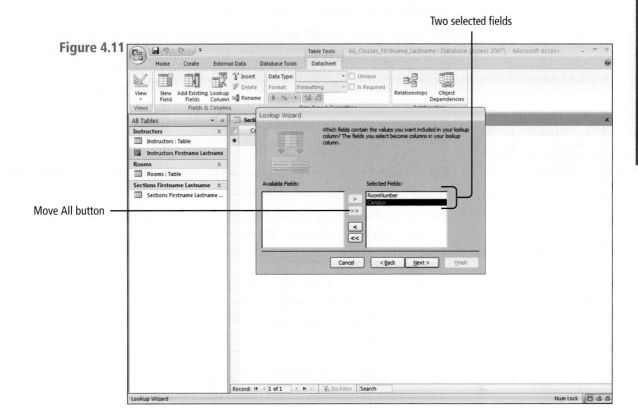

Figure 4.11

Two selected fields

Move All button

5 Click **Next**. For sort **1**, click the **arrow**, and then click **Campus**. For sort **2**, click **RoomNumber**.

The Boise classrooms display before the Portland classrooms.

6 Click **Next** two times, be sure that **RoomNumber** is selected, and then click **Next**.

The room numbers will be stored in the Sections table.

7 In the **What label would you like for your lookup column?** box, type **Room** and then click **Finish**.

A lookup field named Room is added to the table and is selected in the append row.

8 In the **Room** field, click the **arrow**.

Two columns display—one for room numbers, and the other for campuses.

9 Press Esc to close the combo box without selecting any values.

10 Switch to Design View and click in the **Room** row. Under **Field Properties**, be sure that the **Lookup tab** is still active. Click the **Display Control** box, click the displayed **arrow**, and then click **List Box**.

In Datasheet View, a list box displays as a combo box. Later in this project, you will create a form that will display this lookup field as a list box.

11 **Save** 🔲 the table, and leave it open for the next activity.

Activity 4.6 Creating an Input Mask Using a Wizard

The Input Mask Wizard provides several pre-built input masks for commonly recognized data formats such as telephone numbers, Social Security numbers, and dates and times. The wizard then provides screens that enable you to modify and test the input mask. The Input Mask Wizard is a good method to learn how Input Masks work before trying to write one manually. In this activity, you will use the Input Mask Wizard to create an input mask for the date that a class starts.

1 With the **Sections** table open in Design View, add a new field named **StartDate** and assign it the **Date/Time** data type.

2 Under **Field Properties** for **StartDate**, click the **General tab**, and then click in the **Input Mask** box. At the right of the box, click the displayed **Build** button 🔳, and then in the displayed **Input Mask Wizard** dialog box, click **Yes**.

The Input Mask Wizard asks to save the table, and then asks you to choose which input mask best matches how you want the data to look. The wizard lists each input mask and provides an example for each.

3 Click **Medium Date** and click **Next**. Press Tab two times. In the **Try It** text box, type **05jan09** and compare your screen with Figure 4.12.

The characters needed for this input mask are written by the wizard and display in the Input Mask box. The Placeholder character arrow enables you to assign a different placeholder character. *Placeholder characters* are the characters that the user can actually change during data entry. By default, the placeholder character for this input mask is the underscore character. The Try It box shows the results of applying the input mask.

Input mask

Figure 4.12

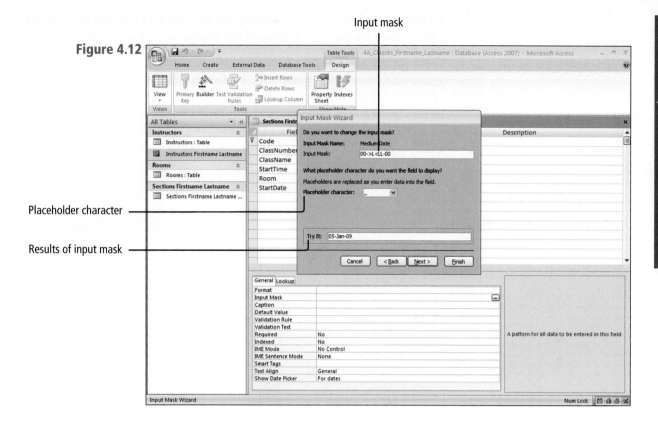

Placeholder character

Results of input mask

---

4 In the **Try It** box, click the first character, and then try to type the letter **n** one time.

This input mask requires numbers in the first two placeholders and will not allow you to enter anything other than a number.

5 Click the **Placeholder character arrow**, and then click **#**. Press Tab one time and type **05jan09**

The placeholder character is replaced as you type.

6 Click **Next**, and then click **Finish**.

The input mask characters are inserted into the StartDate field's Input Mask property.

7 Save 🖫 the table, and leave it open for the next activity.

Activity 4.7 Creating a Custom Input Mask

Often business data must conform to a standard structure unique to that business. In these cases, input masks can be created manually. In this activity, you will create an input mask that ensures that all class names are three capital letters followed by a hyphen followed by three numbers.

1 With the **Sections** table open in Design View, click in the **StartDate row** and compare your screen with Figure 4.13.

All input masks contain three sections, each separated by a semi-colon. Only the first section is required and contains the actual mask characters. Recall that placeholder characters are the characters that can be replaced during data entry. The other type of character that goes in this section is called a *literal character*. A literal character is a character that you do not want the end user to change during data entry, such as the parentheses that might surround an area code.

The second section in an input mask lets you decide if the literal characters should be saved in the table with the data. If this value is set to 0, for example, a phone number would be stored as (555)555-55555. If the second section is set to 1, this same phone number would be stored as 5555555555. The third section of an input mask provides the default placeholder character.

Default placeholder character

Figure 4.13

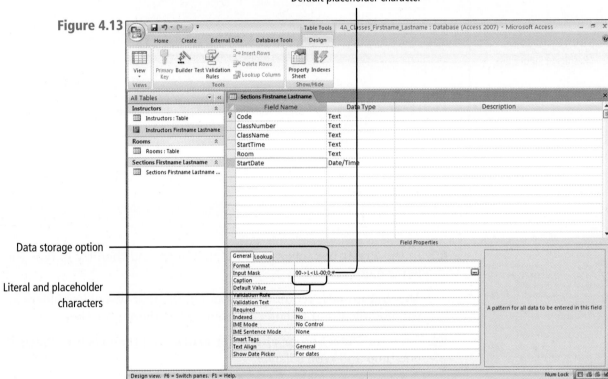

Data storage option

Literal and placeholder characters

▇2▇ Click the **ClassNumber row**. Under **Field Properties**, click the **Input Mask** text box, and then type **>LLL\-000**

The first section of the input mask is complete. During data entry, the end user must enter three letters and three digits. The letters will be converted to uppercase, and because it is a literal character, the hyphen will be placed between the letters and digits.

▇3▇ After the last character of the input mask, type **;0**

Each section of an input mask is separated by semicolons. The zero tells Access to include the hyphen when it stores this data.

▇4▇ After the last character of the input mask, type **;***

The third section is complete. In a new record, each L and 0 in the first section will first display as an asterisk.

▇5▇ **Save** 🖫 the table and switch to Datasheet View. In the **Code** field, type **FOR250AA** and press Tab

▇6▇ In the **ClassNumber** field, type **for250** and press Tab.

The input mask converts the entry to FOR-250.

7 In the **ClassName** field, type **Digital Forensics and Data Recovery** and press Tab.

8 In the **StartTime** field, type **5** and press Tab. Click the **Room arrow**, scroll down and click **214 Boise**, and then press Tab.

Data in combo boxes can be accessed using either the keyboard or the mouse. Although the Room and Building displayed in the Room combo box, only the room number will be stored in the table.

9 In the **StartDate** field, type **06feb09** and press Tab. Double-click the border between the **ClassNumber** and **ClassName** column headers. Double-click the border between the **ClassName** and **StartTime** column headers, and then compare your screen with Figure 4.14.

The entire class name displays and the date *displays* as 2/6/2009. The data is *stored* as a single number such as 37979.875. Access calculates the date from this number, and then formats it according to the field's Format property. The StartTime field's **Format property** is set to General Date. A field's format is an interpretation of the underlying data stored in the table.

Figure 4.14

General Date format

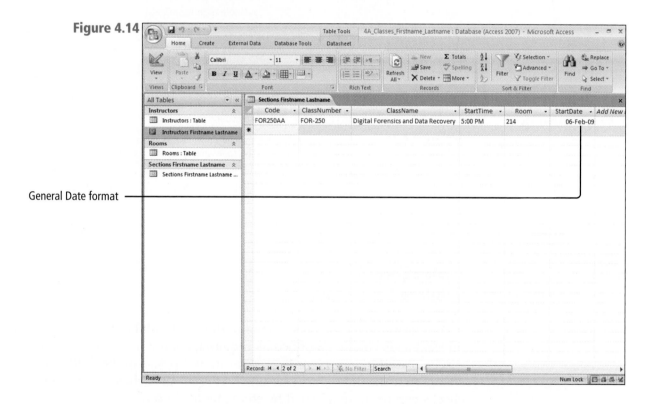

10 Click the **StartDate** column header. Click the **Datasheet tab**. In the **Data Type & Formatting group**, change the **Format** to **Medium Date**.

The date displays as 06-Feb-2009.

11 **Save** the table, and leave it open for the next activity.

More Knowledge

Creating Custom Input Masks

The true power of input masks are the special meanings assigned to placeholder characters. In a Medium Date input mask, 00\->L<LL\-00;0;#, the placeholder characters are 0's and L's. Each 0 in the mask requires the user to enter a single digit. For each L, a letter is required. Special symbols can be used with placeholder characters. Placing > in front of an L converts the following letters to uppercase. Placing < before an L converts the rest of the letters to lowercase. Literal characters are typically preceded by a backslash. For example, \ places a hyphen into the mask as a literal character that cannot be changed by the user. Common characters used in input masks are shown in the table in Figure 4.15.

Common Input Mask Characters

Character	Meaning
0	A single digit is required.
9	A single digit is optional.
L	A single letter is required.
?	A single letter is optional.
A	A single letter or digit is required.
a	A single letter or digit is optional.
&	Any character is required (spaces are characters).
C	Any character is optional.
PASSWORD	Displays them as asterisks(*).
\	The following character will be a literal character.
>	All characters that follow change to uppercase.
<	All characters that follow change to lowercase.

Figure 4.15

Objective 3
Validate Data Input

Access provides many tools to ensure that only valid data is placed into tables. Fields can be identified as required, commonly assigned values can be placed in new records by default, and rules can be written to ensure that the data meets specified criteria. All of these data input checks can be accomplished by changing field properties.

Activity 4.8 Classifying Fields as Required

By default, the only field in a table in which a user must enter a value is the primary key. To require the end-user to enter a value into a different field, one or two properties must be changed, depending on the field's data type. In this activity, you will set two fields as required fields.

1 With the **Sections** table open in Datasheet View, click the **ClassNumber** column header.

2 On the **Datasheet tab**, in the **Data Type & Formatting group**, click the **Is Required** check box.

3 Switch to Design View, and then click the **ClassNumber row**. Compare your screen with Figure 4.16.

The Required property is set to Yes and the Allow Zero Length property is set to No. When a field's **Required property** is set to Yes, that field must contain an entry. The **Allow Zero Length property** determines if an entry can have zero characters. If this property is present, it should be set to No to make the field required.

Figure 4.16

Required property
Allow Zero Length property

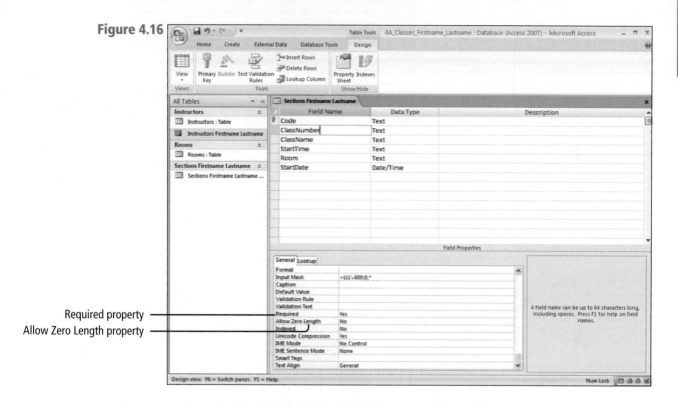

4 Display the **Field Properties** for **ClassName**, double-click the **Required** box, and then double-click the **Allow Zero Length** box.

The Required property changes to Yes and the Allow Zero Length property is set to No.

5 **Save** the table and compare your screen with Figure 4.17.

A message box displays a warning that **data integrity** rules have changed. Data integrity means that data is entered and stored according to its intended use. Access lets you decide if you want to test the existing data. By clicking Yes, Access checks to see if data is in all of the required fields. In a database that already has many records, this may take quite a bit of time. That is why it is important to establish your field properties using small sets of sample data.

Figure 4.17

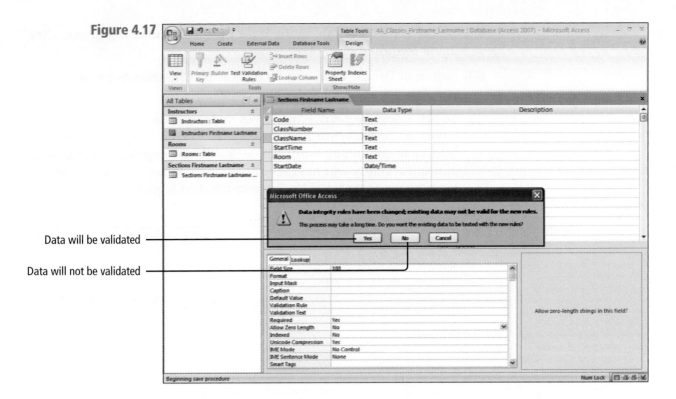

Data will be validated

Data will not be validated

6 In the message box, click **Yes** and keep the table open for the next activity.

Access tests for data integrity by checking that all of the required fields have data in them.

Activity 4.9 Assigning Default Values to Fields

For some fields, a certain value is entered more than any other value. When this happens, setting a default value saves time during data entry. The end-user can skip the field when the default value is the correct entry, or enter a different value if needed. In this activity, you will add a field to store the day of the week that a class meets and set a default value for that field.

1 With the **Sections** table open in Design View, add a new field named **DayofWeek** and assign the **Text** data type.

2 Under **Field Properties**, click in the **Field Size** box, and then type **15**

3 Under **Field Properties**, click in the **Default** box, and then type **Fri**

4 **Save** 🖫 the table and switch to Datasheet View. **Close** « the **Navigation Pane** and compare your screen with Figure 4.18.

Because most classes are held on Fridays, this value will display by default in the append row. Because the first class record has already been entered, the DayofWeek field for that record will need to be entered manually.

Figure 4.18

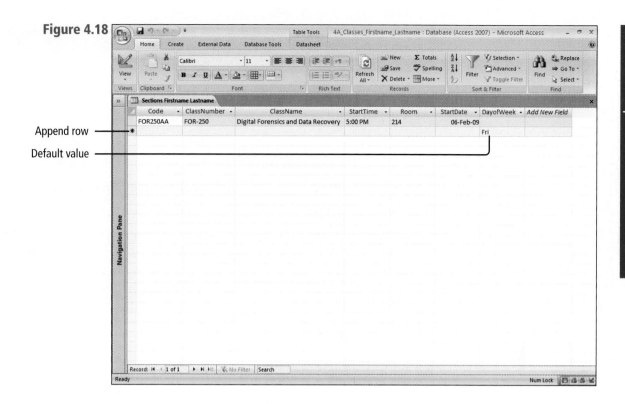

Append row

Default value

5 In the first record, under **DayofWeek**, type **Fri** and press Tab.

The append row becomes the active record.

6 Enter the following new record:

Code	ClassNumber	ClassName	StartTime	Room	StartDate	DayofWeek
MIS100AA	MIS 100	Introduction to Information Systems	9:00 AM	212 (Portland)	13-Feb-09	Fri

7 Leave the table open for the next activity.

Activity 4.10 Setting Validation Properties

The **Validation Rule property** provides another method to ensure that data entered into a table is valid. A Validation Rule property is used to test values for accuracy as they are entered into a table. If an entry fails the test, an error message displays and the value cannot be entered into the table. Custom error messages are written in the field's **Validation Text property**. The Validation Text property provides a custom message when the validation rule has been violated. In this activity you will write a validation rule so that classes meet only on Wednesdays through Saturdays.

Access provides a powerful set of validation rules. These rules are similar to the criteria entered in queries. Examples of common validation rules are shown in the table in Figure 4.19.

Common Validation Rules

Validation Rule	Meaning
>0	Number must be greater than zero
BETWEEN 0 And 1	Number must be between zero and one
<#01/01/2009#	Date must be before 2009
>=#01/01/2009# And <#01/01/2010#	Date must occur during 2009
"Male" Or "Female"	Value must be either Male or Female
Like "[A-Z*@[A-Z].gov"	Value must be a government web site
[ShipDate]<=[OrderDate]+30	Value in ShipDate field must be within 30 days of value in OrderDate field
Len([Passwd])>7	Value in Passwd field must have more than 7 characters

Figure 4.19

1 With the **Sections** table open, switch to Design View and display the field properties for **DayofWeek**.

2 Under **Field Properties**, click in the **Validation Rule** box, and then type **"Wed" Or "Thu" Or "Fri" Or "Sat"**

This rule determines that any data entered into this field must be one of the four values. This rule is an example of a **business rule.** Business rules describe how a business is run. Valid data must follow these business rules. Recall from the scenario that the business offers classes Wednesdays through Saturdays. The validation rule will help enforce this business rule.

3 **Save** 🔲 the table. In the message box that displays, click **Yes**, and then switch to Datasheet View.

The data that we entered in previous activities has passed the validation test.

4 In the append row, enter the following record:

Code	Class Number	ClassName	StartTime	Room	StartDate	DayofWeek
MIS101AA	MIS-101	Database Theory and Design	1:00 PM	212 (Portland)	14-Feb-09	Thu

5 In the record just entered, change **DayofWeek** to **Mon** press ⟨Tab⟩, and then compare your screen with Figure 4.20.

A message box warns that the data entered into the field did not pass the data integrity test. The message shows the actual validation rule and field name but is not very user-friendly. This message box can be customized.

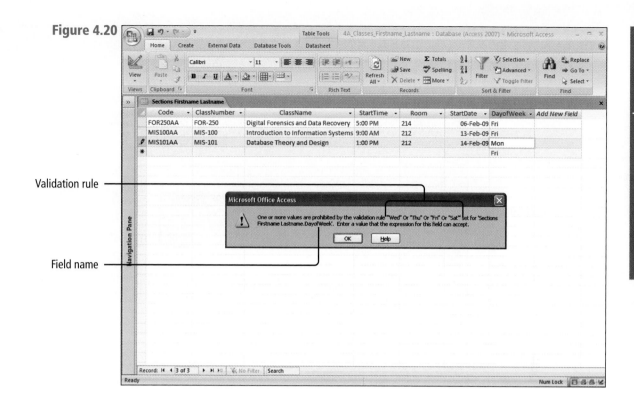

Figure 4.20

Validation rule

Field name

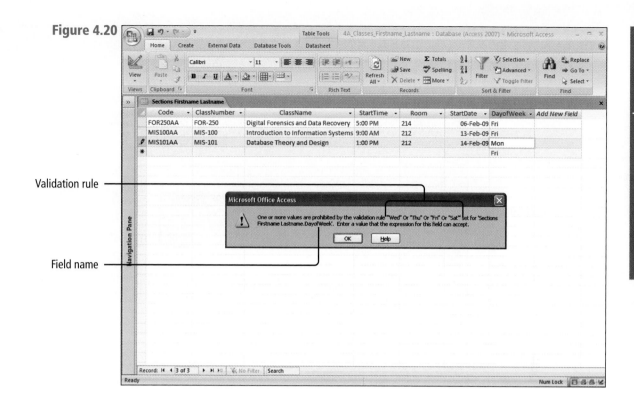

6 Click **OK** and in the **DayofWeek** field, replace the existing text with **Sat** and then press Tab.

No warning displays because the new value has passed the validation test.

7 Switch to Design View and display the field properties for **DayofWeek**. In the **Validation Text** box, type the following sentence: **The day must be Wed, Thu, Fri, or Sat.**

Text should be entered that informs the user what type of data the field requires.

8 **Save** the table and switch to Datasheet View. In the first record, change the **DayofWeek** to **Friday** and then press Tab. Compare your screen with Figure 4.21.

The message you entered in the Validation Text property displays in the message box.

Figure 4.21

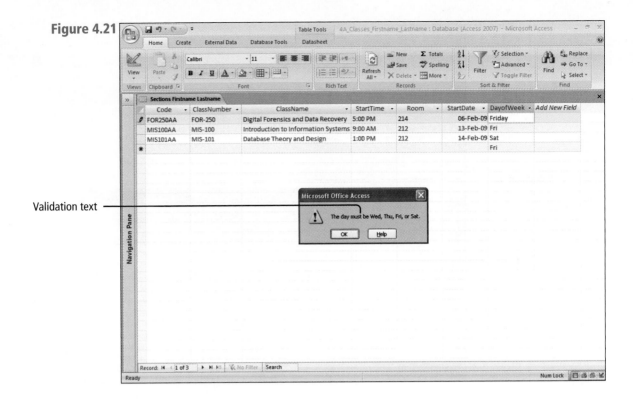

Validation text

9 Click **OK**, and then press Esc to return to the original value.

10 **Close** ☒ the table.

Activity 4.11 Testing a Validation System in a Form

Typically, data is entered into forms, not directly into tables as you have been doing so far in this project. Because the end-users will be entering data in forms, it is important that you test your validation system using a form. In this activity, you will create a form for the Sections table and test your data validation system by entering data using the form.

1 **Open** ⏩ the **Navigation Pane** and click the **Sections** table. Click the **Create tab,** and then in the **Forms group**, click the **Form** button.

A new form is created and opened in Layout View.

2 In the **AutoFormat group**, click the **More arrow**, and then click the **Civic** AutoFormat. Click in the **ClassName** text box, and then drag to resize the width of the control. The control should be just wide enough to display the entire class name.

All of the control widths are adjusted.

3 Click the **ClassName** text box and drag the lower border up so that the control is one line tall. Repeat this technique so that the **StartTime** text box is one line tall.

4 Switch to Form View. At the bottom of the form window, click the **New (blank) record** button 🖀 and compare your screen with Figure 4.22.

A blank form displays so that a new record can be entered. StartTime is a combo box, Room displays as a list box, and the default value for DayofWeek is already entered.

Figure 4.22

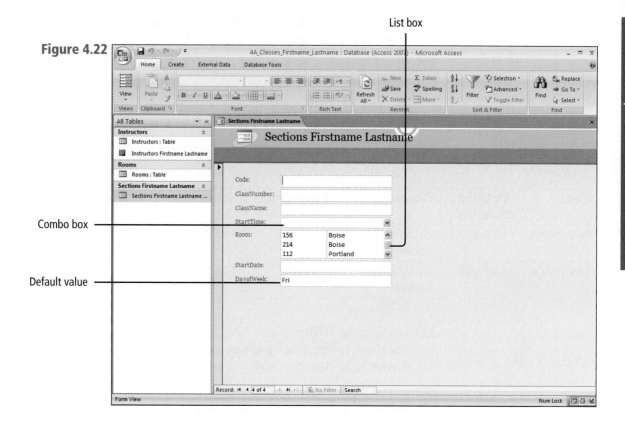

List box

Combo box

Default value

5 **Save** 🔒 the form, accept **Sections Firstname Lastname** in the displayed **Save As** dialog box, and click **OK**.

The new form is listed in the Navigation Pane.

6 In the **Code** field, type **NET101BA** and press Tab. In the **ClassNumber** field, type **net101** and press Tab.

The input mask converts the letters to uppercase and inserts the hyphen for you. The input mask will not allow the data to be stored until it conforms to the structure specified in the input mask.

7 In the **ClassName** field, type **Network Design** and press Tab. In the **StartTime** field, type **5** and press Tab.

Because StartTime is a lookup field, Access provides a combo box in the form. The end-user can click one of the choices or enter a new time in the blank space at the top of the list.

8 In the **Room** field, press ↓ until **212 Portland** is selected, and then press Tab.

By using the Tab and arrow keys, you are able to enter data without using the mouse. Keeping both hands on the keyboard speeds data entry.

9 In the **StartDate** field, type **2/**

The input mask will not allow the date to be entered in this format.

10 Press ←Bksp, type **18feb09** and then press Tab. In the **DayofWeek** field, type **Wednesday** and press Tab.

Data integrity rules have been violated and the validation text displays in a message box.

11 In the display message, click **OK**. In the **DayofWeek** field, replace the entry with **Wed** and press Tab.

The record is stored in the table and the form displays a new blank record. Entire records can be entered without ever using the mouse.

12 Using the techniques you have just practiced, add the following records without using the mouse:

Code	Catalog Number	ClassName	StartTime	Room	StartDate	DayofWeek
SRV152BA	SRV-152	Apache Web Server	9:00 AM	145 (Boise)	20-Feb-09	Fri
SRV152CA	SRV-152	Apache Web Server	9:00 AM	112 (Portland)	21-Feb-09	Sat

13 Display the **Office** menu , point to **Print**, and then click **Print Preview**. In the **Page Layout group**, click the **Margins button arrow**, and click **Normal**.

14 In the **Page Layout group**, click the **Columns** button. Under **Grid Settings**, in the N**umber of Columns** box, replace the value with **2** Under **Column Size**, in **Width**, replace the value with **3.5"** and then click **OK**.

15 If your instructor has asked you to print this project, click **Print**.

16 **Save** and then **Close** ☒ the form. **Exit Access** to close the database and to quit Access.

End **You have completed Project 4A** ────────────

Project 4B **Registration**

The MIS Technical Training Institute needs a database that will track their courses and the students enrolled them. In Activities 4.13 through 4.25, you will work with the tables that store information about their classes, the times those classes are offered, and the students who will enroll in these classes. When you are done, you will have a relational database that can be used to register students into classes. Your final output will be a form, query, and report that will look similar to Figure 4.23.

For Project 4B, you will need the following file:

a04B_Registration

**You will save your database as
4B_Registration_Firstname_Lastname**

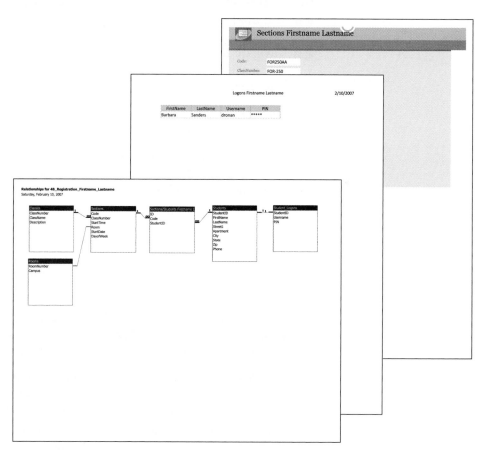

Figure 4.23
Project 4B—Registration

Objective 4
Create Indexes and Change Sort Order

In a database, data must often be searched and sorted. In a typical business database, tables will contain *thousands* of rows. Searching and sorting a large table is very time-consuming. Databases use **indexes** to speed searching and sorting. The **Indexed property** creates a second, more efficient table that is quickly searched or sorted. Access does not show you the actual index tables, but it does build and use them. Indexes can slow data entry because as data is entered, the table as well as the table's indexes are updated. Therefore, indexes should be built only for fields that will be searched or sorted often.

Activity 4.12 Creating an Index to Optimize Sorting Data

By default, tables are sorted by their primary key. Some tables need to be sorted using a field other than their primary keys. In a large database, these fields should be indexed. In this activity, you will build an index for a field that stores student last names.

1 Navigate to the location where you are storing the student files for this project. Right-click **a04B_Registration**, and then click **Copy** from the shortcut menu.

2 Open the **Access Chapter 4** folder and paste the copied file. Rename the file **4B_Registration_Firstname_Lastname**

3 Open **4B_Registration_Firstname_Lastname** in Access 2007. If necessary, in the Message bar, click Options. Click Enable this content, and then click OK.

4 Open the **Navigation Pane**, and then open the **Students** table in Datasheet View.

The students are sorted by the primary key, StudentID. In the forms, queries, and reports that will use this table, the data will typically need to be sorted by the students' last names.

5 Switch to Design View and click the **LastName row**. Under **Field Properties**, click the **Indexed** text box. Click the displayed **arrow** and compare your screen with Figure 4.24.

The Yes (Duplicates OK) option will create an index that enables duplicate values to exist. Because a student may have the same last name as another student, this choice is the best option. The other option, Yes (No Duplicates), builds an index where every value in that field must be unique in the table.

Figure 4.24

Yes (No Duplicates) option

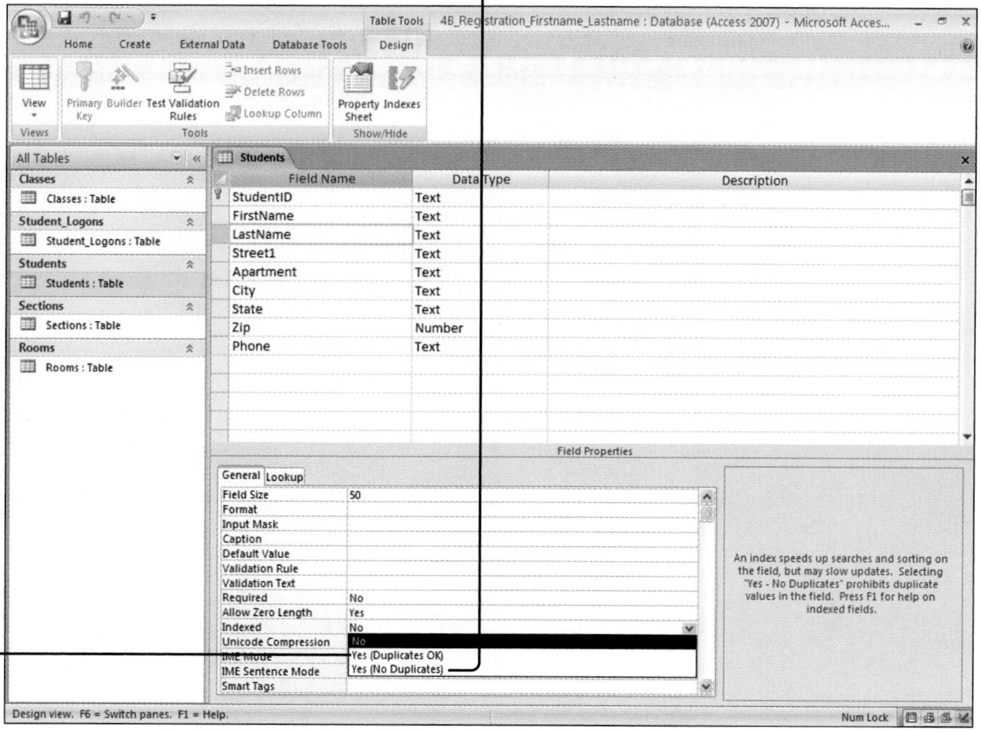

Yes (Duplicates OK) option

6 Click **Yes (Duplicates OK)**, and then **Save** the table.

The index is built during the save operation.

7 Switch to Datasheet View. Click the **LastName** column header. In the **Find group**, click the **Find** button. In the displayed **Find and Replace** dialog box, in the **Find What** box, type **Golden** and then press Enter.

The first instance of Golden in the LastName field is quickly found.

8 Click **Cancel** to close the **Find and Replace** dialog box. Right-click the **LastName** column header and in the displayed shortcut menu, click **Sort A to Z**.

The field's index was used to sort the table by the student's last name.

9 **Save** the table and switch to Design View. On the **Design tab**, in the **Show/Hide group**, click the **Property Sheet** button, and then compare your screen with Figure 4.25.

The table's Property Sheet displays. In the Order By property, the LastName field is designated as the default sort order.

Table Property Sheet

Figure 4.25

Default sort order

10 Close [X] the **Property Sheet** and **Close** [X] the table.

Activity 4.13 Creating an Index to Maintain Data Integrity

An index can be built to ensure that a field's value is unique among all records in a table. This is useful when that field is not the table's primary key, yet each record needs to hold unique value in that table. In this activity, you will create an index that ensures that each user name is a unique value.

1 Open the **Student_Logons** table in Design View. Click in the **Username row**. Under **Field Properties**, change the **Indexed** property for this field to **Yes (No Duplicates)**.

This type of index will ensure that each student has a unique user name. This is the same type of index used for a primary key.

2 Display the field properties for the **PIN** field, click in the **Input Mask** text box, and then type **Password**

The Password input mask displays all of the Password's characters as asterisks, but stores the actual password in the table.

3 Save [💾] the table, and then switch to Datasheet View. At the bottom of the table, click the **New (blank) record** [button] button.

4 In the append row, for **StudentID**, enter **998-16-3283** and press [Tab]. In the **Username** field, type **kamote** and press [Tab].

This user name is already used and will create a duplicate value. However, Access will not check for duplicate values until you are completely done entering data into the record.

5 In the **Password** field, type **12345** Press ⌨Tab and compare your screen with Figure 4.26.

Because there are two identical user names, Access will not store this record in the table.

Figure 4.26

6 Click **OK** and change the **Username** to **damoter** and press ⌨Tab two times.

The new user name is a unique value and the record's data is stored in the table.

7 **Close** ⌫ the table.

Objective 5
Create Relationships Between Tables

Many programs—including Word and Excel—can store data in tables. The true power of using a database program instead of Word or Excel is its capability to *relate* tables. Recall that a **relationship** is an association between two tables that is established using a field common to both tables. Recall also that relationships between tables can be created several ways. When a lookup field is created, a relationship is established. Queries, forms, and reports can also establish relationships between tables. None of those methods will enforce **referential integrity**. Recall that referential integrity refers to the rules used to preserve valid data in the relationship when records are entered, edited, or deleted.

Related fields do not need to have the same names, but they do need to have the same data type. The only exception is when one of the fields is an AutoNumber. In that case, the related field must be a number and both fields must have the same Field Size property.

Activity 4.14 Establishing a One-to-One Relationship

When a table has numerous fields, or certain data needs to be isolated for security purposes, the table can be divided into smaller tables. The smaller tables are then related using a **one-to-one relationship**. In a one-to-one relationship, the common field used to join the tables must have one, and only one, matching record in the other table. This type of relationship is rare and only used in limited situations. In this activity, you will create a one-to-one relationship between the Students and Student_Logons tables.

1 Click the **Database Tools tab**, and in the **Show/Hide group**, click the **Relationships** button.

2 In the **Relationships group**, click the **Show Table** button, and in the displayed **Show Table** dialog box, click **Students**, and then click **Add**. Click **Student_Logons**, click **Add**, and then **Close** the **Show Table** dialog box.

To create a relationship, the two tables must be added to the Relationships window.

Note — Removing Tables from the Relationships Window

Access will enable you to place more than one copy of a table into the Relationships Window. If you need to remove a table, right-click the table, and then click Hide Table. Alternatively, click the table title bar and press [Delete].

3 Move the pointer over the lower border of the **Students** table. When the [↕] pointer displays, drag down until the **Phone** field displays. Compare your screen with Figure 4.27.

Every student in this table has a matching record in the Students table. For security purposes, each student's logon data has been isolated from the data stored in the Students table. The two tables need to be joined in a one-to-one relationship. Both tables have the StudentID field in common.

Figure 4.27

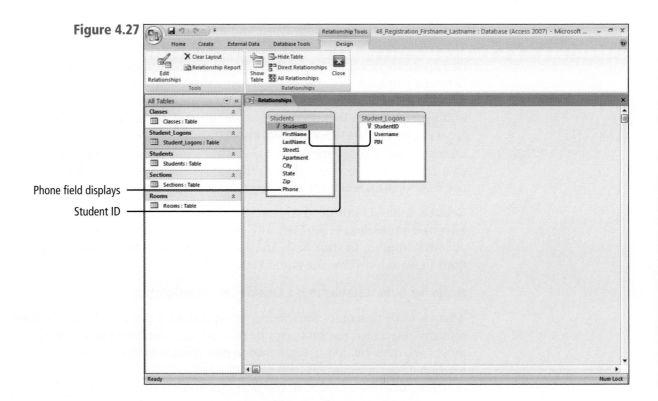

Phone field displays

Student ID

4 In the **Students** table, place the pointer over **StudentID**. Click and drag **StudentID** to the right so that is directly over **StudentID** in the **Student_Logons** table, and then release the mouse button. Compare your screen with Figure 4.28.

The Edit Relationships dialog box shows that StudentID will be used to relate the two tables and provides options for the relationship. One-to-one relationships are established only if the fields used to relate both tables are primary keys or are indexed with no duplicates.

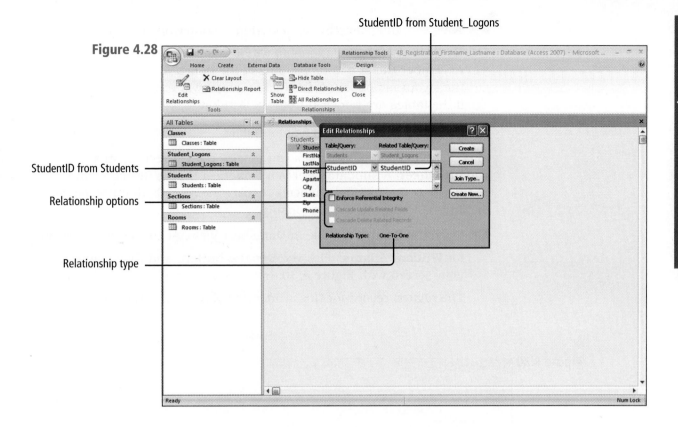

StudentID from Student_Logons

Figure 4.28

StudentID from Students

Relationship options

Relationship type

5 Click the **Enforce Referential Integrity** check box, click **Create**, and then compare your screen with Figure 4.29.

The relationship is created. Access displays the relationship as a line joining the tables with a number one on each side of the line.

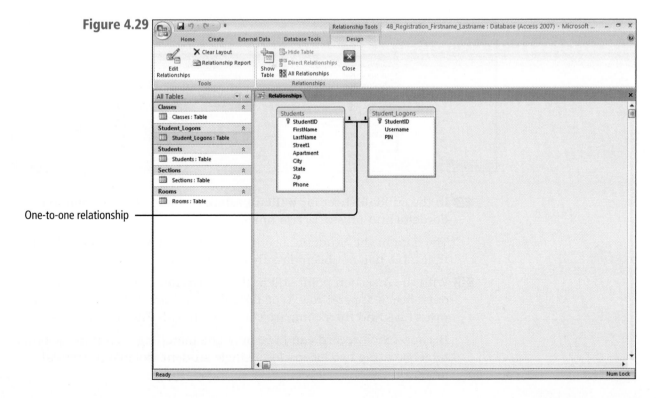

Figure 4.29

One-to-one relationship

6 Save 🖫 and leave the Relationships window open.

The layout of the Relationship window is saved so that Access can remember the size and positions of the tables within the window. If the layout is not saved, the relationships will remain in place, even if the tables are removed from the window.

Activity 4.15 Working with Related Tables

In Design View, Access enables you to view related records in a *subdatasheet*. A subdatasheet is a datasheet that is nested within another datasheet. Subdatasheets display the records that are joined to the first table through a relationship.

1 Open the **Students** table in Datasheet View. At the left of the record for **William Adams**, click the **Expand** button, and then compare your screen with Figure 4.30.

The related record for this student displays in a subdatasheet.

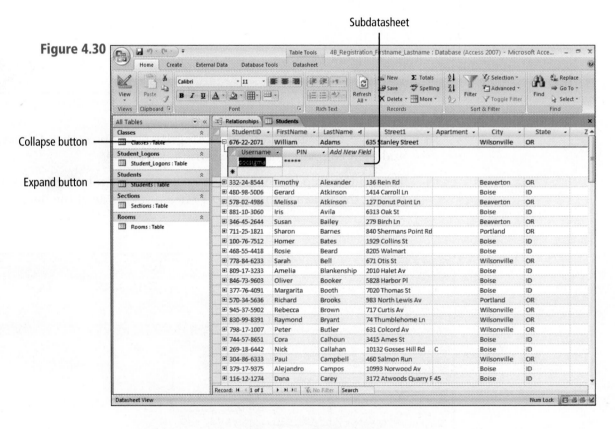

Figure 4.30

2 In the subdatasheet for **William Adams**, change the **Username** to **docdelta** and press Tab two times.

The data in the Student Logons table has been updated even though that table has not been directly opened.

3 With the insertion point still in the **Username** column of the sub-datasheet's append row, type **docdelta2** and press Tab. Type **12345** press Tab, and then compare your screen with Figure 4.31.

Because each record can have only one matching record in the other table, creating two logons for a single student violates referential integrity.

Figure 4.31

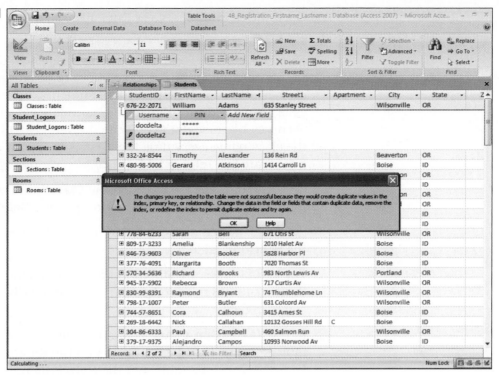

4 Click **OK** to close the message box, and then press Esc to cancel the data entry. **Close** ⊠ the **Students** table.

5 Open the **Student_Logons** table in Datasheet View. Click the **Username** column heading, and then in the **Find** group, click **Find**.

6 In the **Find What** box, type **docdelta** and press Enter.

7 **Close** the **Find and Replace** dialog box and **Expand** ⧽ the subdatasheet for docdelta.

The record for William Adams displays in the subdatasheet.

8 In the subdatasheet for **docdelta**, change the **Street1** value to **4543 E 5th St**

The new address is stored in the Students table.

9 **Close** ⊠ the **Student_Logons** table.

Activity 4.16 Creating a One-to-Many Relationship

Recall that a ***one-to-many relationship*** is the most common type of relationship in a relational database. In a one-to-many relationship, the common field in the first table is typically the table's primary key, although it could be an indexed field that does not allow duplicate values. In the second table, the related field is called a ***foreign key***. Recall that foreign keys are always on the "many" side of the relationship. Establishing proper one-to-many relationships provides the means to maintain accurate and timely information. In this activity, you will create a one-to-many relationship between the Classes and Sections tables.

1 Open the **Sections** table in Datasheet View.

This table will store one record each time a class is offered. With the current structure, this table will have repeated data. For example, the class name for MIS-100 will have to be entered every time the class is offered to a new group of students. In a database, this is called **data redundancy**. Data redundancy decreases efficiency and accuracy because data is repeated unnecessarily. Instead of entering the class name every time the class is taught, it should be stored in a separate but related table.

2 Click the **Datasheet tab**. Click the **ClassName** column header, and then in the **Fields & Columns group**, click **Delete**.

In the displayed message box, click **Yes** to delete the field. **Close** ⊠ the **Sections** table.

The class names are stored in the Classes table. The Classes and Sections tables need to be related using the ClassNumber field as the common field.

3 In the **Navigation Pane**, locate the **Classes** table. Drag the **Classes** table from the **Navigation Pane** into the **Relationships** window. Drag the **Sections** table into the **Relationships** window.

4 **Close** the **Navigation Pane**. In the **Relationships** window, click the title bar of **Student_Logons** table, drag it to the upper right corner of the window, and release the mouse. Use this technique to position the three other tables as shown in Figure 4.32.

Figure 4.32

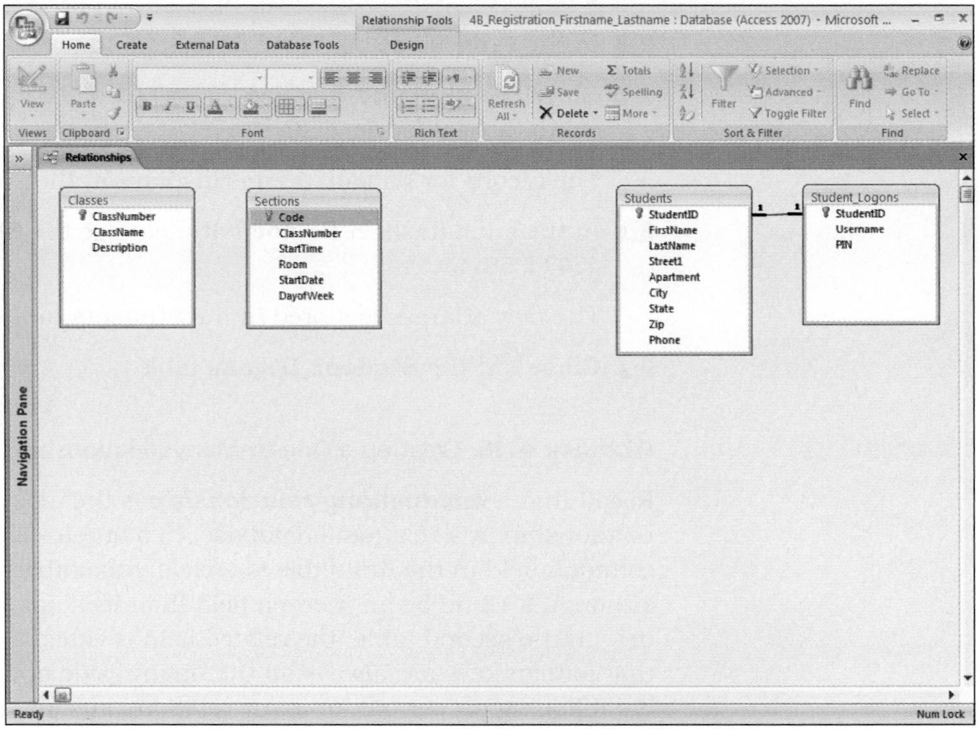

5 Using one of the techniques that you have practiced, add the **Rooms** table to the **Relationships** window. Position the table as shown in Figure 4.33.

The Rooms field in the Sections table is a lookup field that looks up values from the Rooms table. When a lookup field is created, an *indeterminate relationship* is established. An indeterminate relationship is a relationship that cannot enforce referential integrity. In the Relationships window, Access displays this type of relationship as a single line between the related tables.

Figure 4.33

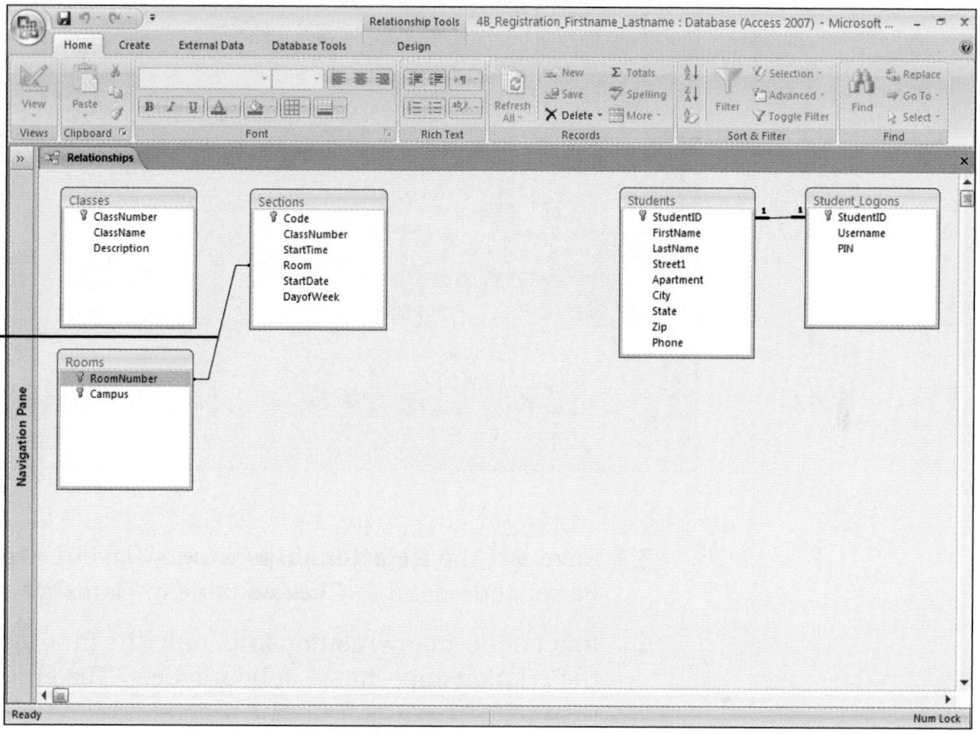

Indeterminate relationship

6 If necessary, close the **Navigation Pane**. Drag the **ClassNumber** field from the **Classes** table and drop it on the **ClassNumber** field in the **Sections** table.

The Relationships dialog box displays, indicating that a one-to-many relationship will be created.

7 Select the **Enforce Referential Integrity** check box, and then select the **Cascade Update Fields** check box. Do not select the **Cascade Delete Related Records** check box.

In a *cascading update*, whenever the data in the first table is changed, all the related occurrences of the data in the second table are also changed. With a *cascading delete*, deleting a record in the first table will cause all matching records in the second table to also be deleted. If *Cascade Delete Related Records* was selected, deleting a class from the Classes table would delete all past records of when that class had been taught.

8 In the **Edit Relationships** dialog box, click **Create**, and then compare your screen with Figure 4.34.

The one-to-many relationship displays in the Relationships window.

Figure 4.34

One-to-many relationship

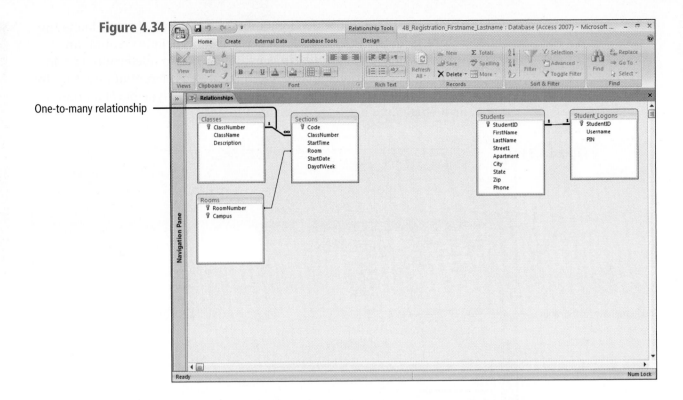

9 Save ⊟ the **Relationships** window layout, **Open** the **Navigation Pane**, and open the **Classes** table in Datasheet View.

In a one-to-many relationship, only the first table—the one side of the relationship—has a subdatasheet. The subdatasheet lists all the related records from the second table—the many side of the relationship.

10 In the subdatasheet's append row, add the following sections for FOR-250:

Code	StartTime	Room	StartDate	DayofWeek
FOR250CA	1:00 PM	218	03-Apr-09	Fri
FOR250DA	9:00 AM	218	10-Jul-09	Fri

Room 218 is not a room listed in the Rooms table. Recall the relationship between the Sections table and the Rooms table does not enforce referential integrity. If this was a one-to-many relationship, the new room number would not be allowed.

11 For **ClassNumber** FOR-250, change the **ClassName** to **Digital Forensics and Data Recovery**

By storing the class name in the related Classes table, every section of this class will now use the new name by changing only one record. Had the class name been still stored in the Sections table, you would have needed to change the class name in three records.

12 Close ☒ the table.

Activity 4.17 Creating a Many-to-Many Relationship

In a *many-to-many relationship*, a record can match many records in the second table and a record in the second table can match many records from the first table. In this activity, you will create a many-to-many relationship between the Sections and Students tables.

1 If it is not already open, open the **Relationships** window, and then **Close** ⟨«⟩ the **Navigation Pane**.

To register students into a class, the Sections table and the Students table need to be joined in a relationship. Because a student can take many classes and a class can have many students, this relationship will be a many-to-many relationship.

2 Click the **Create tab**. In the **Tables group**, click the **Table Design** button.

3 Using the techniques you have practiced, add the following fields to the new table:

Field Name	Data Type	Description
ID	AutoNumber	Primary Key
Code	Text	Foreign Key
StudentID	Text	Foreign Key

4 Set **ID** as the **Primary Key**, and then click **Save**. In the displayed **Save As** dialog box, name the table **Sections/Students Firstname Lastname** and click **OK**.

5 **Close** ⟨X⟩ the table. Using one of the techniques you have practiced in this project, add the **Sections/Students** table to the **Relationships** window.

6 In the **Relationships** window, position the **Sections/Students Firstname Lastname** table between **Sections** and **Students**.

In the strictest sense, a many-to-many relationship cannot be created. Instead, the primary keys from each table are placed into a third table called a *junction table*. Junction tables join the two outer tables with two one-to-many relationships. Together, all three tables function as a many-to-many relationship. The Sections/Students table will be a junction table.

7 Click the **Design tab**, and then in the **Tools group**, click the **Edit Relationships** button, and then in the displayed **Edit Relationships** dialog box, click the **Create New** button.

The Create New dialog box is another method used to create a relationship.

8 Under **Left Table Name**, click the **arrow**, and then click **Sections**. Under **Right Table Name**, click the **arrow**, and then click **Sections/Students**. For both the **Left Column Name** and **Right Column Name** boxes, click **Code**, and then compare your screen with Figure 4.35

Figure 4.35

Right table and column names

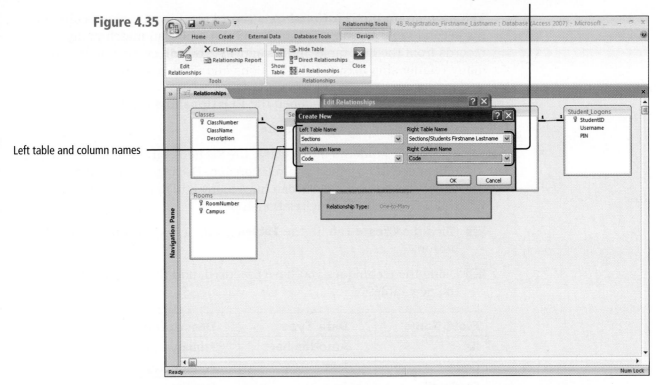

Left table and column names

9 Click **OK**. Select the **Enforce Referential Integrity**, **Cascade Update Related Fields**, and **Cascade Delete Related Records** check boxes, and then click **Create**.

A one-to-many relationship is created.

10 From the **Students** table, drag and drop the **StudentID** field onto the **StudentID** field in the **Sections/Students** table. Select the **Enforce Referential Integrity**, **Cascade Update Related Fields**, and **Cascade Delete Related Records** check boxes. Click **Create** and then compare your screen with Figure 4.36.

The many-to-many relationship is formed by joining each table to the junction table using one-to-many relationships.

Junction table

Figure 4.36

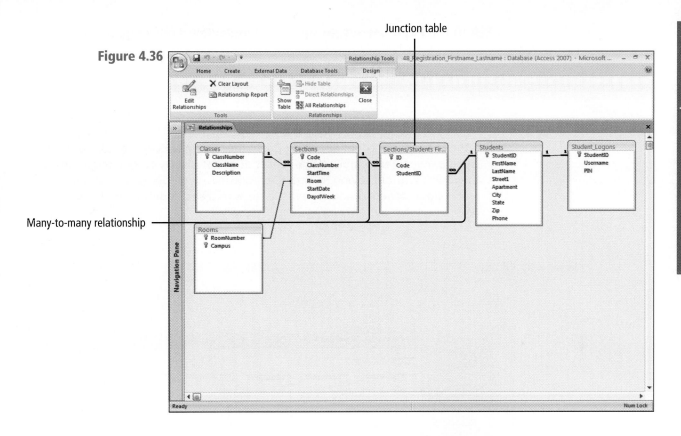

Many-to-many relationship

11 Click **Save** and leave the **Relationships** window open for the next activity.

Objective 6
Create Queries, Forms, and Reports from Related Tables

In relational databases, the queries, forms, and reports based on related tables can access data from the related tables. This data can be shaped and grouped, and even repeated, without having to place redundant data in the underlying tables. For example, a report that lists the students enrolled in each class section can include all of the information from the related students table.

Activity 4.18 Creating a Relationships Report

The Relationships window can be printed in a report. The *relationships report* is a special report showing the current layout of the Relationships window. This report is useful for database designers. In this activity, you will create a relationships report for the relationships you created earlier in this project.

1 With the **Relationships** window still open, in the **Tools group**, click the **Relationship Report** button.

A report is created and opened in Print Preview.

2 In the **Zoom group**, click the upper portion of the **Zoom** button.

The first page now fits the screen.

3 In the **Page Layout group**, click **Landscape** and compare your screen with Figure 4.37.

The report should now fit on one page.

Alert!	Does your report not fit on one page?
	If the entire report does not fit on one page, you may have placed too much space between each table. If the report does not display on one page, close the report without saving it. In the Relationships window, position your tables closer together and repeat the steps to create a new relationships report.

Figure 4.37

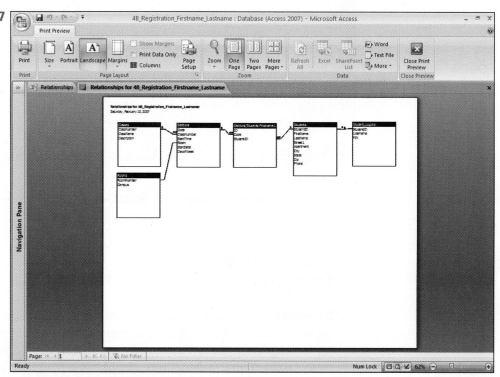

4 Click **Save** 🖫 and in the displayed **Save As** dialog box, accept the suggested name by clicking **OK**.

5 If your instructor wants you to print this project, print the report.

6 **Close** the Print Preview view. **Close** ✖ the report. **Close** ✖ the **Relationships** window, and then expand 》 the **Navigation Pane**.

Activity 4.19 Creating a Query Using Related Tables

Data from more than one table can be queried. Recall that a **query** is the method used to extract information from the database. To display information from more than one table, queries match the values in the two fields that join the tables. In Access, the relationship defined in the Relationships window will also display in the query's Design View. In this activity, you will create a query that uses related data from two related tables.

1 Click the **Create tab**. In the **Other group**, click the **Query Design** button.

A new query is created and the Show Table dialog displays.

2 In the **Show Table** dialog box, double-click **Students**, and then double-click **Student_Logons**. Close the **Show Table** dialog box and compare your screen with Figure 4.38.

The two tables are added to the query, and the one-to-one relationship displays much like it did in the Relationships window.

Figure 4.38

One-to-one relationship

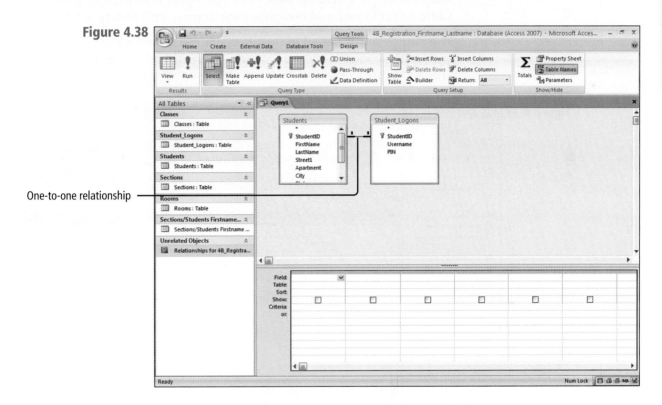

3 In the **Students** table, double-click **FirstName**, and then double-click **LastName**. In the **Student_Logons** table, double-click **Username** and **PIN**.

Four fields are added to the query. By matching the Student ID fields, the query can display the data from both tables.

4 In the **Criteria** row for the **LastName** column, type **Sanders** and then in the **Results group**, click the **Run** button.

The logon information for Barbara Sanders displays.

5 **Save** the query, and name it **Logons Firstname Lastname**

6 If your instructor asks you to print this project, from the **Office** menu , click **Print**, and then retrieve your printout from the printer.

7 **Close** the query.

Activity 4.20 Creating a Form Using Related Tables

In a relational database, a single form can be used to enter data from more than one table. **Subforms** are forms inserted within another form, and are often used for tables in a one-to-many relationship. Subforms typically display all the records related to the record being viewed in the main form. In this activity, you will create a form and subform based on the Sections table.

1 In the **Navigation Pane**, click the **Sections** table. Click the **Create tab**, and in the **Forms group**, click the **Form** button. Apply the **Civic** AutoFormat and compare your screen with Figure 4.39.

The subform will list all of the students registered for the FOR250AA section that starts on Feb. 6, 2009. There are currently no students enrolled in this class.

Figure 4.39

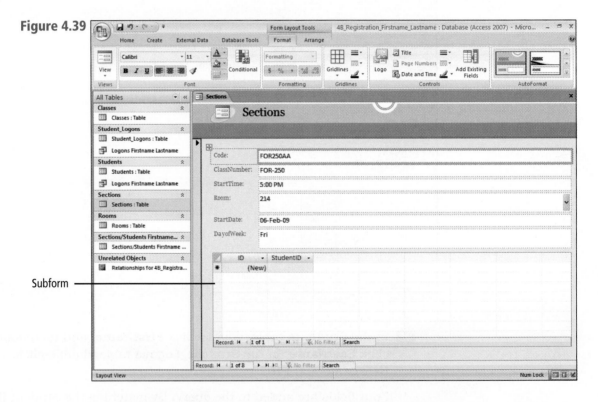

Subform

2 Switch to Form View and in the append row of the subform, under **StudentID**, type **101-29-8307** and then press ⏎ Tab two times. Repeat the technique just practiced to enroll the following students into the class.

ID	StudentID
(AutoNumber)	798-17-1007
(AutoNumber)	128-38-9699
(AutoNumber)	183-24-1031
(AutoNumber)	350-50-1786
(AutoNumber)	998-16-3283

Six students have been enrolled in section FOR250AA.

3 Switch to Layout View, double-click the **Form title** text box, and change the title to **Sections Firstname Lastname**

4 Click the subform so that it is selected, and decrease and move its right border so that only the first two columns display. Decrease the width of the **Code** text box so it is the same width as the subform.

All of the text boxes in the main form are resized and the subform's datasheet fits its contents better.

5 Display the **Office** menu , point to **Print**, and then click **Print Preview**. In the **Page Layout group**, click the **Columns** button. Under **Column Size**, in the **Width** box, replace the value with **7.5"** and then click **OK**.

6 Click **Save** . Name the form **Registration Form Firstname Lastname** and then click **OK**. Click the **Close Print Preview** button.

7 If your instructor asks you to print this project, click **Print**. Under **Print Range**, click the **Selected Record(s)** option button, and then click **OK**.

8 **Close** ☒ the form. If asked to save changes, click Yes.

9 **Exit Access**.

End **You have completed Project 4B** ———————

There's More You Can Do!

From My Computer, navigate to the student files that accompany this textbook. In the folder **02_theres_more_you_can_do**, locate and open the folder for this chapter. Open and print the instructions for this project, which are provided to you in Adobe PDF format.

Try It! 1—Add a Custom Entry to the Quick Part Gallery

Content-Based Assessments

Access

chapterfour

Summary

Setting proper field properties ensures that a database contains valid information. Data is structured and tested using an Input Mask or Validation Rule. Lookup fields speed data entry by retrieving data from a table or list, and then displaying in a combo box or list box. Other properties, such as the Caption property, provide a user friendly label for field names.

A relational database groups similar data into tables and then relates those tables using common fields. Depending on the nature of the data, these relationships can be one-to-one, one-to-many, or many-to-many. Indexes speed searching and sorting and can be created when a field that is not a primary key must contain a unique value. With the proper relationships in place, forms, queries, and reports use the relationships to access data from more than one table.

Key Terms

The ⊙ symbol represents Key Terms found on the Student CD in the 02_theres_more_you_can_do folder for this chapter.

Content-Based Assessments

Matching

Match each term in the second column with its correct definition in the first column by writing the letter of the term on the blank line in front of the correct definition.

____ **1.** Characteristics of a field that control how the field will display and how the data can be entered in the field.

____ **2.** A data type that can be assigned to any field that will hold one of only two values.

____ **3.** The row where new records or values are entered.

____ **4.** A field property that specifies the name of a table or query or the typed list that actually stores the list of values to be looked up.

____ **5.** Data that is entered and stored according to its intended use.

____ **6.** A field property that tests values for accuracy as they are entered into a table.

____ **7.** A field property that provides a custom message when the validation rule has been violated

____ **8.** An Access field property that creates a second, more efficient table that can be quickly searched or sorted.

____ **9.** A set of rules that Access uses to ensure that the data between related tables is valid.

A Append

B Data integrity

C Field properties

D Foreign key

E Indeterminate

F Indexed

G Many-to-many

H One-to-many

I One-to-one

J Referential integrity

K Row source

L Subdatasheet

M Validation Rule

N Validation Text

O Yes/No

____ **10.** A relationship where each record must match have one identical match in the other table.

____ **11.** A datasheet that is nested within another datasheet.

____ **12.** The most common type of relationship in Access.

____ **13.** A field that is joined to a primary key in another table for the purpose of creating a relationship.

____ **14.** A relationship that cannot enforce referential integrity.

____ **15.** A relationship where a record can match more than one record in a second table and a record in the second table can match more than one record from the first table.

Content-Based Assessments

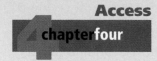
Fill in the Blank

Write the correct answer in the space provided.

1. The field attribute that determines what kind of values will be stored in a field is called the _____ _____.

2. Any data already entered into a new record is called the _____ value.

3. To store pictures, Office files, and even small executable programs, the _____ data type is used.

4. To retrieve values from another table or a value list, use a(n) _____ field.

5. A box that has an arrow that when clicked displays a list of items is called a _____ box.

6. A box that displays several values without having to click an arrow is a(n) _____ box.

7. To control the structure of the data entered in the field, a(n) _____ _____ is used.

8. In an input mask, the end-user cannot change the _____ character during data entry.

9. In an input mask, the end-user can change the _____ character during data entry.

10. Underlying data stored in the table is interpreted and displayed according to the field's _____ property.

11. A database must follow how the business is run, which are referred to as business _____.

12. An association between two tables that is established using a field common to both tables is called a(n) _____.

13. In a relationship, the option where deleting a record in the first table will cause all matching records in the second table to also be deleted, is called a(n) _____ delete.

14. A table that joins two outer tables to form a many-to-many relationship is called a(n) _____ _____.

15. A form that is inserted within another form is called a(n) _____.

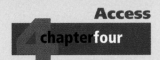

Access

chapterfour

Skills Review

Project 4C — Rooms

In this project, you will apply the skills you practiced from the Objectives in Project 4A.

Objectives: 1. *Customize Table Fields;* **2.** *Structure Data Input;* **3.** *Validate Data Input.*

In the following Skills Review, you will design two tables that will track campus and room information for MIS Technical Training Institute. The company has a business rule that all room numbers must begin with a letter signifying which campus that room belongs to. You will create an input mask and validation rule to enforce this policy. You will test your design changes using sample data. Your table and form will look similar to the ones shown in Figure 4.40.

> **For Project 4C, you will need the following files:**
>
> a04C_Rooms
> a04C_Boise

You will save your database as
4C_Rooms_Firstname_Lastname

Figure 4.40

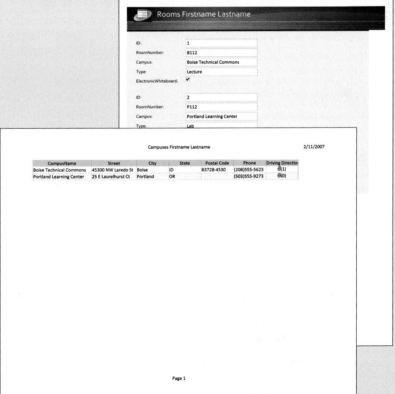

(Project 4C–Rooms continues on the next page)

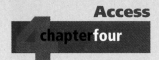
(Project 4C–Rooms continued)

1. From the student files that accompany this textbook, locate the file **a04C_Rooms**. **Copy** and **Paste** the file to your **Access Chapter 4** folder. Rename the file **4C_Rooms_Firstname_Lastname**

2. Open **4C_Rooms_Firstname_Lastname** in Access 2007. Enable the content and open the **Navigation Pane**.

3. In the **Navigation Pane**, right-click **Campuses** and in the displayed shortcut menu, click **Rename**. Change name of the table to **Campuses Firstname Lastname** and press Enter. Right-click the **Campuses Firstname Lastname** table and in the displayed shortcut menu, click **Design View**.

4. In the **Field Name column**, click in the **Postal Code row**. Under **Field Properties**, click in the **Input Mask** box. At the right of the box, click the displayed **Build** button. In the **Input Mask Wizard** dialog box, click **Zip Code**, and then click **Next** two times. Click the **With the symbols in the mask** option button, and then click **Finish**.

5. In the first empty **Field Name row**, type **Directions** and then press Tab. Click the displayed **arrow**, click **Attachment**, and then press Tab. Under **Field Properties**, click in the **Caption** box, and then type **Driving Directions**

6. On the Quick Access toolbar, click the **Save** button, and then in the **Views group**, click the **Datasheet View** button.

7. In the first record, click in the **State** field, and then press Tab. Type **837284530** and then press Tab. The input mask adds the hyphen to the postal code.

8. In the **Boise** campus record, double-click the **Driving Directions** field. In the displayed **Attachments** dialog box, click **Add**. Navigate to the student files that accompany this textbook, and then click the **a04C_Boise** Word document. Click **Open**, and then click **OK** to close the dialog box.

9. Display the **Office** menu, point to **Print**, and then click **Print Preview**. In the **Page Layout** group, click the **Landscape** button. If your instructor asks you to print this project, click **Print**.

10. Click the **Close Print Preview** button and close the table. In the **Navigation Pane**, right-click the **Rooms** table, and then click **Rename**. Change name of the table to **Rooms Firstname Lastname** and press Enter.

11. Open **Rooms** in Design View. Click the **RoomNumber row**, and then in the **Input Mask** box, enter **>L000;0;#** This will create a mask with a capital letter followed by three digits.

12. In the **Validation Rule** for **RoomNumber**, type **Like "B*" Or Like "P*"** This rule requires that the first value to be a "B" or a "P". In the **Validation Text** box, type **The room number must be a B or P followed by 3 numbers.**

13. In the **Required** box for **RoomNumber**, double-click to change the value to **Yes**, and then double-click to change the **Allow Zero Length** box to **No**.

14. Click in the **Campus row**, click the **Data Type arrow**, and then click **Lookup Wizard**. In the

(Project 4C–Rooms continues on the next page)

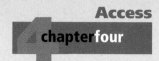

(Project 4C–Rooms continued)

displayed **Lookup Wizard** dialog box, click **Next** two times. Under **Available Fields**, **CampusName** should already be selected. Click the **Move** button one time, click **Next** two times, and then click **Finish**. When asked to save the table, click **Yes**.

15. Click the **Default Value** box for **Campus** and type **Boise Technical Commons**

16. In the **Type row**, click in the **Data Type** box, and then change its data type to **Lookup Wizard**. In the first screen of the displayed wizard, click the **I will type in the values that I want** option button, and then click **Next**. In the field below **Col1**, type **Lab** and then press Tab. Type **Lecture** press Tab, and then type **Lecture/Lab** Click **Finish** to close the wizard.

17. Click the **ElectronicWhiteboard** field, and then change the **Data Type** to **Yes/No**.

18. **Save** your changes, and then close the table. Click the **Create tab**. If necessary, in the **Navigation Pane**, click the **Rooms** table. In the **Forms group**, click the **Form** button.

19. Close the **Navigation Pane**. In the **Views group**, click the **View** button, and then use the form to enter the following records:

ID	RoomNumber	Campus	Type	ElectronicWhiteboard
1	B112	Boise Technical Commons	Lecture	Yes(checked)
2	P112	Portland Learning Center	Lab	No(unchecked)
3	B145	Boise Technical Commons	Lecture/Lab	Yes(checked)

20. Click the **View** button and on the **Format tab**, in the **AutoFormat group**, click the **More** button. In the second row, third column, click the **Module** AutoFormat. With the **ID** text box selected, drag the right border so that the text box controls are approximately 2 inches wide. Click **Save**, name the form **Rooms Form Firstname Lastname** and click **OK**.

21. Display the **Office** menu, point to **Print**, and then click **Print Preview**. Click the **Columns** button, and then under **Column Size**, change the **Width** to **7.5"** and then click **OK**. If your instructor asks you to print this project, click **Print**.

22. **Save** your changes, close the form, and then **Exit** Access.

 You have completed Project 4C _____

Skills Review

Project 4D—Schedule

In this project, you will apply the skills you practiced from the Objectives in Project 4B.

Objectives: 4. *Create Indexes and Change Sort Order;* **5.** *Create Relationships Between Tables;* **6.** *Create Forms and Reports with Related Tables.*

In the following Skills Review, you will create new relationships in the MIS Technical Training Institute database. The company needs a way to schedule classes that may meet at different times and in more than one room. To test your relationships, you will create a form and enter sample data. Your completed relationships report and form will look similar to Figure 4.41.

For Project 4D, you will need the following file:

a04D_Schedule

You will save your database as
4D_Schedule_Firstname_Lastname

Figure 4.41

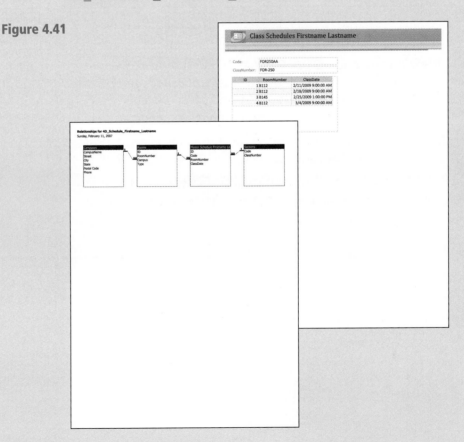

(Project 4D–Schedule continues on the next page)

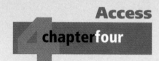

(Project 4D–Schedule continued)

1. From the student files that accompany this textbook, locate the file **a04D_Schedule**. **Copy** and **Paste** the file to your **Access Chapter 4** folder. Rename the file **4D_Schedule_Firstname_Lastname**

2. Open **4D_Schedule_Firstname_Lastname** in Access 2007. Enable the content and open the **Navigation Pane**.

3. Click the **Database Tools tab**. In the **Show/Hide group**, click **Relationships**. The line connecting the campus fields reveals that a lookup field is used. Click the relationship line between **Campuses** and **Rooms**. In the **Tools group**, click the **Edit Relationships** button.

4. In the displayed **Edit Relationships** dialog box, select the **Enforce Referential Integrity** check box, and then select the **Cascade Update Related Fields** and **Cascade Delete Related Records** check boxes. Click **OK** and notice the one-to-many relationship between the Campuses and Rooms tables.

5. **Save** your changes, and close the **Relationships** window. In the **Navigation Pane**, right-click the **Rooms** table, and from the shortcut menu, click **Design View**.

6. Click in the **RoomNumber row**, and under **Field Properties**, click the **Indexed** box. At the right of the box, click the **arrow** and click **Yes (No Duplicates)**. **Save** your changes, and then close the table.

7. Click the **Create tab**. In the **Tables group**, click the **Table Design** button. Using the techniques you have practiced in previous projects, add the following fields to the table.

Field Name	Data Type	Description
ID	AutoNumber	Primary Key
Code	Text	Foreign Key
RoomNumber	Text	Foreign Key
ClassDate	Date/Time	Date and start time of class

8. Set **ID** as the **Primary Key**, and then click the **ClassDate row**. Under **Field Properties**, click the **Format** box, click the displayed **arrow**, and then click **General Date**.

9. **Save** your changes. Under **Table Name**, type Master Schedule Firstname Lastname click **OK**, and then close the table.

10. Click the **Database Tools tab**, and then in the **Show/Hide group**, click the **Relationships** button. On the **Design tab**, in the **Relationships group**, click the **Show Table** button. In the displayed **Show Table** dialog box, double-click the **Master Schedule** table, double-click the **Sections** table, and then click the **Close** button.

11. In the **Relationships** window, drag **RoomNumber** from the **Rooms** table and drop it on the **RoomNumber** field in the **Master Schedule** table. Select the **Enforce Referential Integrity**, **Cascade Update Related Fields**, and **Cascade Delete Related Records** check boxes, and then click **Create**.

(Project 4D–Schedule continues on the next page)

Skills Review

(Project 4D–Schedule continued)

12. Use the techniques you have just practiced to create a one-to-many relationship between the **Sections** and **Master Schedule** tables. Use **Code** as the common field and select the same options as in the previous step. The many-to-many relationship between Rooms and Sections enables a class to meet in more than one room.

13. **Save** your changes, and then from the **Tools group**, click the **Relationships Report** button. Click the **Save** button, and in the displayed **Save As** dialog box, click **OK**. If your instructor asks you to print this project, click the **Print** button.

14. Close the Relationships Report. **Save** your changes, and then close the **Relationships** window.

15. In the **Navigation Pane**, click the **Sections** table. Click the **Create tab**, and then in the **Forms group**, click the **Form** button.

16. On the **Format tab**, in the **AutoFormat group**, click the **More** button. In the fourth row, first column, click the **Office** AutoFormat. In the form title, double-click **Sections**, select the title text, and then type **Class Schedules Firstname Lastname**

17. Click the subform and then drag the right border so that only two columns of the data table display. Click the **Code** text box control, and drag so that it is as wide as the subform.

18. On the **Format tab**, in the **Views group**, click the **View** button. In the Subform, click below the **RoomNumber** column header. Type **B112** press Tab, type **2/11/09 9a** and then press Tab. Notice that the ClassDate field is too narrow.

19. Place the mouse over the right border of the **RoomNumber** column and double-click. The column's width is expanded to fit the contents. Repeat this technique to widen the **ClassDate** column.

20. Use the techniques that you have practiced to schedule three more weekly meetings of the FOR250AA class section:

ID	RoomNumber	ClassDate
(AutoNumber)	B112	2/18/09 9:00:00 AM
(AutoNumber)	B145	2/25/09 1:00:00 PM
(AutoNumber)	B112	3/4/09 9:00:00 AM

21. **Save** your changes. In the **Save As** dialog box, under **Form Name**, type **Class Schedules Firstname Lastname** and then click **OK**. From the **Office** menu, point to **Print** and click **Print Preview**. Click the **Columns** button, and then under **Column Size**, change the **Width** to **7.5"** Click **Save** and then click the **Close Print Preview** button.

22. If your instructor asks you to print this project, from the **Office** menu, click **Print**. Under **Print Range** click the **Selected Records(s)** option button, and then click **OK** to print the first page of the form.

23. Close the form. **Exit** Access.

 You have completed Project 4D———————————

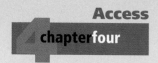

Mastering Access

Project 4E — Instructors

In this project, you will apply the skills you practiced from the objectives in Project 4A.

Objectives: 1. *Customize Table Fields;* **2.** *Structure Data Input;* **3.** *Validate Data Input.*

In the following Mastering Access project, you will edit three tables for MIS Technical Training Institute. The tables will be used to track instructor log on data and class information. Your completed table and two forms will look similar to Figure 4.42.

For Project 4E, you will need the following file:

a04E_Instructors

You will save your database as 4E_Instructors_Firstname_Lastname

Figure 4.42

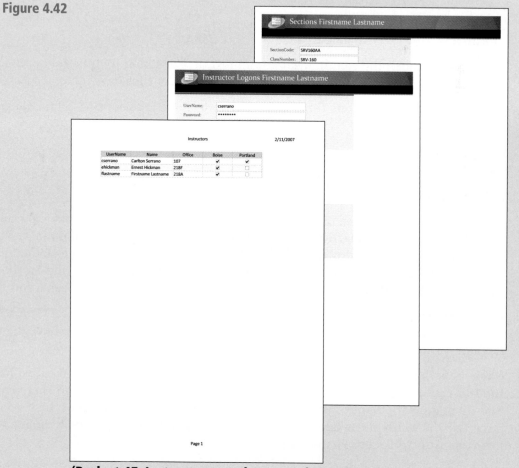

(Project 4E–Instructors continues on the next page)

Content-Based Assessments

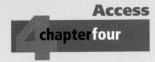
(Project 4E–Instructors continued)

1. From the student files that accompany this textbook, locate the file **a04E_Instructors**. **Copy** and **Paste** the file to your **Access Chapter 4** folder. Rename the file **4E_Instructors_ Firstname_Lastname**

2. Open **4E_Instructors_Firstname_Lastname**, enable the content, and open the **Navigation Pane**. Open the **Instructors** table in Design View. For the **InstructorName** field, change the **Caption** field property to **Name**

3. Add the following fields to the table:

Field Name	Data Type
Boise	Yes/No
Portland	Yes/No

4. Enter the following records into the **Instructors** table. For the last record, enter your own name as an instructor. Your UserName should be the first letter of your first name followed by your last name:

UserName	Name	Office	Boise	Portland
cserrano	Carlton Serrano	107	Yes	Yes
ehickman	Ernest Hickman	218F	Yes	No
flastname	Firstname Lastname	218A	Yes	No

5. If necessary, widen the columns so that all text displays, and then **Save** the table. If your instructor asks you to print this project, print the table. Close the table.

6. Open the **InstructorLogons** table in Design View. For the **Password** field, change the following field properties:

Field Size	12
Required	Yes
Allow Zero Length	No

7. For the **Password** field, use the Input Mask Wizard to assign the **Password** input mask. For the same field, assign a **Validation Rule** that requires the password to contain more than five characters. (Hint: To write the rule, adapt one of the Common Validation Rules found in Project 4B.) Because the Field Size property is 12, the password must be between 6 and 12 characters. Assign the following **Validation Text** field property: **The password must be between 6 and 12 characters.**

8. In the **SecretQuestion** field, start the **Lookup Wizard**. Lookup the **SecretQuestion** field found in the **SecretQuestions** table. Accept all other wizard defaults. For the **SecretQuestion** field's **Default Value** field property, enter **"What is your mother's maiden name?"**

9. **Save** your changes, and then close the table. Use the **Form** button to create a form based on the **InstructorLogons** table. Change the form's title to **Instructor Logons Firstname Lastname** and then apply the **Paper** AutoFormat located in the second column of the second row. Decrease the width of the **SecretQuestion** text box so that it is about **4 inches** wide. **Save** the form as **InstructorLogons Firstname Lastname**

(Project 4E–Instructors continues on the next page)

Content-Based Assessments

Access

Mastering Access

(Project 4E–Instructors continued)

10. Use the form to enter the following records. For the third record, use the username that you assigned to your record in the Instructors table:

UserName	Password	Secret Question	Secret Answer
cserrano	c@tman34	What is your mother's maiden name?	Brown
ehickman	g0ld1gger	What is your favorite movie?	Goldfinger
flastname	REv3rb	What is your favorite book?	The Magus

11. Open the form in **Print Preview**, and then change the **Column Size Width** to 6″ If your instructor asks you to print this project, print the form. **Save** your changes, and then close the form.

12. Open the **Sections** table in Design View. For the **SectionCode** field, create an **Input Mask** for the following data structure: three uppercase letters followed by three digits followed by two more uppercase letters. Assign # as the placeholder character.

13. For the **DayofWeek** field, use the **Lookup Wizard** to create a lookup field. For the lookup values, use the following data as a typed list: **Wednesday Thursday Friday Saturday** and then accept all other wizard default settings.

14. **Save** your changes, and then close the table. Use the **Form** button to create a form based on the **Sections** table. Change the form's title to **Sections Firstname Lastname** and then apply the **Paper** AutoFormat. Change the width of the **SectionCode** text box so that it is about **2 inches** wide, and then **Save** the form as **Sections Firstname Lastname**

15. Use the form to enter the following records:

SectionCode	ClassNumber	DayofWeek
SRV160AA	SRV-160	Thursday
SRV160BA	SRV-160	Saturday
XML101AA	XML-101	Friday

16. Open the form in **Print Preview** and the change the **Column Size Width** to 5″ If your instructor asks you to print this project, click **Print**.

17. **Save** the form, close the form, and then **Exit** Access.

 You have completed Project 4E —————————————

Content-Based Assessments

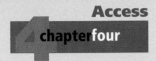
Project 4F—Team Teaching

In this project, you will apply the skills you practiced from the Objectives in Project 4B.

Objectives: 4. *Create Indexes and Change Sort Order;* **5.** *Create Relationships Between Tables;* **6.** *Create Forms and Reports with Related Tables.*

In the following Mastering Access project, you will expand the MIS Technical Training Institute database to track instructors who teach as a team. A single class can be taught by more than one instructor and an instructor can teach more than one class. Your completed form and two reports will look similar to Figure 4.43.

For Project 4F, you will need the following file:

a04F_Team_Teaching

You will save your database as 4F_Team_Teaching_Firstname_Lastname

Figure 4.43

(Project 4F–Team Teaching continues on the next page)

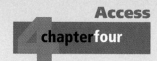

(Project 4F–Team Teaching continued)

1. From the student files that accompany this textbook, locate the file **a04F_Team_Teaching**. Copy and paste the file to your **Access Chapter 4** folder. Rename the file **4F_Team_Teaching_ Firstname_Lastname**

2. Open **4F_Team_Teaching_Firstname_Lastname**, enable the content, and open the **Navigation Pane**. In the **Sections** table, set the **Indexed** field property of the **ClassNumber** field to **Yes (Duplicates OK)**. **Save** your changes, and then close the table.

3. In the **Instructors** table, set the **Indexed** field property of the **UserName** field to **Yes (No Duplicates)**. **Save** and close the table.

4. Open the **Relationships** window, and then add the following tables in this order: **InstructorLogons**, **Instructors**, and **Sections**.

5. Create a one-to-one relationship between the **InstructorLogons** and the **Instructors** tables using **UserName** as the common field. Enforce referential integrity but do not select the cascade update or cascade delete options. **Save** the layout of the Relationships window.

6. Use the **InstructorLogons** table's datasheet and subdatasheet to add the following instructors. For the second instructor, use your own name. Your UserName should be the first letter of your first name followed by your last name:

UserName	Password	InstructorID	Fname	LName	Office
gchapman	sw@ns0ng	808	Graham	Chapman	218C
flastname	abC1234	909	Firstname	Lastname	218C

7. Close the **InstructorLogons** table, and then create a new table to act as a junction table. Add an **AutoNumber** field named **ID** and use it as the primary key. Add two more fields with the same names and data types as the primary key in the **Instructors** and **Sections** tables. Hint: Look in the open **Relationships** window for these field names. **Save** the table as Instructors/Sections Firstname Lastname and then close the table.

8. In the **Relationships** window, add the **Instructors/Sections** table. Rearrange the tables so that **Instructors/Sections** is between the **Instructors** and **Sections** tables. Create a many-to-many relationship between **Instructors** and **Sections** using **Instructors/Sections** as the junction table. For both one-to-many relationships, enforce referential integrity and select the option to cascade changes when fields are updated.

9. Create a relationships report, and then save the report with the name provided by Access. If your instructor asks you to print this project, print the relationships report. Close the report, and then close the **Relationships** window.

10. Use the **Form** button to create a form for the **Sections** table. Change the form's title to **Sections Firstname Lastname** apply the **Verve** AutoFormat located in the fourth column of the last row. Change the width of the subform so that one empty column displays, and then change the width of the **SectionCode** text box so that it is as wide as the subform.

11. Save the form as **Sections Firstname Lastname** Switch to Form View and in the subform, add an InstructorID of **808** In the main form, navigate to the next record (**SectionCode** FOR250CA). In

(Project 4F–Team Teaching continues on the next page)

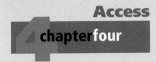

(Project 4F–Team Teaching continued)

the subform, add the following **InstructorID** values: **808** and **909** The many-to-many relationship enables the company to track sections that are taught by more than one instructor.

12. Display the form in **Print Preview** and the change the **Column Size Width** to **5" Save** and then close Print Preview.

13. If your instructor asks you to print this project, be sure the record for For250CA still displays, and then from the **Office** menu, click **Print**. Under **Print Range** click the **Selected Records(s)** option button, and then click **OK** to print the second record of the form.

14. Close the form and then create a new query that answers the following question: What is the teaching schedule for Graham Chapman? Add these tables to the query: **Instructors**, **Instructors/Sections**, and **Sections**.

15. Right-click the indeterminate relationship line between the **Instructors** and **Sections** tables, click **Delete**, and then add the following fields to the query in this order: **Fname**, **LName**, **ClassNumber**, **StartTime**, **DayofWeek**, **StartDate**, and **Room**. As the last field, add the **InstructorID** field from the **Instructors/Sections** table.

16. Set the **InstructorID** field criteria to equal **808** and clear that column's **Show** check box. Run the query and notice that the instructor's two classes display. **Save** the query as **Teaching Schedule Firstname Lastname** and then close the query.

17. Use the **Report** button to create a report based on the **Teaching Schedules** query. Apply the **Verve** AutoFormat. Resize the columns to fit their contents. When you are done, the report should fit on one page. **Save** the report as **Teaching Schedules Firstname Lastname** If your instructor asks you to print this project, print the report.

18. **Close** the report, and then **Exit** Access.

 You have completed Project 4F _____

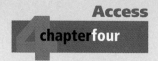

Project 4G—Companies

In this project, you will apply the following Objectives found in Projects 4A and 4B.

Objectives: 1. *Customize Table Fields;* **2.** *Structure Data Input;* **3.** *Validate Data Input;* **4.** *Create Indexes and Change Sort Order;* **5.** *Create Relationships Between Tables;* **6.** *Create Forms and Reports with Related Tables.*

In the following Mastering Access project, you will expand the MIS Technical Training Institute database to track data about the companies that enroll their employees in classes. Depending on the number of students enrolled by a company, different class and consulting fees will be assigned. Your completed relationships report and form will look similar to Figure 4.44.

For Project 4G, you will need the following files:

a04G_Companies
a04G_DS_Contract.pdf

**You will save your database as
4G_Companies_Firstname_Lastname**

Figure 4.44

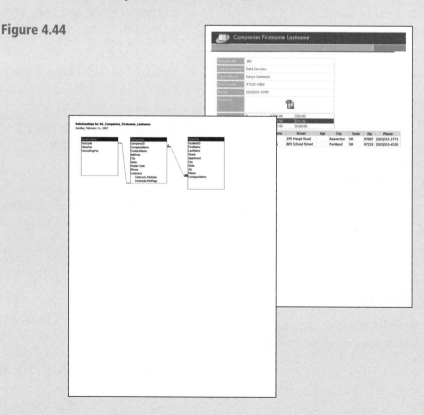

(Project 4G–Companies continues on the next page)

Content-Based Assessments

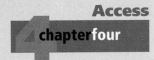

Access
chapterfour

Mastering Access

(Project 4G–Companies continued)

1. From the student files that accompany this textbook, locate the file **a04G_Companies**. Copy and paste the file to your **Access Chapter 4** folder. Rename the file **4G_Companies_Firstname_Lastname**

2. Open **4G_Companies_Firstname_Lastname**, enable content, and open the **Navigation pane.** For the **Students** table, change the **Apartment** field **Caption** property to **Apt**

3. Add a new field named **CompanyName** and then set the **Data Type** to **Text** For the field just created, change the **Default Value** property to **Self** and the **Indexed** property to **Yes (Duplicates OK)**.

4. Switch to Datasheet View and enter the following data in the **CompanyName** field:

StudentID	CompanyName
109-56-8438	Lancer Networking
110-80-1693	Data Services
116-12-1274	Lancer Networking
127-75-8752	Self
128-38-9699	Data Services

5. In the **Students** table, set **CompanyName** as a required field, **Save**, and then close the table.

6. For the **FeeSchedule** table, change both the **ClassFee** and **ConsultingFee** data type to **Currency**. For the **ConsultingFee** field, write a validation rule that requires the amount to be between 50 and 150 dollars. (Hint: Refer to the Common Validation Rules from Project 4B.) For the **Validation Text** property, type **Consulting Fee must be between $50 and $150.**

7. In the **FeeSchedule** table, enter the following records. When you are done, **Save** and close the table:

FeeCode	ClassFee	ConsultingFee
A	$250.00	$50.00
B	$350.00	$75.00
C	$500.00	$150.00

8. For the **Companies** table, index the **CompanyName** field so that duplicate values are not allowed.

9. For the **Postal Code** field, use a wizard to create the default **Input Mask** for **Zip Code**. For the **Phone** field, use a wizard to create the default **Input Mask** for **Phone Number**.

10. Add a new field named **Contracts** that can be used to store attachments.

11. Create a new field called **Rate** and assign the **LookupWizard** data type. Look up the values from the **FeeSchedule** table. Include the **FeeCode**, **ClassFee**, and **ConsultingFee** fields. In the wizard, do not sort and uncheck the **Hide the key column** check box. Accept all remaining wizard defaults.

12. For the **Rate** field, change the **Display Control** to a list box. Save the table, and then add the following record. Close the table when you are done:

CompanyID	Company Name	Remaining Fields
999	Self	Leave Blank

13. Create a one-to-many relationship between the **Companies** and **Students** tables using **Company Name** as the common field. Enforce referential integrity and set the relationship to cascade update fields and cascade delete records.

14. Create a relationships report. If your instructor asks you to print this project, print the report. Close the report, and then save it using the name displayed in the **Save As** dialog box. In the **Relationships**

(Project 4G–Companies continues on the next page)

Content-Based Assessments

(Project 4G–Companies continued)

window, **Save** your changes, and then close the window.

15. Use the **Form** button to create a form based on the **Companies** table. Assign the **Median** AutoFormat located on the second column of the third row, and then change the form title to **Companies Firstname Lastname**

16. In the subform datasheet, resize the column widths so that all of the columns display. In the main form, move the right border of the **City** text box so that it aligns with the border between the **Street** and **Apt** columns in the subform datasheet. Delete the **Address**, **City**, and **State** fields, click the subform, and then drag the subform's **Selector** button up so that the subform is directly under the main form.

17. In Form View, display the record for *Data Services*. Double-click the **Contracts** field, attach the file **a04G_DS_Contract.pdf** located in the student files that accompany this textbook, and then set the rate for this company to **B $350.00/$75.00**.

18. **Save** the form as **Companies Firstname Lastname** Open it in **Print Preview**, and then change the **Column Size Width** to **7.5" Save** your changes and then close Print Preview. If your instructor asks you to print this project, be sure that the first record still displays, and then from the **Office** menu, click **Print**. In the displayed **Print** dialog box, under **Print Range**, click the **Selected Record(s)** option button, and then click **OK**.

19. **Close** the form, and then **Exit** Access.

End **You have completed Project 4G** ——————————————

Content-Based Assessments

Mastering Access

Project 4H — Grades

In this project, you will apply the following Objectives found in Projects 4A and 4B.

Objectives: 1. *Customize Table Fields;* **2.** *Structure Data Input;* **4.** *Create Indexes and Change Sort Order;* **5.** *Create Relationships Between Tables;* **6.** *Create Forms and Reports with Related Tables.*

In the following Mastering Access project, you will expand the MIS Technical Training Institute database to track student progress. The companies that send their employees, and pay for these classes, will be able to log on to the database and check if their employees have successfully completed a class. MISTTI will also be able to track which classes have been paid for. You will test your information system using sample data. Your completed reports will look similar to Figure 4.45.

For Project 4H, you will need the following file:

a04H_Grades

**You will save your database as
4H_Grades_Firstname_Lastname**

Figure 4.45

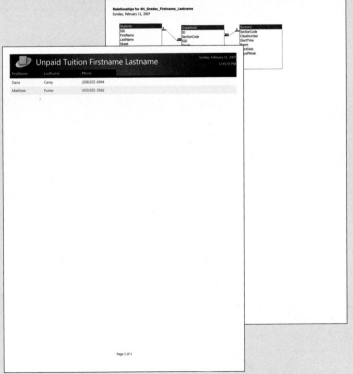

(Project 4H–Grades continues on the next page)

Content-Based Assessments

(Project 4H–Grades continued)

1. From the student files that accompany this textbook, locate the file **a04H_Grades**. Copy and paste the file to your **Access Chapter 4** folder. Rename the file 4H_Grades_Firstname_Lastname

2. Open **4Grades_Firstname_Lastname**, enable the content, and then open the **Navigation Pane**. For the **Students** table, change the **SID** field **Caption** property to Student ID

3. For the **SID** field, create an input mask that requires three digits, followed by a hyphen, two digits, another hyphen, and then four more digits. Include the hyphen in the data's value and use # for the default placeholder character.

4. For the **Phone** field, use a wizard to create the default input mask for **Phone Number**. **Save** your changes, and then add the following records using your own name for the second record:

Student ID	First Name	Last Name	Street	City	State	Zip	Phone	Company Name
958-26-4681	Paul	Andrews	805 East Acensio Road	Portland	OR	97233	(503)555-4520	Data Services
123-45-6789	Firstname	Lastname	555 State Street	Boise	ID	83722	(208)555-5555	Paragon Financial

5. Close the **Students** table, and then open the **Gradebook** table in Design View. For the **SID** field, create an index that allows duplicate values.

6. Create a new field named **Grade** and assign the **Lookup Wizard** data type. For the values to lookup, enter the following list:

   Col1

   Passed

   Failed

   Did not attend

7. Create a new field named **TuitionPaid** and assign it the **Yes/No** data type. **Save** your changes, and then close the table.

8. Create a many-to-many relationship between the **Students** and **Sections** tables relating the primary key from each table to the appropriate field in the **Gradebook** table. For the one-to-many relationships, enforce referential integrity but do not select the two cascade options.

9. Use the **Sections** table datasheet and subdatasheet to enter the following grades for **SectionCode** *FOR250AA*. When you are done, close the table:

ID	SID	Grade	TuitionPaid
(AutoNumber)	109-56-.8438	Passed	Yes
(AutoNumber)	110-80-1693	Passed	Yes
(AutoNumber)	116-12-1274	Failed	No
(AutoNumber)	127-75-8752	Did not attend	No
(AutoNumber)	958-26-4681	Passed	Yes

(Project 4H–Grades continues on the next page)

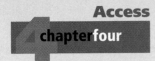

(Project 4H–Grades continued)

10. Create a query that answers this question: *Which students listed in the Gradebook table have unpaid tuition?* Include the student's **FirstName**, **LastName**, and **Phone** fields, and from the **Gradebook** table, include the **TuitionPaid** field. Enter the criteria necessary to answer the question, and then run the query. **Save** the query as **Unpaid Tuition Firstname Lastname** and then close the query.

11. Use the **Report** button to create a report based on the **Unpaid Tuition** query. Assign the **Windows Vista** AutoFormat, located on the last column of the last row. Delete the **TuitionPaid** field from the report, and then resize the column widths of the three remaining controls to better fit their contents.

12. **Save** the report using the name suggested in the **Save As** dialog box. If your instructor asks you to print this project, print the report. Close the report.

13. Create a one-to-one relationship between the **Companies** and the **Company_Logons** tables using each table's primary key as the common field. For the relationship, enforce referential integrity, cascade update related fields, and cascade delete related records.

14. In the **Relationships** window, arrange the tables as shown in Figure 4.45, and then create a relationships report. **Save** the report using the name suggested in the **Save As** dialog box. If your instructor asks you to print this project, print the relationships report.

15. Close the report, **Save** the **Relationships** window, and then **Exit** Access.

 You have completed Project 4H

Content-Based Assessments

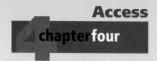
Mastering Access

Project 4I — Certifications

In this project, you will apply the skills you practiced from all the Objectives in Projects 4A and 4B.

Objectives: 1. *Customize Table Fields;* **2.** *Structure Data Input;* **3.** *Validate Data Input;* **4.** *Create Indexes and Change Sort Order;* **5.** *Create Relationships Between Tables;* **6.** *Create Forms and Reports with Related Tables.*

In the following Mastering Access project, you will continue improving the MIS Technical Training Institute database and add tables that can track instructor qualifications and certifications. You will test your information system using sample data. Your completed reports will look similar to Figure 4.46.

For Project 4I, you will need the following files:

a04I_Certifications
a04I_MCP
a04I_IC3

You will save your database as
4I_Certifications_Firstname_Lastname

Figure 4.46

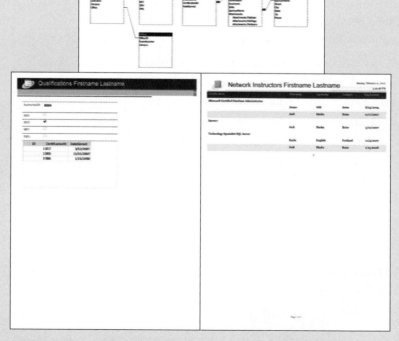

(Project 4I–Certifications continues on the next page)

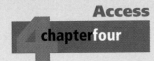
(Project 4I–Certifications continued)

1. From the student files that accompany this textbook, locate the file **a04I_Certifications**. **Copy** and **Paste** the file to your **Access Chapter 4** folder. Rename the file **4I_Certifications_ Firstname_Lastname**

2. Open **4I_Certifications_Firstname_Lastname**, enable the content, and open the **Navigation Pane.** For the **Instructors** table, change the **InstructorID** field **Field Size** property to **4** and then create an **Input Mask** that structures the data as an uppercase letter followed by three digits. In the input mask, assign an underscore as the default placeholder character.

3. Add a field named **Campus** and assign a data type that looks up values from a list. For the list, type the following values: **Boise** and **Portland** For the **Campus** field, set the **Default Value** property to **Boise**

4. Add a field named **Office** and assign a data type that looks up the **RoomNumber** and **Campus** fields found in the **Offices** table. Change the **Control Display** to **List Box**, and then **Save** and close the table.

5. Create a new table and add the following fields:

Field Name	Data Type
InstructorID	Text
MIS	Yes/No
NET	Yes/No
SRV	Yes/No
XML	Yes/No

6. Set **InstructorID** as the primary key, **Save** the table with the name **Qualifications Firstname Lastname** and then close the table.

7. Create a one-to-one relationship between the **Instructors** and **Qualifications** tables using each table's primary key as the common field. For the relationship, enforce referential integrity, cascade update, and cascade delete.

8. Use the **Instructors** table's datasheet and subdatasheet to add the following instructors and their respective qualifications. Close the table when you are done:

InstructorID	Firstname	Lastname	Campus	Office	MIS	NET	SRV	XML
P001	Carlton	Serrano	Portland	107	Yes	No	No	Yes
B002	Ernest	Hickman	Boise	218A	No	No	Yes	No
P003	Joey	Booth	Portland	105	Yes	No	Yes	No
B004	Judi	Marks	Boise	218A	No	Yes	No	No
B005	James	Mill	Boise	218B	Yes	Yes	No	No
P006	Kayla	English	Portland	109	No	Yes	No	No
B007	Margarita	Patel	Boise	218B	Yes	No	No	Yes

9. In the **Certifications** table, after the **SponsorName** field, add an attachment field named **Attachments** and then change the field's **Caption** property to **Logo**

(Project 4I–Certifications continues on the next page)

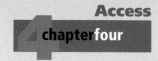
(Project 4I–Certifications continued)

10. Save the changes to the **Certifications** table, and then attach the following logos, which are located in the student files that accompany this textbook:

CertificationID	File Name
001	a04I_MCP
008	a04I_IC3

11. Close the **Certifications** table, and then open the **Sponsors** table in Design View. In the **SponsorName** field, create an index with no duplicate values so that the field can be used in a one-to-many relationship. **Save** your changes, and then close the table.

12. Create a new table with the following fields:

Field Name	Data Type
ID	AutoNumber
InstructorID	Text
CertificationID	Text
DateEarned	Date/Time

13. Assign **ID** as the primary key, and then for the **DateEarned** field, set the **Format** property to **Short Date**. For the **DateEarned** field, write a **Validation Rule** property that requires all dates be later than 12/31/2001. Hint: Adapt one of the Common Validation Properties found Project 4B. For the **Validation Text** property, enter **Certification must be earned after year 2001**.

14. Save the table with the name **Instructor Certs Firstname Lastname** In the **DateEarned** field, use a wizard to set the **Input Mask** property to **Short Date**, and make the field a required field. In the **DateEarned** field, create an index that allows duplicate values, and then close the table.

15. In the **Relationships** window, add the following tables: **Offices**, **Instructor Certs**, **Certifications**, and **Sponsors**. Arrange the tables similar to the layout shown in Figure 4.46, and then **Save** the layout.

16. Create a one-to-many relationship between the **Certifications** and **Sponsors** tables using **SponsorName** as the common field. For the relationship, enforce referential integrity, cascade update, and cascade delete.

17. Create a many-to-many relationship between the **Qualifications** and **Certifications** tables using **Instructor Certs** as the junction table. For the first relationship, use **InstructorID** for the common field, and for the second relationship, use **CertificationID** for the common field. For both relationships, enforce referential integrity, cascade update, and cascade delete.

18. Create a relationships report. **Save** the report using the name provided in the displayed **Save As** dialog box, and then change the orientation to **Landscape**. If your instructor asks you to print this project, print the relationships report. Click the **Save** button, close the report, and then close the **Relationships** window.

19. Use the **Form** button to create a form based on the **Qualifications** table. Assign the **Urban** AutoFormat located in the third column of the last row. **Save** the form as **Qualifications Firstname Lastname**

(Project 4I–Certifications continues on the next page)

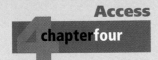

(Project 4I–Certifications continued)

20. Decrease the width of the subform so that one blank column displays and then align the right border of the **InstructorID** text box with the right edge of the subform. **Save** changes, and then use the form and subform to enter the following data:

InstructorID	ID	CertificationID	DateEarned
B004	(AutoNumber)	017	11/11/2007
B004	(AutoNumber)	003	03/12/2007
B004	(AutoNumber)	006	01/15/2008
B005	(AutoNumber)	003	08/15/2005
P006	(AutoNumber)	006	12/04/2007

21. Open the form in **Print Preview** and change the **Column Size Width** to 6" Click **Save,** and then close Print Preview. If your instructor asks you to print this project, navigate to the record for Instructor *B004*, and then from the **Office** menu, click **Print**. In the displayed **Print** dialog box, under **Print Range**, click the **Selected Record(s)** option button, and then click **OK**.

22. Close the form, and then create a query in Design View that answers this question: *Which instructors can teach the server classes and what certifications do they have?* Add the **Instructors**, **Qualifications**, **Instructors Certs**, and **Certifications** tables to the query, and add these fields in this order: **Firstname**, **Lastname**, **Campus**, **NET**, **Date Earned**, and **Certification**.

23. Add criteria so that the query returns only the records where the **NET** field is Yes, and then run the query. **Save** the query with the name **Network Instructors Firstname Lastname** and then close the query.

24. Use the **Report** button to create a report based on the **Network Instructors** query. Apply the **Urban** AutoFormat, delete the **NET** column, and then resize the fields to fit their contents. When you are done, the report should fit on one page.

25. On the **Format tab**, in the **Grouping & Totals group**, click the **Group & Sort** button. Under the form, in the **Group, Sort, and Total** pane, click the **Add a Group** button, and then click **Certification**. **Save** the report using the name suggested in the displayed **Save As** dialog box. If your instructor asks you to print this project, print the report.

26. Close the **Group, Sort, and Total Pane**, close the report, and then **Exit** Access.

 End **You have completed Project 4I** ——————————————————

Content-Based Assessments

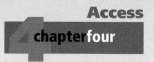

Business Running Case

Project 4J—Business Running Case

In this project, you will apply the skills you practiced from the Objectives in Projects 4A and 4B.

From My Computer, navigate to the student files that accompany this textbook. In the folder **03_business_running_case**, locate and open the folder for this chapter. Open and print the instructions for this project, which are provided to you in Adobe PDF format. Follow the instructions and use the skills you have gained thus far to assist Jennifer Nelson in meeting the challenges of owning and running her business.

 You have completed Project 4J ————————————

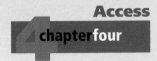

Rubric

The following outcomes-based assessments are *open-ended assessments*. That is, there is no specific correct result; your result will depend on your approach to the information provided. Make *Professional Quality* your goal. Use the following scoring rubric to guide you in *how* to approach the problem and then to evaluate *how well* your approach solves the problem.

The *criteria*—Software Mastery, Content, Format and Layout, and Process—represent the knowledge and skills you have gained that you can apply to solving the problem. The *levels of performance*—Professional Quality, Approaching Professional Quality, or Needs Quality Improvements—help you and your instructor evaluate your result.

	Your completed project is of Professional Quality if you:	Your completed project is Approaching Professional Quality if you:	Your completed project Needs Quality Improvements if you:
1-Software Mastery	Choose and apply the most appropriate skills, tools, and features and identify efficient methods to solve the problem.	Choose and apply some appropriate skills, tools, and features, but not in the most efficient manner.	Choose inappropriate skills, tools, or features, or are inefficient in solving the problem.
2-Content	Construct a solution that is clear and well organized, contains content that is accurate, appropriate to the audience and purpose, and is complete. Provide a solution that contains no errors of spelling, grammar, or style.	Construct a solution in which some components are unclear, poorly organized, inconsistent, or incomplete. Misjudge the needs of the audience. Have some errors in spelling, grammar, or style, but the errors do not detract from comprehension.	Construct a solution that is unclear, incomplete, or poorly organized, containing some inaccurate or inappropriate content; and contains many errors of spelling, grammar, or style. Do not solve the problem.
3-Format and Layout	Format and arrange all elements to communicate information and ideas, clarify function, illustrate relationships, and indicate relative importance.	Apply appropriate format and layout features to some elements, but not others. Overuse features, causing minor distraction.	Apply format and layout that does not communicate information or ideas clearly. Do not use format and layout features to clarify function, illustrate relationships, or indicate relative importance. Use available features excessively, causing distraction.
4-Process	Use an organized approach that integrates planning, development, self-assessment, revision, and reflection.	Demonstrate an organized approach in some areas, but not others; or, use an insufficient process of organization throughout	Do not use an organized approach to solve the problem.

Outcomes-Based Assessments

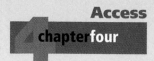
Problem Solving

Project 4K—Qualifications

In this project, you will construct a solution by applying any combination of the skills you practiced from the Objectives in Projects 4A and 4B.

For Project 4K, you will need the following file:

a04K_Qualifications

You will save your database as
4K_Qualifications_Firstname_Lastname

MIS Technical Training Institute needs a better way to track the professional certifications that qualify instructors to teach their classes. In this project, you will create a many-to-many relationship, and then enter data using a form that relies on that relationship. Copy a04K_Qualifications and paste it into your Access Chapter 4 folder, and then save the file as **4K_Qualifications_Firstname_Lastname**

Relate the Classes and Certifications tables following this scenario: A single certification may qualify an instructor to teach one or more classes and a single class may have one or more certifications that would qualify an instructor to teach that course. Name the junction table that is required for this type of relationship **Classes/Certs Firstname Lastname** For the relationship, be sure to enforce referential integrity. When you are done, create a relationships report.

Use the Form button to create a form and subform based on the Certifications table. Name the form and change the title to **Qualifications Firstname Lastname** Resize and apply an AutoFormat so that the form better displays on the screen. Use the form and subform to enter the following qualifications:

CertificationID	ClassNumber(s)
001	NET-101
002	NET-202
003	MIS-101
	MIS-102
	SRV-154

Submit the project as directed.

End **You have completed Project 4K** —————

Problem Solving

Project 4L—Attendance

In this project, you will construct a solution by applying any combination of the skills you practiced from the Objectives in Projects 4A and 4B.

For Project 4L, you will need the following file:

New blank Access database

You will save your database as
4L_Attendance_Firstname_Lastname

A networking instructor at MIS Technical Training Institute has asked you to create a database to help track weekly attendance in his class. You will create a table and edit field properties to speed data entry and to maintain data integrity. To start, create a new database with the name **4L_Attendance_Firstname_Lastname** and save it in your Access Chapter 4 folder.

Create a new table that will store the following information: a student ID number, student name, student phone, and a digital photo of each student. Look at the data that you will be putting into the table, and then create an appropriate input mask for the student ID and phone fields. Set the name fields as required, and then create an index for the last name field.

Add five more fields labeled Week 1, Week 2, Week 3, Week 4, and Week 5. Convert each of these five fields into a lookup field that looks up these three values: Present, Absent, Late. You can either type the list or make a table to store these values. Save the table with the name **NET-101 Students Firstname Lastname**

Create a form based on the Attendance table. Resize the controls and apply an appropriate AutoFormat. Save the form as **NET-101 Attendance Firstname Lastname** Use the form to enter the following records for the first week of class, and then submit the database as directed by your instructor:

Student ID	First Name	Last Name	Phone	Week 1	Photo and Weeks 2 through 5
711-25-1821	Sharon	Barnes	(503) 555-1433	Present	Leave Blank
729-10-2771	Linda	Hernandez	(503) 555-3673	Present	Leave Blank
737-58-4047	Kristi	Evans	(503) 555-5313	Present	Leave Blank
740-75-2549	Faye	Wiley	(503) 555-7244	Present	Leave Blank
744-57-8651	Cora	Calhoun	(503) 555-5930	Absent	Leave Blank
747-49-8180	Matt	Pacheco	(503) 555-4366	Present	Leave Blank
749-92-8717	Shannon	Henson	(503) 555-9055	Late	Leave Blank
757-26-1001	Michael	Evans	(503) 555-7281	Present	Leave Blank

End You have completed Project 4L

Outcomes-Based Assessments

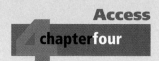

Problem Solving

Project 4M — Evaluation

In this project, you will construct a solution by applying any combination of the skills you practiced from the Objectives in Projects 4A and 4B.

> **For Project 4M, you will need the following file:**
>
> a04M_Gradebook

You will save your database as
4M_Gradebook_Firstname_Lastname

An instructor at MIS Technical Training Institute has asked you to create a database to track grades for her classes. You will need to build relationships between tables, enter sample data, and then create a query and report. To start, copy a04M_Gradebook into your Access Chapter 4 folder, and then rename the new file **4M_Gradebook_Firstname_Lastname**

Build a new table named **Gradebook Firstname Lastname** In the table, add the appropriate foreign keys so that the table can be used as a junction table in a many-to-many relationship between the Students and Classes tables. Add fields with the following names: **Quiz 1, Quiz 2, Project,** and **Final**. Write a validation rule that requires the four grade fields to be a number between 0 and 100. Write an appropriate warning message if any value fails the validation's test for data integrity.

Create a many-to-many relationship between Classes and Students and then add sample data into the tables. Enter sample grades for at least two students in at least two different classes (for a total of at least four records). Create a relationships report.

Create a query that displays the student first and last names and all of their grades. Save the query as **Grades Firstname Lastname** Use the report button to create a report based on the Grades query. Resize the report controls and format the report so that it prints on one page. Save the report using the name provided by Access. Submit the database as directed by your instructor.

End **You have completed Project 4M** ——————

Outcomes-Based Assessments

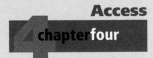

Access

chapterfour

Problem Solving

Project 4N — Computer Support

In this project, you will construct a solution by applying any combination of the skills you practiced from the Objectives in Projects 4A and 4B.

> **For Project 4N, you will need the following file:**
>
> a04N_Work_Orders

**You will save your database as
4N_Work_Orders_Firstname_Lastname**

The computer support staff at MIS Technical Training Institute needs to track work orders. To start, copy a04N_Work_Orders into your Access Chapter 4 folder, and then rename the new file **4N_Work_Orders_ Firstname_Lastname**

Open the database and view the data in the table. Decide what field properties could be changed to improve speed and accuracy during data entry. Create input masks for the Work Order ID, Employee ID, and the two date fields. The two technicians should be a lookup value. Change the properties for the Technician field so that the values must be either Rick or Mary, and then set the default value to Rick. Display an appropriate message if a different value is entered.

Create a form based on the table. Size and format the form to display more effectively. Change the form title to **Work Orders Firstname Lastname** and then save the form with the name **Work Orders Firstname Lastname** Submit the project as directed by your instructor.

 You have completed Project 4N _____

Outcomes-Based Assessments

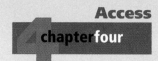
Problem Solving

Project 4O — Inventory

In this project, you will construct a solution by applying any combination of the skills you practiced from the Objectives in Projects 4A and 4B.

> **For Project 4O, you will need the following file:**
>
> New blank Access database

You will save your database as
4O_Inventory_Firstname_Lastname

In this project, you will build a database to track inventory for MIS Technical Training Institute. To start, create a new database with the name **4O_Inventory_Firstname_Lastname** and save it in your Access Chapter 4 folder. Create a table to track information about the two buildings, one in Portland and the other in Boise. Include fields for the addresses and phone numbers for each campus. Create another table to track information for rooms including the room number and seating capacity. Create a third table that lists the inventory that would go into a classroom. Include an inventory number, name, date acquired, and condition. For all the tables, include the fields necessary to relate the three tables in relationships that enforce referential integrity, and then create the relationships between the three tables. Test your database by populating each table with sample data. Include at least two records per table. When you are done, create a relationships report. Submit the project as directed by your instructor.

End **You have completed Project 4O** ——————

Outcomes-Based Assessments

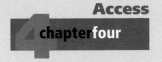

 You and *GO!*

Project 4P—You and *GO!*

In this project, you will construct a solution by applying any combination of the Objectives found in Projects 4A and 4B.

From My Computer, navigate to the student files that accompany this textbook. In the folder **04_you_and_go**, locate and open the folder for this chapter. Open and print the instructions for this project, which are provided to you in Adobe PDF format. Follow the instructions to create a music inventory database.

 You have completed Project 4P ——————————

GO! with Help

Project 4Q—*GO!* with Help

When you assign a field the Yes/No data type, instead of displaying a check box, you can change the display control to a text box, and enter a custom format. A custom format allows values other than Yes/No, True/False, or On/Off and can provide a custom format for each value. In this project, you will explore creating a custom format for the Yes/No data type.

1 **Start** Access. Click the **Microsoft Office Access Help** button.

2 In the **Search** box, type **Yes/No Data Type** and then click **Search**.

3 In the **Access Help** window, in the **Results** list, click **Format Property – Yes/No Data Type**. Read the introduction, click the links to learn more about check boxes and text boxes, and then learn about predefined formats and how to create a custom format.

4 If you want to print a copy of the information, click the **Print** button in the upper portion of the **Access Help** window.

5 Close the **Help** window, and then **Exit** Access.

 You have completed Project 4Q ——————————

5 chapterfive

Automating Data Entry with Forms

OBJECTIVES

At the end of this chapter, you will be able to:

1. Create Forms with Subforms
2. Create Forms with Specials Views

OUTCOMES

Mastering these objectives will enable you to:

PROJECT 5A
Create Forms with Subforms and Custom Views

3. Build a Form in Design View
4. Add Controls to Forms
5. Use Advanced Formatting Tools

PROJECT 5B
Design Forms with Custom Controls

Rock Ridge Lighting

Rock Ridge Lighting is a leading manufacturer of indoor fluorescent lighting products. The company's founder, Harriett Johnson, started manufacturing fluorescent light fixtures for a large building contractor. Now the company has several product lines and distributes its products through commercial retailers throughout the western United States. Recently, the company has hired two new sales directors to manage the company's recent expansion into Midwestern states. Due to their energy saving designs, Rock Ridge Lighting expects strong demand for their innovative lighting products.

Automating Data Entry with Forms

Access provides several options for how the data in a form will display. These different views help the user enter data, especially when decisions need to be made during data entry. For example, when the form data is related to data in another table, it may be useful to see the related records in the same form. Recall that a table displays data in a datasheet while forms typically use a form view, which displays only one record at a time. Access provides forms that combine the advantages of both the Datasheet and Form Views. Multiple forms or pages are also viewed by providing a row of tabs along the top of a form.

In addition to labels and text boxes, several other types of controls are added to forms. These controls include combo boxes, buttons, option buttons, and charts. Some controls aid data entry; others perform actions when they are clicked, and still others provide useful views of the table's data. These controls are available to the form designer when working in Design View. After the desired controls are added to a form, the form is enhanced using special formatting techniques.

Project 5A **Sales Force**

Rock Ridge Lighting needs a way to track its sales force, which consists of Sales Directors and Sales Representatives. The Sales manager oversees the regional Sales Directors, who each oversee a group of Sales Representatives. The company's sales force needs a form to assign territories and dealers to their Sales Representatives, and the Sales Representatives need a form to write notes when they contact their assigned dealers. In this project, you will create several forms using a variety of layouts and styles. The sales force will choose the layout and format that they prefer to work with. Your printed forms will look similar to Figure 5.1.

For Project 5A, you will need the following files:

a05A_Sales_Force
a05A_Logo

You will save your database as
5A_Sales_Force_Firstname_Lastname

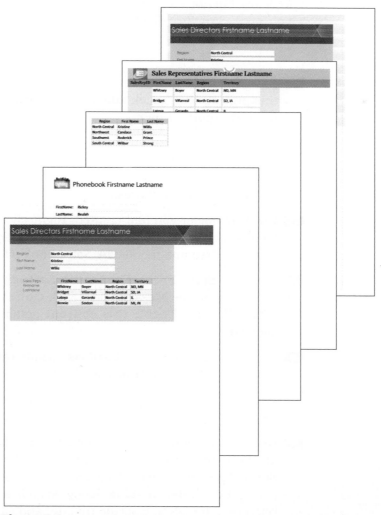

Figure 5.1
Project 5A—Sales Force

Objective 1
Create Forms with Subforms

When working with data in a relational database, a **subform** is used to display data from related tables. A subform is a form that is nested inside another form. The other form is often called the **main form**. Access provides several methods for creating, formatting, and viewing subforms.

Activity 5.1 Creating One-to-Many Relationships

Before creating a subform, create a relationship between the two tables on which the main form and subform will be based. The main form will display data from the *one* side of the relationship, and the subform will display data from the *many* side of the relationship. In this activity, you will establish relationships between the database tables.

Note — Comparing Your Screen with the Figures in This Textbook

Your screen will match the figures shown in this textbook if you set your screen resolution to 1024 × 768. At other resolutions, your screen will closely resemble, but not match, the figures shown. To view your screen's resolution, on the Windows desktop, right-click in a blank area, click Properties, and then click the Settings tab.

---

1 Navigate to the location where you are storing the student files for this project. Right-click **a05A_Sales_Force**, and then click **Copy** from the shortcut menu.

2 Navigate to the location where you are saving your files for this project, such as your USB drive. Right-click a blank area and from the shortcut menu, point to **New**, and then click **New Folder**. Type **Access Chapter 5** and press Enter.

3 Open the folder you just created. Right-click and from the shortcut menu, click **Paste**. Right-click the copied file, and then click **Rename**. Rename the file 5A_Sales_Force_Firstname_Lastname

4 Open **5A_Sales_Force_Firstname_Lastname** in Access 2007. If necessary, in the **Message bar**, click **Options**. Open the **Navigation Pane**. Click the **Enable this content** option button, and then click **OK**.

5 On the Ribbon, click the **Database Tools tab**. In the **Show/Hide group**, click the **Relationships** button.

Three of the tables used by the company's sales force display in the Relationships window.

6 Use the techniques that you have practiced in earlier projects to create a one-to-many relationship between the **Sales Directors** and **Sales Reps** tables using **Region** as the common field. In the displayed **Edit Relationships** dialog box, click the options to enforce referential integrity, cascade update, and cascade delete.

7 Create a one-to-many relationship between the **Sales Reps** and **Dealers** tables using **SalesRepID** as the common field. In the displayed **Edit Relationships** dialog box, click the options to enforce referential integrity, cascade update, and cascade delete, and then click **Create**. Compare your screen with Figure 5.2.

Figure 5.2

One-to-many relationships

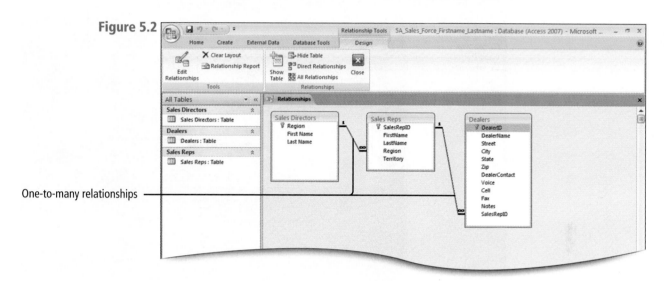

8 **Save** 🖫 the relationships, and then close ☒ the **Relationships** window.

Activity 5.2 Creating a Form and Subform Using the Form Wizard

In this activity, you will use the Form Wizard to create a form and subform that will enable the sales manager to manage both the regional sales directors and their subordinate sales representatives on the same form.

1 Click the **Create tab**. In the **Forms group**, click the **More Forms** button, and then click **Form Wizard**.

2 In the displayed **Form Wizard** dialog box, under **Tables/Queries**, click the **arrow**, click **Table: Sales Directors**, and then click the **All Fields** button >> .

3 Under **Tables/Queries**, click the **arrow**, click **Table: Sales Reps**, use the **One Field** button > to move the following fields into **Selected Fields**: **FirstName**, **LastName**, **Region**, and **Territory**. Compare your screen with Figure 5.3.

When fields from two or more related tables are selected in the Form Wizard, the wizard assigns the fields from the many side of the relationship to a subform. The Region field will be used to link the form and subform. Because the Region field is common to both tables, the wizard inserts the table name followed by a period before both instances of the Region field name.

Figure 5.3

Region field from
Sales Directors table

Region field from
Sales Reps table

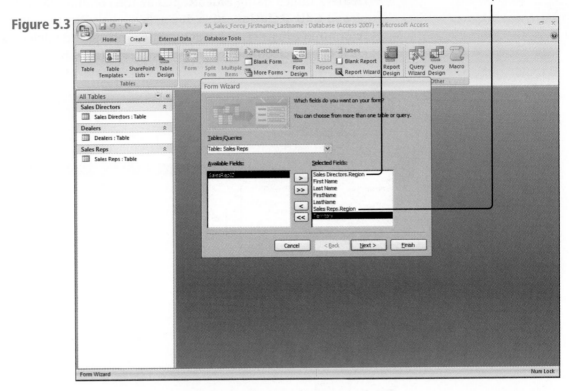

4 Click **Next** and compare your screen with Figure 5.4.

The Form Wizard's remaining screens provide options for the layout and format of the form and subform. A preview of the main form and subform is provided, along with options for viewing the data differently.

Figure 5.4

Table for main form

Form and Subform preview

Linked forms option

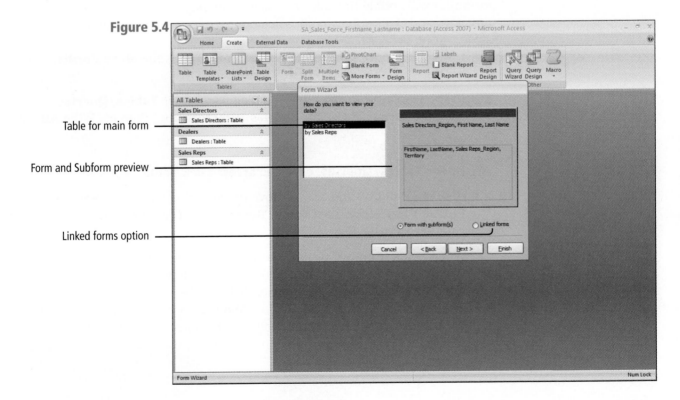

5 Without changing any view options, click **Next**.

The wizard provides two layout options for the subform, *Tabular* and *Datasheet*. The datasheet layout provides a simple datasheet for the subform, whereas the tabular option applies the formatting of the main form.

6 With the **Datasheet** option button selected, click **Next**, and then click the **Verve** style.

7 Click **Next**, and then in the **Form** box, replace the existing text with **Sales Directors Firstname Lastname** Click in the **Subform** box and replace the existing text with **Sales Reps Firstname Lastname**

8 Be sure the **Open the form to view or enter information** option button is selected, and then click **Finish**.

9 Switch to Layout View, and then apply the **Verve AutoFormat**—the fourth choice in the last row. Switch to Form View, and then compare your screen with Figure 5.5.

Additional Verve style formatting is applied. The wizard saves the main form and subform with the names you provided. The main form displays the Northwest sales director record; the subform displays all of the sales representatives assigned to her. Some of the subform's columns do not display without using the subform's scroll bar. The subform's navigation buttons move between records in the subform's datasheet; the main form's navigation buttons are used to display the different sales directors.

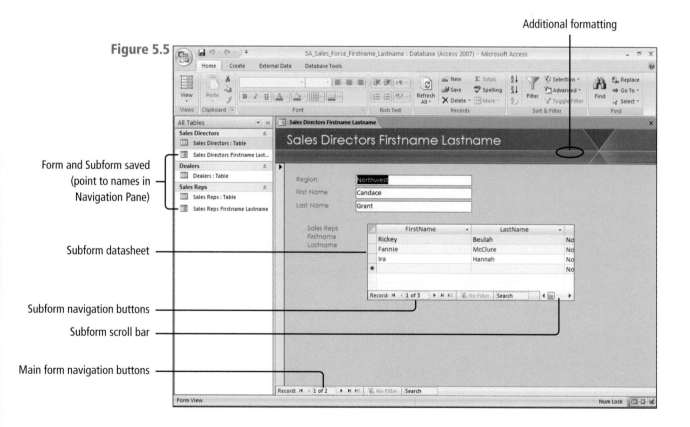

Figure 5.5

Additional formatting

Form and Subform saved
(point to names in
Navigation Pane)

Subform datasheet

Subform navigation buttons

Subform scroll bar

Main form navigation buttons

10 In the subform, position the pointer on the border between the **FirstName** and **Lastname column** headers and double-click. Repeat this technique to resize the three remaining columns.

The column widths resize to fit the contents of each column and all of the columns display without scrolling.

11 In the navigation buttons for the main form, click the **Next record** button ▶.

The form displays the Southwest Sales Director, and the subform displays his assigned Sales Representatives.

12 In the navigation buttons for the main form, click the **New (blank) record** button, and then in the main form, add the following sales director:

Region	First Name	Last Name
North Central	**Kristine**	**Willis**

The subform's Region column displays North Central by default. However, some of the text may not display.

13 In the subform, use the technique you have practiced to resize the width of the **Region column** to fit its contents.

14 With the **North Central** region still displayed in the main form, add the following sales representatives to the subform, and then compare your screen with Figure 5.6:

First Name	Last Name	Region	Territory
Whitney	**Boyer**	**North Central**	**ND, MN**
Bridget	**Villarreal**	**North Central**	**SD, IA**
Latoya	**Gerardo**	**North Central**	**IL**
Bennie	**Sexton**	**North Central**	**MI, IN**

Figure 5.6

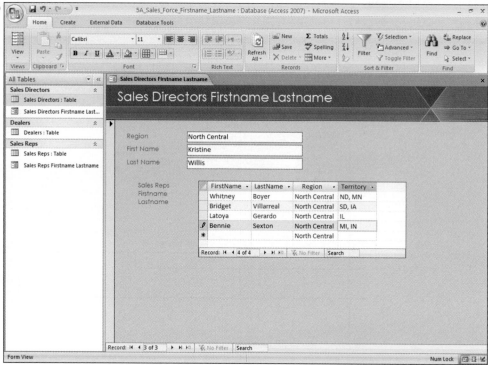

15 Check your *Chapter Assignment Sheet* or your *Course Syllabus* or consult your instructor to determine how you are to submit the results of this project. If your instructor asks you to print this project, from the **Office** menu, click **Print**. Under **Print Range**, click the **Selected Record(s)** option button, and then click **OK**.

16 **Save** 🖫 your work, and then close the form and subform.

Activity 5.3 Creating a Form Using the Blank Form Tool

The ***Blank Form tool*** provides an efficient way to build a form in Layout View. The Blank Form tool is especially useful when you need a form that will contain a subset of a table's available fields. In this activity you will use the Blank Form tool to create a form that displays just the phone contact data from the Dealers table.

1 On the Ribbon, click the **Create tab**, and then in the **Forms group**, click the **Blank Form** button.

A blank form opens in Layout View, and the Field List pane displays.

2 In the **Field List** pane, click **Show all tables**, and for the **Dealers** table, click the **Expand** button ⊞.

3 In the **Field List**, double-click the following fields in this order: **DealerName**, **DealerContact**, **Voice**, **Cell**, **Notes**, and **SalesRepID**. When you are done, compare your screen with Figure 5.7.

A label and text box is added to the form in the order that the fields were clicked.

Figure 5.7

Field List pane   Dealers table fields

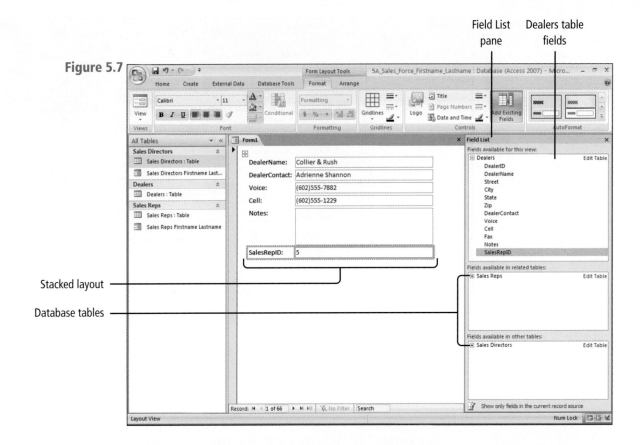

Stacked layout

Database tables

4 In the **Controls group**, click the **Title** button, type **Dealer** and then apply the **Module** AutoFormat, which is the third choice in the second row of the gallery.

5 Close ☒ the **Field List** pane, and then click the **Save** button 🖫. In the displayed **Save As** dialog box, in the **Form Name** box, type **Dealers Firstname Lastname** and then click **OK**.

6 Click anywhere in the data grid, and then click the data grid's displayed **Layout Selector** ⊞. Drag the control group down so that the **DealerName** controls are no longer over the dark shaded area created by the Module AutoFormat.

7 **Save** 🖫 your work, and then close the form.

Activity 5.4 Adding a Subform Using the Subform Control

An existing form is added to another form as a subform using the Subform control. To use this technique, the main form and subform need to be based on related tables. The form and subform are created separately, and then combined using the Subform control. In this activity, you will create the main form, and then use the Subform control to add the Dealers form that you created earlier. Sales Representatives will use the form and subform when making calls to their assigned dealers.

1 Click the **Create tab**, and then in the **Forms group**, click the **Blank Form** button.

2 In the **Field List**, expand the **Sales Reps** table, double-click the **SalesRepID** field, and then compare your screen with Figure 5.8.

Because the Sales Reps table is related to the Dealers and Sales Directors tables, the Field List displays those tables in a separate area.

Figure 5.8

Related tables ——————————

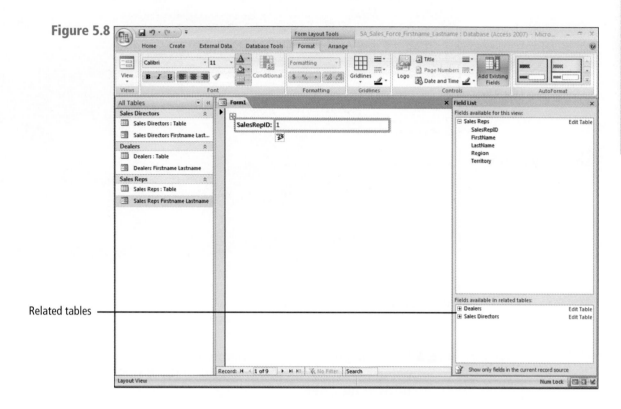

3 Double-click to add the **FirstName** field, and then add the **LastName** field to the form. Close ⊠ the **Field List** pane, and then save the form with the name **Phonebook Firstname Lastname**

4 In the **Views group**, click the **View button arrow**, click **Design View**, and then compare your screen with Figure 5.9.

In Design View, the Ribbon displays the Form Design Tools. In the Design tab, many control buttons are available that are not available in Layout View, including the Subform/Subreport button. In the design area, the Vertical ruler displays at the left, and the horizontal ruler displays at the top. Gridlines extend to help you position controls on the form. Between the gridlines, grid dots display to help you position controls between gridlines.

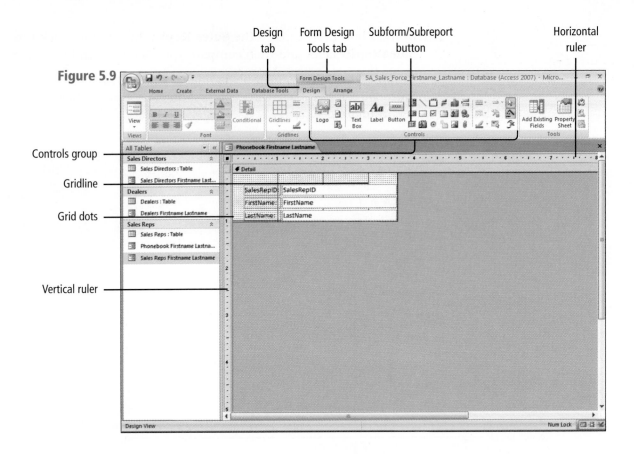

Figure 5.9

Design tab · **Form Design Tools tab** · **Subform/Subreport button** · **Horizontal ruler**

Controls group

Gridline

Grid dots

Vertical ruler

5 Place the pointer over the right edge of the form. When the ↔ pointer displays, drag to the right to the **6 inch mark on the horizontal ruler**.

Note — Displaying Rulers in Design View

If your display does not show rulers along the upper and left sides of the form, click the Arrange tab, and then in the Show/Hide group, click the Ruler button.

6 Using the technique you just practiced, drag the lower edge of the form until it is aligned with the **5 inch mark on the vertical ruler** to make room for a subform.

7 In the **Controls group**, click the **Subform/Subreport** button.

The pointer changes to the Subform/Subreport pointer. The subform will be placed at the location of the + sign on the pointer when the left mouse button is clicked.

8 Align the + sign of the pointer at the **.5 inch mark on the horizontal ruler** and three grid dots below the **LastName** control, and then click one time to display the Subform Wizard.

9 In the displayed **Subform Wizard** dialog box, click the **Use an existing form** option button, click the **Dealers** form that you created in an earlier activity, and then click **Next**.

The wizard asks which fields will link the two forms. The relationship's common field, SalesRepID, is used by default.

10 Click **Next**, click **Finish**, and then compare your screen with Figure 5.10.

The Dealers form created in an earlier activity displays as a subform. You will format the form and subform in the next activity.

Main form

Figure 5.10

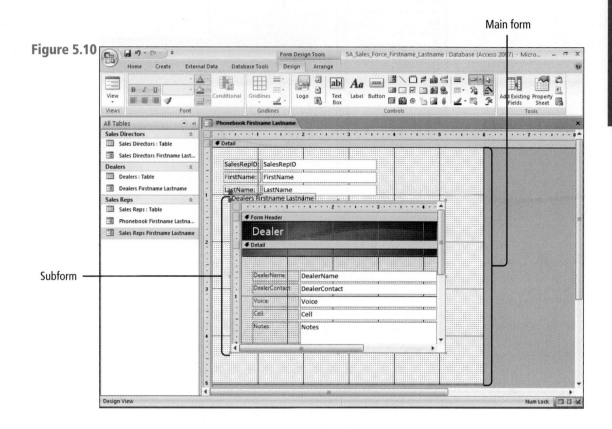

Subform

11 **Save** the form and subform, and leave them open for the next activity.

Activity 5.5 Formatting a Form and Subform in Layout View

Subforms can be formatted in Form View, Layout View, and Design View. Layout View provides a more accurate preview than Design View. No matter which view is used to format a subform, the end result should always be tested in Form View. In this activity, you will format a form in Layout View, and then test your changes in Form View.

1 With the **Phonebook** form and its subform still open, in the **Views group**, click the **Form View** button, and then compare your screen with Figure 5.11.

All of the subform fields display correctly in Form View. The subform has a label control positioned above the subform.

Subform label control

Figure 5.11

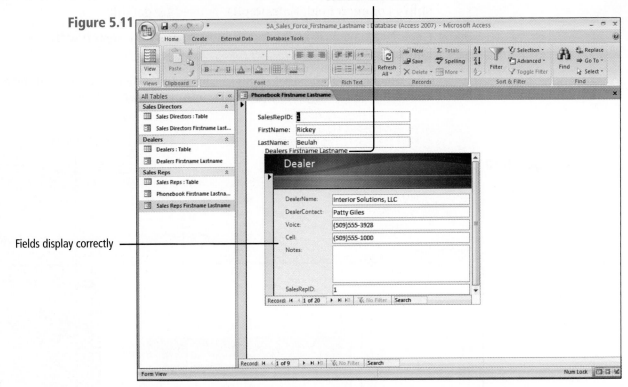

Fields display correctly

2 In the **Views group**, click the **Layout View** button, click the sub-form's label control, and then press [Delete] to delete the label.

3 In the **Controls group**, click the **Logo** button, and then in the displayed **Insert Picture** dialog box, navigate to the student files that accompany this project. Click **a05A_Logo**, and then click **OK**.

The Form Header is expanded and the image is inserted into the Form Header.

4 In the **Controls group**, click the **Title** button. Notice that the main form's name is inserted as a label in the Form Header.

5 Click any blank area of the form, and then click the main form's title control so that it is selected. Press [↓] four times.

Controls are moved more precisely using the arrow keys instead of dragging them with the mouse.

6 Click the **Arrange tab**. In the main form, click the **SalesRepID** text box control, and then in the **Tools group**, click the **Property Sheet** button.

The *Property Sheet* for the SalesRepID text box control displays. Recall that the Property Sheet is a list of characteristics for controls on a form or report in which you make precision changes to each property associated with the control.

7 On the Property Sheet's **Format tab**, locate the **Visible** property, and then double-click its box. Alternatively, click in the Visible property box, click the displayed arrow, and then click No.

The Visible property changes to No. The control remains on the form, but it will not be visible in Form View.

8 In the subform, click the **SalesRepID** text box control, use the technique just practiced to set its **Visible** property to **No**, and then compare your screen with Figure 5.12.

By hiding these controls, they are still used to link the form and subform while preventing the sales representatives from changing their assigned IDs.

Figure 5.12

Hidden controls

9 Double-click the subform's title control, and then change the existing text to **Assigned Dealers**

10 Use the technique just practiced to change the **DealerName:** label to **Dealer:** and then the **DealerContact:** label to **Contact:**

11 Click the **Dealer:** label control to select it, press and hold down Shift, click the four remaining label controls, and then release Shift.

All five labels are selected. Using this technique, multiple items are edited at one time.

12 In the **Property Sheet**, click the **Text Align** box, click the displayed **arrow**, and then click **Right**. Notice that all formatting options available on the Ribbon are also available in the Property Sheet.

13 **Save** your work, and then switch to Form View. In the subform's navigation bar, click the **Next record** button.

The record for Becker Enterprises displays in the subform.

14 In the **Notes** field, type the following sales call notes: **2/04/2009: They are interested in adding three of our product lines. Call again next week.** Compare your form with Figure 5.13.

Figure 5.13

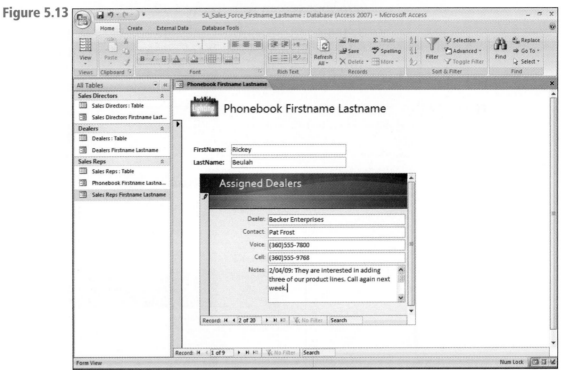

15 If your instructor asks you to print this project, from the **Office** menu [icon], click **Print**. Under **Print Range**, click in the **From** box and type **1** In the **To** box, type **1** and then click **OK**.

16 Close the form and leave the database open for the next activity.

Objective 2
Create Forms with Special Views

Recall that a datasheet displays multiple records in rows and columns. Most forms, on the other hand, display only one record at a time so that data is entered more efficiently and accurately. Access provides two special form views which combine the features of both a datasheet and a typical form view. The advantages of both views are provided in a single form.

Activity 5.6 Creating a Split Form

A **split form** gives you two views of the same data, a form view and a datasheet view. You use the datasheet to quickly navigate the table, and then use the form to enter or edit records. Both forms stay synchronized as you enter data. In this activity, you will create a split form that the Sales Manager will use to track Sales Directors.

1 In the **Navigation Pane**, click the **Sales Directors** table one time. On the Ribbon, click the **Create tab**, and then in the **Forms** group, click **Split Form**.

2 **Close** the **Property Sheet** if necessary and apply the Civic AutoFormat, which is the last choice in the first row of the gallery. Compare your screen with Figure 5.14.

A new form is created with a form view at the top and a datasheet below.

Figure 5.14

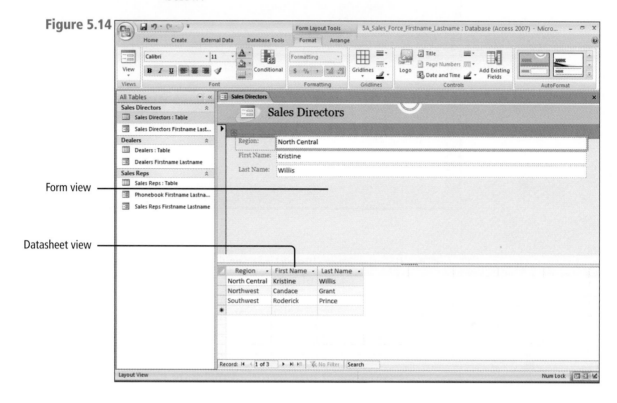

Form view

Datasheet view

3 Using techniques practiced in earlier activities, change the form's title to **Sales Directors Firstname Lastname**

4 Switch to Design View, and then close ⊠ the **Navigation Pane**. Click to select the **Region** text box control, and then drag the control's right border to place the right edge of the control at **4.5 inches on the horizontal ruler**.

5 In the **Controls group**, click the **Date & Time** button ⊞. In the displayed **Date and Time** dialog box, if necessary click to select both the Include Date and Include Time check boxes. Under **Include Date**, click the third option button. Under **Include Time,** click the second option button, and then click **OK**.

The date and time controls are inserted into the Form Header.

6 On the Quick Access toolbar, click the **Save** button ⊞. In the displayed **Save As** dialog box, in the **Form Name** box, type **Sales Directors Split Firstname Lastname** and then click **OK**.

7 Switch to Form View, and then compare your screen with Figure 5.15.

Figure 5.15

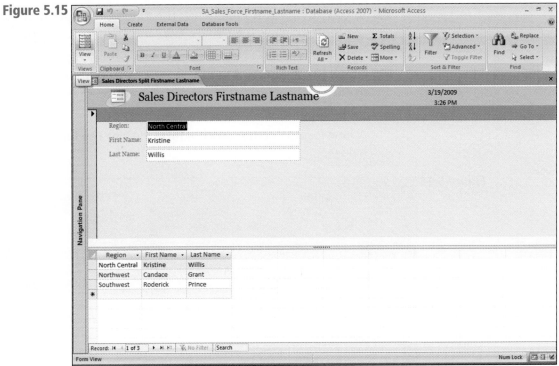

8 Click the **New (blank) record** button, click in the **Region** text box, and then enter the following record:

Region	First Name	Last Name
South Central	**Wilbur**	**Strong**

As you enter a new record in the main form, the data is also inserted into the datasheet.

9 From the **Office** menu , point to **Print**, and then click **Print Preview**.

Only the datasheet prints in a split form.

10 If your instructor has asked you to print this project, click the **Print** button .

11 **Save** your work, close the **Print Preview** and then close the form.

Activity 5.7 Creating a Multiple Items Form

If you want a form to display more than one record at a time and need more formatting options than are offered in Datasheet View, then a *multiple items form* should be used. A multiple items form displays the records in rows and columns much like a datasheet, but provides many of the customization and formatting options found only in a form layout. In this activity, you will create a multiple items form that the Sales Directors will use to track Sales Representatives.

1 Open 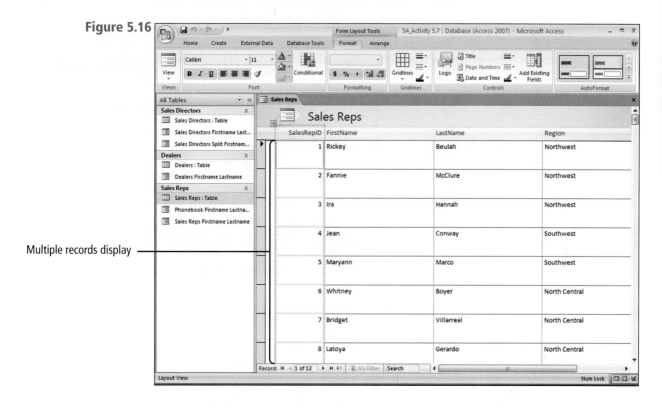 the **Navigation Pane**. Click the **Sales Reps** table one time. Click the **Create tab**, and then in the **Forms group**, click the **Multiple Items** button. A form that shows several records on one screen displays, as shown in Figure 5.16.

Figure 5.16

Multiple records display

2 Apply the **Civic** AutoFormat, and then change the form's title text to **Sales Representatives Firstname Lastname**

3 Click the **Save** button. In the displayed **Save As** dialog box, click in the **Form Name** box, type **Sales Reps Multiple Firstname Lastname** and then click **OK**.

4 Click in the first row, and then click the displayed **Layout Selector** to select all the data labels and text box controls. Click the **Arrange tab**, and then in the **Position group**, click the **Size to Fit** button.

5 Click in the **Region column**, and in the **Tools group**, click the **Property Sheet** button. On the **Format tab**, replace the **Width** property with **1** and then press Enter.

6 Under **Selection type**, click the **arrow**, and then scroll to and click **Territory** to display the properties for the Territory text box control.

7 Using the technique you just practiced, set the width of the **Territory** text box to **1.5**

8 In the **Property Sheet**, display the properties for the **SalesRepID** text box. On the **Format tab**, change the **Visible** property to **No**

Because the SalesRepID field has the AutoNumber data type, the end-user will not need to see the label and text box during data entry.

9 Using the technique you just practiced, display the properties for **Label1**—the label associated with the Sales Rep ID column—and then change its **Visible** property to **No**

10 In the **Property Sheet**, display the properties for the **FirstName** text box. Change the **Height** property to **0.35"** **Close** the **Property Sheet**, and then compare your screen with Figure 5.17.

The table's primary key field and label do not display, the last two column widths have changed, and the row heights have changed.

SalesRepID label and control not visible   Text box height set to .35"

Figure 5.17

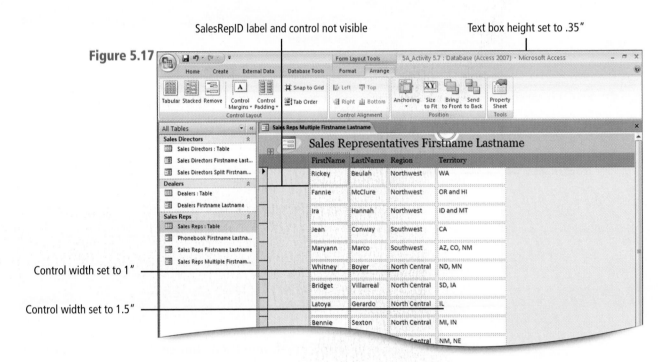

Control width set to 1"

Control width set to 1.5"

11 Switch to Form View. Use the form to assign two new sales representatives in the South Central region:

First Name	Last Name	Region	Territory
Garry	Carillo	South Central	NM, NE
Geoffrey	Kent	South Central	TX

12 On the **Home tab**, in the **Sort & Filter group**, click the **Advanced Filter Options** button, and then click **Advanced Filter/Sort**.

Recall that the displayed Advanced Filter design grid is similar to the Query design grid.

13 Double-click **Region** to add it to the design grid. In the **Region column Criteria row**, type **North Central** In the **or row**, type **South Central** and then in the **Sort & Filter group**, click the **Toggle Filter** button.

The filter is applied, and only the sales reps from the new North Central and South Central regions display in the Multiple Items form.

14 If your instructor asks you to print this project, print the form with the advanced filter in place.

15 With the filter in place, **Save** 🖫 your changes, and then close the form.

Activity 5.8 Creating a Form with Tabbed Pages

A *tabbed form* displays a row of tabs at the top of the form, and each tab displays a different form or page. Tabbed forms provide the end-user an easy way to open and work with several forms at once. Columbia Lighting is considering using a tabbed interface. In this activity, you will create a form with two tabs—one tab will track the Sales Force and the other tab will track Dealers.

1 Click the **Create tab**, and then and in the **Forms group**, click the **Form Design** button.

2 In the **Controls group**, click the **Tab Control** button 🗔.

3 Place the plus sign (+) of the Tab Control pointer 🗔 in the upper left corner of the **Detail** section.

The insertion displays as a + sign with the Tab Control icon.

4 Drag from the upper left corner of the **Detail** section down to **4 inches on the vertical ruler**, and then over to **6 inches on the horizontal ruler**. Compare your screen with Figure 5.18.

A 6 x 4 inch tab control is inserted into the form. The tab control displays two pages with Page1 on top.

2 tabbed pages

Figure 5.18

6 x 4 inch tab control

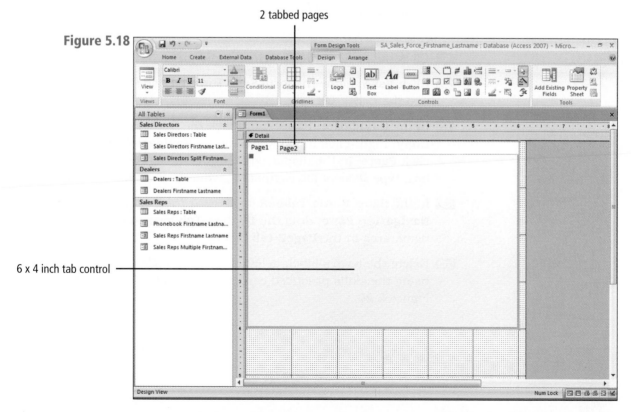

5 From the **Navigation Pane**, drag the **Sales Directors** form and place it over the blank area in the **Page1** tab control. Place the pointer in the upper left corner of the displayed black rectangle, and then release the left mouse button. Compare your screen with Figure 5.19.

The form and subform are inserted into the Page1 tab. The form's label displays above the form.

Form   Subform

Figure 5.19

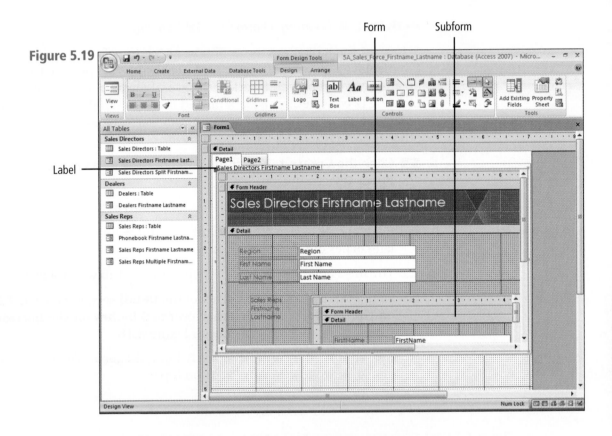

Label

6 Click the form's label to select it and press Delete.

7 Click **Save**, name the form **Sales Force Tabbed Firstname Lastname** and then click **OK**.

8 In the **Navigation Pane**, right-click the **Dealers** form and then click **Copy**. Right-click a blank area of the **Navigation Pane**, and then click **Paste**. In the displayed **Paste As** dialog box, in the Form Name box, type **Dealers Tab Firstname Lastname** and then click **OK**.

9 In the **Sales Force Tabbed** form, click the **Page2 tab**. From the **Navigation Pane**, drag the **Dealers Tab** form and place it over the blank area in the **Page2 tab** control.

10 Delete the form's label, delete the form's **Title** text box, and then using the skills practiced earlier, position the form as shown in Figure 5.20.

Figure 5.20

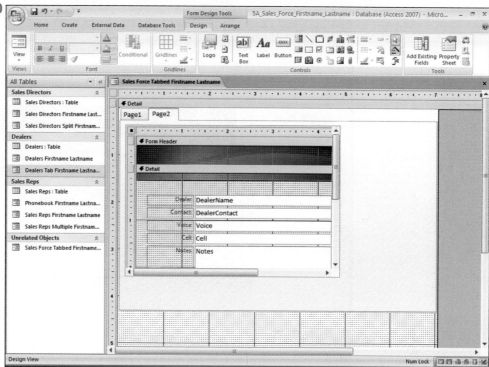

11 In the **Tools group**, click the **Property Sheet** button. Click the **Selection type arrow**, and then click **Form**. In the **Format tab**, change the **Default View** property to **Datasheet**.

12 Click the **Page1 tab** to display its properties. In the **Format tab**, change the **Caption** property to **Sales** Click the **Page2 tab**, and then change the **Caption** property to **Dealers** and then close the **Property Sheet**.

13 Save the form, switch to Form View, and then compare your screen with Figure 5.21.

Figure 5.21

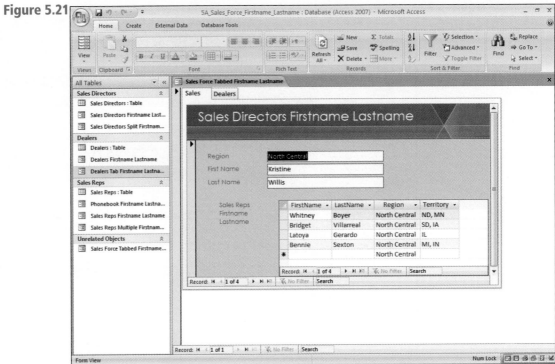

14 In the subform for the *Northwest* director, add the following Sales Representative:

First Name	Last Name	Region	Territory
David	Koz	Northwest	AK

15 If your instructor asks you to print this project, with the Northwest director still displayed, from the **Office** menu , click **Print**. Under **Print Range**, click in the **From** box and type **1** In the **To** box, type **1** and then click **OK**.

16 Click **Save**, close the form, and then **Exit** Access.

End You have completed Project 5A ————————

Project 5B Opportunities

Rock Ridge Lighting needs a form that their Sales department can use to track sales opportunities. In this project, you will build a form with several custom controls that are accessible only in Design View. You will then use special formatting to enhance the form's usability. Your final output will be a form similar to Figure 5.22.

For Project 5B, you will need the following file:

a05B_Opportunities

**You will save your database as
5B_Opportunities_Firstname_Lastname**

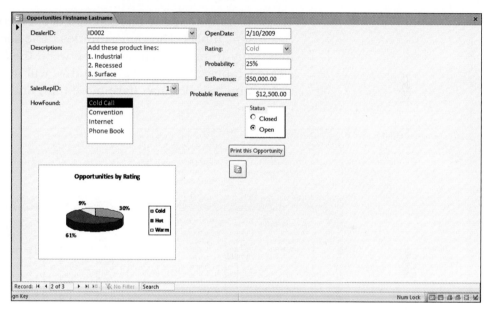

Figure 5.22
Project 5B—Opportunities

Objective 3
Build a Form in Design View

In earlier projects, you have used Design View to perform tasks that cannot be done in Layout View. In Design View, the form is not actually running and data does not display. Because no data displays, control source properties can be typed directly into a textbox without having to use the Property Sheet. When building forms, Design View provides more controls, such as labels, lines, and images. Design View also provides greater control over the form's sections—the Form Header, Detail section, and Form Footer.

Activity 5.9 Building a Form in Design View

When controls are added in Design View, each control is positioned, resized, and formatted independently from the other controls. This is especially helpful when you plan to build a form that needs a layout that differs from the strict columns provided in Layout View. In this activity, you will build a form in Design View.

1 Navigate to the location of the student files for this project. Right-click **a05B_Opportunities**, and then from the shortcut menu, click **Copy**.

2 Navigate to the **Access Chapter 5** folder, right-click and from the displayed shortcut menu, click **Paste**. Rename the file **5B_Opportunities_Firstname_Lastname**

3 Open **5B_Opportunities_Firstname_Lastname** in Access 2007. If necessary, in the **Message** bar, click **Options**. Select Enable this content, and then click **OK**.

4 On the Ribbon, click the **Database Tools tab**, and in the **Show/Hide group**, click **Relationships**, and then compare your screen with Figure 5.23.

There is a one-to-many relationship between the Sales Directors and Sales Reps tables. The Opportunities table serves as a junction table in a many-to-many relationship between the Sales Reps and the Dealers tables. A Sales Representative will have many sales opportunities, and a dealer may have more than one opportunity.

Figure 5.23

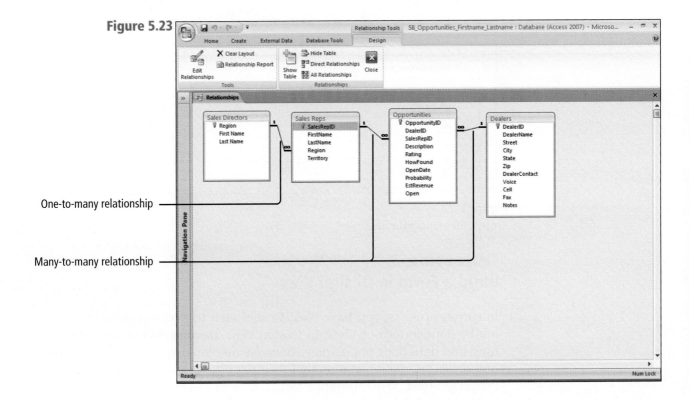

One-to-many relationship

Many-to-many relationship

5 Without making any changes, close the **Relationships** window. Click the **Create tab**, and then in the **Forms** group, click the **Form Design** button.

6 In the **Tools group**, click the **Add Existing Fields** button. In the displayed **Field List** pane, click **Show all tables**, and expand the **Opportunities** table.

7 From the **Opportunities** table in the **Field List** pane, double-click the **DealerID** field. In the **Field List** pane, double-click each of these fields in the following order, and then compare your screen with Figure 5.24: **Description**, **SalesRepID**, and **HowFound**.

A label and text box displays for each field added to the form.

Text box controls

Figure 5.24

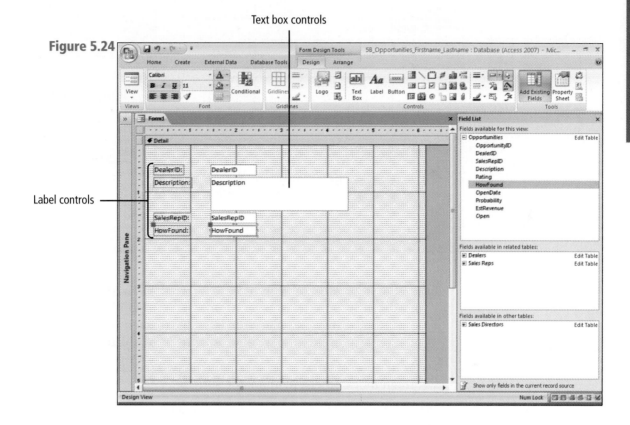

Label controls

8 Click the **Description** text box, and then place the pointer over the right border. When the pointer changes to ⟷, drag to the left. When the control's right edge is over the **3 inch vertical gridline**, release the left mouse button.

The controls are *arranged* the same as a stacked layout, but unlike a stacked layout, each control can be resized and moved independently of the others.

9 Drag the **OpenDate** field into the **Detail** section so that the left edge of the field's text box is at **4.5 inches on the horizontal ruler** and about two dots from the top of the **Detail** section. Compare your screen with Figure 5.25.

A second column of controls has been started.

Figure 5.25

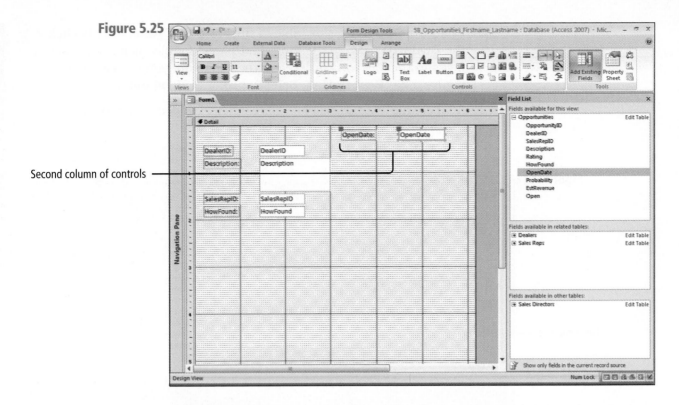

Second column of controls

10 Using the technique you have just practiced, add the following fields in the order given. Drop each control about four dots below the one inserted earlier, and place the left edge of each text box near the 4.5 inch mark on the upper ruler: **Rating**, **Probability** and **EstRevenue**.

Your controls may not be exactly aligned or spaced. You will align them more precisely in a later activity.

11 Close the **Field List** pane. Click the **Arrange tab**, and then in the **Show/Hide group**, click the **Page Header/Footer** button.

The Page Header section displays above the Detail section. Recall that a Page Header displays information at the top of every printed page, and that controls in a Page Footer will display at the bottom each printed page.

12 Scroll down to display the **Page Footer** section. Click the **Design tab**, and then in the **Controls group**, click the **Label** button. In the **Page Footer**, click in the upper left corner, and then type **5B_ Opportunities_Firstname_Lastname**

13 Place the pointer at the lower edge of the **Detail** section. When the pointer displays, drag up, and when the selection line is at the **4.5 inch mark on the vertical ruler**, release the left mouse button.

14 Click **Save**, and then in the displayed **Save As** dialog box, in the **Form Name** box, type **Opportunities Firstname Lastname** and then click **OK**. Leave the form open for the next activity.

Activity 5.10 Aligning Controls using Arrange Tools

In Design View, aligning controls using the mouse is difficult. Access provides many tools for precisely aligning controls on a form without having to use the mouse. In this activity, you will use alignment and spacing tools to position controls in the Opportunity form.

1 With the **Opportunities** form open, switch to Layout View. Apply the **Solstice** AutoFormat, which is the last choice in row 4 of the gallery.

2 Switch to Design View and click the **OpenDate** text box. While holding the ⇧Shift key, click the **OpenDate** label, **DealerID** text box, and then the **DealerID** label. Be careful not to move the mouse while clicking.

3 Click **Arrange tab**. With the four controls still selected, in the **Control Alignment group**, click the **Top** button.

The tops of the controls are now precisely aligned. Control alignments are quickly adjusted using the alignment tools in the Control Alignment group.

4 Starting directly below the **How Found** text box, drag up and to the left. When the pointer is above the **DealerID** label, release the left mouse button, and then compare your screen with Figure 5.26.

Four labels and four text boxes are selected.

Figure 5.26

Four label and four text box controls are selected

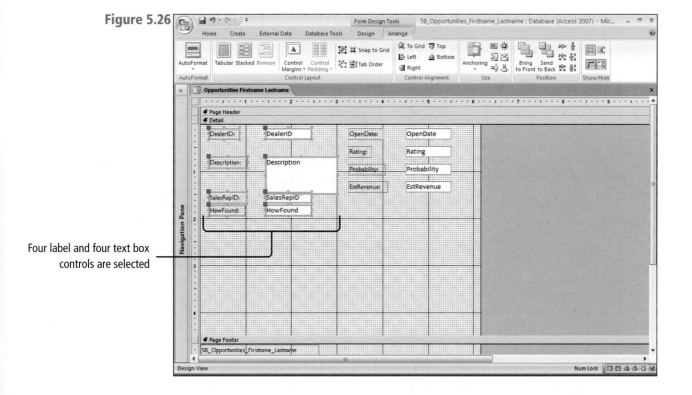

5 With the eight controls still selected, in the **Position group**, click the **Make Vertical Spacing Equal** button 🔲.

The controls now have the same amount of space between them.

6 In the **Position group**, click the **Decrease Vertical Spacing** button 🔲 until there is no space between the controls. Click the **Increase Vertical Spacing** button 🔲 two times.

The four controls are precisely spaced.

7 Click any blank area in the **Detail** section, and then use one of the multiple selection techniques that you have practiced to select the **Open Date**, **Rating**, **Probability**, and **EstRevenue** text boxes.

8 With the four controls still selected, in the **Control Layout group**, click the **Stacked** button. Notice that four labels and four textboxes are now selected.

The controls are aligned in a *stacked layout*. In a stacked layout, labels and text boxes are arranged vertically with a label to the right of each text box. Access also provides a *tabular layout*. In a tabular layout, controls are arranged in rows and columns like a table. With both layouts, the controls are positioned and sized as a single group. For example, changing the width of one text box will also change the width of the other text boxes in the group.

9 With the eight controls still selected, in the **Control Layout group**, click the **Remove** button.

The controls retain the same layout, but each control can now be resized and positioned independently.

10 With the eight controls still selected, press the ➡ until the left edges of the labels are aligned with the **4 inch vertical gridline**.

11 With the eight controls still selected, use the techniques practiced in earlier steps to increase the vertical spacing one time and compare your screen with Figure 5.27.

The labels are aligned on their right borders and the text boxes all have an equal amount of vertical spacing between them.

Figure 5.27

Equal vertical spacing

Label controls are aligned

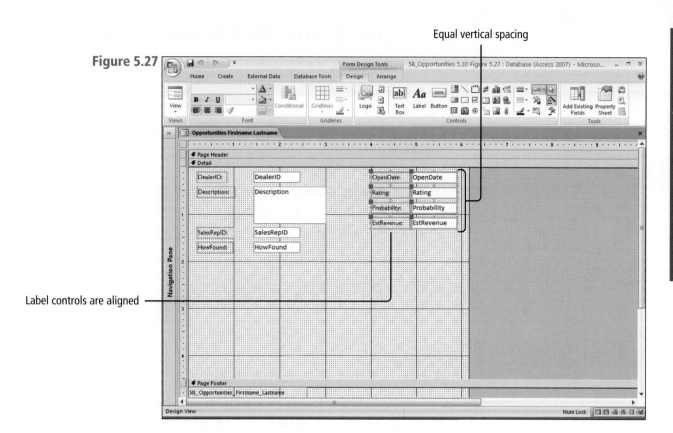

12 Click **Save** 🖫 , and leave the form open for the next activity.

More Knowledge

Setting Tab Order

In a form, the *tab order* is the order in which fields are navigated when the Tab key is pressed. When creating a custom form, the tab order must sometimes be adjusted to match the order in which fields are displayed. The Tab Order dialog box can be open in the Arrange tab when working in Design View. To remove a field from the tab order, set its Tab Stop property to No.

Objective 4
Add Controls to Forms

You have already worked with many controls in earlier projects: labels, text boxes, tabs, subforms, combo boxes, and list boxes. Access provides several other controls that improve how a form displays and functions. Most of these controls are typically added while working in Design View.

Activity 5.11 Creating a Combo Box with Data from a Related Table

Recall that when a form includes values that are a primary key in a related table, only one value needs to be entered into the form and all of the corresponding data in the related table will be available. Listing these foreign keys in a combo box helps the end user enter the correct values from the related table. When the data in the combo box is based on a field in a related table, the related value from both tables may be edited within the combo box. In this activity, you will add and format combo boxes for the two fields in the Opportunities form that are primary keys in related tables.

1 With the **Opportunities** form still open in Design View, right-click the **DealerID** text box, and from the shortcut menu, point to **Change To**, and then click **ComboBox**.

2 Open the **Property Sheet**, click the **Data tab**, and click the **Row Source** box. Click the displayed **arrow**, and then click **Dealers**.

The combo box will list the DealerID values from the Dealers table.

3 In the **Property Sheet**, click the **Format tab**, and then change the **Column Count** to **2**

In the combo box, the first two fields from the Dealer's table will display—*DealerID* and *Dealer Name*.

4 In the **Property Sheet**, change the **Column Widths** property to **.5** Set the **List Rows** property to **10** and then in the **Width** property, type **2.4**

5 Click the **Form View** button, click the **DealerID combo box arrow**, and then compare your screen with Figure 5.28.

The combo box lists the first 10 records from the Dealers table and displays a scroll bar to view the other records. The first column displays the DealerID field and the second column displays the Dealer Name field. A new DealerID can be added by typing in the upper row of the combo box.

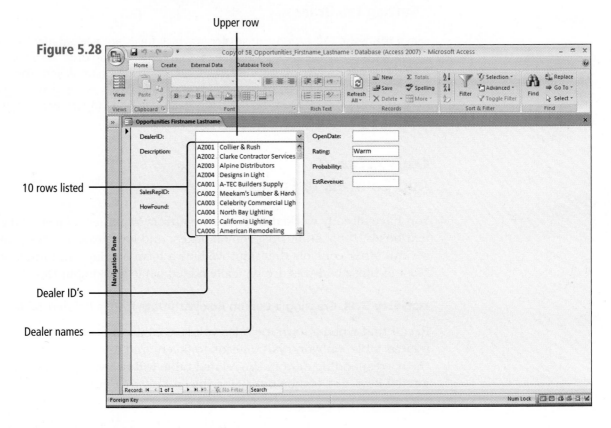

Figure 5.28

6 Return to Design View. Using the technique just practiced, change the **SalesRepID** text box into a **Combo Box**.

7 In the Property Sheet's **Data tab**, select the **Sales Reps** table as the **Row Source** property for **SalesRepID**.

8 In the **Property Sheet**, click the **Format tab**, change the **Column Count** to **3** and the **Column Widths** property to **.5** Set the **List Rows** property to **9** and for the **Width** property, type **2**

9 In the **Property Sheet**, click the **Data tab**, and then change the **Limit to List** property to **Yes**

With the Limit to List property set to *Yes*, a Sales Rep ID that is not already listed may not be entered in the combo box's upper row.

10 In the **Property Sheet**, click the **Other tab**, and then in the **ControlTipText** property, type **Enter existing Sales Reps only.**

11 Switch to Form View, click the **SalesRepID arrow**, pause briefly, and then compare your screen with Figure 5.29.

A control tip displays the message you entered.

Figure 5.29

ControlTip Text —

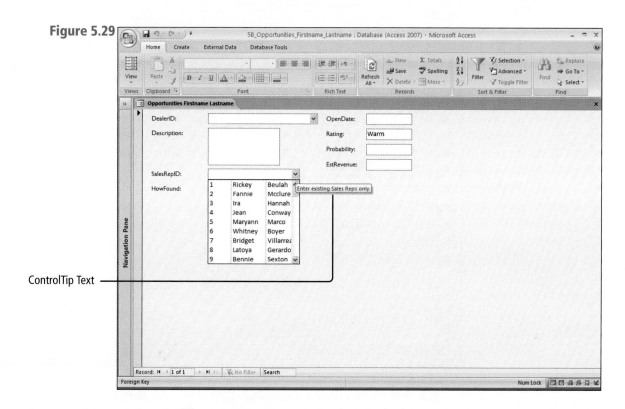

12 Click **Save** , and then leave the form open for the next activity.

Activity 5.12 Adding a List Box and Combo Box

A combo box or list box speeds data entry for fields that will contain a limited set of values. In a form, any text box may be converted to a list box or combo box. In a form, a combo box or list box uses values from an unrelated table or a typed list. In this activity, you will create a combo box and list box that looks up values from a typed list.

1 With the **Opportunities** form still open, switch to Design View, right-click the **How Found** text box, and from the shortcut menu, point to **Change To**, and then click **List Box**.

The control increases in size to allow room for a list of values.

2 Display the properties for the **How Found** text box, and click the **Data tab**. Click the **Row Source Type** box, click the displayed **arrow**, and then click **Value List**.

3 Click in the **Row Source** box, and then click the displayed **Build** 🔲 button. In the displayed **Edit List Items** dialog box, type **Cold Call** and press [Enter], and then type **Convention** Complete the list by typing **Internet** and then **Phone Book**

4 In the **Edit List Items** dialog box, click the **Default Value arrow**, click **Cold Call,** and then click **OK**. Switch to Form View and compare your screen to Figure 5.30. Notice that the list box displays the typed list and Cold Call is selected by default.

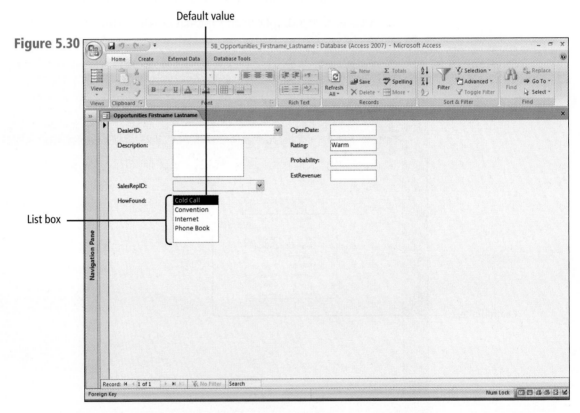

Figure 5.30

5 Return to Design View and right-click the **Rating** text box. From the displayed shortcut menu, point to **Change To**, and then click **Combo Box**.

6 In the **Property Sheet**, with the properties for the **Rating** combo box displayed, click the **Data tab**, click the **Row Source Type arrow**, and then click **Value List**.

7 Click in the **Row Source** property text box, and then click the **Build** 🔲 button. In the displayed **Edit List Items** dialog box, set the default value to **Hot**, and then click **OK**.

8 **Save** 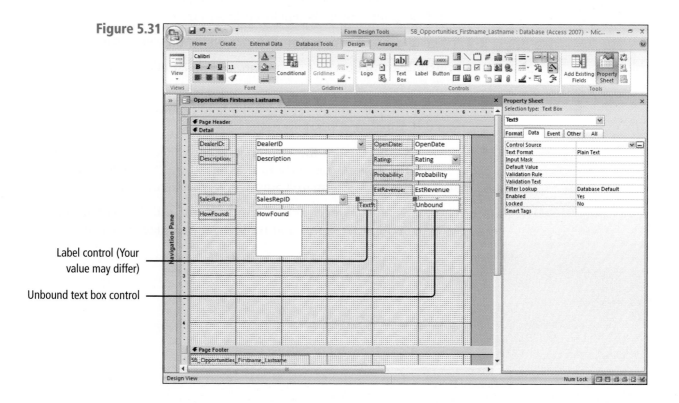 the form, and then switch to Form View. Notice that the Rating combo box displays *Hot* as the default value.

9 Leave the form open for the next activity.

Activity 5.13 Adding a Calculated Control

Recall that a calculated control displays the results of a calculation. To create a calculated control, an **expression** is entered into the Control Source property. An expression is any combination of field names, properties, constants, or operators. In Access, an **operator** performs a specific function such as multiplying, comparing two values, or testing if a condition is true or false. In this activity, you will add a calculated control that multiplies the value in the Probability field by the value in the Estimated Revenue field.

1 With the **Opportunities** form still open, switch to Design View.

2 In the **Controls group**, click the **Text Box** button, and then below the **EstRevenue** text box, drag to create a control the same width and height as the **EstRevenue** text box. Compare your screen to Figure 5.31.

The new text box is an **unbound control**. Any control that doesn't have a source of data, such as a field from a table, is called an unbound control.

Figure 5.31

Label control (Your value may differ)

Unbound text box control

3 With the new text box still selected, in the **Property Sheet**, click the **Data tab**, and then if necessary, click in the Control Source box. In the **Control Source** box, click the displayed **Build** button and compare your screen with Figure 5.32.

The Expression Builder dialog box displays. The **Expression Builder** provides easy access to the fields and controls in a database along with common operators. The database objects display in the left column and the control list for the currently selected object displays in the middle column.

Figure 5.32

Logical operators —

Mathematical operators —

Database objects —

List of fields and controls —

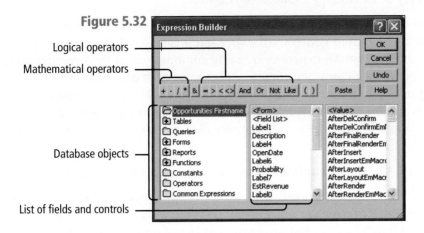

☐4 In the displayed **Expression Builder** dialog box, click the **Equals** operator button ☐. In the middle column, which lists fields and controls, locate the **Probability** field, and then double-click the field.

The Expression Builder displays =[Probability]. In a calculated control, field names must be enclosed in square brackets.

☐5 In the displayed **Expression Builder** dialog box, click the **multiplication** operator ☐ button. In the list of controls, double-click **EstRevenue**.

The Expression Builder encloses the field names in brackets and displays =[Probability]*[EstRevenue]

☐6 Click **OK**, and then in the **Property Sheet**, click the **Format tab**. Change the **Format** property to **Currency**, and then click any blank area in the form. Compare your screen with Figure 5.33.

The control is no longer an unbound control and the expression that you created in the Expression Builder now displays in the text box.

Figure 5.33

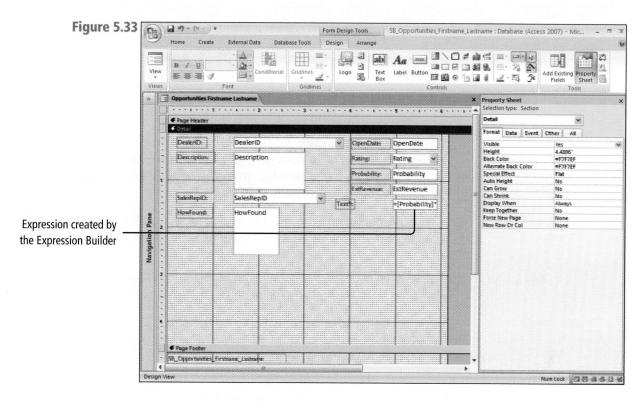

Expression created by the Expression Builder

7 Click the **Arrange tab**, and then reapply the **Solstice** AutoFormat. Click in the label control for the calculated text box and replace the existing text with **Probable Revenue:**

8 Click the **Home tab**, click the **Form View** button, and then enter the following data into the form:

DealerID	AZ003	Open Date	02/02/2009
Description	Store has asked for a presentation.	Rating	Hot
Sales Rep ID	5	Probability	85
How Found	Phone Book	Est. Revenue	100,000

The calculated control displays the result of the expression that you entered as the control source, $85,000.00.

9 Save 💾 your work and leave the form open for the next activity.

Activity 5.14 Adding an Option Button Group

A Yes/No field may be represented on a form in an **option group**. An option group displays a set of option buttons where only one option button may be selected at a time. Option groups are **bound controls**. A bound control is any control whose data source is a field in a table or query. In that way, when an option is selected, the selected option's value is stored in the table. In this activity, you will create an option button group to store the Open field, which can be Yes or No.

1 With the **Opportunities** form still open, switch to Design View.

2 Click the **Design tab**, and in the **Tools group**, click **Add Existing Fields**. Drag the **Open** field from the **Field List** pane to an area below the **HowFound** list box.

By default, the control for a Yes/No field displays as a check box.

3 In the **Controls group**, click the **Option Group** button and place the pointer at **4.5 inches on the horizontal ruler** and about two grid dots below the **Probable Revenue** text box. Click one time, and then compare your screen with Figure 5.34.

The Option Group Wizard displays. The wizard will create an option button for each label name inserted in the Label Names column.

Figure 5.34

Label Names column ——

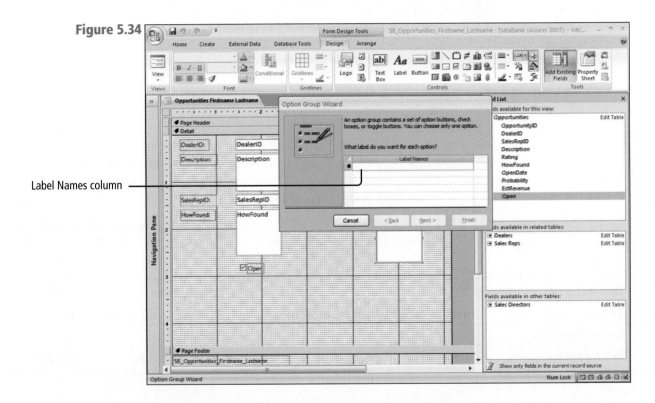

4 In the **Label Names column**, type **Closed** Press ⎡Tab⎦, and then type **Open**

5 Click **Next**, click the **Yes, the default choice is arrow**, and then click **Open**.

6 Click **Next**, and then in the **Values column** for the **Closed row**, type **0** and then in the **Values column** for the **Open row**, type **-1**

In a Yes/No field, Access stores a -1 for Yes and 0 if the value is No.

7 Click **Next**. Click the **Store the value in this field** option button, click the down arrow, and then click **Open**.

The option group is now bound to the Open Yes/No field.

8 Click **Next** and compare your screen with Figure 5.35.

Option groups display as three control types: option buttons, check boxes, or toggle buttons. Access provides a variety of border styles. For each option that you click, a sample displays.

Control types

Figure 5.35

Sample format

Border styles

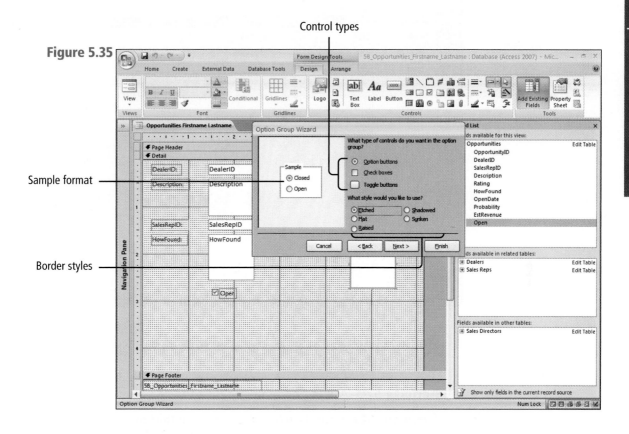

9 Click each of the control type options and notice the sample format for each. Click each style and notice the changes in the sample. When you are done, click the **Option buttons** and the **Raised** border style, and then click **Next**.

10 Under **What caption do you want for the option group?**, type **Status** and then click **Finish**.

The option group displays below the Probable Revenue controls. The original Open check box and label are no longer needed on the form.

11 With the entire option group selected, press ← and → as needed so that the option group is directly below the **Probable Revenue** text box.

12 With the entire option group still selected, press ↑ or ↓ as needed so that the **Status** label is about two grid dots below the **Probable Revenue** text box.

13 With the entire option group still selected, display the **Property Sheet**, click the **Other tab**, and then change the **Name** property to **Status**

Renaming a control with a meaningful name will make it easier to identify the control as you continue working with the form.

14 Click the original **Open** label and check box, and then press Delete.

15 Switch to Form View and compare your screen with Figure 5.36.

The option group displays with a raised border effect.

Figure 5.36

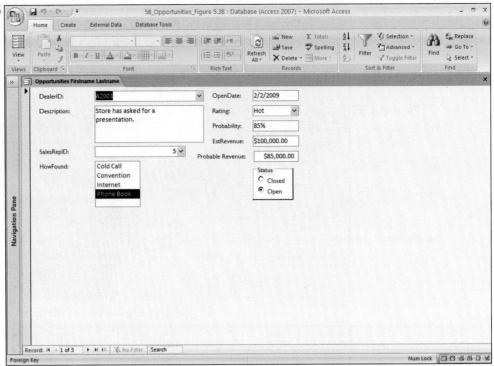

16 Switch to Design View, click **Save**, and then leave the form open for the next activity.

Activity 5.15 Adding a Command Button

A ***command button*** is used to start an action or set of actions. Common actions on a form command button include applying a filter, closing the form, and printing a form. In this activity, you will add a command button that prints the form when clicked and another button that will refresh the form data.

1 With the **Opportunities** form still open in Design View, in the **Controls group**, click the **Button (Form Control)** button. Place the

pointer at **4.5 inches on the horizontal ruler** and about four dots below the **Status** option group created in the earlier activity. Click one time, and then compare your screen with Figure 5.37.

The Command Button Wizard displays. In the left column, actions are divided into categories. In the right column, the actions for the selected category display.

Actions for the selected category

Figure 5.37

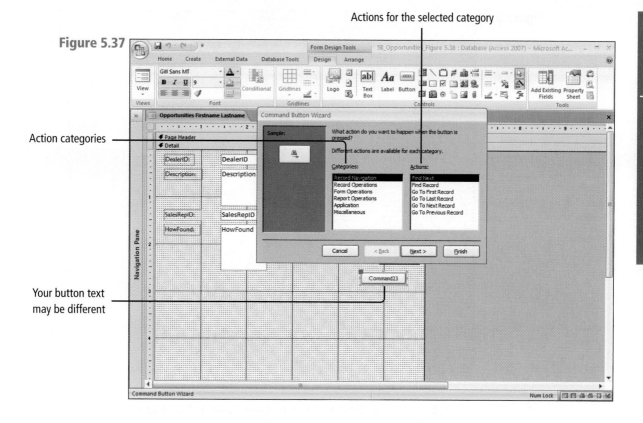

Action categories

Your button text
may be different

▣ Under **Categories**, click **Form Operations**, and then under **Actions**, click **Print Current Form**.

▣ Click **Next**, and then compare your screen with Figure 5.38.

The Command Button Wizard provides two options for the format of the command button—a rectangular button with text or a picture. A sample is provided on the left. The Browse button provides the option of using a custom picture.

Figure 5.38

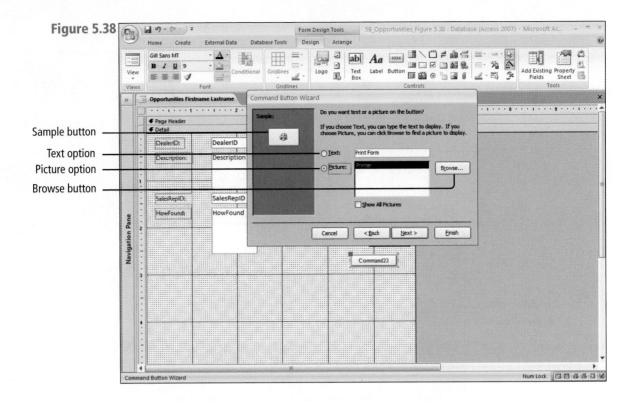

Sample button
Text option
Picture option
Browse button

4 Click the **Text** option button, and in the **Text** box, change the text to **Print this Opportunity** and notice that the new text is displayed in the sample.

5 Click **Next** and in the **A meaningful name will help you to refer to the button later** box, type **PrintOppForm** and then click **Finish**.

The new button displays below the Status option group.

6 Using the techniques you just practiced, insert a command button at **4.5 inches on the horizontal ruler** and about 2 grid dots below the **Print** button created earlier.

7 Under **Categories**, click **Form Operations**, and then under **Actions**, click **Refresh Form Data**, and then click **Finish**.

A picture button with the Refresh form icon is inserted.

8 **Save** your work, switch to Form View, and then click the **Print this Opportunity** button.

The Print dialog box displays.

9 In the displayed **Print** dialog box, click **Cancel**.

10 Use the form to add the following sales opportunities:

DealerID	ID002	Open Date	2/10/2009
Description	Store is considering carrying our product lines.	Rating	Cold
Sales Rep ID	1	Probability	25
How Found	Cold Call	Est. Revenue	50,000
		Probable Revenue	(Calculated Field)
		Status	Open

DealerID	WA003	Open Date	2/9/2009
Description	Store is considering expanding into contractor sales.	Rating	Warm
Sales Rep ID	3	Probability	50
How Found	Cold Call	Est. Revenue	15,000
		Probable Revenue	(Calculated Field)
		Status	Open

11 Leave the form open for the next activity.

Activity 5.16 Inserting a Chart

Charts provide an alternative view of the data entered into a form. In Access, the chart control provides many of the same options as in other Microsoft Office applications such as Word and Excel. In Access, the chart's values are typically based on the values in a table. In this activity, you will insert a pie chart into the Opportunities form.

1 With the **Opportunities** form still open, switch to Design View.

2 In the **Controls group**, click the **Insert Chart** button. Place the pointer at **3 inches on the vertical ruler**, and about **0.5 inches on the horizontal ruler**. Click one time, and then compare your screen with Figure 5.39.

A new chart control is inserted into the form, and the Chart Wizard displays.

Figure 5.39

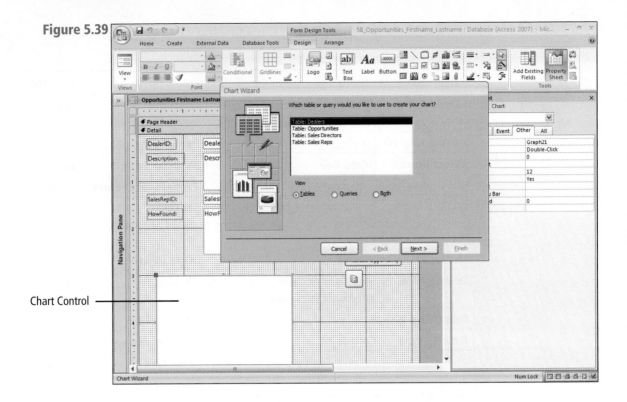

Chart Control

3 In the displayed **Chart Wizard**, click **Table: Opportunities**, and then click **Next**.

4 Using the techniques that you have practiced, move the **Rating** and **EstRevenue** fields into the **Fields for Chart** column.

5 Click **Next**, and then click the **3-D Pie Chart** button—the second chart in the last row.

The wizard displays information about 3-D pie charts.

6 Click **Next**, click the **Preview Chart** button, and then compare your screen with Figure 5.40.

The Sample Preview displays. The chart displays the total estimated revenue grouped by the rating: Cold, Warm, or Hot.

Figure 5.40

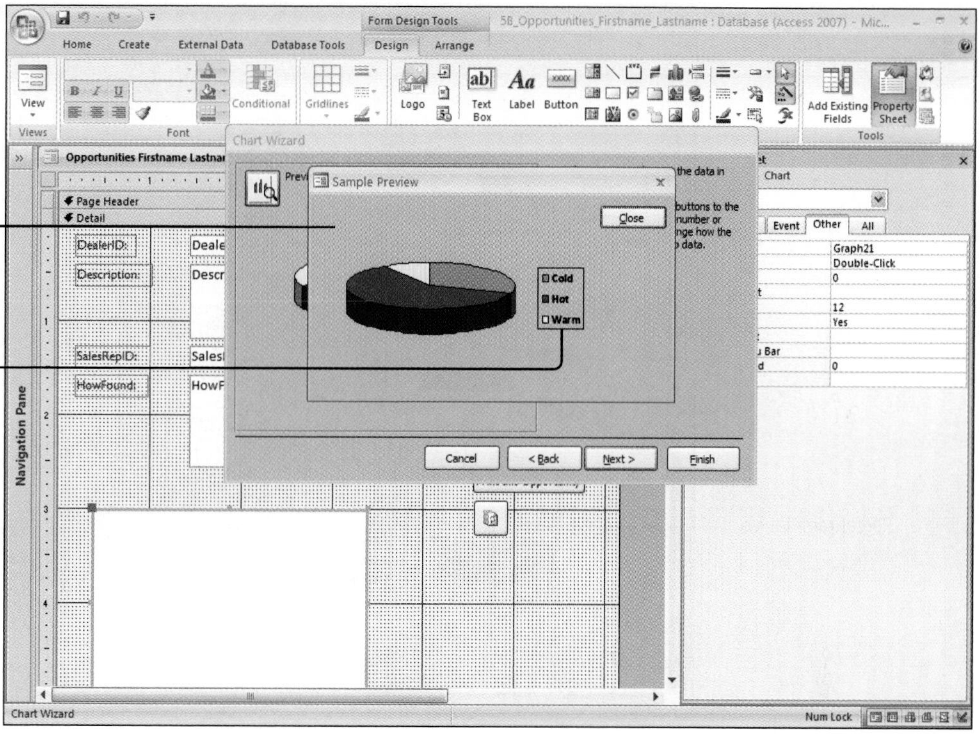

Sample Preview

Ratings

7 In the **Sample Preview** dialog box, click the **Close** button, and then in the **Chart Wizard**, click **Next**.

The wizard asks if you want the chart to change with each record displayed. The company wants the total estimated revenue to display in the chart, not the revenue for each particular record.

8 Under **Form Fields**, click the first **arrow**, and then click **<No Field>**. Under **Chart Fields**, click the first **arrow**, and then click **<No Field>**.

9 Click **Next**, and in the **What title would you like for you chart?** box, replace the existing text with **Opportunities by Rating**

10 Click **Finish**, and then switch to Form View.

The actual chart data displays only in Layout View or Form View.

11 Right-click the chart and in the displayed shortcut menu, point to **Chart Object**, and then click **Edit**.

12 Right-click a blank area in the chart, and then click **Chart Options**. In the displayed **Chart Options** dialog box, click the **Data Labels tab**, and then under **Label Contains**, click the **Percentage** check box.

13 Click **OK** to close the dialog box. Click a blank area of the form, and then compare your screen with Figure 5.41.

The percentage labels display.

14 **Save** your changes, and leave the form open for the next activity.

Figure 5.41

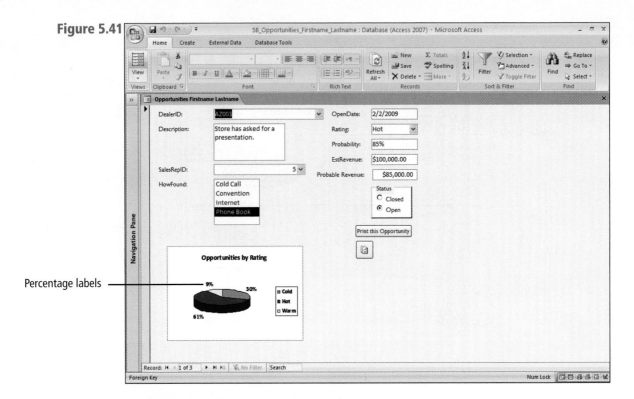

Percentage labels

Objective 5
Use Advanced Formatting Tools

A form should be formatted in a way that will help its users enter data. Access provides formatting options that emphasize data as it is entered. Formatting helps the user to better recognize and understand the data, which results in more accurate data and better decision making for those who will use the data.

Activity 5.17 Applying Conditional Formatting

Access provides a way to change the formatting of a field depending on the value in the current record. In Access, a **conditional format** is a format that displays only when one or more conditions are true. In this activity, you will apply conditional formatting to the Rating field in the Opportunities form.

1 In the open **Opportunities** form, switch to Layout View, and then click the **Rating** combo box control. In the **Font group**, click the **Conditional** button, and then compare your screen with Figure 5.42.

The Conditional Formatting dialog box displays. The **default formatting** is the format that will display if none of the conditions are met. Under Condition 1, the condition rules are defined in boxes and the formatting is set using the formatting buttons. A preview is provided for each format.

Figure 5.42

Condition rules

Default format

Preview

Formatting buttons

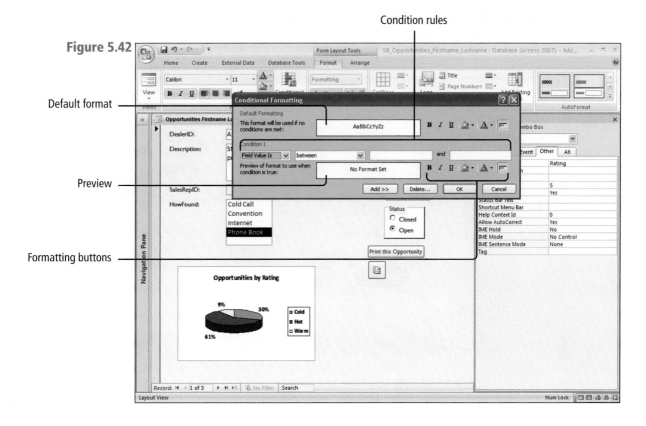

2 Under **Default Formatting**, click the **Font/Fore Color button arrow** , and then in the displayed color palette, click the fourth color in the first row—a shade of blue. Notice that a preview of the new default font color displays.

3 Under **Condition 1**, click the second **arrow**, and then click **equal to**.

4 Under **Condition 1**, click in the third box, and then type **Hot**

5 Click the **Bold** button , and then click the **Font/Fore Color button arrow** . In the displayed color palette, click the first color in the last row, a shade of red.

If the Rating field value is *Hot*, the text will display red and bold.

6 In the **Conditional Formatting** dialog box, click the **Add** button to add a second condition.

7 Under **Condition 2**, change the second box to **equal to**, and then in the third box, type **Cold**

8 Under **Condition 2**, set the **Font/Fore Color** to the second color in the second row, a shade of gray, and then compare your screen with Figure 5.43.

Figure 5.43

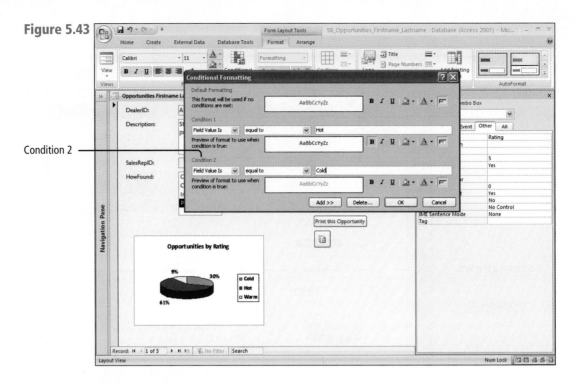

Condition 2

9 Click **OK** to close the displayed dialog box, and then switch to Form View. Navigate through the three records, and check that the conditional formatting is working.

If the rating is hot, then the format will be red and bold. If the rating is Cold, then the font color will be gray. Otherwise, the font color will be dark blue.

10 **Save** your work, and then close the form.

Activity 5.18 Applying Rich Text Formatting to Data

In a label, text box, and most other controls, all the displayed text must use the same format. When applying bold for example, the bold cannot be applied to just one word in the text. For a memo field, however, individual words or phrases can be formatted separately.

1 **Open** the **Navigation Pane**, right-click the **Opportunities** table, and then from the displayed shortcut menu, click **Design View**.

2 Display the field properties for the **Description** field. Under **Field Properties**, click the **Text Format** box, click the displayed arrow, and then click **Rich Text**. Read the message that displays, and then click **Yes**.

The message warns that the field will be converted to *rich text*. Rich text is text that is formatted with options common to many programs such as Word, Excel, and PowerPoint. A few of these options include font type, bold, center, and bullets.

3 Click **Save**, and then close the table.

4 Open the **Opportunities** form in Layout View. Click the **Description** text box, and then open the **Property Sheet**.

5 In the **Property Sheet**, click the **Data tab**, and then change the **Text Format** property to **Rich Text**.

The Description control will now *display* the Rich Text data that is stored in the table as Rich Text.

6 In the **Property Sheet**, click the **Format tab**, and then change the **Width** property of the **Description** text box to **2.4**

7 Switch to Form View and navigate to the second record, the one with the **DealerID** of *ID002* and dated 2/10/2009.

8 In the **Description** field, replace all of the text with the following. Type the text on four lines as shown:

Add these product lines:

Industrial

Recessed

Surface

9 In the **Description** field, select the three product lines typed earlier, and in the **Rich Text group**, click the **Numbering** button ▤. Compare your screen to Figure 5.44.

The three items display as a numbered list. This type of formatting is not possible when Plain Text is assigned in the Text Format property.

Figure 5.44

Numbered list

10 If your instructor asks you to print this project, display record 2 with a **DealerID** of *ID002*, and then click the **Print this Opportunity** button that you created earlier. In the **Print** dialog box, under **Print Range**, click the **Selected Record(s)** option button, and then click **OK**.

11 Click **Save**, close the form, and then **Exit** Access.

End You have completed Project 5B

There's More You Can Do!

From My Computer, navigate to the student files that accompany this textbook. In the folder **02_theres_more_you_can_do**, locate and open the folder for this chapter. Open and print the instructions for this project, which are provided to you in Adobe PDF format.

Try It! 1—Add an ActiveX Control to a Form

Content-Based Assessments

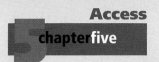

Summary

Forms provide the end-user an efficient way to enter data into tables. Access provides several methods for creating forms and subforms. After being created, those forms and subforms are then edited using either Layout View or Design View. Other formats for forms include Split forms, Multiple View forms, and Tabbed forms.

When creating forms, Design View provides alignment tools and controls not found in Layout View. These controls include combo boxes, calculated controls, option button groups, command buttons, and charts. Access also provides special formatting tools such as conditional formatting and Rich Text formatting.

Key Terms

The *θ* symbol represents Key Terms found on the Student CD in the 02_theres_more_you_can_do folder for this chapter.

Matching

Match each term in the second column with its correct definition in the first column by writing the letter of the term on the blank line in front of the correct definition.

_____ **1.** A form that is nested inside another form.

_____ **2.** A form that has another form nested within it.

_____ **3.** In a form or report, a layout where labels and text boxes are arranged vertically with a label to the left of each text box.

_____ **4.** In a form or report, a layout where labels and text boxes are arranged in rows and columns.

_____ **5.** A list of characteristics for controls in which you make precision changes to each characteristic assigned to the control.

_____ **6.** A form that gives you two views of the same data: a form view and a datasheet view.

_____ **7.** A form that displays records in rows and columns like a datasheet, but provides formatting options found only in form layout.

_____ **8.** Any combination of field names, properties, constants, or operators.

_____ **9.** A symbol in an expression that performs a specific function such as multiplying, comparing two values, or testing if a condition is true or false.

_____ **10.** Any control that doesn't have a source of data.

_____ **11.** Any control whose data source is a field in a table or query.

_____ **12.** A control used to start an action or set of actions.

_____ **13.** A format that displays only when one or more conditions are true.

_____ **14.** In a conditional format, the formatting that will display if none of the other conditions are met.

_____ **15.** Text that is formatted with options common to many programs such as Word, Excel, and PowerPoint.

A Bound control

B Command button

C Conditional format

D Default formatting

E Expression

F Main form

G Multiple Items form

H Operator

I Property Sheet

J Rich text

K Split form

L Stacked layout

M Subform

N Tabular layout

O Unbound control

Content-Based Assessments

Fill in the Blank

Write the correct answer in the space provided.

1. A form that is nested inside another form is called a(n) _____.

2. The tool used to build a custom form in Layout View is called the _____ _____ _____.

3. In a form or report, when labels and text boxes are arranged vertically with a label to the left of each text box, it is arranged in the _____ _____.

4. In a form or report, when labels and text boxes are arranged in rows and columns, it is arranged in the _____ _____.

5. A list of characteristics for controls on a form or report in which you make precision changes to each property associated with the control can be found in the _____ _____.

6. A form that gives you both a form view and a datasheet view is called a(n) _____ _____.

7. A form that displays a row of tabs at the top of the form, and each tab displays a different form or page is called a(n) _____ _____.

8. A combination of field names, properties, constants, or operators is called a(n) _____.

9. A control that doesn't have a source of data is called a(n) _____ _____.

10. The dialog box that builds expressions with easy access to fields, controls, and common operators is the _____ _____.

11. A set of option buttons where only one option button may be selected at a time is called a(n) _____ _____.

12. A control that starts an action or set of actions when clicked is the _____ _____.

13. A format that displays only when one or more conditions are true is called a(n) _____.

14. The format that will display if none of the conditions are met in a conditional format is called the _____ _____.

15. Text that is formatted with options common to many programs such as Word, Excel, and PowerPoint uses _____ _____.

Content-Based Assessments

Project 5C—Part Suppliers

In this project, you will apply the skills you practiced from the Objectives in Project 5A.

Objectives: 1. *Create Forms with Subforms;* **2.** *Create Forms with Specials Views.*

In the following Skills Review, you will create three forms for Rock Ridge to track the small parts that they use to manufacture their lighting products. You will create a form and subform that lists each supplier and the parts that each one supplies. You will also create a form with a split view and another with a multiple items view. Your forms will look similar to Figure 5.45.

> ### For Project 5C, you will need the following files:
>
> a05C_Part_Suppliers
> a05C_Logo

You will save your database as
5C_Part_Suppliers_Firstname_Lastname

Figure 5.45

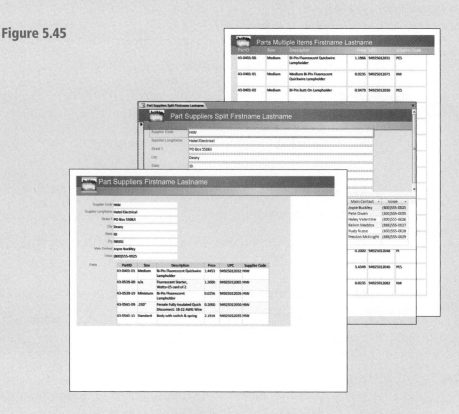

(Project 5C–Part Suppliers continues on the next page)

Content-Based Assessments

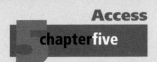

(Project 5C–Part Suppliers continued)

1. From the student files that accompany this textbook, locate the file **a05C_Part_Suppliers**. **Copy** and **Paste** the file to your **Access Chapter 5** folder. Rename the file 5C_Part_Suppliers_Firstname_Lastname

2. Open **5C_Part_Suppliers_Firstname_Lastname** in Access 2007. Enable the content and open the **Navigation Pane**.

3. Click the **Database Tools tab**, and in the **Show/Hide group**, click the **Relationships** button. Create a one-to-many relationship using **Supplier Code** as the common field. Select the **Enforce Referential Integrity** check box, click the **Create** button, and then **Close** the **Relationships** window.

4. Click the **Create tab**. In the **Forms group**, click the **More Forms** button, and then click **Form Wizard**. In the displayed **Form Wizard** dialog box, be sure that **Table: Parts Suppliers** is selected, and then click the **Move All** button to add all of the fields from the **Parts Suppliers** table. Use the technique that you just practiced to add all of the fields from the **Parts** table.

5. Click the **Next** button four times. In the **Form** box, change the name to **Part Suppliers Firstname Lastname** and then click **Finish**.

6. Switch to Layout View, and then apply the **Northwind** style located in the last column and third row of the **AutoFormat** gallery.

7. Switch to Design View. In the **Controls group**, click the **Logo** button, and then in displayed **Insert Picture** dialog box, navigate to the student files that came with this project. Click **a05C_Logo**, and then click **OK**.

8. In the **Form Header**, move the **Title** control to the right of the logo you just inserted. Click the **Parts** subform to select it, and then use the ⬆ arrow to move the subform so that it is approximately three grid dots below the **Voice** label and text box.

9. In the main form, click each of the eight label controls while holding ⇧ Shift. With all eight labels selected, on the **Home tab**, in the **Font group**, click the **Align Text Right** button.

10. Switch to Layout View. In the subform, select all of the columns and double-click the border between the **PartID** and **Size** column headers. Click in the **Description column**, and then decrease its width so that only the first three words in the first record display. In subform datasheet, in the row selector area to the left of the **Part ID** column, place the pointer on the border between the two rows and drag down so that two lines display in each row. Increase the width of the **UPC** column so that each code displays on one line.

11. **Save** your work, and then switch to Form View. From the **Office** menu, point to **Print** and then click **Print Preview**. In the **Page Layout group**, click the **Landscape** button, and then click **Close Print Preview**.

12. If your instructor asks you to print this project, with the first record displayed in the main form, click **Print**. In the displayed **Print Dialog** box, click **Selected Record(s)** and then click **OK**.

13. **Save** your work, and then close the form. In the **Navigation Pane**, click to select the **Part Suppliers** table, click the **Create tab**, and then in the **Forms group**, click the **Split Form** button.

(Project 5C–Part Suppliers continues on the next page)

Content-Based Assessments

Access
chapter**five**

Skills Review

(Project 5C–Part Suppliers continued)

14. Apply the **Northwind** AutoFormat, change the title to **Part Suppliers Split Firstname Lastname** and then insert a logo using the file **a05C_Logo**.

15. Open the form in **Print Preview**. Change the orientation to **Landscape**, and then **Close Print Preview**. Recall that with a Split form, only the datasheet prints. If your instructor asks you to print this project, print the form.

16. Save the form with the name **Part Suppliers Split Firstname Lastname** and then close the form. In the **Navigation Pane**, click to select the **Parts** table, click the **Create tab**, and then in the **Forms group**, click the **Multiple Items** button.

17. Apply the **Northwind** AutoFormat, change the title to **Parts Multiple Items Firstname Lastname** and insert a logo using the file **a05C_Logo**.

18. Use the technique practiced in earlier projects to resize each column to better fit the displayed text. When you are done, all of the columns should display without having to close the **Navigation Pane**.

19. Save the form with the name **Parts Multiple Firstname Lastname** If your instructor asks you to print this project, switch to Form View and print page one of the form.

20. Close the form and **Exit** Access.

End You have completed Project 5C

Access
chapterfive

Skills Review

Project 5D — Metals

In this project, you will apply the skills you practiced from the Objectives in Project 5B.

Objectives: 3. *Build a Form in Design View;* **4.** *Add Controls to Forms;* **5.** *Use Advanced Formatting Tools.*

In the following Skills Review, you will build two forms to help Rock Ridge Lighting track data about the metals used to manufacture fluorescent lighting fixtures. The first form will be used to track rolled metal, a common raw material in manufacturing. The other form tracks the quantities of metals in common aluminum alloys. Your completed forms will look similar to Figure 5.46.

For Project 5D, you will need the following file:

a05D_Metals

You will save your database as
5D_Metals_Firstname_Lastname

Figure 5.46

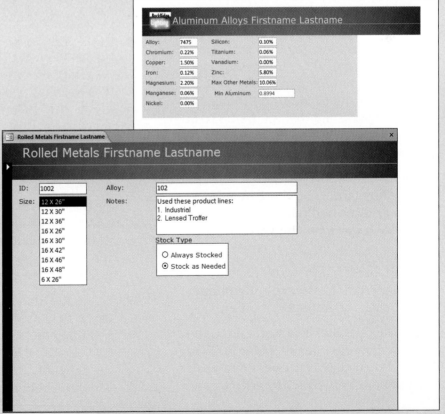

(Project 5D–Metals continues on the next page)

Access

chapterfive

Skills Review

(Project 5D–Metals continued)

1. From the student files that accompany this textbook, locate the file **a05D_Metals**. **Copy** and then **Paste** the file to your **Access Chapter 5** folder. Rename the file 5D_Metals_Firstname_Lastname

2. Open **5D_Metals_Firstname_Lastname** in Access 2007. Enable the content and open the **Navigation Pane**.

3. Click the **Create tab**, and in the **Forms group**, click the **Form Design** button. In the **Tools group**, click the **Add Existing Fields** button. Click **Show all tables**, expand the **Rolled Metals** table, and then double-click the following fields in this order: **ID**, **Size**, **Alloy**, **Notes**, and **Common Stock**.

4. Close the **Field List** pane, and then drag the right edge of the form so that it is aligned with the **7 inch mark on the horizontal ruler**.

5. Drag to select the **ID** and **Size** labels and text boxes, click the **Arrange tab**, and then in the **Control Layout group**, click the **Stacked** button. Drag to select the **Alloy**, **Notes**, and **Common Stock** labels and text boxes, and then in the **Control Layout group**, click the **Stacked** button.

6. Place the pointer over the middle of the **Alloy** label and drag so that the left border of the **Alloy** label is on the **2 inch horizontal gridline** and the top border is at the **.5 inch mark on the vertical ruler**.

7. With the controls moved earlier still selected, press ⇧Shift while clicking the **ID** text box. From the **Control Alignment group**, click the **Align Top** button.

8. Right-click the **Size** text box, and in the displayed shortcut menu, point to **Change To**, and then click **List Box**. Right-click the **Size** text box, click **Properties**, and

then click the Property Sheet **Data tab**. Click the **Row Source arrow**, click **Rolled Metals Sizes**, and then close the Property Sheet.

9. Delete the **Common Stock** label and text box. Click the **Design tab**, and in the **Controls group**, click the **Option Group** button. Click below the **Notes** text box, and in the displayed **Option Group Wizard**, under **Label Names**, type Always Stocked and in the next row, type Stock as Needed

10. Click **Next** two times. In the **Always Stocked row**, under **Values**, type -1 and then in the **Stock as Needed row**, type 0 Click **Next**, click the **Store the value in this field arrow**, and then click **Common Stock**. Click **Next** two times, and then in the **What caption do you want for the option group** box, type Stock Type: and then click **Finish**.

11. While pressing ⇧Shift, click the **ID**, **Alloy**, and **Notes** text boxes; click the **Size** combo box; and then the **Stock Type** option group label. With the controls selected, in the **Controls group**, click the **Line Color button arrow**, and then click **Dark Red**—the first color on the last row under **Standard Colors**.

12. Save the form with the name **Rolled Metals Firstname Lastname** Switch to Layout View, and in the **Controls group**, click the **Title** button. In the **AutoFormat group**, apply the **Aspect** style—the fourth choice in the first row of the gallery.

13. Select the **Size** label, and drag its left border to the left so that the all of the text, including the colon, display on one line. Click the **Size** list box, and then increase the height so that all of the sizes display without scrolling.

(Project 5D–Metals continues on the next page)

Content-Based Assessments

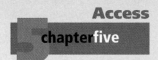
(Project 5D–Metals continued)

14. Select the option group label and use the arrow keys to move the label above the option group as shown in Figure 5.46. Reposition the **Stock Type** option group so that it is aligned with the **Notes** text box as shown in Figure 5.46.

15. Switch to Form View, and in the **Notes** field for the first record, select **Industrial** and **Lensed Troffer**. In the **Rich Text group**, click the **Numbering** button. If your instructor asks you to print this project, click **Print**, click the **Selected Record(s)** option button, and click **OK**. Save your work and close the form.

16. Open the **Aluminum Alloys** form in Design View. In the **Controls group**, click the **Text Box** button. Position the pointer below the lower left corner of the **Max Other Metals** text box and click.

17. Click the unbound control's label, delete the existing text, and then type **Min Aluminum:** Click in the unbound control's text box, and type **=1-[Max Other Metals]**

18. With the insertion point still in the text box, from the **Font group**, click the **Conditional** button. Under **Condition 1**, click the **arrow** for the second box, and then click **less than**. In the third box, type **.93** Under **Condition 1**, click the **Font/Fore Color button arrow**, click the first color in the last row, a dark red, and then click **OK**.

19. In the **Form Header**, change the title to **Aluminum Alloys Firstname Lastname** Save your work, and then switch to Form View. Navigate to the last record. The **Min Aluminum** value should be *0.8994*, and should display in dark red.

20. If your instructor asks you to print this project, be sure that the last record is still displayed, click **Print**, click the **Selected Record(s)** option button, and then click **OK**.

21. Save your work and close the form. **Exit** Access.

End **You have completed Project 5D** ——————————————

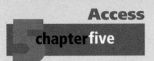

Mastering Access

Project 5E—Lamps

In this project, you will apply the skills you practiced from the Objectives in Project 5A.

Objectives: 1. *Create Forms with Subforms;* **2.** *Create Forms with Specials Views.*

In the following Mastering Access project, you will create forms that track the fluorescent lamps used by Rock Ridge Lighting. You will create a form with a subform, and you will also place two forms into a single form with a tabbed interface. Your completed forms will look similar to Figure 5.47.

For Project 5E, you will need the following files:

a05E_Lamps
a05E_Logo

**You will save your database as
5E_Lamps_Firstname_Lastname**

Figure 5.47

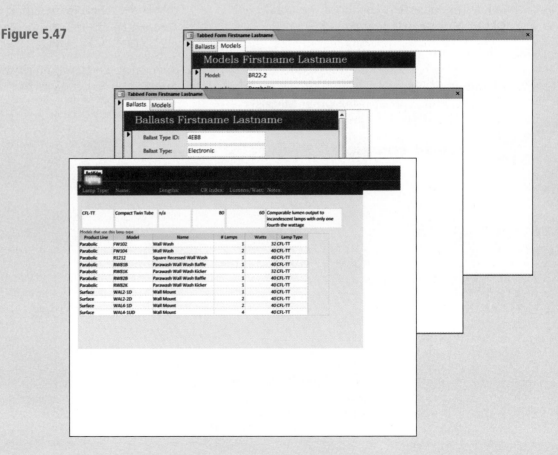

(Project 5E–Lamps continues on the next page)

Content-Based Assessments

(Project 5E–Lamps continued)

1. From the student files that accompany this textbook, locate the file **a05E_Lamps**. **Copy** and then **Paste** the file to your **Access Chapter 5** folder. Rename the file 5E_Lamps_Firstname_Lastname Open **5E_Lamps_Firstname_Lastname** and enable the content.

2. Create a one-to-many relationship between the **Lamp Types** and **Ballasts** tables, using **Lamp Type** as the common field, and then enforce referential integrity. Create a one-to-many relationship between the **Lamp Types** and **Models** tables, using **Lamp Type** as the common field, and then enforce referential integrity.

3. Start a new form using the **Form Design** tool. Open the **Field List**, and from the **Lamp Types** table, double click to add the following fields in this order: **Lamp Type**, **Name**, **Lengths**, **Coloring Rendering Index**, **Lumens/Watt**, and **Notes**. Select all of the controls just added and apply the **Tabular** layout.

4. Switch to Layout View and close the Field List. From the **AutoFormat gallery**, apply the **Origin** style—the fourth style in the fourth row. Click the Layout Selector button, and then drag the Layout Selector to the left to position the controls near the left edge of the form.

5. Adjust the width of the **Name** text box so that its values display on one line. Adjust the width of the **Notes** text box so that the first record's text displays on three lines. Decrease the height of the **Notes** text box, so that it displays three lines of text.

6. Save the form with the name **Lamp Types Firstname Lastname**, add a **Logo** control using the file a05E_Logo, and then insert a **Title** control with the text provided by

Access. Click the **Notes** label, and then press ⬇ to move all of the labels below the logo.

7. Switch to Design View. Increase the height of the **Detail** section so that it is about **4 inches** tall, and then use the **Subform/Subreport** control to place a subform near the left edge of the **Detail** section, about four grid dots below the **1 inch horizontal gridline**. For the subform, choose the **Models Subform**, accept the next two wizard defaults, and then name the subform **Models that use this lamp type** Finish the Subform Wizard.

8. Resize the subform so its lower edge is at **4 inches on the vertical ruler**. Move the subform's right edge to the **8 inch gridline**.

9. In the subform, double-click the empty blue area to open the **Property Sheet** for the subform. On the **Format tab**, change the **Default View** property to **Datasheet**.

10. Switch to Form View, and then open the form in **Print Preview**. Change the **Page Layout** to **Landscape**, and then **Close Print Preview**. Save the form. If your instructor asks you to print this project, navigate to the first record, and then print just the **Selected Record(s)**. Close the form.

11. Create a new form in Design View, and then insert a tab control that is 6 inches wide and 5 inches tall. From the **Navigation Pane**, drag the **Ballasts** form and drop it into the **Page1** tab. Delete the **Ballasts** label, and then, if necessary, move the form to the upper left corner of the tab control.

12. In the form, change the title to **Ballasts Firstname Lastname** On the tab control, double-click **Page1**. In the displayed

(Project 5E–Lamps continues on the next page)

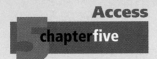

(Project 5E–Lamps continued)

Property Sheet, change the **Caption** property to **Ballasts**

13. Add the **Models** form to the **Page2** tab control. Change the **Page2** caption to **Models** and then change the form's title to **Models Firstname Lastname**

14. Delete the **Models** label, and then position the form in the upper left corner of the tab control. Change the height of the **Models**

form so that its lower edge is at **3.5 inches on the vertical ruler**. Click **Save**, saving the form as **Tabbed Form Firstname Lastname** and then click **OK**.

15. If your instructor asks you to print this project, print page 1 of the **Ballasts** form, and then print page 1 of the **Models** form.

16. Close the form and **Exit** Access.

End **You have completed Project 5E**

Mastering Access

Project 5F—Models

In this project, you will apply the skills you practiced from the Objectives in Project 5B.

Objectives: 3. *Build a Form in Design View;* **4.** *Add Controls to Forms;* **5.** *Use Advanced Formatting Tools.*

In the following Mastering Access project, you will create a form to track the various fluorescent lighting models manufactured by Rock Ridge Lighting. You will build the form in Design View, add specialized controls to the form, and apply custom formatting. Your completed form will look similar to Figure 5.48.

> ### For Project 5F, you will need the following files:
>
> a05F_Models
> a05F_Logo

You will save your database as
5F_Models_Firstname_Lastname

Figure 5.48

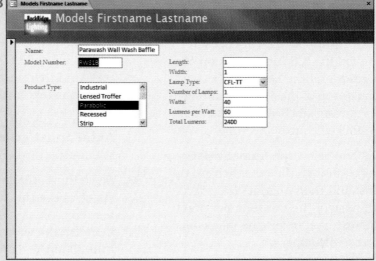

(Project 5F–Models continues on the next page)

Content-Based Assessments

Mastering Access

(Project 5F–Models continued)

1. From the student files that accompany this textbook, locate the file **a05F_Models**. **Copy** and then **Paste** the file to your **Access Chapter 5** folder. Rename the file 5F_Models_Firstname_Lastname

2. Open **5F_Models_Firstname_Lastname** and enable the content. Create a new form in Design View. Using the **Field List**, double-click to add these fields from the **Models** table in the following order: **Model Number**, **Name**, **Product Type**, **Length**, **Width**, **Lamp Type**, **Number of Lamps**, and **Watts**.

3. In the **Field List**, expand the **Lamp Types** table and double-click the **Lumens per Watt** field to add it to the form. Close the **Field List**, and then save the form as Models Firstname Lastname

4. Select the **Length**, **Width**, **Lamp Type**, **Number of Lamps**, **Watts**, and **Lumens per Watt** label and text box controls, and then apply the **Stacked** control layout. Move the stacked control group so the left edges of the labels are on the **3.5 inch mark on the horizontal ruler** and the **Length** label is aligned with the top of the **Model Number** text box. For the six labels and textboxes, remove the stacked control layout.

5. Insert a text box below the **Lumens per Watt** text box. Change the label text to **Total Lumens:** and then align its left edge with the left edge of the **Lumens per Watt** label. In the text box, insert the following control source: =[Number of Lamps]*[Watts]*[Lumens per Watt]

6. Apply **Conditional Formatting** to the calculated control you just created. For **Condition 1**, apply the sixth color on the last row of the **Font/Fore Color** palette if the field value is **between 5000** and **10000** For **Condition 2**, apply the third color on the last row of the **Font/Fore Color** palette if the field value is **greater than 10000**

7. Select all of the text boxes in the form's right column, and in the **Control Alignment group**, align the left edges of each control. Select all of the text boxes and labels in the form's right column, and in the **Position group**, remove all of the vertical spacing.

8. Change the **Product Type** text box to a list box that displays the **Product Type** field from the **Product Types** table.

9. Change the **Lamp Type** text box to a combo box that displays the **Lamp Type** field from the **Lamp Types** table.

10. Increase the width of the **Product Type** list box so that its right edge is at the **3 inch grid line**.

11. Insert a logo using **a05F_Logo** located with the student files that came with this text, and then insert the **Title** control using the text suggested by Access.

12. Switch to Layout View, and then use the **AutoFormat gallery** to apply the **Apex** style—the third choice in the first row.

13. Move the **Name** label and text box into the space above the **Model Number** label and text box. Navigate to **Record 4**, and then increase the width of the **Name** text box so that all of the data displays.

14. **Save** your work. If your instructor asks you to print this project, print page 1 of the form.

15. Close the form and then **Exit** Access.

End You have completed Project 5F

Content-Based Assessments

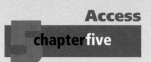

Mastering Access

Project 5G — Dealers

In this project, you will apply the skills you practiced from the Objectives in Projects 5A and 5B.

Objectives: 1. *Create Forms with Subforms;* **2.** *Create Forms with Specials Views;* **3.** *Build a Form in Design View;* **4.** *Add Controls to Forms;* **5.** *Use Advanced Formatting Tools.*

In the following Mastering Access project, you will create two forms to track the dealers that sell the products made by Rock Ridge Lighting. First, you will create a form using the Blank Form method, and then you will insert a chart. In the second form, you will create a split form that makes navigating the data easier. Your completed forms will look similar to Figure 5.49.

For Project 5G, you will need the following files:

a05G_Dealers

a05G_Logo

You will save your database as
5G_Dealers_Firstname_Lastname

Figure 5.49

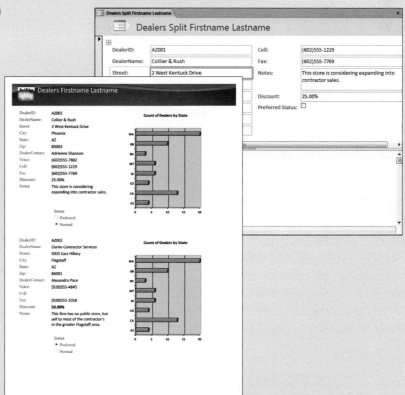

(Project 5G–Dealers continues on the next page)

(Project 5G–Dealers continued)

1. From the student files that accompany this textbook, locate the file **a05G_Dealers**. **Copy** and then **Paste** the file to your **Access Chapter 5** folder. Rename the file 5G_Dealers_Firstname_Lastname

2. Open **5G_Dealers_Firstname_Lastname** and enable the content. Create a new form using the **Blank Form** tool, and then double-click each field name to add all of the fields from the **Dealers** table in the order given in the Field List.

3. Move the **Discount** label and text box so that it comes before the **Notes** label and text box.

4. In the **Discount** text box, apply the following **Conditional Format**: In **Condition 1**, the text should be **Bold** if the field value is **greater than .25** Test by viewing record 2.

5. Save the form as **Dealers Firstname Lastname** and then in Design View change the **State** field to a combo box that looks up the **State** field from the **States** table.

6. Adjust the width of the **DealerID** text box so that the right edge is under the **3.5 inch mark on the horizontal ruler**. Select all the labels and text boxes, remove the stacked layout, and then click the **Decrease Vertical Spacing** button one time.

7. Delete the **Preferred Status** label and text box, and in the space created, insert an **Option Group** control. In the displayed **Option Group Wizard**, under **Label Names**, type Preferred and Normal Set the default choice to **Normal**, the **Value** for **Preferred** to **-1** and the **Value** for **Normal** to **0** Store the value in the **Preferred Status** field. For the option group style,

accept the default settings; for the caption, type **Status** and then finish the wizard.

8. Add a **Chart** control near the top of the form and on the **4 inch vertical grid line**. In the displayed **Chart Wizard**, use the **Dealers** table, and then add the **State** and **DealerID** fields to the chart. Select the **3-D Cylinder Bar Chart** style—the third style in the second row. In the wizard's next step, drag the **DealerID** field from the **Series** box into the **Data** box, and be sure that the **State** field is in the **Axis** box. In the wizard's next step, under **Form Fields** and under **Chart Fields**, click **<No Field>**. In the wizard's next step, change the chart title to **Count of Dealers by State** and do not display a legend. Finish the wizard.

9. Using the rulers as a guide, resize the chart so that it is three inches wide and four inches tall.

10. Switch to Layout View. Insert a **Logo** control using the file **a05G_Logo** that came with your text. Insert the **Title** control using the text suggested by Access, and then apply the **Flow AutoFormat**—the last style in the second row. Move the chart down, if necessary, so that it is below the shading created by the Flow style.

11. If your instructor asks you to print this project, print page 1 of the form.

12. **Save** and then close the form. Create a **Split Form** based on the **Dealers** table. Save the form with the name **Dealers Split Firstname Lastname** and then change the title to **Dealers Split Firstname Lastname**

13. In the datasheet in the lower part of the form, select the **Street** column. Scroll to

(Project 5G–Dealers continues on the next page)

Content-Based Assessments

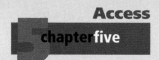
Mastering Access

(Project 5G–Dealers continued)

the end of the columns and while holding click the **Preferred Status** column header. Right-click any selected column header, and then in the displayed shortcut menu, click **Hide Columns**. The datasheet will be used for form navigation, so only the first two columns need to display.

14. If your instructor asks you to print this project, print page 1 of the split form. Recall that only the datasheet will print.

15. **Save** your work, close the form, and then **Exit** Access.

End **You have completed Project 5G** ———————————————————

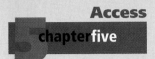

Mastering Access

Project 5H — Invoices

In this project, you will apply the skills you practiced from the Objectives in Projects 5A and 5B.

Objectives: 1. *Create Forms with Subforms;* **3.** *Build a Form in Design View;* **4.** *Add Controls to Forms.*

In the following Mastering Access project, you will design a form for Rock Ridge Lighting that generates Invoices. You will add calculated controls to a form, and then add that form to another form as a subform. You will then test your form and subform by entering data. Your completed form will look similar to Figure 5.50.

For Project 5H, you will need the following file:

a05H_Invoices

**You will save your database as
5H_Invoices_Firstname_Lastname**

Figure 5.50

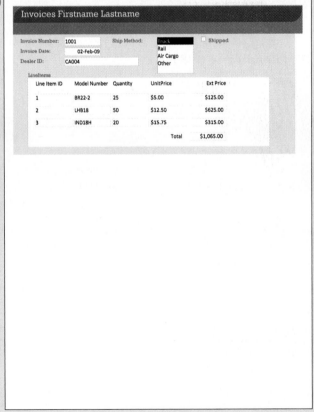

(Project 5H–Invoices continues on the next page)

Content-Based Assessments

(Project 5H–Invoices continued)

1. From the student files that accompany this textbook, locate the file **a05H_Invoices**. **Copy** and **Paste** the file to your **Access Chapter 5** folder. Rename the file 5H_Invoices_Firstname_Lastname

2. Open **5H_Invoices_Firstname_Lastname** and enable the content. Open the **LineItems** form in Design View, and then change the **Text6** label to **Ext Price**

3. In the **Unbound** text box, insert the following control source: **=[Quantity]*[UnitPrice]**

4. Change the **Visible** property of the **Invoice Number** text box to **No**. With the Property Sheet open, select the entire **Form**, and change its **Default View** property to **Continuous Forms**.

5. In the **Form Footer**, add a text box aligned with the **Ext Price** text box. Change the label to **Total** and then move the label to the right so that it is two grid dots from its text box.

6. In the **Unbound** text box, insert the following control source: **=Sum([Quantity]* [UnitPrice])** Switch to Form View and check that the total is *750*. Save your work, and then close the form.

7. Create a new form in Design View. In the **Field List**, double-click each field name to add all the fields from the **Invoices** table in the order listed.

8. Move the **Ship Method** label and text box so that the left edge of the text box is on the **4 inch vertical gridline**. Move the **Shipped** check box and label so that the right edge of the label is on the **6 inch vertical gridline**.

9. Select the label and text box controls for **Invoice Number**, **Ship Method**, and **Shipped**, and then in the **Control Alignment group**, align their top edges. If

necessary, align the **Shipped** check box with its label.

10. Change the **Ship Method** text box to a list box, and then change its **Row Source Type** to **Value List**. For the **Row Source** property, provide the following values: **Truck Rail Air Cargo** and **Other** and then set the default value to **Truck**.

11. Change the **DealerID** text box to a combo box. Set the **Row Source** to the **Dealers** table. In the **Format tab**, change the **Column Count** to **2** and the **Column Widths** to **.5** Resize the combo box so that the right edge is at the **3.5 inch mark on the horizontal ruler**.

12. **Save** the form as **Invoices Firstname Lastname** and then insert the **Title** control, using the text provided by Access. Add a **Subform/Subreport** control at the **1.5 inch mark on the vertical ruler** and the **.5 inch mark on the horizontal ruler**. In the **Subform Wizard**, use the **LineItems** form as the subform, and then accept all other wizard defaults.

13. Switch to Layout View. Decrease the width of the subform to better fit its contents and increase the height so that three rows display. Apply the **Foundry** style, the first choice in the third row of the **AutoFormat** gallery. For the **Ext Price** and **Total** text boxes, apply the **Currency** format.

14. Save your work and switch to Form View. For **Invoice Number** *1001*, add the following line item:

LineItem ID	Description	Quantity	UnitPrice
3	IND18H	20	15.75

15. If your instructor asks you to print this project, print just the selected record.

16. **Save** the form, and then **Exit** Access.

End **You have completed Project 5H**

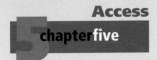

Mastering Access

Project 5I — Metal Suppliers

In this project, you will apply the skills you practiced from all the Objectives in Projects 5A and 5B.

Objectives: 1. *Create Forms with Subforms;* **2.** *Create Forms with Specials Views;* **3.** *Build a Form in Design View;* **4.** *Add Controls to Forms;* **5.** *Use Advanced Formatting Tools.*

In the following Mastering Access project, you will create several forms for Rock Ridge Lighting. You will use the Form Wizard to create a form with a subform and then insert that form and subform as a subform in a *third* form. Another form will be used to display a chart. Finally, you will place two forms into a single form with a tabbed interface. Your completed forms will look similar to Figure 5.51.

For Project 5I, you will need the following file:

a05I_Metal_Suppliers

**You will save your database as
5I_Metal_Suppliers_Firstname_Lastname**

Figure 5.51

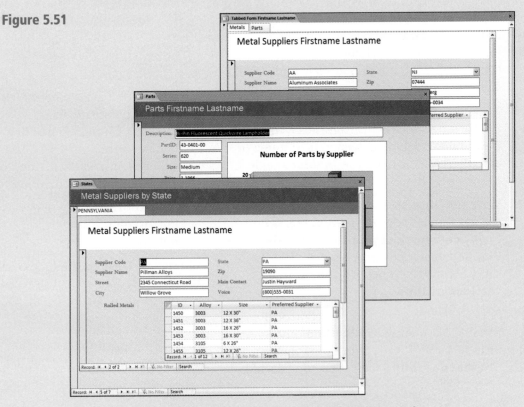

(Project 5I–Metal Suppliers continues on the next page)

Content-Based Assessments

(Project 5I–Metal Suppliers continued)

1. From the student files that accompany this textbook, locate the file **a05I_Metal_Suppliers**. **Copy** and **Paste** the file to your **Access Chapter 5** folder. Rename the file 5I_Metal_Suppliers_Firstname_Lastname

2. Open **5I_Metal_Suppliers_Firstname_Lastname** and enable the content. Create a one-to-many relationship between the **States** and **Metal Suppliers** tables using **State** as the common field. For the relationship, enforce referential integrity. Create a one-to-many relationship between the **Metal Suppliers** and **Rolled Materials** tables using **Supplier Code** and **Preferred Supplier** as the common fields. For the relationship, enforce referential integrity.

3. Start the **Form Wizard**, add all of the fields from the **Metal Suppliers** table, and then add all of the fields from the **Rolled Metals** table. In the **Form Wizard**, move to the *style* step and apply the **None** style. In the next step, name the main form **Metal Suppliers Firstname Lastname** and then finish the wizard.

4. In Design View, select the **Supplier Code** label and place its right edge at the **1.5 inch mark on the horizontal ruler**. Place the right edge of the **Supplier Code** text box at the **3.5 inch mark on the horizontal ruler**.

5. In the main form, select all of the labels and text boxes and remove the **Stacked** layout. Select the labels and text boxes for **State**, **Zip**, **Main Contact**, and **Voice**, and then apply the **Stacked** layout. Move the stacked controls to the right of the **Supplier Code** text box. Place the right edge of the labels on the **5 inch vertical grid line**, and then align the tops of the **Supplier Code** label and text box and the **State** label and text box.

6. Change the **State** text box to a combo box that looks up the **State** field from the **States** table.

7. Apply **Conditional** formatting so that if the **State** field is *not* equal to **WA** the font style is bold and the font color is the red shade located in the second column in the last row of the **Font/Fore Color** palette.

8. Click the **Detail** section bar, and then from the **AutoFormat gallery** click the **Equity** style—the fourth style in the second row. The style is applied only to the Detail section. Move the subform up so that it is about three grid dots below the **City** text box. Switch to Form View and resize the subform's columns to better fit their contents. Save and then close the form.

9. Open the **States** form in Design View. The text box on the right will be used to link another form and its subform, but does not need to be displayed. Set its **Visible** property to **No**.

10. Below the **StateName** text box, at **.5 inches on the vertical and horizontal rulers**, insert a subform control. For the data, use the **Metal Suppliers** form that you created earlier and accept all other wizard defaults.

11. Resize the subform just inserted so that its lower edge is at the **4.5 inch mark on the outer vertical ruler**. Resize main form so that its lower edge is at the **5 inch mark on the outer vertical ruler**.

12. For the subform just inserted, delete its **Metal Suppliers** label. In Layout View, apply the **Equity AutoFormat**.

13. **Save** your work, and then switch to Form View. Navigate to the suppliers records for *Pennsylvania*, and then in the subform, navigate to the record for *Pillman Alloys*.

(Project 5I–Metal Suppliers continues on the next page)

Content-Based Assessments

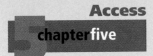
Mastering Access

(Project 5I–Metal Suppliers continued)

Change the **Main Contact** to **Justin Hayward** If your instructor asks you to print this project, display the record for *Pennsylvania* and print the selected record.

14. Save your work, and then close the form. Open the **Parts** form in Design View, and change the title to **Parts Firstname Lastname**

15. In the blank area below the **Description** text box, insert a **Chart** control. In the **Chart Wizard** select the **Parts** table and in the next screen add the **SupplierCode** field, and then the **PartID** field. Select the **3-D Column Chart**, and then in the next screen, move the **PartID** field into the **Data** area. In the next screen, select **<No Field>** under both **Form Fields** and **Chart Fields**. In the next screen, title the chart **Number of Parts by Supplier** and do not display a legend. Finish the wizard.

16. Resize the chart so the lower edge is on the **4 inch horizontal gridline** and the right edge is on the **7 inch vertical gridline**.

17. Add a command button below the **Supplier Code** text box. The button should **Refresh Form Data** when clicked,

and display the text **Refresh Chart** Accept all other **Command Button Wizard** defaults.

18. Save the form. If your instructor asks you to print this project, print just the first record. Close the form.

19. Create new form in Design View. Increase the width of the form to **7.5 inches**. In the upper, left corner of the **Detail** section, add a **Tab** control. Resize the tab control so that it is **5** inches tall and **7.5** inches wide.

20. In the first tab, drag the **Metal Suppliers** form that you created earlier. Delete the form's label and position the form into the tab's upper left corner.

21. In the second tab, drag the **Parts** form that you edited earlier. Delete the form's label and position the form into the tab's upper left corner.

22. Change the first tab's **Caption** property to **Metals** and the second tab's **Caption** property to **Parts**

23. **Save** the form as **Tabbed Form Firstname Lastname** Close the form, and then **Exit** Access.

 You have completed Project 5I

Content-Based Assessments

Project 5J — Business Running Case

In this project, you will apply the skills you practiced from all the Objectives in Projects 5A and 5B.

From My Computer, navigate to the student files that accompany this textbook. In the folder **03_business_running_case**, locate and open the folder for this chapter. Open and print the instructions for this project, which are provided to you in Adobe PDF format. Follow the instructions and use the skills you have gained thus far to assist Jennifer Nelson meet the challenges of owning and running her business.

 You have completed Project 5J ——————————————

Rubric

The following outcomes-based assessments are *open-ended assessments*. That is, there is no specific correct result; your result will depend on your approach to the information provided. Make *professional quality* your goal. Use the following scoring rubric to guide you in *how* to approach the problem and then to evaluate *how well* your approach solves the problem.

The *criteria*—Software Mastery, Content, Format and Layout, and Process—represent the knowledge and skills you have gained that you can apply to solving the problem. The *levels of performance*—Professional Quality, Approaching Professional Quality, or Needs Quality Improvement—help you and your instructor evaluate your result.

	Your completed project is of Professional Quality if you:	Your completed project is Approaching Professional Quality if you:	Your completed project Needs Quality Improvements if you:
1-Software Mastery	Choose and apply the most appropriate skills, tools, and features and identify efficient methods to solve the problem.	Choose and apply some appropriate skills, tools, and features, but not in the most efficient manner.	Choose inappropriate skills, tools, or features, or are inefficient in solving the problem.
2-Content	Construct a solution that is clear and well organized, contains content that is accurate, appropriate to the audience and purpose, and is complete. Provide a solution that contains no errors of spelling, grammar, or style.	Construct a solution in which some components are unclear, poorly organized, inconsistent, or incomplete. Misjudge the needs of the audience. Have some errors in spelling, grammar, or style, but the errors do not detract from comprehension.	Construct a solution that is unclear, incomplete, or poorly organized, containing some inaccurate or inappropriate content; and contains many errors of spelling, grammar, or style. Do not solve the problem.
3-Format and Layout	Format and arrange all elements to communicate information and ideas, clarify function, illustrate relationships, and indicate relative importance.	Apply appropriate format and layout features to some elements, but not others. Overuse features, causing minor distraction.	Apply format and layout that does not communicate information or ideas clearly. Do not use format and layout features to clarify function, illustrate relationships, or indicate relative importance. Use available features excessively, causing distraction.
4-Process	Use an organized approach that integrates planning, development, self-assessment, revision, and reflection.	Demonstrate an organized approach in some areas, but not others; or, use an insufficient process of organization throughout	Do not use an organized approach to solve the problem.

Outcomes-Based Assessments

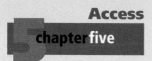

Access

chapter five

Problem Solving

Project 5K — Purchase Orders

In this project, you will construct a solution by applying any combination of the skills you practiced from the Objectives in Projects 5A and 5B.

> **For Project 5K, you will need the following file:**
>
> a05K_Purchase_Orders

You will save your database as
5K_Purchase_Orders_Firstname_Lastname

In this project you will create relationships, and then build a form and subform that can be used to create purchase orders for Rock Ridge Lighting. Copy **a05K_Purchase_Orders** and paste it into your Access chapter 5 folder. Rename the file **5K_Purchase_Orders_Firstname_Lastname**

In the Relationships window, add the database's four tables. When two tables share a common field, use that field to create a one-to-many relationship that enforces referential integrity.

Create a form based on the Line Items Table. Apply a Tabular layout for the form. The form's labels should be in a single row across the bottom of the Form Header and the text box controls should be in a single row at the top of the Detail section. Change the Part ID text box into a combo box that displays the Part ID and Description values from the Parts table. Add a control that calculates the extended price for the line item. Set the form's Default View property to Continuous Forms. In the Form Footer, add a control that calculates the total of the extended prices.

Create a form that includes all of the fields from the Purchase Orders table, and, as a subform, the Line Items form that you created earlier. Change the Supplier Code to a combo box that displays the Supplier Code and Supplier Name from the Part Suppliers table. Use the techniques practiced in this chapter to format, size and arrange the controls in both forms to create an attractive layout. Test the form the form and subform by creating three new purchase orders from three different suppliers. Create your own prices for the parts. Submit the project as directed.

End **You have completed Project 5K** ————————————

Outcomes-Based Assessments

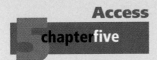

Access
chapterfive

Problem Solving

Project 5L—Lighting Comparisons

In this project, you will construct a solution by applying any combination of the skills you practiced from the Objectives in Projects 5A and 5B.

For Project 5L, you will need the following file:

a05L_Lamp_Comparisons

**You will save your database as
5L_Lamp_Comparisons_Firstname_Lastname**

Rock Ridge Lighting needs a form that compares the properties of incandescent lights with those of fluorescent light. In this project you will build a one-to-many relationship with a table that uses two fields for the primary key and then you will create a form and subform based on that relationship. Copy **a05L_Lamp_Comparisons** and paste it into your Access Chapter 5 folder. Rename the file **5L_Lamp_Comparisons_Firstname_Lastname**

Add the two database tables into the Relationships window. Use both the Incandescent Type and Incandescent Watts fields to create one-to-many a relationship between the two tables that enforces referential integrity.

Build a form and subform based on the two tables. The subform should display all of the equivalent fluorescent lamps for the incandescent lamp displayed in the main form. In the main form, add a control that calculates the lumens per watt (Lumens divided by Watts). In the subform, add a control that calculates the lumens per watt for each fluorescent lamp. For both calculated controls, provide a suitable label and add conditional formatting that makes the lamps that are highly energy efficient stand out from those that are not. Format the forms in an attractive manner and arrange the controls into an effective layout. In the subform, hide the Incandescent Type and Incandescent Watts columns. Title the form and submit the database as directed by your instructor.

End **You have completed Project 5L** ——————

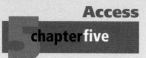

Problem Solving

Project 5M — Steel Properties

In this project, you will construct a solution by applying any combination of the skills you practiced from the Objectives in Projects 5A and 5B.

For Project 5M, you will need the following file:

a05M_Steel_Properties

You will save your database as
5M_Steel_Properties_Firstname_Lastname

Rock Ridge Lighting has asked you to make forms with charts displaying properties of four types of steel used to manufacture their lighting products: Alloy, Carbon, Stainless, and Tool. To start, copy **a05M_Steel_Properties** into your Access Chapter 5 folder, and then rename the new file **5M_Steel_Properties_Firstname_Lastname**

Create a form based on the Steel Properties table. Add a chart displaying the Hardness values for each of the four types of metals. For the data, display both the lower and upper limit. Choose a suitable chart type, have the chart display the values for the whole table without changing from record to record, title the chart **Hardness (Brinell 3000kg)** and do not display a legend. Title the form **Hardness Firstname Lastname** Position and resize the controls to make a visually appealing form.

Create another form based on the Steel Properties table. Add a chart displaying the Tensile Strength values for the four types of metals. Display both the lower and upper limit. Choose a suitable chart type, have the chart display the values for the whole table without changing from record to record, title the chart **Tensile Strength (MPa)** and do not display a legend. Title the form **Tensile Strength Firstname Lastname** Position and resize the controls to make a visually appealing form and chart.

Create a new form with a tabbed interface. In the first tab, add one of the forms created earlier and in the other tab, add the other form created earlier. Resize and position the forms to display all of their contents and rename the two tabs as appropriate. Save the form as **Steel Properties Firstname Lastname** Submit the database as directed by your instructor.

End **You have completed Project 5M** ——————

Outcomes-Based Assessments

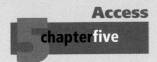
Problem Solving

Project 5N—Lamp Suppliers

In this project, you will construct a solution by applying any combination of the skills you practiced from the Objectives in Projects 5A and 5B.

For Project 5N, you will need the following file:

a05N_Lamp_Suppliers

**You will save your database as
5N_Lamp_Suppliers_Firstname_Lastname**

Rock Ridge Lighting needs forms to track the different types of fluorescent lamps and the companies that supply them. To start, copy **a05N_Lamp_Suppliers** into your Access Chapter 5 folder, and then rename the new file **5N_Lamp_Suppliers_Firstname_Lastname**

Create a one-to-many relationship between the Lamp Suppliers and Lamps tables that enforces referential integrity. Create a form and subform based on this relationship. Resize the main form controls to fit their contents and then move the subform to that it is to the right of the main form controls. Resize the subform data table so that all of the lamps provided by each supplier display when viewed in Form View. Format the form and subform as appropriate, and add your name to the title. Save the form as **Lamp Suppliers Firstname Lastname**

Create multiple items form based on the Lamp Suppliers table. Apply an appropriate AutoFormat, and resize the form's controls to display without scrolling. Change the row heights so that the text displays on a single line. Add your name to the title, and then save the form as **Lamp Suppliers Multiple Firstname Lastname**

Create a split form based on the Lamps table. Apply an appropriate AutoFormat, and then reposition the controls as needed. Add your name to the title, and then save the form as **Lamps Split Firstname Lastname** Submit the database as directed by your instructor.

End You have completed Project 5N _____

Outcomes-Based Assessments

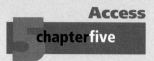

Access
chapterfive

Problem Solving

Project 5O — Employees

In this project, you will construct a solution by applying any combination of the skills you practiced from the Objectives in Projects 5A and 5B.

For Project 5O, you will need the following file:

a05O_Employees

You will save your database as
5O_Employees_Firstname_Lastname

In this project, you will create a form to track the employees that work for Rock Ridge Lighting. To start, copy **a05O_Employees** into your Access Chapter folder, and then rename the new file **5O_Employees_Firstname_Lastname**

Create a form based on the Employees table. Apply an appropriate AutoFormat, position and resize the controls to match the form's content, and add your name to the form's title. Change the *Department* text box into a combo box that looks up the 11 departments from either a table or a typed list. Add an option group with two option buttons with label names of **Full-Time** and **Part-Time** The Full-Time option should be stored in the Full-Time field as a *Yes* value and the Part-Time option should be stored as a *No* value. Name the option group's frame **Status** and then delete the Full-Time check box and label.

Add a text box that calculates each employee's length of employment. Hint: For the expression, subtract the HireDate value from **Date()** and then divide by 365. Change the label text to **Years Employed** For the text box control, add conditional formatting so that the value displays in bold and green for employees who have been employed five or more years. Format the text box so that no decimals display. Save the form as **Employees Firstname Lastname** and submit the project as directed by your instructor.

 You have completed Project 5O ————————————

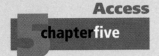

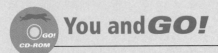

You and *GO!*

In this project, you will construct a solution by applying any combination of the Objectives found in Projects 5A and 5B.

From My Computer, navigate to the student files that accompany this textbook. In the folder **04_you_and_go**, locate and open the folder for this chapter. Open and print the instructions for this project, which are provided to you in Adobe PDF format. Follow the instructions to create a form to enter records for a database of personal music.

 You have completed Project 5O ————————————————

GO! with Help

A form and subform is also called a one-to-many form. When several one-to-many relationships exist, it is possible to add two subforms to a main form. The main form can contain two subforms or the first subform can contain the second subform.

1 Start **Access**. Click the **Microsoft Office Access Help** button.

2 In the **Search** box, type **two subforms** and then click **Search**.

3 In the **Access Help** window, from the **Results** list, click **Create a form that contains a subform (a one-to-many form)**. In the displayed help page, click the **Create a form that contains two subforms** link. Read the section to learn how two subforms can be inserted into a single main form. Read the next section to learn how a subform can be nested inside another subform.

4 If you want to print a copy of the information, click the Print button at the top of Access Help window.

5 Close the **Help** window, and then **Exit** Access.

 You have completed Project 5Q ————————————————

6 chaptersix

Customizing Data Output with Reports

OBJECTIVES

At the end of this chapter, you will be able to:

OUTCOMES

Mastering these objectives will enable you to:

1. Build Reports Based on Queries
2. Export a Report and Create a Labels Report

PROJECT 6A
Create and Export Reports from Queries

3. Create a Subreport Using Design Tools
4. Summarize Report Data
5. Create a Report with an Interactive Filter

PROJECT 6B
Group, Summarize, and Filter Report Data

The Petite Book

The Petite Book buys and sells first edition children's books, vintage travel books, and other rare books. The company's oldest and largest stores are in Corvalis, Oregon and Seattle, Washington. A third store in Post Falls, Idaho was opened three years ago. The company recently started selling books to customers throughout the world by adding an online store on the Internet. Because the online store offers the inventory from all three stores, The Petite Book is developing a central database to track inventory, in-store sales, online sales, and employees.

Customizing Data Output with Reports

Recall that in a database, reports are the most common format for data output. Business reports typically provide data that has been filtered and shaped for a specific business need. When building reports, a query is often created first and then the report is based on that query. Reports can be output to several types of media including regular paper, labels, email, and electronic Web pages.

An effective report displays just the desired data. Instead of presenting all of the records in a table, the data typically needs to be filtered according to the needs of the business. The information is often easier to understand when it is divided into groups. Totals, averages, and other statistics are added to provide a summary of the data presented in the report.

Project 6A **Orders**

The Petite Book needs to track online book orders. Each day, the company wants reports that list what books have been ordered from their online store. Because the books offered online are actually located at one of the three stores, each store will need its own custom report. Each store will then pull the books listed on their report and ship them to the online customer. In this project, you will create the queries, reports, and shipping labels needed to fulfill the online orders. Your printed forms will look similar to Figure 6.1.

For Project 6A, you will need the following files:

a06A_Orders
a06A_Logo

You will save your database as
6A_Orders_Firstname_Lastname

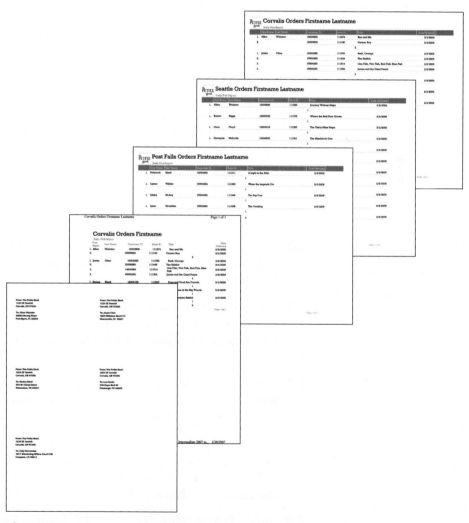

Figure 6.1
Project 6A—Orders

Objective 1
Build Reports Based on Queries

Often, a table by itself does not provide the information needed to build the desired report. You may want to include data from a related table in the *recordset*. A recordset is the name given to all of the records in a particular set of records, such as the records that are displayed when a query is run. You may also want to summarize the data from the table before including it in the report. In these cases, a query should be built that provides the exact data you desire. That query is then used as the recordset for the report.

Activity 6.1 Building a Select Query

Recall that a *select query* is a database object that retrieves (selects) specific data from one or more tables and displays the specified data in Datasheet view. In this activity, you will use the Simple Query Wizard to select all of the books from the Corvalis store that need to be shipped to online customers.

Note — Comparing Your Screen with the Figures in This Textbook

Your screen will match the figures shown in this textbook if you set you screen resolution to 1024 x 768. At other resolutions, your screen will closely resemble, but not match, the figures shown. To view your screen's resolution, on the Windows desktop, right-click in a blank area, click Properties, and then click the Settings tab.

---

1 Navigate to the location of the student files for this project. Right-click **a06A_Orders**, and then from the shortcut menu, click **Copy**.

2 Navigate to the location where you are saving your files for this project, such as your USB drive, and create a **New Folder** named **Access Chapter 6**

3 Open the folder, paste the database, and then, using your own first and last names, rename the file **6A_Orders_Firstname_Lastname** Open **6A_Orders_Firstname_Lastname** in Access 2007, and then enable the content.

4 Click the **Create tab**, and then in the **Other group**, click the **Query Wizard** button. In the displayed **New Query** dialog box, be sure that **Simple Query Wizard** is selected and click **OK**.

5 In the displayed **Simple Query Wizard** dialog box, under **Tables/Queries**, be sure that **Table: Books** is selected. Move the following fields into **Selected Fields**: **Book ID**, **Title**, **Location**, **Customer ID**, **Date Ordered**, and **Shipped**.

6 Under **Tables/Queries**, click the **Tables: Customers** table, and then move the following fields into **Selected Fields**: **First Name** and **Last Name**.

7 Click **Next** two times, and then under **What title do you want for your query?**, replace the existing text with **Corvalis Orders Firstname Lastname** Click **Finish** and compare your screen with Figure 6.2.

All books that have a matching record in the Customers table display in the datasheet, including the books that have already been shipped.

Figure 6.2

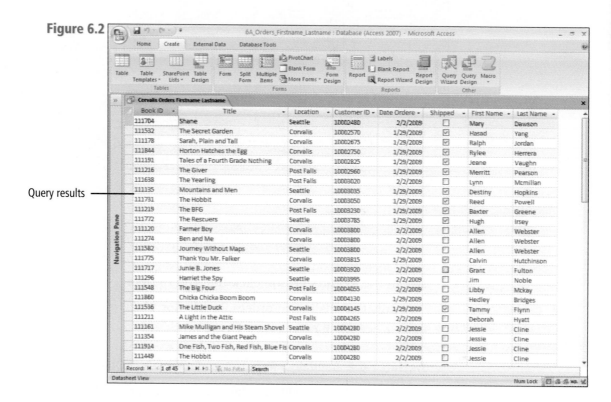

Query results ——

8 Click the **Home tab**. In the **Views group**, click the **Design View** button.

9 In the **Location column**, click in the **Criteria** box, and then type **Corvalis** In the **Criteria** box of the **Date Ordered column**, type **Is Not Null** In the **Criteria** box of the **Shipped column**, type **No** and then compare your screen with Figure 6.3.

The query will return only the records where all three criteria are true. This is sometimes referred to as an **_AND condition_**. Recall that an AND condition is a logical test that compares two conditions, and returns true only when both of those conditions are true.

Figure 6.3

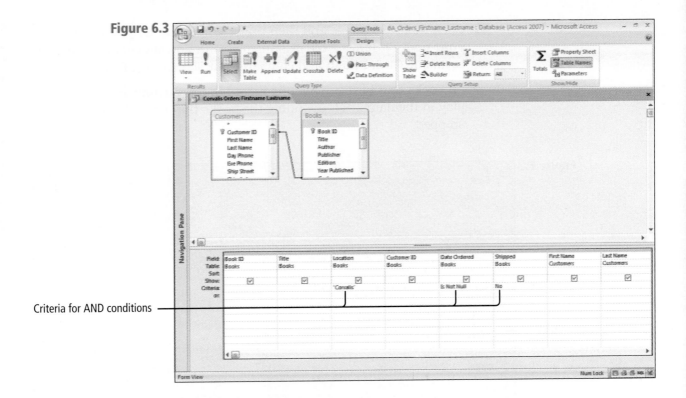

Criteria for AND conditions

🔟 In the **Results group**, click the **Run** button.

Only the unshipped orders for the Corvalis store display.

11 Click **Save** 💾, and then **Close** the query.

Activity 6.2 Building a Report Based on a Select Query

In this activity, you will use the Report Wizard to build a report based on the Corvalis query that you created.

1 On the Ribbon, click the **Create tab**, and then in the **Reports group**, click the **Report Wizard** button.

2 Click the **Tables/Queries arrow**, and then click **Query: Corvalis Orders**.

The fields from the Corvalis query that you created earlier display in Available Fields.

3 Using the techniques you practiced earlier, **Move** ▷ the following fields to **Selected Fields** in this order: **Book ID**, **Title**, **Customer ID**, **Date Ordered**, **First Name**, and **Last Name**.

4 Click **Next**. Under **How do you want to view your data?**, click **by Customers**, and then compare your screen with Figure 6.4.

A group has been added to the report. In an Access form or report, a *group* organizes records by a common value and enables the addition of summary data for each group. For example, grouping by Customers will group all the books purchased by a customer as one group, and enables you to calculate totals for each customer.

Figure 6.4

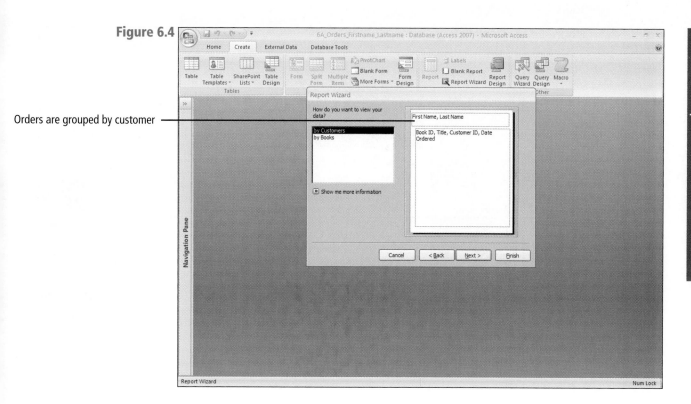

Orders are grouped by customer ———

5 Click **Next**. No additional grouping levels are needed, so click **Next** again. Click the **Sort arrow**, and then click **Customer ID**.

6 Click **Next**. Under **Layout**, click the **Block** option button. Under **Orientation**, click **Landscape**, be sure that **Adjust the field width so all fields fit on a page** check box is selected, and then click **Next**.

7 Under **What style would you like?**, click **Foundry**, and then click **Next**. Under **What title do you want for your report?**, type **Corvalis Orders Firstname Lastname** Click **Finish**, and if necessary, in the Zoom group, click the One Page button. Compare your screen with Figure 6.5.

The report displays in Print Preview. The Date Ordered field is too narrow. The report will need to be formatted before it is ready to print.

Figure 6.5

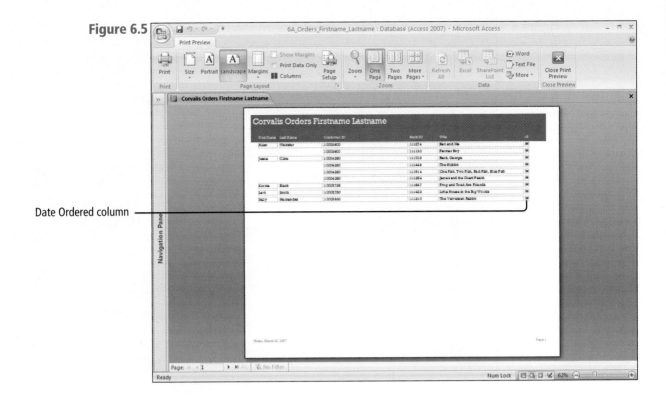

Date Ordered column

8 **Close** Print Preview and, if necessary, switch to Design view. Click a blank area of the report, and then click the **Customer ID** text box. Adjust the width of the **Customer ID column** so that its right edge aligns with the **4-inch vertical gridline**.

9 If necessary, **Close** the Property Sheet or Field List. Adjust the width of the **Date Ordered** text box so that its right edge is aligned with the **9-inch vertical gridline**.

10 In the **Page Footer**, move the control that calculates the page number so that its right edge is at the **9-inch vertical gridline**.

11 Change the width of the report to **10 inches**. Click **Save** 🖫 and leave the report open for the next activity.

Activity 6.3 Adding Line Numbers and a Record Count

In this activity, you will add controls that count the number of books ordered by each customer. You will then create a calculated control that provides a unique line number for each record displayed in the report.

1 With the **Corvalis Orders** report open, switch to Layout view, and apply the **Foundry AutoFormat**—the first choice in the third row.

Applying an AutoFormat in Layout view adds additional formatting that was not applied when the AutoFormat was applied in the Report Wizard.

2 Select the **Book ID** text box. In the **Grouping & Totals group**, click the **Totals** button, and then click **Count Records**. Compare your screen with Figure 6.6.

The total number of books ordered by each customer displays as well as the total number of books that need to be shipped.

Figure 6.6

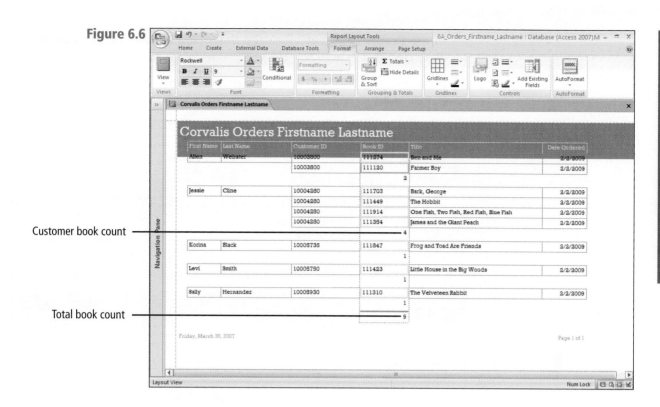

Customer book count

Total book count

3 Click the **Layout Selector** button, and then press → eight times.

4 Switch to Design view. In the **Tools group**, click the **Property Sheet** button. Click the **Selection arrow**, scroll, and then click **Detail** to display the properties for the Detail section.

5 In the **Property Sheet**, click the **Format tab**, and then change the **Height** property to **1**

6 In the **Controls group**, click the **Text Box** button, and then in the **Detail Section**, click anywhere in the blank area below the **First Name** text box.

A text box and a label control are inserted.

7 Click in the label control, and then press Delete.

8 Click the text box control. In the **Property Sheet**, click the **Other tab**, and then change the **Name** property to **LineNumber**.

9 Click the **Data tab**, change the **Running Sum** property to **Over Group**. In the **Control Source** box, type **=1**

A *running sum* is a calculation that accumulates from record to record. On your report, the first record will display a 1 and each record that follows adds one more to the total. In this way, each record will be assigned a unique line number starting.

10 Click the **Format tab**. In the **Format** property box, type **#**. Be sure to include the period.

This property will place a period after each line number.

11 Set the **Width** property to **.25** and then press Enter.

12 Position the **LineNumber** text box to the left of the **First Name** text box.

13 In the **Property Sheet**, click the **Selection arrow**, locate, and then click **Detail**. Change the **Height** property to **.25**

14 Switch to Report view, and then compare your screen with Figure 6.7.

A line number displays for each book ordered by each customer. The line numbers will increase accuracy during the order fulfillment process.

Figure 6.7

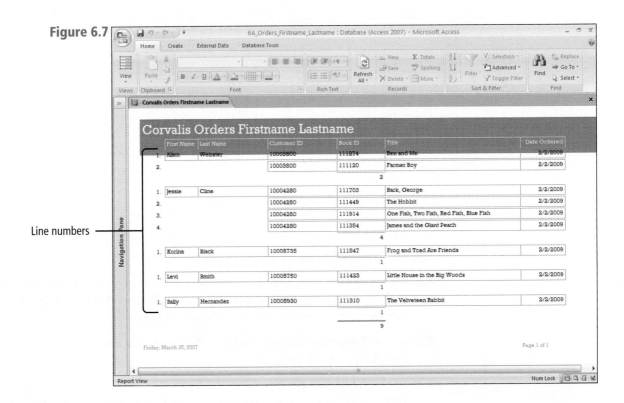

Line numbers

15 Save 🖫 your work, and leave the report open for the next activity.

Activity 6.4 Optimizing a Report for Black-and-White Printing

When printing reports for their own staff, many businesses prefer to print in black and white. In these cases, reports should be optimized for black-and-white printing, and formatting should be changed so that less ink is needed to print the report. In this activity, you will optimize the Corvalis Orders report for cost-effective, black-and-white printing.

1 With the **Corvalis Orders** report open, switch to Design view. Open the **Property Sheet** if necessary and display the properties for Report.

2 In the **Property Sheet**, click the **Format tab**, locate the **Picture** box, and then replace the text *(image)* with **(none)** Press Enter, and then in the displayed message, click **Yes**.

3 Click the report title text box. In the **Font group**, click the **Font Color** button ⬛ ▾, and then click **Automatic**.

4 In the **Property Sheet**, display the properties for **ReportHeader**, and change the **Back Color** property to **#FFFFFF**

This changes the background color to white, which will reduce the amount of ink needed to print the report.

5 In the **Controls group**, click the **Logo** button. Navigate to the student files for this chapter. Click **a06A_Logo**, and then click **OK**.

6 Position the logo in the upper left corner of the report, and then move the title control to the right of the logo.

7 In the **Controls group**, click the **Label** button $\boxed{Aa}$, and then click in the blank space to the right of the logo and below the report title. Type **Daily Pick Report** and then click a blank area of the report.

A pick report is a report that lists what books must be pulled for shipping.

8 Change the width of the **Daily Pick Report** label so that its right edge is on the **2-inch vertical gridline**.

9 **Close** the **Property Sheet**. Click the **LineNumber** text box that you created earlier. While holding down $\boxed{\triangle \text{Shift}}$, click the following text box controls: **First Name**, **Last Name**, **Customer ID**, **Book ID**, **Title**, and **Date Ordered**.

Seven controls are selected and are ready to be formatted as a group.

10 In the **Gridlines group**, click the **Gridlines** button, and then click **Bottom**.

11 In the **Controls group**, click the **Select All** button $\boxed{}$. In the **Gridlines group**, click the **Color button arrow**, and then click **Automatic**. In the **Controls group**, click the **Line Type** button $\boxed{}$, and then click the **Transparent** type, which is the first choice listed.

12 Switch to Print Preview and compare your screen with Figure 6.8.

Bottom gridlines help workers to focus on one record at a time.

Figure 6.8

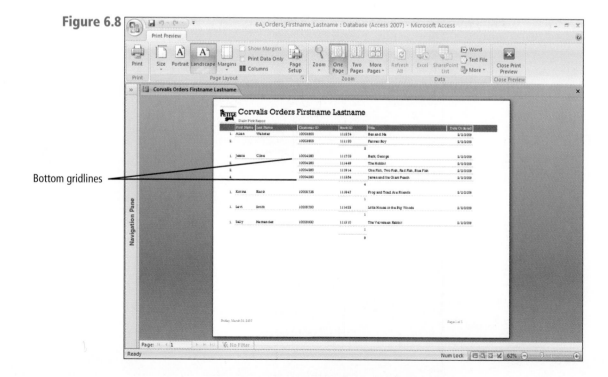

Bottom gridlines

13 If your instructor asks you to print this project, print the report.

14 **Close** Print Preview, **Save** 🖫 your work, and then **Close** the report.

Activity 6.5 Building and Modifying Queries Using Copy and Paste

After a query is finished, the query can be copied, pasted, and then adjusted to select different records. In this activity, you will copy the Corvalis query and modify it to select books that need to be shipped from the Post Falls and Seattle stores.

1 Open the Navigation Pane if necessary. In the **Navigation Pane**, click the **All Tables arrow**, and then click **Object Type**. Right-click the **Corvalis Orders** query and from the displayed shortcut menu, click **Copy**.

2 Right-click a blank area in the **Navigation Pane**, and from the shortcut menu, click **Paste**.

The new query needs a different name because two queries cannot share the same name.

3 In the displayed **Paste As** dialog box, under **Query Name**, type **Seattle Orders Firstname Lastname** and then click **OK**.

4 Using the technique you just practiced, **Paste** the **Corvalis Orders** query again and name the new query **Post Falls Orders Firstname Lastname**

5 Right-click the **Seattle Orders** query, and from the displayed shortcut menu, click **Design View**.

6 In the **Criteria row** for the **Location column**, change the criteria to **Seattle**

7 **Run** the query and compare your screen with Figure 6.9.

The books that need to be shipped from the Seattle store display.

Figure 6.9

Seattle orders

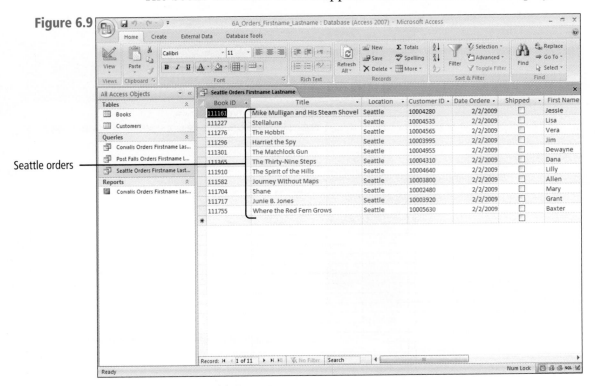

8 Save 🖫 , and then **Close** the query.

9 Using the techniques you just practiced, open the **Post Falls Orders** query in Design view and change the **Location** criteria to **Post Falls**

10 **Run** the query.

The books that need to be shipped from the Post Falls store display.

11 Save 🖫 , and then **Close** the query.

Activity 6.6 Building and Modifying Reports Using Copy and Paste

Reports based on queries can be copied, pasted, and then adjusted to display the results of a different query. In this activity, you will copy the report created earlier to provide daily pick reports for the Post Falls and Seattle stores. Each report will use the queries that you created earlier.

1 Right-click the **Corvalis Orders** report, and from the displayed shortcut menu, click **Copy**.

2 Right-click a blank area in the **Navigation Pane**, and from the shortcut menu, click **Paste**.

The new report needs a different name because two reports cannot share the same name.

3 In the displayed **Paste As** dialog box, under **Report Name**, type **Seattle Orders Firstname Lastname** and click **OK**.

4 Using the technique you just practiced, **Paste** again, and then name the new report **Post Falls Orders Firstname Lastname**

5 Right-click the **Seattle Orders** report, and from the displayed shortcut menu, click **Design View**.

The report inherits all of the layout and formatting that you created in the Corvalis report.

6 In the **Tools area**, click the **Property Sheet** button, and then compare your screen with Figure 6.10.

The black square in the upper left corner of the report indicates that the entire report is currently selected. When working with reports in Design view, clicking this Report Selector button selects the entire report.

Figure 6.10

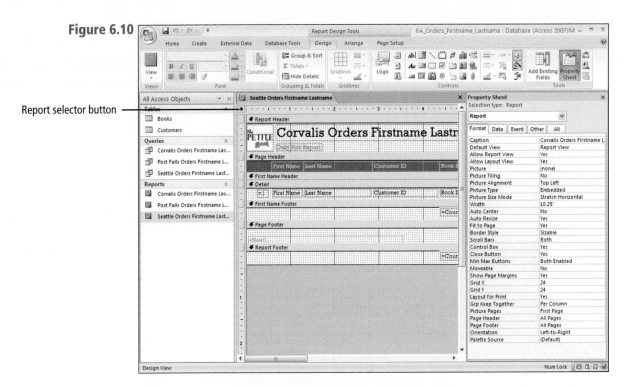

Report selector button

7 In the **Property Sheet**, click the **Format tab**, change the **Caption** property to **Seattle Orders Firstname Lastname**

8 In the **Property Sheet**, click the **Data tab**. Click the **Record Source arrow**, and then click the **Seattle Orders** query.

A **record source** is the table or query that provides the underlying data for a form or report.

9 In the **Report Header**, change the **Title** text box to **Seattle Orders Firstname Lastname** Switch to Report view, and then compare your screen with Figure 6.11.

The report displays the 11 picks for the Seattle store.

Figure 6.11

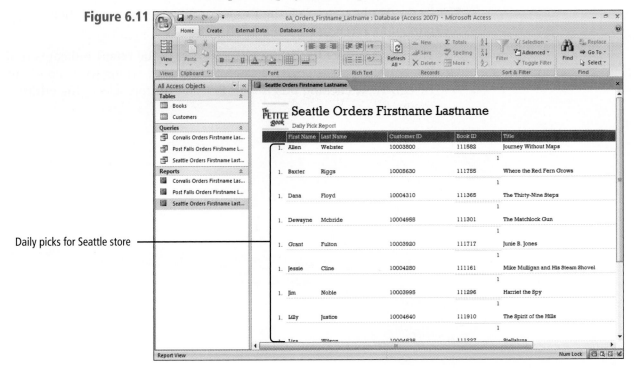

Daily picks for Seattle store

10 If your instructor asks you to print this project, print the report.

11 **Save** 🖫 your work, and then **Close** the report.

12 Open the **Post Falls Orders** report in Design view, and then change **Record Source** property to the **Post Falls Orders** query.

13 Click the **Format tab**, and then change the report's **Caption** property to **Post Falls Orders Firstname Lastname**

14 Change the **Title** text box to **Post Falls Orders Firstname Lastname** and then switch to Report view.

The four picks for the Post Falls store display.

15 If your instructor asks you to print this project, print the report.

16 **Save** 🖫 your work, and then **Close** the report.

Objective 2
Export a Report and Create a Labels Report

The three reports that you created earlier are all designed to be printed. These printed reports will be sent to the Accounting department. The stores, however, will need quicker access to the reports. Access can export the reports in several formats, including Web pages. The Petite Book will be able to post the reports on their internal Web site for immediate viewing. The Petite Book also needs shipping labels that they can attach to the packages that are shipped each day. Access will create label reports to match several types of labels.

Activity 6.7 Exporting Reports as Web Pages

Access reports can be saved as HTML documents. An ***HTML document*** is a text document written in Hypertext Markup Language that displays in a Web browser. In this activity, you will export the Corvalis daily pick report as a Web page. Because The Petite Book will export this report to its Web server every day, you will save the export steps.

1 Open the **Corvalis Orders** report in Report view.

2 Click the **External Data tab**, and in the **Export group**, click the **More** button, and then click **HTML Document**. Compare your screen with Figure 6.12.

The Export - HTML Document displays. The export process will create several new files. The location and name of the new Web page display in the File name box. This is changed by clicking the Browse button. The only export option that is available is the option to open the page in a Web browser after the export is complete.

Figure 6.12

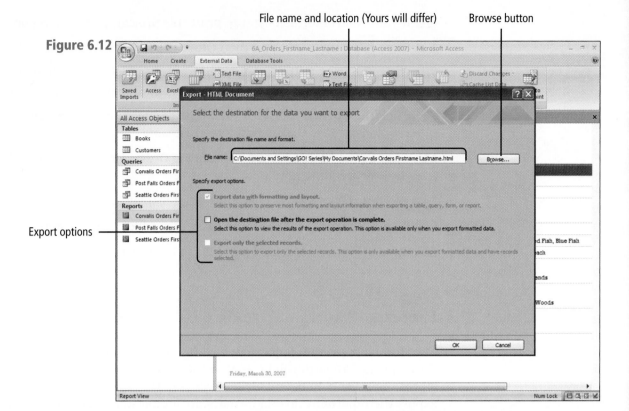

Export options

3 Click the **Browse** button. In the displayed **File Save** dialog box, under **Save in**, navigate to your **Access Chapter 6** folder. Change the **File name** to **6A_Corvalis_Orders_Firstname_Lastname.html** and then click **Save**.

In the File name box, the location and name of the Web page has changed. The underscores were used because Web page files should not have spaces in their names.

4 In the **Export - HTML Document** dialog box, select the **Open the destination file after the export operation is complete** check box, and then click **OK**.

5 In the displayed **HTML Output Options** dialog box, accept the default settings by clicking **OK**. In the displayed Web browser, click the Maximize button if necessary, and then compare your screen with Figure 6.13.

The Corvalis report displays in your computer's default Web browser. Most of the formatting is the same, but the bottom gridlines do not display. The formatting options for Web pages are not as flexible as an Access report.

Figure 6.13

Web browser

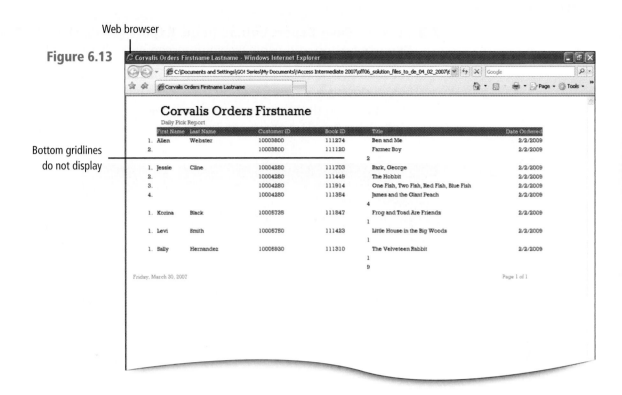

Bottom gridlines
do not display

6 If your instructor asks you to print this project, print the Web page.

7 **Close** the Web browser window. In the displayed **Export - HTML Document** dialog box, click the **Save export steps** check box, and then compare your screen with Figure 6.14.

Saving the export steps will save time when the report is exported each day. The name of this saved export can be changed. The Create Outlook Task check box enables you to setup the export steps as a recurring task in Outlook.

Figure 6.14

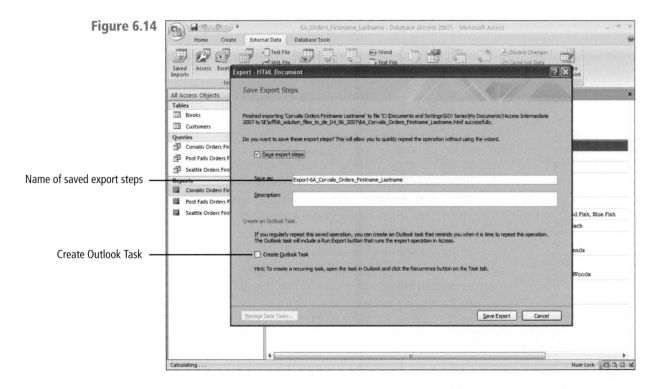

Name of saved export steps

Create Outlook Task

8 Click the **Save Export** button. In the **Export group**, click the **Saved Exports** button and compare your screen with Figure 6.15.

The data task specification is listed in the Manage Data Tasks dialog box. A **data task specification** saves the steps needed to import or export data so that the import or export can be performed by clicking a single button. The report can be exported by clicking the Run button.

Figure 6.15

Saved export ——

Run button ——

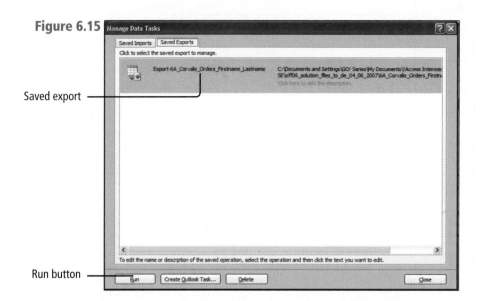

9 Click the **Close** button, and then **Close** the report.

More Knowledge

Setting a Saved Export as an Outlook Task

For any data task specification, the Create Outlook Task option will place a new task in the user's Outlook Tasks folder. In Outlook, the new task can be set to recur as needed and then provide a reminder to run the export. In our scenario, a Corvalis Orders Outlook task could be set to remind the user to export the report each weekday morning.

Activity 6.8 Creating an Aggregate Function Query

In this exercise, you will create a query with an aggregate function that lists customer data for the customers who have ordered books. Recall that an **aggregate function** calculates statistics such as totals, averages, and counts based on a group of records. In a query, the **Group by function** is an aggregate function that returns one record for each unique value in the column that the function is applied. This function prevents the unique value from being listed more than one time in the query. In the query you are building, the Group by function will be used to list each customer with open orders one time, even though a customer may have more than one book ordered.

1 Using the technique you practiced earlier, **Copy** and **Paste** the **Corvalis Orders** query, and then name the new query **Corvalis Labels Firstname Lastname**

2 Open the **Corvalis Labels** query in Design view.

3 Move the pointer to the top of the **Book ID column**. When the ⬇ pointer displays, click to select the column.

4 Press Delete to remove the field from the query. Use this technique to delete the **Title** field.

5 **Close** the **Navigation Pane**. In the displayed **Customers** field list, double-click the **Ship Street** field to add it to the query. Use this technique to add the following fields in this order: **Ship Apt**, **Ship City**, **Ship State**, and **Ship Postal Code**.

6 **Save** 🖫 your work, **Run** the query, and then compare your screen with Figure 6.16.

Customers who ordered more than one book are listed two times. The Petite Book needs each customer to be listed only once.

Figure 6.16

Customer listed two times —

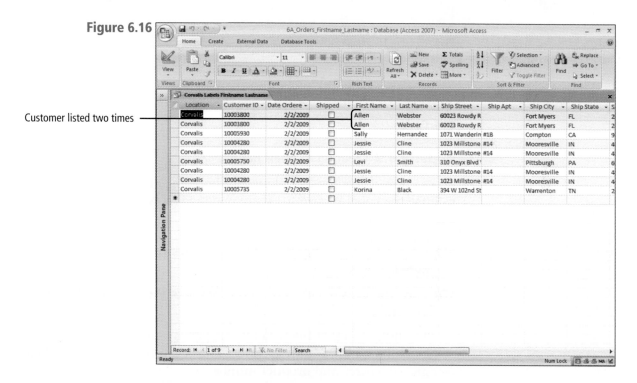

7 Switch to Design view. Right-click anywhere in the query design grid, and from the displayed shortcut menu, click **Totals**.

The Total row is inserted into the query and each column is assigned the default value of Group By.

8 **Save** 🖫 your work, **Run** the query, and compare your screen with Figure 6.17.

The Group By aggregate function lists each customer only one time.

Figure 6.17

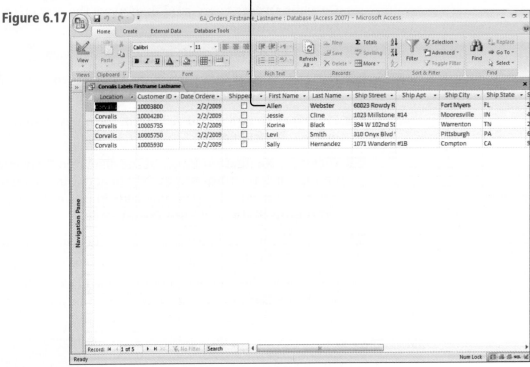

9 **Close** the query.

Activity 6.9 Creating a Labels Report

Access provides many techniques for creating labels. In this activity, you
will use the Label Wizard to create mailing labels based on the Corvalis
Labels query that you created earlier.

1 **Open** ⟩⟩ the **Navigation Pane** and click to select the **Corvalis
Labels** query.

2 Click the **Create tab**, and in the **Reports group**, click the **Labels**
button.

The first screen of the Label Wizard asks you to select the type of
label that you want to use. Most labels can be identified by their
manufacturer and product number.

3 Be sure that the **Filter by manufacturer** box displays **Avery**, and
then under **Product number**, scroll down and click **Avery USA
8164**.

4 Click **Next**. Click the **Font name arrow**, scroll down, and then click
Eras Demi ITC. Click **Next** and compare your screen with
Figure 6.18.

The insertion point is in the first line of the prototype label. The label
is constructed by typing text and moving available fields into the
Prototype label.

First line of label

Figure 6.18

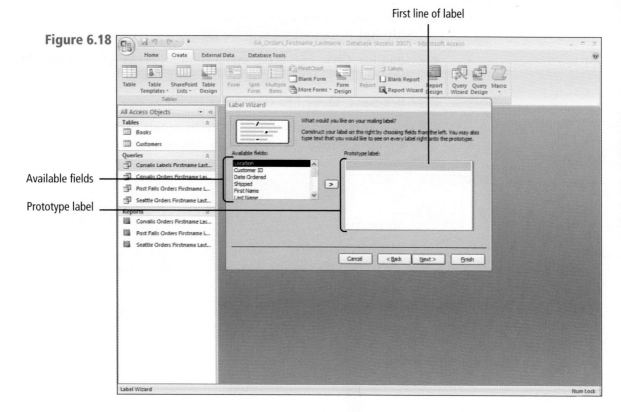

Available fields

Prototype label

5 Type the following using three lines as shown:

From: The Petite Book
1224 SE Yamhill
Corvalis, OR 97205

6 Press Enter two times, type **To:** and press Spacebar.

7 Under **Available fields**, double-click **First Name**, press Spacebar one time, and then **Move** ☑ the **Last Name** field. Compare your screen with Figure 6.19.

The first three lines display the company's return address. The fifth line will display the customer's first and last name. Notice the space between the two name fields.

Figure 6.19

Space between names

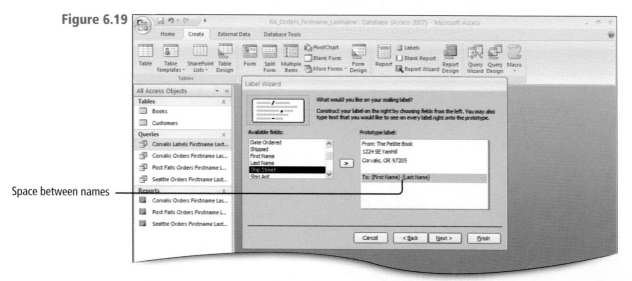

8 Press [Enter], and then add the **Ship Street** field. Press [Spacebar], add the **Ship Apt** field, and then press [Enter].

9 Add **Ship City,** and then type a comma. Press [Spacebar], add **Ship State**, press [Spacebar], and then add **Ship Postal Code**.

10 Click **Next**. Move **[>]** **Customer ID** under **Sort by.**

11 Click **Next**, name the report **Corvalis Labels Firstname Lastname** and then click **Finish**. Compare your screen with Figure 6.20.

Figure 6.20

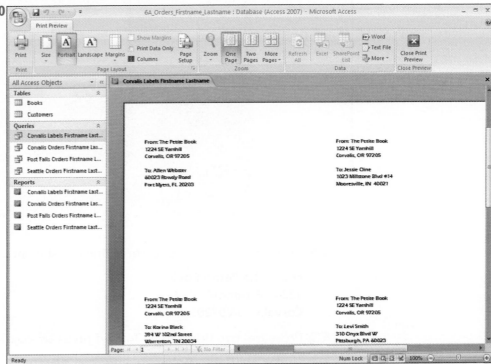

12 If your instructor asks you print this project, print the labels report. Most printers will not print labels until a sheet of labels is inserted into one of the printer trays. Check with your instructor to see how to tell your printer to print the labels on plain paper instead of a sheet of labels.

13 **Close** Print Preview, **Close** the report, and **Exit** Access.

End **You have completed Project 6A**

Project 6B **Sales**

The Petite Book needs several sales reports. In this project, you will filter, group, and summarize the sales data from the Books and Customers table to create three different reports. Your final output will be a report similar to Figure 6.21.

For Project 6B, you will need the following files:

a06B_Sales
a06B_Logo

You will save your database as
6B_Sales_Firstname_Lastname

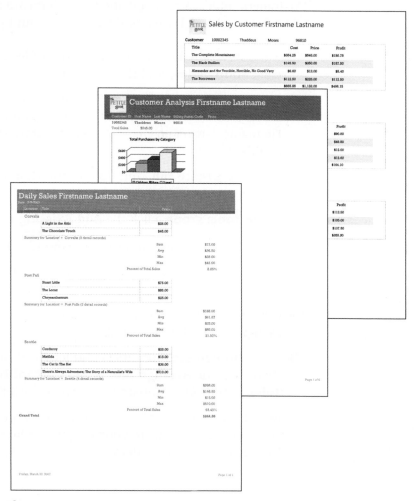

Figure 6.21
Project 6B—Sales

Objective 3
Create a Subreport Using Design Tools

In your previous projects, you practiced creating reports in Layout view. At times, creating the report in Design view is more effective. Design view provides more controls, better precision, and greater flexibility when building a report. When a report is open in Design view, the Ribbon buttons work much the same way they did when you created custom forms in Design view. Reports support the same types of controls, including labels, text boxes, charts, and calculated controls.

Activity 6.10 Creating a Report Using Report Design

The Report Design tool creates a new, blank report. The report opens in Design view, and you add fields and other controls as needed. The Petite Book needs a custom report that lists only a few fields from the Customers table. In this activity, you will create a report in Design view, add labels and text boxes, and then format and position the controls.

1 Navigate to the location of the student files for this project. Right-click **a06B_Sales**, and then from the shortcut menu, click **Copy**.

2 Open your **Access Chapter 6** folder, paste the database, and then using your own first and last names, rename the file **6B_Sales_Firstname_Lastname** Open **6B_Sales_Firstname_Lastname** and enable the content.

3 Click the **Create tab**, and then in the **Reports group**, click the **Report Design** button.

4 In the **Tools group**, click the **Add Existing Fields** button. If necessary, click Show all tables, and then expand ⊞ the Customers table.

5 Double-click to add the following fields in this order: **Customer ID**, **First Name**, **Last Name**, and **Billing Postal Code**.

6 Click **Save** 🖫, name the report **Sales by Customer Firstname Lastname** and then click **OK**.

7 Drag through the four labels and four text boxes to select them, and then click the **Arrange tab**. In the **Control Layout group**, click the **Tabular** button. Compare your screen with Figure 6.22.

Recall that a Tabular layout arranges each field in a column and each record in a row. In your report, the labels move into the Page Header as column headers.

Figure 6.22

Labels in Page Header ⎯⎯⎯⎯

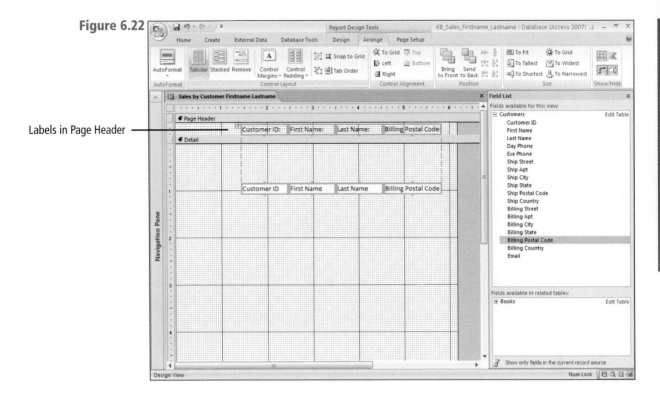

8 With the tabular control group still selected, in the **Control Layout group**, click **Remove**.

Removing a Stacked layout or Tabular layout enables each control to be positioned independently of the others. Recall that a stacked layout arranges labels in a vertical column and places the text boxes to the left of each label.

9 Drag through the four text box controls to select them. Press ⬆ until the four controls are about one grid dot from the top of the Detail section. With the four text boxes still selected, press ⬅ so that the left edge of the **Customer ID** text box is at the **1-inch vertical gridline**.

10 Click the **Design tab**, and then in the **Controls group**, click the **Label** button 🄰🄰. Click in the upper left corner of the Detail section and type: **Customer**

11 Click a blank area of the report.

A green triangle in the label control displays.

12 Click the label that you just created, click the displayed **Error Checking Options** button ⬦, and compare your screen with Figure 6.23.

Access suggests there is an error because the label is not associated with any control and suggests possible actions to take.

Figure 6.23

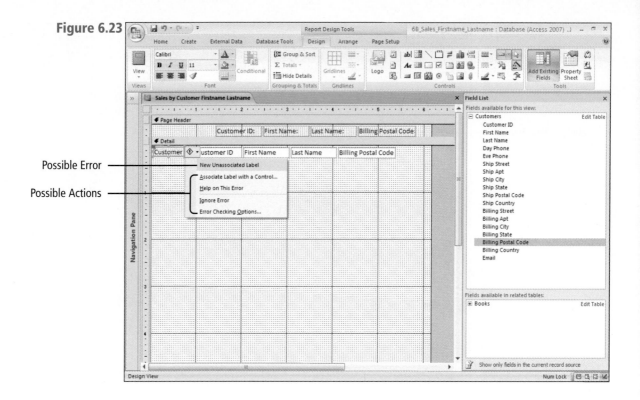

Possible Error

Possible Actions

13 From the displayed **Error Checking Options** menu, click **Ignore Error**.

The label does not need to be associated with any particular text box in the report.

14 With the **Customer** label still selected, in the **Font group**, click the **Bold** button [B], and then change the **Font Size** [11▾] to **12**. Increase the label's width so that all of its text displays.

15 **Save** [🖫] your work and leave the report open for the next activity.

Activity 6.11 Creating a Subreport Using the SubReport Wizard

When two tables share a one-to-many relationship, the *many* side of the relationship can be included as a subreport. A **subreport** is a report that is nested inside another report. The Petite Book needs the Sales by Customer report to include all of the books that the customer has ordered. Because the Books table of is on the *many* side of a relationship with the Customers table, the list of books will be included as a subreport. In this activity, you will use the Subform/Subreport control to insert a subreport, and then use the SubReport Wizard to create the subreport.

1 With the **Sales by Customer** report still open in Design view, in the **Controls group**, click the **Subform/Subreport** button. Position the pointer about one grid dot below the **Customer** label and about one grid dot from the report's left edge, and then click.

2 In the displayed **SubReport Wizard** dialog box, click **Next**. From the **Books** table, use the **Move** [>] button to include the following fields in this order: **Title**, **Cost**, **Price**, and **Customer ID**.

3 Click **Next,** two times. Name the subreport **Books subreport Firstname Lastname** click **Finish**. In the upper left corner of the report, click the **green triangle**, and then click the displayed **Error** button. Compare your screen with Figure 6.24.

The subreport is inserted into the report. The wizard applies whatever AutoFormat was last used, which may not be the Foundry AutoFormat shown in the figure. The error message indicates that the report width is too narrow. This will be adjusted in a later activity.

Subreport (Your formatting may differ)

Figure 6.24

Error message

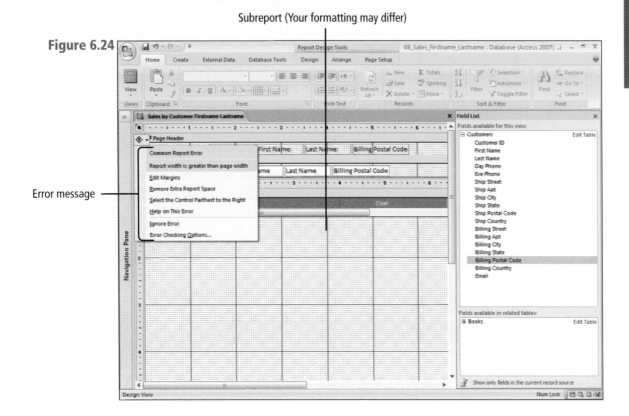

4 Click a blank area of the report. Click the **Subreport** label, and then press Delete.

5 Click the **Design tab** and in the **Controls group**, click the **Logo** button. Locate the student files for this project, and then insert the file **a06B_Logo**.

6 In the **Controls group**, click the **Title** button 🔲.

The title is inserted and displays the Report name.

7 Double-click the **Page Header** section bar to display its properties in the **Property Sheet**. In the **Property Sheet**, on the **Format tab**, change the **Visible** property to **No**.

8 **Save** 🔲 your work and leave the report open for the next activity.

Activity 6.12 Formatting a Report and Subreport

In this activity, you will format the report and subreport. You will edit the subreport in its own window.

1 With the **Sales by Customer** report open in Design view, right-click the subreport and from the shortcut menu, click **Subreport in New Window**.

2 Switch to Layout view, and then apply the **Foundry AutoFormat**— the first choice in the third row. **Close** the **Property Sheet**, and then compare your screen with Figure 6.25.

Formatting a subreport in its own window provides more precision and options than trying to format it while it is in the main report window. The main report remains open while you edit the subreport.

Main report   Subreport

Figure 6.25

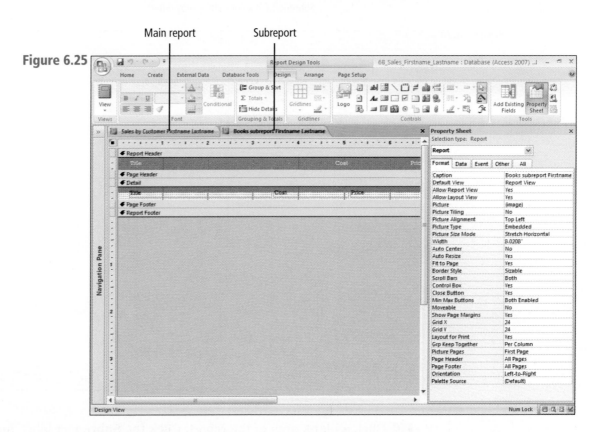

3 Switch to Design view. In the **Report Header**, select all four labels, and in the **Font group**, change the **Font Color** to **Automatic**. With all four labels still selected, in the **Font Group**, click the **Font Size arrow**, and then click **10**.

4 Display the properties for the **Report Header**, and then change its **Back Color** property to **#FFFFFF**

5 Display the properties for the **Cost** text box. Change its **Width** property to **.75** Use this technique to change the **Width** property of the **Price** text box to **.75**

6 Display the properties for the **Report**, and then change the report's **Width** property to **7**

7 Change the report's **Picture** property to **(none)** Press **Enter**, and then click **Yes** in the displayed message box.

8 Click the **Detail** section bar, and then in the **Font group**, click the **Alternate Fill/Back Color** button. Under **Access Theme Colors**, click **Light Label Text**—the second color in the first row.

9 Click the **Title** label, and then click the **Layout Selector**. Click the **Arrange tab**, and then in the **Control Layout group**, click the **Remove** button.

10 In the **Report Header**, click a blank area, and then delete the **Customer ID** label.

11 **Close** the **Property Sheet**. Change the width of the **Customer ID** text box so that its right edge is aligned at **5.25 inches on the horizontal ruler**.

12 Drag the **Customer ID** text box so that its left edge is aligned at **6.5 inches on the horizontal ruler**. Compare your screen with Figure 6.26.

In the next activity, a new text box will be inserted in the space created.

Space for new text box

Figure 6.26

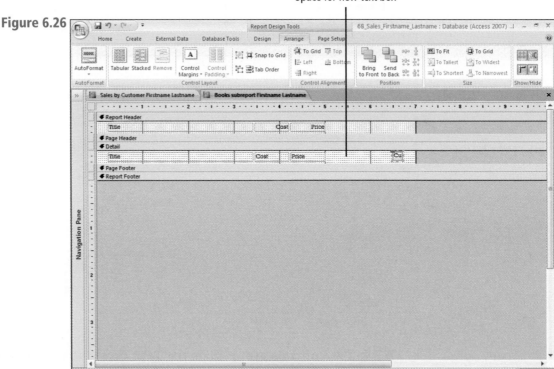

13 Display the properties for the **Customer ID** text box, and then change its **Visible** property to **No**.

The Customer ID will link the main report with the subreport, but it will not display in the printout.

14 **Save** your work and leave the Subreport window open for the next activity.

Activity 6.13 Adding Calculated Controls

The Petite Book would like the Sales by Customer report to include the profits. In this project, you will add a calculated control to display the profit made from each book. Recall that a calculated control displays the results of a calculation. You will also provide the total price, total cost, and total profit for each customer.

1 With **Books subreport** still open in its own window, click the **Cost** text box, and then click the **Design tab**. In the **Grouping & Totals group**, click the **Totals** button, and then click **Sum**.

2 Use the technique just practiced to add the **Sum** totals to the **Price column**, and then compare your screen with Figure 6.27.

In the Report footer, two calculated controls display column totals, one for the Cost column and the other for the Price column.

Total Cost calculated control

Figure 6.27

Total Price calculated control

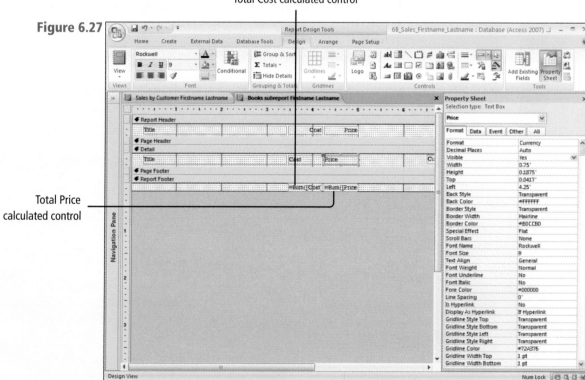

3 In the **Controls group**, click the **Text Box** button. Place the pointer about two grid dots to the right of the **Price** text box and about one grid dot from the top of the **Detail** section, and then click.

4 Type **=[Price]-[Cost]** and press Enter. Decrease the text box control's width so that its right edge is on the **6-inch vertical gridline**.

5 Click the label for the calculated control just inserted, and then press Delete.

6 In the **Report Header**, use the techniques practiced earlier to insert a new label to the right of the **Price** label, and then type the text **Profit**

7 Click a blank area of the report, and then click the **Profit** label. In the **Font group**, click the **Align Text Right** button. In the **Font group**, click the **Font Color** button, and then click **Automatic**.

8 For the label just inserted, increase the width so that the right edge is on the **6-inch vertical gridline**.

9 In the **Report Header**, select all four labels, click the **Arrange tab**, and in the **Control Alignment group**, click the **Top** button. Compare your screen with Figure 6.28.

Figure 6.28

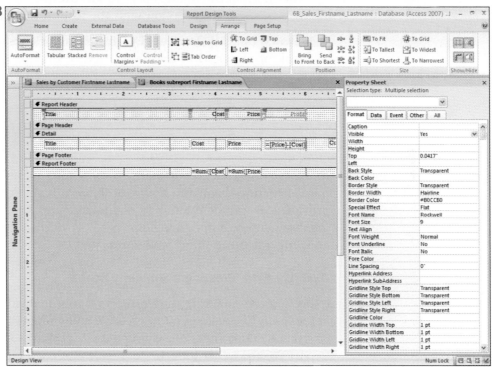

10 In the **Report Footer**, use the techniques practiced earlier to insert a text box to the right of the text box that calculates the total of the **Price** column. For the expression, type **=Sum([Price])-Sum([Cost])**

11 Delete the calculated control's label and then decrease the width of the text box so that its right edge is on the **6-inch vertical gridline**. Align the top of the control with the top of the text box with the expression **=Sum[Price]**.

12 Click the **=[Price]-[Cost]** text box, and then in the **Font group**, click the **Conditional** button. Using techniques practiced in Project 5A, Objective 5, create a condition where the **Font/Fore Color** displays as **Magenta**—the first color in the last row—if the value is greater than **500**

13 Select all four calculated controls, one in the **Detail** section and three in the **Report Footer**, and in the **Property Sheet**, change the **Format** property to **Currency**.

14 **Save** your work and **Close** the subreport window.

Alert!

Does the subreport displays as a blank rectangle?

The subreport may display as a blank rectangle as you change views. If you need to work with the subreport again, open it in its own window. Often, the subreport will display after changing to Report view and then back to Design or Layout view.

15 Close the **Property Sheet**. Change the width of the subform so that its right edge is at the **7.5-inches on the horizontal ruler**. Change the width of the main report to **7.5 inches**, and then align the bottom of the **Detail** section with the **2-inch horizontal gridline**.

16 Switch to Print Preview. If your instructor asks you to print this project, print page 1 of the report.

17 **Save** 🖫 your work, and then **Close** the report.

Objective 4
Summarize Report Data

In a large database, reports may display too much detail. Personnel in management typically do not want to see a high level of detail. Access provides several techniques to summarize and filter report data, including summary options, using charts to provide a visual summary, and applying advanced filters and sorts.

Activity 6.14 Creating a Summary Report

Information is easier to understand when it is divided into groups. The Petite Book has asked you to create a sales report that shows sales grouped by customer. You will use the Summary Options tool within the Report Wizard to list just the total sales for each customer.

1 With **6B_Sales** still open, click the **Create tab**, and in the **Reports group**, click the **Report Wizard** button.

2 In the displayed **Report Wizard** dialog box, click **Table: Customers** and use the **Move** button ⊳ to add the following fields in this order: **Customer ID**, **First Name**, **Last Name**, and **Billing Postal Code**.

3 Under **Tables/Queries**, click **Table: Books**, add the **Price** field, and then click **Next** three times.

4 Click the **What sort order and summary information do you want for detail records? arrow**, click **Price**, and then click the **Ascending** button so that it displays as **Descending**.

5 Click the **Summary Options** button. In the **Price row**, click the **Sum** check box, and then under **Show**, click the **Summary Only** option button.

6 Click **OK** to return to the **Report Wizard**, and then click **Next** two times. If necessary, click the Foundry style. Click **Next**.

7 Under **What title do you want for your report?**, type **Customer Analysis Firstname Lastname** Click **Finish** and compare your screen with Figure 6.29.

The report displays the total of the Price field for each customer. The price field is too narrow to display the entire number, so Access displays pound signs instead. The individual books purchased by each customer do not display.

Figure 6.29

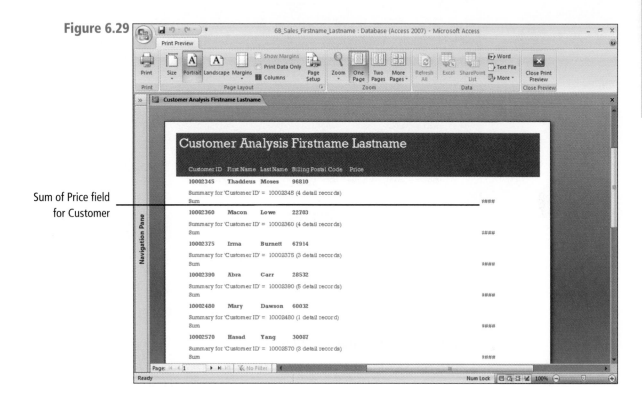

Sum of Price field for Customer

8 **Close** Print Preview and switch to Layout view. Click the text box that begins with the text *Summary for 'Customer ID'* and then press Delete.

9 Double-click the **Sum** label, and replace the existing text with **Total Sales** and then press Enter.

10 Resize the **Price** text box so that the pound signs—#—no longer display in any of the text boxes.

11 Move the **Price** text box so that it is to the right of the **Total Sales** label and below the **First Name** and **Last Name columns**, and then compare your screen with Figure 6.30.

Figure 6.30

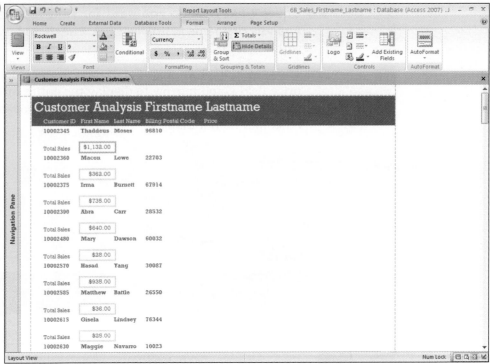

12 Select the **Total Sales** label, and then press ⬆ four times.

13 Select the **Price** text box, and then press ⬆ four times.

14 **Save** 🖫 your work and leave the report open for the next activity.

Activity 6.15 Inserting a Chart

Charts provide visual meaning that is often hard to see when data is arranged in rows and columns. The Petite Book would like a chart that shows the total books ordered by each customer grouped by the three categories that they sell: Children, Travel, and Rare. In this activity, you will insert a chart into the report.

1 With the **Customer Analysis** report still open, switch to Design view. Double-click the **Customer ID Footer** to display it properties. In the **Property Sheet**, change the **Height** property to **2.5**

2 In the **Controls group**, click the **Insert Chart** button 📊. Position the Chart pointer 📊 below the **Totals Sales** label, and then click.

3 In the displayed **Chart Wizard** dialog box, be sure that **Table: Books** is selected, and then click **Next**.

4 Under **Which fields contain the data you want for the chart**, move **Price** and then **Category** into **Fields for Chart**, and then click **Next**.

5 Click the **3-D Column Chart**—the second chart type in the first row—and then click **Next**.

6 Click the **Preview Chart** button.

7 Click **Close**, and then click **Next**. Be sure that **Customer ID** displays under both **Report Fields** and **Chart Fields**, and then click **Next**.

8 Title the chart **Total Purchases by Category** Click **Finish**, and then compare your screen with Figure 6.31.

Design view does not display actual data, so an alternate chart displays.

Figure 6.31

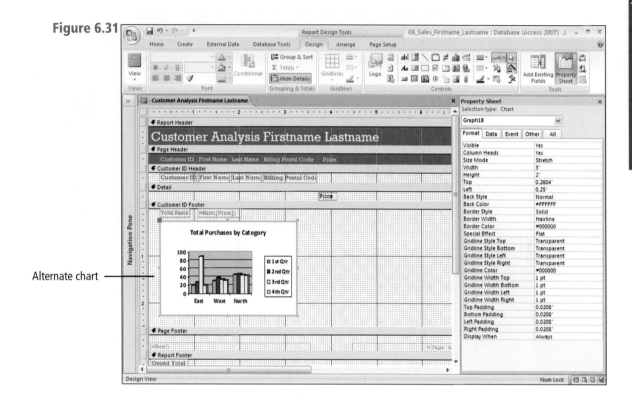

Alternate chart

Activity 6.16 Editing a Chart

Access uses a separate program called Microsoft Chart to create charts. In this activity, you start Microsoft Chart and edit the chart you created in the earlier activity.

1 With the **Customer Analysis** report still open in Design view, right-click the chart. From the shortcut menu, point to **Chart Object**, and then click **Edit**. Compare your screen with Figure 6.32.

The Microsoft Chart program is started. Above the chart, the Chart toolbar displays, and below the chart, a datasheet displays.

Chart toolbar

Figure 6.32

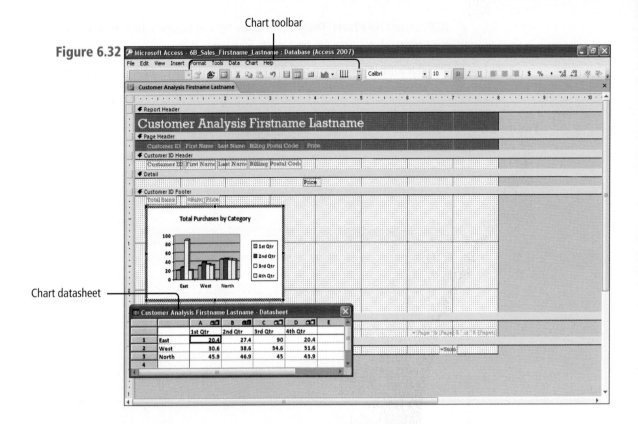

Chart datasheet

2 On the **Chart** toolbar, click the **By Row** button.

The totals for each category will display in across the chart's horizontal axis.

3 Right-click a blank area in the chart, and from the displayed shortcut menu, click **Chart Options**.

4 In the displayed **Chart Options** dialog box, click the **Axes tab**, and then clear the **Category (X) axis** check box.

The labels along the X axis will no longer display.

5 Click the **Legend tab**. Under **Placement**, click the **Bottom** option button, and then click **OK**.

6 Right-click the **Z axis**, which is the vertical axis at the left of the chart, and click **Format Axis**.

In a 3-D chart, the *Z-axis* replaces the Y-axis as the value axis. Recall that the *value axis* is a numerical scale on the left side of a chart that shows the range of numbers for the data points.

7 In the displayed **Format Axis** dialog box, click the **Number tab**. Under **Category**, click **Currency**, set the **Decimal places** to **0**, and then click **OK**.

8 On the **Chart** toolbar, click the **Chart Object arrow**, and then click **Walls**. On the **Chart** toolbar, click the **Format Walls** button.

All chart objects can be selected using this method.

9 In the displayed **Format Walls** dialog box, under **Border**, click the **None** option button. Under **Area**, click the **None** option button, and then click **OK**.

The chart's background changes from gray to white.

10 Click a blank area in the report, switch to Report view, and then compare your screen with Figure 6.33.

A different chart displays for each customer.

Figure 6.33

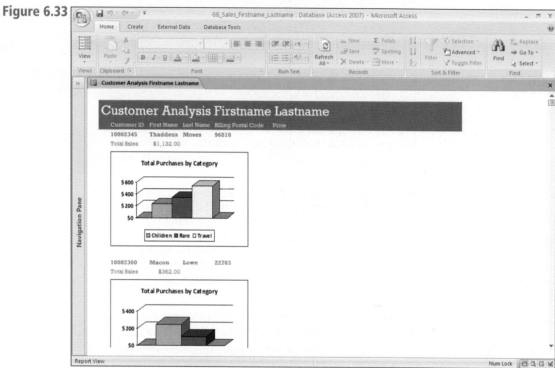

11 **Save** [icon] your work and leave the report open for the next activity.

Activity 6.17 Filtering and Printing a Report

In earlier projects, you built queries to filter the data, and then built reports based on those queries. When a report is built without an underlying query, the Advanced Filter/Sort should be used to filter and sort the data. In this project, you will add a filter to the Customer Analysis report using the Advanced Filter/Sort tool.

1 With the **Customer Analysis** report still open in Report view, in the **Sort & Filter group**, click the **Advanced** button, and then click **Advanced Filter/Sort**.

A new query opens in Design view.

2 In the list of fields, double-click the **Price** field to add it to the design grid.

3 In the **Criteria** box for the **Price column**, type **>350**

Only customers who have spent more than 350 dollars will display in the report.

4 In the **Sort & Filter group**, click the **Toggle Filter** button, and then compare your screen with Figure 6.34.

The Report view window displays only the desired records. The query is named and saved, but does not display in the Navigation Pane.

Filtered records   Filter query

Figure 6.34

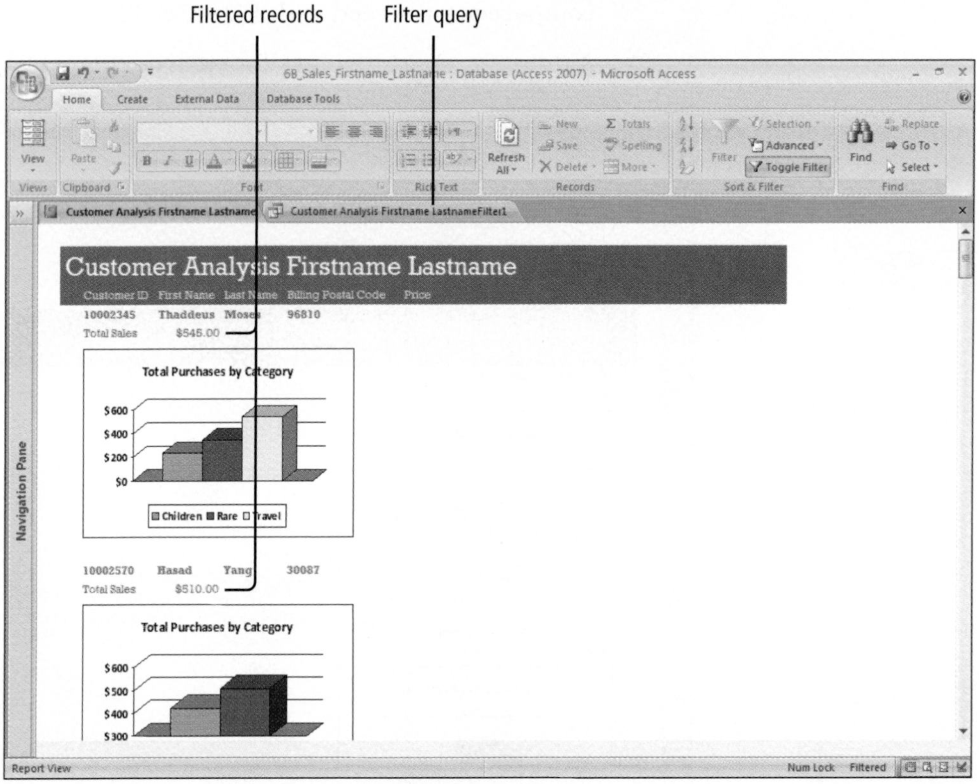

5 Switch to Design view. In the **Controls group**, click the **Logo** button, and then add the file **a06B_Logo**.

6 Position the **Title** control so that it is to the right of the logo.

7 In the **Grouping & Totals group**, click **Group & Sort**.

The Group, Sort, and Total pane displays at the bottom of the window.

8 In the displayed **Group, Sort, and Total** pane, click **More**.

9 Click the **do not keep group together on one page arrow**, and then click **keep whole group together on one page**.

The *keep whole group together on one page* option will prevent a customer's data from printing on two pages.

10 Switch to Print Preview, click the **Last Page** button ⏭, and if necessary, click the One Page button. Compare your screen with Figure 6.35.

With the filter in place, there are eight pages in the report. Notice that the Grand Total text box is too narrow.

Figure 6.35

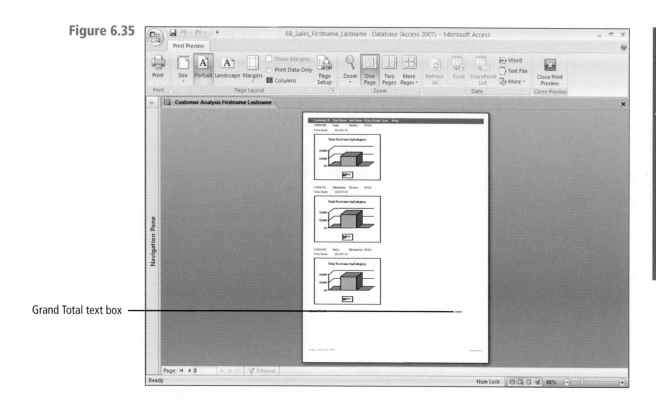

Grand Total text box ——

[11] **Close** Print Preview, and then switch to Layout view. **Close** the **Property Sheet** and then **Close** the **Group, Sort, and Total** pane.

[12] Scroll to the bottom of the report and then widen the **Grand Total** text box so that all its text displays.

[13] If your instructor asks you to print this project, print page 1 of the Report.

[14] **Save** 🖫 your work, and then **Close** the report.

Objective 5
Create a Report with an Interactive Filter

Earlier, you practiced creating filters for forms and reports using the Advanced Filter tool. So far, you have typed the criteria needed to create the filter after the report was opened. With an *interactive filter*, Access prompts the user for input when the report is opened and then filters the report based on the user's input.

Activity 6.18 Building a Daily Sales Report

In this activity, you will create a daily sales report using the Report Wizard. You will group the data by location and provide summary statistics for each location. *Summary statistics* describe groups of data by calculating totals, averages, minimums, and maximums.

[1] With **6B_Sales** still open, click the **Create tab**, and then click the **Report Wizard** button.

[2] From the **Books** table, add the following fields in this order: **Title**, **Price**, **Date Ordered**, and **Location**.

3 Click **Next**. Under **Do you want to add any grouping levels?**, click **Location**, and then click the **Move** button $\boxed{>}$.

4 Click **Next**, and then click the **Summary Options** button. Select the **Sum**, **Avg**, **Min**, and **Max** check boxes, check **Calculate percent of total for sums**, and then click **OK**.

5 Click **Next** two times, click the **None** style, and then click **Next**.

6 Title the report **Daily Sales Firstname Lastname** Click **Finish**, and then compare your screen with Figure 6.36.

The Price and Dated Ordered columns are too narrow and all of the books are listed, including ones that have not been sold. You will filter this list in the next activity.

Price text box   Date Ordered text box

Figure 6.36

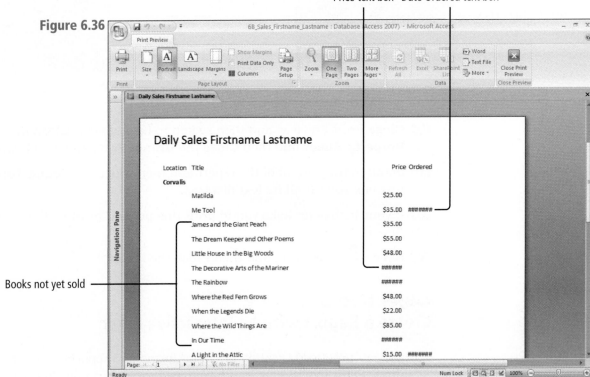

Books not yet sold

7 **Close** Print Preview to switch to Design view. In the **Location Header**, increase the width of the **Location** text box so that its right edge is on the **1-inch vertical gridline**.

8 In the **Detail** section, change the width of the **Price** text box so that the left edge is aligned with at **4.5 inches on the horizontal ruler**. Widen the **Date Ordered** text box so that its right edge is on the **7-inch vertical gridline**.

9 In the **Location Footer**, increase the width of the calculated control for *Sum* so that its left edge is at **5.5 inches on the horizontal ruler**. Repeat this technique to increase the width for these calculated controls: *Avg, Min, Max*, and *Standard*.

10 In the **Location Footer**, change the text of the **Standard** label to Percent of Total Sales

11 In the **Location Footer**, move the following labels one grid dot to the left of their corresponding calculated controls, and then compare your screen with Figure 6.37: **Sum**, **Avg**, **Min**, **Max**, and **Percent of Total Sales**.

Figure 6.37

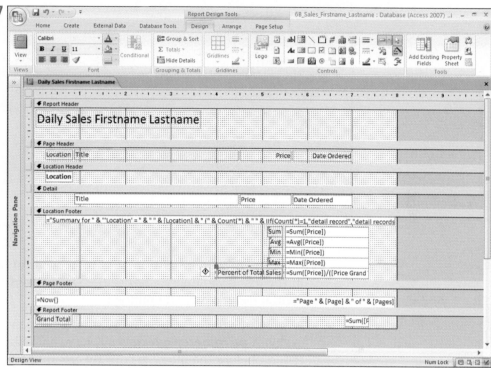

12 **Save** 🖫 your work and switch to Report view. Leave the report open for the next activity.

Activity 6.19 Creating a Filter That Asks for User Input

The Petite Book needs the Daily Sales report to display sales for only one day. Instead of creating a new query or filter each time the report is run, you will create a filter that asks the user to type the desired date each day the report is opened. The report will display the sales for the date typed by the user.

1 With the **Daily Sales** report still open in Report view, in the **Sort & Filter group**, click the **Advanced** button, and then click **Advanced Filter/Sort**.

2 Add the **Date Ordered** field to the query's first column. In the **Date Ordered Criteria** box, type **=02/03/09**

3 In the **Sort & Filter group**, click the **Toggle Filter** button, and then compare your screen with Figure 6.38.

Only the books that sold on the specified date display.

Figure 6.38

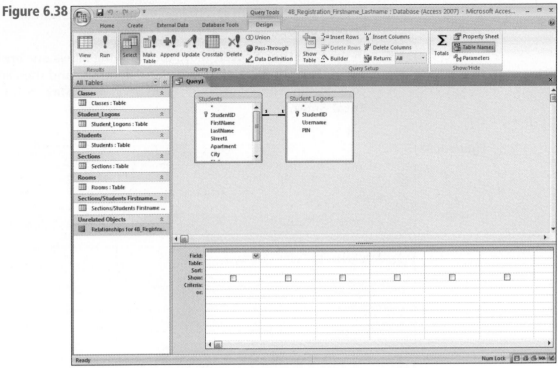

4 Click the **Advanced** button, and then click **Advanced Filter/Sort**. In the displayed query, change the **Date Ordered Criteria** box to **=[Enter desired date: dd/mm/yy]**

Placing this message inside square brackets creates a parameter query. A **_parameter query_** is a query that asks the user to type the criteria before the query is run. By creating a parameter query, the Sales Report can display sales for any date entered by the user.

5 Click the **Toggle Filter** button, and then compare your screen with Figure 6.39.

The text placed within the square brackets displays in the Enter Parameter Value dialog box.

Figure 6.39

Text from query ——

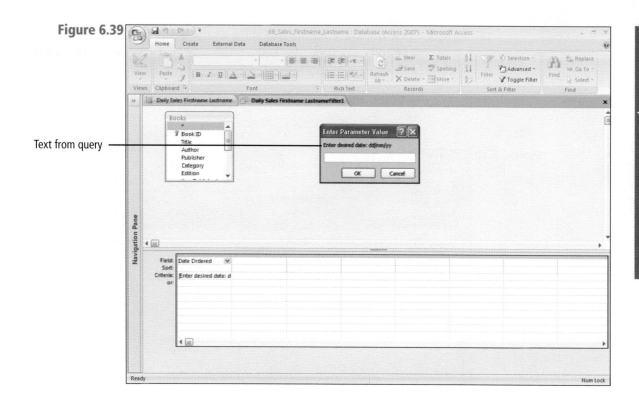

6 In the displayed **Enter Parameter Value** dialog box, type **02/04/09** and then click **OK**.

The sales for 02/04/2009 display. Currently, the user must click the Toggle Filter button after the report is opened to run the parameter query. The Petite Book would like the query to run when the report is first opened.

7 Switch to Design view, and in the **Tools group**, click the **Property Sheet** button. In the **Property Sheet**, select **Report**, and then click the **Data tab**.

The Filter property displays the parameter query that you created using the Advanced Filter tool.

8 Change the **Filter on Load** property to **Yes**

9 Display the properties for the **Date Ordered** label and set its **Visible** property to **No**. Click the **Date Ordered** text box, and then set its **Visible** property to **No**.

10 In the **Controls group**, click the **Text Box** button, and then in the **Report Header**, click on the **5-inch vertical gridline**.

11 In the label, replace the text with **Date:** and then in the **Font group**, click the **Align Text Right** button. In the text box, type **=[Date Ordered]**

12 Switch to Layout view. In the displayed **Enter Parameter Value** dialog box, type **02/05/09** and then click **OK**.

13 In the **AutoFormat group**, apply the **Foundry AutoFormat**—the first choice on the third row of the gallery.

14 Click the **Date** label, and then in the **Font group**, change the **Font Size** to **8**. Position the **Date** label and text box below the **Title** text box, as shown in Figure 6.40.

The column labels move down to make room for the Date label and text box.

Figure 6.40

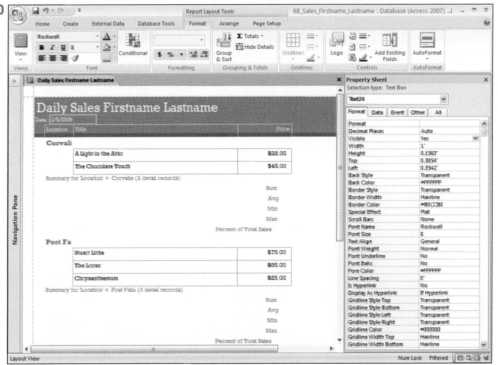

15 Click the **Location** text box, change the **Font Size** to **10**, and then remove the **Bold** format.

16 **Close** the Property Sheet. Scroll to the bottom of the report, and increase the width of the **Grand Total** text box, so that the entire amount displays.

17 If your instructor asks you to print this project, print the report with the current filter in place.

18 **Save** 🔲 your work, **Close** the report and **Exit** Access.

End **You have completed Project 6B** _____

There's More You Can Do!

From My Computer, navigate to the student files that accompany this textbook. In the folder **02_theres_more_you_can_do**, locate and open the folder for this chapter. Open and print the instructions for this project, which are provided to you in Adobe PDF format.

Try It! 1—Create a Report from a Crosstab Query

In this Try It! exercise, you will add and ActiveX control to a form.

Content-Based Assessments

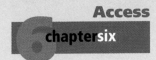
Summary

You have practiced shaping data and presenting that data in reports. Basing a report on a query gives your report the power and flexibility of queries to filter and summarize the data. Existing queries and reports are often copied and then adapted to quickly create new reports. Adding objects such as calculated controls and charts further enhances the report. Grouping data in a report and subreport provides another effective method to display data. For increased flexibility, interactive filters ask the user for input and the results are then based on that input. Once a report is created, it can be printed or exported into several file types such as Web pages.

Key Terms

Content-Based Assessments

Matching

Match each term in the second column with its correct definition in the first column by writing the letter of the term on the blank line in front of the correct definition.

_____ **1.** A name given to all the records displayed when a query is run.

_____ **2.** A database object that retrieves specific data from one or more tables and displays it in Datasheet view.

_____ **3.** A logical test that compares two conditions.

_____ **4.** A calculation that accumulates from record to record.

_____ **5.** The table or query that provides the underlying data for a form or report.

_____ **6.** A text document that displays in a Web browser.

_____ **7.** The saved steps for an import or export procedure.

_____ **8.** In a query, these calculate statistics for groups of records.

_____ **9.** Returns one record for each unique value in a query column.

_____ **10.** A report nested inside another report.

_____ **11.** The value axis in a 3-D chart.

_____ **12.** A vertical numerical scale in a 2-D or 3-D chart.

_____ **13.** Prompts the user for input and selects records based on that input.

_____ **14.** Numerical descriptions of groups of data such as totals, averages, and maximums.

_____ **15.** A query that asks the user to type the criteria before the query is run.

A Aggregate function

B AND condition

C Data task specification

D Group

E Group by function

F HTML document

G Interactive filter

H Parameter query

I Record source

J Recordset

K Running sum

L Select query

M Subreport

N Summary statistics

O Value axis

P Z-axis

Content-Based Assessments

Fill in the Blank

Write the correct answer in the space provided.

1. The name given to all of the records displayed in a query or filter is called a(n) _____.

2. A logical test that compares two conditions and returns true only if both of them are true is a(n) _____ _____.

3. Records organized by a common field are called a _____.

4. A calculation that accumulates from record to record is called a(n) _____ _____.

5. The table or query that provides the underlying data for a form or report is called a(n) _____ _____.

6. A text document meant to be displayed in a Web browser is called a(n) _____ _____.

7. The saved steps need to perform an import or export with a single click is called a(n) _____ _____ _____.

8. Statistics calculated on a group of records in a query use a(n) _____ _____.

9. An aggregate function that returns one record for each unique value is the _____ _____ _____.

10. A report nested within another report is a(n) _____.

11. The value axis on a 3-D chart is the _____.

12. A numerical scale on a vertical axis on any chart is the _____ _____.

13. A filter that prompts the user for input is called a(n) _____ filter.

14. Numerical descriptions of groups of data are called _____ _____.

15. A query that prompts the user for input is called a(n) _____ _____.

Content-Based Assessments

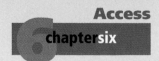

Skills Review

Project 6C—Customers

In this project, you will apply the skills you practiced from the Objectives in Project 6A.

Objectives: 1. *Build Reports Based on Queries;* **2.** *Export a Report and Create a Labels Report.*

In the following Skills Review, you will create a report showing total purchases for each customer who has purchased children's books. You will then create two label reports. You will base the first report on a query that filters the customers who have purchased travel books. You will copy the query and report to create a second report that lists customers who have purchased rare books. Your reports will look similar to Figure 6.41.

For Project 6C, you will need the following file:

a06C_Customers

You will save your database as
6C_Customers_Firstname_Lastname

Figure 6.41

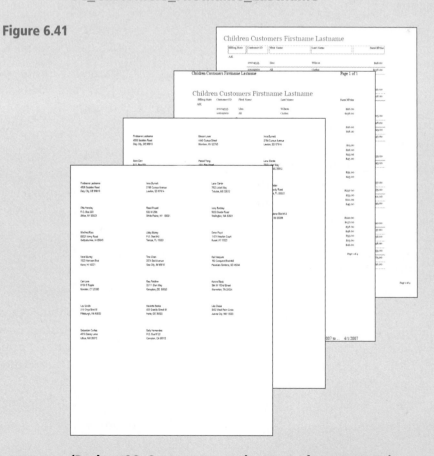

(Project 6C–Customers continues on the next page)

Content-Based Assessments

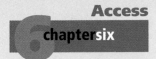
(Project 6C–Customers continued)

1. From the student files that accompany this textbook, locate the file **a06C_Customers**. Copy, and then paste the file to your **Access Chapter 6** folder. Rename the file 6C_Customers_Firstname_Lastname

2. Open **6C_Customers_Firstname_ Lastname**, enable the content, and then open the **Navigation Pane**. In the **Navigation Pane**, click the **All Tables arrow**, and then click **Object Type**.

3. Open the **Customers** table in Datasheet view. In the first record, with a **Customer ID** of 10002345, replace *Firstname* and *Lastname* with your own name, and then close the table.

4. Open the **Children Customers** query, and then switch to Design view. In the **Criteria row** for **Category**, type **Children**

5. Right-click the **Customer ID column**, and from the displayed shortcut menu, click **Totals**. In the **Price** column, click the **Total** box. Click the displayed **Total arrow**, and then click **Sum**.

6. In the **Results group**, click the **Run** button. **Save** and **Close** the query.

7. Click the **Create tab**, and then in the **Reports group**, click the **Report Wizard** button. In the displayed **Report Wizard** dialog box, move the following fields from the Children Customers query in this order: **Customer ID**, **First Name**, **Last Name**, **Billing State**, and **SumOfPrice**.

8. Click **Next**. Under **Do you want to add any grouping levels**, double-click **Billing State**. Click **Next** four times. Under **What Title do you want for your report?**, replace the existing text with **Children Customers Firstname Lastname** and then click **Finish**.

9. **Close** Print Preview and then switch to Layout view. Click the **AutoFormat**

button, and then click **Civic**—the last choice in the first row.

10. Click the **Customer ID** label. In the **Grouping & Totals group**, click the **Totals button**, and then click **Count Records**.

11. With the **Customer ID** label still selected, while holding down ⇧ Shift, click the following labels: **Billing State**, **First Name**, **Last Name**, and **SumOfPrice**. In the **Font group**, click the **Font Color button arrow**, and then click **Automatic**.

12. Place the pointer in the shaded area to the left of the **Billing State** label, and then click. With the entire label area selected, in the **Font group**, click the **Fill/Back Color button arrow**, and then click **White**.

13. **Save** the report. If your instructor asks you to print this project, print page one of the report. **Close** the report.

14. Open the **Travel Customers** query, and then switch to Design view. In the **Criteria row** for **Category**, type **Travel**

15. Right-click the **Customer ID column**, and from the displayed shortcut menu, click **Totals**.

16. In the **Results group**, click the **Run** button. **Save** and **Close** the query.

17. In the **Navigation Pane,** be sure the **Travel Customers** query is still selected. Click the **Create tab**. In the **Reports group**, click the **Labels** button.

18. In the displayed **Label Wizard**, be sure that **Filter by manufacturer** displays *Avery*. Under **Product Number**, scroll, and then click **Avery USA 5160**.

19. Click **Next** two times. Move **First Name** into the **Prototype label**, add a space, and then add **Last Name** into the **Prototype label**.

(Project 6C–Customers continues on the next page)

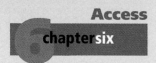
(Project 6C–Customers continued)

20. Press [Enter], and then in the second line of the **Prototype label**, add the **Billing Street** field, a space, and then the **Billing Apt** fields.

21. On the third line of the **Prototype label**, add the **Billing City**, type a comma followed by a space, and then add the **Billing State**. Add a space, and then add the **Billing Postal Code**.

22. Click **Next** two times, name the report **Travel Customers Firstname Lastname** and then click **Finish**. If your instructor asks you to print this project, print the report.

23. **Close** Print Preview, and then **Close** the report. In the **Navigation Pane**, be sure that the **Children Customers** report is selected. Click the **External Data tab**. In the **Export group**, click the **More** button, and then click **HTML Document**.

24. Click the **Browse** button, and then navigate to the location of your **Access Chapter 6** folder. In the **File name** box, type 6C_Customers_Firstname_Lastname and then click **Save**.

25. Click the **Open the destination file after the export operation is complete** check box, and then click **OK** two times. If your instructor asks you to print this project, print the Web page. **Close** the Web browser. In the **Export - HTML Document** dialog box, click the **Close** button.

26. In the **Navigation Pane**, right click the **Travel Customers** query, and then from the displayed shortcut menu, click **Copy**.

27. Right-click a blank area in the **Navigation Pane**, and then click **Paste**. Name the query **Rare Customers Firstname Lastname** and then click **OK**.

28. Use the techniques you just practiced to **Copy** and **Paste** the **Travel Customers** report. Name the pasted report **Rare Customers Firstname Lastname**

29. Open the **Rare Customers** query in Design view. Change the **Category Criteria** to Rare Click **Save**, and then **Close** the query.

30. Open the **Rare Customers** report in Design view. In the **Tools group**, click the **Property Sheet** button. If necessary, click the **Selection type arrow**, and then click **Report**.

31. Click the **Data tab**, click the **Record Source arrow**, and then click **Rare Customers Firstname Lastname**.

32. Click **Save**, and then switch to Print Preview. If your instructor asks you to print this project, print the report.

33. **Close** the report and **Exit** Access.

End **You have completed Project 6C**

Content-Based Assessments

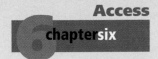

Skills Review

Project 6D — Categories

In this project, you will apply the skills you practiced from the Objectives in Project 6B.

Objectives: 3. *Create a Subreport Using Design Tools;* **4.** *Summarize Report Data;* **5.** *Create a Report with an Interactive Filter.*

In the following Skills Review, you will create a report for management that analyzes sales for each of the three major categories. You will insert a subreport, calculate totals for each customer, insert a chart, and create an interactive filter that asks the user to pick which category to report on. Your completed report will look similar to Figure 6.42.

For Project 6D, you will need the following file:

a06D_Categories

**You will save your database as
6D_Categories_Firstname_Lastname**

Figure 6.42

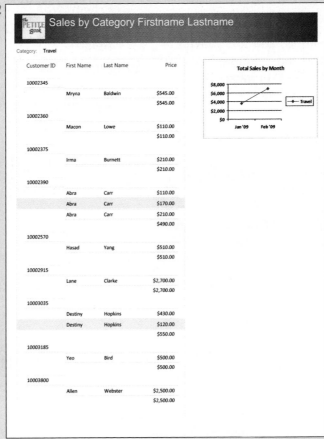

(Project 6D–Categories continues on the next page)

Content-Based Assessments

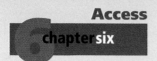
(Project 6D–Categories continued)

1. From the student files that accompany this textbook, locate the file **a06D_Categories**. Copy and then paste the file to your **Access Chapter 6** folder. Rename the file 6D_Categories_Firstname_Lastname

2. Open **6D_Categories_Firstname_ Lastname**, enable the content, and open the **Navigation Pane**.

3. Open the **Sales by Category** report and switch to Design view. In the **Report Header**, change the **Title** text box to **Sales by Category Firstname Lastname**

4. In the **Controls group**, click the **Subform/Subreport** button. Place the pointer two grid dots below the **Category** label and one grid dot from the report's left edge, and then click.

5. In the displayed **SubReport Wizard**, click **Next**. Add the following fields from the **Customers** table in this order: **Customer ID**, **First Name**, and **Last Name**. Add the following fields from the **Books** table in this order: **Price** and **Category**.

6. Click **Next** two times, name the Subreport **Customers subreport Firstname Lastname** and then click **Finish**.

7. Click any blank area in the main report, click the subreport's label, and then press ⌀Delete⌀.

8. Right-click the subreport, and from the displayed shortcut menu, click **Subreport in New Window**.

9. Double-click the **Category** text box. On the displayed **Property Sheet**, on the **Format tab**, change the **Visible** property to **No**. **Close** the **Navigation Pane**, click the **Category** label, and then change its **Visible** property to **No**.

10. **Close** the **Property Sheet**, and then switch to Layout view. Apply the **Access 2007 AutoFormat**, which is the second choice in the gallery. Select the subreport's four labels, and change the **Font Size** to **10**.

11. Switch to Design view. Change the width of the **Customer ID** text box and label so that the right edge is aligned with the **1.25 inch mark on the horizontal ruler**. Change the width of the **Price** text box and label so that their right edges are aligned with **6 inches on the horizontal ruler**.

12. Change the width of the **First Name column** controls so their right edges are aligned with **2.25 inches on the horizontal ruler**. Change the width of the **Last Name column** controls so their right edges are aligned with **3.5 inches on the horizontal ruler**. Change the width of the **Price column** controls so their right edges are aligned with the **4.25 inches on the horizontal ruler**.

13. Click **Save**, and then close the subreport window. In the main report, change the width of the subreport so that its right edge is aligned with **4.5 inches on the horizontal ruler**.

14. In the **Controls group**, click the **Insert Chart** button. Place the pointer on the **5-inch vertical gridline** and aligned with the top of the subreport, and then click.

15. In the displayed **Chart Wizard** dialog box, under **View**, click the **Queries** option button, and then click **Next**. **Move** the following fields into **Fields for Chart** in this order: **Date Ordered**, **Price**, and **Category**.

16. Click **Next**. Click the **Line Chart** button—the third choice in the third row. Click

(Project 6D–Categories continues on the next page)

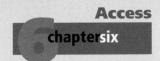

(Project 6D–Categories continued)

Next three times. Under **What title would you like for your chart?**, replace the existing text with **Total Sales by Month**

17. Click **Finish**. Right-click the chart. From the displayed shortcut menu, point to **Chart Object**, and then click **Edit**.

18. Right-click the vertical **value axis**, and from the displayed shortcut menu, click **Format Axis**. In the displayed **Format Axis** dialog box, click the **Number tab**. Under **Category**, click **Currency**. Under **Decimal places**, change the value to **0**, and then click **OK**.

19. Click a blank area of the report, and then switch to Layout view. Right-click a **Customer ID** text box, and from the short-cut menu, click **Group On Customer ID**.

20. Right-click the **Price** text box, and from the shortcut menu, point to **Total Price**, and then click **Sum**.

21. Switch to Report view, and then click the **Category** text box. In the **Sort & Filter group**, click the **Advanced** button, and then click **Advanced Filter/Sort**.

22. In the displayed query, add the **Category** field to the design grid. In the **Criteria row** for **Category**, type **[Type a category]**

23. In the **Sort & Filter group**, click the **Toggle Filter** button. In the displayed **Enter Parameter Value** dialog box, type **Children** and then click **OK**. The chart will appear blank while Access calculates the charts for each user.

24. Switch to Design view and in the **Tools group**, click **Property Sheet**. Display the properties for **Report**. Click the **Data tab**, and then change the **Filter On Load** property to **Yes**.

25. Click **Save**, and if a message displays, click **Yes**. Switch to Print Preview. In the displayed **Enter Parameter Value** dialog box, type **Travel** and then click **OK**.

26. If your instructor asks you to print this project, print the first page of the report.

27. **Save** your work and **Close** the report. From the **Office** menu, click **Exit** Access.

End **You have completed Project 6D** _____

Content-Based Assessments

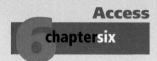
Mastering Access

Project 6E — Discounts

In this project, you will apply the skills you practiced from the Objectives in Project 6A.

Objectives: 1. *Build Reports Based on Queries;* **2.** *Export a Report and Create a Labels Report.*

In the following Mastering Access project, you will create a query to calculate discounted prices for the Corvalis store. After creating a report based on that query, you will use Copy and Paste to create a similar report for the Seattle store. You will export the Seattle report as a Web page. Your completed reports will look similar to Figure 6.43.

> **For Project 6E, you will need the following file:**
>
> a06E_Discounts

**You will save your database as
6E_Discounts_Firstname_Lastname**

Figure 6.43

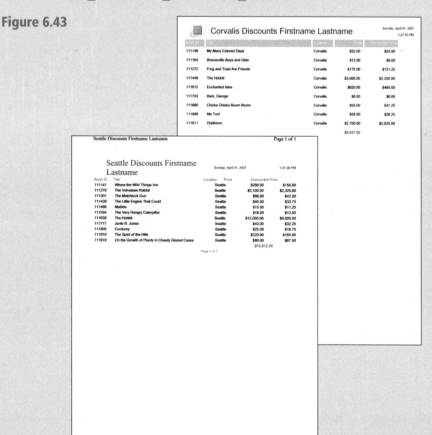

(Project 6E–Discounts continues on the next page)

Content-Based Assessments

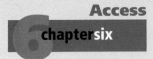

Mastering Access

(Project 6E–Mastering Access continued)

1. From the student files that accompany this textbook, locate the file **a06E_Discounts**. Copy, and then paste the file to your **Access Chapter 6** folder. Rename the file **6E_Discounts_Firstname_Lastname** Open **6E_Discounts_Firstname_Lastname** and enable the content.

2. On the **Create tab**, start the **Simple Query Wizard**. Use the wizard to add the following fields in this order: **Book ID**, **Title**, **Location**, **Price**, **Date Acquired**, and **Date Ordered**. Name the query **Corvalis Discounts Firstname Lastname** and finish the wizard.

3. Switch to Design view and add the following calculated field: **Discounted Price:[Price]*.75**

4. Add the following criteria:

	Location	Date Acquired	Date Ordered
Criteria	Corvalis	<3/31/2007	Is Not Null

5. Run the query. **Save**, and then **Close** the query.

6. In the **Navigation Pane**, select the **Corvalis Discounts** query. In the **Create tab,** click the **Report** button.

7. With the report open in Layout view, delete the **Date Acquired** field, and then delete the **Date Ordered** field. For the **Discounted Price** text box, apply the **Currency** format.

8. Apply the **Northwind** AutoFormat, which is the last choice in the gallery's third row. Resize the report's columns to better fit their contents. Be sure the report is one page wide.

9. If your instructor asks you to print this project, print the report.

10. **Save** the report with the name suggested by Access, and then **Close** the report.

11. **Copy**, and then **Paste** the **Corvalis Discounts** query. Name the new query **Seattle Discounts Firstname Lastname Copy**, and then **paste** the **Corvalis Discounts** report. Name the new report **Seattle Discounts Firstname Lastname**

12. Open the **Seattle Discounts** query and change the **Location Criteria** to **Seattle** Open the **Seattle Discounts** report and change the **Record Source** property to the **Seattle Discounts** query.

13. Change the report's title to **Seattle Discounts Firstname Lastname**

14. **Save** the report, and then **Close** the report. Export the **Seattle Discount** report as an **HTML Document**. Name the report **6E_Discounts_Firsname_Lastname** and be sure save it in your **Access Chapter 6** folder. **Exit** Access.

15. If your instructor asks you to print this project, open the HTML document created earlier in a Web browser and print the Web page. When you are done, close the browser.

End **You have completed Project 6E**

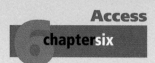

Access
chapter**six**

Mastering Access

Project 6F — Employees

In this project, you will apply the skills you practiced from the Objectives in Project 6B.

Objectives: 3. *Create a Subreport Using Design Tools;* **4.** *Summarize Report Data;* **5.** *Create a Report with an Interactive Filter.*

In the following Mastering Access project, you will add a subreport to a report, edit the subreport in a new window, and then add an interactive filter to the main report. Your completed report will look similar to Figure 6.44.

> ### For Project 6F, you will need the following file:
>
> a06F_Employees

**You will save your database as
6F_Employees_Firstname_Lastname**

Figure 6.44

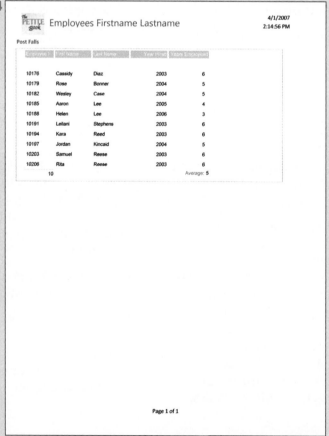

(Project 6F–Employees continues on the next page)

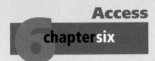
(Project 6F–Employees continued)

1. From the student files that accompany this textbook, locate the file **a06F_Employees**. Copy and then paste the file to your **Access Chapter 6** folder. Rename the file **6F_Employees_Firstname_Lastname**

2. Open **6F_Employees_Firstname_Lastname** and enable the content. Open the **Employees** report in Design view and change the title to **Employees Firstname Lastname**

3. Use the **Subform/Subreport** tool to insert a subreport below the **Store Name** text box. Use the **SubReport Wizard** to add the following fields from the **Employees** table in the following order: **Employee ID**, **First Name**, **Last Name**, **Year Hired**, and **Store Name**. Click **Next** two times, name the subreport **Employees subreport Firstname Lastname** and then **Finish** the wizard.

4. Delete the **Subreport's** label, and then open the subreport in its own window. Change width of the **Employee ID** label and text box so that its right edge is on the **1-inch vertical gridline**. Repeat this technique to change the widths of the following controls:

Label and Text Box	Right Edge/Vertical Gridline
First Name	2 inch
Last Name	3 inch
Year Hired	4 inch

5. Display the properties for the **Store Name** text box. Set its **Width** property to **.25** and its **Visible** property to **No**. With the **Store Name** controls still selected, **Remove** the Tabular Layout for the two controls. Delete the **Store Name** label, and then position the **Store Name** text box near the right edge of the report. The text box will link

the report and subreport, but will not need to be displayed in the subreport.

6. In the **Detail** section, between the **4-** and **5-inch vertical gridlines**, insert a text box control. Delete the label and in the text box, insert the following: **=2009-[Year Hired]**

7. In the **Report Header** section, between the **4-** and **5-inch vertical gridlines**, insert a label control, with the text **Years Employed** Vertically align the label with the **Year Hired** label. Click the **Year Hired** label, in the **Font group**, click the **Format Painter** button, and then click the **Years Employed** label.

8. Use the **Property Sheet** to set the **Height** property of the **Report Header** to **.5**

9. Click the **Employee ID** text box, in the **Grouping & Totals group**, apply **Count Records**.

10. In the **Report Footer**, on the **5-inch vertical gridline,** insert a text box. Change the label text to **Average:** In the text box, type **=2009-Avg([Year Hired])** Position the label so that it is one grid dot to the left of the text box.

11. Switch to Layout view. For the *=Avg* calculated control at the bottom of the report, in the **Formatting group**, assign the **Fixed** format, and then remove the decimals. In the **Font group**, click the **Align Text Left** button.

12. Select the **Years Employed** text box, and then click the **Align Text Right** button.

13. **Save** the subreport, and then **Close** its window. In the main report, switch to Report view. Click the **Store Name** text box, open **Advanced Filter/Sort**, and then add **Store Name** to the displayed query.

(Project 6F–Employees continues on the next page)

Content-Based Assessments

(Project 6F–Employees continued)

14. For the filter **Criteria**, type **[Enter a store name]** and then apply the filter. For the parameter, type **Seattle**

15. Switch to Design view and change the **Filter On Load** property so that the filter is applied when the report is opened.

16. Switch to Print Preview. For the criteria, type **Post Falls** If your instructor asks you to print this project, print the report for *Post Falls*.

17. **Close** Print Preview, **Save** the report, and then **Exit** Access.

End **You have completed Project 6F**

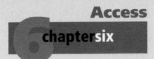

Mastering Access

Project 6G — Inventory

In this project, you will apply the skills you practiced from the Objectives in Projects 6A and 6B.

Objectives: 1. *Build Reports Based on Queries;* **4.** *Summarize Report Data;* **5.** *Create a Report with an Interactive Filter.*

In the following Mastering Access project, you will create a query to filter the desired records and then build a report based on that query. Your completed report will look similar to Figure 6.45.

For Project 6G, you will need the following file:

a06G_Inventory

**You will save your database as
6G_Inventory_Firstname_Lastname**

Figure 6.45

Inventory Firstname Lastname				
Post Falls				
A Bad Case of Stripes	111756	$19.25	$35.00	$15.75
A Wind in the Door	111627	$19.25	$35.00	$15.75
Brideshead Revisited	111391	$2,325.00	$3,100.00	$775.00
Bronzeville Boys and Girls	111384	$6.60	$12.00	$5.40
Call For the Dead	111701	$2,255.00	$4,100.00	$1,845.00
Camera Obscura	111446	$2,025.00	$2,700.00	$675.00
Charlie and the Chocolate Factory	111444	$22.00	$40.00	$18.00
Dear Mr. Henshaw	111908	$15.40	$28.00	$12.60
Just Grandma and Me	111481	$20.90	$38.00	$17.10
Just Me and My Dad	111669	$24.70	$38.00	$13.30
Lady Chatterly's Lover	111668	$2,255.00	$4,100.00	$1,845.00
Misty of Chincoteague	111404	$9.00	$18.00	$9.00
Sideways Stories from Wayside School	111422	$6.60	$12.00	$5.40
Tacky The Penguin	111897	$13.50	$18.00	$4.50
The Big Sleep	111776	$2,310.00	$4,200.00	$1,890.00
The Black Stallion	111874	$97.90	$178.00	$80.10
The Giver	111509	$16.90	$26.00	$9.10
The Giving Tree	111466	$19.50	$26.00	$6.50
The Jungle Books	111720	$552.50	$850.00	$297.50
The Pigman	111368	$17.60	$32.00	$14.40
The Polar Express	111839	$22.75	$35.00	$12.25
The Secret Garden	111494	$123.75	$225.00	$101.25
The Secret Garden	111527	$137.50	$275.00	$137.50
The Secret of the Indian	111564	$41.25	$75.00	$33.75
The Sneetches	111604	$55.25	$85.00	$29.75
The Thin Man	111857	$2,500.00	$5,000.00	$2,500.00
The Three Voyages of Edmond Halley in the Paramore, 1698-1701	111804	$90.00	$120.00	$30.00
The Yearling	111650	$41.25	$75.00	$33.75
To Kill a Mockingbird	111614	$495.00	$900.00	$405.00
Trade and Trade Centers of History	111553	$178.75	$275.00	$96.25
	30	$15,717.10	$26,651.00	$10,933.90

Wednesday, March 18, 2009   Page 1 of 1

(Project 6G–Inventory continues on the next page)

Content-Based Assessments

Access

Mastering Access

(Project 6G–Inventory continued)

1. From the student files that accompany this textbook, locate the file **a06G_Inventory**. Copy, and then paste the file to your **Access Chapter 6** folder. Rename the file **6G_Inventory_Firstname_Lastname**

2. Open **6G_Dealers_Firstname_Lastname** and enable the content. Create a new query with the following fields from the **Books** table: **Book ID**, **Title**, **Store Name**, **Cost**, **Price**, and **Date Ordered**. Name the query **Inventory Firstname Lastname**

3. In the **Date Ordered** criteria, type **Is Null** In the first empty column of the query, add this calculated field: **Profit:[Price]-[Cost] Run** the query, click **Save**, and then **Close** the query.

4. Start the **Report Wizard** and select the following fields from the **Inventory** query: **Book ID**, **Title**, **Cost**, **Price**, and **Profit**. In the wizard, do not add any grouping levels, sort by **Title** in **Ascending** order, and then click **Finish**.

5. Switch to Layout view and apply the **Paper AutoFormat**, which is the second choice on the second row of the gallery.

6. Using Figure 6.45 as your guide, resize the width of the columns to better fit their contents. Be sure the report's width remains on one page.

7. Use the **Totals** tool to provide the following summary statistics: a count of the **Book ID** field, the total of the **Cost** field, the total of the **Price** field, and the total of the **Profit** field.

8. In the calculated field for the **Profit** column, apply the **Currency** format.

9. Switch to Design view. Set the **Height** property for the **Report Header** to .75 Below the title, insert a text box. Delete the label, and then in the text box, type **=[Store Name]**

10. Switch to Layout view. For the **Store Name** text box, change the **Font Size** to **12,** and then apply **Bold**. Resize the text box to display all its text and then position the label as shown in Figure 6.45.

11. **Save** and **Close** the report. Open the **Inventory** query in Design view, and then in the **Store Name** criteria type **[Which store?]**

12. **Save** and **Close** the query. Open the **Inventory** report in Print Preview. For the parameter, type **Post Falls**

13. If your instructor asks you to print this project, print the report for *Post Falls*.

14. **Close** the report and then **Exit** Access.

End **You have completed Project 6G** ─────────────

Content-Based Assessments

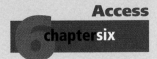

Access
chaptersix

Mastering Access

Project 6H — Invoices

In this project, you will apply the skills you practiced from the Objectives in Projects 6A and 6B.

Objectives: 2. *Export a Report and Create a Labels Report.* **4.** *Summarize Report Data.*

In the following Mastering Access project, you will create a report for the store owner. Your report will display summary statistics for each store, but not the underlying details. You will add a chart to the report and then export the report as a Web page. Your completed reports will look similar to Figure 6.46.

> **For Project 6H, you will need the following file:**
>
> a06H_Statistics

**You will save your database as
6H_Statistics_Firstname_Lastname**

Figure 6.46

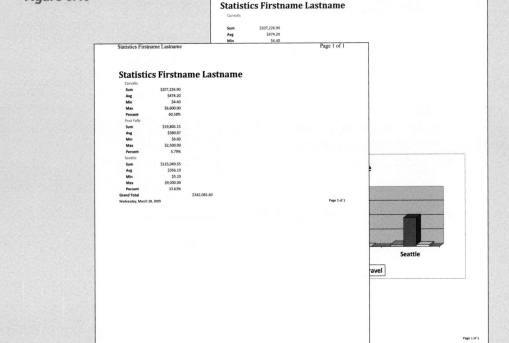

(Project 6H–Invoices continues on the next page)

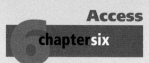

(Project 6H–Invoices continued)

1. From the student files that accompany this textbook, locate the file **a06H_Statistics**. Copy, and then paste the file to your **Access Chapter 6** folder. Rename the file 6H_Statistics_Firstname_Lastname

2. Open **6H_Statistics_Firstname_ Lastname** and enable the content.

3. Start the **Report Wizard** and add the following fields from the **Books** table: **Cost**, and **Store Name**.

4. Click **Next** two times and click the **Summary Options** button. Select all four summary values, click the **Summary only** option button, and select the **Calculate percent of total for sums** check box.

5. Close the **Summary Options** dialog box and click **Next** two times. Under **Report AutoFormats**, be sure that **Office** is selected, and then click **Next**. Name the report **Statistics Firstname Lastname** and then click **Finish**.

6. Switch to Design view. With the **Store Name** and **Cost** controls still selected, **Remove** the Tabular Layout. In the **Page Header**, delete the two labels, and then change the Page Header's height to **0**. In the **Detail** section, delete the **Cost** text box, and then change the Detail section's height to **0**.

7. In the **Store Name Footer**, delete the text box beginning = "*Summary for*. Select the five remaining text boxes and change their width so that their left sides are aligned with the **2-inch vertical gridline**.

8. With the five controls still selected, use the ← key to place the controls between the **1-** and **2-inch vertical gridlines**. In the label

with the text *Standard*, change the text to **Percent**

9. Increase the height of the **Report Footer** to approximately **4 inches** and insert a chart control. Use the Chart Wizard to select **Category**, **Cost**, and **Store Name** from the Books table for the chart fields. Choose the **3-D Column Chart**, and move the next screen.

10. Below the sample chart, move **Store Name** into the **Axis** box. To the right of the sample chart, move **Category** into the **Series** box. Move to the next step of the wizard and then select **<No Field>** for both the **Report Fields** and the **Chart Fields**. Move to the last screen of the wizard, type the title **Books by Store** and then click **Finish**.

11. Start **Microsoft Chart** so that the chart can be edited. Use the **Chart Options** dialog box to position the legend below the chart.

12. Switch to Layout view. Resize the chart so that it fills the empty space between the **Grand Total** and the **Date** and **Page Number** in the Page Footer.

13. Increase the width of the **Grand Total** text box so that all of the text displays.

14. If your instructor asks you to print this project, print the report.

15. **Save** your work, and then **Close** the report. Export the report as an **HTML Document** named 6H_Statistics_Firstname_ Lastname and then **Exit** Access.

16. If your instructor asks you to print this project, open the Web page in a browser and print.

End **You have completed Project 6H** ————————————

Content-Based Assessments

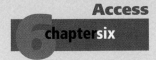
Project 6I — Authors

In this project, you will apply the skills you practiced from all the Objectives in Projects 6A and 6B.

Objectives: 1. *Build Reports Based on Queries;* **2.** *Export a Report and Create a Labels Report;* **3.** *Create a Subreport Using Design Tools;* **4.** *Summarize Report Data;* **5.** *Create a Report with an Interactive Filter.*

In the following Mastering Access project, you will create two reports with information about authors and which of their works are available for sale at The Petite Book. Both reports will be based on queries with interactive filters. The first report will use a subreport to list each of the books by each author, and the second report will list only the summary statistics for each author. Your completed reports will look similar to Figure 6.47.

For Project 6I, you will need the following file:

a06I_Authors

**You will save your database as
6I_Authors_Firstname_Lastname**

Figure 6.47

(Project 6I–Authors continues on the next page)

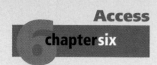
(Project 6I–Authors continued)

1. From the student files that accompany this textbook, locate the file **a06I_Authors**. Copy, and then paste the file to your **Access Chapter 6** folder. Rename the file **6I_Authors_Firstname_Lastname**

2. Open **6I_Authors_Firstname_Lastname** and enable the content. Create a new query in Design view and add the following fields from the **Books** table: **Author**, **Category**, and **Customer ID**.

3. In the query, display the **Total row**. For the **Category Criteria**, type **[Enter a category]** For the **Customer ID Criteria**, type **Is Not Null**

4. **Save** the query as **Author List Firstname Lastname** and then close the query.

5. Start the **Report Wizard**, and from the **Author List** query, add the **Author** field. Click **Next** three times, apply the **Office** style, and then click **Finish**. For the report's parameter, type **Rare**

6. Switch to Design view and increase the width of the **Author** label and text box so that the right edge is aligned with **2.5 inches on the horizontal ruler**.

7. Use the **Property Sheet** to set the **Height** of the **Detail** section to **2** Insert a **Subform/Subreport** control two grid dots below the **Author** text box and aligned with the left edge of the **Author** text box.

8. Use the displayed **SubReport Wizard** to include the following fields from the **Books** table: **Title**, **Author**, **Price**, and **Store Name**. Accept all remaining wizard defaults.

9. Delete the subreport's label, and then change the subreport height so that it fills the remaining space in the Detail section.

10. For the **Author** label and text box in the subreport, set their **Visible** property to **No**, and then set the width of the **Author** text box to **.15**

11. Switch to Layout view, and then for the parameter, enter **Rare** Apply the **Equity AutoFormat**—the fourth choice on the second row. Move the right edge of the subreport so that it is inside page 1 of the report.

12. In the subreport, select the **Title** text box, and then in the **Grouping & Totals group**, add a control that counts the records. Select the **Price** text box, and then in the **Grouping & Totals group**, add a control that calculates the total for that column.

13. Switch to Report view. Add an **Advanced Filter/Sort** that displays the books for "Christie, Agatha" Apply the filter. If your instructor asks you to print this project, print the report with the filter in place.

14. **Save** and then **Close** the **Author List** report. **Copy**, and then **paste** the **Author List** query that you created earlier. Name the new query **Author Summary Firstname Lastname**

15. Open the **Author Summary** query in Design view and add the **Year Published** and **Price** fields to the query. **Save**, and then **Close** the query.

16. Use the Report Wizard to create a report with the following fields from the **Author Summary** query: **Author**, **Category**, **Year Published**, and **Price**. Group by the **Author** field. In **Summary Options**, include the average of the **Year Published** field, the total of the **Price** field, and check the **Summary Only** option button. In the Wizard, apply the **Equity** style and accept

(Project 6I–Authors continues on the next page)

Content-Based Assessments

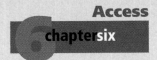
(Project 6I–Authors continued)

all other wizard defaults. For the parameter, enter **Rare**

17. In Design view, select all the controls in the **Page Header**, **Author Header** and **Detail** sections, and then remove the stacked layout. In the **Page Header**, delete the four labels. In the **Page Header**, insert a text box with its left edge aligned with the **1-inch vertical gridline**. Change the **Font Color** of both the label and text box to white. Change the label text to **Category:** and then in the text box enter **=[Category]**

18. Increase the width of the **Author** text box so that its right edge is on the **3-inch vertical gridline**.

19. Change the **Sum** label text to **Total Inventory** and the **Avg** label text to **Average Year Published**

20. In the **Author Footer**, move the **=Sum** calculated text box to the left so that its right

edge is aligned with **2.5 inches on the horizontal ruler**. Move the **=Avg** calculated text box to the left so that its right edge is aligned with **2.5 inches on the horizontal ruler**.

21. In the **Report Footer**, increase the width of the **=Sum** calculated text box so that its left edge is aligned with the **4-inch vertical gridline**.

22. Switch to Layout view and for the parameter, enter **Rare** For the text box starting, **Summary for 'Author'** apply **Italic**. Increase the width of the **Total Inventory** text box by dragging the left edge until all of the text displays.

23. **Save** the report and then switch to Report view. If your instructor asks you to print this project, print page 1 of the report.

24. **Close** the report and **Exit** Access.

End **You have completed Project 6I**

Content-Based Assessments

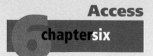

Business Running Case

Project 6J — Business Running Case

In this project, you will apply the skills you practiced from all the Objectives in Projects 6A and 6B.

From My Computer, navigate to the student files that accompany this textbook. In the folder **03_business_running_case**, locate and open the folder for this chapter. Open and print the instructions for this project, which are provided to you in Adobe PDF format. Follow the instructions and use the skills you have gained thus far to assist Jennifer Nelson meet the challenges of owning and running her business.

End **You have completed Project 6J** ——————————

Outcomes-Based Assessments

Rubric

The following outcomes-based assessments are *open-ended assessments*. That is, there is no specific correct result; your result will depend on your approach to the information provided. Make *Professional Quality* your goal. Use the following scoring rubric to guide you in *how* to approach the problem and then to evaluate *how well* your approach solves the problem.

The *criteria*—Software Mastery, Content, Format and Layout, and Process—represent the knowledge and skills you have gained that you can apply to solving the problem. The *levels of performance*—Professional Quality, Approaching Professional Quality, or Needs Quality Improvement—help you and your instructor evaluate your result.

	Your completed project is of Professional Quality if you:	Your completed project is Approaching Professional Quality if you:	Your completed project Needs Quality Improvements if you:
1-Software Mastery	Choose and apply the most appropriate skills, tools, and features and identify efficient methods to solve the problem.	Choose and apply some appropriate skills, tools, and features, but not in the most efficient manner.	Choose inappropriate skills, tools, or features, or are inefficient in solving the problem.
2-Content	Construct a solution that is clear and well organized, contains content that is accurate, appropriate to the audience and purpose, and is complete. Provide a solution that contains no errors of spelling, grammar, or style.	Construct a solution in which some components are unclear, poorly organized, inconsistent, or incomplete. Misjudge the needs of the audience. Have some errors in spelling, grammar, or style, but the errors do not detract from comprehension.	Construct a solution that is unclear, incomplete, or poorly organized, containing some inaccurate or inappropriate content; and contains many errors of spelling, grammar, or style. Do not solve the problem.
3-Format and Layout	Format and arrange all elements to communicate information and ideas, clarify function, illustrate relationships, and indicate relative importance.	Apply appropriate format and layout features to some elements, but not others. Overuse features, causing minor distraction.	Apply format and layout that does not communicate information or ideas clearly. Do not use format and layout features to clarify function, illustrate relationships, or indicate relative importance. Use available features excessively, causing distraction.
4-Process	Use an organized approach that integrates planning, development, self-assessment, revision, and reflection.	Demonstrate an organized approach in some areas, but not others; or, use an insufficient process of organization throughout	Do not use an organized approach to solve the problem.

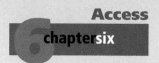

Problem Solving

Project 6K — Publishers

In this project, you will construct a solution by applying any combination of the skills you practiced from the Objectives in Projects 6A and 6B.

For Project 6K, you will need the following file:

a06K_Publishers

**You will save your database as
6K_Publishers_Firstname_Lastname**

The Petite Book needs a report that lists available books for each publisher. In this project you will create a query to filter records and then build a report based on that query. You will then apply an additional filter after the report is created. Copy a06K_Publishers and paste it into your Access Chapter 6 folder. Rename the file as **6K_Publishers_Firstname_Lastname**

Create a query that lists each Publisher, Title, Author, Price, Date Ordered, and Location. Insert criteria so that only the books with no value in the Date Ordered field are selected. Save the query as **Book List Firstname Lastname**

Create a new report with all of the fields from the Book List query except for the Date Ordered field. Group by the Publisher field. Add the title **Books by Publisher Firstname Lastname** and then apply the AutoFormat of your choice. Remove the stacked layout, and then resize and position the reports controls to make an effective printout. Apply a filter so that only the list for Avon Books displays. Save the report as **Publishers Firstname Lastname**

Submit the project as directed.

End **You have completed Project 6K** ——————

Outcomes-Based Assessments

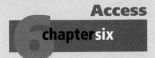
Problem Solving

Project 6L — Labels

In this project, you will construct a solution by applying any combination of the skills you practiced from the Objectives in Projects 6A and 6B.

> **For Project 6L, you will need the following file:**
>
> a06L_Labels
>
> **You will save your database as**
> **6L_Labels_Firstname_Lastname**

The Petite Book needs a report that creates mailing labels for their employees. In this project you will create the labels report and then add an interactive filter. Copy a06L_Labels and paste it into your Access Chapter 6 folder. Rename the file **6L_Labels_Firstname_Lastname**

In the Employees table, add yourself as an employee at the Post Falls store. Use your own name. Create a labels report using any 1-inch-by-2⅝-inch standard label. In the prototype label, choose and arrange the fields as needed to create a mailing label. For the report, add an interactive filter that asks the user to enter a store name and then displays the labels for all the employees at that store. Set the filter to run when the report is first opened. For the parameter, enter **Post Falls** and then save the labels report with the filter in place.

Submit the database as directed by your instructor.

 You have completed Project 6L ————————————

Problem Solving

Project 6M — Chart

In this project, you will construct a solution by applying any combination of the skills you practiced from the Objectives in Projects 6A and 6B.

For Project 6M, you will need the following file:

a06M_Chart

**You will save your database as
6M_Chart_Firstname_Lastname**

The Petite Book has asked you to create a chart comparing the net value of the inventory at each store. To start, copy a06M_Chart into your Access Chapter 6 folder, and then rename the new file **6M_Chart_Firstname_Lastname**

Create an aggregate function query that calculates the total of the Cost field for each store. Add criteria to select only books that have not been ordered. If done correctly, the Corvalis store should total 169,991.00 and the Post Falls store should total 15,717.10. Create a report based on the query. In the report footer, add a pie chart with three slices, one for each store's total from the query. For the chart, do not display a legend and title the chart appropriately. For the chart data label, include both the store name and the percentage each contributes. Format the report as needed.

Submit the database as directed by your instructor.

End You have completed Project 6M————————————

Outcomes-Based Assessments

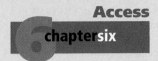
Problem Solving

Project 6N — Awards

In this project, you will construct a solution by applying any combination of the skills you practiced from the Objectives in Projects 6A and 6B.

For Project 6N, you will need the following file:

a06N_Awards

**You will save your database as
6N_Awards_Firstname_Lastname**

The Petite Book needs reports listing what books are for sale that have won the Newberry and Caldecott awards. To start, copy a06N_Awards into your Access Chapter 6 folder, and then rename the new file **6N_Awards_Firstname_Lastname**

Create a query that lists the titles, authors, and prices of every book that has been awarded the Newberry award and limit the selection to the Corvalis store. Add a calculated field labeled *Discounted Price* that decreases the regular price by 15 percent. Add criteria so that only books without an order date are selected. Create a report based on the query. Insert an appropriate title and apply the AutoFormat of your choice. Position and resize the report controls to make an effective presentation. Be sure all the columns fit within a single page width.

Copy the query and report and then adjust the query and report so that the report lists the Newberry books from the Seattle store. Copy the query and report and then adjust each so that the report lists the Newberry books from the Post Falls store. Export the three reports as Web pages.

Submit the database as directed by your instructor.

 You have completed Project 6N _____

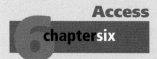

Problem Solving

Project 6O — Books by Age

In this project, you will construct a solution by applying any combination of the skills you practiced from the Objectives in Projects 6A and 6B.

For Project 6O, you will need the following file:

a06O_Books_by_Age

**You will save your database as
6O_Books_by_Age_Firstname_Lastname**

In this project, you will create a parameter query that takes two inputs from the user and then build a report based on that query. To start, copy a06O_Books_by_Age into your Access Chapter 6 folder, and then rename the new file **6O_Books_by_Age_Firstname_Lastname**

Create a query that selects the Book ID, Title, Author, and Publisher fields. Add the Year Published field. For the Year Published criteria, add a parameter that asks the user to type a year. Have the query select all books published before the year input by the user. Test your query. Add the Store Name field. Add a second parameter that asks the user to type the store name. Test that the query selects just the books from the store input by the user and older than the year input by the user.

Create a report based on the query. Title the report appropriately and apply the AutoFormat of your choice. In the Report Header, add a text box that displays the store name entered by the user. For the text box label, enter **Store:** In the Detail section, do not display the Store Name text box or its label. Position and resize the controls to make an effective report. Be sure the report is not wider than one page.

Submit the project as directed by your instructor.

 End **You have completed Project 6O** ————————————

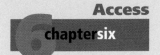

Access

You and *GO!*

In this project, you will construct a solution by applying any combination of the Objectives found in Projects 6A and 6B.

From My Computer, navigate to the student files that accompany this textbook. In the folder **04_you_and_go**, locate and open the folder for this chapter. Open and print the instructions for this project, which are provided to you in Adobe PDF format. Follow the instructions to create a music collection inventory.

 End **You have completed Project 6P** ———————————

GO! with Help

Access reports are often distributed electronically. Electronic file formats include HTML documents, PDF documents, and rich text. These are easily distributed via email.

1 Start **Access**. Click the **Microsoft Office Access Help** button.

2 In the **Search** box, type **electronic reports** and then click **Search**.

3 In the **Access Help** window, from the **Results** list, click **Distribute a report electronically**. In the displayed help page, click the **Distribute a report by using the E-mail command** link. Read the section to learn how to distribute reports using email.

4 If you want to print a copy of the information, click the Print button at the top of Access Help window.

5 **Close** the Help window, and then **Exit** Access.

 End **You have completed Project 6Q** ———————————

Glossary

Aggregate function calculates statistics such as totals, averages, and counts based on a group of records.

Allow Zero Length property An Access field property that determines if an entry can have zero characters.

AND condition A condition in which only records where both specified values are present in the selected fields.

Append row Row in an Access table where new records or values are entered.

Ascending order A sorting order that arranges text in alphabetical order (A to Z) or numbers from the lowest to highest number.

Attachment data type An Access field used to store pictures, Office files, and even small executable programs.

AutoNumber An Access feature that sequentially numbers entered records creating a unique number for each record; useful for data that has no distinct field that could be considered unique.

Between. . . And operator A comparison operator that looks for values within a range.

Blank database A database that has no data and has no database tools; you create the data and the tools as you need them.

Blank Form tool An efficient way to build a form in Layout View.

Blank Report tool An Access feature with which you can create a report from scratch by adding the fields you want in the order you want them to appear.

Bound The term used to describe objects and controls that are based on data that is stored in tables.

Bound control Any control whose data source is a field in a table or query.

Business rules Rules that describe how a business is run.

Calculated controls Controls whose source of data is an expression—typically a formula—rather than a field.

Caption property An Access field property that provides an alternate display text for database objects.

Cascading delete A data integrity option where deleting a record in the first table will cause all matching records in the second table to also be deleted.

Cascading update A data integrity option where the data in the first table is changed, and all the related occurrences of the data in the second table are also changed.

Cell The box formed by the intersection of a row and a column in a datasheet.

Combo box A control that provides an arrow that when clicked displays a list of items from which the user can choose.

Command button A control used to start an action or set of actions.

Common fields Fields that contain the same data in more than one table.

Comparison operators Symbols that evaluate each field value to determine if it is the same (=), greater than (>), less than (<), or in between a range of values as specified by the criteria.

Compound criteria Multiple conditions in a query or filter.

Conditional format (Access) A format that displays only when one or more conditions are true.

Controls Objects on a form or report that display data, perform actions, and let you view and work with information.

Control layout The grouped arrangement of controls on a form or report.

Criteria Conditions that identify the specific records you are looking for.

Data Facts about people, events, things, or ideas.

Data entry The action of typing the record data into a database.

Data integrity Data is entered and stored according to its intended use.

Data redundancy Data that is repeated unnecessarily in a database table.

Data source The table or tables from which a query gets its data.

Data task specification The saved steps needed to import or export data so that the import or export can be performed by clicking a single button.

Data type The characteristic that defines the kind of data that can be entered into a field, such as numbers, text, or dates.

Database An organized collection of facts about people, events, things, or ideas related to a particular topic or purpose.

Datasheet view The Access view that displays an object organized in a format of columns and rows similar to an Excel spreadsheet.

Date control A control on a form or report that inserts the current date each time the form or report is opened.

DBMS An acronym for database management system.

Default formatting In a conditional format, the format that will display if none of the conditions are met.

Default values The values that will automatically display in a new record.

Descending order A sorting order that arranges text in reverse alphabetical (Z to A) order or numbers from the highest to the lowest number.

Design grid The lower pane of the Query window, which displays the design of the query.

Design view The Access view that displays the underlying structure of an object.

Detail section The section of a form or report that displays the records from the underlying table or query.

Dialog box A window containing commands or that asks you to make a decision.

End users People who enter data using forms and use the information found in queries in reports.

Expression Any combination of field names, properties, constants, or operators.

Expression Builder A dialog box that builds expressions with easy access to fields, controls, and common operators.

Field A category that describes each piece of data stored in a table.

Field list A list of the field names in a table.

Field properties Characteristics of a field that control how the field will display and how the data can be entered in the field.

Filter By Form An Access command that filters the records in a form based on one or more fields, or based on more than one value in the same field.

Filter By Selection An Access command that retrieves only the records that contain the value in the selected field.

Filtering The process of displaying only a portion of the total records (a subset) based on matching specific value.

Foreign key The field that is included in the related table so that it can be joined to the primary key in another table for the purpose of creating a relationship.

Form An Access object with which you can enter, edit, or display data from a table or a query; a window for displaying and collecting information.

Format property A field property that interprets the underlying data stored in the table, which may be different than the actual data.

Form footer Information at the bottom of the screen in Form view that is printed after the last detail section on the last page.

Form header Information, such as a form's title, which displays at the top of the screen in Form view, and that is printed at the top of the first page when records are printed as forms.

Form tool The Access tool that creates a form with a single mouse click, and that includes all the fields from the underlying data source (table or query).

Group Organizes records by a common value and allows the addition of summary data for each group.

Group by function An aggregate function that returns one record for each unique value in the column that the function is applied.

Group footer Displays the field label by which the summarized data has been grouped.

Group header Information printed at the beginning of each new group of records, for example the group name.

Group, Sort, and Total pane A pane that opens at the bottom of your screen in which you can control how information is sorted and grouped in a report; provides the most flexibility for adding or modifying groups, sort orders, or totals options on a report.

HTML Document A text document written in Hypertext Markup Language that displays in a Web browser.

Indeterminate relationship A relationship that cannot enforce referential integrity.

Indexed property An Access field property that creates a second, more efficient table that can be quickly searched or sorted.

Information Data that has been organized in a useful manner.

Inner Join In a query datasheet based on related tables, a record from the left table displays only if there is a matching record in the other table.

Innermost sort field When sorting on multiple fields in datasheet view, the field that will be used for the second level of sorting.

Input Mask property An Access field property used to control the structure of the data entered in the field.

Interactive filter Prompts the user for input when the report is opened and then filters the report based on the users input.

Is Not Null A criteria that searches for fields that are not empty.

Is Null A criteria that searches for fields that are empty.

Join line In the Relationships window, the line joining two tables that visually indicates the related field and the type of relationship.

Join Type A relationship option that determines how unmatched records should display in a query.

Junction table A table in a many-to-many relationship used to join the two outer tables with two one-to-many relationships.

Label control A control on a form or report that contains descriptive information, typically a field name.

Landscape orientation A print layout in which the printed page is wider than it is tall.

Layout selector A small symbol that displays in the upper left corner of a selected control layout, and with which you can move the entire group of controls.

Layout view The Access view in which you can make changes to a form or to a report while the form is running—the data from the underlying record source displays.

Left outer join In a query datasheet based on related tables, every record in the left table displays even if there is no matching record in the other table.

List box A control that displays several values without having to click an arrow.

Literal character A character in an input mask that you do not want the end user to change during data entry.

Logical operators The criteria of AND and OR used to enter criteria for the same field or different fields; AND requires that both conditions be met and OR requires that either condition be met.

Lookup field An Access data type that retrieves values from another table or a value list.

Lookup Wizard A wizard that automatically fills in the correct field properties needed to perform a lookup.

Main form A form that has a subform nested within it.

Many-to-many relationship A relationship where a record can match many records in a second table and a record in the second table can match many records from the first table.

Message Bar The area directly below the Ribbon that displays information such as security alerts when there is potentially unsafe, active content in an Office 2007 document that you open.

Microsoft ActiveX control A pre-built program designed to run inside of multiple programs.

Microsoft Visual Basic for Applications (VBA) A programming language designed to extend the capabilities of Microsoft Office applications.

Microsoft Web Browser An ActiveX control that displays a Web page inside another application such as an Access form, Word document, or PowerPoint presentation.

Multiple column lookup field A lookup field that displays more than one column of data.

Multiple Items form A form that displays records in rows and columns similar to a datasheet, but provides formatting options found only in form layout.

Navigation Pane The area of the Access window that displays and organizes the names of the objects in a database; from here you open objects for use.

Object window The portion of the Access window that displays open objects.

Objects The basic parts of a database, which includes tables, forms, queries, reports, and macros.

OLE An abbreviation for *object linking and embedding*, a technology for transferring and sharing information among applications.

One-to-many relationship A relationship between two tables where one record in the first table corresponds to many records in the second table—the most common type of relationship in Access.

One-to-one relationship A relationship where each record in the first table has one, and only one, matching record in the second table.

Operator A symbol in an expression that performs a specific function such as multiplying, comparing two values, or testing if a condition is true or false.

Option group A set of option buttons where only one option button may be selected at a time.

OR condition A condition in which only records where one of two values is present in the selected field.

Outermost sort field When sorting on multiple fields in datasheet view, the field that will be used for the first level of sorting.

Page footer Information printed at the end of every page in a report; used to print page numbers or other information that you want to appear at the bottom of every report page.

Page header Information printed at the top of every page of a report.

Page number control A control on a form or report that inserts the page numbers of the pages when displayed in Print Preview or when printed.

Parameter query A query that asks the user to type the criteria before the query is run.

Placeholder characters The characters that the user can actually change in an input mask.

Populate The action of filling a database table with records.

Portrait orientation A print layout in which the printed page is taller than it is wide.

Primary key The field that uniquely identifies a record in a table—for example, a Student ID number at a college.

Programming comment Text in a program that helps the person writing the program that is usually ignored when the program is run.

Property sheet A list of characteristics for controls on a form or report in which you make precision changes to each property associated with the control.

Query A database object that retrieves specific data from one or more tables and then displays the specified data in Datasheet View.

Record All of the categories of data pertaining to one person, place, thing, event, or idea.

Record selector The bar on the left side of a form with which you can select the entire record.

Record selector box The small box at the left of a record in datasheet view which, when clicked, selects the entire record.

Record source The table or query that provides the underlying data for a form or report

Recordset The name given to all of the records in a given set of records, such as the records that are displayed when a query is run.

Referential integrity A set of rules that Access uses to ensure that the data between related tables is valid.

Relational database A type of database in which the tables in the database can relate or connect to other tables through common fields.

Relationship An association that is established between two tables using common fields.

Relationships report A special report showing the current layout of the Relationships window.

Report A database object that summarizes the fields and records from a table, or from a query, in an easy-to-read format suitable for printing.

Report footer Information that is printed once at the end of a report; used to print report totals or other summary information for the entire report.

Report header Information printed once at the beginning of a report; used for logos, titles, and dates.

Report tool The Access feature that creates a report with one mouse click, and which displays all the fields and records from the record source that you choose—a quick way to look at the underlying data.

Report Wizard An Access feature with which you can create a report by answering a series of questions; Access designs the report based on your answers.

Required property A field property that requires data be entered into the field.

Rich text Text that is formatted with options common to many programs such as Word, Excel, and PowerPoint.

Right outer join In a query based on related tables, every record in the right table displays even if there is no matching record in the other table.

Row source property A field property that specifies the name of a table or query or the typed list that actually stores the list of values to be looked up.

Run The process in which Access searches the records in the table(s) included in a query design, finds the records that match the specified criteria, and then displays those records in a datasheet; only the fields that have been included in the query design display.

Running Sum A calculation that accumulates from record to record.

Section bar A gray bar in a form or report that identifies and separates one section from another; used to select the section and to change the size of the adjacent section.

Select Query A database object that retrieves (selects) specific data from one or more tables and then displays the specified data in datasheet view.

Simple select query Another name for a select query.

Sizing handles The small boxes around the edge of a control indicating the control is selected and that can be adjusted to resize the selected control.

Sorting The process of arranging data in a specific order based on the value in each field.

Split form A form that gives you two views of the same data: a form view and a datasheet view.

Spotlight The area in the opening Access program screen that displays content from Microsoft's Web site.

Stacked layout In a form or report, labels and text boxes are arranged vertically with a label to left of each text box.

Subdatasheet A datasheet that is nested within another datasheet.

Subform Forms inserted within another form that are often used for tables in a one-to-many relationship.

Subreport A report that is nested inside another report.

Subset A portion of the total records available.

Summary statistics Numerical descriptions of groups of data such as totals, averages, minimums, and maximums.

Tab order The order in which the insertion point moves from one field to the next in a form when you press the Tab key.

Tabbed form A form that displays a row of tabs at the top of the form, and each tab displays a different form or page.

Table The Access object that stores your data organized in an arrangement of columns and rows.

Table area The upper pane of the Query window, which displays the field lists for tables that are used in the query.

Table design The number of fields, and the type of content within each field, in an Access table.

Table template A pre-built table format for common topics such as contacts, issues, and tasks.

Tables and Views category An arrangement of objects in the Navigation Pane in which the objects are grouped by the table to which they are related.

Tabular layout In a form or report, labels and text boxes are arranged in rows and columns.

Template A pre-formatted database designed for a specific purpose.

Text box control The graphical object on a form or report that displays the data from the underlying table or query; a text box control is known as a bound control because its source data comes from a table or a query.

Text string A sequence of characters, which when used in query criteria, much be matched.

Trust Center (Access) An area of the Access program where you can view the security and privacy settings for your Access installation.

Unbound control Any control that doesn't have a source of data.

Validation Rule property A field property that tests values for accuracy as they are entered into a table.

Validation Text property A field property that provides a custom message when the validation rule has been violated.

Value axis A numerical scale on the left side of a chart that shows the range of numbers for the data points.

VBA sub procedure A group of instructions used to manipulate controls.

Wildcard character In a query, a character that serves as a placeholder for one or more unknown characters in your criteria.

Wizard A feature in Microsoft Office programs that walks you step by step through a process.

Yes/No data type A data type that can be assigned to any field that will hold only two values, typically Yes/No, On/Off/ or True/False.

Z-axis The value axis in a 3-D chart.

Zoom The action of increasing or decreasing the viewing area of the screen.

Index

The CD symbol represents Index entries found on the CD (See CD file name for page numbers).